Methods and materials for
Secondary school physical education

San Diego County Schools.

Greensboro, N. C., City Schools.

THIRD EDITION

Methods and materials for
Secondary school physical education

CHARLES A. BUCHER, A.B., M.A., Ed.D.

Professor of Education, New York University, New York, N. Y.

CONSTANCE R. KOENIG, B.A., M.S. in Education

The Peabody Demonstration School of George Peabody College for Teachers, Nashville, Tenn.

with

MILTON BARNHARD, B.S., M.A.

Yonkers Public Schools, Yonkers, N. Y.

With 293 illustrations

The C. V. Mosby Company

Saint Louis   1970

Department of Education, Wellington, New Zealand.

Department of Education, Wellington, New Zealand.

Department of Education, Wellington, New Zealand.

Hurst-Euless-Bedford Public
Schools, Hurst, Texas.

Preface

Education is changing rapidly in a changing society. Physical education should also be changing if it is to keep abreast of the times. It should not change for change itself but because we are living in a different world where the student, the teacher, the learning process, and the materials for teaching are also changing. The curriculum reform movement has brought about such innovations as the "new physics," the "new math," and the "new social studies." New types of educational tools have revolutionized the teaching process. The academic pace has been stepped up in most schools. Research has created new knowledge. The theory of learning is better understood. The computer makes old ways of scheduling classes and storing knowledge obsolete. The behavioral sciences have come into their own.

What has affected education in general should result in a different type of physical education. The conceptualization of subject matter presents a challenge to physical educators. New audiovisual techniques provide us with more effective ways of teaching motor skills. A better understanding of learning theory, especially as related to motor learning, offers help in the scientific teaching of skills. More knowledge about the atypical student indicates that physical education can make a greater contribution to all students, including the culturally disadvantaged, mentally retarded, and physically handicapped. The impact of movement education is being felt throughout the country.

To keep up with our changing society, changing education, and changing physical education, this book has been completely

Walt Whitman High School, South Huntington Schools, New York.

Mount Pleasant Senior High School, Wilmington, Del.

revised. There are new chapters to meet the needs of the times: The Secondary School in a Changing Society, The Physical Educator and Teaching Style, The Teaching-Learning Process, Methods and Materials for Teaching the Atypical Student, and Methods and Materials for Movement Education. The authors would like to thank Miss Myra Goldman for her thinking and help in the writing of these chapters. In addition to these new chapters others have received a major overhaul, including Developing the Goals of Physical Education, Developing the Curriculum, The Beginning Teacher, Methods of Teaching, and Resources and Materials for Teaching.

We feel that the reader of this book will be well informed about the changing world of which he is a part and the role that physical education can play in the educational process.

Charles A. Bucher
Constance R. Koenig
Milton Barnhard

Contents

part two

The program

part three

The teacher

part four

Teaching physical education

14 Methods and materials for teaching the atypical student, 252

15 Methods and materials for developing physical fitness, 276

16 Methods and materials for movement education, 289

part five

Class management and control

part six

Evaluation

part seven

Records and forms for physical education

Introduction

Manchester Public Schools, Manchester, N. H.

West High School, Davenport, Iowa.

Manchester Public Schools, Manchester, N. H.

Manchester Public Schools, Manchester, N. H.

The secondary school in a changing society

Our modern society is dynamic, flexible, demanding, materialistic, and self-centered. As recently as ten years ago, a society that possessed these characteristics might have been condemned. Instead, the world of today is an exciting place in which to live, learn, and teach. The meaning of the word "society" encompasses not only people but also those factors such as machines, goods and services, and facilities which influence people.

With the 1957 launching of the Russian sputnik and subsequent space probes by the United States, society entered an era hallmarked by the development of highly sophisticated machinery. The turn-of-the-century flight of the Wright brothers was the initial impetus in freeing man from his earthbound environment. The space age is freeing man from the confines of his own atmosphere and has permitted him to reach into outer space, even to the moon, and to probe the depths of the seas. This era has had an increasingly profound influence on society. The skilled working man has had to become a highly trained technician, and the professional has had to become a specialist in a wide variety of interrelated fields. Widespread use of computers, the children of the space age, has increased the pace of life. More people need more education to understand and control the machines that are the core of modern life. Each highly complicated electronic vehicle that is launched into space or dropped into the sea is the result of increased technology and of the refinement of the machines of science, industry, and education.

Our world becomes more complicated year after year. Not only are there many problems that affect us domestically, such as the need for more education, increasing specialization among vocations, and a faster living pace, but international problems seem to be becoming more complex.

Only a little over ten years ago, our world was a relatively uncomplicated place in which to live, become educated, and earn a living. There were brief periods of world peace, and domestic and international unrest were not in the forefront of the news. Students in colleges and universities were willing to adapt themselves to required courses and curriculums in order to achieve a good job and a steady income. Today's college-age youth realize that colleges and universities must change as the world changes, and are calling for improvements in curriculum, faculty, and administration. The activism and militancy of the college student have affected the

3

passivity of secondary school youth, who also are no longer content to endure outdated pedagogy. We have a "new" secondary school student, and we are rapidly giving him "new" secondary schools geared to the needs of his tomorrow.

Today's secondary school youth live in a computer-card world. They have never known international peace or domestic stability, but instead they are intimately familiar with a constantly fluctuating society, community change and upheaval, electronic marvels, and educational evolution. It is not technology *per se* that has brought about the changes in secondary schools, but the effect technology has had on all the factors that combine to influence and control secondary education. Society at large, the changing structure of communities, the student and his parents, educators, administrators, and the schools themselves are all intimate parts of educational evolution.

THE CHANGING STRUCTURE OF SOCIETY

Today's society is, for most people, an open one that tends to be materialistic and adventuresome. People have become highly mobile, and there is more money available to be spent on more and more consumer goods and services. Increased ease of ownership of private automobiles has helped to motivate many families to travel extensively, and this has in turn resulted in the continuing construction of coast-to-coast and border-to-border superhighway systems that have effectively made the country "smaller."

This last decade has been marked by increased suburbanization. The desire for a middle-class mode of living has resulted in a great exodus of people from the large cities. Still others, having already attained middle-class status or better, have chosen to leave the cities to seek out the supposedly quieter, more stable, and relatively more peaceful life of the suburbs. Many former urbanites prefer to commute many hours to work rather than live in the crowded, industrialized cities. The cities are now largely the domain of the lower socioeconomic groups, who cannot leave because the suburbs cannot house or employ them, or because they find that society has effectively closed the door on upward mobility.

Our society is becoming more, rather than less, structured in spite of civil rights legislation that includes open housing measures. Suburbanites have learned to safeguard their residents-only beaches and recreational facilities and members-only clubs. The modern schools and recreational facilities we read about are manifestations of suburban growth where there is land to build modern structures and the money to support them. Our cities are typically becoming more and more populated by those who cannot support, and thus do not have, the schools and other advantages that epitomize the privileges and expectations of the suburban dweller.

The length of the working day for the average professional man and for the skilled worker is, in effect, increasing. The worker and the professional man must remain abreast of new technological advances in order to maintain job efficiency and effectiveness. Additional time spent in commuting to job or office adds to the length of the working day and reduces the number of hours that can be spent in socialization or recreation. The technology that brought television to all reaches of society also fostered the age of the spectator. For the suburbanite with his many opportunities for active recreation, and the urbanite with his lack of them, the television set dispenses recreation vicariously through expanded scheduling of sports events. Many people in our society are gradually forgetting how to play as they increasingly allow modern technology to do their playing for them.

Society is also becoming more internationally minded. New communications media, such as Telstar and its sister satellites, have helped to bring the world and even the moon into every home. News is relayed, at the time it happens, from country to country, shrinking the size of the world and making international understanding a possibility. The youth of today are especially concerned with the whole aspect of international understanding, and are actively demonstrating this feeling through involvement, while in secondary schools, in United Nations clubs and international relations clubs. Many older youth have turned to Peace Corps service or are assisting in other humanitarian activities.

Our wealthy, knowledgeable, mobile, and highly automated society is still fighting the ills of poverty, discrimination, and unemployment. There are many people in this affluent society who live in poverty, lack money for adequate medical care, attend schools that do not meet their educational needs, and rarely venture outside their own neighborhoods. Additionally, lack of adequate education and training prohibits these individuals from obtaining employment. Many of them are fortunate enough to succeed—to rise out of their ghetto existence and attain a limited measure of social mobility. However, the technology that has been a boon to most of American society has only served to drive the lower socioeconomic classes farther away from the mainstream of society and is denying them a chance at the good life.

The changing society and education

Education is one of the most important facets of modern life. There is an emphasis on providing education for everyone regardless of age or social class, and many more people than ever before are thinking in terms of continuing their education beyond secondary school. A minimal education, they realize, is of limited practical value in the demanding job market of the computer age. At the same time, increased applications for college admission have caused many four-year institutions to raise their entrance standards to keep enrollments at a manageable level. This has had a concomitant effect on the secondary schools, since they have been forced to raise their academic standards to ensure that their students can meet college admission requirements. Our newly education-conscious society has helped to bring about the construction of many new community and junior colleges and technical schools that are successfully meeting the demand for "education for all."

It is at the secondary school level that the most startling educational changes are coming about. Some of the implications of the computer age for education have already been realized. The earliest teaching

Fig. 1. Educators planning. (Peabody Demonstration School, George Peabody College for Teachers, Nashville, Tenn.)

machines, in the form of manual Skinner boxes, have already been superseded by complex electronic devices such as talking typewriters, video-tape and instant play-back machines, recording and playback hardware, and the machinery specific to the language laboratory. Operation COM-PU/TEL, for example, is a Chicago-based computer network that links twenty-five secondary schools and colleges in two states to its machinery. By utilizing telephone lines, each school can independently program instruction in computer science for its students. Similar computer networks link schools in other states, and even tie in East Coast schools with computers based on the West Coast.[1]

The use of electronic equipment has allowed the learner to proceed at his own pace in many curricular areas. Where electronic equipment is utilized, the teacher is freed to decrease mass instruction time while increasing individual instruction time. Thus, the teacher can introduce new material more effectively and efficiently, and can supplement group instruction with individualized machine instruction.

In many secondary schools scheduling of classes and room and teacher assignments are programmed by computers. Register-keeping, once a time-consuming task, is also adaptable to computerization, giving the teacher additional hours of teaching time. However, the most profound influence of the computer age has occurred in the curriculum itself. Static and classic curricula have been forced to undergo extensive revision and continued evaluation. Not only the sciences, but the languages and social sciences as well, are updating all phases of their courses to meet the advancing tide of programmed instruction.

Some secondary schools, however, do not have any of the hardware of the computer age, even though the computer has become increasingly important as an aid to education. Secondary schools that fail to keep up with modern educational methodology cannot hope to offer their students a competitive education by adhering to outdated educational processes. The full implications of the computer age for general education will not be known until society finds that it has exhausted the last frontiers of knowledge.

The changing society and physical education

Physical education has so far failed to realistically meet the challenge of today's

Fig. 2. The changing society and physical education. (Walt Whitman High School, South Huntington Schools, New York.)

technology. While there are, and have been, many computer-related implications for physical education, this machinery has not been utilized in the teaching-learning process.

Researchers in physical education have used new electronic gadgetry, but only in a very limited fashion. The known effects of space and ocean exploration on the physiology and psychology of man have prompted much scholarly research by physical, behavioral, and social scientists. The knowledge they contribute holds many implications for changes in emphases in physical education curricula, but the challenge has not been taken up.

Our secondary school physical education programs too frequently lapse back into traditional patterns, apparently with no emphasis on meeting the computer age head-on. Physical fitness has been emphasized for several years. Movement education is being embraced as a "new" form of physical education. Presently, some physical educators seem to be content to maintain the status quo while the rest of education passes them by.

Physical education needs to be revised in the light of the computer age. This could mean such things as programmed textbooks, audiovisual aids, the full use of specially adapted teaching machines, and a conceptual approach to physical education as an equal partner in the process of modern education and educational technology.

THE CHANGING STRUCTURE OF COMMUNITIES

A community is a place where people live and function as a largely homogeneous group, with their own schools, shops, and parks. It may be a section of a large city, or an entire suburban town. While larger cities have traditionally been subdivided into wards or districts for political expediency, it is only recently that the citizens of these districts have begun to become more interested in assuming the responsibility for the life in their community. Neighborhood

groups in many large cities are currently seeking a greater voice in managing the affairs of their schools, especially those aspects related to curriculum and administration. In many suburbs, recent referendums to increase tax limits to gain money needed to run the schools have been defeated. Ten years ago, most taxpayers fully supported their schools, but many now feel that the schools are not adequate to modern needs, and they are unwilling to pay higher taxes without the guarantee of educational reform.

Educators as well as community members are aware of the climate that surrounds education and the educational systems of today. Many new or expanding communities attract home buyers or apartment renters by constructing carefully planned educational parks. These parks contain modern elementary and secondary schools as well as recreational facilities that are the core of these new communities and one of the vital focuses of community life. Planning assures that these educational parks will fulfill community needs for years to come, in spite of the construction of additional dwelling units and resultant increases in school enrollments.

In still other newly developing suburban communities there has been no such careful planning. The need and demand for housing has far outstripped the supply of building lots, and recreational lands have been laid waste by housing developments. A secondary school student in such a community may have to commute many miles to a regional high school or attend a vastly overcrowded school in his own community.

The move to suburbia has not relieved the population density of the cities. More and more members of the lower socioeconomic groups move into the cities each day in search of better housing, higher paying jobs, and better schools for their children. Their efforts are largely unrewarded. This great influx of people leads to crowded tenements and unemployment, and city schools that serve the lower socioeconomic groups are typically old, overcrowded, and inadequately staffed.

There is a rising civic interest in education and in providing a better education for all children regardless of where they live. The federal government is pouring financial aid into the schools through its aid-to-education programs, but many cities and towns of all sizes are finding that even this aid, when combined with their own limited financial resources, is not enough to secure adequate personnel or to build facilities that are required even for present needs.

The changing community and education

Many suburbs boast futuristic secondary schools. Community planners and architects and builders specializing in school construction have developed new materials, new plant layouts, and new exteriors especially suited to modern-day secondary education. Geodesic domes and bubble-topped structures have made their appearance along with schools-in-the-round and schools that are completely submerged below the ground.[2] These structures afford more flexibility, can accommodate more students, and are in general lighter and brighter than traditional architectural designs. Where building space has been at a premium, additions to existing secondary schools have been placed under athletic fields or under structurally sound portions of buildings. These subterranean structures are artificially lighted, soundproofed, and air-conditioned. The city of New York has recently opened several secondary schools that are above ground, but windowless. These totally air-conditioned structures help to keep out street noises that would distract students from the learning process.

Other communities have supported the construction of rambling structures that have separate wings for science, mathematics, physical education, and the other divisions of the school. With such an arrangement students must walk farther between classes, but shop noises, for example, do not intrude on the quiet needed by students in language laboratories. This type of structure also allows needed sections to be opened for community use on evenings and weekends, while other sections of the school can remain closed off from access.

Still other communities are involved in the process known as bussing. Both de facto and intentional segregation have created a plethora of unequal educational facilities in suburbs and cities alike. Many larger suburbs have a divisional line between socioeconomic classes and have their own problems with ghettolike conditions. They may have two secondary schools serving the community, but the better of the two, the least crowded, and the best staffed is likely to serve the upper socioeconomic groups. Civic concern, sometimes prodded by court order, may dictate that an equal number of students from all areas of the city or town attend each of the secondary schools, and that the schools be made as equal as possible in staff, equipment, and facilities. Many civic groups and parents' organizations have been opposed to bussing because many students must ride long distances on a bus between home and school twice each day. A rural school district in Colorado, which must of necessity bus all its pupils, has faced the problem of bussing realistically by installing audiovisual equipment and individual headphones in its school buses. Youngsters may choose from a wide variety of age-level instructional tapes on preassigned channels or select regular AM-band, live radio broadcasts on another channel, or they may choose not to listen at all. As a further option, this school district has installed three additional channels that students can reserve for their individual study of preselected tapes. When this specially equipped bus is not transporting students, it is used as a mobile classroom.[3]

Innovations in the building of contemporary schools and the problems of providing an equal education for all students are not the only concerns of the various communities. Lay people today are calling for dedicated professionals to teach in their schools and dedicated people to administer them. Parent and community organizations are demanding adequately trained, professional educators who will devote themselves to understanding the needs of the communities in which they teach.

The influx of the culturally disadvantaged into the urban schools has created other unforeseen problems for school boards, administrators, and teachers. Frequent bussing of students and the lack of adequate staff in ghetto schools have created problems in giving the urban student an adequate education. Many urban schools find that obtaining and keeping qualified staff is their biggest problem. Experienced teachers are often unwilling to teach in difficult situations, and new teachers are ill equipped to cope with many of the problems that arise in the urban setting. This implies not only that our urban schools and school systems must prove that they are capable of providing for the educational needs of the city child but that they must also be able to staff their schools with qualified personnel who are willing and able to teach under adverse conditions.

The changing community and physical education

When new secondary schools are constructed the physical education facilities become a major concern because they are often the single most expensive item in the budget. Recent trends, however, have been to construct physical education facilities that can be opened to community use when school is not in session. A community is generally less than willing to pay for extensive and expensive facilities that will see only limited use.

The construction of new physical education facilities and the expansion of existing ones have met with community opposition in many cases. This resistance may be due to parental interest in courses of an academic nature that help to determine college admission, the nationwide focus on

science and mathematics, or general community apathy toward physical education as an important part of the curriculum. Affluent communities in which the citizenry has unlimited access to a variety of recreational facilities tend to oppose the added construction of secondary school physical education facilities beyond a bare minimum because they do not see any justified need for elaborate plants. Other communities view physical education as a frill added to the school curriculum. Opposition to modernization or expansion of physical education facilities may also come from administrators or school budget directors who either hold the same opinions as the community at large or who look with alarm on the necessary increase in personnel to staff any additional facilities.

Physical educators must be cognizant of community needs and interests and must themselves elicit community support. This can be done only through the program that is offered, and through the physical educator's willingness to become an active member of the community in which he teaches. Good community relations, and eventually community support, are developed and furthered in this way. When new facilities are proposed, the physical educator should take the initiative in making certain that the new physical education facility will be adequate and still modern many years into the future. He should take an active part in the planning and design of such facilities so that they can be used by the community as well as the school.

When completely new facilities for physical education are constructed, they often follow a rather unique but proved arrangement. Swimming pools and tennis courts are frequently placed under air-supported structures at some distance from the main school building but in close proximity to playing fields. Additionally, communities have found that air-supported structures can, if planned well in advance, be converted to multiple use. For example, the tennis courts used in spring and summer may be flooded and used for ice skating in winter. The air-supported bubble over the swimming pool and tennis courts is often removed in warmer weather, and heating is easily piped in, in colder temperatures. The gymnasium building itself, with lockers, office space, and possibly a classroom or two, will be erected adjacent to the other physical education facilities.

No longer are secondary schools built with a single open gymnasium that must be shared by both girls' and boys' classes. Modern construction almost always includes either two full-size gymnasiums or a single oversized facility that can be divided by a motor-driven door. Some of these large gymnasiums can be divided into four smaller rooms, affording adequate numbers of indoor stations for indoor seasons. Additional features of modern gymnasiums often include rooms for correc-

Fig. 3. Good facilities help to make a good secondary school. **A,** Main gymnasium—2 teaching stations—overhead rolling aluminum door. **B,** Upper balcony gymnasium. **C,** Indoor track, golf, and baseball area. **D,** Six-lane swimming pool. **E,** Field house and other facilities. (**A-D,** West High School, Davenport, Iowa; courtesy Louis C. Kingscott & Associates, Inc., Kalamazoo, Mich. **E,** Bethesda Public Schools, Bethesda, Md.; courtesy McLeod and Ferrara Architects, Washington, D. C.)

tives, weight training, and wrestling, as well as small dance studios adjacent to, but entirely separate from, the gymnasiums. Built-in sound systems and projection facilities are more and more becoming commonplace parts of new or modernized physical education facilities.

Outdoor facilities have also come in for their share of updating. New methods of seeding and new materials designed for outdoor use have facilitated rapid drainage after rainstorms, and have helped to make such facilities as running tracks usable virtually the full year.

Not all secondary schools have new facilities, and not all secondary schools with inadequate and outdated facilities can look forward to community support for new facilities. Many secondary schools will have to struggle for many years with overcrowded and inadequate physical plants. Community character determines the educational support available, and the construction of new educational and physical education facilities depends on the community's educational outlook on the whole.

THE CHANGING STUDENT

The students who are attending our secondary schools today have never known a world at peace. Their world is one of materialism and of immediate need gratification. Today's student lives in an open society that did not exist ten years ago. He is a questing individual whose environment includes many examples of moral decay, as evidenced by drug abuse, changing sexual mores, and an ever-increasing crime rate. Domestic and international ferment are facts of life for today's adolescent, who desperately needs guidance in coping with the world in which he lives.

Today's youth is concerned with his individuality and his place in the world as an individual. Social and political activism appeal to modern adolescents because they help him to establish himself as a part of society. Student militancy, especially among secondary school youth, is a fairly recent phenomenon and has not received the wide attention lavished on the militant and activist college youth. Yet secondary school students have mimicked their elders and demonstrated for educational reforms just as vocally. Chief among the secondary school students' causes have been curriculum revisions and decreased administrative censorship of student publications. Where secondary school newspapers once reported only sterile school news, they now editorialize on national and world events and run feature articles concerned with the latest student causes the world over.

Today's adolescent is not content with mere obedience to parental controls, and he actively seeks the freedom to direct the course of his own life. The new adolescent has had a profound effect on all of education, causing educators to take a new and hard look at educational methodology, procedures, objectives, and curricula. Discontent with what was not being taught has led to new, experimental curricula and new courses. Educators have been forced to realize that their programs of instruction lack the ability to teach the student about the world as it really is. The implications of this new voice for education has had a far-reaching effect that is only beginning to be felt.

The changing student and education

To today's adolescent the individual and what becomes of him is extremely important. Within the environment of the school, these courses geared to today are the ones in which the adolescent is interested and from which he learns. The adolescent usually is not as interested in what the world was like yesterday as in what it is like today, and what this means to him as an individual.

Education as a whole is beginning to develop courses that adolescents can understand and interpret in the light of themselves. Those few courses which are not making use of the new media, new methodologies, and new curricula are, in effect, teaching the adolescent in a foreign language that he will never be able to understand.

Education is becoming profoundly aware of the student and his individual needs, and of his creativity. Educators have begun to realize that creativity and individuality are enhanced when an individual takes on some of the responsibility for his own educational progress. Teaching machines, educational television, and language laboratories all cater to individual differences, adapting education to the student rather than the reverse. Courses in history and languages, for example, which were once only dry textbook and memorization courses, have been made into living adventures through the use of individual instructional media.[4]

Flexible and modular schedules have been developed that allow students to spend longer blocks of time in courses that stimulate and challenge them. Blocks of free time are arranged in some secondary schools so that students can pursue independent projects or participate in seminar or discussion groups. An increased emphasis on guidance and counseling in the secondary school has helped to uncover the real needs of students so that schedules and courses can be better adapted to them.

If a course does not interest today's ado-lescent, does not identify with him as an individual, or does not speak directly to him, he tends to endure it but will not attempt to pursue it beyond the formal requirements. Science clubs and language clubs are usually full of youngsters who attend them not because they must but because they have chosen to be there. They are motivated because their individuality is recognized and respected.

The changing student and physical education

To prosper in today's secondary schools, physical education must become more intellectual. It should be based on a conceptual approach, and must appeal to the individuality of the adolescent. At the same time, it must challenge his creativity.

The physical educator has typically been a sounding board for students, and guidance of the student has been one of his most important tasks. Most physical educators, however, have not capitalized on this rapport in building meaningful programs. The open society of today demands that secondary school physical education provide an outlet for excess energy and that it provide limitless opportunities for self-expression and creativity.

Today's student presents a challenge to

Fig. 4. The changing student and physical education. (Spartanburg High School, Spartanburg, S. C.)

the physical educator, not only in the area of understanding the student, but also in regard to providing a program worthy of today's student. Physical education, through its tenacity in the use of traditional methodology, is presently guilty of failing to make a worthwhile contribution to today's youth. The average secondary school physical educator often is concerned with educating his students physically while losing sight of the mind the body houses.

To appeal to and motivate today's youth, physical education needs to shift more toward an intellectual emphasis. Years ago, young girls were dissuaded from seeking careers in physical education because the name of the field alone made their mothers think of gross musculature and possible masculinization. Among some of today's adolescent girls this stereotype persists, and it persists basically because physical education in most of today's secondary schools is exactly the same as it was for their mothers years ago. Physical education does not, in many schools, answer the needs of today's youth of either sex.

New curricula in physical education and the use of new media and textbooks can help in bringing physical education up-to-date. Some schools have done just this, while others have even attempted college-type elective programs, but this trend is very limited. Perhaps physical education will make its best move toward modernity by training teachers of physical education who can talk to adolescents in their own language, understand their world, and make physical education an essential and desirable part of that world.

THE CHANGING TEACHER

While the professions have for many years declined to align themselves with labor unions, alignment has now become a very prevalent direction in education. Many teachers have become dissatisfied with the slow gains made by the National Education Association, the major professional organization for public school teachers in the United States. Professionals in many fields outside of teaching are now seeking to accelerate their progress by employing the highly organized and effective union structure.

Frequently, newspapers carry items concerned with strikes and work stoppages by teachers. These tactics are not limited to the United States but are increasingly becoming an international phenomenon. The motives for walkouts are often centered around salary demands, but the desire for general improvement of the profession and the people served by it is also a strong motive—, and it is sometimes the prime motive resulting in strikes by teachers.

Professional militancy can either devastate or enhance the process of general education. Where teacher strikes have occurred, teaching days have been lost and the educational continuity destroyed for the students. However, positive action has resulted from many of these walkouts. Some school systems have agreed to reduce the size of classes, decrease the amount of paper work required of teachers, and eliminate many nonteaching duties that cut into instructional time. Improved working conditions help to improve the effectiveness of the educator: smaller classes allow for more individualized instruction, and reductions in nonteaching assignments free the teacher to prepare and conduct more effective lessons. Of late, even the National Education Association has begun to approve of a greater degree of teacher militancy based on its analyses of educational gains made by these tactics.

The changing teacher and education

Today's teachers are more flexible, more knowledgeable, and more attuned to the whole panorama of education than any past generation of teachers. Much of this improvement, of course, has been born of the necessity to learn to cope with the new mathematics, the new social studies, and the new approaches to the other areas of the curriculum.

The teacher of today voluntarily attends in-service courses and seeks a higher edu-

Fig. 5. The changing teacher of physical education. (Ames High School, Ames, Iowa.)

cation in quest of becoming a better educator. He is better read in all fields, attends more concerts and plays, and is more likely to participate actively in community affairs than was the teacher of ten years ago. Student militancy has motivated the teacher to speak out and be heard not only as a professional but as a citizen of the community. The educator does not hold the untouchable place in society that he once did, but instead he has gained the more important status of an equal citizen.

Within the confines of the school the teacher has been able to become more of an equal partner with administrators. It is the teacher who knows the educational pulse of the students most intimately, and the teacher in cooperation with the students can effectively help to translate their educational needs and interests to the administrators. Educators have had to drop their role of omnipotence in the light of the "new" student. They are now moving closer to the ideal of becoming guides through the educational process rather than retaining their timeworn position as dictators of this process. The "new" teacher has accepted the student as a coequal in the process of education.

The new physical educator

The implications of teacher militancy for physical education parallel those for general education. Physical educators have traditionally taught larger-than-average classes and have been responsible for many nonteaching functions, such as proctoring of study halls, monitoring of the lunchroom, and supervising of buses. While teacher militancy has been effective as far as general educators are concerned, the nonteaching load of physical educators has not been lightened to any appreciable extent. Administrators tend to feel that someone must take on the nonteaching duties that abound in any school, and if paraprofessionals cannot be hired for these functions, they usually devolve to the physical educator. These duties must be eliminated from the physical educator's routine so that he will be able to turn himself fully to the task of physical education. The diversion of energies resulting from administrative decree undermines the physical education program in many secondary schools. The necessity of using the physical educator in a variety of roles has been one of the causes of overly large classes.

Many secondary school physical educators have had to reexamine their roles in the light of student needs, but their adaptation to the new student has been somewhat slower than that of general educators. Physical educators have generally been able to maintain close contact with their students, but they have not as yet had to cope with the "new" student as well as a "new" type of physical education. Thus, the physical educator will be one of the last members of the education profession to assume the new role of educational guide unless the field quickly accepts the challenge of formulating a modern approach to physical education.

THE NEW SCHOOLS

Today's secondary schools have been characterized as having a new technology, a new student, and a new kind of educator. A new society and new communities have assisted in bringing about these new schools. However, there are other, equally important changes, a few of which are briefly discussed here, that have helped to give another new focus to public education. These changes are discussed in greater detail in other chapters of this text.

Nongraded schools

The nongraded school concept can be used effectively on all grade levels. In a nongraded school there are no grade labels placed on the classes, freeing the student to learn and advance at his own pace.[2] In a secondary school, a student might be placed in a beginning mathematics class during his first year of attendance, but at the same time might attend an advanced language class made up largely of students who were in their final year of attendance. This procedure encourages each student to work at his own capacity and allows for upward movement to more advanced levels as soon as sufficient achievement has been attained. This system permits more advanced students to work more rapidly, while slower learners can spend additional time on fundamentals. This approach

effectively recognizes and caters to individual needs and differences.

Nongrading is also adaptable to physical education classes. Students can be placed in classes by ability and moved to more advanced sections as they improve and indicate that they are ready to accept the more difficult challenge.

Team teaching

Two or more teachers working cooperatively together to instruct a common group of students comprises the team-teaching approach. On the secondary school level a class of seventy-five chemistry students may attend a common lecture given by one member of the team, and then divide into smaller discussion, seminar, or laboratory groups led by other members of the team. One teacher acts as coordinator for the team, but all the teachers combine to plan lessons and schedules. The team teaching approach affords many opportunities for individualized instruction.

Physical educators have utilized the team teaching approach to great advantage. They have found it possible to show films or give lectures to large classes, and then to divide into smaller sections for skill practice and/or discussions.

Educating the disadvantaged

Project Head Start, although its worth is presently being questioned, has been directed toward disadvantaged children of prekindergarten age. This program was designed to give these youngsters some of the skills they will need to help them adjust to a formal school experience. Some communities have also given special assistance to disadvantaged youngsters in elementary school through Project Mid-Start, while the Upward Bound program is aimed at culturally disadvantaged youngsters of secondary school age who have demonstrated that they have the potential to continue on to college providing they have extra help. Still other federally funded projects included aid to migrant children through the

Fig. 6. Team teaching. **A,** Small group instruction in weight training. **B,** Small group instruction in wrestling. **C,** Small group instruction in gymnastics. **D,** The large group technique as utilized in physical education classes. Each period begins with the large group warm-up before the breakdown into smaller segments determined by the nature of the activity. (Evergreen Park High School, Evergreen Park, Ill.)

Migrant Amendment to Title I of the Elementary and Secondary Education Act.

Each of the above projects makes special provisions for the teaching of physical education. Swimming instruction and recreational sports are vital parts of each of them.

POINTS TO REMEMBER

1. The implications of the space age for today's world
2. The effect of technology on education
3. The characteristics of the new society, the new communities, the new student, the new teacher, and the new schools

PROBLEMS TO THINK THROUGH

1. What are the implications of programmed learning for physical education?
2. What constitutes a meaningful education for today's student?
3. How must physical education change in order to become more relevant to today's student?

CASE STUDY FOR ANALYSIS

Select a single piece of electronic hardware that is used today as an aid to general education. Trace its development and show how it is used in various ways in the classroom. Give its applications for physical education.

EXERCISES FOR REVIEW

1. Trace the growth of the computer age from 1957 to the present.
2. Show how changes in society have affected education and physical education from 1960 to the present time.
3. Interview ten secondary school students to find out whether they think they are receiving a relevant education. Analyze their comments critically.
4. Compare your own secondary school experience with the new approaches to secondary school education.

5. Develop an essay that shows how student militancy affects the complacency of educators.
6. Devise a computer-age secondary school curriculum for physical education.

REFERENCES

1. deGrazia, Alfred, and Sohn, David A.: Revolution in teaching: new theory, technology, and curricula, New York, 1964, Bantam Books.
2. Goodlad, John I., and Anderson, Robert H.: The nongraded elementary school, New York, 1963, Harcourt, Brace & World, Inc.
3. Hoffman, Milton: A new way of bussing students, American Education **4:**14, 1968.
4. Oliva, Peter: The secondary school today, Cleveland, 1967, The World Publishing Co.

SELECTED READINGS

Annual Education Review, The New York Times, Friday, Jan. 12, 1968.
Blubaugh, Ronald: School bells for migrants, American Education **4:**5, 1968.
DeBoer, John J.: The "new" English, The Educational Forum **32:**393, 1968.
Keats, John: The sheepskin psychosis, New York, 1963, Dell Publishing Co., Inc.
Paterson, Franklin: High schools for a free society, Glencoe, Ill., 1960, The Free Press.
Peluso, Anthony P.: An answer for a dime, American Education **4:**28, 1968.

The setting
for teaching

Chandler Street Junior High School, Worcester, Mass.

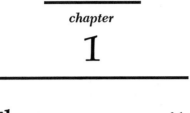

chapter

1

The community

The physical education program, as in many ways all education, is a product of the community in which it exists. The community is that subdivision of people, homes, and businesses which makes up a school district. It may coincide with the geographical limits of a city, town, or village, such as San Diego, California, or Denver, Colorado; or it may include two or more political subdivisions, such as the Bedford School District, which includes the towns of Bedford, New Castle, North Castle, and Pound Ridge, New York.

In any event, the local community plays an important part in the philosophy and formulation of the school program. A knowledge of the community is of importance to the teacher so that he or she may better prepare for the experiences to be encountered.

What is the structural organization of the community? What factors play a part in the financing of the schools? In regard to the schools, who is responsible to the citizens of the community? What influencing factors should be considered in establishing a philosophy of education? How is the physical education program affected by the community.

In this chapter these and other problems as they relate to the schools and specifically to physical education will be discussed so that teachers may be better able to understand and work with their particular situations.

COMMUNITY RELATIONS POLICIES FOR THE PHYSICAL EDUCATOR

The relations between the physical educator and the community are affected by many divergent interactions varying widely in scope, complexity, and intensity. The implications for the physical educator are of great depth and latitude, ranging from the seemingly innocuous task of answering the telephone to being able to effectively utilize public communications media. Because of the inherent dissimilarities in communities, any discussion here must be relatively broad in scope. Some policies which the physical educator should think about very carefully in his relations with the community in which his school is located include the following:

1. *The physical educator should work closely with the community in goal setting, planning, and subsequent program evaluation.* Although the "how" of the school operation is essentially the responsibility of the professional physical educator, he should constructively enlist the abilities, interests, and drives of persons in the community in respect to many school activities of which he is a part. By utilizing citizen cooperation at its highest level, better programs can be developed, community needs can more readily be met, citizen involvement in activities such as parent-teacher associations and neighborhood clubs can be enhanced, and greater public interest can be gained.

2. *The physical educator must be guided by the knowledge that public reaction to school personnel and practices creates the basis for community approval or rejection of many aspects of school affairs.* The physical educator should familiarize himself with the community's traditions, beliefs, resources, and limitations, and, most important, with its people. In working with the community, the physical educator must use integrity in all of his relations and must be efficient in his daily functions and services, for these have significant value.

3. *The school, actively assisted by the physical educator, should offer learning opportunities that meet the needs of the community as well as its students.* Within legal limitations, and rules and regulations of the Board of Education, the physical educator should assist in making the school a community center by helping to provide recreational and educational activities for adults as well as children and youth. Furthermore, the physical educator should

participate in community efforts and activities in the capacity of a resource person. Finally, the physical educator should utilize appropriate community facilities and resources to enhance his program of physical education in the school.

4. *The physical educator should develop his program with the community in mind and flavor it with acceptable habits, customs, traditions, ideals, resources, and problems of the community.* In order to accomplish his task most effectively, the physical educator should familiarize himself with such things as the community's historical background, social pursuits, economic status, political philosophy, leaders, and channels of organized communication.

5. *In order to be most effective in community relations the physical educator must develop professional skills to make his role effective and his contributions as extensive as possible.* The physical educator should be capable of utilizing available communications media in his community,

Fig. 1-1. The physical educator should develop his program with the community in mind. Group from Crystal Springs Camp in Griffith Park Pool. (Youth Services Section, Los Angeles City Schools, Los Angeles, Calif.)

make adjustments and improvements to meet changing needs, maintain continual communication with various groups, and keep school and community leaders informed regarding his school and community activities.

COMMUNITY STRUCTURE

Through a knowledge of the composition and governing bodies of the community, the teacher will be better able to understand the problems facing the community. It is also true that any suggestions for improvement of the curriculum, school plant, facilities, number of personnel, or school philosophy will be more meaningful when they are based upon local community conditions. It is necessary, therefore, to investigate and obtain information about the community, evaluate these facts in the light of professional knowledge, and plan a course of action.

Size

Is your community a compact industrial area, such as Scranton, Pennsylvania, or does it sprawl over the countryside, as does Berkeley, California? The answer to this question has much significance for the school and the physical education program. In a compact area, for instance, there is little or no transportation problem. After-school activities such as intramurals and varsity team practice are not greatly affected, because public transportation is available to take students home. In the sprawling community, lack of public transportation can be a deterrent to the conduct of many activities. Solutions to these transportation problems may include convincing school authorities to provide extra transportation, enlisting the aid of the local parent-teacher association, and coordinating efforts with other departments, such as music or dramatics, thereby involving

Fig. 1-2. Working with community agencies—an important responsibility of physical education. (Public Relations Department, National Council, Y. M. C. A.)

enough students to warrant extra transportation.

Another problem of community size involves future growth, particularly with regard to the current exodus to suburbia. Has your community reached its peak growth, or is it still expanding? Do your facilities amply provide for the number of students you are now handling? What are the plans for the future regarding new facilities? Do these plans properly provide for physical education space, facilities, and teaching stations?

In an eastern community two elementary schools were constructed. It was expected that one of the schools would have a number of vacant rooms during its first two years of operation, while housing classes from kindergarten through grade 7. By the time of occupancy, however, there had been such an increase in the population that school authorities were unable to keep any rooms vacant. In each of the following three years, in fact, a grade was moved out of the school. After the completion of a new secondary school building, a community-wide realignment plan was effected. This plan enabled the schools to more adequately serve its local residents.

Type

Are you going to teach in a predominantly residential community such as Darien, Connecticut, or Berkley, Michigan? If so, you may assume that the parents will take time to inquire about and be in on the planning for education. Active and interested parents are a great help to the school when they put their energies to work in helping the administrators and teachers. Interested parents can help the physical education program by supporting its activities, helping to obtain new facilities, equipment, and supplies, and gaining an understanding of the program. In an industrial community or in a culturally disadvantaged one, residents may be less inclined or may have less time to concern themselves with education. In Flint, Michigan, however, a public interest in education has

brought more people into the schools at night than during the day.

Flint has developed the school-community idea to the point where each school has an evening center and most have gymnasiums that are at least 100 by 100 feet in area, as well as other community rooms. In addition to the evening recreation centers, there are a child health program, in-service training for teachers, an outdoor camp, Big Sister organization, adult education programs, tots and teens groups, a stepping-stone program, and other programs.

This program was begun in 1935 by the Mott Foundation in cooperation with the Flint Board of Education. Its purposes are threefold: (1) to make possible the maximum utilization of school buildings and school facilities as well as other community resources—personnel, material, and organizations; (2) to act as a pilot project in testing and demonstrating to the local board of education and other communities the possibilities of what may be accomplished; and (3) to stimulate, by demonstrating what can be done, constructive influences not only in this community but eventually in other parts of the state, the nation, and the world.

The values of the Flint program are obvious. Important also are the attitudes of the taxpayers when they are able to see and use the buildings for which they pay. Flint was blessed with the Mott Foundation, but most communities can achieve community-centered schools for very little extra cost.

You may find yourself in an industrial or business community like Flint, Michigan, but where the village, town, or city does not have a positive attitude toward education. There may be little room for playing fields and recreational areas. There may be a large populace of older residents who no longer have school-age children. The attitude of the public is of great importance because many residents may feel little sympathy for public school problems, particularly since most solutions to the problems involve an increase in taxes.

Fig. 1-3. Parents are interested in the school's physical education program.

In addition to the older residents, there are those parents who send their children to private or parochial schools and who have no desire to pay twice for education. They must pay their taxes, which are used for public education, but they have a vested interest in minimizing these payments.

Although there are always many parents interested in the schools and their problems, the support of a majority of the population is necessary. This requires public interpretation. In Flint this positive attitude has been achieved through a community-centered program. In Norfolk, Virginia, an interest has been manifested in education through a program of health instruction, activity instruction, and intramurals. This program developed because of close cooperation in the fields of health and physical education, which led to an integrated core of instruction.

If community support is not present, it is the responsibility of the school and of every individual in the school to foster it through careful planning.

Governing body

There are three main types of governing body which determine the form of local government: the mayor-council, the commission, and the city manager.

The *mayor-council plan* places primary control of administrative matters in the hands of an elected mayor. The council, elected by the citizens, handles local legislation. There are variations in the organization of this plan. Some communities have a dominant mayor, others divide the responsibilities of the mayor and the council relatively equally, and still others have a weak mayor, with the majority of the duties being handled by or through the council. The mayor-council plan is still the most prevalent. The majority of small cities use it in one form or another, as do such large cities as New York, Boston, San Francisco, and Detroit.

The *commission plan* has had its period of rise and is now generally regarded as being in eclipse. The city of Galveston made this plan popular just after the turn of the century. There were five commissioners elected by the people. One was designated as mayor, but only for the purpose of presiding at the meetings. He had no veto power and only a proportionate share of the administration with the other commissioners. This type of plan is still used by some municipalities, but its popularity is on the wane.

The *city manager plan* is growing the most rapidly of any type of city government. In this plan, a career man trained in public administration is appointed by the council. He is responsible for the conduct of municipal administration. There are variations in this plan, such as that wherein the council keeps certain appointment rights. The majority of plans leave only two duties in the hands of the council: (1) the right to pass necessary ordinances and resolutions, and (2) the right to select the city manager. The trend in many municipalities is toward the city manager type of government.

The rise of the city manager plan has numerous implications for education. The concentration of powers in a professional person (the manager is supposed to be nonpartisan and is generally chosen from an approved list) usually brings about wider use of modern administrative procedures which generally are credited with unusually effective standards of modern administration.

The implications of the governmental structure, whether it is city, village, town, or other type, in your community for the school and the physical education program are numerous. Knowing it well will provide an understanding of the following:

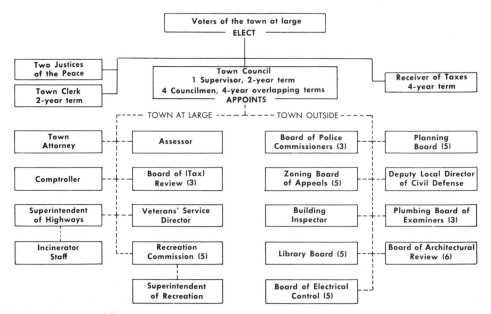

Fig. 1-4. Structure of town government.

1. The chain of responsibility—that is, who the local district leaders are and what they have to do with appropriated moneys
2. The use of modern governmental structure—that is, the degree to which the community is operating under an archaic form of patronage or an efficient modern structure that attempts to cut unnecessary costs and meet today's challenges
3. The pressure points in the community structure—that is, how public sentiment for needed school expenditures can best be made known and brought to bear on local officials

It is your responsibility as a teacher as well as a member of the community to know as much as possible about your local government.

Board of education

The board of education, or school board or committee, as it is known in some areas, is the administrative unit whose responsibility it is to develop policies for the educational program in the local schools. Some communities have a single commissioner of education, but the vast majority of cities and districts retain the board plan. This is true in spite of the widespread movement to single-headed departmental control in such areas as police, fire, health, etc. This may be because of the reasonable success of the board plan and the caliber of board members, who are able to remain aloof from local politics. Whatever the reasons, the board plan appears to be here to stay, especially since most educators seem to prefer this type of administration.

A board of education may be financially independent, allowing it to fix its own tax rate within limits set by the state, and to spend the money as it sees fit. In many cities of more than 25,000 people, as well as in some smaller communities, the boards are financially independent. When a board is fiscally dependent, it recommends the amount it needs to cover the cost of its budget, but the municipal administration decides upon the amount the board will receive. If the full amount is not given, the board must reduce, eliminate, or adjust budget items to fit the amount allotted.

It is important for the physical educator to keep the board aware of problems facing the teacher and to recommend some realistic solutions. It is necessary to channel this information through the principal, director or supervisor, or superintendent.

Composition. Boards of education for school districts evolve from acts of state legislatures. In most cities, boards are elected by the voters. There are places, however, where the mayor appoints members. Regardless of how they obtain their positions, their terms vary from one year to about four years. The usual term is three to four years. Terms are frequently overlapped to ensure continuity in membership.

Size. Boards of education are gradually diminishing in size, from the thirty- and forty-member boards of yesteryear to the five- and nine-member boards seen most commonly today. The number of board members ranges from the three who represent a small local district, to fifteen members, who constitute the board in some large cities. The smaller boards of today seem to produce better results by working more efficiently and with greater harmony. As a rule, most members serve without compensation, although very nominal salaries are given in certain areas.

The National School Boards Association has indicated the following characteristics of school boards in forty-two cities throughout the nation having more than 300,000 population.

Most of these school boards have seven, five, or nine members, in that order. Three cities have boards with fifteen members. The composition of school board members (3% of whom are women and 13% of whom are Negroes) is broken down as follows: businessmen, 103; lawyers, 66; housewives, 51; physicians, 22; ministers, 11; and college professors, 8.

Most of the 137,000 members of the nation's 25,000 school boards are elected. Among the large cities, only Philadelphia, Pittsburgh, and Washington, D. C., choose boards through a committee of court judges. In Boston, Detroit, Los Angeles, and St. Louis, school boards are elected.

Duties. The board of education's responsibilities may be summed up as follows:

Establishes policies and legislates
    Curriculum—including physical education curriculum (in accordance with certain state regulations)
    School calendar—including time and days when interscholastic contests may or may not be played
    School entrance age—set by the state in some areas
Provides means for carrying out policies
    Prepares budget—including salary scale, arrangements for time off or extra pay for coaching, and policy regarding coaching duties
    Hires superintendent and other personnel (upon recommendation of the superintendent)
    Votes tax levies, if fiscally independent, or recommends adequate levies to those who have the fiscal responsibility
    Plans and executes building and maintenance program (within limits mentioned above)—including new physical education plants and facilities
Sees that policies are efficiently carried out
    Visits schools
    Receives oral and written reports on progress

The board also represents the public in the preparation of its policies and budgets, interpreting to the public the needs of the school in terms of plant, facilities, and working conditions. Although there are some specific duties and responsibilities of boards of education and of superintendents, there is no exact line where the duties of the board end and those of the superintendent begin. This must be worked out together toward a common goal. The superintendent of schools, however, is the professional education leader, and members of the board of education are lay personnel. This, of course, has implications for the responsibilities of each.

There is a growing awareness among professional and lay leaders alike of the need for reform in respect to school board operations. Reforms have been advocated by such an important group as the New York Committee on Educational Leadership and are receiving support in some of the more progressive sections of the country. These reforms include (1) the transfer of all administrative functions that encumber school board operations to the superintendent of schools, (2) better procedures for screening school board members so that the "office seeks the man rather than the man seeking the office," (3) elimination of the annual public vote on the school budget where required and substitution of budget hearings in its place, and (4) improved procedures for selecting superintendents of schools.

Neighbors

Good neighbors are necessary, whether one is speaking of the family next door or of a near-by community. The current trend toward centralized, or consolidated, school districts is dependent upon good neighborliness. According to James B. Conant, President Emeritus of Harvard University and author of *The American High School Today*, this trend must continue if high schools are to function properly. Dr. Conant says that any high school with a graduating class of less than 100 is unable to do its job. Since only a small percentage of each class have the aptitude for advanced studies, and since these pupils must be challenged and their programs enriched, it becomes financially necessary to have larger schools. In order to be able to organize classes and to hire competent teachers for these gifted pupils, there must be enough students to warrant spending the money to maintain advanced classes. Therefore, Dr. Conant contends, the number one problem is the elimination of the small high school by district reorganization.[1]

The implications for physical education are similar. The small school may not be able to afford the plant, facilities, and personnel necessary to conduct a satisfactory program. In centralization, or consolidation, the duplication of two or three small, inadequate plants can be eliminated and one adequate, fully staffed plant created.

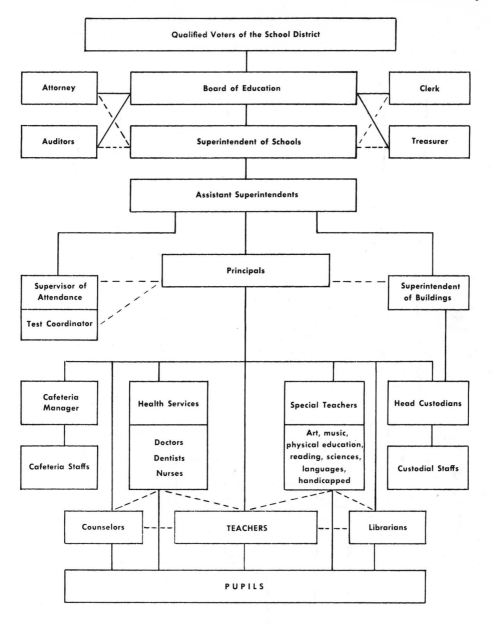

Fig. 1-5. Structure of school system relationships.

A nearby community can also help by providing an example of what can be done in certain educational areas. Being able to point to a part of a program that has been successfully accepted elsewhere may help in establishing a similar program. For instance, the successful inclusion of the trampoline in the program of a neighboring school can be used to help convince administrators of its feasibility, lack of danger under proper supervision, and value in a program. Bringing in educators from the neighboring community to explain what has been done and how it has helped would certainly make it easier to achieve the objective.

COMMUNITY FACTORS INFLUENCING EDUCATION

There are many factors that have a bearing upon the school system and the program within the school. These factors could be termed external, in that they are related to influences outside the school and the teacher-pupil relationship. Their importance, however, cannot be overemphasized. In the pages that follow some of them will be discussed, and the implications they have for education and the possible means of working with them will be mentioned.

Economic conditions

One of the great problems facing every community today is how to obtain enough money to close the gap between the amount and quality of education that is needed and the financial support that is available. The following factors that determine the cost of education are listed by the National Education Association: the rise in enrollments, the problem of securing an adequate number of teachers at salaries high enough to attract and hold them, the need for counseling and guidance, the need for adequate facilities, equipment, etc., the need for enough classrooms to implement a modern program, and the need to lift poverty-stricken districts to a respectable level of support.

The community that is able and willing to meet the needs will have a good educational system. In relation to physical education, this means good physical plants—both indoors and out—and enough qualified personnel to administer a sound, safe, and varied class program; an inclusive intramural program; a full interscholastic program; and a practical adapted program.

In the community that is not able to afford what it should have, there are lower salaries, larger classes, less equipment and supplies, fewer personnel, and limited intramural and interscholastic programs. Possible sources of revenue are indicated below.

1. Local property taxes. This source of revenue, however, is reaching the breaking point, with many communities unwilling to approve the necessary funds for the constantly rising costs of education. Recently, in one state approximately 45% of all referendums pertaining to the construction of new buildings or the addition or renovation of old ones were defeated during one year.

2. Other local taxes. Sales or other nuisance taxes are being used or considered in many communities. Opposition is so great that it is obvious that other sources must be found.

3. State aid. State aid as a reliable source has also reached a breaking point and can certainly not be expected to offer much help to local communities under present tax structures.

4. Federal aid. Dr. Conant sees only two possible solutions: massive federal aid or a radical revision in state and federal tax structures. The question of federal aid has often been pushed aside by claims that federal aid would mean federal control. A former senator from Oregon contended that federal aid must be forthcoming. In answer to those who contend that this will mean control, he notes the following facts about federal expenditures that did not lead to federal intervention: (a) federal aid through Works Progress Administration for 6,687 elementary schools and secondary schools, (b) construction of 5,900 schools and modernization of 33,000 others under Works Progress Administration, and (c) the millions of dollars given states for land-grant colleges under the Morrill Act of 1890.

The problem has no easy solution, but the implications for physical education, as for all education, are monumental. The economy of a community may have particular impact upon the physical education program. In an economically weak situation, the classes are apt to be overcrowded, with far too many students for an effective teaching-learning situation. There may be inadequate locker and shower facilities, as well as inadequate teaching stations both indoors and out. Equipment may be worn or inadequate, and new equipment may be difficult to obtain. In a situation where students may be employed after school, it may be difficult to operate an intramural program. Lack of staff may dictate that physical education personnel assume a variety of nonteaching duties, such as lunch hour supervision, and study hall and bus duty. In a community where the schools enjoy strong economic support, the reverse will be true in proportion to economic standing in relation to school expenditures.

Religious groups

Fifty to one hundred years ago, religious groups had a great and direct influence upon the administration of a community's affairs, including the program in the schools. In recent years the separation of church and state has been more faithfully followed, to a point where the influence of religious groups is now much less and more indirect.

The *church school* has grown rapidly. Many children spend part or all of their school life without going to a public school. With conditions as crowded as they are in many public schools, this helps alleviate further overcrowding. Support for public education, however, is understandably less from this group.

Some religious groups frown upon certain activities which a school endorses. This may include social dancing, Saturday or Sunday athletic contests, and family-life courses. The attitude of some religious groups toward social dancing may cause one or more of the students to drop out of the class activity. Where the particular church is large enough, it may mean a complete breakdown of one aspect of the program, even though it is needed and wanted by the other students. The prohibition on participation in athletics on the Sabbath may also affect planning of school activities in some parts of the country. In the realm of family-life or sex education courses, some religious groups have been outspoken opponents of incorporating courses of this kind in school programs.

In order to meet these religious problems, the physical educator must base the program on educationally sound principles. The teacher should be certain that the school administration is supporting the program. If a question arises, he should be prepared to explain his program at a meeting of representatives of the community's churches and to listen carefully for valid criticisms and suggestions.

Politics

The politics of a community affects its schools. In communities where school boards are appointed, selection of board members may be made on the basis of merit and qualifications for the job. In

Fig. 1-6. The economy of a community has an impact on the physical education program. (Walt Whitman High School, South Huntington Schools, New York.)

other instances, appointments are made on the basis of political patronage. Where board members are elected, the entire voting community has a voice in who runs the schools. However, this system may also have drawbacks. Interested candidates who will do a good job run and often win election. However, aspiring politicians often run for the school board and then use their position as a stepping-stone in their careers. The process of education is frequently only a minor consideration to such politically motivated individuals. Further, in a community that favors one political party over another, the candidates of that party, rather than the best man for the job, may be elected.

Not only the school board, but local politicians as well, may have a voice in running the schools of a community. The local press and radio, through editorial comment, reflect local political views in regard to the schools. It is the school board, however, that hires and fires teachers, approves budgets, and decides on new construction. The teacher is ultimately responsible to the school board, which, as a group, is responsible to the community.

Strong support of a school board by the community will be reflected in the physical education program. Qualified staff will be hired, and they will teach in a healthful environment and, if satisfactory, be retained for further service. Budget requests and appropriations are most likely to be honored where the school board receives community support and in turn supports its teachers and their programs. Where the school board is ineffective and inefficient because it is politically maneuvered, all of education suffers.

Climate

Another consideration is the geographical location of the community. Planning must take the following aspects into consideration.

1. Amount of time it will be possible to be out-of-doors. It would be unreasonable to spend large amounts of money in equip-

ping and maintaining an oversized gymnasium, to the detriment of the outdoor facilities, in southern California or Florida, where the amount of time spent out-of-doors will be much greater than that indoors. Conversely, in the northern states more time will be spent inside because of the weather.

2. Activities that will be of interest to local residents. The inclusion of and emphasis on skiing and ice skating in the program in northern states would certainly be understandable, while more emphasis on tennis would be reasonable in Arizona and Texas. This does not exclude ice skating from the program in the South or the Southwest, although facilities would have to be available. The emphasis on winter sports in the South, however, would not approximate that in the northern section of the country.

It is necessary to determine the activities and interests of the community as they relate to the climate and make efficient use of funds in the light of it.

Sociological and cultural backgrounds

The composition of the community has a bearing upon the physical education program. The races or nationalities, wealth or lack of it, educational backgrounds, and ages of the residents are just a few of the sociological and cultural factors that should be considered when planning a program.

The program in a low socioeconomic area should include many opportunities for very active participation as an outlet for aggressive tendencies that may be more apparent in this type of area. In requiring proper gymnasium attire it is important to recognize that some pupils may not have the money to purchase sneakers or gym suits. It may be possible to stockpile uniforms as pupils outgrow them. It is necessary, however, to be tactful when making them available to pupils. It is also important that showers be taken as often as possible because some of the pupils may not have other opportunities to take baths.

Your community residents may be college graduates and fairly well-to-do. The physical education program should make use of the educational interests of these fathers and mothers to encourage support for programs, facilities, special equipment, and supplies. The program may include individual activities such as golf, tennis, and archery, since the students will probably be able to make use of these skills out of school.

The great problem of meeting the needs of children from varied backgrounds presents a challenge to the teacher, in working not only with his or her pupils but with their parents as well. It is therefore important to know the parents of the community. Such a knowledge could come from an analysis of the following items concerning the parents: (1) interest in the parent-teacher association, (2) participation in various organizations that are important in the community (groups such as the League of Women Voters, garden clubs, and Junior League may indicate a higher educational background and socioeconomic status), (3) participation in hobbies and leisure-time activities (golf and tennis clubs and riding stables may indicate a higher socioeconomic area), (4) interest in school sports activities, which may indicate interest and potential support if properly channeled by the physical educator, and (5) the desire to conform (the danger lies in the possibility of conforming to mediocrity).

Differences in taste, attitude, and race or nationality are minimized in the gymnasium and on the athletic field. Breaking down false beliefs, recognizing ability, and giving a feeling of belonging can be easily accomplished in the field of sports. The physical educator can help combat the harmful social and cultural variances within the community by means of a good program.

Attitude toward education

Is the community willing and able to support the schools? How have they voted in recent referendums relating to school expansion or expenditures? Do they regularly cut the school's operating budget? If they have, it is possible that the community is either unable or unwilling to meet desirable educational expenses.

A beginning physical education teacher should be conscious of the handicap of working where the equipment and supplies are old or in short supply, classes are overcrowded, or facilities are inadequate. The amount of relief that can be expected is largely dependent upon the attitude of the members of the community as evidenced by recent trends in voting on school budgets and referendums.

Another aspect worth noting is the degree of acceptance of educational trends approved and used in other communities or sections of the country. For instance, are antiquated strength tests, an excessive amount of formal work such as calisthenics, or heavy apparatus being used? Is the term "physical training" still used? The answers to these questions indicate attitudes of the community and schools that may have a part in the eventual success of the physical education program.

Pressure groups

A pressure group can be defined as an organization or group of people working to achieve a common goal. There are groups or organizations in every community that attempt to bring pressure to bear in order to elect a certain candidate, repair a street, reduce a tax, or perhaps change the physical education program. Examples of pressure groups are a dads' club desiring to sponsor a football league, a church group wanting to eliminate social dancing in the school, and a citizens' group trying to rally support for a school referendum.

Not all pressure groups try to tear down the program. In fact, quite the opposite is true. It is possible that one of your strongest allies in combating the goals of one pressure group will be another group. It is also true that many organizations believe they are helping the physical education program by their actions when in reality they are doing a great disservice to the students. For example, a fraternal organization that gives expensive prizes or awards or sponsors a football league at the elementary school level usually does so out of a desire to be of service to the community and the school. It is only by fostering an understanding of the possible harm that can be caused that the physical educator can effectively combat these influences.

When a physical education teacher is a member of the community, ideas are often discussed informally with him. This provides a good opportunity to encourage, dissuade, or rechannel a group of interested community members. Speaking at meetings, interpreting a good program, and sending home happy, understanding students are probably the best ways to combat undesirable group pressures.

A PICTURE OF ONE COMMUNITY

The following is a description of a community as it was viewed by one of my graduate students. It describes what it is like to teach in the community, the major aspects of community life that play an important role in the teacher's life, and the implications for the performance of physical education duties.

The community is basically a residential area in which industry remains on a very limited scale and is not a major function of community life. The school district is 18 years old, and its growth has paralleled the internal growth of the community. Presently the district includes seven elementary schools (kindergarten to grade 6), two junior high schools (grades 7 to 9) and one senior high school (grades 10 to 12). Plans are being made for an additional elementary school. The schools are all modern, well-designed complexes, and the beginning teacher will find all the necessary educational facilities available, from the simple art supplies to educational television. The community has several recreational parks that are available to students after school and on weekends, but the majority of recreational and physical activity is confined to the school program. The population is almost exclusively middle class, with homes ranging in price from $18,000 to $30,000. A portion of the population commutes daily to the city for employment, while the rest find their jobs in the local area. The average income is approximately $10,000. The community is thus not exceptionally wealthy, but the standard of living is the same throughout the district, and there are very few culturally disadvantaged families in the area.

All denominations of religion are found within the community, the predominant ones being Jewish and Roman Catholic. Religion plays an important role in the physical educator's duties, especially in the area of scheduling after-school activities such as intramural and interscholastic events. Denominations hold religious instruction after school during the week, and parents insist that their children attend the classes. Intramural activities must be held during school hours or after school on days free from religious instruction periods to ensure equal participation for all concerned. Coaches of interscholastic athletics must give consideration to religious obligations when scheduling practice sessions and not penalize athletes who must miss practice to attend a religious meeting. The physical educator must plan his program to allow for religious holidays during the school year, because school is not held in the community on major Jewish and Roman Catholic holidays.

As previously stated, the socioeconomic level of the community is predominantly middle class. The school tax rate is high, and yet the community has always supported school building proposals and teacher salary increases. Teacher salaries are on a par with other districts in the area, and the community consistently approves new and better benefits to improve the working conditions of their teachers.

The socioeconomic level of the community must be considered by the teacher in the performance of his duties. The scheduling of trips and requiring students to purchase certain materials for class must be planned according to what the average family can actually afford. The socioeconomic level of the community enables the majority of students to be available after school for activities, since they are not required to work in order to help support their families. The availability of students for intramural and interscholastic participation has a great bearing on the physical education program.

The students and parents of the community are very much interested in athletic competition, and participation is extensive in all phases of the after-school physical education program. The beginning physical educator must be prepared to undertake work in both the intramural and the interscholastic athletic programs. The community has a well established Little League and church league program that are in constant need of prefessional physical educators, and the beginning teacher might find this a good opportunity for additional experience and employment. The socioeconomic level of the community does not hinder the educational process, and the community is willing to support any program to improve the educational system as the need arises.

The school board of education is understanding and sympathetic to problems of education, and the community shows a high degree of interest in all school board activities. School board members are firm believers in a complete physical education program, and is always supporting the improvement of physical education facilities in the schools. The physical educator can make a valid request for more equipment needed for a specific activity and this equipment will be appropriated if the need is substantiated. The school board works in close conjunction with the individual school's parent-teacher associations. The community PTA's are very active, promoting a good rapport between parents and teachers. Physical education is discussed periodically at PTA meetings, and physical educators play an important role in all meetings because of the introduction of sex education in the community schools. Physical education teachers will teach sex education in the school system, and they are currently involved with presenting the program of instruction to the community PTA's for understanding and approval. The beginning teacher in this community should become involved with and informed about the PTA and school board of education, as they play a major role in his life.

The beginning teacher will find himself involved socially with the community at various times during the school year. Parties, dinner, and dances are prevalent in the community, and parent-teacher socializing is encouraged. Teachers will periodically be asked to speak at community functions, and it is the teacher's professional responsibility to do justice to the profession when these speaking opportunities do arise. Physical educators are involved with a community organization called the Dads Club, which works to assist the school's interscholastic athletic program. The Dads Club gives assistance to the community and to the school's physical education program by raising needed money, holding athletic award dinners, giving out athletic scholarships, and supervising school athletic contests. All physical educators in the district work in close cooperation with the Dads Club, and a beginning teacher will find himself working professionally and socially with this community organization. The social atmosphere of the community is congenial, and it plays an important role in the teacher's life.

The community and the teachers form a solid working relationship that is needed for the success of the overall educational system in the district. The community demands a superior performance by all the teachers, and the community shows a deep admiration and respect for the professional teacher. The beginning teacher must anticipate some minor discrepancies and problems that are inherent in a typical community that is young and expanding. These minor difficulties are all overcome because both the community and the teachers have better education as their goal, and all their energies are devoted to making the community educational system a more rewarding experience for all concerned. The community life plays an important role in the teacher's life, and the beginning teacher must explore this community life to draw implications for his own life, both professional and personal. The teacher is also a very important part of the community, because in this typical community, which is basically residential, the educational system is the single most important portion of community life.

STATE AND NATIONAL INFLUENCE

Education is a state function. The state legislature is responsible for education. Although most states follow similar administrative structures, they differ in details. In every state there is usually a commissioner or superintendent of education as well as a board of education.

State departments of education emphasize cooperative planning. They do not serve merely as law-enforcement agencies. Although most states have the power to change school districts, they prefer to leave as much choice as possible to the local districts; however, they will bring pressure to bear where necessary. They are always ready to provide consultant services to help in the solution of local problems.

Recently, at the request of an eastern city, the state department of education conducted a school survey in that city. The recommendations included in the survey covered many aspects of education. The imminent threat of the withdrawal of state aid was one of the factors that hastened the city's compliance with many of the basic recommendations made in the survey. In the field of physical education the survey resulted in the addition of teachers, an increase in allocation for supplies, and the expediting of plans for reconditioning and enlarging existing physical plants.

A knowledge of the minimum state standards will enable the beginning teacher to determine whether the school has provided the educational essentials. If the recommended standards have not been met, an attempt to make improvements should be made. Since one responsibility of state departments of education is to improve physical education programs, consultants are usually available to local schools and districts for (1) evaluation of program content, (2) assistance in curriculum revision, (3) guidance in problem situations, and (4) assistance in public relations. State department representatives will usually work to find ways of improving the profession, curriculum, standards, and facilities.

Since the Constitution of the United States does not carry any provision for federal education, the state has assumed the responsibility. The state has limited its own action primarily to guidance and the specification of minimum requirements, leaving a major part of the obligation of education in the hands of the local district and thus placing more responsibility on the physical educator to constantly interpret his program.

ALLIED FIELDS

The fields of recreation and health are closely allied to physical education. The positions that are established to handle these responsibilities may or may not be within the department of physical education. It is obvious that cooperation is necessary regardless of the local structure. The city of Norfolk, Virginia, has shown how the objectives of education can better be reached through close cooperation in the fields of health and physical education. Flint, Michigan, has proved extensively the values of cooperation in the fields of recreation and physical education. The accomplishments made through mutual effort can be limitless when a community sets its mind to the task.

Recreation

Before discussing recreation, it is first necessary to define it. Recreation is a leisure-time activity—that is, an activity that is performed during nonworking hours. It is enjoyable and wholesome—something that contributes to one's satisfaction and happiness. It is voluntary—something in which the individual participates because he desires to do so.

There are many types of recreational activities. There are those which challenge the mind and those which challenge the body. There are those which call for cooperative effort and those which involve only the individual. Integrated physical educa-

tion and recreation programs can be of great value to each other in at least the following ways: (1) programming, in which recreation programs are used as a testing ground for skills learned in physical education class; (2) extension of the intramural program; (3) facility construction, in which duplication is avoided by constructing one unit to serve both the school and after-school programs; and (4) economies, in which common use is made of personnel, supplies, and equipment.

There are different means of coordinating physical education and recreation. In one Minnesota city, the administration of community recreation is vested in a board composed of one appointed representative from each city ward, one member-at-large and three ex-officio members representing the school board, park board, and common council. In one California city the superintendent of recreation coordinates and administers the recreation program, and the costs are borne by the board of recreation, the board of education, and the city. In other areas similar plans are in effect, varying in many details except the important one, which is coordination, or cooperation.

Communities that have minimized the duplication of personnel and established a person or board responsible for recreation and physical education list the following values: (1) dollar savings, resulting from lack of duplication of facilities and use of the same personnel; (2) stronger programs, with continuity of school and out-of-school activities; and (3) greater participation, resulting in better understanding of programs and better public relations.

In some communities the recreation board and the school board have no administrative tie, and although they work together on particular activities or problems, they also have their differences, with no ready means of working them out. The importance of cooperation between physical education and recreation programs cannot be overemphasized.

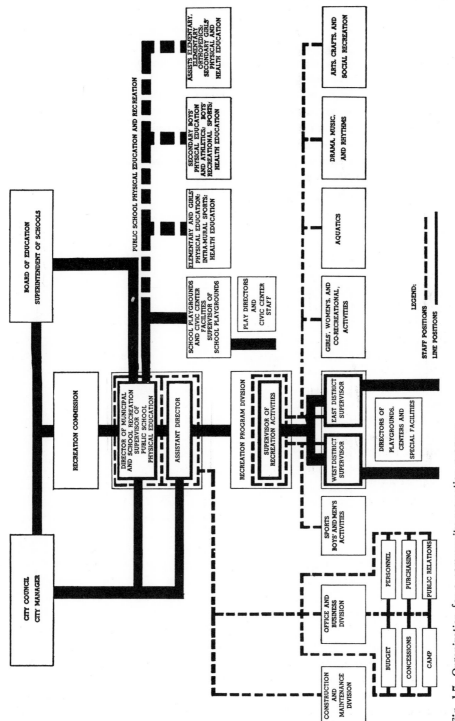

Fig. 1-7. Organization for a community recreation program.

NUMBER OF OCCASIONS OF PARTICIPATION IN OUTDOOR SUMMER RECREATION

1960 COMPARED WITH 1976 AND 2000 (BY MILLIONS)

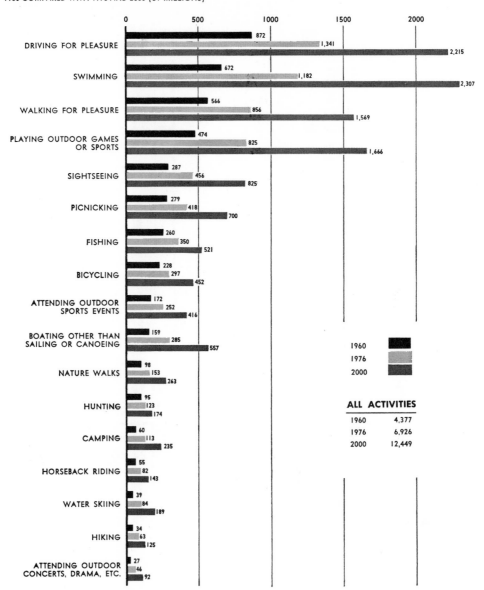

Fig. 1-8. The recreational activities that will be most popular among Americans in the year 2000. (A Report to the President and to the Congress by the Outdoor Recreation Resources Review Commission: Outdoor Recreation in America, Washington, D. C., January, 1962, Superintendent of Documents.)

Health

The fields of health and physical education share much in common, although they are two separate entities. It is only in recent years that the differences have become more commonly recognized. There were times when the job of health was everyone's job—from members of the mathematics department to the custodial staff—and so it was really no one's job. Today, some states have moved so far as to certify people in the field of health educa-

Fig. 1-9. Health education. (San Diego County Schools, San Diego, Calif.)

tion, while other communities have put the responsibility in the hands of the director or supervisor of health and physical education. The degree to which this person is able to coordinate and guide is an important factor in establishing a good program. This is especially true when one realizes that a school health council may include any or all of the following: school principal, physician, dentist, nurse, health educator, teacher of physical education, teachers of biology and home economics, psychologist, members of guidance staff, teacher for the physically handicapped, nutritionist, dental hygienist, custodian, student representatives, parent representatives, and representatives from community health organizations.

In some communities cooperative health services may be organized by a school health coordinating council. In other communities a joint cooperative plan involves the park board, board of education, board of health, and volunteer agencies. School health policies are formulated by the board of education and rendered by the town health department.

Coordination in the fields of health and physical education results in the following: (1) better total education—using coordinated means to reach the goals; (2) better program planning—avoiding duplication and providing more available hands to operate a complete program; (3) minimizing of clerical work in handling special problems, which is more economical and provides readily available records; and (4) more prompt and complete follow-up of remediable defects, through sound and convenient use of physical education and health personnel. Coordination and cooperation are obviously the key to better health and physical education programs.

POINTS TO REMEMBER

1. There are many different types of communities.
2. The nature of each type of community has many implications for physical education.
3. Many community factors—including economic conditions, religious groups, climate,

sociological and cultural backgrounds, attitude toward education, and pressure groups
—affect education and physical education.
4. The state departments of education serve the local community through assistance, guidance, and evaluation.
5. There is a vital need for cooperation between physical education, health, and recreation.

PROBLEMS TO THINK THROUGH

1. What are the advantages to the physical education department in a community where the board of education is fiscally independent? Fiscally dependent?
2. What would you, as the physical educator, do in a community where there is a movement to organize a Pop Warner Football League?
3. What can you, as a physical educator, do to combat the attitude of a community which believes that taxes are too high and that the physical education budget should therefore be cut, since it is not a "solid" subject?
4. What are the implications for physical education in the drive to consolidate or centralize small school districts?

CASE STUDY FOR ANALYSIS

Select a community (where you live or where you attended high school) and indicate the sources of all money used for education. Would it be possible to secure additional money from the same sources? Analyze other potential sources of financial aid and the effects of these new sources upon the taxpayer and the schools.

EXERCISES FOR REVIEW

1. Describe the composition of the board of education in your community and the powers and qualifications of the members.
2. What are the pressure groups in your community that may affect the physical education program?
3. List possible religious factors that could affect your program.
4. What effect does climate have upon the physical education program in the secondary schools?

5. List five facets of a program of physical education that are successfully performed in communities near your own.

REFERENCE

1. Conant, James B.: The American high school today, New York, 1959, McGraw-Hill Book Co., Inc.

SELECTED READINGS

Blount, Nathan S., and Klausmeier, Herbert J.: Teaching in the secondary school, ed. 3, New York, 1968, Harper & Row, Publishers.

Bucher, Charles A.: The administration of school and college health and physical education programs, ed. 4, St. Louis, 1967, The C. V. Mosby Co.

Bucher, Charles A.: Foundations of physical education, ed. 5, St. Louis, 1968, The C. V. Mosby Co.

Callahan, Sterling G.: Successful teaching in secondary schools, Glenview, Ill., 1966, Scott, Foresman & Co.

Conant, James B.: The American high school today, New York, 1959, McGraw-Hill Book Co., Inc.

Culbertson, Jack A., et al.: Trends and issues in the development of a science of administration, Eugene, Oregon, Center for the Advanced Study of Educational Administration, University of Oregon.

Halpin, Andrew W.: Administrative theory in education, New York, 1958, The Macmillan Co.

Morphet, Edgar L., et al.: Educational organization and administration, Englewood Cliffs, N. J., 1967, Prentice-Hall, Inc.

Morris, Van Cleve: Physical Education and the Philosophy of Education, Journal of Health, Physical Education, and Recreation **17:**21, March, 1956.

Mott Foundation: The Mott Foundation Program, Flint, Mich., 1959, Board of Education.

Oliva, Peter F.: The secondary school today, Cleveland, 1967, The World Publishing Co.

Physical fitness elements in recreation—suggestions for community programs, Washington, D. C., 1962, President's Council on Physical Fitness.

Report of the National Conference on School Recreation; School Recreation, Washington, D. C., 1959, American Association for Health, Physical Education, and Recreation.

Simon, Herbert A.: Administrative behavior, New York, 1957, The Free Press.

Thompson, James D., editor: Approaches to organizational design, Pittsburgh, 1966, University of Pittsburgh Press.

chapter 2

The school

The school has the responsibility of educating tomorrow's citizens. Although the goals of education are similar, the means to the end will differ from one school system to another. In this chapter a picture will be presented of the organization and structure of schools, so that the beginning teacher of physical education can be better prepared to take his or her place in the educational system.

STRUCTURE
School district

A school district is that subdivision which is responsible to the state for the administration of public education. Districts vary greatly in size and function. They may be formed on township and city lines, according to elementary or secondary levels, or by other divisions. The trend is away from having many, overlapping, ineffectual districts and toward the use of larger, more effective districts. The National Education Association reports that in the decade from 1948 to 1958 the number of school districts in the United States dropped from nearly 102,000 to 48,043. In recent years the number of school districts has been reduced; at the present time there are approximately 30,000.

Since public education is not mentioned in the Constitution of the federal government, the state has assumed this obligation. Local school districts operate under authority granted by the state. The school district, which is administered by a board of education, is therefore legally responsible to all the people of the state—not to those of the school district only. The fact that a great amount of local freedom is allowed does not alter the legal responsibility. The school board's duties are explained in Chapter 1, on the community. The agents of the board, such as superintendents and principals, are the administrators who concern themselves directly with school problems. Their duties will be discussed in detail in this chapter.

The implications of district reorganization bode well for physical education. As districts become larger, their ability to support and maintain proper physical education plants, personnel, equipment, and supplies should increase—hence, the probability of a more comprehensive program.

School system

The size of the system dictates the number and type of duties its school administrators have. In a small system the superintendent performs many separate functions. In a larger system he is concerned primarily with coordination and public relations, while the many details are handled by assistant or deputy superintendents, department heads, subject supervisors, and principals.

The pattern of school organization at the

elementary and secondary levels is in a period of transition. Some of the present patterns of school organization are as follows:

1. The traditional high school, or 8-4, system. Under this type of organization the four-year high school is preceded by the eight-year elementary school.

2. The combined junior and senior high school, or 6-6 or 7-5, plan. Under this type of organization the junior and senior high schools are combined under one principal.

3. The three-year junior high school, or 6-3-3, system. Under this plan the junior high school is grouped separately under one principal. Although the junior high school usually includes grades 7 to 9, there are exceptions to this type of organization.

4. The four-year high school, or 6-2-4, system. Under this plan the four-year high school is similar to the traditional high

school in organization, and the junior high school consists of two grades.

5. The middle school, or 4-4-4, plan. This type of organization is a new development that retains the old high school idea but groups the early elementary grades together, and has grades 5 to 8 in one unit.

There are many arguments that can be set forth for each plan of school organization. The physical, psychological, and sociological aspects of the school setting and of child growth and development, the need for effective communication between schools, the range of subjects, the facilities provided, and the preparation of teachers are all pertinent to the type of administrative organization selected. One survey of 366 unified school systems with pupil enrollment of 12,000 or more, conducted by the Educational Research Service, showed that 71% of these school systems were or-

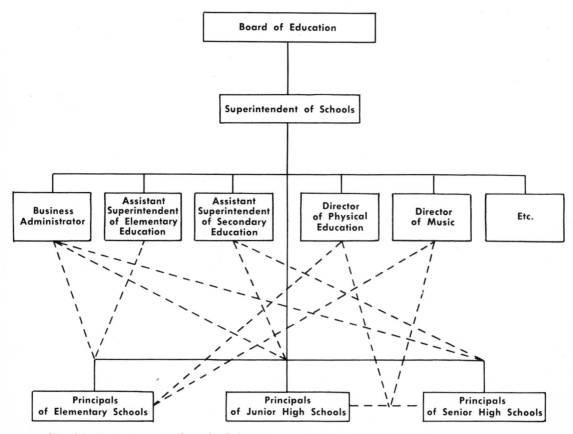

Fig. 2-1. Basic structure of a school district.

ganized on the 6-3-3 plan, 10% on the 8-4 organization, and 6% on a 6-2-4 pattern. Other patterns included 7-5, 6-6, 5-3-4, and 7-2-3.

The school organization pattern is strongly affected by the physical plant facilities. The plan that best meets the needs of a particular system is the one that makes maximum use of the available personnel and facilities in meeting the objectives of education.

Elementary school

In the elementary school the pupil is with one teacher most of each school day. The only change comes when a specialist handles the class for a period one or more times each week. These specialists may include the physical educator, music teacher, science teacher, art instructor, and an occasional resource person. In most elementary schools the principal is the only administrator with whom the child comes in contact.

In very small rural schools one teacher often instructs grades one through six—in the same classroom.

In some elementary schools all physical education is handled by the classroom teacher. In other situations a physical education teacher may meet with the elementary class weekly or biweekly and prepare a program for the classroom teacher to use during the intervening days. In other elementary schools the physical education specialist sees the children two or three times weekly and is able to establish a pattern, which simplifies the job of the classroom teacher in continuing the program.

Middle school

One pattern of organization being considered by many school systems today is the middle school concept. Most simply stated, a middle school is for boys and girls between the elementary and high school

Fig. 2-2. Elementary school program. (Madison Elementary School, Spokane, Wash.)

years—grades, 6, 7, and 8, and sometimes 5. New York City, for example, which has the nation's largest school system, has decided to eliminate junior high schools, replacing them with middle schools having a grouping by grades 5 to 8 or 6 to 8. The secondary schools have become comprehensive high schools. Other places that have embarked on the middle school pattern are Bridgewater, Massachusetts; Bedford Public Schools in Mount Kisco, New York; Sarasota County, Florida; Saginaw, Michigan; Easton, Connecticut; and Independence, Ohio.

Some of the advantages of the middle school include the opportunity for more departmentalization, better stimulation of students, special teachers and special programs, and better student grouping.

Some of the disadvantages of the middle school include the lack of evidence to support its value, the social adjustment problems occurring when ninth graders are placed with twelfth graders, the possibility that youngsters in the middle school will be pushed too hard academically and socially, and the necessity of altering administrative techniques and procedures.

Secondary school

The junior high school is usually composed of grades seven, eight, and nine, and the senior high school is composed of grades ten, eleven, and twelve.

It is difficult to present a picture of a typical secondary school because of the variety in the size of the schools. They will range from small rural schools with fewer than a hundred pupils to large city schools that house student bodies numbering in the thousands. There are, however, certain *basic factors* that are true regardless of size or location:

1. Secondary education is usually coeducational.
2. Guidance is offered in most schools by specially trained personnel.
3. Extracurricular activities are an important part of the program.

4. Secondary schools are prepared to offer terminal education as well as college preparation.
5. Individual courses of study are prepared for the students.
6. Teachers are specialists in subject areas.

There are many *handicaps in the small high school* that have brought about the present tendency toward centralization and consolidation. Some of them are listed below:

1. Meager curriculum offerings—inability to hire teachers for small groups of gifted children
2. Inadequate equipment—such as library, gymnasium, shops, laboratories, etc.—due to lack of funds for these expensive items
3. Inferior opportunities for social development—small number of children of comparable age and interests
4. Inferior staff—lower pay scale and living conditions, due to lack of funds available[1]

The *larger high schools* are generally able to offer a much more varied curriculum. Many educators have pointed to the necessity of challenging our gifted pupils and bringing along the slower ones. In the large high school the opportunity to meet these and other objectives is more readily present. Dr. Conant,[2] among recommendations in his survey of American high schools, calls attention to these needs:

1. More counseling
2. Individual programs
3. Grouping according to ability
4. Consideration for slow readers
5. Programs for the academically talented
6. Prerequisites for advanced courses
7. An academic honors list
8. A developmental reading program
9. More foreign languages and sciences

The opportunity to meet children's needs is greater in a larger school—one with a graduating class of at least one hundred pupils. In a large school there are usually

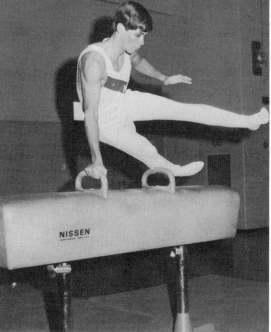

Fig. 2-3. Physical education in the secondary school. (Mount Pleasant Senior High School, Wilmington, Del.)

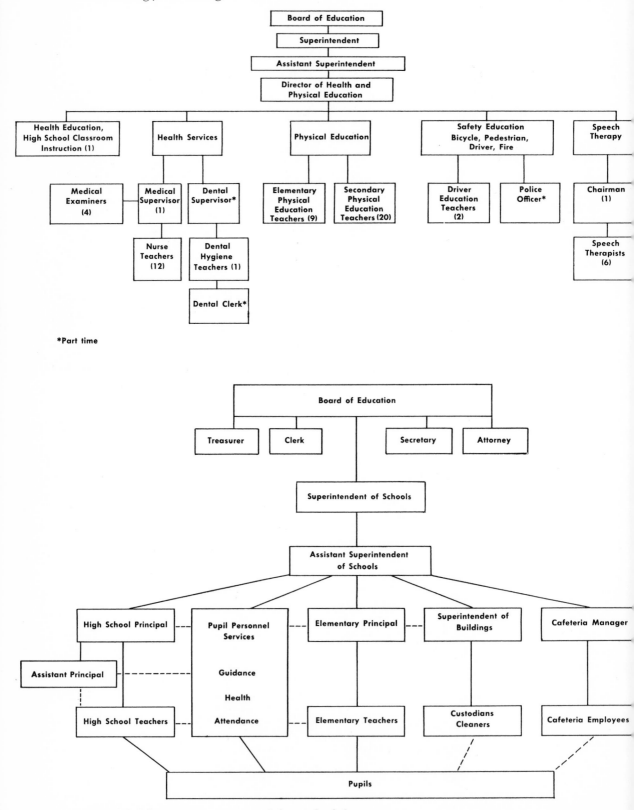

Fig. 2-4. Administrative structure of three school districts.

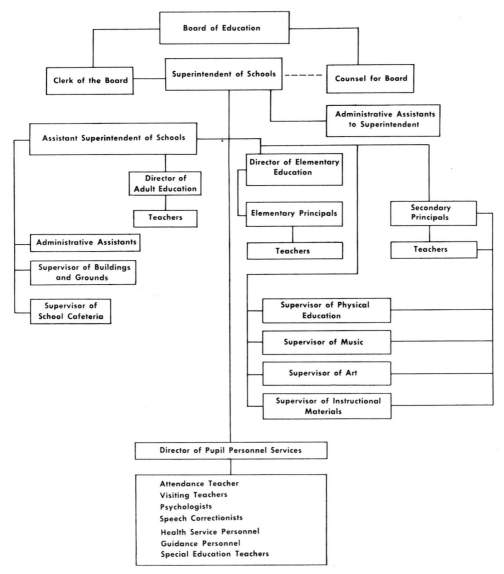

Fig. 2-4, cont'd. For legend see opposite page.

enough gifted pupils to fill a special class. The more experienced and better teachers are attracted to the larger school by better salaries and working conditions. The curriculum is more varied because full-time teachers are hired to teach the slow readers and the languages, sciences, and other needed courses. Guidance personnel are also more readily available.

Specialists almost always handle the physical education program on the secondary level. In some junior high schools the arrangements are similar to the elementary school procedure, but more and more schools are using physical educators to handle the entire program, as they do in senior high schools.

PERSONNEL

Responsibility for the operation of the local schools rests with the board of education. The board hires a professional educator to administer the school system. This practice is about 130 years old. It started when education grew to be more than could be handled by the existing town officials. Now, as then, administrators attempt to solve the ever-present problems of public education.

Superintendent

The chief school official hired to supervise a school system is the superintendent. In a small community he may double as the principal of a high school and may be referred to as the district supervising principal. In larger communities he has an office staff and possibly an assistant to handle his myriad responsibilities. In large cities or towns he has numerous assistants, deputies, or associates to assist in the various duties. (See Fig. 2-1.) Included in the superintendent's charge are these responsibilities:

1. School organization—establishes the school structure for the system
2. Curriculum development—establishes groups to conduct curriculum revisions in all areas
3. Personnel recommendations—recommends to the board those individuals needed to fill vacancies.
4. Administration of all the school plants and facilities—supervises maintenance, construction, and repair of all plants and facilities
5. Budgetary recommendations—submits budget recommendations to the board of education
6. School-community relations—fosters good public relations through public appearances, meetings, and so forth
7. Advice—advises the board regarding policy changes, procedures, and practices, presenting educationally sound, workable suggestions
8. Publicity—keeps the board informed, giving reports on educational trends and notice of special school activities

To assist in these responsibilities and make recommendations to the superintendent there may be any or all of the following individuals as part of the administrative organization in the school system: assist-

ants of secondary education and/or elementary education; business administrators; school health assistants; personnel assistants; public relations assistants; curriculum assistants; and directors of special areas such as art, music, library, industrial arts, physical education, and buildings and maintenance.

It takes dynamic, intelligent leadership to meet today's demands, increased as they are by more pupils, greatly expanded programs, and new plants.

Principal

In each school within any system, the principal is the chief administrator. His duties vary, depending upon the size of the school. In a small building he may teach some classes in addition to his supervisory and administrative responsibilities. In larger schools he not only is relieved of his teaching duties but also has some administrative assistants. They may include an assistant principal, guidance personnel, department heads, deans of girls and/or boys, and a custodial head. (See Fig. 2-5.)

The principal's responsibilities are similar to the superintendent's. They consist of executing the educational policy as outlined by the superintendent, directing the instructional program, promoting harmony and a democratic feeling within the faculty, encouraging and directing good school-community relationships, and supervising the maintenance of the physical plant.

It is usually difficult for a principal to know all the pupils in a large high school, but as a rule the pupil-administrator relationship will be much better when the principal is able to know his pupils personally. Many administrators drop in at a rehearsal, team practice, or sports event not only to observe the teacher but also to let the students know that he is interested in their activities.

The principal works closely, also, with the parents. He plays an important role in the local Parent-Teacher Association and in community affairs. He meets with parents to discuss student problems regarding college, grades, or discipline, or he acts as the intermediary to bring parents and teachers together to discuss these problems. The work of principals is time consuming and tedious.

One of the responsibilities of a principal is to establish a democratic administration. This means that faculty members have an obligation to participate in the formulation of policies. Of course, it is the principal's decision to use or to discard any suggestions, but it is the successful and wise administrator who listens to faculty suggestions—whether in open meetings, through committees, or in personal conferences. Faculty committees are usually appointed by the principal to work with specific problems such as grading, graduation, discipline, and the honor society. The committees present their recommendations to the faculty and the principal, to be used in the formulation of school policies. A knowledge of the formation and the functioning of these committees can be invaluable to

the new teacher. It is also important to know the function and frequency of staff meetings and the channels through which problems, questions, and suggestions may be presented. Knowing how to approach the supervisor can play an important part in the satisfactory adjustment of the beginning teacher.

Department heads

Depending upon the size of a school system, there may be heads of special subject matter areas. In large systems these administrators are necessary because it would be impossible for the superintendent to supervise and direct all the personnel. These heads assist the superintendent by coordinating the work of all the teachers in their special fields.

Similarly, in the larger high schools there are department heads to assist the principal in his duties. These people usually teach a number of classes, but their assignment also includes supervision, organization, and guidance. In smaller schools a

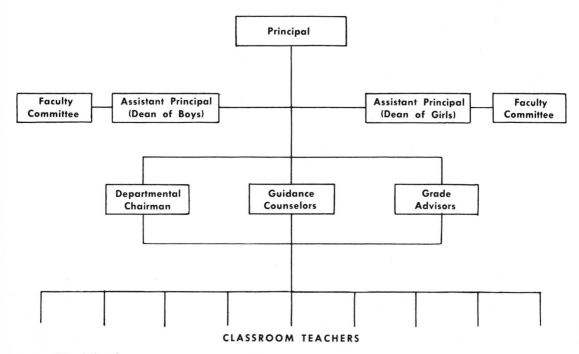

Fig. 2-5. Administrative structure of a secondary school.

department representative is often appointed by the principal to act as a liaison between the administration and the department when it is inconvenient to meet with the faculty as a whole.

In the field of physical education it is the usual practice in the larger school systems to have a director or supervisor who coordinates the work and supervises all the physical education teachers. In the smaller systems the superintendent or an assistant in charge of secondary or elementary education may supervise the physical education teachers.

Teachers

Teachers are hired by the board of education upon recommendation from the superintendent. A recommendation generally comes from a principal or department head.

In small schools a teacher often must teach two subjects, and possibly on two levels. This situation is not usually prevalent in larger schools. Physical education teachers on the secondary level usually administer the program in one school. In some systems they may have to teach in more than one school. On the elementary level physical education teachers, like other elementary teachers of special subjects, often teach in several schools.

It is becoming more common to use specialists in health to handle all health instruction; however, in many systems the physical education teacher still doubles as the health teacher—and possibly as the driver education teacher, as well. Specific problems and details that the new physical education teacher must face are discussed in other chapters.

Custodians

Responsibility for the maintenance of the building rests with the principal. It is customary for a principal to delegate this responsibility to a head custodian. The importance of this aid to good teaching becomes very evident when the temperature is too high or seats are in disrepair and conditions are not satisfactory for good learning. A means of communication from the teacher to the custodians is usually established so that these environmental factors can be quickly controlled and kept at optimum standards.

The school's custodians are often the physical educator's best friends and allies. Where they are treated with respect, the gymnasium and locker and shower rooms will be kept in spotless condition. Frequently, the custodians are also responsible for maintaining the playing fields and for marking lines. If the physical educator takes cognizance of these individuals, his work can be made much easier. Where good relationships exist, the custodians will go out of their way to help repair a piece of equipment, to build a special item, or to mow the field an extra time. Poor teacher-custodian relations can have disastrous effects on the entire physical education program.

Specialists

Once again, the size of a system usually determines how many specialists will be part of the professional staff and just what their duties will be.

Medical staff. A large system may have a full-time physician in charge of the nurses and part-time physicians who assist in the yearly examinations, follow-up of remediable defects, examination of athletic team participants, etc. The medical staff in a smaller system may consist of a nurse who is assisted for a few hours weekly by a local physician.

Some schools authorize the nurse as the only person who can excuse a student from a physical education class for the day. She can assist the physical education department by observing and referring students who need advanced medical or dental treatment. She also has knowledge of those students in need of a modified program, and can act as a liaison between the physical education department and the family physician. The school nurse is an invalu-

Fig. 2-6. The school physician. (San Diego County Schools, San Diego, Calif.)

able resource person as a member of the physical education team.

Supervisory personnel. The range in this area will be from numerous assistants in the large system to a superintendent or supervising principal who is the primary supervisor in a small school.

Curriculum specialists. Responsibility for the curriculum may be placed in the hands of committees of classroom teachers, or it may be delegated to curriculum specialists who organize and supervise all revisions.

Guidance specialists. Professional workers in guidance may include psychologists as well as other guidance personnel. Some students manifest various behavioral and/or emotional problems. The school guidance counselors have dossiers on each student and can guide the physical educator in the most effective way of handling a particular problem. The guidance people are usually backed up by school psychologists and social case workers, who may have, or who can obtain, further helpful information. The physical educator should seek the assistance of these people before disciplining any student too severely. A mishandled problem can create further problems, especially where a chronically disruptive pupil is concerned.

Because of their unique position in the school, the guidance counselors are often in a good position to observe and evaluate the physical education programs. They frequently receive the student's point of view in counseling interviews and can relate nonconfidential comments to the physical educator.

Business administrator. The details of business administration may be assigned either to an individual or to a staff responsible for the maintenance and repair of all plants, as well as the preparation and distribution of all supplies, texts, or equipment.

Cafeteria personnel. Supervision may be handled on an individual basis in each school, or it may be handled through a head dietitian responsible directly to the superintendent.

FACILITIES

A good educational program does not need an ideal plant, nor does an ideal plant guarantee a good program; however, they complement each other. School construction is a major problem in the United States. Since the physical education department is one of the most expensive items in the school, this problem is of particular interest to the physical educator. Multiple use of the physical education areas, such as the gymnasium, playing fields, and pool, undoubtedly engenders more support from the voting public for school construction. This implies the use of the facilities during evenings, weekends, holidays, and summers, in addition to school hours. Some communities that make extensive use of their school plants are Oakland, California; Spokane, Washington; and Norwich, Connecticut. In these areas public reaction to educational expenditures is generally more favorable than the national average. This is undoubtedly true because many of the residents themselves are involved in the use of the school building, have a better understanding of where their money goes and are therefore more inclined to support educational referendums.

Multiple use of facilities is not a panacea for education but has implications for the physical education teacher. Extensive use of facilities and proper interpretation to the public may help alleviate some of the problems relating to plant and facilities.

CURRICULA

Today's secondary schools vary greatly in the type of courses offered and in size and organization. If the trend toward centralization and consolidation of districts continues, it will help most schools to offer comprehensive programs and greatly raise the level of education.

There are three basic curricula offered on the secondary level. Some schools offer all three, which is a good, comprehensive program. Others offer only one or two of these types.

General. The general curriculum is usually a terminal education program. It meets state requirements for graduation and covers the basic courses in English, history, science, mathematics, physical education, art, and music.

College preparatory. This program includes the same courses as above, at an advanced level, plus added units in any or all of the following subjects required for college entrance or used for advanced standing: foreign languages, sciences, mathematics, music, and art.

Vocational education. The vocational curriculum includes basic courses in English, history, practical mathematics, and physical education, as well as specialized courses in such vocational areas as bookkeeping, typing, welding, auto mechanics, food trades, and designing.

In most schools grades seven and eight follow the required courses; grade nine allows for some exploration; and the tenth, eleventh, and twelfth grades allow the student to follow his chosen course of study. This pattern is usually selected through the joint effort of the pupil, parents, and guidance personnel.

In some small schools the choice may be limited; therefore, a student may be forced into a pattern he would not select if given a choice. In some larger cities special schools meet the needs for special courses. In many cities there are schools that concentrate in a particular area, such as science, music and art, machine and metal trades, aviation, and food trades.

The type of course a student follows in high school has no bearing upon the amount of physical education required. It is generally accepted that this instruction is necessary for all students.

KEYS TO SUCCESS IN PHYSICAL EDUCATION

Indicated below are some characteristics of a secondary school that are essential for good education and good physical education.

Administrative philosophy and policies

The administrator of a secondary school may or may not view the physical education program with favor. His feeling of the worth of physical education in his school often has a very direct influence on the program. Where the administration values physical education, it will be easier to schedule homogeneous classes, and physical education will not be the last class to be scheduled. Where the administration is cooperative, the physical education program will be put on a par with academic courses. The administration sets the policies in regard to uniforms, excuses, and the grading system. The teacher must abide by these policies. The administration also assigns extra duties to teachers. Where physical education is given its rightful place in the curriculum, the physical education teacher has a minimum of extra duties during the school day. Lack of a homeroom means time to ready the equipment for the day. Lack of study halls and lunch duty frees the physical education teacher for teaching, and lack of afternoon bus duty allows time for the conduct of a good intramural program. In any case, the physical education program must be conducted within the existing administrative framework.

Use of the democratic process. The principal should use the democratic process in his relations with his staff as well as with the students and allow them a voice through elected representatives.

Faculty relationships. The teachers should work together not only to coordinate subject matter but also to support and coordinate those special events which are so much a part of school life. The efforts of all teachers should be harmonized to culminate successfully a music festival, school dance, general organization membership drive, athletic event, or other school-sponsored project.

Many faculty lounges are no more than gossip and rumor dens. The faculty lunchroom may be almost as bad, if not worse. However, the physical educator must strive to maintain good and cooperative relationships with the rest of the faculty. Social conversation with other faculty members allows for an interchange of ideas. Understandings are developed and concepts formed about other areas of the curriculum. It is also here that the physical educator can articulate the relationship of his program to the rest of the school. The physical educator should always maintain his professional ethics and refuse to discuss confidential information about students or to participate in a discussion that is concerned with gossip about students, other teachers, or the administration.

Teacher-parent relationships. When teacher-parent relationships are good, parents believe that they can approach their child's teacher to discuss any problem, and the teacher believes that he or she can call on parents for assistance when necessary. The relationship is one of mutual respect, providing the basis for a frank discussion between parent and teacher of problems and possible solutions.

Some secondary schools welcome parents on visiting nights, host them at concerts and plays, and have strong parent-teacher associations. Other schools only see the parents when an urgent disciplinary matter is involved.

To know the parents helps the teacher to understand the child. By joining the parent-teacher association and attending its meetings and socials, the teacher is able to meet the parents in a relaxed and informal atmosphere. It is here that the teacher can explain his program and answer any questions the parents may have. The physical education program in a secondary school thrives on good public relations, and they start with the parents of the community.

Teacher-pupil relationships. When teacher-pupil relationships are good, mutual respect exists between pupils and teachers. The teacher is aware of the need and the methods for earning this respect from his or her pupils and, therefore, is the one to foster this feeling. He or she is able to establish rapport with pupils, which greatly contributes to the success of his or her program.

Besides teaching his students, the physical educator must know and guide them, and try to inspire them. In some schools, student respect for teachers is totally lacking, and good discipline is difficult at best to maintain. Safety alone requires that physical education classes be well-disciplined. A new teacher must be especially cognizant of the fact that students will test him. They want to know how he will react to disrespect, horseplay in class, and bad conduct in general. Where the school administration has set strong behavior policies, the teacher will receive backing in maintaining these standards. Where behavior policies are weak, the teacher must set his own high standards and be consistent in applying them.

A martinet never develops close rapport with his students. The good disciplinarian who respects and knows his students as individuals will be able to develop good rapport. Discipline must be tempered with understanding and respect for the student.

Good teacher-student relationships also develop in, and are carried over to, areas outside the classroom. The teacher who at-

Fig. 2-7. Good teacher-pupil relationships are essential to good education. (San Diego City Schools, San Diego, Calif.)

tends football games and concerts and helps to chaperone dances and social affairs has the opportunity to develop a working and companionable relationship with his students. Students will respond in kind to respect, understanding, and interest.

Size. A school should be of sufficient size to economically offer a comprehensive program. It has been stated that there are too many school districts. There should be only half as many, to obtain financial stability and to provide schools of economical size.

PHYSICAL EDUCATION IN THE SCHOOL

In order for beginning teachers to better meet their responsibilities, it is necessary to understand the place of the physical education department in the school and the responsibilities of the personnel in the department.

Structure

The positions of physical educators sometimes have more complications than those of other teachers. As teachers, they will be under the direct supervision of the principal of the school. In many systems, however, there is a director or supervisor of physical education who represents the superintendent of schools in his special area. One would expect this supervisor to have direct control over the members of his department. This is not usually the case. Although the director is responsible for the coordination of all physical education in the system, his or her role is primarily that of an advisor to the principal and superintendent. The relationship of physical education instructors, their director, and the principal is a delicate one and should be understood by the new teacher so that he or she may avoid the obvious pitfalls. The beginning teacher should find out the chain of responsibilities in his system. (See Fig. 2-8.)

Personnel

In the field of physical education, the responsibilities of the personnel will depend upon the size of the system. In a small school one person may handle all the physical education duties from kindergarten through the twelfth grade. In other

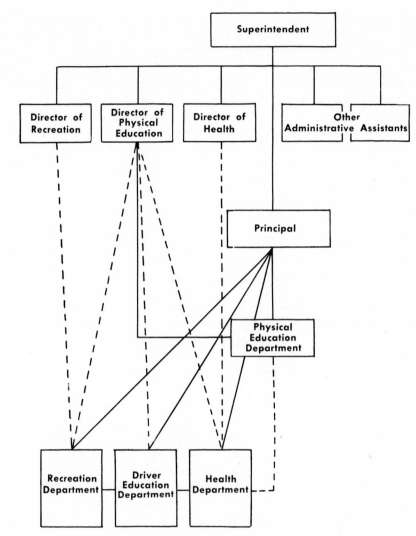

Fig. 2-8. Administrative structure of physical education in a school system.

communities, the responsibilities may be divided by director, chairman, and teachers.

Director or supervisor. There is a trend that recognizes the necessity for one person to oversee and coordinate all physical education in a school system. In at least one state, a physical educator may become certified as a Director of Health, Physical Education, and Recreation. His responsibilities are to help establish policy; see that it is carried out; organize and administer girls' and boys' physical education programs at all levels; check facilities; coordi-

nate programs; supervise teachers; help prepare the budget; organize all athletic programs, including scheduling—as well as arranging for officials, transportation, equipment, and insurance; and assume responsibility for all equipment and supplies. In some communities, these responsibilities are divided between the coach at the high school and an assistant or deputy superintendent.

The director's areas of responsibility include the following duties when he has been charged with the fields of physical education, health, and recreation.

General duties of the director

1. Implement standards established by the state department of education and the local board of education.

2. Interview possible candidates for positions in the special areas and make recommendations for these positions.

3. Work closely with the assistant superintendent in charge of business affairs, the assistant superintendent in charge of instruction, and subject matter and classroom teachers.

4. Coordinate areas of health, physical education, and recreation.

5. Supervise all inside and outside facilities and equipment and supplies concerned with special areas (this responsibility includes maintenance, safety, and replacement operations).

6. Maintain liaison with community groups—for example, hold educational meetings with doctors and dentists to interpret and improve the school health program, schedule school facilities for community groups, and serve on various community committees for youth needs.

7. Prepare periodic reports regarding areas of activity.

8. Coordinate school civil defense activities in some school systems.

9. Serve on the school health council.

Physical education duties of the director

1. Supervise total physical education program (class, adapted, intramurals, extramurals, and varsity interscholastic athletics).

2. Administer schedules, practice and game facilities, insurance, and equipment.

3. Maintain liaison with county, district, and state professional groups.

4. Upgrade program in general.

Health duties of the director

1. Supervise health services, including supervision of school nurse-teachers and dental hygiene teachers, coordination of the work of school physicians, preparation of guides and policies for the program of health services, organization of health projects, and obtaining of proper equipment and supplies.

2. Supervise health science instruction, including supervision of health education programs throughout the school system, preparation of curriculum guides and research studies, and upgrading of the program in general.

3. Promote healthful school living through general supervision of the school plant, attention to psychological aspects of the school program, and making of recommendations for improvement.

Recreation duties of the director

1. Supervise various aspects of recreation program, including, in addition to the school program, summer and vacation playgrounds, teen centers, etc.

2. Obtain, where necessary, facilities, equipment, personnel, and supplies.

3. Plan and administer the recreation program.

Chairman. The chairman of a department is usually appointed by the superintendent of schools. In some schools there is no formal department head; an individual is appointed by the principal to act as representative of the department. In most instances this person is the immediate supervisor of the physical education teachers. Part of his or her responsibilities may be to assist in the evaluation of a new teacher's performance. Such a teacher may teach a full program and receive extra compensation for duties rendered, may be relieved of some or all teaching responsibilities to allow time for administrative duties, or may merely be the department representative and have no supervisory responsibilities. He may be the athletic director, which means that he will arrange for and plan all interscholastic athletics. However, this may or may not be in addition to the responsibilities assigned to him as the department head.

Teachers. The teacher of physical education will handle the physical education classes, assist in curriculum evaluation, make suggestions for the improvement of the program, handle the intramural and interscholastic programs, and assume other obligations to the school that fall to the lot of every teacher.

In a small secondary school, the physical education program may be conducted by only one teacher for the girls, and one for the boys. In such a situation, each teacher must assume total responsibility for all areas of the program, including teaching, care of equipment, budget making, and directing intramural and extramural programs, as well as assuming any other responsibilities that may accrue from being all things to all phases of the job.

In a large secondary school in a large school system, there are frequently several male and several female physical educators. One of these teachers may serve as department chairman, and in turn be responsible to a supervisor of physical educa-

tion who serves the entire school system. In this kind of hierarchy, each teacher is usually asked to assume the responsibility for a particular area, such as equipment maintenance or the ordering of library materials and audiovisual aids. This arrangement fragments the operation of the overall program but frees each teacher to devote more time to teaching. Similarly, department chairmen and city supervisors can devote more time to serving as resource people and to general supervision of the program.

The new physical education teacher. Two of the main responsibilities confronting a new physical education teacher are to be accepted (1) as part of the total school and (2) as an important part of the physical education department.

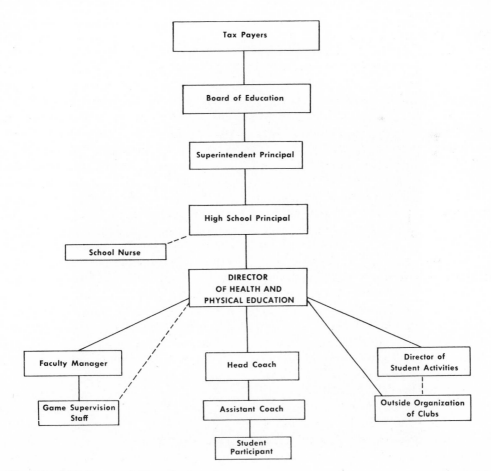

Fig. 2-9. Athletic organization chart.

1. Part of the total school picture. Some teachers look upon the physical education instructor with a certain amount of envy. Whose name is in the paper most often? To whom do almost all the children react favorably? Who is affectionately called "Coach"? Who is usually given the biggest hand when introduced in assembly? Who is most often called upon to assist the administration? Many times it is the physical educator.

One way in which a physical educator may gain the respect of his colleagues is to do his share of the so-called boring, routine jobs that are so much a part of the school day. These may involve distribution of supplies, detention assignments, lunchroom duty, or graduation practice. It is well worth the effort to shoulder one's share of the day's responsibilities.

As a member of a school, the physical educator should show an interest in school activities and projects of all kinds. There is always something to be done, such as helping with the annual concert, the dramatic presentation, or the magazine drive, as well as participating in parent-teacher association meetings, staff meetings, and even faculty social functions. The physical educator should know the teachers in his school so that they will have the opportunity to gain a new respect for and understanding of the physical education department. This could very well lead to a more honest evaluation of the physical education program and to new supporters for its rightful place in the school curriculum.

2. Member of the physical education department. As is true for any new worker, it is necessary for the physical educator to

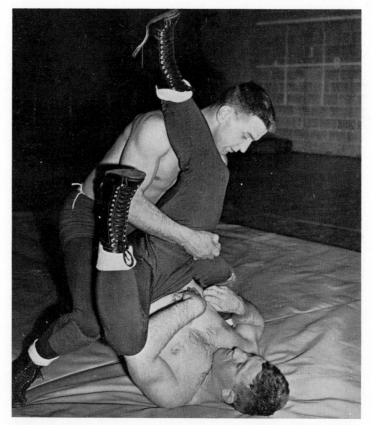

Phil H. Webber, Seattle

Fig. 2-10. Interscholastic athletics.

prove to his peers his capability, flexibility, and sincerity. To do this he must do his job as best he can and respect the experience and seniority of his colleagues. He should not be afraid to speak his mind, but should remember that his colleagues have experienced what he has only studied about. He should consider the whole picture, observe carefully and thoroughly, and have positive, realistic suggestions when discussing any facet of the program that he believes could stand improvement.

Interscholastic athletics

The interscholastic athletic part of the physical education program usually involves much controversy. In the early 1950's the college basketball scandals roared into the headlines; in the late 50's, with attention on "Sputnik," the demands for more science and mathematics were the vogue. During that period the advocates of fewer interscholastic programs were vociferous. Fortunately, there were many voices raised in defense of the need and value of physical education in general and interscholastic sports in particular. The battle still rages. It is especially necessary, therefore, that physical educators use educationally sound principles in the performance of their duties so that they are able to defend their program by action and words at all times.

It is unfortunately true that there are some coaches who go to extremes in the handling of their teams. These men drive their teams unmercifully, attempt to pressure teachers to keep boys eligible, believe they have to win at any cost, and devote too much of their time and energy to their teams—to the detriment of their physical education classes. These people do not help to advance the cause of physical education.

It is important to have an interscholastic sports program in its proper place in the total program. It has great value in that it challenges the athletically gifted child, kindles and keeps aflame the spirit of a student body, and unites the members of a school and gives them a proud feeling of belonging, in addition to having many other worthwhile aspects. It is, however, only one part of a physical education program.

Interpreting physical education*

Too often the physical educator or coach is considered apart from the educational staff. The faculty is educating the

---

*See Chapter 8.

E. F. Marten, Seattle

Fig. 2-11. Interscholastic athletics.

child—the physical educator is exercising him.

The challenge of this attitude must be met by the physical educator. He must have a sound philosophy of education and an understanding of the place of physical education in the development and growth of the child. He must be exemplary in the performance of his duties. He should not be afraid to speak his mind at faculty gatherings; in fact, other faculty members should show that they are aware of and interested in the total education of the child. This interpreting of physical education must be directed not only to faculty members but to the community as a whole.

The physical educator has many means of interpreting the program at his disposal. Speaking at meetings of the Parent-Teacher Association, Rotary, Elks, Masons, Kiwanis, and other clubs is an accepted and effective method of presentation. Physical education demonstrations, sports nights, and athletic contests can also afford good publicity.

The best selling point, however, is the student in the physical education class. If pupils understand why they spend hours on the playground or in the gymnasium, their reactions and comments at home are the best means of interpreting the program to parents. In order to accomplish this, however, students must receive more than a chance to play ball. There must be an understanding of the accumulated values of a well-rounded program. Students, then, can be the physical educator's best salesmen. If they are educated well, the opportunity to do an even better job will generally be forthcoming because of increased school and community support.

POINTS TO REMEMBER

1. The structure of a school district.
2. The personnel involved in education.
3. The types and characteristics of secondary schools.
4. The place of the physical education department in the total school picture.
5. The new physical education teacher as a member of the department and the school.
6. The problems inherent in a poorly conceived philosophy of interscholastic sports.
7. The means of interpreting physical education to fellow teachers.
8. The means of interpreting physical education to the public.

PROBLEMS TO THINK THROUGH

1. What are the values of having a department chairman? How large should a department be to have a chairman?
2. What are some of the considerations that face a new teacher?
3. How may a coach avoid alienating members of the school faculty?
4. What are the advantages of a secondary school that has a graduating class of 100 pupils?
5. What value would a director or supervisor of physical education be to a school system?

CASE STUDY FOR ANALYSIS

Every teacher is responsible to his or her principal. Many physical education teachers are also supervised by a department chairman and/or a director or supervisor of physical education who represents the superintendent of schools. Analyze the chain of responsibility of all physical education teachers in a school system containing one senior high school, one junior high school, and four elementary schools. Consider possible friction points between the supervisory personnel. How can physical education teachers avoid difficulty in their relationships with their supervisors?

EXERCISES FOR REVIEW

1. What are the responsibilities of the superintendent of schools regarding physical education?
2. How may the physical education teacher best interpret his program to the general public?
3. To whom may the new physical education teacher turn for help and guidance? Indicate the specific areas needing assistance and the individuals who may be of greatest value.
4. Prepare a speech that you could use to interpret physical education to a parent-teacher association, men's club, or sports night dinner.

REFERENCES

1. Douglass, Harl, and Grieder, Calvin: American public education, New York, 1948, The Ronald Press Co.
2. Conant, James B.: The American high school today, New York, 1959, McGraw-Hill Book Co., Inc.

SELECTED READINGS

Alberty, Harold B., and Alberty, Elsie J.: Reorganizing the high school curriculum, ed. 3, New York, 1962, The Macmillan Co.

American Association of School Administrators: Staff Relations in School Administration, 33rd yearbook, Washington, D. C., 1955, The Association.

Blount, Nathan S., and Klausmeir, Herbert J.: Teaching in the secondary school, ed. 3, New York, 1968, Harper & Row, Publishers.

Bucher, Charles A.: The administration of school and college health and physical education programs, ed. 4, St. Louis, 1967, The C. V. Mosby Co.

Bucher, Charles A.: Foundations of physical education, ed. 5, St. Louis, 1968, The C. V. Mosby Co.

Callahan, Sterling G.: Successful teaching in secondary schools, Glenview, Ill., 1966, Scott, Foresman & Co.

Conant, James B.: The American high school today, New York, 1959, McGraw-Hill Book Co., Inc.

Cowell, Charles C., and Hazleton, Helen W.: Curriculum designs in physical education, Englewood Cliffs, N. J., 1955, Prentice-Hall, Inc.

National Association of Secondary-School Principals: Health, physical education, and recreation in the secondary school, Washington, D. C., May, 1960, The Association.

Oliva, Peter F.: The secondary school today, Cleveland, 1967, The World Publishing Co.

Patterson, Franklin: High schools for a free society, Glencoe, Ill., 1960, The Free Press.

The student
in the
secondary school

Teachers in today's secondary schools face student populations quite different from those found many years ago. Both teen-agers and their environments have undergone extensive changes that need to be understood because of their implications for teaching.

Approximately a hundred years ago the Bureau of the Census found that only two out of every one hundred persons 17 years of age graduated from high school. By the mid-1960's seventy-two persons out of one hundred were graduating. This difference acquires even greater magnitude when it is realized that a century ago only 815,000 people were included in this 17-year-old category, while in this decade the Bureau estimates that there are 3,670,000 17-year-olds.[1] As populations increase, so do school enrollments, thereby making the teen-agers of today compete against far greater numbers and struggle under more complex pressures than ever before.

National attention is being focused on this adolescent struggle for existence, and it is this increased interest in the teen-ager which has brought about further changes in his environment, other than the population increase. For example, the Children's

Bureau in Washington, D. C., recently formed an Ad Hoc Committee on Cooperative Planning for Youth, whose chief function is to consider the variety of problems and conditions facing today's youth. This group of experts have discussed teen-age living in both rural and urban communities, and some of their suggestions will undoubtedly bring about educational improvements.[2]

In New York a research institute is currently studying adolescents in terms of their buying power, for teen-agers have become a lucrative economic market, and their trade is avidly sought by manufacturers. Teen-agers respond by lavishly spending their considerable allowances on cosmetics, bizarre clothing, and jewelry. They are spending approximately thirty billion dollars per year at the present time.[3]

Another interesting project has been initiated by the United States Office of Education, entitled Project Public Information, wherein students in several communities are evaluating their own secondary school curricula to suggest changes. Results of this study should be very interesting to all educators.[4]

From these few examples it may be seen

Fig. 3-1. The secondary school student. (Guymon Junior High School, Guymon, Okla.)

that today's student is being studied while he studies, and is being influenced while he himself tries to exert influence. The student has achieved a unique importance in the structure of education, and it is this individual which the teacher must try to understand. The forces and pressures being exerted upon the adolescent while he is undergoing an important phase of personal growth and development all combine to make this a very difficult period of adjustment, and the teacher must try to assist the student in every way possible.

What should a teacher expect to find in a secondary school population?

In a school of 500 students a teacher should be prepared to find 500 different individuals, each one advancing through various stages of the adolescent process, and each one at a different level of development. While over 50% of the students may be college-bound, others require education to fit them immediately for life.

Secondary-school students will have a variety of cultural backgrounds and bring with them a vast assortment of needs, fears, hopes, abilities, and problems. Those individuals who require special attention—the mentally retarded, the culturally disadvantaged, and the physically handicapped—must be identified in order that programs may be tailored to meet their needs. At the present time the federal government is spending increased sums of money on special education programs for these individu-

als. Yet less than one half of the five million handicapped persons are receiving the special programs they require. Many of these students are still enrolled in public secondary schools. Physical educators have a very real responsibility for providing these students with an opportunity to develop their physical capacities equal to the opportunity provided for regular students. This may be done through the adapted program of physical education or through assignments within the regular class program. The individualization of teaching can best accomplish the goals.*

What is the role of the school?

The school must identify and recognize the individual nature of each student. It must strive to help all secondary school

---

*Chapter 14 discusses the different types of atypical students and the contribution that physical education can make to each.

students to find themselves, for this is the central problem of adolescence. The development of self-esteem and the identification of the self are vital concerns of every teen-ager. Too often schools provide threats (through class distinctions and values and unrealistic standards of behavior) rather than reassurances to students. Too often schools demand conformity rather than independence of thought and action. If the purpose of the school is to develop future worthy citizens, it must start by helping them to feel worthy and competent within themselves.

The physical education program provides excellent opportunities for the development of these needed competencies. The feeling of importance derived from team, group, or squad membership, the feeling of freedom of expression in movement, and the pride in accomplishment when points are scored for a team are all competencies that are natural outcomes of physical education activities. More important, however, is the recognition of the self as defined by a body concept developed through participation in a well-balanced program. Recent research indicates a close relationship be-

SCHOOL — LIKES AND DISLIKES

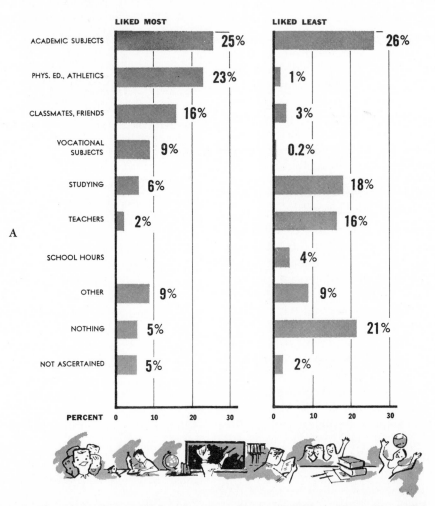

Fig. 3-2, A. The 14- to 18-year-old boy has many likes and dislikes. (From Boys' Clubs of America: Report on the national survey of members aged 14 to 18—needs and interests of adolescent Boys' Club members, New York, 1960.)

tween a body concept and a self concept in terms of the confidence needed to face life. The individual who feels satisfied with his body in terms of its ability to move, to express, to attract, to feel, and to react is more apt to feel satisfied with his total adjustment to life. On the other hand, the unhappy student is frequently one who is dissatisfied with his own body image. Physical educators have a vital responsibility for the development of healthy attitudes toward the body and should therefore provide the necessary experiences through well-planned and well-executed programs.

Understanding the complex changes of adolescence is a large task, both for students and for teachers. The implications for teaching are many because of the relationship between the student's development and his achievements in education. It will be the purpose of this chapter to describe the physical, social, emotional, and intellectual changes that take place in the adolescent and also to indicate the specific implications for teaching physical education which these changes produce.

PHYSICAL DEVELOPMENT

The secondary school student passes through four stages of development generally labeled preadolescence, early adolescence, middle adolescence, and late adolescence. It should be understood that each individual develops according to his own

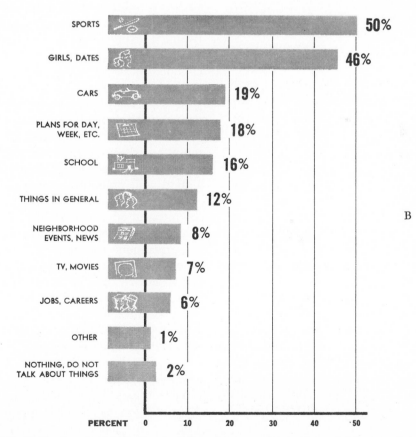

Fig. 3-2, B. Topics of conversation in informal groups (percentages total more than 100% because boys gave more than one response). Sports, girls, and cars are the topics of most of the conversations of adolescent boys. (From Boys' Clubs of America: Report on the national survey of members aged 14 to 18—needs and interests of adolescent Boys' Club members, New York, 1960.)

Table 1. Stages of development*

	Girls	*Boys*
Preadolescence or childhood	11-13	13-15
Early adolescence	13-15	15-17
Middle adolescence	15-18	17-19
Late adolescence	18-21	19-21

*From Cole, Luella: Psychology of adolescence, New York, 1954, Rinehart & Co., Inc., p. 4.

growth pattern, but, in general, the stages may be identified at certain age levels.

The classification of adolescent development offered in Table 1 is a guide to the use of these terms throughout the discussions in this chapter of physical, emotional, social, and intellectual development.

Because of the complexity of adolescent physical development and the differentiation between boys and girls, it is necessary to consider each phase of their growth separately. Height and weight, skeletal changes, and primary and secondary sex changes will be discussed, with the differences in boys and girls explained at each level of development. The implications for physical education will also be included in the discussion.

Height and weight

Probably the most obvious physical changes during adolescence occur in height and weight. These changes can be accounted for by increased hormone production, which in turn causes the sudden growth spurt of the preadolescent and early adolescent period.

Girls 11 to 13 years old become taller than boys of the same ages but then show slower increases in height until late adolescence. A rapid increase in weight also takes place at this time or following the growth in height. Girls are frequently heavier than boys at ages 12 to 14 years, but with the onset of menstruation a leveling-off period occurs.

The sudden growth spurt in boys does not come until approximately two years after that of the girls, and it continues to a

greater extent until around 20 years of age. Boys show an even greater increase in weight and also continue this gain for a longer period than do girls.

These changes have definite implications for the physical education program. First, boys and girls have a real concern for their physical development. Participation and total involvement in physical education activities provides an opportunity for them to forget their own self-concerns and to lose themselves in the enjoyment of the game.

Second, in regard to regular class activities in which height is an important factor, as in volleyball or basketball, it may be advisable to distribute the tallest boys and girls among the squads for the best playing results. Also, the coeducational program at the junior high level, where differences in sizes are most obvious, must be carefully organized to minimize any undue embarrassment experienced by both boys and girls. Dancing activities may be difficult to conduct because the boys are shorter than the girls, whereas relays, games of low organization, badminton, volleyball, and similar activities may have great success. However, it should be noted that in communities where social dancing is established and promoted for this age level, this activity will probably meet with success.

One of the most important factors that the physical education teacher should consider is the personal self-consciousness and embarrassment suffered by teen-agers in regard to their physical development. This is particularly true in physical education classes, where emphasis is placed on physical skills and bodily coordination. Students who are concerned with overweight or underweight conditions frequently seek excuses from class participation, showers, or exercise because of their discomfort, fatigue, and ineptitude. The teacher of physical education has a real opportunity for guidance in such cases by offering suggestions on healthful nutrition and proper exercise. A sincere interest and understanding of individual problems can direct the

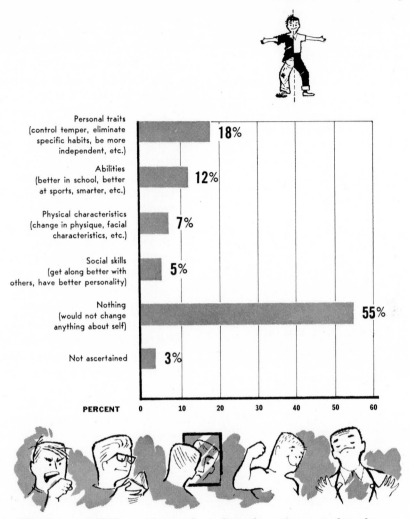

Fig. 3-3. What boys would like to change about themselves. Four out of ten boys would like to change something about themselves. (From Boys' Clubs of America: Report on the national survey of members aged 14 to 18—needs and interests of adolescent Boys' Club members, New York, 1960.)

student's self-interest toward a solution of his problems and motivate him to put forth increased effort.

Skeletal changes

Some of the adolescent increases in height and weight may be attributed to inner changes in the skeletal structures (the bones), which cause differences in body proportions at this time.

The bones of the growing youth change in length and breadth as well as in density (mass). Studies of x-ray films show that a definite relationship may be found be- tween skeletal age and age of puberty. In other words, a child's bony growth con- tinues at approximately the same rate and time as other facets of his development and is complete when the sexual function is mature.

These skeletal changes cause differences in body proportions common in adoles- cence. The long bones of the arms and legs are extended, with accompanying growth of the superimposed muscles. Facial con- tours change, and as the nose lengthens, the hairline changes and the second molars appear.

Several implications for physical education are involved here. With these constant changes occurring in their skeletal framework, adolescents need considerable exercise for their large muscles in order to maintain competent physical skills. The teacher must use caution, however, during strenuous activities and guard against fatigue and strain in this age group. Adolescents also need a broad understanding of the changes taking place in order to offset disappointment and discontent when skills suddenly seem less effective.

In relation to the competitive aspects of the intramural and interscholastic programs, especially among early adolescents, skeletal growth, muscle strain, and fatigue should be considered. Physical educators must, of course, follow state regulations in regard to competition, but in this connection it may be helpful to note what Kuhlen[5] says:

> Excessive exertion, as is apt to occur in highly competitive sports, is probably bad hygiene at any age. It is desirable to play safe, to keep athletic competition at pubescence at a safe level, and organize teams so that no undue strain is placed on one individual and so that the beneficial effects to physical education will accrue to a larger number.*

Primary and secondary sex changes

Besides the sudden spurt in height and weight, the next most obvious adolescent change is in their sex characteristics. There are two levels of changes to be considered here: the primary sex changes, which involve the reproductive organs, and the secondary sex characteristics, which include those traits generally attributed to masculine and feminine appearances. Growth of facial hair on boys and breast development in girls are examples of secondary sex characteristics.

The primary sex change in girls is the development of the organs of reproduction (ovaries and fallopian tubes), which signal their maturation with the onset of the menstrual cycle. This signpost of adult function is of major importance to growing girls and usually occurs between the ages of 12 and 14 years, although it may be earlier or later in a minority of cases.

The implications of this cycle in teaching physical education are many. In the first place it is essential that a healthy attitude toward menstruation be fostered by requiring all students to dress for classes and to participate in some, if not all, the activities. Girls should not be allowed to pamper themselves on these occasions but should learn to lead a regular, normally active life. There are, of course, exceptional cases—girls who are under a doctor's care and who may need rest at this time.

Instruction in proper hygiene and cleanliness, as well as in helpful exercise to relieve tensions, is another area wherein the physical education teacher can do great service to adolescent girls. Special provisions for showering may have to be made, however, to spare them real embarrassment. In schools where individual stall showers and dressing areas are provided there is no problem, but in other instances girls having their menstrual period may need to shower earlier or to substitute a sponge type of bath for a shower at the end of class.

The reproductive organs of boys (penis and testes) do not mature until approximately two years later than girls' reproductive organs, or around the ages of 14 to 16 years. Because growth of the male organs is external in nature, overdevelopment or underdevelopment is often a cause for much self-concern. Teachers should show care and understanding and should foster on the part of all students an attitude of acceptance of individual variations. Locker room antics and teasing about this personal characteristic can develop an unhealthy dislike for physical education and should not be permitted.

The main female secondary sex characteristic that develops in adolescence is the mammary gland. Other minor changes in-

---

*From Kuhlen, Raymond G.: The psychology of adolescent development, New York, 1952, Harper & Brothers, p. 37.

clude growth of pubic and axillary hair, settling of the voice, and broadening of the hips. These changes begin the slow process of development at around 10 years of age and continue long after the menarche.

In boys the changes termed secondary sex characteristics are similar to those of the girls: pubic and axillary hair, plus facial hair, as well as a deepening of the voice, broadening of the shoulders, and development of a waistline. These changes generally appear around the age of 12 years and continue into late adolescence.

The teacher of physical education should recognize the great importance these changes have in the minds of the students and the deep concern they feel about their growth and development. The teacher should help the students to understand the process of growth itself, and he should guide their thinking toward an appreciation of individual differences.

The teacher should also assist students in overcoming some of the problems that usually accompany sex changes. Acne, caused by the increase in glandular activity, and body odors, for example, may both be discussed by the physical education teacher, and hints may be given for improving these conditions. Group instruction on personal cleanliness and hygiene and individual, personal consultations in extreme cases are services that the teacher can perform for adolescents.

Other systemic changes

Other physiological systems undergo further development along with the previously mentioned areas of growth. The circulatory system, which includes the heart and blood vessels, continues to grow steadily during adolescence. This growth may be identified by a normal increase in blood pressures. However, the pulse rate seems to decrease in adolescence, although girls maintain a higher rate of speed than boys.

Respiratory system changes are also evident in adolescence, as seen by measurements of vital capacity. Large increases are registered in both boys and girls from ages 10 to 14 years, with a subsequent slowing down in girls' capacities, while boys' capacities continue to increase.

The digestive organs continue to grow during this time, necessitating more and more daily nourishment and thereby making greater demands on the adolescent body.

The nervous system is more fully developed before adolescence than the other systems, but there is thought to be an increase in the complexity of brain connections, with a subsequent increase in the types of thought processes. These developments continue until late adolescence.

Systemic changes should be considered as part of the total adolescent developmental picture, each having some bearing on the teaching program. In regard to the respiratory and circulatory changes, adolescent students should be watched carefully for signs of fatigue and exhaustion. Their appetites are usually large because of changes in digestion, but improper food habits are generally prevalent, and students need guidance in this respect. The further development of the nervous system, with increases in the types of thought processes, has implications for the knowledge and appreciation which adolescent students can now achieve. The teaching program may therefore be geared to more advanced aspects of strategy, rules, and philosophical ideas.

Basic motor skills

Consideration of the basic motor skills and their development during adolescence is a very important concern of the physical education teacher. The following observations[6] seem to hold true:

1. Balance. Young boys perform better in this area than girls and continue their improvement of this skill in adolescence, while girls show little actual improvement.

2. Accuracy. Girls are usually better

Fig. 3-4. Motor skills—an essential consideration for the physical education teacher. **A,** Straddle vault. **B,** Uneven parallel bar freize. **C,** Yogi handstand in free movement routine. **D,** Wolf vault. **E,** Flank vault. (Colorado Springs Public Schools, Colorado Springs, Colo.)

than boys in this skill throughout adolescent development.

3. Agility. Girls are more agile than boys until around 13 years of age, at which time boys surpass the girls in this respect.

4. Control. Girls perform with more control than boys in early adolescence. Then the boys become superior after the age of 14.

5. Strength. Boys are always superior to girls in strength, but a greater degree of differentiation is seen with their maturity.

Basic motor skills are an essential part of the program in physical education. Therefore, changes in adolescent performance of these skills have definite implications for teaching. For girls emphasis should be placed on continuing improvement in balance, agility, control, and strength. Boys need to work, particularly in the early years, on accuracy, agility, and control, while in later years stress should be placed on their ability to achieve accuracy.

The differences in basic motor skill performances should be kept in mind when different aspects of the program are planned. With coeducational groups, for instance, activities requiring strength would not be chosen because of boys' superiority. When expected athletic performances of students are estimated, these same skill differences and changes should be considered. The teacher should realize that a change in students' interests and satisfactions takes place as their motor skills change and develop. In motivating students, therefore, different techniques will be necessary at each age level.

Health aspects[*]

Although adolescence is sometimes described as one of the healthiest periods of life, a study[7] of illnesses and problems of secondary school students is quite revealing to teachers.

Figures gathered from nineteen clinics across the United States indicate that the most frequent diagnoses of adolescent patients include the following:

Obesity	74%
Acne	63%
Allergy	42%
Seizures	31%
Orthopedic problems	31%

The physical education program should consider what contributions it might make, through its curriculum, to alleviate the number one problem, obesity. At the same time, physical education teachers should realize that injuries, along with upper respiratory infections, are frequent problems for their students, and consider what steps need to be taken to ensure student safety and freedom from exposure to disease.

It is also interesting to note that although the death rate among adolescents is low, accidents cause about 50% of their deaths, and two thirds of these are motor vehicle accidents.[4] These statistics are particularly significant for teachers of driver training courses.

A comparatively new problem in high schools in the larger urban areas across the country involves pregnancy in high school girls. In many instances it is the girl's physical education teacher who first recognizes the symptoms, and therefore she should be aware of the type of help currently available in the schools for such students.

Although the health and vitality of adolescents are usually good, every teacher should be aware of other aspects of student life that may cause difficulties.

The physical education teacher should take advantage of every opportunity to offer guidance in health matters. The need

[*]See also discussion on health goals, p. 89.

for proper diet, rest, and exercise is easily related to athletic performance, and discussions of these factors can be very valuable. Guidance in proper body mechanics and posture, which is also a responsibility of the physical education teacher, is very important to adolescent health. Every program of physical education should contain a unit or series of classes devoted to postural studies for the identification of defects and improvement of postural conditions.

Fitness aspects

It is of utmost importance that physical fitness be an objective of the physical education program in junior and senior high schools. Students undergoing the constant process of change need to pay particular attention to achieving and maintaining a high level of fitness. It is at this stage in their development when a true appreciation of activity and fitness for its own sake is formulated. Fitness will be discussed further in Chapter 15. However, it should be emphasized here that the physical education teacher has a very great responsibility in this regard, for it is in this field alone where physical fitness may be promoted in the school.

The physical development of the adolescent is a very complex process. Its close association with the physical education program makes it essential that teachers understand thoroughly the various aspects of growth and development in order to meet the needs of the adolescent and help him to understand better the process which is taking place.

EMOTIONAL DEVELOPMENT

The emotional development of the adolescent is just as complex as his physical development, but it is not as easily defined or measured because there is no exact pattern of development to follow. To discuss this phase of adolescence it will be necessary to picture briefly the basic human emotions and the adolescent adjustments

Fig. 3-5. Physical fitness is an objective of physical education. (Oconomowoc Senior High School, Oconomowoc, Wis.)

and responses that are distinguishable from those of childhood and adulthood.

Basic human emotions. It must first be realized that the adolescent, like human beings of any age, experiences the three basic emotions: fear, anger, and joy, and their variations. It is in the stimulus exciting an emotion and in the response to a particular situation that the growing adolescent differs from other age groups.

Adolescent responses. Adolescent responses tend to be extreme in nature. Members of this age group are either highly excited or greatly depressed, and rapid changes of mood are typical. For this reason adolescence is sometimes described as a period of heightened emotionality.

Adolescents develop emotionally at the same time that physical, social, and intellectual maturation is taking place. Signs of extreme emotional responsiveness may be seen as early as the preadolescent stage, and the developmental process continues

slowly, with completion in late adolescence. Boys mature approximately two years later than girls in this respect as well as in other phases of development.

The heightened emotional responses of adolescents can best be understood in terms of the changing needs which cause them and which in themselves form a pattern of emotional development. A study of these adolescent needs, therefore, is necessary in order to interpret their relationship to physical education.

Adolescent needs

The emotions of adolescents are aroused in response to the adjustment needs peculiar to their stage of development. They must adjust to a changing physical state, to a heterosexual interest, and to an environment free from parental control.[8] Other adolescent needs that must be satisfied are shared by all human beings. They include security, achievement, affection, adventure, and well-being. Adolescents, however, in satisfying these needs, find methods which are limited to their particular age group and which undergo changes as different stages of development are reached. It is this transition in satisfaction-producing factors which provides a clue to adolescent emotional development and which should be studied individually in respect to each student's needs.

Affection. The early adolescent seeks many friendships with individuals of the same sex, whereas in middle adolescence friendships for the opposite sex begin. These friendships become even stronger in late adolescence, while friends of the same sex continue to hold interest. Also in late adolescence relationships with adults are more friendly as authority relaxes, and eventually friendships with the same sex dwindle in number as they deepen in intensity.

Problems in regard to affection usually arise either from fears centered around the making or losing of friends or from conflicts with them. Still others may stem from a desire for continued affection from parents, which is in conflict with a simultaneous need for independence from them.

All teachers need to understand the basic problems faced by teen-agers in reference to their need for affection. Physical education teachers should provide many socializing situations in which friendships with everyone may be fostered and should further the process of adjustment to the opposite sex through coeducational activities.

Achievement. In early adolescence achievement is realized through success in many and varied interests and hobbies. In middle and late adolescence, as interests center upon fewer, more important areas, achievement is sensed through accomplishments in these areas. These later interests usually stem from the adult role which the adolescent determines is most suitable for him, and success is felt as this ideal approaches reality.

Problems of adolescents generally stem from lack of achievement in the areas of interest at each age level. For example, receiving good grades in school becomes a problem when an interest in a college education is aroused.

Teachers of physical education should realize that many students find satisfaction in superior performance and achievement in their field. For those students who have difficulty performing in physical education, the teacher should try to provide a program varied enough so that in some particular activity or sport a sense of accomplishment may be derived.

Adventure. In early adolescence the variety of interests in many different areas provides much satisfaction of the need for adventure. Striking out on one's own with the new freedom which age permits provides much excitement in middle adolescence, and this same satisfaction is present in late adolescence.

The major problem occurs when satisfaction of this need for adventure is gained from improper experiences, as seen in the juvenile crimes of today.

In physical education this need for excitement and adventure may easily be satisfied through the challenge and thrills of sports and competition. The program should therefore be set up on a broad scale in order to provide satisfaction through after-school activities for as many students as possible.

Security. The early adolescent seeks security in his social world through the gang or crowd. The middle adolescent finds similar satisfaction in smaller groups or cliques, and the late adolescent begins to be satisfied with more adult relationships, having found security within himself.

The main problem that creates insecurity in the adolescent lies within himself. Because of the uncertainties life holds for him and the doubts he has of his own success, the adolescent does not dare to rely upon himself. Instead, he seeks security in whatever else he can find: the gang, the club, the world of books or music, or some other facet of life.

The physical education teacher has a very real responsibility toward the security of students in all activities. All students should feel at ease in the gymnasium, and this goal may be accomplished by giving concrete instructions and establishing definite procedures and regulations so that students will know exactly what is expected of them. This, together with consistency in handling routine procedures, discipline problems, and other everyday occurrences, ensures feelings of security in physical education.

Sense of well-being. A sense of well-being is brought about by adjusting the picture of the self through various mechanisms. Adolescents employ the same methods as all human personalities: rationalization, blame, compensation, and use of excuses, to name a few.

Superiority in physical pursuits provides one outlet for adjusting the self-picture of individuals who have difficulty in academic work. Students who can achieve in some area of physical education naturally augment their sense of well-being or sense of worth. Elementary classroom teachers have said that the key to all learning is making a child feel good about himself in regard to whatever he is trying to do. Surely this same principle applies to students of all ages.

Physical education teachers should be aware of the abnormal extremes to which human personalities may go when overrationalizing or overcompensating. When the teacher recognizes these extreme cases he should make the proper referrals to the school psychologist for study. In this way the teacher does a service to students who need help in regaining their sense of well-being.

Adjustment to physical change. The adjustment to the changing physical self has been discussed previously in this chapter. From the emotional standpoint it should be emphasized again that this is a source of great concern to all adolescents.

Adjustment to heterosexual interest. This discussion will be expanded in the section on social development, but the close relationship of heterosexual interest to emotional responses should be pointed out here. Many adolescent fears and worries center around this particular phase of development, necessitating a real contribution on the part of the physical education program through coeducational activities to relieve tensions.

Freedom from parental control. In adolescence there is a particular need to gain freedom from parental control, yet the conflicts in treatment given adolescents by adults cause many problems.

Fig. 3-6. Adolescents need a sense of well-being. (Walt Whitman High School, South Huntington Schools, New York.)

At home adolescents begin to assume adultlike responsibilities in relation to doing household chores, baby-sitting, holding part-time jobs, and having an increased allowance. At the same time, however, they still are restricted in many things, such as using the family car, dating, and observing curfews. These discrepancies in treatment frequently seem senseless to the adolescent and are difficult to reconcile.

At school this dichotomy—treating adolescents partially as adults and partially as children—continues. Rules and regulations are established about smoking, dances, and conduct, while at the same time the students are allowed to run the school government, athletic organizations, and other school activities.

To help adolescents feel secure in themselves, without depending on parental or other adult controls, the physical education teacher should try to offer many opportunities for the development of self-responsibility, self-discipline, and self-reliance. This may be done through assignment of leadership positions and through class planning of rules and regulations of conduct. Students who are allowed to mutually formulate their standards of behavior better understand the necessity for having them and follow them more willingly.

An understanding of the many adolescent worries and needs helps the physical education teacher make provisions in the program to overcome these emotional difficulties. It is also important that additional problems be avoided in the school situation, and the teacher who understands possible areas of concern, such as security, is better able to provide a healthy teaching situation. Students who are emotionally upset learn little, and they need help in controlling emotional responses. It is the responsibility of teachers to assist them in achieving this goal.

SOCIAL DEVELOPMENT

Social development can be thought of in terms of the adolescent's relationships with friends of his own sex, with friends of the

Fig. 3-7. In early adolescence, the individual finds a place in the social world by becoming part of a large group, which usually consists of age-mates of the same sex. (San Diego County Schools, San Diego, Calif.)

opposite sex, and with adults. In each of these areas different stages of growth are found, appearing later in boys than in girls, and to a different degree. The developmental process itself is based on the adolescent's desire to break away from his parents and to assume selfhood in his social world.

Relationships with his own sex

In early adolescence the individual finds a place in the social world by becoming part of a large group, which usually consists of age-mates of the same sex. This occurs with girls in junior high school, and somewhat later, perhaps in the ninth or tenth grade, with boys. Groupings usually evolve from similar school classes, neighborhoods, and social backgrounds. They provide standards of behavior, such as manner of dress and talk, as well as opportunities to learn how to act with people in different situations.

In middle adolescence the dictates of the peer groups continue to be strong. However, the crowds break down into smaller, more cohesive cliques that promote snobbishness and prejudices not usually found in the larger groupings. With girls these close friendships maintain an extreme importance that continues into the college years, while boys seldom rely as completely on friendships.

There are two important implications for physical education stemming from this phase of adolescent social development. One concerns leadership and the other, clique formations.

Because the development of *leadership* qualities is a fundamental phase of physical education, the program should provide many opportunities for promoting and guiding good leaders. The formation of leaders' clubs in junior and senior high school provides a structured situation wherein leadership qualities may be developed and practiced by many interested members. Learning to select good leaders may also be considered an outcome of physical education, and this factor should

have carry-over value into out-of-school group activities.

Another phase of the physical education program that should have carry-over value in adolescent circles relates to the injurious aspects of *clique formations*. The socializing phases of physical education activities, such as the teamwork entailed, should point out the equalities of all individuals and promote consideration for and cooperation with people of all races and religions. The harmful effects of ostracizing a few people—so frequently found in small-clique formations—should be discussed during class organization, with the hope that desirable extracurricular practices will be followed.

Relationships with opposite sex

In early adolescence, between the ages of 10 and 12 years, boys and girls generally exhibit an antagonistic attitude toward one another.

In middle adolescence, girls at 13 and 14, who are now developing physically, begin to take an active interest in boys, parties, and mixed social functions. Boys, however, remain uninterested in girls. Between 14 and 16 years of age boys return this interest in the opposite sex, and social activities consume a great deal of an adolescent's time and energies. It is usually at this point that pairs begin to develop. By the age of 16 or 17, adolescent adjustments to members of the opposite sex are nearly complete.[6]

The development of an interest in the opposite sex has two important implications in the physical education program: the planning of coeducational activities and the individual class program.

Coeducational activities for the early adolescent in junior high school should provide an opportunity for relaxed socialization, in which no undue embarrassment is felt. At this level boys and girls are at various stages of development, ranging from no interest to too much interest in the opposite sex. Activities should therefore be those already familiar to the students, such as badminton, volleyball, tennis, or recreational games. Knowing the activity helps the adolescent overcome the fear of socializing. Simple mass dancing activities may be successful when well organized and taught, particularly in communities that promote social activities in junior high school.

The senior high school coeducational program, on the other hand, may be instructional as well as recreational, and it should provide learning experiences that will have carryover value when students complete their education. Bowling, golf, and other individual sports may be introduced at this level if facilities permit.

The individual program of physical education must change somewhat along with this changing heterosexual drive. Younger girls love to play all kinds of games, but with physical development comes an increased desire for attractiveness, grace, poise, and balance, rather than extreme physical prowess. This aspect of their interests can and should be served in the teaching program, with dance and fitness activities stressing these goals. The motivation of boys does not change as much as that of girls because of their keen interest in competition and the stress placed on athletic achievements for popularity. This holds true for boys at all age levels, and the physical education teacher should capitalize on this natural motivational device.

Relationships with adults

Preadolescents usually accept adult authority, whereas early adolescents begin to be resentful. The latter try to assert themselves above such authority, except in cases of hero worship. In middle and late adolescence the students become more receptive to adult helpfulness and seek advice from those who represent fields in which they are strongly interested. Then at the end of adolescence adults are met on a more friendly basis, and the socially mature individual finds that he can enjoy casual friendship with everyone.

This change in the adolescent-adult relationship has two important implications for physical education. One concerns class management and the other, the problem of hero worship.

Because the younger adolescent tends to be resentful of adult authority, the physical educator should try to have members of a class manage themselves as much as possible. Through guided group planning the adolescent can set proper standards of behavior for himself and others, and therefore he has no reason to rebel. Students are then motivating themselves and providing self-direction—both of which are educational goals as well as developmental goals of adolescents.

In regard to the second factor, hero worship, it should be pointed out that in physical education, where an informal teacher-pupil relationship is likely to be maintained, hero worship and infatuations easily develop. This can become a serious problem for the student involved, for such strong feelings often become very time-consuming and thought-consuming, to the detriment of the individual. If such an attachment develops, the wise teacher remains objective and tries to be friendly and helpful and at the same time remote in his relationships with the student. Fortunately these infatuations are usually short-lived, and when they are properly handled no personal misunderstandings or ill-feelings result.

The social development of the adolescent is of great importance both to him and to the school. The physical educator should assist in as many ways as possible in this development in all three aspects: relationships with friends of the same sex, with those of the opposite sex, and with adults.

INTELLECTUAL DEVELOPMENT

The adolescent does not go through a great intellectual growth spurt or change as in other phases of development. At this time there seems to be an expansion of powers, however, as well as an increase in capacities. The continuing growth toward intellectual maturity is extremely varied in individuals, with a high degree of this development being reached at any time between the ages of 16 and 25 years.[6] Boys and girls are alike in this respect, and the wide range of ages points out the individualized nature of intellectual growth.

Adolescent intellectual advancement may be discussed in reference to four general areas: memory, concentration, imagination, and reasoning power. The power of memory, which is so strong in childhood, seems to decrease in adolescence. Actually, however, it is the adolescent's lack of interest in making use of his capacity to memorize which causes this decline.

The powers of an adolescent to concentrate increase, particularly in regard to areas of work in which he is greatly interested. The adolescent's ability to use his imagination also increases at this time. Of greatest importance in relation to his schoolwork is the distinct increase in adolescent powers of reasoning and judging. It is this phase of intellectual development which distinguishes his growth away from his childish ideas and permits him to generalize from his experiences to formulate moral values and knowledge, together with a philosophy of life.

The importance of this intellectual development of adolescents to the physical education program lies in its relationship to teaching methods and the influences exerted by the teacher.

In regard to the first point, teaching methods, the teacher must be sure to consider the variation of intellectual abilities when presenting instructions and explanations. As students progress through high school, the material presented in physical education class should require more and more reasoning power and judgment. Thought questions should be included in tests rather than simple true-false or multiple-choice types. Strategy and game concepts should become a part of the teaching program, for adolescents are now able to understand more fully this phase of physical education activities.

The teacher should also make use of teaching methods that promote creative thinking on the part of adolescent students. Units on modern dance obviously foster creative thinking in girls, but sports units for both boys and girls may be constructed to take advantage of improved adolescent powers of imagination and thinking. Students should have an opportunity to work out team plays in basketball, for example, or to develop their own exercise patterns, drill formations, or football plays. The teacher can use the problem-solving technique to accomplish this, asking the students to think out some specific solution to a given game situation.

The other important aspect of adolescent intellectual development that affects the physical education teacher lies in the student-teacher relationship. Because adolescence is the period in which adult attitudes, moral values, and a philosophy of life become formalized, the teacher of physical education should exemplify those ideals which are most suitable to mature living. For example, the physical education teacher should try to promote positive attitudes toward health and physical fitness: a desire to maintain good health, a desire to continue physical pursuits for enjoyment, and an appreciation for the outcomes of physical exercise. As an influence on adolescent moral values, on their concepts of right and wrong, and on their prejudices, which are now taking final shape, the physical education teacher should have clearly defined values that are consistently applied and worthy of imitation by the students. The ideals of respect for all individuals, no matter how different they may be, should be promoted in physical education, together with the real meaning of sportsmanship.

The philosophy of life that shapes an individual's outlook and actions is also formulated during adolescence. Religious doubts and philosophical questioning are increasing concerns of the adolescent. Physical education teachers never know when their actions, thoughts, or beliefs may be idealized or when guidance and advice may be sought. They must therefore be ready to serve and to answer students to the best of their abilities, and must recognize that many values are best learned from example.[9]

POINTS TO REMEMBER

1. The process of adolescent physical development and the stages undergone are different in boys and girls, and each individual follows his own particular growth pattern.
2. The emotional responses of adolescents are different from those of adults because of their varying needs.
3. Social development in adolescence is recognizable by the changes in relationships with friends and adults.
4. Intellectual growth is experienced during adolescence and plays an important part in mature living.
5. The process of growth and development in adolescents has many implications for the physical education program.

PROBLEMS TO THINK THROUGH

1. How can we motivate high school girls in physical activities when social interests are uppermost in their minds?
2. How can we capitalize on the varying interests exhibited in junior high school students?
3. How can we promote and further good social relationships in junior high school students when heterosexual interests develop?
4. How can we develop in students an understanding of the physical growth that takes place during adolescence?
5. How can we develop good habits of cleanliness and proper hygiene techniques during early adolescence?
6. How can we prevent cliques from controlling or damaging class and afterschool activities?
7. How can we capitalize on the heightened interests and abilities of the older high school pupils?
8. How can we further the development of leadership techniques in students not usually given opportunities to demonstrate them?
9. How can we relieve extreme emotional tensions that develop during adolescence?
10. How can we promote attitudes of honesty, fair play, and consideration of others?

CASE STUDY FOR ANALYSIS

Tina was the rather unfortunate nickname given to a very large eighth grade girl, recently moved into a small community. Physical education classes met twice a week for all eighth grade girls, and once a week with boys and girls together. Embarrassment over both her size and her lack of abilities in physical activities forced her to try every conceivable technique to be excused from class, especially the coeducational class, where she was completely ill at ease. How should Tina be motivated to enter into activities in order to derive the benefits she so badly needs?

EXERCISES FOR REVIEW

1. What points of good grooming should be emphasized with junior high school girls? Boys?
2. What steps should be followed in helping a student whose emotional adjustment is questionable, in a school where a nurse is not in daily attendance?
3. How would procedures regarding monthly periods be outlined to a class of seventh grade girls?
4. In what way could proper class and locker room management benefit the ostracized high school boy?
5. What adolescent individuals in the modern world of sports should be singled out as examples of athletic achievement?
6. What advice should be given the adolescent youth, ordinarily proficient in physical activities, who finds himself falling below par?

REFERENCES

1. United States Department of Health, Education, and Welfare: Digest of Educational Statistics 1966, Washington, D. C., 1966, U. S. Government Printing Office.
2. United States Department of Health, Education, and Welfare: Dialogue on adolescence, Washington, D. C., 1967, U. S. Government Printing Office.
3. Rand, Lester: Teen-agers and money, National Education Association Journal **56:**5, 1967.
4. Guernsey, John: Teens sound off, American Education **3:**8, 1967.
5. Kuhlen, Raymond G.: The psychology of adolescent development, New York, 1952, Harper & Brothers.
6. Cole, Luella: Psychology of adolescence, New York, 1954, Rinehart & Co., Inc.
7. Gallagher, J. Roswell: Medical care of the adolescent, ed. 2, New York, 1966, Appleton-Century-Crofts.

8. Malm, Marguerite, and Jamison, Olis G.: Adolescence, New York, 1952, McGraw-Hill Book Co.
9. Garrison, Karl C.: Psychology of adolescence, Englewood Cliffs, N. J., 1956, Prentice-Hall, Inc.

SELECTED READINGS

American Association for Health, Physical Education, and Recreation: The growing years—adolescence, fifth yearbook, Washington, D. C., 1962, The Association.

Carroll, Herbert A.: Mental hygiene, the dynamics of adjustment, Englewood Cliffs, N. J., 1956, Prentice-Hall, Inc.

Cole, Luella: Psychology of adolescence, New York, 1954, Rinehart & Co., Inc.

Frank, Lawrence K., and Frank, Mary: Your adolescent at home and in school, New York, 1956, The Viking Press, Inc.

Friedenberg, Edgar Z.: Coming of age in America, New York, 1965, Random House, Inc.

Friedenberg, Edgar Z.: The vanishing adolescent, Boston, 1959, Beacon Press.

Gallagher, J. Roswell: Medical care of the adolescent, ed. 2, New York, 1966, Appleton-Century-Crofts.

Garrison, Karl C.: Psychology of adolescence, ed. 2, Englewood Cliffs, N. J., 1959, Prentice-Hall, Inc.

Havighurst, Robert J.: Human development and education, New York, 1953, Longmans, Green & Co.

Hurlock, Elizabeth A.: Adolescent development, New York, 1955, McGraw-Hill Book Co.

Kuhlen, Raymond G.: The psychology of adolescent development, New York, 1952, Harper & Brothers.

Malm, Marguerite, and Jamison, Olis G.: Adolescence, New York, 1952, McGraw-Hill Book Co.

Oliva, Peter F., The secondary school today, Cleveland, 1967, The World Publishing Co.

Research Division, National Education Association: Student behavior in secondary schools, 1964, Washington, D. C., 1965, The Association.

Research Division, National Education Association: What teachers think, Washington, D. C., September, 1965, The Association.

Steinhaus, Arthur H.: Toward an understanding of health and physical education, Dubuque, Iowa, 1963, W. C. Brown Co.

United States Department of Health, Education, and Welfare: Dialogue on Adolescence, Washington, D. C., 1967, U. S. Government Printing Office.

United States Department of Health, Education, and Welfare: Digest of Educational Statistics 1966, Washington, D. C., 1966, U. S. Government Printing Office.

BOOKLETS, PAMPHLETS, AND ARTICLES

Berman, Sidney: On middle-class teen-agers, National Education Association Journal **54**:17, Feb., 1965.

Blumenfeld, Warren S., and Remmers, H. H.: Sports preferences of high school students as defined by reported participation, The Research Quarterly **36**:205, May, 1966.

Guernsey, John: Teens sound off, American Education **3**:24, Sept., 1967.

Hannah, John A.: Education for the jet age, The Education Digest **29**:3, Jan., 1964.

Johnson, Harry: Let's teach kids, Journal of Health, Physical Education, and Recreation **37**:65, Sept., 1966.

Lawrence, Trudys: Appraisal of emotional health at the secondary school level, The Research Quarterly **37**: May, 1966.

Murphy, Gardner: What can youth tell us about their potentialities? The Bulletin of the National Association of secondary-school principals, pp. 10-34, May, 1966.

Pearl, Arthur: On disadvantaged teen-agers, National Education Association Journal **54**:19, Feb., 1965.

Rand, Lester: Teen-agers and money, National Education Association Journal **56**:34, May, 1967.

Schmuck, Richard: Concerns of contemporary adolescents, The Bulletin of the National Association of Secondary-School Principals **49**:19, April, 1965.

Strom, Susan: The schools and the pregnant teen-ager, Saturday Review, p. 80, Sept. 16, 1967.

Ulrich, Celeste: The tomorrow mind, Journal of Health, Physical Education, and Recreation **35**:17, Oct., 1964.

United States Department of Health, Education, and Welfare: Dialogue on adolescence, Washington, D. C., 1967, U. S. Government Printing Office.

Zion, Leela C.: Body concept as it relates to self-concept, Research Quarterly **36**:490, Dec., 1965.

The program

Ellensburg Public Schools, Ellensburg, Wash.

4

Developing the goals
of
physical education

Many parents are confused about the real worth of games and sports as part of the school program. Over the years the authors have had the opportunity to discuss physical education with many people. Some of their comments reflect this confusion: "It's exercise done to command." "A matter of arms and legs and good intentions." "Something that entertains the students—a necessary evil." "A good device to keep the kids off the street." "Just an extracurricular activity—a frill, a fad." "It certainly isn't part of the educational program—merely an appendage." "Too much time should not be devoted to it—above all, don't take time away from learning science and mathematics."

If physical education and play do not mean more than these comments indicate, they should be abolished from the school program. After all, there are more than 100,000 leaders getting paid nearly one-half billion dollars annually in this specialized field today. Approximately 60,000,000 school children are being exposed to their programs. Gymnasiums, swimming pools, playgrounds, and recreational facilities are being constructed at a cost of billions of dollars to taxpayers. An up-to-date gymna-

sium costs at least $300,000 and a 75-foot swimming pool $75,000; even the basketball that the kids bounce up and down the floor costs $25. The average gymnasium is one of the most costly parts of the school building and takes up space equivalent to ten to fourteen classrooms. Why pay all these teachers, construct these expensive facilities, and take up valuable space unless they are going to produce results—unless they are an important phase of education?

Parents are demanding the answers to such questions. They have become vitally interested in their children's education. This interest has mushroomed until today there are over 15,000,000 members of parent-teacher associations throughout the country. They want to make sure their children have the benefits of worthwhile educational experiences. They vote money only for those things they consider sound.

As these parents scan the educational programs of their communities, they should become increasingly aware that children do not learn, grow, and develop only during those hours spent at their desks in reading, writing, and working with paper and pencil. There are other

times that may be even more important—
time spent in taking a trip to the zoo, going
to camp, making a doghouse, attending a
dance, and yes, playing on the field, in the
gymnasium, or in the swimming pool.

KNOWLEDGE OF OBJECTIVES—
AN IMPORTANT CONSIDERATION

Upon the shoulders of the teacher of
physical education rests the responsibility
for interpreting to students, their parents,
and the public in general the objectives of
their specialized field. This responsibility
cannot be met unless the teacher understands clearly the goals of education, students, and physical education. Furthermore, all these goals must be compatible
with and must contribute to the educational development of each boy and girl in
the secondary school.

Each student of physical education and
each teacher in the schools should know
the objectives they are trying to reach.
These aims represent the worth of this specialized field, they show the contribution
that can be made to young and old alike,
and they provide a guide for action in our
day-to-day programs.

It is impossible for a teacher of physical
education to do a worthy educational job
unless he or she knows the objectives of the
field and how they fit into the total education picture. Trying to work without such
vital information would be analogous to a
carpenter's trying to build a house without
blueprints to guide him.

THE DEVELOPMENT OF GOALS
FOR ACCOMPLISHMENT IN
THE PHYSICAL EDUCATION
PROGRAM

The physical educator in the secondary
school should use a logical, step-by-step
approach for arriving at the goals he
wishes to accomplish in his program. The
following steps are suggested as a specific
way in which goals may be determined.
Each step is presented in a form of a question, and the questions proceed from
general to specific considerations.

What is the purpose of education?

The physical educator should be aware
of the purposes for which formal institutions of learning exist. This nation has
basic objectives for educational programs
that are well-grounded in democratic ideals. Some of these objectives, discussed
later in this chapter, were formulated by
the Educational Policies Commission.

The physical educator should next determine how physical education can best
help to accomplish the basic goals of education. Furthermore, he should recognize
the place of physical education in the total
sphere of general education. As will be
discussed later, physical education makes a
contribution to the physical, mental, emotional, and social development of the student.

What is the school's philosophy of
education?

Physical education goals should be in
keeping with the philosophy of education
within the school where the physical educator works. Therefore, the physical educator should be familiar with the goals of
education of his secondary school and relate them to his physical education program. A careful study of the school's goals
should be made, and where there is doubt
in regard to the school's philosophy, it
should be clarified through discussions
with the administration. Most schools have
specific goals of accomplishment that have
been put in writing. If not, there should be
some research to identify existing goals.
One school, for example, points out that it
has as its goals the following: "To promote
healthful living by developing physical fitness, emotional stability, and appreciation
of the ideals of good sportsmanship. . . . In
our entire program we consciously support
good physical and mental health habits,
which are specifically taught in physical education, family living. . . . Through
sports and other extracurricular activities
we encourage participation in and enjoyment of rewarding recreational activities."

What are the needs and interests of the students?

The physical education program is for the students, and thus their needs and interests are a vital consideration. These needs and interests may be determined in a number of ways and by using a variety of resources, including school records, observation of students, talks with parents, making inventory of students' interests and suggestions, examining the literature that specifically relates to this subject, studying the professional research, and talking with specialists in the school program, such as the school physician, the nurse, and the guidance counselor. Any program that is developed should be compatible with the needs and interests of the students in a specific school. The procedure of studying students carefully should be a continuous one so that the goals are flexible and meet the changing needs of the students.

Fig. 4-1. The needs and interests of students are important considerations in physical education. (Maui High School, Hamakuapoko-Paia, Hawaii.)

What are the influencing factors relating to such items as facilities, state regulations, and staff?

A basic premise for the development of physical education goals is that they must be established within the framework of factors that are essential for their accomplishment. For example, it would not be a worthwhile goal to indicate that each student should know how to swim, if there is no swimming pool or water available for such instruction, or if a state regulation does not permit the use of a trampolene, it would be foolish to list such an activity as a goal. Individualized instruction in many activities is not possible without adequate staff. In addition, there are other influencing factors, such as climate, local school regulations, equipment available, and administrative philosophy, that must receive the attention of the physical educator in the development of goals.

What does the nature of the community indicate is the type of program that is needed?

The community itself—its social, economic, political, and physical makeup—should play an important role in the development of goals. For example, Americans are becoming aware that a different type of education is needed in the "ghetto" and poverty areas of this country than in suburbia. The program must be geared to the boys and girls who dwell in these neighborhoods. The fact that they are physically, emotionally, socially, and educationally disadvantaged has implications for education. The fact that many of the students are anti-intellectual must be taken into consideration. Ethnic considerations are pertinent.

The physical education program has particular value and can make a valuable contribution to many boys and girls if it is related particularly to the conditions that exist in their communities and to the type of educational program needed to meet their needs and interests.

A consideration of the community is also

important from the standpoint that its support and cooperation are needed if an excellent program of physical education is to be developed.

What is the physical educator's personal philosophy of education and physical education?

After all the previous steps have been taken into careful consideration, the physical educator should give thought to his own personal philosophy of education and physical education. His training, experience, and thought have resulted in a realization of what is valuable, what is educational, and the type of program that will make the greatest contribution to young people. When the first five steps, plus the development of a personal philosophy, are synthesized, they should provide a valid formula which, when implemented, will result in an excellent physical education program.

OBJECTIVES OF GENERAL EDUCATION

The teacher of physical education must be concerned with general educational goals before thinking of the goals of his or her special field. Since physical education is a part of general education, it is important to understand the purposes of education—why schools, teachers, and curricula exist. Physical education is one part of the educational program, as is geography, science, mathematics, foreign languages, or art. Each field of specialization needs to keep its sights on the purposes of general education if it is to justify its rightful place in the schools. If each area of specialization in secondary education established its own objectives irrespective of the overall goals of education, chaos would result, and programs of education would probably conflict and become distorted, depriving the students of a well-balanced educational experience. Therefore, each area of learning must realize that it is a part of the whole, and that the whole is greater than the sum of its parts.

For purposes of this discussion the goals of general education set forth by the Educational Policies Commission[1] may be used. This influential policy-forming group points out that there are four major categories of educational objectives: (1) self-realization, (2) human relationship, (3) economic efficiency, and (4) civic responsibility.

The objectives of self-realization are concerned with helping the individual to become all that he is capable of becoming. For example, education should help each boy and girl to speak, read, and write effectively, to acquire fundamental knowledge and habits concerned with healthful living, and to develop ability to use leisure time in a wholesome manner.

The objectives of human relations are concerned with assisting the individual to fully understand and relate to his function as a human being working cooperatively with other human beings. Thus, education should help to develop such things as an appreciation of the home, friendships, courtesy, the value of human welfare, and the ability to work harmoniously with one's fellowmen.

The objectives of economic efficiency relate to the individual as both a producer and a worker and also as a buyer and a consumer. Therefore, these objectives stress, on the one hand, such things as the importance of good workmanship, selecting one's vocation carefully, occupational adjustment, appreciation, and efficiency and, on the other hand, such things as consumer judgment, buying, and protection.

The objectives of civic responsibility pertain to the function of the individual in a law-abiding society. These goals apply to such things as the citizen's responsibility to his fellowmen, to his country, and to the world; his responsibility for being tolerant, scientific, critical, sympathetic, and cooperative as a member of a free society; and his responsibility for developing an unswerving loyalty to the democratic way of life.

The four categories of objectives outlined by the Educational Policies Commission point to the overall purposes of education. The goals of physical education, therefore, must be compatible with and reinforce these objectives. The education that takes place at the gymnasium, playground, dance studio, swimming pool, and other play facilities can contribute much to the accomplishment of these worthy objectives.

GOALS FOR SECONDARY SCHOOL STUDENTS

The teacher of physical education, in addition to understanding and appreciating the goals of general education, must also be familiar with the goals that are peculiar to boys and girls who are pursuing their secondary school education. General educational goals and physical education objectives must be interpreted and delineated in terms of what the student needs at each stage of development and at each educational level through which he passes. At the secondary level the teacher should be aware of the developmental goals that boys and girls are accomplishing and continually try to utilize the physical education program as a means of helping the young person to accomplish these worthy goals. Some of the developmental goals of the secondary school student include the following:

1. *Understanding of self.* He understands himself physically, mentally, emotionally, and socially—how each aspect of self is reflected in his personality, and how he should strive for integration of the various aspects of self so that he functions harmoniously as a whole.

2. *Feeling of security.* He has security because he has developed skills for such tasks as protecting himself against danger, earning a living, and meeting his physical needs. He has security within himself, and this sense of security embraces such conditions as being loved, possessing self-confidence, and having a feeling of belonging.

3. *Realistic attitude.* He has discovered his abilities and interests, has grown in understanding of himself, and knows his needs and capabilities. He is realistic in his self-appraisal and accepts himself for what he is. He deals with situations and problems with honesty and objectivity.

4. *Self-sufficiency.* He becomes increasingly self-sufficient. He develops a fund of skills and interests that free him from dependency on his family and group. He is increasingly able to make his own decisions, do original thinking, and work out his own plans.

5. *Flexibility.* He profits from the thinking and experiences of others and is tolerant and understanding of the feelings of other people.

6. *Social-mindedness.* He establishes satisfying relationships with boys and girls his own age and with parents and adults, serves as a participating citizen in both school and community, learns about the social environment, gains experience in group living, and learns to respect the rights of others. He conforms to the standards of acceptable behavior.

7. *Balance.* He has a variety of interests —he is not interested in only one activity, such as basketball or reading, but develops a variety of interests that may include sports, drama, music, and history.

8. *Sense of personal worth.* He has self-respect and self-esteem. He has a sense of pride, achievement, mastery, usefulness, and success.

9. *Emotional stability.* He is able to control himself and adjusts to changes in a more mature manner.

10. *Intellectual improvement.* He develops basic mental skills, acquires knowledge, learns about natural and physical environment, acquires better understanding of the scientific approach to learning, grows in ability to listen, read, think, speak, and write, and is motivated by learning.

11. *Value consciousness.* He appreciates what is right and wrong and the importance of striving for excellence, scholarly behavior, and proper ethical conduct.

If the boy or girl in secondary school can achieve these developmental tasks be-

Fig. 4-2. A secondary school student has the developmental goal of seeking balance—she has a variety of interests. (Peabody Demonstration School, George Peabody College for Teachers, Nashville, Tenn.)

Fig. 4-3. Organic development refers to the building of physical power in the student. Students pair up in teams to conduct exercises designed to build strong bodies. (South Camp Drake Junior High School.)

fore completing this phase of education, he or she will have gone a long way toward becoming an educated and well-adjusted person and thus lay the foundations for productive, happy, and healthful living. Physical education can play an important role in helping each young person to be successful in accomplishing these goals.

MAJOR OBJECTIVES OF PHYSICAL EDUCATION

The general objectives of physical education are usually stated in broad terms, with no distinction made for boys or girls. The physical education profession has selected, through its leading authorities, the general objectives of organic development, interpretive development, neuromuscular development, and personal-social adjustment.

Organic development

Organic development refers to the building of physical power through development of the various organic systems of the body. It is concerned with a state of vigorous health and physical fitness. Physical power is built into the individual partially through participation in a program of physical activities. Such participation, if engaged in wisely and adapted to the needs of the individual, results in the ability to sustain adaptive effort, to recover, and to resist fatigue. The value of this objective is that an individual will be more active, have better performance, and be healthier if the organic systems of the body are functioning properly. Physical activity helps these organs to function properly. Through vigorous muscular activity the heart provides better nourishment for the body and the person is able to perform work for a longer period of time with less expenditure of energy. Such a condition is necessary for a vigorous and abundant life. Throughout the entire day a person is continually in need of vitality, strength, endurance, and stamina—both to perform routine tasks and to meet emergencies. A well-planned physical education program can help equip the student with these essential items.

Neuromuscular development

Neuromuscular skills are concerned with proficiency in the performance of physical activities. They include the coordination, rhythm, accuracy, and poise that lead to excellence in executing various

Fig. 4-4. Neuromuscular skills are concerned with proficiency in the performance of physical activities. (Little Rock Public Schools, Little Rock, Ark.)

games, sports, and physical skills. Neuromuscular development is concerned with cutting down waste motion, with performing physical acts in a proficient, graceful, and esthetic manner, and with utilizing as little energy as possible in the process. This has implications for one's work, play, and any other activity requiring physical movement. This objective is sometimes referred to as "motor" development, a name that is derived from the relationship between a nerve or nerve fiber that connects the central nervous system, or a ganglion, and a muscle. As a consequence of the impulse thus transmitted, movement results. The impulse the nerve delivers is known as the motor impulse.

Motor, or neuromuscular, development is very essential to physical education. With increased cortical control of the body there is less waste motion; consequently, coordination and skill are increased. Greater skill and proficiency and fewer errors mean more enjoyment of the activity and a greater desire to engage in it. It is human nature to like to do those things in which one excels. It is very important to the physical education profession, to the individual, and to society in general, to develop many and varied skills in the individual. In this way, the desire and motivation will be present to spend time regularly in activities that will result in a more totally fit population.

Interpretive development

Interpretive development involves knowledge, judgment, and appreciation attendant on performing physical activities. It is concerned with an accumulation of knowledge essential to enriched living and the ability to think and to interpret situations continually encountered in day-to-day living. The accumulation of knowledge takes place when the person gains information concerning the body, the importance of exercise, the need for a well-balanced diet, and the values of good health attitudes and habits.

Interpretive development also includes knowledge of the importance of sanitation, factors in regard to disease prevention, community and school agencies that provide health services, rules and regulations in regard to various games and allied activities, techniques and strategies involved in organized play, human relations, and many other items useful in living a full life. The

Fig. 4-5. Gaining knowledge of out-of-door activities. (San Diego County Schools, San Diego, Calif.)

ability to think and to interpret situations is developed through many experiences in games and sports. These experiences foster a sense of values, alertness, the ability to diagnose a situation under tense conditions, the ability to make a decision quickly and wisely under highly emotional conditions, and the ability to interpret human actions. A body of knowledge is stored away so that it can be called upon at some future time to help in making discriminatory judgments, discerning right from wrong, and distinguishing the logical from the illogical.

Personal-social development

Personal-social development entails adjustment both to self and to others and development of desirable standards of conduct essential to good citizenship. It represents one of the main contributions of physical education to modern society. Through physical activities the individual, under qualified leadership, can be aided in making adjustments. Physical education carries its own drive. Most children and youth do not have to be motivated to engage in many of the activities that are offered. They want to participate as a result of their own free choice and as a result of an inner drive that propels them into action. Under such conditions rules can be established and a framework of conduct set forth, and the individual will conform in order to participate. Good human relations are developed when there is respect for

Table 2. Frequency of physical education objectives from authoritative sources[*]

	Organic development	Interpretive development	Neuromuscular development	Personal-social adjustment
AAHPER	X		X	X
Bookwalters	X	X		X
Brace	X	X	X	X
Brownell-Hagman	X	X	X	X
Bucher	X	X	X	X
Clarke	X			X
Cowell-Hazelton	X	X	X	X
Daniels	X		X	X
Davis-Lawther		X	X	
Duncan-Johnson	X	X	X	X
Evans-Gans	X	X	X	X
Hughes-French	X	X	X	X
Irwin	X	X	X	X
Knapp-Hagman	X	X	X	X
Kozman et al.	X	X	X	X
LaPorte		X	X	X
Larson-Hill	X	X	X	X
LaSalle	X	X	X	X
Mathews	X			X
McCloy	X	X	X	X
Miller-Whitcomb	X	X		X
Nash-Hetherington	X	X	X	X
Neilson-Van Hagen	X	X	X	X
Nixon-Cozens	X		X	X
Oberteuffer	X	X	X	X
O'Keefe-Aldrich	X	X	X	X
Salt et al.	X	X	X	X
Seaton et al.	X	X	X	X
Sharman	X	X	X	
Staley	X			X
Vannier-Fait	X	X	X	X
Voltmer-Esslinger	X	X	X	X
Williams	X		X	X

*From Adams, Miller K.: Principles for determining high school grading procedures in physical education for boys, doctoral thesis, New York University, 1959.

ability, one's desires are subordinated to the will of the group, aid is given to the less-skilled and weaker players, and the realization exists that cooperation is essential to the success of society. Physical education further aids in developing a feeling of belonging, regard for the rules of sportsmanship and fair play, courtesy, sympathy, truthfulness, fairness, honesty, and respect for authority. All are essential to good human relations—one of the most important keys to a peaceful and democratic world.

Adams'[2] research concerning the objectives of physical education has enabled him to indicate the frequency with which a selected list of leaders in physical education endorse these objectives. Table 2 demonstrates the unanimity of opinion with respect to the objectives.

OBJECTIVES IN TERMS OF SCIENTIFIC PRINCIPLES

Principles that support objectives and provide a scientific foundation for them have been set forth by Adams[2] after his research into the thinking of many of the outstanding leaders in the field:

1. Education is a total mind-body relationship involving the whole organism. The concept of "oneness of mind and body" follows the tenets of Gestalt psychology and is generally accepted by the majority of physical education authorities.

2. Physical education is one phase of the total process of education. Physical education has the same goal and aim as education—a well-rounded development and growth for all children and youth in a democratic society. Its immediate and general objectives contribute to the aims of modern education.

3. Physical activity is essential to optimum growth and development. Big-muscle activity contributes to the development of the organic systems. Optimum growth and development are contingent upon this development.

4. Physical education contributes to training for a wise use of leisure time. Many of the activities taught in physical education can become a hobby or interest field for wholesome recreation during leisure. Tennis, golf, swimming, archery, and badminton are a few of the many activities suited to these needs.

5. Physical education offers opportunities for leadership training. No other subject in the curriculum is so rich in opportunities for training in leadership. Nearly every activity in the physical education program calls for student direction. This leadership may be assigned, earned, and rotated among the students.

6. Physical education offers opportunities for self-expression and creativity. Every child needs to express himself; the variety of activities in the physical education program affords many opportunities for creativity and self-expression. The modern dance program in college and high school is an example of creativity through self-expression.

7. Physical education offers opportunities for esthetic and cultural development. Activities in physical education are often a positive source both of esthetic appreciations and of artistic production for the participant. The popularity of sports and athletics in America is in itself an expression of the mores of the people—the indication of a culture of sport-loving millions.

8. Physical education provides opportunities for release and training of the emotions (sportsmanship). The vigorous contact games in physical activity, with their keen competition, present a give-and-take that both releases and trains the emotions.

9. Physical education provides opportunities for character and personality development. Strong ties, loyalty, team spirit, and group effort are much in evidence in team sports. This is a valuable contribution to the development of character and personality. The daily adjustments to teammates and opponents become a laboratory in personal-social adjustment.

10. Physical education offers a wide range of activities for motor skill development. The variety of activities offered in the physical education program presents numerous skill opportunities for pupils of different interests. The skills mastered vary with the student's interest and amount of practice put into the activity.

11. Physical education provides opportunities for the development of health and safety habits. The teacher of physical education instructs the pupils in habits of health and safety—and the games and contests are played under conditions conducive to learning safety practices.

12. Physical education provides opportunities for mental development. The learning of game rules, techniques, and strategies, as well as the judgments necessary to good play in competitive games, require interpretive development.

13. Physical education provides opportunities for the development of the organic systems of the body. Muscular activity develops physical fitness and endurance, which in turn step up the functioning of the vis-

ceral organs. This increased functioning of the visceral organs results in better organic development and better health.

14. Physical education provides for experiences that contribute to the democratic processes. The physical education class is conducted in a manner to allow the pupils to take part in the planning and carrying out of the class activities.

15. Physical education has its basis in the sciences of biology, psychology, and sociology. The program is planned by teachers and administrators who draw upon these sciences for a realistic and effective program.

16. Physical education is based on human needs. Activity is recognized as one of the important human needs. Modern living with its sedentary aspects presents a challenge to physical education.

17. Play is an instinctive urge or drive that can become an asset in the learning process. The dynamic quality of play can be utilized to instill in youngsters proper forms of conduct and behavior.*

*From Adams, Miller K.: Principles for Determining High School Grading Procedures in Physical Education for Boys, doctoral thesis, New York University, 1959.

LEADERSHIP—THE KEY TO ACCOMPLISHMENT OF PROFESSIONAL OBJECTIVES

Leadership is essential in the field of physical education if the goals that have been set for this profession are to be realized. The most elaborate facilities can be provided and the necessary materials can be at hand; but unless there are qualified leaders available, programs will fail. These leaders must have certain general and specific qualifications if they are to do an acceptable piece of work. Leaders will be better able to accomplish physical education objectives if they possess the following qualities:

1. Sound judgment, logical thinking, common sense, and the ability to discriminate right from wrong.

2. Functional use of written and oral English. Since the use of English is so essential in effectively presenting programs

Fig. 4-6. Good leadership is essential to the accomplishment of physical education goals. (Hartsdale Public Schools, Hartsdale, N. Y.)

to the public, this qualification is required. In addition, because physical education leaders are emulated by the thousands of youths who engage in their programs, they must set a good example by using correct English.

3. Acceptable health. Leaders should be free from any physical or mental defects that would prevent successful leadership. Because of the important part a leader plays in shaping the lives of those under his leadership, persons with any health handicap that would adversely affect the consumer of the product should not be a part of this profession. Leaders should be in a state of buoyant, robust health in order that they may carry out their duties regularly and effectively. They should be able to teach by doing and to participate in the activities they recommend to others. Good health is essential if this function is to be performed effectively. Most important, however, the physical education leader should be an example for the profession that stresses the importance of a healthy body.

4. Pleasant personality. Such traits as enthusiasm, friendliness, cheerfulness, industry, cooperation, dependability, self-control, integrity, and likeableness are essential to working with people in a manner that will ensure the success of the programs concerned.

5. Interest in and understanding of human beings. Leaders should be familiar with the needs of the atypical as well as the normal individual. They should be conscious of the interests and capacities of those with whom they will work. The leader should enjoy working with people. He or she should get along well with others, be interested in people, be able to obtain their respect, and be able to adapt to various social settings. Such qualities as patience, loyalty, tactfulness, sympathetic attitude, sincerity, friendliness, tolerance, reliability, and a good temperament are some of the essential attributes to develop if this qualification is to be met.

6. A sincere interest in the work. Leaders should be willing to contribute generously of time and effort to the advancement of the profession. Individuals must believe in what they are doing and conscientiously strive to promote their work so that more people may share its benefits.

7. Skill in many of the activities that constitute the program. Skill is essential in appreciating and demonstrating good performance, instilling confidence, knowing the work that constitutes the profession, and adequately interpreting the program to the public.

8. Technical training. Specialized training is essential for the field of physical education. An understanding of the fundamental sciences and of scientific principles in the areas of philosophy, administration, and methods and materials, in addition to many other areas of knowledge, is necessary to the development of physical educators.

The qualifications that have been listed are essential to one who desires to become a leader. Physical education work has appeal to many, but not all are qualified to become leaders in this endeavor. Only those who meet the essential qualifications should be considered. In the hands of good leadership, methods and materials may be used effectively and wisely.

Physical education leaders often remark that inadequate facilities are preventing them from doing a job, that it is impossible to have a good program without essential indoor and outdoor equipment, and that the program is not recognized because of these deficiencies.

Acres of beautiful green grass, spacious gymnasiums, and special equipment for sports and other physical education activities are very helpful. Other things being equal, they result in programs that better meet the needs and interests of the public than do programs that have poor resources. However, one must strive to do an effective job with what is available. Programs must be built on the status quo while effort is expended to obtain more and better facilities. Many needs can be satisfied by improvising and by obtaining auxiliary playing fields and space to tide over an emergency period. Doing an effective job with what is available is one of the best ways to stimulate good public relations to the point where additional facilities will be provided. The public must recognize the need for the program and how it is helping to build a better community. When the community is able to see how it can be further aided by additional facilities, the response will be greater. This will not be the situation if the leader exhibits apathy, indifference, and lassitude because ample resources are not provided.

There is an increasing need for better qualified leaders in physical education. There must be a stringent selective policy for all preprofessional students, and standards must be established which allow only qualified individuals to become members of the profession. Only in this way will it be possible to adequately meet the needs and interests of the public, obtain their respect and enthusiasm for this work, and realize the potentialities of this great profession.

The fact that many undergraduate students and leaders in physical education do not have sufficient knowledge of the many activities that comprise their programs presents a problem. This applies to any student recently graduated from college whose training did not cover the entire area he has been assigned to teach as well as to the person who has not received formal training in the work being done. Better professional preparation in our colleges and in-service education in the schools will help in solving the problem.

Another problem encountered by many professional leaders is that of large instructional groups. Under these conditions the ratio of leaders to participants is usually very low—a few leaders are responsible for many students. In order to do a good instructional job under such conditions, many important factors cannot be overlooked. There must be advance planning that takes into consideration all the equip-ment, visual aids, and other materials that will be needed. There must be good organization of the class, of materials, and of other essential items. Good teaching methods and proper techniques must be utilized. Safety precautions must be stressed. These items deserve attention even in smaller classes but must have special attention in large groups.

IMPORTANCE OF METHODS AND MATERIALS IN REALIZING PHYSICAL EDUCATION OBJECTIVES

Where do methods and materials fit into the total picture of leadership and teaching of physical education? The goals of physical education are worthy ones and should be accomplished in the most economical, thorough, and beneficial way possible. Since the activities that comprise physical education are the media through which the objectives are to be achieved, they should be taught by utilizing the best methods of organization and presentation that can be compiled. The methods and materials that are used should represent the experience and training of those who have worked with these activities for many years and who, through their training and experience, know the method that is most effective under various situations. The use of such methods and materials will result in the best teaching and learning situations, with consequent interest, acquisition of knowledge and skill, and proper attitudes on the part of the learner-participant. In this way individuals will experience the enriched living which members of this profession know will come from such activities. The consumers of the programs will find that their total fitness for living has increased, their relations with their fellowmen have been improved, their community has benefited, and they have developed their own personal skills and resources for leisure to an extent that was never before realized.

This book shows how activities may be presented with a minimum of equipment. Improvisations, sport and game variations, and teaching aids and materials that provide the best results under existing circumstances are set forth. The material allows for the presentation of activities in situations where limiting factors such as inadequate facilities are present. Also included are various techniques of presenting activities, teaching, and evaluating, as well as other aids that are useful in program development.

POINTS TO REMEMBER

1. An understanding of the goals of physical education.
2. Importance of knowing the objectives of physical education.
3. Scientific principles upon which physical education programs need to be based.
4. The role of the leader in accomplishing the objectives of physical education.
5. Importance of methods and materials in achieving the objectives of physical education.

PROBLEMS TO THINK THROUGH

1. Why is a teacher who does not know the objectives of his or her profession somewhat like a ship without a rudder?
2. Why should the goals of physical education give support to and help accomplish general education goals?

CASE STUDY FOR ANALYSIS

Select a secondary school and study the program of physical education to determine how well this educational system is accomplishing the four major goals of our profession.

EXERCISES FOR REVIEW

1. Read four professional books in the field of physical education and list and discuss the goals of physical education as described by the authors.
2. Categorize the specific values of physical education under each of the four major objectives.

3. What areas of knowledge should a student have in regard to physical education?
4. Describe a physically educated boy and a physically educated girl.
5. Why is leadership so important in the achievement of educational objectives?

REFERENCES

1. Educational Policies Commission: Policies for education in American democracy, Washington, D. C., 1946, National Education Association and American Association of School Administrators.
2. Adams, Miller K.: Principles for determining high school grading procedures in physical education for boys, doctoral thesis, New York University, 1959.

SELECTED READINGS

Blount, Nathan S., and Klausmeier: Teaching in the secondary school, ed. 3, New York, 1968, Harper & Row, Publishers.
Brown, Camille, and Cassidy, Rosalind: Theory in physical education, Philadelphia, 1963, Lea & Febiger.
Bucher, Charles A.: The administration of school and college health and physical education programs, ed. 4, St. Louis, 1967, The C. V. Mosby Co.
Bucher, Charles A.: Foundations of physical education, ed. 5, St. Louis, 1968, The C. V. Mosby Co.
Bucher, Charles A., and Reade, Evelyn: Physical education and health in the elementary school, New York, 1970, The Macmillan Co.
Cowell, Charles C., and Hazelton, Helen W.: Curriculum designs in physical education, Englewood Cliffs, N. J., 1955, Prentice-Hall, Inc.
Cratty, Bryant J.: Social dimensions of physical activity, Englewood Cliffs, N. J., 1967, Prentice-Hall, Inc.
Halsey, Elizabeth: Inquiry and invention in physical education, Philadelphia, 1964, Lea & Febiger.
Hetherington, Clark W.: School program in physical education, New York, 1922, World Book Co.
National Association of Secondary-School Principals: Health, physical education, and recreation in the secondary school, Washington, D. C., May, 1960, The Association.
Report of the President's Commission on National Goals: Goals for Americans, New York, 1960, A Spectrum Book.
Webster, Randolph W.: Philosophy of physical education, Dubuque, Iowa, 1965, Wm. C. Brown Co.

chapter 5

Health goals that can be accomplished through physical education

Physical education has a direct relationship to the health of secondary school boys and girls. The ultimate objective of any health program is to maintain and improve the health of the youngsters in our schools. This refers to all aspects of health, including physical, mental, emotional, and social. It applies to human beings regardless of race, color, economic status, creed, or national origin. The school has the responsibility to see that all students achieve and maintain optimum health, not only from a legal point of view, but also from the standpoint that the educational experience will be much more meaningful if optimum health exists. A child learns easier and better when in a state of good health.

The physical educator will find many teachable moments when it is possible to contribute to the achievement of health goals. The opportunity is provided to impart scientifically accurate information that will contribute to better health habits on the part of students when they ask: "Why will it be necessary to take showers?" "Must we bring clean towels?" "Why must uniforms be clean?" The physical educator is trained in the biological sciences. This foundational science information provides

him with accurate factual information on various health subjects that have a direct bearing on the health of students.

The physical educator can see that the health services of the school and community are understood and utilized by the students in the physical education program, whether they involve emergency care, health appraisal, communicable disease control, or other health measures.

The physical educator should provide an environment that promotes health, growth, and learning. For example, he should cooperate with the custodian in providing safe and sanitary facilities that meet acceptable health standards; in providing proper ventilation, heating, and lighting in the settings for his activities; in seeing that all equipment is in a safe and clean condition; and in providing a proper social and emotional atmosphere for the conduct of his program. He should conduct regular inspections of facilities and equipment, institute rules that will promote safety in various activities, establish procedures to be followed in the event of illness or injury to participants, and provide proper insurance protection.

The physical educator should be cogni-

Fig. 5-1. The physical educator should be cognizant of the health of students. (Ellensburg Public Schools, Ellensburg, Wash.)

zant of the health of students in the conduct of his program, being continually alert to their health practices and encouraging them to improve. He should take an interest in each student's total physical, emotional, social, and mental health.

Physical educators can help in the attainment of several specific objectives which the health program is attempting to accomplish in our schools. They are (1) to provide boys and girls with *health knowledge* that is reliable and based on scientific facts, (2) to help young people develop desirable *health attitudes,* and (3) to stimulate students to develop desirable *health practices.* This chapter outlines some specific ways in which the physical educator may help in the achievement of these worthy objectives.

HEALTH KNOWLEDGE

Physical educators have many opportunities to present and interpret scientific health data for purposes of personal guidance. Such information will help students to recognize health problems and to solve them by utilizing information that is valid and helpful. It also will serve as a basis for the formation of desirable health attitudes.

In today's complex society there are many choices confronting a boy or girl in regard to factors that affect his or her health. A reliable store of knowledge is essential to making sound decisions.

Young people should know such things as how their bodies function, causes of infections, methods of preventing disease, factors that contribute to and maintain health, and the role of the community in the health program. Such knowledge will help boys and girls to live correctly, help them to protect their bodies against harm and infection, and impress upon them the responsibility for their own health and the health of others.

Presentation of facts about health varies with different age groups and educational levels. For young children in the early grades there should be an attempt to provide experiences that will show the importance of living healthfully. Such settings as the cafeteria, lavatory, and medical examination room offer excellent opportunities for such learning. When a boy or girl becomes a secondary school student, the underlying reasons for following certain health practices and ways of living can be presented. Some of the areas of health

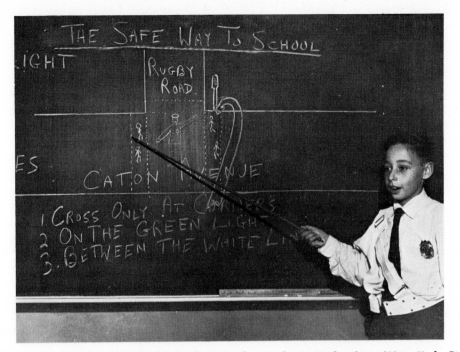

Fig. 5-2. Education should try to develop sound attitudes toward safety. (New York City Schools.)

knowledge that should be understood by students and can be presented by physical educators include nutrition, the need for rest, sleep, exercise, and protection of the body against changing temperature conditions, contagious disease control, the dangers of self-medication, and community resources for health.

The following are a few areas of health knowledge that can be imparted by physical educators at the secondary school level:

1. Safety education as applied to physical education activities
2. Accident prevention as applied to physical education activities
3. Dangers of self-medication
4. How to dress for warmth, comfort, and protection
5. Sanitary practices involved in physical education participation
6. Available community health services
7. Organic systems of the human body
8. Good body mechanics
9. Physical limitation and fatigue
10. Effect of depressants upon the human body
11. Effect of stimulants upon the human body
12. Structures of the human body
13. How to safeguard eyes and vision
14. Physical defects and how to correct or live with them
15. Communicable and noncommunicable diseases and minor health disorders—how to prevent and control
16. Nutrition and weight control
17. Good grooming
18. Importance of an adequate and a balanced use of free time for relaxation and recreation
19. Relationship between exercise and good health
20. Need for physical activity to develop and strengthen the body
21. First aid procedures
22. Amount of sleep and rest a student needs
23. Necessity and importance of the medical examination

24. Physical fitness and health
25. First aid

HEALTH ATTITUDES

Health attitudes refer to the health interests of persons or the motives behind health practices. All the health knowledge that can be accumulated will have little worth unless the student is interested and motivated to apply this knowledge to everyday living. Proper health attitudes, motives, drives, or impulses will cause a boy or girl to seek out scientific knowledge and utilize it as a guide to living. This interest, drive, or motivation must be dynamic to the point where it results in behavior changes.

The physical education program should be directed toward developing those attitudes which will result in optimum health.

Students should have an interest in and be motivated toward possessing a state of buoyant health, feeling fit and strong, being well rested and well fed, having wholesome thoughts free from anger, jealousy, hate, and worry, and possessing adequate physical power to perform life's routine tasks. If they have the right attitudes toward health knowledge, healthful living, and such health services as medical examinations, proper health practices will be followed. Health should not be an end in itself except in cases of severe illness. Health is a means to an end—it aids in achieving noble purposes and living an enriched life.

Another factor that motivates boys and girls to good health is the desire to avoid the pain and disturbances that accompany ill health. They do not like toothaches,

Fig. 5-3. Physical educators can help students to understand how one's body can function best. (Hurst-Euless-Bedford Public Schools, Hurst, Texas.)

headaches, or indigestion because of the pain or distraction involved. However, developing health attitudes in a negative manner, through fear of pain or other disagreeable conditions, is not as desirable as the positive approach to achieving proper health attitudes.

A strong argument for developing proper attitudes or interests centers around the goals the students are trying to achieve in life and the manner in which optimum health is an aid in achieving such goals. This is the strongest incentive or interest that can be developed in the individual. A great artist, an outstanding businessman, or a famed dancer is greatly benefited by good health. It is important that the study, training, hard work, trials, and obstacles encountered be met successfully. Optimum health will aid in the accomplishment of such goals. As Jennings, the biologist, has pointed out, the mind can attend to only one thing at a time. If attention is focused on a headache or an ulcer, it cannot be satisfactorily focused on essential work that has to be done.

Some of the health attitudes which the physical educator can help to develop include an interest in the following:

1. Attaining and maintaining good health
2. Obtaining accurate scientific information concerning health
3. Forming proper nutrition and eating habits
4. Preventing accidents
5. Recognizing the roles of physical activity, sleep, rest, and relaxation in physical fitness
6. Separating health fact from fancy
7. Understanding one's physical limitations
8. Correcting any remediable body defects
9. Developing good health habits
10. Evaluating one's health habits and making needed changes
11. Understanding how one's body can function to utmost capacity
12. Using the body in an efficient, graceful manner in sports activities and daily life
13. Mastering and enjoying a wide range of physical activities
14. Providing for play and large-muscle activities, as well as daily relaxation, in order to realize optimum achievement in physical and mental well-being
15. Knowing how various organic systems of the body work together
16. Acknowledging health responsibility as a member of a school, community, and family
17. Accepting reasonable responsibility in keeping the school, home, and community environment neat and clean
18. Participating in social and play activities with others
19. Being a good sportsman and taking failures and successes in stride
20. Learning to accept physical handicaps of self and others
21. Recognizing the effects of alcohol, narcotics, and tobacco on performance in physical activities

HEALTH PRACTICES

Desirable health practices represent the application to one's routine of living of those habits which are best, according to the most qualified thinking in the field. An individual's health practices will, to a large extent, determine his state of health. Harmful practices or habits, such as failure to obtain proper rest or exercise, overeating, overdrinking, and oversmoking, as well as the failure to observe certain precautions against contracting disease, will often result in poor health.

Knowledge does not necessarily ensure good health practices. An individual may have at his command all the statistics concerning the dangers of speeding on the highway; yet this information is useless unless it is applied. The health of an individual can be affected only as he applies that which is known. At the same time, knowledge will not usually be applied unless an incentive, interest, or attitude exists that impels its application. It is important, therefore, to see the close relationship that exists among health knowledge, health attitudes, and health practices. One contributes to the other.

Listed below are a few health practices with which every physical educator teaching at the secondary school level should be especially concerned:

1. To prevent the spread of infection, insist that each member of an athletic team and/or physical education class have an individual towel and drinking cup, and personal articles of clothing.

2. To prevent the spread of infection (colds, influenza, mumps, measles, etc.), do not allow students to exercise or engage in a strenuous workout while an infection is still resident.

3. Give proper first-aid treatment promptly to floor or mat burns or other abrasions and wounds encountered in physical activity.

4. Have a physician present at all in-terscholastic contests in which the injury hazard is great.

5. Do not allow a player to reenter a game following a severe injury, particularly when unconsciousness or injury to the head or spine has occurred.

6. Work closely with the medical adviser and health department in all matters that are medical in nature, such as treating infected wounds. Honor all excuses from physicians.

7. Maintain a sanitary environment in the locker and shower rooms, gymnasium, swimming pools, and other facilities of the physical education department.

8. Insist on clean clothing, towels, etc. for all types of physical education activities.

9. Discuss with physicians, the medical society, nurses, and other qualified persons the school policy that should govern excuses from physical education for health reasons.

10. Encourage students with colds and other illnesses to remain home.

Fig. 5-4. A physical education class. (Maui High School, Hamakuapoko-Paia, Hawaii.)

11. Make the health and welfare of students the primary considerations in planning all physical education and athletic programs.

12. See that students have adequate medical examinations if they participate in any of the various phases of the physical education program.

13. Conduct an athletic program in which contests are adapted to the physical capacities and other needs of the student.

14. Plan the playing seasons for athletics so that they will be of a reasonable duration, with no post-season contests. Make sure that players are well conditioned before competition is conducted.

15. Do not require girls to participate in the same highly organized and competitive athletic experiences as boys, and omit from their program heavy lifting, jumping from high places, and other activities that require hard landings in a vertical position.

16. Encourage all boys and girls to receive proper sleep, rest, and nutrition and to develop other desirable health practices essential to good physical performance and sound health.

17. Do not include boxing as part of the physical education program.

18. Be qualified in first aid.

19. In planning classes, allow sufficient time to permit change of clothing and showering.

20. Provide an opportunity for each student to participate in physical education class and the intramural sports program.

21. Give appropriate guidance to community groups sponsoring organized competitive athletics.

22. Offer a wide variety of activities based upon students' interests and needs.

23. Group students for participation on the basis of their abilities and needs.

SELECTED METHODS OF TEACHING HEALTH KNOWLEDGE, ATTITUDES, AND PRACTICES

Some methods of teaching health information to students are as follows.

Discussions. The classroom, gymnasium,

athletic field, and other places where students gather offer many desirable moments for presenting and discussing important health information.

Example. A teacher's example is a very powerful method.

Films and other visual aids. Many excellent health films are available from state departments of health, voluntary health agencies, universities, and professional associations.

Reading assignments. There is a considerable amount of health material available, in pamphlet form as well as in book form. The author's high school physical education text, entitled *Physical Education for Life,** contains several chapters on health matters relating to the physical education program. By being selective, a teacher of physical education can assign readings that will give meaning to the health principles he or she is trying to impart.

Speakers. The school doctor, team physician, outstanding community personality, professional sportsman, or other person can be brought in from time to time to accent the importance of health.

Special projects. Health Days, Physical Fitness Weeks, Clean-up Week, Work Day, and other projects can be utilized to focus attention on various aspects of health.

Awards. An award in the form of a letter, certificate, or other form of recognition can be given to the healthiest student or to the boy or girl who ranks highest on the physical fitness tests, on a health knowledge examination, etc.

Experiments. An actual experiment such as feeding two rats different diets will work wonders in putting across health information to students.

PRINCIPLES TO KEEP IN MIND IN FURTHERING HEALTH OBJECTIVES

1. Physical activities should be included in the program only as the pupils' health status warrants. This means that such factors as students' strength, organic or func-

---

*See Selected Readings.

Fig. 5-5. Health experiment in nutrition. (San Diego County Schools, San Diego, Calif.)

tional disorders, muscular development, physical disabilities, and coordination, as ascertained through medical examinations, are taken into consideration.

2. All students should participate in the physical education program.

3. Class size should be sufficiently small to permit effective instruction and activity. A general guide would be to enroll not more than forty pupils in a class.

4. Every precautionary measure possible should be taken to provide for safety and to prevent accidents.

5. The intramural, extramural, and interscholastic athletic programs should be laboratory periods for the class instructional program and should be conducted in the light of the welfare and health interests of those who participate.

6. Every school should have a well-defined plan that provides for the proper medical and health considerations of each pupil. This means that there should be well-thought-through policies governing procedures for prevention of disease, emergency care in event of accidents, environmental sanitation, medical examinations, etc.

7. The physical education program should establish and enforce sound hygienic standards.

8. The physical education teacher should be sure that each student understands the roles of eating, smoking, and the use of alcoholic beverages in physical performance.

9. Each teacher of physical education should have an understanding and an appreciation of the school health program and a desire to further the health of his or her pupils.

POINTS TO REMEMBER

1. An understanding of the relationship of physical education to the health of the student
2. An appreciation of ways in which the physical educator can contribute to the health of the student
3. Health facts that physical education can teach to students
4. Health attitudes that physical educators can help to develop in students
5. Health practices that physical educators can help to develop in students
6. Effective techniques and means of presenting health information

CASE STUDY FOR ANALYSIS

Through a program of testing and observation, determine the amount of scientific health knowledge possessed by a high school boy and girl, their attitudes toward health, and the health practices that are a part of their daily routine. Analyze this health information in light of the contribution a physical educator can make.

EXERCISES FOR REVIEW

1. What are some of the outstanding objectives of any school health program?
2. What should each secondary school student know about his or her body?
3. What is the relationship of attitudes to health practices?
4. What are some methods of motivating high school boys and girls to develop good health practices?
5. Why is it better to use the "positive" approach in the teaching of health?
6. Discuss and illustrate five methods of presenting health information to students.
7. Prepare a list of basic principles essential to making physical education a dynamic force in furthering the health of secondary school students.

SELECTED READINGS

American Association for Health, Physical Education, and Recreation: Children in focus, their health and activity, 1954 yearbook, Washington, D. C., 1954, The Association.

American Association of School Administrators: Health in schools, 20th yearbook, Washington, D. C., 1951, National Education Association.

Bucher, Charles A.: Administration of school and college health and physical education programs, ed. 4, St. Louis, 1967, The C. V. Mosby Co.

Bucher, Charles A.: Physical education for life, St. Louis, 1969, Webster Division, McGraw-Hill Book Co.

Bucher, Charles A., Olsen, Einar A., and Willgoose, Carl E.: The foundations of health, New York, 1967, Appleton-Century-Crofts.

Irwin, Leslie W., and Mayshark, Cyrus: Health education in secondary schools, St. Louis, 1964, The C. V. Mosby Co.

Joint Committee on Health Problems in Education of the National Education Association and the American Medical Association: The physical educator asks about health, Washington, D. C., 1951, National Education Association.

Kilander, H. Frederick: School health education, New York, 1968, The Macmillan Co.

National Committee on School Health Policies: Suggested school health policies, ed. 4, Washington, D. C., 1964, National Education Association.

Nemir, Alma: The school health program, Philadelphia, 1963, W. B. Saunders Co.

Oberteuffer, Delbert, and Beyrer, Mary K.: School health education, New York, 1966, Harper & Row, Publishers.

The physical education program*

*P*hysical education is an integral part of the total education process and has as its aim the development of physically, mentally, emotionally, and socially fit citizens through the medium of physical activities that have been selected with a view to realizing these outcomes. This is the definition of physical education that is recommended for this important field of endeavor.

1. *Physical education should be an integral part of the total system of education.* Its value is determined by its contributions to the objectives of education in general. It is one part of the total educational process and, therefore, must contribute to the achievement of the objectives of general education.

2. *Physical education should promote the optimum physical, mental, emotional, moral, and social development of each student as a contributing member of a free and democratic society.* It is concerned not only with training the physical self but with the mental, social, and emotional selves of human development. Its worth is associated with such things as health, organic efficiency, character, and personality.

It helps each pupil in the process of normal growth and natural development.

3. *A study of needs and interests of students is essential in determining the type of program content and methods for a physical education program.* The program does not exist apart from the student. The program must be made to fit the needs and interests of students—not the students made to fit the program.

Components of the secondary school physical education program have been listed by many authors and under a variety of terms. The four components of the school physical · education program used here are those proposed by Bucher: (1) the basic instructional class program, (2) the adapted program, (3) the intramural and extramural programs, and (4) the interschool program.

THE BASIC INSTRUCTIONAL CLASS PROGRAM

Where sound basic instructional class programs of physical education exist, they have been developed on the basis of the physical, social, mental, and emotional needs of the students. A broad and varied program of activities, both outdoor and indoor, progressively arranged and adapted to the capacities and abilities of each student, is offered.

*Parts of this chapter have been adapted from material in Bucher, Charles A.: Administration of school and college health and physical education programs, ed. 4, St. Louis, 1967, The C. V. Mosby Co.

Fig. 6-1. Physical education class is a place to teach skills. (Oconomowoc Senior High School, Oconomowoc, Wis.)

Fig. 6-2. Instruction should be basic and interesting.

Following are some important considerations for the basic instructional class program of physical education at the secondary level for both boys and girls.

Instructional in nature

1. *The physical education class is a place to teach the skills, strategy, appreciation, understanding, knowledge, rules, regulations, and other material and information that are part of the program.* It is not a place for free play, intramurals, and varsity competition. It is a place for instruction. Every minute of the class period should be devoted to teaching boys and girls the skills and subject matter of physical education.

2. *Instruction should be basic and inter-*

esting. Skills should be broken down into simple components and taught so that each individual may understand clearly what he or she is expected to accomplish and at the same time how it should be done. Utilization of demonstrations, loop films, models, slide films, posters, and other visual aids and materials can help to make the instruction more meaningful and interesting.

3. *Instruction should be progressive.* There should be a definite progression from the simple to the complex skills. Just as a student progresses in mathematics from simple arithmetic to algebra, geometry, and calculus, so in physical education the pupil should progress from basic skills and materials to more complex and involved skills and strategies.

4. *Instruction should involve definite standards.* Students should be expected to reach certain standards of achievement in the class program. A reasonable amount of skill—whether it is in swimming, tennis, or another activity—should be mastered, depending upon individual differences. Laxity and indifference to achievement should not be tolerated any more in physical education than in any other subject area in the curriculum. When boys and girls graduate from high school they should have met definite standards which indicate that they are *physically educated.*

5. *Instruction should involve more than physical activity.* All physical education classes do not have to be held in the gymnasium where physical activity predominates. A reasonable proportion of class time, perhaps as much as 10% to 20%, can be devoted to discussions, lectures, and meaningful classroom activity. Good coaches often have chalktalks for their players, in which they study rules and regulations, strategies, execution of skills, and other materials that are essential to playing the game effectively. This same principle can be applied to the physical education class period. There is a subject matter content that the student needs to know and understand. Physical activity

should not be conducted in a vacuum—for if it is, it has no meaning and will not be applied when the youngster leaves the class and school. As the student understands more fully the importance of sports and activities in life, what happens to the body during exercise, the history of the various activities in which he or she engages, and the role of physical activity in the culture of the world, the class takes on new meaning and physical education takes on new respect and prestige.

6. *A textbook should be used.* Just as other subjects in the secondary school program utilize textbooks in their courses, so can physical education profitably use a textbook. Assignments can be made, discussions held, and tests given—all of which will provide the student with a much more meaningful learning experience. Physical education should not be a "snap" course. It has content, and knowledge and appreciation are to be gained from this subject just as they are, for example, in American history. The author recently completed a high school physical education textbook for student use—*Physical Education for Life.**

7. *There should be records.* Adequate records should be kept by the instructor to provide tangible evidence of the degree to which objectives are being met by the students. This means that data on physical fitness, skill achievement, knowledge of rules and other information, and social conduct—such as sportsmanship—should be a part of the record.

8. *There should be homework.* It is just as reasonable to assign homework in physical education as in general science. There is much subject matter to be learned and many skills to be mastered. If teachers would require their students to work on various activity skills and knowledge outside of class, there would be more time in class for meaningful teaching.

9. *Each student should have a health examination before participating in the physical education program.* An annual

---

* See Selected Readings.

health examination should be regarded as a minimum essential to determining the amount and nature of physical activity that best meets each student's needs.

10. *The teaching load of physical educators should be determined not only by the number of instructional class periods assigned but also by the total number of activities handled by the teacher both in class and outside of class.* To do efficient work a teacher should have a normal work load—not an overload. Some professional standards have established that class instruction should not exceed five hours, or the equivalent of five class periods per day.

Required of all students

Physical education represents a need of every child, just as do English, social studies, and other school experiences. Physical education became part of the school offering as a required subject to satisfy such a need and therefore should be continued on the same basis.

All students should take physical education. No one should be excused. If a boy or girl can come to school, he or she should be required to attend physical education class. At the same time, this presupposes that a program adapted to the needs of *all* pupils is provided.

The student is compelled to take so many required courses that elective courses are limited, if not entirely eliminated. If physical education is not required, many students will not have the opportunity to partake of this program because of the pressures placed on them by the required courses. In addition, the student looks upon those subjects that are required as being the most important and the most necessary for success. If physical education is not on the required list, it becomes a subject of second-rate importance in the eyes of students.

Various subjects in the curriculum would not be provided for unless they were required. This is probably true of physical education. Until state legislatures passed laws requiring physical education,

this subject was ignored by many school administrators. If physical education were on an elective basis, it could be crowded out of the school curriculum in many communities. Either the subject would not be offered at all or it would have to be eliminated because of low enrollment.

Even under a required program, physical education is not fulfilling its potentialities for meeting the physical, social, and mental needs of students in most schools. If an elective program were instituted, deficiencies and shortages would increase, thus further handicapping the attempt to meet the welfare and needs of the student.

The physical educator should try very hard to convince administrators, school boards, and the public in general of the place of his special subject in the curriculum of the secondary school. Only as this is done will the subject occupy an important place in the school and become a required offering that is respected.

Daily period

On the secondary level there should be a daily period for physical education. Although this does not exist in many schools at the present time, it should be a goal toward which all leaders should work. The great amount of subject matter, skills, and activities to be covered and the need for regular participation in physical activities are two good reasons that a daily period is so essential. Dr. James B. Conant, in studying the American school system, has recommended that a daily period of physical education be held for all pupils in grades one through twelve.

Credit

Physical education should be given credit like the other major subject matter offerings. It is included in the curriculum because it contributes to educational outcomes. The credit is justified by the contribution physical education makes to the achievement of goals toward which all of education is working.

E. F. Marten, Seattle

Fig. 6-3. There should be a variety of activities.

Variety of activities

Physical education activities* that should be covered in the secondary school are as follows:

Team games: baseball, softball, basketball, touch football, vollyball, soccer, and field hockey (women only)

Duel and individual sports: track, badminton, table tennis, deck tennis, handball, horseshoes, tennis, archery, golf, and shuffleboard

Rhythms and dancing: social dancing, folk dancing, rhythms, gymnastic dancing, square dancing, tap dancing, and modern dancing

Formal activities: calisthenics and marching

Aquatic activities: swimming, diving, lifesaving, water games

Outdoor winter sports: skating, snow games, ice hockey, skiing, and tobogganing

Gymnastics: tumbling, pyramid building, apparatus, rope climbing, and acrobatics

Other activities: self-testing activities, relays, correctives, camping and outdoor education

In order to best meet the needs of the secondary school student, the types of activities should be wide and varied. Team games of high organization should occupy an increasingly important place at the junior high level and are even more outstanding at the senior high school level. The

*From Bucher, Charles A.: Foundations of physical education, ed. 5, St. Louis, 1968, The C. V. Mosby Co.

junior high and early senior high school programs should be mainly exploratory in nature, offering a wide variety of activities, with the team games modified in nature and presented in the form of lead-up activities. Toward the end of the senior high school years there should be an opportunity to select and specialize in certain activities that will have a carry-over value after formal education ceases. Furthermore, many of the team games and other activities should be offered in a more intensive manner and in larger blocks of time as the student approaches the terminal point of the secondary school. This allows for greater acquisition of skill in selected activities.

As a general rule, boys and girls at the secondary level, including both junior and senior high, can profit greatly from rhythmic activities such as clog, tap, folk, and social dancing; team sports such as soccer, field hockey, softball, baseball, touch football, volleyball, and speedball; individual activities such as track and field, tennis, paddle tennis, badminton, hiking, handball, bowling, archery, and fly casting; many forms of gymnastics, such as tumbling, stunts, and apparatus activities; and

Fig. 6-4. Rich Township High School offers a variety of activities for its students. (Rich Township High School, Park Forrest, Ill.)

various forms of games and relays. These activities will comprise the major portion of the program at the secondary level. Of course, the activities should be adapted to boys and to girls as they are played separately or on a coeducational basis.

THE ADAPTED PROGRAM

The adapted program refers to that phase of physical education which meets the needs of the individual who, because of some physical, mental, or cultural inadequacy, functional defect capable of being improved through exercise, or other defi-

ciency, is temporarily or permanently unable to take part in the regular physical education program. The adapted program can correct faulty body mechanics, develop physical fitness, and provide a meaningful program of physical education for students who may otherwise not be able to benefit from such an experience. The word "adapted" is used here, although in many books and schools this special program is known by other terms, such as "corrective," "individual," "modified," "remedial," "atypical," and "restricted."

Health examinations such as medical or

physical fitness tests often indicate that some of the pupils are not able to participate in regular physical activity programs. The principle of individual differences that applies to education as a whole should also apply to physical education. Physical education leaders believe that as long as a student can come to school, he should be required to participate in physical education classes. Adherence to this tenet means that programs must be adapted to individual needs. Many boys and girls who are recuperating from long illnesses or operations or are suffering other abnormal conditions require special consideration in their program of activities.

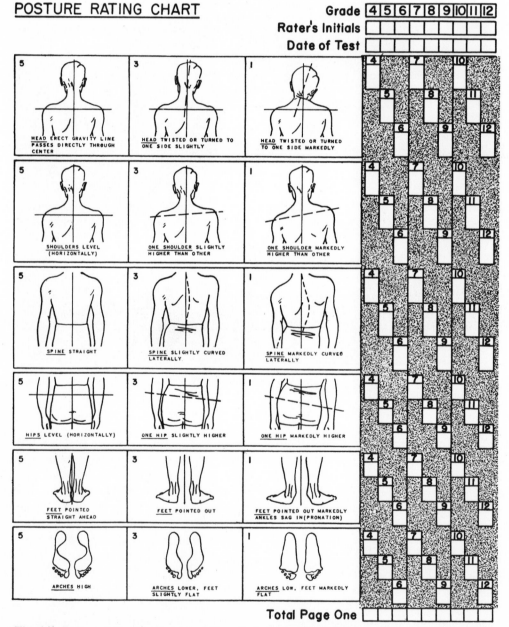

Fig. 6-5. Posture rating chart—part of New York State Physical Fitness Test. (Courtesy Division of Health, Physical Education, and Recreation, State Department of Education, Albany, N. Y.)

It cannot be assumed that all individuals in physical education classes are normal. Unfortunately, many programs are administered on this basis. One estimate indicates that one out of every eight students in our schools is handicapped to the extent that special provision should be made in the educational program.

Special provisions under an adapted type of program also need to be made for such students as the mentally retarded, the physically handicapped, the poorly coordinated, and the culturally disadvantaged in the secondary school population. Cul-

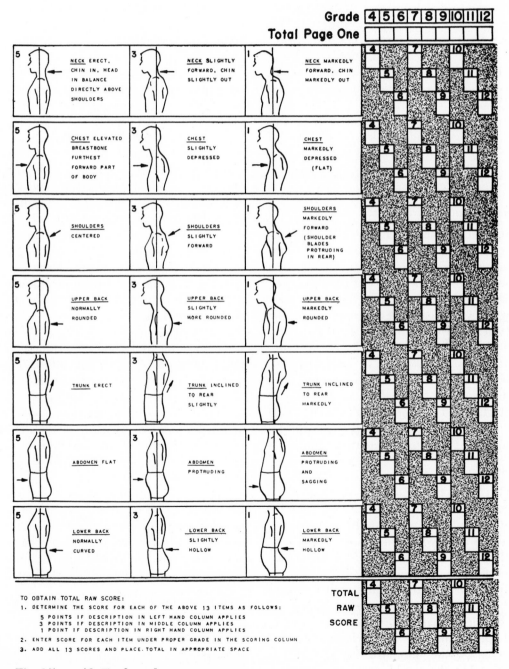

Fig. 6-5, cont'd. For legend see opposite page.

turally disadvantaged students, for example, often have had only a limited physical education experience, either because their families have moved frequently or because they may have attended ghetto schools that did not have adequate facilities and staff for a sound physical education program.

Culturally disadvantaged students benefit from an adapted type of program because they have so often not had prior training in physical education activities, nor have they developed the fitness needed to cope with a regular physical education program.

An adapted physical education program can help these students develop the skills, fitness, and ability they need to find enjoyment and success in sports, games, and recreational activities.

Types of students in adapted program

Students having such atypical physical conditions as the following may profit from an adapted program: (1) faulty body mechanics; (2) nutritional disturbances (overweight or underweight); (3) heart and lung disturbances; (4) postoperative or convalescent problems; (5) hernias, weak and flat feet, menstrual disorders, etc.; (6) nervous instability; (7) poor physical fitness; and (8) crippling conditions (infantile paralysis, etc.); (9) cultural disadvantages; (10) mental retardation; (11) disruptive tendencies; (12) poor coordination; and (13) gifted or creative minds.

Scheduling

There is a feeling among physical education leaders that scheduling handicapped children and youth in separate groups is not always satisfactory. Many educators who have studied this problem believe that the atypical child should receive his physical education along with the normal children and, in order to accommodate his handicap, that the program be modified and special methods of teaching used. In such cases, the administrator should be certain that the modification of the program is physically and psychologically sound for the pupil. Sometimes mental and emotional defects can be minimized if the teacher acquaints other pupils with the general problems of the handicapped child and encourages their cooperation in helping the child to make the right adjustment and maintain his self-esteem and social acceptance. There also seems to be a trend in secondary schools to follow an adapted sports program rather than to have a corrective type of program.

In the larger schools it sometimes has been possible to schedule special classes for children with certain types of abnormalities. This procedure has not always proved satisfactory, however, because of the financial cost and the feeling that boys and girls should be scheduled with normal children for social and psychological reasons. Therefore, including the handicapped in the same classes with other students has become a common practice.

In some smaller schools where there is a staff problem, students needing an adapted program have been scheduled as a separate section within the regular physical education class. In some cases group exercises have been devised, pupils have been encouraged to assist one another in the alleviation of their difficulties. These methods are not always satisfactory, but according to the schools concerned, they are much better than not doing anything about the problem. In other schools atypical pupils have been scheduled during special periods in which individual attention can be given to them.

The procedure followed by any particular school in scheduling students for the adapted program will depend upon its educational philosophy, finances, facilities, and staff available, and should be guided throughout by the needs of the students.

Principles underlying a sound adapted physical education program

1. A thorough medical examination is a prerequisite to assignment to the adapted program.

2. Through the conference technique the teacher can gain from the student much information concerning his or her interests, needs, limitations, and abilities.

3. The program of activities should be adapted to the individual and his or her atypical condition. Special developmental exercises, aquatics, and recreational sports can play an important part in most adapted programs.

4. There should be a periodic evaluation' of student progress.

5. Complete records of each student should be kept. Such information as the nature of the handicapping condition, the recommendation of physician, special activities, interviews, progress, and other pertinent data should be recorded.

6. Excellent teacher-student-nurse-physician-administrator rapport is essential to an effective program.

7. The teacher of adapted physical education should work very closely with medical and guidance personnel.

8. Teachers of adapted physical education should have a sincere interest in handicapped students and should recognize the real challenge in helping them.

INTRAMURAL AND EXTRAMURAL ATHLETIC PROGRAMS

Intramural and extramural activities comprise that phase of the school physical education program which is geared to the abilities and skills of the entire student body and which consists of voluntary participation in games, sports, and other activities. It offers intramural activities within a single school and such extramural activities as "play" and "sports" days that bring together participants from several schools. It is a laboratory period for sports and other activities whose fundamentals have been taught in the physical education class. It affords competition for all types of individuals—the strong and the weak, the skilled and the unskilled, the big and the small. It also includes both sexes, separately and in corecreational programs. It is not characterized by the highly organized features of

Fig. 6-6. Intramural sports. (Hurst-Euless-Bedford Public Schools, Hurst, Texas.)

varsity sports, including their commercialization, many spectators, considerable publicity, and stress on winning. It is a phase of the total physical education program that should receive considerable stress.

Relation to interschool athletics

Both intramural and extramural and varsity interschool athletics are integral phases of the total physical education program, which is made up of the required physical education class program, the adapted program, the intramural and extramural programs, and the varsity interschool athletics program. Each has an important contribution to make to the achievement of physical education objectives. The important thing is to maintain a proper balance so that each phase enhances rather than restricts the other phases of the total program.

Whereas intramural and extramural activities are for the entire student body, varsity interschool athletics are usually for students who have a greater degree of skill. Intramurals are conducted primarily on a

Fig. 6-7. Intramural activities.

school basis, whereas extramural and varsity interschool athletics are conducted on an interschool basis.

There is no conflict between these phases of the program if the facilities, time, personnel, money, and other factors are apportioned according to the degree to which each phase achieves the educational outcomes desired, rather than according to the degree of public appeal and interest stimulated. One should not be designed as a training ground or feeding system for the other. It should be possible for a student to move from one to the other, but this should be incidental in nature, rather than a planned procedure.

If conducted properly, each phase of the program can contribute to the other, and through an overall, well-balanced program, the entire student body will come to respect sports and the great potentials they have for improving physical, mental, social, and emotional growth. When a physical education program is initially developed, it would seem logical to first provide an intramural program for the majority of the students, with the interschool athletics program coming as an outgrowth of the former. The first concern should be for the majority of the students. This is characteristic of the democratic way of life. Although the intramural and extramural athletics program is designed for every student, in practice it generally attracts the poorly skilled and moderately skilled individuals. The skilled person finds his niche in the varsity interschool athletic program.

This has its benefits, in that it is an equalizer for competition.

In junior high school

In the junior high school the main concentration in athletics should be on intramural and extramural activities. It is at this particular level that students are taking a special interest in sports, but at the same time their immaturity makes it unwise to allow them to engage in an interscholastic program. The program at this level should provide for all boys and girls, appeal to the entire student body, be well supervised by a trained physical educator, and be adapted to the needs and interests of the pupils.

The American Association for Health, Physical Education, and Recreation, the Society of State Directors, and many other authoritative and professional groups have gone on record in favor of a broad intramural and extramural junior high athletics program. They believe that it is in the best interests of youth at this age level.

The junior high school provides a setting for developing students' fundamental skills in many sports and activities. It is a time of great energy—and a time when physiological changes and rapid growth are taking place. Youth in junior high schools should have proper outlets to develop in a healthful manner.

In senior high school

At the senior high school level the intramural and extramural athletics program should develop its full potential. At this time the interests and needs of boys and girls require such a program. These students want and need to experience the joy and satisfaction that are a part of playing on a team, excelling in an activity with one's own peers, and developing skill. Every high school should see to it that a broad and varied program is part of the total physical education plan.

The program of intramural and extramural athletics for boys and girls should receive more emphasis than it now has at the senior high school level. It is basic to sound education. It is a setting in which the skills learned and developed in the instructional program can be put to use in a practical situation, with all the fun that comes from such competition. It should form a basis for the utilization of skills that will be used during leisure time, both in the present and in the future. Since this is the time when so many young people, especially girls, lose interest in physical activity, the intramural and extramural program can help to maintain such an interest.

Corecreational activities should play a prominent part in the program. Girls and boys need to participate in common activities. Many of the activities in the high school program adapt themselves well to both sexes. Play and sports days also offer a setting in which both sexes can participate and enjoy worthwhile competition together.

For girls

According to many leaders in the field, intramural and extramural athletics are preferred and emphasized for women over interschool athletics. These leaders point out that certain biological, social, and psychological characteristics of girls and women adapt better to this type of organization and program. The Division of Girls' and Women's Sports of the American Association for Health, Physical Education, and Recreation has stated that sports, when conducted in the right manner, contribute to such desirable outcomes as fitness for living and to the development of the most desirable and attractive qualities of womanhood, including many physical and mental as well as social qualities.

The program should be composed of a wide variety of team and individual sports and other activities that may be played among the girls themselves or in mixed groups. Girls have spearheaded the drive for sports and play days and thus these activities deserve special emphasis. There should be qualified women leaders directing all phases of the program, although men should work very closely with them and lend support and help at every opportunity. Women should officiate in their own activities. Every safeguard should be taken to protect girls from harmful practices. There should be no commercial exploitation or unfavorable publicity attached to the program.

Principles underlying sound intramural and extramural programs

1. The goals of the intramural and extramural programs must be consistent with those of general education and physical education.

2. The supervision of the intramural and extramural programs should be the responsibility of qualified physical education personnel.

3. The planning and conduct of the intramural and extramural programs should be based upon democratic principles and allow for participation by students as well as faculty.

4. The facilities of the entire physical education department should be available for the intramural and extramural programs in order to permit a wide variety of activities and the maximum participation possible.

5. The units of competition in intramural and extramural programs should depend upon such factors as the size of the school, needs and interests of students, natural formation of groups within the school, and other considerations that will lend flavor to the competition.

Fig. 6-8. Interscholastic athletics in basketball. (Central Westchester League, New York.)

6. Tournaments should be so conducted as to permit maximum participation of students.

7. Eligibility requirements should be designed to enable maximum participation of the student body and to protect the health and welfare of the participants.

8. Achievement can be recognized by some token of recognition, but awards should not become a primary motive for participation.

9. Officials should be well qualified so as to promote better play and maintain safety.

THE INTERSCHOLASTIC PROGRAM

Varsity interschool athletics have a definite and important place in senior high school. Whether they should exist at the junior high school level is controversial. Varsity interscholastic competition at the senior high school level can help players achieve a higher standard of mental, moral, social, and physical fitness, provided the overall objectives of physical education are kept in mind.

Varsity interschool athletics represent

Fig. 6-9. Interscholastic athletics in water polo.

an integral part of the total physical education program. They should grow out of the intramural and extramural athletics program. Athletics, with the appeal it has for youth, should be the heart of physical education.

Varsity interscholastic athletics at the junior high school level

There has been considerable discussion in recent years on the advisability of varsity athletic competition at the junior high school level. The resolutions passed by some professional organizations and the stands taken by leaders in the field point to the fact that highly organized interschool athletics programs are questionable as a part of junior high school programs.

There are two sides to the question of junior high school varsity athletics, and at times they both sound convincing. Opponents have offered facts to indicate that it is risky business to permit boys and girls to play varsity interschool athletics at this level of growth and development. Those who favor these activities have shown that programs have been conducted in a safe and sound manner.

Both sides would agree, it seems, that more research is needed to determine the right policy to follow. Probably educators would be on the safe side if they waited until more research has been conducted before encouraging this kind of participation. Above all, the following principles are basic:

1. The main object of athletics should be healthful participation and fun.

2. Every youngster should have opportunities to participate in a varied program of many physical activities and sports both in a physical education class and in intramural and extramural programs. These phases of the total physical education program should receive priority for the junior high schools.

3. Occasional competitive experiences in selected activities on an informal basis such as sports days and play days can be conducted with profit.

4. A complete medical examination is a prerequisite.

5. Proper leadership consists of persons who know and appreciate the physical and emotional limitations of youngsters, the fundamentals of first aid, the sport itself, and how to condition and train players for the activity. A certified physical educator should handle such activities.

Varsity interscholastic athletics at the senior high school level

The high school level is the logical place to start interschool athletics on a more highly organized basis. This is the place where youngsters may find an opportunity to experience exhilarating competition and test their skill against that of teams in neighboring communities.

The following principles should guide the program:

1. High school varsity interscholastic athletics should be voluntary in nature. All students who desire to be on a team should be allowed to play on the squad. In theory no one should ever be cut from the squad. Every attempt should be made to have sufficient junior varsity, or grade "B," "C," and other teams, so that any interested student will have the opportunity to participate at his level of ability.

2. Athletics should be conducted in out-of-school hours. The class period should never be utilized for practice.

3. Players should not be excused from physical education class. Programs may be adapted, but every player can receive some benefit from participating in the class program.

4. The interschool athletic program should be organized and administered with the needs of the participant in mind. What will benefit the spectator should never influence the program.

5. A wide variety of activities based on the needs and interests of students should be offered. The number of students that can be accommodated in a wide variety of sports and other physical education activities should be the basis on which an inter-

school athletic program is founded and developed.

6. The coach should be selected on the basis of his knowledge of the game, ability to teach, understanding of the participant, and character and personality. Some physical education preparation is an essential.

7. Through interschool competition the player should become physically, mentally, emotionally, and socially more fit.

8. One of the first requisites for every participant in an athletics program should be a medical examination to determine physical fitness and capacity to engage in such a program.

9. Everything possible should be done to provide for the safety of the participant.

10. Every school should have a written policy in regard to financial and other responsibilities associated with injuries. The administrator, parents, and players should be thoroughly familiar with the responsibilities of each in regard to injuries.

11. Some form of insurance plan to cover injuries should be in force in all schools.

12. For boys' programs the standards of the National Federation of State High School Athletic Associations should apply, and for girls' programs the principles established by the Division of Girls' and Women's Sports should apply.

13. Officials should be well qualified. They should know the rules and be able to interpret them accurately; recognize their responsibility to the players; be good sportsmen, and be courteous, honest, friendly, cooperative, and impartial; and be able to control the game at all times.

Girls' interschool athletics

The question of highly organized athletics for girls is highly controversial. The problems of too much, too little, and what is a happy medium are frequently raised, with enthusiastic supporters on all sides of the issue. There seems to be a general consensus of opinion that athletics can render a valuable service for girls. The question

arises as to what type of program can best render this service. Girls can develop a better state of total fitness, skills for worthy use of leisure time, and other desirable qualities and attributes, just as boys can. However, it must be recognized that girls are not boys. There are many biological, social, emotional, and other differences that must be taken into consideration.

The girls' program should be concerned especially with the individual sports and activities, as well as with team games. The women in charge and those doing the officiating should be qualified. Official girls' rules should be followed. The girls' games should be separated from the boys', except in coeducational activity, which should occupy an important place in the program. The social aspects should be stressed; jumping and body contact should be limited or eliminated altogether. Health safeguards should be observed, seasons limited, and restrictions enforced on the amount of competition allowed any one girl. Publicity and commercial aspects should be controlled so that the girls are not exploited. The statement on policies and procedures of the Division for Girls' and Women's Sports should be an important reference and guide.

POINTS TO REMEMBER

1. A workable definition of physical education
2. The four components of the physical education program
3. Basic considerations in the required class physical education program
4. Nature and scope of adapted physical education program
5. Characteristics of intramural and extramural physical education program
6. Considerations for an interscholastic athletic program

PROBLEMS TO THINK THROUGH

1. Why is it essential to consider all four components of a program of physical education in order to best meet the needs and interests of all boys and girls?
2. Why is it that many schools do not have an adapted physical education program?
3. Why is it that many schools do not follow

resolutions of professional associations in regard to interscholastic athletic programs?

CASE STUDY FOR ANALYSIS

Select a secondary school and make a careful study of its class, adapted, intramural and extramural, and interschool athletic programs. Make a list of commendable aspects of the school's physical education program and a list of points that are weaknesses and require attention.

EXERCISES FOR REVIEW

1. Define physical education.
2. Why must the class physical education program be instructional in nature?
3. What are some important considerations in developing an effective instructional class program?
4. Make a study of what four physical education leaders say are important characteristics of the class physical education program.
5. Debate the issue Resolved: Interschool athletics should be banned from all junior high schools.

SELECTED READINGS

Brace, David K.: Health and physical education for junior and senior high schools, New York, 1948, A. S. Barnes & Co.

Bucher, Charles A.: Administration of school and college health and physical education programs, ed. 4, St. Louis, 1967, The C. V. Mosby Co.

Bucher, Charles A.: Foundations of physical education, ed. 5, St. Louis, 1968, The C. V. Mosby Co.

Bucher, Charles A.: Physical education for life, St. Louis, 1969, Webster Division, McGraw-Hill Book Co.

Bucher, Charles A., and Reade, Evelyn: Physical education in the modern elementary school, New York, 1970, The Macmillan Co.

Callahan, Sterling G.: Successful teaching in secondary schools, Glenview, Ill., 1966, Scott, Foresman & Co.

Clarke, H. Harrison, and Clarke, David H.: Developmental and adapted physical education, Englewood Cliffs, N. J., 1963, Prentice-Hall, Inc.

Matthews, Donald K., et al.: The science of physical education for handicapped children, New York, 1963, Harper & Brothers.

National Association of Secondary-School Principals: Health, physical education, and recreation in the secondary school, Washington, D. C., May, 1960, The Association.

Nixon, John E., and Jewett, Ann E.: Physical education curriculum, New York, 1964, The Ronald Press Co.

Voltmer, Edward F., and Esslinger, Arthur A.: The organization and administration of physical education, ed. 4, New York, 1967, Appleton-Century-Crofts.

Developing
the
curriculum

The physical education curriculum at the secondary level is gradually undergoing changes that match new developments in other subject matter areas. For example, emphasis on individualized instruction is one of the most significant advancements in the educational picture at the present time. Physical educators, like teachers in all areas, are faced with mapping out curricula that take advantage of new teaching media to develop programs that will meet the newly discovered individual needs.

Physical educators are also finding it necessary to focus on factual material as a part of their instruction, to provide students with a greater understanding of physical education and its unique contribution to their education.

If the new as well as the established goals and objectives of physical education are to be achieved, a worthwhile program for students must first be formulated. A well-developed curriculum is a prerequisite for teaching and learning and the key to successful daily programming. It requires much time and thought from many people to construct an extensive course of study that encompasses the present and future needs of an ever-changing student body and community. However, the results, as evidenced by pupil progress and attainment of goals, are indeed worth the effort.

DEVELOPING THE CURRICULUM
What is a curriculum?

A well-developed physical education curriculum is more than just a course of study or a program of activities. It is a statement of the philosophy behind the physical education program. It is a set of principles guiding the staff in all phases of classroom and extra-class instruction. It is a series of objectives and goals to be achieved by those who learn. It is the program, progressive in nature from year to year, and season to season, providing the best opportunity for education to the majority of students as often as possible. It is the measuring rod beside which the achievements and accomplishments of students and staff alike may be evaluated. The curriculum is all these things—a culmination of the united efforts of the many people who serve to develop it.

Purpose. The purpose of a curriculum is to provide the best type of physical education program possible to students in a particular school situation. Over thirty years ago William Ralph LaPorte headed a committee on Curriculum Research for the

College Physical Education Association. His group formulated a practical program of physical education adaptable to wide variations of geographic and local conditions.[1] Since that time several types of curricula have evolved: *the core program,* consisting of units of study required of all students; *the elective program,* in which students select units of study according to personal preference; *the combined core and elective program;* and *the problem-centered program,* in which students and staff work out selections according to the needs of the group.[2] It is the task of a curriculum committee not only to determine the type of program to be presented but also to construct an appropriate progression of activities in accordance with many other factors needing consideration.

The curriculum committee

The curriculum committee is usually established by the administrator of a school or superintendent of schools and is directed to rewrite or to revise the course of study. The head of the physical education department may serve as chairman of the group to revise the physical education program, or the committee may select its own leader. Other members may include the physical education staff, a representative from the administration, such as a school principal, individuals from the health and recreation departments of the school and/or community, and selected classroom teachers from the elementary grades.

The size of the committee is variable and depends largely upon the size of the school and community to be served. The group may be further enlarged by visiting specialists or consultants in curriculum design who are called in to advise and guide the workshop meetings. In some school systems, developing a new curriculum may be labeled in-service education, and members serving on committees may receive credits toward salary increases for their participation. When university personnel are used as permanent consultants for curriculum workshops, committee members may be able to receive graduate credits for this course of study. Serving on the curriculum committee should be a very rewarding and enriching experience for both new and experienced teachers. Although completion of the study may require a full school year and innumerable after-school meetings, if a worthwhile program of physical education is the result, the entire school system and the community benefit.

Steps in curriculum development

Collection of data. The first step in curriculum construction is a vitally important one. Many facts and details should first be gathered by the committee to serve as a background or foundation upon which to build the new curriculum. Several factors influence a course of study, and they should first be identified, analyzed, and understood. To prepare for constructing a curriculum, therefore, subcommittees should be established to investigate the following areas:

The current program of physical education. The present program of physical education should be evaluated in terms of student achievements and progress. Specific weaknesses and strengths of the program should be identified, and areas for expansion studied. Are students meeting or exceeding minimum physical fitness standards? Are more teachers or teaching stations needed at any level? These and similar questions need answering.

The needs of the students. A curriculum is successful only to the extent that the students benefit from it. They learn, they achieve, they develop, they become better rounded, and they are better prepared to face the future as a result of experiences in physical education. Therefore, it is essential that the basic needs of the students be identified. Two areas require investigation in this respect. Current research findings related to adolescent growth and development should be studied, and a survey of student interests and attitudes should be taken. The results of these two studies of the needs of students should yield much

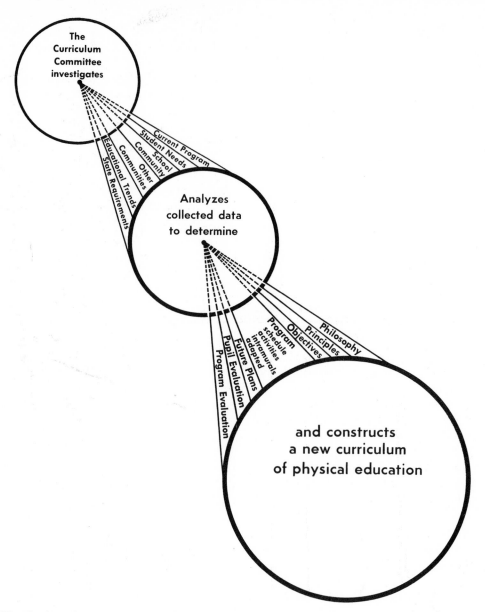

Fig. 7-1. Development of the curriculum.

helpful information and background material.

The school's community. A curriculum should fulfill the specific needs of the school's particular community. It is essential to survey the community in terms of its prospective growth and change, school population expansion, and recreational needs. Similarly, it is important to survey community feelings in regard to the physical education program itself. Would the community approve construction of athletic facilities for increased interscholastic programs, for example? Would it support competitive activities? Is there a desire for adult recreation programs using school facilities? Is there an increasing need for other recreational activities? All these areas should be fully investigated before beginning the actual development of a curriculum, for the information obtained should affect it greatly.

The surrounding communities. The physical education curricula of schools in neighboring communities should be surveyed, as well as those of distant schools similar in size, geographic location, and climate. Much can be learned from the successes of others, and valuable ideas may be gained in this way. For example, if a course in scuba diving has been successful in other schools, the curriculum committee may want to consider such an activity in its own school program.

The current trends in education. A study should be made of recent trends in the field of education in general, as well as in physical education. The latest techniques and methods of teaching, such as team teaching and programmed learning, should be considered. Research findings in relation to the learning process, grouping, and group dynamics should be studied. Information on improved equipment, new resource materials, new films, and new books and games should be collected. It is in this area in particular in which real stimulation and impetus may be found for changing a program. At the same time provisions may be made for professional progress and real contributions to the field of physical education through program experimentation and valuable research.

The state requirements. An investigation of state regulations and requirements should also be made to ensure acceptance of a revised curriculum. At the same time it should be determined if any changes in state standards are anticipated or are in process, in order to fulfill any future specifications that may be enacted.

When the subcommittees have completed studies in each of these six areas and have gathered as many facts and materials as possible, the committee as a whole should then be ready for the next step in curriculum construction.

Analysis of materials. The materials thus collected should be thoroughly discussed and considered by the entire committee, for the information thus obtained should serve as a basis for rebuilding the new curriculum. Recommendations of the subcommittees should be heard, and the committee as a whole should then determine a new philosophy and direction for the program and should outline present and future changes advisable for the total school and community benefit.

Development of the curriculum. When the data have been thoroughly analyzed and the committee has agreed upon the fundamental directions of the new curriculum, smaller working groups should again be appointed for the purpose of actual construction of the curriculum. Using the committee findings as a basis upon which to work, these new committees should prepare the following:

1. A statement of philosophy of the physical education department, compatible with the school's philosophy of general education
2. A set of principles for teaching, incorporating new methods and techniques for use at specific grade levels
3. A set of goals and objectives for students at each grade level
4. An outline of class activities, identifying levels at which new materials should be introduced, to ensure progression within the program
5. A schedule of classes, including suggested size of classes, time allotment, class sessions per week, and teacher assignments
6. An intramural and extramural program, outlining levels at which each type should be initiated, activities to be included, and standards for participation of boys and/or girls
7. An adapted program, including methods of appraisal and referral, and suggested time and types of activities for class sessions
8. A prospectus for the years ahead, suggesting additions needed in facilities and equipment, and increases needed in the teaching staff and budget to accommodate expansion in the activities program and the school population

9. A synthesis of evaluative techniques, covering individual record cards for students at different levels, and methods of reporting and assessing achievement of objectives

10. A technique for the yearly evaluation of the total curriculum and staff, with suggested methods for revision of the curriculum when necessary

It should be noted here that a curriculum does not dictate to a teacher exactly what must be taught during a particular class hour. It serves only as an overall basis for the establishment of the program within a school and offers guidelines for teaching. It provides consistency, progression, and structure for the total physical education program, without binding or stifling the individual and collective creativity of the staff.

Adoption of the curriculum. The committee as a whole should then reconvene to amend and to adopt the resulting curriculum, which should then be sent to the administration for approval and action. A curriculum of physical education should be revised as frequently as the need dictates. In accordance with the method of its construction, it should be reevaluated and amended to bring it up-to-date.

Selection of activities

Whereas the program of physical education itself consists wholly of activities, team sports, individual and dual sports, rhythms, calisthenics, self-testing and leisure-time activities, and so on, particular attention must be focused on the selection of these activities. Those which are finally selected for inclusion in the program should be determined carefully and thoughtfully by the curriculum committee. To provide students with a program consisting merely of popular team sports is neither adequate nor beneficial. Therefore, the following principles are offered as a guideline for determining the activities to be included in a balanced program of physical education.

Physiological principles for determining activities

1. The physical education program should provide ample opportunities for a

E. F. Marten, Seattle

Fig. 7-2. The physical education program should provide for large-muscle activity.

wide range of movements involving the large muscles.

2. The facts related to the growth and development of children are important considerations in curriculum construction.

3. The differences in physical capacities and abilities found among students should be provided for in the program.

4. The physical fitness needs of students must be met by the physical education program.

Physiological characteristics are a major consideration in the selection of activities. It is necessary to understand the physical characteristics of boys and girls at all levels of growth and to meet them in selecting activities. The program must be rewarding for all levels of ability.

Psychological principles for determining activities

1. The physical education program should consist predominantly of natural play activities.

2. Activities should be selected in the light of the psychological age characteristics of the child. For instance, the program should provide more coeducational activities for adolescents, because this type of program meets the needs and interests of this age group.

3. Activities that are valuable in arousing and expressing emotion should be chosen. In the junior high school a varied program of competitive group activities would be advisable.

4. The selection of activities should provide for progression. In the junior high school the fundamentals of tumbling and apparatus work should be taught, along with simple stunts. In the senior high school the student should progress to more advanced work and more challenging combinations.

5. The selection and placement of activities should allow for sufficient time for the skills to be learned reasonably well. It is better to learn three or four basketball skills reasonably well each year than to be exposed to ten in one year and not be able to perform any of them satisfactorily.

E. F. Marten, Seattle

Fig. 7-3. The curriculum should be rich in activities adaptable to use in leisure time.

6. Activities should be selected that best meet the seasonal drives of the students. Football is best taught in the fall, basketball in the winter, and baseball in the spring.

7. Psychologically speaking, the activities should provide a healthy outlet for children; they should be challenging, yet within the students' physical and mental capabilities. The aggressive child who is a problem to the classroom teacher can be placed in a gymnasium where he or she can run, hit the ball, throw, and be thrilled by the excitement of a close competitive contest. A constructive outlet for aggression can often be found on a football field, on a basketball court, or with a field hockey or soccer team. By wisely using the tools of the trade, the physical educator will have a positive effect upon schoolchildren. There must be an opportunity to continually improve and develop knowledge and skills— that is, there must be a progression that will keep interest high and develop abilities to a point where an activity can be enjoyed for the pleasure of doing it correctly.

Sociological principles for determining activities

1. The curriculum should be rich in activities adaptable to use in leisure time. For example, golf, tennis, and swimming should be in the program, if possible.

2. The activities should be selected for their possible contribution to the youth's training for citizenship in a democracy. The opportunity to participate in a team sport, select a captain, and be a member of a cohesive unit should be available with proper teacher guidance.

3. The curriculum should be suited to the ideals of the community as well as to its needs. It will be of value to include square dancing, swimming, or bowling in the curriculum to meet the interests and needs of a community.

4. The activities that are particularly rich in opportunities for individual character training are especially desirable. The self-discipline involved in advanced apparatus work is beneficial to character training.

5. Activities that reflect nationwide interests should be provided in the program. It is important to understand and have a working knowledge of those popular American pastimes—baseball, football, and basketball—because of the values inherent in these team sports and because of their national recognition and acceptance.

WHAT ONE COMMUNITY DID

In White Plains, New York, a community of about 60,000 people, a *Curriculum Guide for Physical Education (K-12)*[3] was developed. The methods and procedures used in organizing the project are worthy of study by other communities. This guide has already been used as a basis for revision in a number of school districts.

The study was made under the guidance of the Director of Physical Education for White Plains. He listed the following ingredients for a curriculum study: an awareness of the need for such a study, the willingness to work on it, and a dedicated interest on the part of the physical education staff. The White Plains Board of Education allotted $750 for the study in order to engage a person well-versed in the field of physical education to act as leader of the workshop. A number of applications were received, and a professor at a nearby university was selected as leader of the group.

The consultant and the director prepared the outline for the study group. It was in the form of a four-month workshop, meeting one evening each week as a group and attended by all members of the physical education staff in the White Plains system. The teachers were divided into committees according to their school level. All male senior high school teachers formed one subcommittee that concerned itself with the physical education program relating to senior high school boys. The other committees were organized in the same manner. Each subcommittee prepared its recommendations, working with the study

Herald Tribune—Kavallines

Fig. 7-4. White Plains, New York, High School cheerleaders.

leader, and presented them to the group as a whole. The entire group discussed and made suggestions to each committee. In the light of these suggestions, and according to an agreed-upon plan for continuity between the levels, each group reworked its recommendations into final form.

All administrative arrangements were handled by the director and leader. During the entire study the director remained in the background. He had made the presentation to the board for the necessary financial outlay. He also secured three credits toward an increment, or salary step, for all the teachers participating in the study. He was available to help with any problems but left the actual outlining to the teachers as much as possible.

The curriculum guide that was developed contains the following:

A general statement—explaining the purpose for and philosophy behind the guide and stating that it was established to fill the framework found in the White Plains system, that it is to be an ongoing project that can be improved from year to year, and that it merely sets minimum essentials

Time requirements—established for kindergarten through twelfth grade in White Plains

Specific objectives—listed for each level (boys and girls together on the primary level, as well as separate objectives for boys and girls on the intermediate, junior high, and senior high school levels) in the physical, neuromuscular, mental, social, and emotional areas

Classification system for activities—including rhythms (dance, marching, and calisthenics); games of low organization; relays; athletic games; apparatus, stunts, and tumbling; individual and dual activities; and aquatics

List of activities provided at each level and time allotment—broken down to number of weeks and percentage of total time for each activity at each grade level

Evaluation—stating the purposes of evaluation and a basis for grading

Cumulative record card

The White Plains curriculum guide will not solve all physical education problems for White Plains or any other community. However, it has placed the physical education program in a more favorable light in the eyes of the residents of that city and undoubtedly makes the staff proud to

E. F. Marten, Seattle

Fig. 7-5. What is the attitude of the community toward interscholastic sports?

know that they are well on their way toward achieving the type of program that each schoolchild should have as part of his or her education.

PLANNING THE TOTAL PROGRAM

The goals of physical education can be achieved only through the teaching process, that is, the execution of a well-made plan. The teacher in the physical education program is the one link between the students and their accomplishment of the goals, and it is therefore the teacher's responsibility to set up the daily learning situation in direct relation to overall objectives. This can be done only through careful and thoughtful planning of every physical education experience, so that it may be a purposeful one for each student and a step toward the attainment of the goals.

Planning the yearly program

The program of study for a single year is based on the overall curriculum, with specific objectives and activities selected according to the grade level. This step in planning is equally as important as the curriculum development. The program for the year must be exact and yet flexible enough to accommodate the changing needs and abilities of the students. Steps in

planning for the year include both selection of objectives and activities, as in developing the curriculum, and evaluation, for only through this last step is the overall program completed.

Objectives. In planning the yearly program teachers must select specific objectives from those outlined in the overall curriculum. Selection is based on the particular age group and developmental status of the class. An overall objective of the goal of physical fitness, for example, may be the development of accuracy. A specific objective based on this factor may be the improvement of accuracy in the lay-up shot for basketball or in pitching across home plate. Similarly, specific objectives should be established for each of the four major goals and activities, and the methods of teaching them should be selected specifically for the purpose of meeting these objectives. Plans must be flexible, however, as some classes may already be proficient in the skills or may learn very quickly, and the teacher must be ready to draw on more difficult specific objectives.

Activities. The activities to be included in a particular year of study are usually outlined in the overall curriculum. However, the teacher must determine the amount of time to be devoted to each ac-

Fig. 7-6. Physical educators should be concerned with the health of students when planning programs. (Roller skating class at Maui High School, Hamakuapoko-Paia, Hawaii.)

Fig. 7-7. A physical education class. (Little Rock Public Schools, Little Rock, Ark.)

tivity, according to the needs and desires of the group. In schools that promote student planning, the teacher may base some decisions on the outcomes of discussions with classes. For example, one class of ninth-grade girls may wish to study field hockey exclusively in the fall, while another group may want to combine field hockey with tennis. However, the teacher must ultimately decide the program for the year—after considering the seasons of the locality, the facilities and equipment available, and the size and needs of the group.

Evaluation. Methods of evaluating the year's work should be planned in advance. Student achievement and program content must be surveyed in terms of the established objectives. Procedures for evaluation are outlined in a separate chapter, but the teacher should realize that planning for this process is an essential part of the yearly plan.

Table 3. Sample physical education program for 36 ninth-grade girls meeting twice weekly

Month and number of weeks		Physical fitness	Physical skills	Knowledge and appreciation	Social development
Sept.	3	Posture	Archery	Archery	Individual respon-
		Strength	Stance	Etiquette	sibilities in class
Oct.	4	Endurance	Technique	Safety	Program planning
		Speed	Hockey	Hockey	Group cooperation
Nov.	1	Agility	Dribble	History	Teamwork
		Accuracy	Drive	Rules	
		Balance	Dodge	Offensive and	
			Lunge	defensive	
			Tackle	strategies	
Total	8		Test	Test	
Nov.	3	Posture	Badminton	Badminton	Partnership
		Balance	Serve	Etiquette	etiquette
Dec.	3	Agility	Forehand	Doubles rules	Improve group re-
		Accuracy	Backhand	Volleyball	lationships and
			Volleyball	History	teamwork
			Single tap	Etiquette	
			Serve	Offensive and	
			Smash	defensive	
			Test	strategies	
				Rules	
				Rotation	
Total	6			Test	
Jan.	4	Endurance	Basketball	Basketball	Teamwork
		Speed	Passes	History	New groups
Feb.	2	Accuracy	Dribble	Offensive and	Leadership
		Balance	Pivot	defensive	
		Agility	Foul-shooting	strategies	
			Goal-shooting	Rules	
			Test	Notebook	
Total	6			Test	
Feb.	2	Strength	Modern dance	Modern dance	Group planning
		Endurance	Types of	History	Creativity
Mar.	3	Balance	movement	Noted	Cooperation
		Agility	Axial	performers	Leadership
		Posture	Swing	Values	
		Poise	Sustained	Purposes	
		Grace	Percussive	Test	
			Locomotor		
			Leaps		
			Skips		
Total	5		Turns		
Apr.	4	Strength	Stunts	Values of	Safety
		Endurance	Tumbling	training	consciousness
		Balance	Apparatus	Olympic	Leadership
		Agility	Parallel bars	performers	Group planning
		Posture	High bar	Safety	Cooperation
			Ladder	procedures	
			Rings	Spotting	
Total	4		Test		

Table 3. Sample physical education program for 36 ninth-grade girls meeting twice weekly—cont'd

Month and number of weeks	Physical fitness	Physical skills	Knowledge and appreciation	Social development
May 4	Strength Endurance	Tennis Forehand	Tennis History	Partnership etiquette
June 3	Agility Speed Accuracy	Backhand Serve Volley	Etiquette Doubles rules	New groups Teamwork Leadership Cooperation
		Softball Base-playing Base-running Batting Bunting Catching Throwing Fielding	Softball History Rules Scoring Base-playing Test	
Total 7		Test		

Table 3 shows a sample yearly program such as may be planned for a class of thirty-six ninth-grade girls meeting twice a week for 45-minute periods. Activities are listed under the particular goal for which they strive.

Planning the unit of teaching

A unit of teaching refers to the period of time during which a particular sport or activity is studied. The program for the year has several units of teaching, some scheduled for six weeks, some for eight weeks, and others for lesser amounts of time. The use of units in teaching physical education is of great importance to the quality of the learning experience. Unit teaching provides direction and structure to each class meeting, and the students recognize each session as being a distinct part of a whole. The physical educator; guided by the unit goals, offers progressive instruction for their attainment, and the students are aware of the purposes of activities within the unit. In planning the unit of teaching the teacher must consider the specific objectives and activities to be included in the sports unit. Because this phase of planning is the basis for daily instruction and the learning experience itself, its extreme importance must not be underestimated.

Objectives. Specific objectives established for the year form the basis of the sub-objectives in the unit plan. There should be sub-objectives relating to all four goals of physical education, for it is these sub-objectives obtained in the unit course of study which are the steppingstones to achievement of overall goals. Following is an example of the way in which objectives may be broken down for a unit: (1) *goal* —physical skill; (2) *objective*—to develop throwing power; (3) *specific objective* (*yearly plan*)—to improve pitching accuracy; and (4) *sub-objective* (*unit plan*)— to pitch fast balls over the plate. Sub-objectives would be established for each of the four goals in this manner, with the age level and developmental needs of the students the determining factor in estimating accomplishment.

Activities. The choice of activities to be included in each unit of study should be made on the basis of the sub-objectives established. Certain principles should be kept in mind while planning the activities, in order to make the unit a complete series of learning experiences.

1. Provide a variety of learning experiences by using different types of activities (relays, games of low organization), techniques (drills, skull sessions), and materials (audiovisual aids, outside reading).

2. Provide activities that are appropriate to the needs, age level, and developmental achievements of the group.

3. Provide activities that are progressive in nature.

4. Provide flexibility in planning so that unforeseen interruptions and delays during the course of the unit do not hinder achievement of unit objectives.

5. Provide a definite form for the unit by introducing new skills and activities on a weekly basis or with each class session (depending upon the frequency of classes), so that students recognize progress within the unit.

6. Provide activities that promote the greatest amount of participation for the greatest number of students by utilizing all facilities and equipment available.

7. Provide for appropriate ending activities in the unit: methods of evaluation based on predetermined, specific objectives, as well as some type of special, climactic activity such as a tournament, demonstration, performance, or similar presentation toward which the work has been building throughout the unit.

Table 4 is a sample unit taken from the yearly plan with its activities and subobjectives.

An alternative to the unit plan, called the day's order, is sometimes used. In this approach the program of activities varies from day to day. However, within a semester of teaching, the same amount of time would be devoted to each activity as in the unit plan. When scheduling problems prevail, this plan facilitates use of gymnasium

Table 4. Sample basketball unit (6 weeks)

	Physical fitness	*Physical skills*	*Knowledge and appreciation*	*Social development*

Week 1	Endurance
	Speed
		Passes
		Dribbling
			History
			Safety
			Rules: ball and
			  line violations
			Assign notebook
				New squads
				Discussion:
				  leadership
				Elect captains

Week 2	Endurance
	Speed
	Agility
		Review passes
		  and dribbling
		New: reverse
		  turn and pivot
			Rules: footwork
			  and fouls
				Group responsibility in drill
				  practice

Week 3	Endurance
	Speed
	Accuracy
	Agility
		Review pivot
		New shots:
		  lay-up, chest,
		  and one-hand
			Offensive
			  techniques
				Safety-shooting
				  practice

Week 4	Endurance
	Speed
	Agility
	Accuracy
	Balance
		Review shooting
		New: foul-
		  shooting
			Defensive
			  techniques
			Planned plays
				Teamwork
				Group planning

Week 5	Endurance
	Speed
	Agility
	Accuracy
	Balance
		Review shooting
		Tournament
			Etiquette in
			  tournament
			Strategy
			Review rules
				Continue group
				  planning and
				  teamwork

Week 6		Evaluation
		  of skills
			Written test
			Notebook due
				Evaluation of social cooperation
				Needs and plans
				  for next unit

space by more than one class, for one group could be working on basketball while the other class concentrates on trampoline or apparatus work at the sidelines.

Planning the daily lesson

The final step necessary in the planning phase of teaching is the actual lesson plan itself. This has as its basis the unit plan of objectives and activities but is a complete analysis of the step-by-step procedures to be followed during each class session. This final plan is probably the most important one, because it represents the real contact with the students and what they should be learning. It therefore needs to be very carefully planned from beginning to end, with many principles followed in selecting procedures and definite objectives established for attainment.

Objectives. Each lesson must have its own set of definite objectives. Unless the teacher knows exactly what should be accomplished during the class period, the students will not know or accomplish the daily objectives. These are drawn from the unit objectives and may or may not be related to all four goals of physical education. Perhaps just two or three goals are touched upon within a single lesson, but in the course of six to eight weeks, all four are represented.

Procedures. A definite outline of all procedures should be written down for each class meeting. The various methods of teaching and the progression from one type of activity to another need to be carefully worked out. The following principles for the daily lesson plan should be helpful in planning procedures for a single class period:

1. Provide maximum participation for all class members. When choosing a method of teaching, the physical educator should consider the size of the class, the facilities and equipment, and the time allotment and select those procedures which allow the greatest amount of practice for the most students.

2. Provide maximum instruction and supervision. The physical educator should select formations and drills that allow instruction for small groups and supervision for the entire class.

3. Provide for the safety of students. Group formations and game situations should be set up in such a way that students are protected from danger. This includes hazards both from stationary equipment and from adjacent practicing groups.

4. Provide for the health of the students. Methods of instruction should be selected in accordance with capacities of students in respect to overexposure, fatigue, and extreme heat or cold.

5. Promote greater student interest and enthusiasm. The physical educator should strive, by varying the teaching patterns (games, drills, relays) and increasing the complexity of the work, to heighten student responses.

6. Provide for the growth and development of the students. The choice of methods should be dependent on the skill levels and accomplishments of the participants, and performances far above or below the estimated limits of their abilities should not be required.

7. Promote learning by proceeding from what is already known by the group to what is unknown. The students will thus be able to understand the relationship of new learnings to that which they have already learned.

8. Provide for self-evaluation by students of their abilities, and for evaluation by the group and the physical educator of their daily accomplishments. In this way improvements and progress are recognized and advancement toward specific goals is kept in mind.

9. Promote carryover values and transfer of learning into daily life situations. Students who learn cooperation and good sportsmanship on the field or in the gymnasium, for example, need help in applying such learning to other experiences. The physical educator should make references to everyday situations to pave the way for transfer of learning.

Platnick's Photo Service, Hempstead, L. I.

Fig. 7-8. Promoting carryover values.

10. Promote creativity on the part of each student. Contributions of new ideas and theories from all the students should be sought by the physical educator. An atmosphere should be established in which all students feel free to express themselves.

One final note in regard to the daily lesson plan is concerned with flexibility. While it is essential that this plan should cover the full time allotted to the class and should be adhered to as closely as possible, the physical educator must be sensitive to the group's response to the procedures. If it is seen that the class tires quickly in a particular drill formation or that one of the procedures is not successful, the physical educator should go on to a different phase of the lesson. It is always wise to plan more than the time allows, so that in such instances valuable time will not be lost for

lack of organization or preparation. During the outdoor season, alternate daily lesson plans should be prepared for use indoors on rainy days. In this way no time is lost because of inclement weather.

A daily lesson plan drawn from the ninth-grade girls' unit on basketball is included as an example (Table 5).

Role of students in class planning

The teacher of physical education should devote some thought to the role of students in program planning. How much opportunity should they have in planning their own course of study?

The answer to this question lies in the philosophy of the department concerning student creativity and free expression. It may be believed that students should share in many phases of the planning or that

Table 5. Sample daily lesson plan, based on the unit plan (Table 4, Week 2)

Date: January 10
Class: Ninth-grade girls

Equipment: 4 basketballs
Time: 45 minutes

Objectives
1. To build endurance
2. To review passes and reverse turn
3. To introduce privots
4. To discuss rules and strategy connected with the pivot
5. To improve participation in group discussion

Procedures	*Organization*	*Time allowance (in minutes)*
1. Change, roll call, and announcements	Squad formations	7
2. Warm-up exercises Stretch, swing, flex, run in place Footwork (stop, start, slide)	Squad formations	5
3. Review Passes Reverse turn	Leader and line	2
4. Introduce pivots Demonstration Explanation Mimetics	Leader and line	3
5. Drills Dribble-pivot-pass Rest; discuss rules and strategy of pivot Dribble-pivot-pass over opponent	Shuttle formation	5
6. Uses in game	Two squads play; others count pivots and reverses; alternate	10
7. Evaluation What has been accomplished? What are uses of pivots? What should be next skill studied? Why should all participate in discussions?	Groups, informal	3
8. Shower and dress		10

they should contribute only to planning within a single unit or part of a unit. Some measure of student contribution should be sought, however, because of the inherent values of increased motivation, understanding, and creativity which it affords.

Motivation. When students assist in making plans for the class work, they are motivated and stimulated to participate to a great extent. They believe that they have a share in the goals and have a genuine desire for their accomplishment.

Understanding. The discussions necessary to bringing out student suggestions require much leadership and guidance from the physical educator. Many of the purposes of physical education should be pointed out to the students at this time to widen their understanding of the program as a whole. In this way their suggestions become consistent with their needs and with the goals of the program.

Creativity. Developing individual creativity is a goal of all education and one that should be included among the physical education objectives. Allowing students to contribute their own ideas and express their feelings is one way in which a creative atmosphere can be produced. While it may be more difficult to promote this type of rapport, it is indeed worthy of the attempt.

Problems. There are certain problems connected with student-teacher planning and the incorporation of the students' ideas into the program. In a large school where use of facilities is tightly scheduled and a prescribed regimen of activities must be followed if all groups are to take advantage of them, students would probably have less say about their yearly curriculum. However, they still could determine various aspects of the units under study, through class discussions. In a small school it is sometimes easier for the teacher to incorporate class suggestions into the program.

Another problem that arises in regard to student planning stems from the type of leadership offered by the teacher. There is a real art to promoting good class discussion to bring out the contributions of all students, and the physical educator must devote much time to planning key questions and ideas. Class suggestions must then be incorporated into the course by the teacher. Teachers should not use class discussion as a mechanism for trying to enforce their own ideas.

INDIVIDUALIZING INSTRUCTION

After incorporating student suggestions into the program, the instructional phases of physical education may be further individualized with the inclusion of variable goals for individual achievement. Inasmuch as each individual student within a class has attained a certain level of ability in a particular sport, the goal for that student should be improvement of his own skill level. Therefore, the student needs freedom to work at his own level of interest and rate of speed. He should strive to improve according to developmental tasks laid out for him by the instructor, based on previous record and performance. For example, in a skill such as pitching a softball or a baseball, proficiency levels for some students might indicate that they require further practice to improve accuracy and

speed, whereas other advanced students may need to advance to practicing various styles of pitching (fast ball, slow ball, inside and outside curves).

In terms of a prescribed curriculum, this may mean that some students are working on advanced skills earlier than suggested on the written guide. It must be remembered, however, that a curriculum is merely an outline, and individual development rarely follows a defined pattern. Therefore, freedom to explore and expand must exist.

When the teacher has completed all phases of planning—for the curriculum, the year, the unit, and the daily lesson—and has incorporated student ideas wherever possible, the time has come to carry out the plan.

NEW IDEAS FOR CURRICULUM REFORM—THE CONCEPTUALIZED APPROACH

The process of education for all youth is undergoing a revolution in many areas of the curriculum. The sciences, mathematics, and languages especially are utilizing new teaching methodology and new technological devices, and are drastically revising their curricula. Today's secondary school students are familiar with concepts and areas of knowledge that formerly were reserved for college-level courses.

Physical educators are well aware that they also must move their profession into this new educational era and that they must adapt physical education to the demands of this era. Physical and health educators have found that today's students require, and react well to, a conceptualized approach to physical and health education, and that this approach to teaching helps to stimulate curriculum reform in these areas.

Today's physical educators realize that their first task is to educate the student about his body and the scientific principles that control the use of the body, and to educate him to use his body effectively and efficiently. The conceptualized approach to the teaching of physical education helps students to better understand how their bodies move and why physical activity is so important in maintaining health and fitness. This approach to teaching physical education integrates the mental aspects with the physical.

In using the conceptualized approach, the teacher serves as a guide rather than a storehouse of information. Students learn, for example, the principles of body leverage, hip rotation, and foot and leg placement in throwing a softball by experimenting. The physical principles involved are best understood when they are ideated by the students themselves. This approach to teaching physical education depends upon the background of the physical educator and his willingness to place much of the burden for learning on the students themselves. This approach, however, also demands that the physical educator utilize a textbook geared to secondary school students and that each student be assigned readings and outside work based on the text and his related experiences in the physical education classroom.

The conceptualized approach to physical education helps students to understand why certain activities are selected for inclusion in the program and why such activities as physical fitness and the lifetime sports receive such great emphasis. This approach to physical education draws the student closer to the program and helps to make physical education activities a respected and pleasurable aspect of the school day.

PROJECTING PHYSICAL EDUCATION INTO THE FUTURE

What will physical education be like for the secondary school student of the future? Based on our knowledge of current advances in education and technology, some tentative projections can be made, but even these will be subject to change in the light of new events and discoveries.

The cost of education is constantly rising, and more and more students will need to be served by the secondary schools.

More physical education facilities will have to be financed and built to accommodate these students, and teaching staffs will have to be increased. New materials, especially plastics, will probably be used extensively for gymnasium floors to reduce the constant need for refinishing and to save on maintenance costs. Synthetics will be utilized on outdoor surfaces to make them more usable for longer portions of the year. Geodesic domes will house multiple-use gymnasiums and auxiliary physical education rooms, and air-supported structures will provide additional teaching stations.

An increasing emphasis on research in physical education will lead to more scientifically formulated curricula. Much of the benefit from this research will result in better programs for the atypical student. The student in regular physical education classes will have a textbook, and he will utilize special audiovisual aids. He will be able to analyze his own performances through instant playback devices housed in physical education projection rooms.

Curricula in the secondary school will be broadened and increased, and students will be given a wider choice in the selection of activities. A wide variety of lifetime sports will be offered, along with physical fitness work, dance, and the usual variety of team and dual sports and activities. Portable pools will help to make swimming instruction a possibility for every student. There will be an emphasis on student-centered learning through the conceptualized approach, and the students will take on an increased responsibility for the program.

As physical education continues to assert itself as an equal partner in the secondary school curriculum, it will gain greater respect. This will help to decrease class size, to give classes a more homogeneous balance, to provide a daily period of physical education for every student, and to release the physical educator from the burden of nonteaching duties. The physical educators themselves will become more expert in their own field, will attend more in-service and graduate courses, and will be more knowledgeable about education in general. This will help physical education to gain full community respect and support.

Athletics will become more educational for both boys and girls. The current trend toward varsity-level competition for secondary school girls will probably continue and intensify, but these programs will be balanced by expanded intramural programs serving the needs and interests of all the students in the school. Intramurals for boys will also be expanded, but interschool competition will place a stronger emphasis on the individual and the effect of competition on him.

As sophisticated communications and transportation media continue to make the world seem smaller, the international aspects of physical education will emerge. More and more students and physical educators will cooperate in international exchange programs, and Olympic and international sports and events will become vital parts of the secondary school program.

We cannot know or predict all the changes the future will bring. We may find that the philosophy and objectives of physical education will have to be drastically revised from year to year. Continued space exploration and reaching the moon may result in significant advances in the understanding of man's physiology and psychology that will affect our programs. Government-sponsored research and pilot physical education programs, changes in professional preparation, and revisions in general education will also have a profound effect on physical education, as will our need to serve disadvantaged students more meaningfully and our efforts to stabilize domestic and world conditions.

POINTS TO REMEMBER

1. Curriculum planning is a group process.
2. The physical educator has a major responsibility in the formulation of a physical education program.
3. A curriculum guide for a school system is a set of minimum standards.

4. There must be understanding of the child and learning laws to produce a valid curriculum.
5. A curriculum study must fit the school system and the society in which it will operate.
6. Activities must be properly selected.
7. Evaluation is a never-ending process for a curriculum.
8. The daily plan, the unit plan, and the yearly plan are all outgrowths of the overall curriculum.

PROBLEMS TO THINK THROUGH

1. How detailed should a curriculum guide be in regard to length of time spent on an activity and items to be covered in a listed activity? Why?
2. Should there be room for initiative by the physical educator working from a curriculum guide? Why?
3. Compare two schools where the same activity may be handled differently. What may make it necessary to handle this activity differently?
4. Why is it important to understand the nature of the child in curriculum planning?
5. What administrative details would limit a curriculum?

CASE STUDY FOR ANALYSIS

Select a secondary grade level (boys or girls) and prepare, in outline form, a curriculum for one twenty-week semester. The school has separate gymnasiums for boys and girls, an outdoor turf area, two teachers for each class of sixty to eigthy pupils, sufficient equipment and supplies for the largest class, and three periods of physical education weekly for each student. Analyze specific objectives, time allotment, activities, and fundamentals. Simulate a school situation by working in committee groups.

EXERCISES FOR REVIEW

1. What steps should be followed in the preparation of a curriculum?
2. How may a physical education teacher make his contribution to a curriculum study?
3. What principles should be considered in the selection of activities for a program?
4. Who may be a part of a curriculum study group?
5. What was the position of the White Plains

director in relation to its study? What other role may the director assume in a curriculum revision group?

6. Plan a six-week unit on badminton for seventh graders.
7. Plan a daily lesson within that unit.

REFERENCES

1. LaPorte, William Ralph: The physical education curriculum, a national program, Los Angeles, 1937, University of Southern California Press.
2. Cassidy, Rosalind Frances: Curriculum development in physical education, New York, 1954, Harper & Brothers.
3. Curriculum guide for physical education (K-12), Board of Education, White Plains, N. Y.

SELECTED READINGS

Bookwalter, Karl W.: Physical education in the secondary schools, Washington, D. C., 1963-1964, Center for Applied Research in Education.

Bucher, Charles A.: Administration of school and college health and physical education programs, ed. 4, St. Louis, 1967, The C. V. Mosby Co.

Bucher, Charles A.: Foundations of physical education, ed. 5, St. Louis, 1968, The C. V. Mosby Co.

Bucher, Charles A., Physical education for life, St. Louis, 1969, Webster Division, McGraw-Hill Book Co.

Bucher, Charles A., and Reade, Evelyn: Physical education and health in the elementary school, ed. 3, New York, 1970, The Macmillan Co.

Conant, James B.: The comprehensive high school, New York, 1967, McGraw-Hill Book Co.

Cowell, Charles C., and Hazelton, H. W.: Curriculum designs in physical education and health, Englewood Cliffs, N. J., 1955, Prentice-Hall, Inc.

Cowell, Charles C., and Schwehn, Hilda M.: Modern principles and methods in secondary school physical education, ed. 2, Boston, 1964, Allyn & Bacon, Inc.

Hughes, W. L., French, E. L., and Lehsten, N. G.: Administration of physical education for schools and colleges, New York, 1962, The Ronald Press Co.

Irwin, Leslie W.: The curriculum in health and physical education, Dubuque, Iowa, 1960, W. C. Brown Co.

Miller, Arthur G., and Massey, Dorothy M.: A dynamic concept of physical education for secondary schools, Englewood Cliffs, N. J., 1963, Prentice-Hall, Inc.

Nash, Jay B., Moench, F. J., and Saurborn, J. B.: Physical education, organization and administration, New York, 1951, A. S. Barnes & Co.

National Association of Secondary School Principals: Secondary education—yesterday, today, and tomorrow, The Bulletin of the NASSP 50:309, April, 1966.

New York State Association of Directors of Health, Physical Education and Recreation: Developing written program guides, New York, 1960, The Directors.

Rusk, Robert R.: An outline of experimental education, New York, 1960, St. Martin's Press, Inc.

Seagoe, Mary V.: A teacher's guide to the learning process, ed. 2, Dubuque, Iowa, 1961, W. C. Brown Co.

Shepard, Natalie M.: Foundations and principles of physical education, New York, 1960, The Ronald Press Co.

Vannier, Maryhelen, and Fait, Hollis: Teaching physical education in secondary schools, ed. 2, Philadelphia, 1964, W. B. Saunders Co.

Voltmer, Edward F., and Esslinger, Arthur A.: The organization and administration of physical education, ed. 4, New York, 1967, Appleton-Century-Crofts.

Williams, Jesse F.: The principles of physical education, ed. 8, Philadelphia, 1964, W. B. Saunders Co.

BOOKLETS, PAMPHLETS, AND ARTICLES

Alexander, William M.: What educational plan for the in-between-ager? National Education Association Journal 55:30, March, 1966.

Bucher, Charles A.: Health, physical education, and academic achievement, National Education Association Journal 54:38, May, 1965.

Bucher, Charles A.: Needed: a new athletic program, The Physical Educator 23:99, Oct., 1966.

Fraleigh, Warren P.: Should physical education be required? The Physical Educator 22:25, March, 1965.

Georgiades, William: Team teaching: a new star, not a meteor, National Education Association Journal 56:14, April, 1967.

Goodlad, John I.: Directions of curriculum change, National Education Association Journal 55:33, Dec., 1966.

Goodlad, John I.: Implications of current curricular change, The North Central Association Quarterly 41:179, Fall, 1966.

Hermann, Don, and Osness, Wayne: A scientific curriculum design for high school physical education, Journal of Health, Physical Education, and Recreation 37:26, March, 1966.

International Council on Health, Physical Education, and Recreation: Questionnaire report part I: Physical education and games in the curriculum, Washington, D. C., 1963, The Council.

National Education Research Division: A new look at the seven cardinal principles of education, National Education Association Journal 56:53. Jan., 1967.

chapter 8

Interpreting the program of physical education

There is an urgent need to interpret physical education to students, academic teachers and other educators, and the public in general. Accurate and significant facts need to be presented to these people so that they will understand the purposes and worth of our profession in the educational process as well as in their personal lives.

Physical education is a misunderstood profession. Surveys conducted among lay persons show that physical education is thought of as "calisthenics done to command," "athletics," "arms and legs and good intentions," or in terms of other misconceptions. Only as physical educators interpret their profession effectively will it be possible to obtain public support and to achieve its goals.

It is vital for teachers, students, parents, and the community-at-large to have a clear understanding of the important place of physical education in general education. This can be accomplished only where there is cooperation within the department, within the school, and within the community. A public that is not informed is not likely to lend its support to furthering physical education.

Teachers, to be effective participants in public relations, must be guided by well-thought-through, sound educational policies. This chapter concerns itself with policies and suggestions that will assist each physical educator to be an effective public relations worker, recognizing that it is his function not only to teach but also to interpret his program and its worth to the various groups of people that are consumers of his product and services.

GENERAL PUBLIC RELATIONS POLICIES FOR PHYSICAL EDUCATION

1. Each school within an educational system should develop its own public relations program, which should be an integral part of the larger school organization.

2. Before attempting to foster good public relations between the school and the community, good internal public relations should be developed, involving students, teaching personnel, nonteaching personnel, and administrators.

3. The public relations program should recognize that there are many kinds of people to be reached, such as pupils, parents, alumni, physicians, and administrators, and that each group requires its own unique procedures and approach for effective results.

4. The public relations program should present an articulate philosophy of physical education that clears away the misconceptions and stresses the objectives and worth of the field through the presentation of scientific evidence.

5. The physical educator should recognize that how he relates to other individuals within and without the department has implications for the public relations program. Consequently, such factors as a pleasing personality and appearance, provision for a healthy physical environment, and harmonious relations with students and parents are very important.

6. Before using communications media, such as radio or television, advanced planning is essential.

7. Evaluation of the effectiveness of the public relations program and the attitudes of the various sectors of the public should be determined through a carefully planned research program.

PUBLIC RELATIONS IN PRACTICE

Fifteen school systems in New York State were questioned about their public relations programs for physical education. They cited these operational factors in the conduct of their program:

1. Each physical education department has an active public relations program in operation.

2. Definite policies are established to guide the public relations program.

3. Responsibility for public relations is shared by all members of the department, with the central authority residing with the director.

4. Many media are used to interpret the program to the numerous groups to be reached.

5. Preparation and planning are essential in the use of all public relations media.

6. The total physical education program in action is recognized as being the most effective medium of public relations.

7. Effort is made to interpret to the public the correct facts concerning physical education.

The fifteen school systems surveyed were asked the question, "What message are you trying to convey to the public?" A compiled list follows of the answers given by the directors of the physical education programs:

1. The aims and objectives of the total physical education program

2. The value of the total physical education program

3. The importance of the program to the student

4. Recognition and achievement of all students in physical education classes and in intramural and extramural activities, and not just in athletics

5. The importance of the physical education program for each child

6. The efforts and energies that are directed toward giving each child a good program of physical education

7. The contributions of the physical education program to all children, not just athletes

8. The fact that even though interschool athletics receive most of the publicity, these activities do not receive priority in the program of physical education

9. The ability of the physical education program to enhance the health and welfare of the student

GROUPS NEEDING INFORMATION

Interpretation, or public relations, is basically concerned with communication. One person has defined it as getting the right facts to the right people at the right time and in the right way. Another has said it is doing good and receiving credit for it. One important consideration, regardless of definition, is to recognize that there are different kinds of people to be reached, and therefore different procedures and techniques are necessary in reaching these various groups. Six important groups that should be contacted are identified below.

Youth

Students in our schools who are exposed to physical education programs should be our best supporters. They should graduate from our schools and depart from our programs feeling that they have been very worthwhile, enjoyable, and educational experiences. They should believe that the subject of physical education needs support and should be recommended to other people. Students grow up to be presidents of boards of education, directors of banks, industrial chairmen, and other important citizens in our communities from coast to coast. The experience they have in physical education will help to determine how much they will support these programs as adults.

Colleagues

Faculty members in other subject matter areas are an important group to reach. The absence of coaches and other physical education personnel at faculty meetings and other academic gatherings frequently results in a lack of adequate communication and interpretation of the program to teachers of history, science, English, and other subjects. Physical education cannot expect to be considered an important part of the school educational program if the department is not represented at important meetings. Physical educators need the support of their colleagues. They should exploit every opportunity to reach these important educators, whether in faculty meetings or in informal discussions in the teachers' room.

Administrators

School administrators make decisions affecting physical education programs, determine budget allocations, approve facility allocations, and in many other ways help or hinder our professional progress. It is important to reach this powerful group and impress them with the contributions of physical education to the total education of the student.

Parents

Mothers and fathers should understand that physical educators contribute to their children's health and welfare. If they believe that their children are receiving a

Fig. 8-1. Students should be our best supporters. A student council meeting.

worthwhile educational experience in physical education, they will be strong supporters, but if they believe that it is a waste of time because of poorly planned programs, they may fail to provide their needed support.

Alumni

The alumni of a school can be a valuable asset to any physical education program, provided they are kept informed.

General public

Of course, the general public, consisting of business and professional people, taxpayers, and other citizens, are interested in their schools. Outstanding educational systems are marks of good communities. Therefore, it is important to interpret to the general public how physical education contributes to a strong educational program.

BASIC CONSIDERATIONS

Following are some basic considerations for reaching the various groups of persons noted above.

Studies and research. The results of investigations of various aspects of the physical education program, such as improvement in the students' physical fitness or skills, are excellent publicity material. These studies should help to place physical education on defensible ground as to its worth in the educational program.

Written material. Newsletters, reports, memoranda, brochures, and other forms of written material that have been accurately and neatly prepared are excellent media for reaching the various groups.

Sound departmental policies. If the department of physical education has given time and study to policies concerning excuses, uniforms, athletic participation, class participation, grades, and other important matters, the wide dissemination of such material will reflect efficiency and a well-functioning program.

Conferences. Student, parent, administrator, or teacher conferences are impor-

tant avenues for explaining purposes of programs, indicating interests, eliminating problems, and planning projects.

Integrated programs. Planning interdepartmental programs is an effective educational and interpretive device. A folk dance festival, for example, which integrates the resources of the physical education, art, music, home economics, history, geography, and other departments is an excellent medium.

Involvement. "As you share you care" is a saying that has much merit. Administrators, townspeople, colleagues, students, and others can be involved in many aspects of the physical education program, ranging from athletics to a "careers day" project.

Internal considerations. Public relations should be considered internally before being developed externally. The support of everyone within the organization, from the top administrator down to the last worker, should be sought. Furthermore, such items as defining the purpose of the program, designating the person or persons responsible, considering the funds available, deciding on the media to be utilized, and procuring the wherewithal to carry on the program should be a first consideration.

Public relations plan. The public relations program should be outlined in writing, and every member of the organization should become familiar with it. The better it is known and understood, the better chance it has of succeeding.

Funds. There should be adequate funds to do the job. Furthermore, the person or persons in charge of the public relations program should be given freedom to spend this money in whatever ways they believe will be most helpful and productive for the organization.

Persons responsible. Individuals assigned to public relations responsibilities should modestly stay in the background, keep abreast of the factors that affect the program, develop a wide acquaintance, and make contacts that will be helpful.

Wide coverage. A good interpretative

program will utilize all available resources and machinery to disseminate information in order to ensure adequate coverage.

Outstanding program. The program of physical education is the most important public relations medium. Good news travels fast but bad news spreads even faster. If the program is good, people will hear about it and, in turn, will give their support and help.

PRINCIPLES OF GOOD PUBLIC RELATIONS

C. O. Jackson, Professor Emeritus of the University of Illinois, lists the following ten principles which he believes are important to carrying out a good program of physical education:

1. *Begin with the best program* of health and PE that you can develop for your students in your situation. Existing time factors, facilities and equipment, aided by your initiative and ingenuity, will help.

2. *Use every opportunity* to acquaint fellow faculty members, other school personnel, with your plans, your special problems. Remember, a good listener makes greater progress, so be sympathetic to *their* problems.

3. *Take every opportunity to speak* to members of the community, individually and in groups, about your program. Talks before PTA groups, civic and fraternal organizations can be of real value in putting your ideas across.

4. *Dress, talk and act* like a respected member of both faculty and community. Your appearance, your personality are selling the program *and* your profession in your classes, at school, elsewhere in the community.

5. *Work with and through the administrator* in getting your ideas approved and accepted. Statements by leaders in education, and in medicine, and discussions of good programs in nearby schools can have nothing but good results.

6. *Sell the editor* of the local newspaper on the value of your program, the news value of the many releases you can give him. Discuss your problems with him, keep him informed of your progress. Even better, write up your problems in short, easy-to-read form for the editor or reporter. He will meet you more than half way if the "meat" of the story is easy to uncover.

7. *Arrange to use some of the educational time* on radio and TV for your program presentation. The complaint in many areas is that not enough such material is available

to even meet requirements set up by the Federal Communications Commission.

8. *Carry on broader, more comprehensive programs* of intramurals, GAA, and recreation as an outgrowth of your in-class program of PE. This is a big step in doing something worthwhile for *all* students.

9. *Plan and carry out demonstrations,* athletic carnivals, play and sport days. Try an annual open house. Parents and townspeople are interested in what their children are doing—give them a good sample.

10. *Remember that good teaching* is the crux of good public relations. Your students are ambassadors of goodwill. If you challenge them, help them in your program, they and their parents will become your strongest supporters. Your program will grow and develop correspondingly.*

INTERPRETIVE MEDIA

Fifteen school systems were surveyed to determine what specific media were utilized by the departments of physical education in interpreting its program to the various groups of people they were attempting to reach. The following media were listed:

Newsletter	Personal contact
School publications	Demonstrations and
Radio	exhibits
Television	Films
Newspaper	Pictures
Posters	Magazines
Letters to parents	Window displays
Public speaking	Brochures
Physical education	Sport days
program	Bulletin boards
Slogans	Professional associations

Some of the media that can be utilized effectively in physical education, along with general principles regarding their use, will be discussed briefly.

Slogans

The strength of a slogan lies in its emotional appeal—it is a distinctive phrase used to signify a purpose.

Slogans should be informational, factual, colorful, appealing, and easily understood and remembered, and they should impel to action.

*From Jackson, C. O.: Ten principles of good conduct, Physical Education and School Athletics Newsletter, Jan. 20, 1957, New London, Conn., Arthur C. Croft Publications.

In addition, slogans should be timely, practical, personal, challenging, simple, based on truth, short, imaginative, and concrete.

They can be used in radio, television, speeches, songs, posters, letterheads, billboards, displays, rallies, exhibits, advertisements, and handbills.

Our nation's political history has been affected by slogans. A few examples: "Walk softly and carry a big stick." "Keep cool with Coolidge." "Make the world safe for democracy." "A chicken in every pot." "54-40 or fight." "Over the top." "Remember the Maine." "Taxation without representation is tyranny."

Slogans have noticeably affected our economic development. A few examples: "It's smart to be thrifty." "We will not be undersold." "What helps business helps you."

Products have used slogans effectively. A few examples: "I'd walk a mile for a Camel." "All the news that's fit to print." "Progress is our most important product." "The pause that refreshes."

Ways of life are reflected in slogans. A few examples: "A stitch in time saves nine." "Time and tide wait for no man." "He who hesitates is lost." "Spare the rod and spoil the child."

Slogans have been used successfully in health, physical education, and recreation. A few examples: "It pays to play." "Give your child's mind his body's support." "Cross at the green, not in between." "Brush today to check decay." "A sound mind in a sound body." "Health, energy, and power are yours." "Fitness—a basic goal of education." "You can't sit and be fit."

Posters

Posters should catch and hold the attention of the viewer.

Posters require an eye-catching design.

Posters should convey a message.

Color is one of the most important agents that help to convey a poster's messages if effectively used.

As a rule, posters should have a short, punchy, well-worded message.

Posters should be simple, interesting, attractive, and convincing and should leave a specific message with the viewer.

Posters should guide an observer's view from one part of the display to the other. This can be done through color, line, and various layout techniques.

Posters should be placed at eye level if possible.

Posters should have good balance, with essential features in the most prominent places.

Radio

A radio program should hold the listeners' attention from start to finish. Many radio stations today broadcast little other than music and news. Programs must fit into such a pattern in order to hold the listeners rather than lose them.

Short programs are good. Very few persons turn on the radio today to listen to a dramatic play or a long discourse on some topic of the day.

The program should be informative and entertaining.

Language must be simple and direct— human interest and anecdotal material are always effective.

It is better to put depth into one idea rather than to cover many ideas and only scratch the surface of each.

Talk *with* rather than *to* the listener. Speak in the listeners' terms.

Know your audience.

Consult with the broadcasters—producers, program directors, etc. Find out the most effective methods for radio broadcasting.

Have a definite message in mind to put across to the public.

Be thoroughly familiar with the method to be used to relay the information: spot announcements, editorials, news broadcasts, reporting of school activities, panels, interviews, plays, quiz programs, etc.

Determine the time of day at which the

most receptive audience would be listening.

Publicize the radio program in advance. This can be done via advertisements, announcements on other broadcasts, school publications, press releases, etc.

Television

Explore the possibility of obtaining free time. The idea of performing a public service will influence some television station managers.

Consult television stations that are reserved for educational purposes.

Be prepared with written plans that can be put into operation immediately. Sometimes one must take advantage of opportunities for television time on short notice. Being ready may make the difference between acceptance or rejection for such an assignment.

Do not overlook the fact that television programming requires rehearsals, preparation of scenery, and other work.

Have boys and girls participate in the program. When youngsters are in the act, the attention of mothers, fathers, aunts, uncles, grandmas, friends, etc. is immediately attracted.

Motion pictures

One of the most powerful means of informing and enlightening the public in regard to physical education is the use of motion pictures.

Good pictures of daily class activity are tangible evidence of the worth of the program to parents and others. They are excellent for PTA groups, civic clubs, etc.

Motion pictures usually receive better audience attention. The situation is not like that in television, where there is opportunity to change to another program.

Before making a film, analyze the potential audience, the message to be conveyed, and other important items.

Survey the entire program of physical education in order to select the most signif-

Chester Studios, Inc., New York

Fig. 8-2. Physical education exhibition. (Yonkers Public Schools, Yonkers, N. Y.)

icant and typical activities to be photographed.

Homemade film depicting daily operation of the school can be useful in interpreting the program to the public.

In a do-it-yourself operation, try to obtain some professional advice—perhaps from a photography club or a camera shop. Use good equipment and material. Nothing is more annoying than watching a poorly planned movie which consists of shots that are blurred or not in proper focus, or going through an unpleasant experience with a projector that does not work properly.

Many films on physical education are available through professional organizations, college and university film libraries, commercial organizations, state departments of education, etc.

Exhibitions and demonstrations

In physical education an exhibition or a demonstration can be a culminating school activity to show what has been accomplished in the program and what students have learned.

Exhibitions and demonstrations can focus public attention on a program and

Fig. 8-3. Physical education demonstration. (Walt Whitman High School, South Huntington Schools, New York.)

stimulate action in support of the program.

Exhibitions can take the form of bulletin board displays, showcases, scrapbooks, drawings, or posters to point up such subjects as physical fitness or some sport or skill. They can also be used to show how expert performers have mastered outstanding skill in a particular sport.

Demonstrations can utilize all the students regardless of skill and also present a picture of what actually goes on in day-to-day classes.

An exhibition, for best results, should be limited to one type of activity or purpose.

Exhibitions should be original, present facts, stimulate participation, provide new ideas, and create action.

Newspaper and magazine articles

Articles can be published in either local papers or periodicals, or in national publications.

Articles should be factual, arouse and secure attention, contain human interest material, and be written in the language of the reader.

Magazines have many advantages since they have excellent color and layout, are read many times by different persons, reach a wide range of people varying in income and intelligence, and are found in many offices and homes.

Know the subject, the ideas to be put across, and the type of persons to be reached; then place the article in a publication that performs these services.

Newspaper material is often read hurriedly. Therefore, the style of writing must take this point into consideration.

Prepare all copy in typewritten form— neat, double-spaced, and on one side of the paper only.

Ideas may be suggested to magazines and newspapers to be staff written.

Letters

Next to personal contact, correspondence is the best interpretive medium.

Letters can be direct, are economical, and may be adapted to any situation.

Letters should be individually typed. It is important to use correct grammar and spelling.

The message contained in the letter should be friendly, cordial, warm, courteous, sincere, enthusiastic, and natural.

Write your letters as though you were speaking to the individual in person.

Letters can be used to announce special programs, to indicate the necessary skills and understandings expected of students, to interpret the objectives desired to be reached, etc.

Letters should be written in terms of the reader's wishes and needs.

Public speaking

Public speaking can be a very effective medium of interpreting. Through public addresses to civic and social groups in the community, public gatherings, professional meetings, and any organizations or groups that desire to know more about the work being performed, a good opportunity is afforded for interpreting the physical education profession to the public.

An effective job must be done in making a public speech, or it may result in poor public relations.

Know the subject to be discussed, have a sincere interest in the topic, and be enthusiastic.

Be direct, straightforward, and well prepared.

Give a brief presentation, and use clear and distinct enunciation.

Prepare an outline of the talk in advance. The talk should be well organized. Use correct English, and have an interesting beginning and conclusion, as well as a theme or central point.

Professional associations

Professional associations on local, state, and national levels can do much to interpret physical education to the public at large.

Professional groups hold meetings to upgrade programs; prepare films, publications, and other materials; establish professional standards; sponsor radio, television, and other programs; publish articles in periodicals; and in many ways inform the community, state, and nation about the physical education profession. They deserve your constant support.

Professional organizations are valuable in reaching boards of education, the general public, colleagues in the profession, other teachers, pupils, and other groups.

Some professional associations to be familiar with are the following:

National Education Association
American Association for Health, Physical Education, and Recreation
National Recreation and Park Association
The American Academy of Physical Education
The American School Health Association
The National College Physical Education Association for Men
The National Association for Physical Education of College Women
The American Physical Therapy Association
The Society of State Directors of Health, Physical Education, and Recreation
American Youth Hostels, Inc.
The Young Women's Christian Association
The Physical Education Society of the Young Men's Christian Association of North America
The Boys' Clubs of America
The National Collegiate Athletic Association
The National Association of Intercollegiate Athletics
The Canadian Association for Health, Physical Education, and Recreation, Inc.
Delta Psi Kappa
Phi Delta Pi
Phi Epsilon Kappa
The American College of Sports Medicine

SOME THINGS EACH PHYSICAL EDUCATOR CAN DO TO INTERPRET HIS FIELD OF PHYSICAL EDUCATION

Following is a brief list of ways in which the physical educator will personally be able to interpret to others the profession of which he is a part:

1. Join professional associations and help them to achieve their goals.

2. Attend faculty meetings after becoming a member of a school staff. Enter into discussions.

3. Become well informed about physical education as a professional field and about education in general.

4. Seek out school administrators, other members of the faculty, and the consumers of physical education's products and services. Help them to better understand the profession of physical education.

5. Understand the scientific foundations underlying physical education: the latest research and new trends and developments. Find out what the latest thinking is and translate it into action at the grassroots level.

6. Develop the best possible program of physical education. Have satisfied children and youth go out from the program.

7. Utilize every opportunity available to sell someone else on the worth of the professional field of endeavor. If the physical educator himself is sold, it will not be difficult to sell someone else.

8. Exploit every medium of communication to put the message across.

9. Think in positive terms. Think success, and the profession's chances of achieving great things will be better assured!

POINTS TO REMEMBER

1. Some of the basic principles underlying a sound program of interpretation and public relations
2. The various groups of people to whom the profession should be interpreted
3. A knowledge and understanding of the following interpretive media: slogans, posters, radio, television, motion pictures, exhibitions, demonstrations, newspapers, magazines, letters, public speaking, and professional associations
4. Some things that can be done to interpret the professional field of physical education

PROBLEMS TO THINK THROUGH

1. What are some of the common misconceptions about physical education? How did these misconceptions originate, and how can they be corrected?
2. What constitutes an adequate public relations program for a secondary school?

CASE STUDY FOR ANALYSIS

Choose some product that has gained national recognition, such as an automobile, cigarette, soap, etc. Do an in-depth study to discover what techniques were used to promote it and to presuade the public to accept this product.

EXERCISES FOR REVIEW

1. Define the term public relations.
2. What are the groups of people with which physical education is most directly concerned?
3. What are five priciples to recognize in interpreting your profession to the public?
4. What do we mean by the statement "As you share you care"?
5. Develop a slogan that can be used to promote physical education.
6. Prepare a poster to stress the importance of physical fitness.
7. Write a series of ten one-minute spot announcements for a radio station.
8. Write a letter that could be used to inform parents about the physical condition of their son or daughter.
9. What is the difference between an exhibition and a demonstration?
10. Write a 500-word magazine article on the topic "It Pays to Play."

SELECTED READINGS

Bernays, Edward L.: Public relations, Norman, Okla., 1952, University of Oklahoma Press.

Bucher, Charles A.: Administration of school and college health and physical education programs, ed. 4, St. Louis, 1967, The C. V. Mosby Co.

Bucher, Charles A.: Foundations of physical education, ed. 5, St. Louis, 1968, The C. V. Mosby Co.

Ciernick, Sylvia: Getting more mileage from school publications, National Education Association Journal 49:24, Feb., 1960.

Fine, Benjamin: Educational publicity, New York, 1943, Harper & Brothers.

Harlow, Rex F., and Black, Marvin M.: Practical public relations, New York, 1947, Harper & Brothers.

Harral, Stewart: Tested public relations for schools, Norman, Okla., 1952, University of Oklahoma Press.

Lesly, Philip (editor): Public relations in action, New York, 1947, Ziff-Davis Publishing Co.

McCloskey, Gordon: Planning the public relations program, National Education Association Journal 49:17, Feb., 1960.

National School Public Relations Association: It starts in the classroom, Washington, D. C., 1951, National Education Association.

National School Public Relations Association: Print it right, Washington, D. C., 1953, National Education Association.

Plackard, Dwight Hilis, and Blackmon, Clifton: Blueprint for public relations, New York, 1947, McGraw-Hill Book Co.

part

three

The teacher

Ellensburg Public Schools, Ellensburg, Wash.

9

Becoming
a
teacher

New teachers in today's modern secondary schools face tasks and responsibilities far different from those faced several years ago. Whereas previously a teacher worked alone to teach the students assigned to him, today's teacher may work with a team of several teachers and with many different groups. Whereas at one time a teacher had only one set of textbooks at his or her disposal, today there are films, television, computers, and programmed materials to assist in teaching. Once the teacher had to rely on subjective judgments to recognize pupil attitudes, aptitudes, and interests, but today's extensive testing programs offer comprehensive guidance information instead. Yet these technological advances have not made the teacher's tasks in education any easier, for they have brought with them additional responsibilities. The teacher must learn how to operate specialized equipment. He or she must keep up with new materials being released, and know when and how to utilize them appropriately.

Teachers presently graduating from professional institutions are being trained to meet these innovations in modern education. First of all, courses of study within their fields of interest are greatly specialized. For example, in physical education a prospective teacher may specialize in such areas as health, the dance, elementary school teaching, or coaching. Moreover, many institutions offer teacher-internship programs in which a student lives and teaches in a community while gaining first-hand teaching experience. Increased knowledge of child development and the learning process has made another substantial contribution to the training of today's teachers.

Yet these improvements in teacher training have not made the teacher's task any easier either, for administrators of modern secondary schools are expecting more productivity from their staff members. Administrators expect the teacher to keep abreast of the great advances in knowledge, application of the latest teaching methods, and utilization of modern equipment. Furthermore, administrators want increased professionalism, through in-service workshops and advance study, plus increased commitments to their field through faculty associations and organizations.

Although the task of teaching has not become any easier, progress in education has brought benefits not only to students but also to the teachers themselves. Today's teachers now enjoy greatly improved standards and practices. Teachers' salaries, for example, have vastly improved from meager wages to an average income of over $6,000 per year. In some sections of the country, of course, the average salary is much higher. Furthermore, many schools now offer valuable fringe benefits in terms of retirement plans, medical and life insurance coverage, and tenure. Teacher organizations such as the National Education Association are developing increased powers to demand improved health standards for children and improved working conditions for teachers, such as lighter class loads, fewer nonteaching duties, and smaller classes.

Teaching is a demanding profession and an ever-changing one. A close look needs to be taken at the changing aspects of the teaching profession—the teacher's responsibilities within the department, to the school, and to the profession, keeping in mind specific relationships to physical education. However, the problems of personal qualifications, job application, and certification generally come first chronologically for those persons entering the profession. Therefore, these topics will be discussed first.

PERSONAL QUALIFICATIONS

The personal qualifications of the physical educator are an extremely important consideration. Administrators regard such characteristics as professionalism, promptness, and the ability to maintain control as attributes of primary importance, while students hold patience, understanding, and fairness as desirable qualities in a teacher.

There is no formula for a successful teacher to follow. The "coach" who is like a father to his boys may be just as highly respected as the one who is a strict disciplinarian and dictator to his team. The woman physical educator who is highly organized and efficient may be just as well liked as the young graduate who can participate with the girls.

Is being "highly respected" and "well liked" the key to successful teaching? Perhaps these characteristics are a part of the overall picture. Certainly maintaining discipline and imparting information well are equally important qualities for the teaching process. The personality traits exhibited by the teacher and the relationship established with the students are the vital links between the subject and its recipients. All four aspects of the teacher's character—physical, social, emotional, and intellectual—should be worthy of emulation by the developing adolescent.

Physical qualifications

The physical educator usually has many more students in classes than do other teachers. Close relationships with students develop through the intramural and interscholastic programs. Because of the number and type of these relationships between student and teacher, it is important that the appearance of the physical educator be worthy of respect and admiration from adolescents. Uniforms should be spotless and all clothing should be neat, clean, appropriate, and in good taste. The association of health, good hygiene, and cleanliness with physical education is so close that the instructor must represent these ideals to the students.

The physical skills and abilities of the physical educator should be exemplary. In order to conduct satisfactory demonstrations and teaching lessons, teachers should be able to perform well in as many areas as possible. This does not mean that they must "star" in all events, but their background of basic coordinations should be well above average.

Social qualifications

Because of the many social objectives of physical education, it is important that the teacher be representative of mature social development.

As a person the teacher should meet

Fig. 9-1. The teacher should be respected. (Richwoods Community High School, Peoria Heights, Ill.)

Fig. 9-2. The teacher should be a stable, mature individual. (Rich Township High School, Park Forest, Ill.)

people easily, mix well, and treat all individuals with respect and consideration. It is these qualities which the teacher emphasizes in the classroom, and the students should therefore be able to recognize them in the teacher.

As a leader the physical educator should strive to control but not dominate the group and to plan with but not for his students. In so doing the qualities of leadership that should be promoted are presented to the students, and they in turn may learn to lead well.

Emotional qualifications

It is important that every teacher be a stable, mature individual, well adjusted to life in his or her chosen occupation. This is particularly true of the physical educator. The nature and tenor of the work require an emotional control and a responsiveness that are not easily defined.

In order to establish effective teaching rapport, the teacher must have patience and understanding mixed with firmness and composure. To meet all the individual problems that arise daily with students—their maladies, their excuses, their upsets—the teacher must offer a sympathetic, understanding ear, indicating to the students a sincere interest in their personal difficulties. In handling the everyday occurrences in the classroom, the teacher should display firmness and quiet confidence, so that the students realize that the situation is well under control.

The many frustrations that beset the physical educator striving for winning teams and competitive excellence must be met with calm self-assurance. Administrative and community pressures should not become so strong that other teaching responsibilities are neglected or that self-concern replaces consideration for the students.

Intellectual and other professional qualifications

Intellectually, the physical educator needs many qualities that are equally important for him both as a teacher and as an influence on young people.

As a teacher the physical educator should be efficiently organized and able to maintain order in handling the myriad administrative details. An ability to express ideas clearly and distinctly both orally and on paper is also important, for students learn from what is imparted to them, and therefore materials must be intelligently presented. A professional manner and outlook enhance the profession itself in the eyes of the students, and this, too, becomes an important aspect of the teacher's personality. The idea that a physical educator is a person of all brawn and no brains is slowly being overcome, and new teachers entering the field should further enhance this newer picture of the teacher as a real educator.

As an influence on young people, the teacher should have many interests both in and out of the field. This is important because it affords more opportunities for sharing the various interests of the students that are contacted daily. As a broader scope of physical education in its relationship to life is presented to the students, the physical educator is respected for more than just coaching abilities or professional skills. In this role of a counselor influencing students in their approach to life, the physical educator should have an outlook worthy of both respect and imitation.

Ideally the physical educator should be a model personality, sharing a deep knowledge and interest in the subject with students who are respected as people and led with sympathetic understanding. The personality which the teacher presents to the students may be as important as the material to be learned. Ideally, also, the physical educator should meet other qualifications and standards in addition to those of a personal nature. A discussion of these and their related problems follows.

PROBLEMS OF CERTIFICATION

Among the many problems encountered by any prospective teacher are those concerning the initial step of becoming properly certified. Often the confusion and red tape involved in finding appropriate information and determining personal status are so disheartening that the new teacher is bewildered before starting. The prospective physical educator is not different from other teachers in this respect, and knowing in advance about state requirements and qualifications can save a great deal of worry and frustration. Certification problems are complicated further by the continuous study and change of specifications.

Certification requirements

All states have established minimum requirements that must be met by prospective teachers before they become legally certified to teach. These certification requirements in teaching correspond to similar requirements in other professions, such as the licensing of doctors and dentists after state or national examinations.

The certification of teachers serves several purposes. The regulations protect schoolchildren by ensuring a high quality of teaching, the employment of only superior and qualified personnel, and unifying teaching standards. The students therefore benefit from these requirements. For teachers, however, the task of meeting the varying state requirements complicates professional preparation and certification procedures.

There are nine general areas in which states have governing regulations for teacher certification. While many states may agree on certain factors, they may disagree on others. The prospective teacher should therefore inquire directly of the state education department, division of teacher certification, for exact requirements. To summarize these nine general areas and the requirements presently established in the fifty states, the following information is presented.

1. *Citizenship.* Approximately thirty states have citizenship requirements or a declaration of intention clause. The teacher must be a citizen of the United States to qualify.

2. *Oath of allegiance or loyalty.* There are about twenty-four states that do not require a loyalty oath for teacher certification. The others usually have a written statement that must be signed.

3. *Age.* The age requirement varies among states. The lowest minimum age is 17 years. In general 18, or 19 years of age is acceptable in states specifying a particular age. Some states have no stipulation in this regard.

4. *Professional preparation.* It is in this area that the greatest differences in state requirements may be found. Several states have particular courses that must be taken by candidates for certification. For example, in Illinois teachers must have studied American government and/or history; in Texas, Texas and federal government; in Utah, school health education; in Wyoming, the United States and Wyoming Constitutions. Some of these special state requirements must be complete before the first year of teaching, while others may be fulfilled within a certain period of time. For example, a course in Rhode Island education may be completed within three years of the first year of teaching in that state.

5. *Recommendation.* A large majority of the states require a teaching candidate to have a recommendation from college or from the last place of employment.

6. *Fee.* A fee for certification, ranging from $1 to $10, is required in a majority of the states.

7. *Health certificate.* A certificate of general health is necessary in many states. Some states require a chest x-ray report instead of or along with this certificate.

8. *Employment.* Candidates from *other* states may need to have secured employment to become certified within some states.

9. *Course of study.* Besides the general areas of state requirements, there are basic and minimum regulations regarding the course of study that must be followed to

qualify for specific certification in physical education. Again, the states disagree in their requirements of hours of study necessary within the subject of physical education.

Because of these curriculum differences and the variation between states in regard to the nine basic factors outlined above, a certificate to teach in one state does not necessarily permit a teacher to teach in a different state. However, reciprocity among states in the same region of the country is a growing reality, particularly for graduates of an accredited teacher preparation program.

A further problem in certification presents itself where localities within a state have specific regulations governing selection of teachers. These are often more rigid than the standards established within the state itself. Detroit and New York City, for example, have their own sets of qualifications that must be met by their teachers, and many southern cities and states require high scores on the National Teacher Examinations. Local regulations usually involve such factors as teacher preparation and experience. An applicant may also be required to pass written and oral examinations for local licensing. Information regarding local teaching requirements may be secured by writing to the board of education in the city in question.

Prospective teachers should try to determine state and local regulations far in advance, if possible. In so doing they may guide their courses of study in college to meet the requirements. They should then send in their records far enough ahead of time to become certified before accepting a position.

Types of certificates

The type and value of certificates issued by the states vary nearly as much as do their regulations. In some states, for example, there are merely two categories of certification, permanent and probationary, while another state may have twenty-two variations of certificates to issue. The cer-

tificate to teach physical education is generally limited to this special field of work, but its validity may be for one year (probationary) or for life. Some states grant temporary, provisional, or emergency certificates to teachers who do not fully meet all requirements, with the understanding that within a certain period of time the candidate will become fully qualified.

The value of the certificate again depends on state regulations. It enables the teacher to teach in any public school system within that state, except those where local standards require further qualifications. It may qualify the teacher to teach in neighboring states, depending on reciprocity agreements. It may also permit him or her to teach in private schools within the state, or at least in private schools seeking state accreditation.

The prospective teacher or the experienced teacher seeking employment in a different state should not let these differences in state requirements and qualifications become a hindrance. An inquiry to the state or local department of education should bring necessary information in time to facilitate certification.

PROBLEMS IN JOB APPLICATION

The next series of problems faced by the prospective teacher revolves around finding a job—writing a proper letter of application, having an interview, and attending to the similar details important in obtaining a teaching position. The superintendent who is forced to choose between two or more candidates for a physical education opening may allow his decision to rest on appearance, on spelling, or on the smallest of details. The applicant should therefore take great care in all phases of the process of finding and obtaining a position.

Letter of application

The prospective teacher usually hears of job openings through friends, the college bureau of appointments, an employment agency, and/or direct application by letter to a specific locale. The letter of application serves as an introduction to the prospective employer and should be carefully constructed to contain appropriate information.

In appearance the letter should be neat, typewritten, and grammatically correct. Pertinent details should be included concisely and yet in such a manner that the personality of the individual is conveyed to the reader. The employer wants to know about the applicant's educational background, experiences related to the field of education, and interests. Personal information such as age and health should also be included, together with names and addresses of references. If possible, the applicant should also state his availability for an interview.

In response to this letter of application the candidate should receive a letter stating either that there are no vacancies or that the position is open and an interview is desired. A printed application form is often included with the latter reply, and it should also be filled out neatly and carefully.

Interview

Interviews of teacher-applicants generally take place at the school itself, providing candidates an opportunity to see the school in action, or at the college of the graduating candidate. In the latter case a field representative of the school system usually interviews several candidates from the college, and a request from the superintendent for a school-visitation type of interview follows.

In either type of interview the prospective teacher should expect to ask and to answer questions of all types, for it is the purpose of the interview to allow the new teacher to learn about the school system, as well as to give the employer an opportunity to screen the applicant.

While the employer is questioning the applicant, he will be observing the teacher's bearing, outlook, speech, personal mannerisms, and general effectiveness as a person. Needless to say, the applicant

should be prompt, well groomed, and neatly dressed for this occasion. The prospective teacher should be ready to answer in a concise and intelligent manner questions about any phase of teaching physical education. What is the most important attribute of a good teacher? What is the philosophy behind the inclusion of physical education in the school curriculum? What are some specific objectives of the program? How are the needs of the children determined? The range of possible questions is very broad, and the candidate can make little actual preparation for them other than to know and sincerely believe in the field of physical education.

The answers given by the applicant at the interview are not the only determining factor in obtaining employment. The employer may judge to some extent on the basis of intelligent questioning by the candidate about the type of education being offered in the school and the community's interest in school affairs. Inquiries about scheduling, class groupings, extramural duties, community activities, and school organizations indicate to the superintendent that the prospective teacher knows what is involved in a teaching position. At the same time the applicant is, of course, determining if this particular school administration is genuinely interested in physical education and if this type of position is the most desirable and suitable in comparison to other available jobs.

There are several types of teaching jobs that the physical educator needs to consider. Is a large or a small school system preferable? In a small school the teacher often has classes from grades one through twelve, while in the larger, multiple-building systems, a position may be limited to elementary, junior high, or senior high teaching. Is teaching in a large, departmentalized situation with several other persons a better position in which to start than one in which the teacher is entirely alone? These are questions that the teacher must settle in his own mind, in terms of his own personal preferences, after several school visitations and interviews have pointed out the differences.

Unfortunately, the prospective teacher does not always receive the position of first choice. A poor impression during the interview or a poor letter of application may make the difference. Other factors also enter into a failure of final appointment. Lateness of application or stiff competition for a high-salaried position may be a determining factor. The teacher seldom knows the real cause of failure.

Appointments are not generally made at the interviews themselves, for the board of education must give final approval, and the applicant should have additional time to think about such an important decision. Later the applicant may receive a letter from the superintendent, saying that the position has been filled, or one with congratulations on his or her appointment and perhaps some type of contractual agreement.

Contractual agreements

Contractual agreements between employer and teacher vary in style, form, and content, but essentially they signify a promise of payment for services rendered. In some areas a single word or handshake is the only type of agreement used, while in other areas a formalized contract carefully specifying duties and assignments is required. Each board of education has its own particular method. However, the prospective teacher should inquire about certain aspects of the agreement in order to know exactly what responsibilities and fringe benefits are contained in it.

Term of employment. The initial contract is usually a provisional one, covering one year of teaching. In many schools there is a two-year or three-year provisional period for new teachers, and at the end of that time a more permanent type of contract may be issued. Some boards of education provide "tenure" for teachers, which means that following the provisional period teachers may be assured of a position in their schools.

Responsibilities. In some instances contracts contain detailed outlines of teaching responsibilities, including, for example, the number of hours of intramural activities or the number of coaching assignments required of the teacher. These duties must be performed by the teacher if he enters into such an agreement, unless unusual circumstances permit exemption.

Release from a contract. Unusual circumstances, such as forced leave of absence or call to military service, may release the teacher from the total contract. This is possible in most cases by application to the board of education. The prospective teacher should realize, however, that except in these unusual situations it is not wise to break an agreement with the board of education. As professionals in the field of education, teachers are expected to be reliable and dependable people, with high ethical standards, and therefore able to live up to agreements.

Salary. Written agreements between teachers and employers usually indicate exact salary arrangements. In most schools a salary scale has been established, with definite regulations governing the placement of teachers on that scale. Years of service or merit usually determine increments in salary, and the prospective teacher should inquire about this aspect of the salary schedule. Where years of service are used as a basis for raises in pay, teachers usually receive regular increments in salary. In schools where a merit plan is in effect, the better teachers usually receive higher pay on the basis of certain standards of teaching that have been established for evaluation of services. A third type of salary schedule has emerged from schools using the team teaching program. In this case the person or persons shouldering major responsibility for a course of study receive higher salaries.

Benefits. Some school systems also establish subsidiary teacher benefits that make them more desirable and attractive places in which to work. Sick leave policies and visitation days are examples of administrative consideration for teacher welfare. Provisions for sabbatical leave, health insurance, and retirement are also benefits that vary among schools and states. The new teacher should try to find out as much as possible about these fringe benefits for teachers in the particular school system offering employment.

When the prospective teacher accepts the appointment offered and signs the contractual agreement, if one is necessary, the benefits and terms are settled and the problems of job application cease. The teacher has now assumed new responsibilities and obligations that must be met. These responsibilities encompass the physical education department itself, the school faculty, the community, and the profession, and are equally important to a successful career.

RESPONSIBILITIES TO THE DEPARTMENT

Whether the school system is large or small, the physical educator has many responsibilities to the department, each of which is essential in administering a successful teaching program. These responsibilities demand the teacher's time and thoughtful consideration, but because they relate directly to the students, the results of the teacher's efforts are apparent.

In a large school

As one member of a team of physical educators, the individual instructor has definite responsibilities in relation to teaching regular classes, conducting the after-school program, and working with other members of the department. In all three areas these duties require constant cooperation and mutual understanding for a smoothly functioning program.

Teaching classes. Each teacher is officially in charge of the instructional program in assigned classes. This responsibility entails far more than just teaching or conducting classes, however. Some of the other duties entailed in class management are the following:

1. Program planning and evaluation
2. Grading and pupil evaluation
3. Testing
4. Motivating (through charts, diagrams, etc.)
5. Checking health problems
6. Counseling on student problems
7. Conferring with students and parents
8. Caring for shared equipment and facilities
9. Maintaining departmental standards in locker room, showers, and gymnasium
10. Keeping records

These duties are performed in cooperation with other members of the department, and the same or similar methods that have been approved for all are used. For example, one teacher would not keep one form of record on a student while another teacher in the same department followed a different system.

Conducting the after-school program. In addition to regular teaching responsibilities, the members of the department share in carrying out the many extra duties that are a natural component of the physical education program. Conducting an after-school program of intramural and extramural activities, as well as interscholastic athletics, involves many details, such as the following:

1. Coaching assignments
2. Scheduling games
3. Handling publicity
4. Scheduling facilities
5. Caring for uniforms and equipment
6. Arranging transportation
7. Handling finances
8. Checking custodial maintenance
9. Ordering awards
10. Keeping records

In a large school a single instructor would not be able to manage all these details alone. With the entire staff working together, however, a well-organized after-school program serving all the students may be effectively conducted.

Working with the staff. Conducting the

after-school program is only one of the ways in which the members of the department cooperate. The director of the department usually considers the staff as a policy-making body that proposes and carries out progressive ideas. They plan together the direction the program will take and share with the administrator of the department the many details of budgeting, scheduling, making inventory, and so forth. In some schools the team teaching approach to physical education has been implemented. In this case the staff cooperates and coordinates all its efforts in order to capitalize on the special abilities of each of its teachers.

Cooperation promotes harmonious relationships among members of the department, and when disagreements or problems arise, they should be handled within the department itself. Ethical standards of conduct indicate that mutual support of colleagues be presented to outsiders and that individual problems of a member be taken to the department chairman first, rather than the principal or superintendent.

The new teacher should realize at the outset the nature of the role he must play as a member of a large school staff. Schools may differ in the actual delegation of the many responsibilities, but the teacher's obligation to share and cooperate remains the same.

In a small school

In a small secondary school it is customary for one man to be responsible for the teaching and handling of the boys' program, and for one woman to take care of the girls' program. While such a situation simplifies the problems of group planning and departmental organization, the same administrative responsibilities outlined for a large school remain, and they must be carried out by these two individuals. Because the number of students served by the program is small, it is possible for one teacher to handle the many details involved in the teaching program and after-school athletics.

A new teacher will find that the job of teaching in a small-school situation requires much coordination between the boys' and girls' departments. The program of physical education is more effective if the instructional procedures and requirements of the two teachers are similar and methods of pupil evaluation agree. Also, their policies on intramural and interscholastic activities should be consistent, with schedules for the use of facilities for these programs mutually arranged.

When problems or difficulties develop between the two departments, concerning the sharing of facilities, for example, the two teachers should try to work out the solutions together. If the answers cannot be found, the teachers should both seek advice from the next higher authority. If there is no officially designated chairman of the department, the school principal would be the person to ask for guidance.

Working together effectively is of primary importance to a smoothly functioning program of physical education in a small-school situation. When the two teachers mutually assist and support each other in all phases of their work, this worthy objective is achieved.

RESPONSIBILITIES TO THE SCHOOL FACULTY

Beyond being a member of a physical education department, a teacher is also a member of a school faculty. This position carries with it many responsibilities related to administering a program of education for children. All teachers must share in this endeavor, which includes three general areas of obligation: upholding school policies, sharing mutual faculty responsibilities, and respecting the educational curriculum.

Upholding school policies

Administration of a secondary school program involves the establishment of well-defined policies concerning all phases of school life: the curriculum, school regulations, homework, activities, and sponsored functions. In most school situations teachers play an important part in regard to these policies.

In a democratically administered school system, the teachers share in the establishment of school policies. Decisions are formulated on the basis of group discussion and majority opinion. The physical educator should share with the other teachers in formulating policies at teachers meetings.

School policies must be upheld by all members of the staff once they are determined. This includes the physical education teacher, who should not expect special privileges for members of varsity teams in respect to academic standards, for example, or request athletic considerations contrary to school regulations.

Sharing mutual responsibilities

In large and small school systems alike, the faculty shares many administrative duties. These are essential to a sound educational program, although they have no relationship to the school curriculum, and are a necessary component of school administration.

For example, there are many instances in which a teacher is called upon to act as a supervisor or sponsor of student activities. Teachers may be required to take bus duty or cafeteria supervision, or to be responsible for noon-hour activities. Homerooms, study halls, club activities, and student council are all additional responsibilities, and the physical educator should expect to serve with the other teachers in any of these areas.

In many schools, faculty committees are established to study current educational problems, such as education for the gifted or elementary foreign language teaching. Committees to handle administrative details such as class scheduling, grouping, or safety may also be set up. Membership in these committees is usually voluntary, but all teachers are expected to serve in some capacity. While the conduct of the after-school program may make it difficult for the physical educator to attend committee meetings, every effort should be made to share in this phase of school organization.

Respecting the curriculum

Just as the physical educator should support the methods and procedures of his colleagues within the department, so should he or she uphold and respect those of the other teachers in all areas of education. The teacher should exhibit a genuine and sincere interest in all phases of the curriculum and respect the work and accomplishments of the other teachers.

In return, the physical educator can expect from other teachers similar respect and appreciation of the work being accomplished by the department. This regard should be deserved, however. Teachers in other subject areas do not necessarily evaluate the physical education program in the same manner that physical educators would. Instead of rating program content with which they are unfamiliar, other teachers tend to value the teacher's seriousness of approach to teaching, the manner in which the instructor fulfills educational responsibilities, the concern shown for student welfare, and general attitudes toward the profession.

The physical educator who meets all these responsibilities as a member of the teaching staff actually promotes appreciation for physical education as a profession.

There is one further obligation of physical educators, which is directly connected with their particular field and deserves special mention at this time. Good working relations with members of the school custodial staff are of vital importance to the program and are clearly as important as relations with other teachers. The service of the custodians in gymnasium maintenance and in care of equipment adds significantly to the quality of physical education and should not be forgotten.

RESPONSIBILITIES TO THE PROFESSION

Membership in a profession such as physical education carries with it certain responsibilities which the new teacher should expect and accept. They are concerned mainly with professional advancement for the teacher and the growth of the profession itself.

Professional organizations

Professional associations are the media through which members mutually assist each other in achieving benefits for the group and promoting advancement.

As an educator, the physical education teacher should join the educational organizations available in his particular district or local area. This includes the faculty association, the local education association, and the country or district group, whichever organization has been formed. It is also considered the mark of a professional to join the state education association and the National Education Association. Membership in these associations is usually made available to the teacher through the school office at the beginning of each school year.

Physical educators should also join their own special local and state organizations, and the American Association for Health, Physical Education, and Recreation. It is through these channels that the teacher is able to keep up with the latest advancements within the profession. There are also specialized organizations on the local level for coaches, women, or teachers of a particular activity. It is in these local, small groups that the greatest benefits are derived, for the members have the opportunity to know each other well and share mutually in the problems and issues at stake.

Membership in these associations is made possible through literature sent to the school in each locale, in most cases. If not, teachers in neighboring districts are ready to provide the necessary information to newcomers.

Professional advancement

Membership in various associations is not the only professional responsibility of the physical educator. To reap the greatest benefits and to aid in advancing the profes-

sion itself, each member must make valuable contributions.

These associations are usually organized into committees that function in a particular area, such as planning, research, fitness, and publications. Working on these committees can be a very satisfying and rewarding experience, and one that should not be missed.

Even greater contributions to the profession as a whole can be made through research on problems in the field. Sharing results or findings on a particular method of teaching or testing is a real service to other members that should be willingly performed.

Personal advancement

Continued study for personal growth and development is another major responsibility of every member of a profession. The physical education teacher has two developmental paths open: in-service education and graduate study.

In-service education takes many forms within the school system and neighboring districts. It is found in individual and staff conferences, and in workshops, clinics, and study institutes. Planning sessions, orientation programs, and interschool visitations are all phases of in-service education. Any opportunity in which teachers join together with associates to consider school problems is considered to be in-service education. Real values stemming from these sessions are seen when teachers change and grow together for the improvement of the school program and the profession.

Graduate study is the other method of personal, professional advancement. Some of the purposes of graduate study include the development of a higher degree of competence and the development of the ability to evaluate, interpret, and draw conclusions from the scholarly work of others.

There are several types of graduate degrees available to the physical education teacher.

1. Master's degree. A master's degree in physical education usually requires one

year of study beyond a bachelor's degree. In some universities a thesis is part of the required program for a degree, while in other schools several related extra credits or a comprehensive examination is required in its place.

2. Doctor of philosophy, doctor of education, or doctor of physical education. The doctoral degrees usually require three or four more years of study. In the curriculum for a doctorate a formal dissertation or document is a requisite.

Some institutions offer a professional or specialist's certificate for thirty hours of graduate work above the completion of the master's program.

The prospective teacher of physical education should realize that a professional attitude is another important responsibility that must be developed through associations and study programs with other professionals. In this way the teacher makes a valuable contribution to himself or herself and to the profession as a whole.

RESPONSIBILITIES TO THE COMMUNITY

Another responsibility of importance to the physical educator relates to the relationship established with the community. This is a two-way association, for the support a physical education teacher gains for the program depends largely upon the program itself and the way the citizens interpret it. The responsibilities of the physical education department in promoting this community relationship are three: presenting a sound program, joining community-sponsored activities, and supporting community standards.

Presenting a sound program

The physical educator is employed by a community's board of education to teach physical education in the finest manner possible. The program of physical education can be a comprehensive source of good public relations between a school and its community because of the many contacts that are a natural by-product of this program. It is in this field that an entire student body is excited by interscholastic competitive activities, and parents, too, share in these enjoyable events. Through the intramural programs, the demonstrations, and the testing program the parents become very much aware of and interested in the total program of physical education. The entire school administration benefits from a sound physical education program because of community interest; therefore, it is essential that the program be thoughtfully planned, presented, and evaluated.

Fig. 9-3. The physical educator has responsibility to become part of the community. (Lincoln High School, Yonkers, N.Y.)

Joining community activities

The physical educator has definite obligations to become a part of the community by joining selected community organizations, including the parent-teacher association. Furthermore, because of the close association between recreational activities and physical education, the teachers often are called to conduct evening programs and assist in sponsoring special events. While sharing in these activities the teacher has an opportunity to know the people of the community and what it is that they want from their schools. This is an advantage to the school, for it must serve its own particular community. At the same time the physical educator helps the school administration by serving as an interpreter of its philosophy to the community and helping the people understand what the schools are trying to do.

Serving the community in which they teach is a responsibility that must be met by all teachers. Good school-community relations are of primary importance to a school that is meeting the needs of its students. The physical educator must do his share by contributing in as many ways as possible, and the results will bring greater support to his program.

Supporting community standards

Throughout the many associations established with community citizens the physical educator should support and honor the standards expected of teachers in that particular community where they are in accordance with high professional standards. It is important to remember that relating school gossip or information of a personal nature about a particular student does not earn respect for a teacher in the schools, but that by wiser action the respect and status of teachers may be upheld in the community.

CODE OF ETHICS

The teacher is far more than just a teacher of physical education. His or her responsibilities extend to all relationships established with people, and all actions are governed in almost every area by a code of professional ethics. Many important principles in this code of ethics have been pointed out in relation to particular situations. The suggested code of the National Education Association and endorsed by the American Association for Health, Physical Education, and Recreation is presented here in its entirety for a more complete explanation of accepted standards. It should be kept in mind when reading this code that it represents the combined thinking of experienced leaders in the field and therefore should be respected. Furthermore, it provides a framework of guidelines for all professional physical educators, thereby guaranteeing the professional freedom it is designed to preserve.

CODE OF ETHICS
OF THE EDUCATION PROFESSION*

Preamble

The educator believes in the worth and dignity of man. He recognizes the supreme importance of the pursuit of truth, devotion to excellence, and the nurture of democratic citizenship. He regards as essential to these goals the protection of freedom to learn and to teach and the guarantee of equal educational opportunity for all. The educator accepts his responsibility to practice his profession according to the highest ethical standards.

The educator recognizes the magnitude of the responsibility he has accepted in choosing a career in education, and engages himself, individually and collectively with other educators, to judge his colleagues, and to be judged by them, in accordance with the provisions of this code.

Principle I
Commitment to the Students

The educator measures his success by the progress of each student toward realization of his potential as a worthy and effective citizen. The educator therefore works to stimulate the spirit of inquiry, the acquisition of knowledge and understanding, and the thoughtful formulation of worthy goals.

In fulfilling his obligation to the student, the educator—

---

*Recommended for Adoption by the Representative Assembly of the National Education Association, July, 1968, by the NEA Committee on Professional Ethics, the NEA Commission on Professional Rights and Responsibilities, and the NEA Board of Directors.

1. Shall not without just cause restrain the student from independent action in his pursuit of learning, and shall not without just cause deny the student access to varying points of view.

2. Shall not deliberately suppress or distort subject matter for which he bears responsibility.

3. Shall make reasonable effort to protect the student from conditions harmful to learning or to health and safety.

4. Shall conduct professional business in such a way that he does not expose the student to unnecessary embarrassment or disparagement.

5. Shall not on the ground of race, color, creed, or national origin exclude any student from participation in or deny him benefits under any program, nor grant any discriminatory consideration or advantage.

6. Shall not use professional relationships with students for private advantage.

7. Shall keep in confidence information that has been obtained in the course of professional service, unless disclosure serves professional purposes or is required by law.

8. Shall not tutor for remuneration students assigned to his classes, unless no other qualified teacher is reasonably available.

Principle II
Commitment to the Public

The educator believes that patriotism in its highest form requires dedication to the principles of our democratic heritage. He shares with all other citizens the responsibility for the development of sound public policy and assumes full political and citizenship responsibilities. The educator bears particular responsibility for the development of policy relating to the extension of educational opportunities for all and for interpreting educational programs and policies to the public.

In fulfilling his obligation to the public, the educator—

1. Shall not misrepresent an institution or organization with which he is affiliated, and shall take adequate precautions to distinguish between his personal and institutional or organizational views.

2. Shall not knowingly distort or misrepresent the facts concerning educational matters in direct and indirect public expressions.

3. Shall not interfere with a colleague's exercise of political and citizenship rights and responsibilities.

4. Shall not use institutional privileges for private gain or to promote political candidates or partisan political activities.

5. Shall accept no gratuities, gifts, or favors that might impair or appear to impair professional judgment, nor offer any favor, service, or thing of value to obtain special advantage.

Principle III
Commitment to the Profession

The educator believes that the quality of the services of the education profession directly influences the nation and its citizens. He therefore exerts every effort to raise professional standards, to improve his service, to promote a climate in which the exercise of professional judgment is encouraged, and to achieve conditions which attract persons worthy of the trust to careers in education. Aware of the value of united effort, he contributes actively to the support, planning, and programs of professional organizations.

In fulfilling his obligation to the profession, the educator—

1. Shall not discriminate on grounds of race, color, creed, or national origin for membership in professional organizations, nor interfere with the free participation of colleagues in the affairs of their association.

2. Shall accord just and equitable treatment to all members of the profession in the exercise of their professional rights and responsibilities.

3. Shall not use coercive means or promise special treatment in order to influence professional decisions of colleagues.

4. Shall withhold and safeguard information acquired about colleagues in the course of employment, unless disclosure serves professional purposes.

5. Shall not refuse to participate in a professional inquiry when requested by an appriate professional association.

6. Shall provide upon the request of the aggrieved party a written statement of specific reason for recommendations that lead to the denial of increments, significant changes in employment, or termination of employment.

7. Shall not misrepresent his professional qualifications.

8. Shall not knowingly distort evaluations of colleagues.

Principle IV
Commitment to Professional Employment Practices

The educator regards the employment agreement as a pledge to be executed both in spirit and in fact in a manner consistent with the highest ideals of professional service. He believes that sound professional personnel relationships with governing boards are built upon personal integrity, dignity, and mutual respect. The educator discourages the practice of his profession by unqualified persons.

In fulfilling his obligation to professional employment practices, the educator—

1. Shall apply for, accept, offer, or assign a position or responsibility on the basis of professional preparation and legal qualifications.

2. Shall apply for a specific position only when it is known to be vacant, and shall refrain from underbidding or commenting adversely about other candidates.

3. Shall not knowingly withhold information regarding a position from an applicant, or misrepresent an assignment or conditions of employment.

4. Shall give prompt notice to the employing agency of any change in availability of service, and the employing agent shall give prompt notice of change in availability or nature of a position.

5. Shall not accept a position when so requested by the appropriate professional organization.

6. Shall adhere to the terms of a contract or appointment, unless these terms have been legally terminated, falsely represented, or substantially altered by unilateral action of the employing agency.

7. Shall conduct professional business through channels, when available, that have been jointly approved by the professional organization and the employing agency.

8. Shall not delegate assigned tasks to unqualified personnel.

9. Shall permit no commercial exploitation of his professional position.

10. Shall use time granted for the purpose for which it is intended.

POINTS TO REMEMBER

1. Physical educators must fulfill personal and educational requirements to become certified to teach. These requirements vary throughout the states, as do the types of certificates issued.

2. Certain personality and character traits help make a teacher more effective in teaching and associating with students and colleagues.

3. A physical educator's relationship to the students is very important for effective teaching and guidance.

4. A physical education teacher's relationships with other teachers, the administration, the profession, and the community have an important bearing on the respect he earns for himself as a professional person and for his program.

5. A physical educator is governed by a code of ethics that protects him and other members of the profession by suggested standards of behavior.

PROBLEMS TO THINK THROUGH

1. When is a teacher not a teacher?

2. What personal qualities are most important for a teacher of physical education—

qualities that may not be as essential in teaching other areas?

3. With whom would a new physical education teacher discuss a disagreement relating to procedures in marking students (a) in a small school? (b) in a large school? With whom would he not discuss it?

4. In August a new teacher receives another job offer at a higher salary in a preferred locale. What course of action should be taken, if any?

5. What community clubs or agencies have a direct interest in the school physical education program? How would the teacher who lives outside the school's community indicate an interest in the activities of such groups?

6. An after-school intramural game conflicts with a special faculty committee meeting. The physical education teacher, as a member of this committee, must choose where his time will be spent. What factors enter into his decision?

CASE STUDY FOR ANALYSIS

The new physical education teacher has been asked by his experienced co-worker to help referee an important eighth grade intramural soccer championship game. The game ends in a tie, and rather than reschedule another playoff or play another quarter, his colleague rules that the team winning two out of three penalty kicks will win. The new teacher senses the keen disappointment felt by the team members with this ruling and does not agree with his superior's decision in this case. What, if anything, should he do?

EXERCISES FOR REVIEW

1. What specific information should be included in an application to a superintendent of schools? Write a sample letter.

2. Investigate the requirements for teaching in another state and determine in what ways these requirements are being met, if they are, and in what ways professional preparation may be lacking.

3. What questions may a candidate for a physical education position in a large school system expect to be asked during an interview with the administrator?

4. What school policies should this candidate inquire about during this interview?

5. A school system is planning to build a

second junior high school and the administrator asks the physical education department to share in the formulation of plans for the physical education facilities. What steps would a new teacher take in order to offer real assistance in this project?

6. A new physical education teacher discovers that the community fathers run a highly competitive Little League program. If this teacher disagrees with the type of management the program is receiving, what procedures would he follow to combat this community enterprise?

7. List some outside interest and hobbies that would add to the professional growth of a physical educator.

8. In what areas of teaching physical education would further scientific research be particularly valuable?

9. In what ways does a professional code of ethics protect the teacher of physical education?

10. What responsibilities to the profession of physical education would be most difficult for a teacher to meet?

SELECTED READINGS

American Association for Health, Physical Education, and Recreation: Developing democratic human relations through health education, physical education, and recreation, Washington, D. C., 1951, The Association.

American Association for Health, Physical Education, and Recreation: Professional preparation in health education, physical education, recreation education, Washington, D. C., 1962, The Association.

Bucher, Charles A.: Administration of school and college health and physical education programs, ed. 4, St. Louis, 1967, The C. V. Mosby Co.

Bucher, Charles A.: Foundations of physical education, ed. 5, St. Louis, 1968, The C. V. Mosby Co.

Bucher, Charles A.: Physical education for life, St. Louis, 1969, Webster Division, McGraw-Hill Book Co.

Filbin, Robert L., and Vogel, Stefan: So you're going to be a teacher, Great Neck, N. Y., 1962, Barron's Educational Series, Inc.

Lieberman, Myron: Education as a profession, Englewood Cliffs, N. J., 1956, Prentice-Hall, Inc.

Morris, Van Cleve, and others: Becoming an educator, Boston, 1963, Houghton Mifflin Co.

National Association of Secondary School Principals: Health, physical education, and recreation in the secondary school, Washington, D. C., 1960, The Association.

Shepard, Natalie Marie: Foundations and principles of physical education, New York, 1960, The Ronald Press Co.

Skinner, B. F.: The technology of teaching, New York, 1968, Appleton-Century-Crofts.

Snyder, Raymond A., and Scott, Harry A.: Professional preparation in health, physical education and recreation, New York, 1954, McGraw-Hill Book Co.

Stiles, Lindley J. (editor): The teacher's role in American society, fourteenth yearbook of the John Dewey Society, New York, 1957, Harper & Brothers.

Stinnett, T. M.: The profession of teaching, New York, 1962, The Center for Applied Research in Education, Inc.

Stinnett, T. M., and Haskew, Laurence D.: Teaching in American schools, New York, 1962, Harcourt, Brace & World, Inc.

BOOKLETS, PAMPHLETS, AND ARTICLES

Batchelder, Richard D.: Unionism versus professionalism in teaching, National Education Association Journal **55**:18, April, 1966.

Carr, William G.: An international Magna Carta for teachers, National Education Association Journal **55**:42, Dec., 1966.

Coplan, Arlo H.: The ugly gym teacher, The Physical Educator **21**:106, Oct., 1964.

Crawford, Wayne H.: Are you ready to teach? Journal of Health, Physical Education, and Recreation **36**:87, Jan. 1965.

Davis, Hazel: Profile of the American public school teacher, National Education Association Journal **56**:12, May 1967.

Denemark, George W.: The teacher and his staff, National Education Association **55**:17, Dec., 1966.

Drew, A. Gwendolyn: Certification of coaches, Journal of Health, Physical Education, and Recreation **37**:77, April, 1966.

Field, David: Bringing teacher and job together, Journal of Health, Physical Education, and Recreation **36**:33, Feb., 1965.

Finlayson, Anne: A consumer's position on teacher preparation, Journal of Health, Physical Education, and Recreation **35**:39, May, 1964.

Hanby, Kenneth R., and Belka, David E.: Beginning teacher tips in health and physical education, The Physical Educator **21**:107, Oct., 1964.

Howe, Harold, II: A nation of amateurs, School & Society **94**:448, Dec. 10, 1966.

Hunter, Madeline C.: The agony and the ecstasy of teaching, National Education Association Journal **56**:36, Feb., 1967.

International Council on Health, Physical Education, and Recreation, part III: Status of teachers of physical education, Washington, D. C., 1963, The Council.

Melaro, Constance L., and Davies, Don: Comments on teacher certification, National Education Association Journal **55**:18, Sept., 1966.

National Education Association: Profiles of excellence, Washington, D. C., 1966, The Association.

National Education Association: Conditions of work for quality teaching, National Education Association Journal **54**:33, March, 1965.

Rock, Donald A., and Hemphill, John K.: Profile of the junior-high principal, Report of the Junior High-School Principalship, National Association of Secondary-School Principals, Washington, D. C., 1966, The Association.

Schooling, H. W.: Teacher-administrator relation-ships, National Education Association Journal 54:32, 1965.

Simandle, Sidney: Certification across state lines, National Education Association Journal 55:56, Dec., 1965.

The beginning
teacher

As the day of birth is one of the most critical for the newborn baby, so is the first year of teaching one of the most critical for the newly trained teacher. The neophyte instructor has spent four or more years in college, learning a great amount of theory from professors, talking about what to do when discipline problems arise with students, and discussing how to function with inadequate facilities. Now he or she finds himself or herself on the job in the classroom or gymnasium faced with a live and restless group of students. These boys and girls know that an inexperienced teacher is handling the class, and many seek opportunities to disprove all the theory that has been learned in four years of training. The big test has come. Will the beginning teacher be successful in meeting the challenge? Will the class be organized for effective instruction? Will the teaching techniques that have been mastered be equal to the practical situation that now exists? The answer to these and similar questions depends upon many factors, including whether or not the beginning teacher has been alerted to some of the problems that may arise and some of the procedures that may be followed in handling them. This chapter is aimed at helping the new teacher meet problems that are encountered the first year on the job. Although the problems of the beginning teacher are infinite, it is believed that many are common and that recommendations by experienced teachers will assist him or her in successfully completing the first critical year of teaching.

There is a high turnover rate of first-year teachers. While some teachers change jobs after the first year to improve their status, others leave the profession because of dissatisfaction and discouragement, and because they have found the job of adjusting to the hard realities of teaching too difficult for them to master. Several research studies have been conducted to determine the reasons teachers give for job satisfaction or dissatisfaction. They include such items as teacher-administrator factors, physical conditions, teacher-community factors, teacher-faculty factors, teacher-student and teacher-parent factors, and salary and security factors. An example of such a study is one by Wey,[1] conducted several years ago but still true today, involving ninety-five beginning teachers who graduated from Appalachian State Teachers College. The research involved the identification of 2,537 difficulties encountered by the teachers. The three areas into which these difficulties were grouped were (1) difficulties related to personal characteristics, (2) difficulties related to instructional activities, and (3) difficulties related to community environment and relationships. Most of the difficulties pertained to (1) pupil control, (2) teaching assignment, (3) adaptation to pupil needs, (4) records and reports, (5) deficiencies in equipment, (6) teacher-principal relationships, and (7) personality.

Kleinman[2] studied the relationship between job selection by beginning teachers in which he compiled factors that affected teacher adjustment and then had a jury select the ones that were most critical to this adjustment. The thirty-five factors selected were as follows:*

1. Status of teachers in the community
2. Salary ranges for personnel in the school or school system
3. The teaching load involved
4. Attitude of the population toward education
5. Special demands by the community on teachers
6. Sufficiency, diversity, and appropriateness of materials of instruction
7. Administrative and supervisory personnel to whom the teacher is directly responsible
8. Cost of housing facilities available in the community
9. Special repressions by the community on teacher conduct
10. Attitude of the community toward the school program, curriculum, practices, and other related educational issues
11. Adequacy of housing facilities available in the community
12. Time allotted for attending professional conferences
13. Size and number of increments for each salary range
14. School policies and practices related to promotion of staff members within the school system
15. Teacher freedom to experiment in the classroom with instructional methods and content
16. Assigned extra duties during the school day
17. Opportunities for teachers to participate in the social life of the community as well as in civic service functions
18. Procedures utilized in the evaluation of teacher competence
19. Assigned extra duties after school hours
20. Role of the teacher in determining rules and regulations related to classroom management
21. Responsibilities and degree of participation by school personnel in the evaluation and planning of the instructional program
22. School policies and practices related to teacher class load
23. School policies and practices related to "extra" teacher assignments during the school day
24. Recommended and/or prevailing teaching methods utilized in the school or school system
25. Personnel responsible for the selection and organization of courses, content, units, and/or experiences
26. Number and types of clerical duties and reports required of teachers
27. School policies and practices related to introducing new teachers to their particular responsibilities
28. Assigned duties related to the "extracurricular" program
29. Types of housing facilities available in the community
30. Merit increments, bonuses, and salary incentives for evidence of professional growth
31. School policies and practices related to assisting worthy staff members to achieve recognition and advancement within the profession
32. Size, location, and suitability of classroom
33. School policies and practices related to after-school teacher assignments
34. School policies and practices related to distribution of teacher "load"
35. Custodial staff cooperation with the professional staff

It is readily evident from the research conducted that problems of beginning teachers are numerous and varied. It would be of great value to the new teacher to study each of these problems in as much detail as possible and the meaning they have in relation to adjusting satisfactorily to the job.

Many of the problems of teachers are "across the board" types of difficulties affecting all teachers regardless of subject-matter affiliation. However, the teacher of physical education encounters some problems that are due to the nature of his or her special field of endeavor. Some of the more

---

*From Kleinman, Lou: The relationship between job selection by beginning teachers and subsequent teacher adjustment, doctoral thesis, New York University, 1959, pp. 92-94.

common problems of beginning physical education teachers that have been identified through research are associated with the following:

Discipline
Facilities
Adjustment to the school
Class organization
Student hostilities toward the program
Methods of teaching
Legal liability
Numbers of students in class
Insufficient space
Equipment
Behavior problems
Introduction of new ideas and techniques
Intellectually inferior label associated with physical education
Program planning
Status
Role of physical education in education
Personal relationships
Interscholastic athletics
Budget
Scheduling
Grouping in classes
Time allotment
Insurance

Many problems of the beginning physical education teacher appear to recur over and over again and can be grouped into two classifications, personal and professional problems, and administrative problems. Before discussing some of these problems it seems important to consider how selecting the right position and having a better understanding of the school, community, and job into which the new teacher is going will reduce or alleviate the problems.

ELIMINATING SOME PROBLEMS BEFORE ASSUMING THE JOB

The teacher should carefully evaluate the position before accepting such a responsibility. Unfortunately, some teachers accept positions in schools and communities in which they do not fit or belong and, consequently, where problems are bound to arise. If one is going to be unhappy and ineffective on the job, it may be better not to accept such a position in the first place. The many complex factors related to proper adjustment on the job are usually associated with the nature of the person, the

nature of the environment, and the interaction of the two. It is therefore important to the candidate for a teaching position to carefully weigh the available position and his or her abilities and personal characteristics for handling this position effectively. If this is done, many of the problems will be foreseen, and the qualities and preparation needed to handle them successfully will be evaluated realistically.

Advance considerations

Two advance considerations important to the beginning teacher before assuming the job are knowledge of the conditions of employment and pertinent factors about the school and community.

Knowledge of conditions of employment. It is imperative for the new teacher to understand the numerous details, duties, and responsibilities that he or she is about to assume, including a knowledge of classes to be handled, sports to be coached, clubs to be sponsored, homeroom assignments, study halls, length of the school day, after-school obligations, compensation to be received, salary schedules in force, sick leave, tenure, sabbaticals, health insurance, and other pertinent facts. Only as the teacher has a clear understanding of the responsibilities will he or she be able to prepare sufficiently, both mentally and physically, for the position. Information can be obtained from other teachers, members of the administration, and/or school literature that contains pertinent school policies.

Lack of advance knowledge of unfavorable working conditions has caused many teachers to be unhappy in their positions. The following are some of the conditions most often mentioned:

1. Classes are too large.
2. The work week is too long.
3. The daily schedule is too long.
4. Clerical duties are excessive.
5. Community demands for out-of-school activities are too heavy.

In some studies it has been shown that the teacher is required on the average to

Fig. 10-1. Physical education classes should not be too large. (Oconomowoc Senior High School, Oconomowoc, Wis.)

spend approximately an hour each day in nonteaching, schooltime duties. Many school systems are attempting to minimize and will undoubtedly eliminate some of the unfavorable conditions. The beginning teacher should not become discouraged but should understand these problems and be prepared to meet them.

The importance of ample preparation and knowledge of conditions of employment cannot be overemphasized. Teachers who know and understand the conditions into which they are entering are less likely to be discouraged when they do not meet the optimum or theoretical standards they have been studying in college.

Pertinent factors about the school and community. A beginning teacher should have a thorough knowledge of the school and community of which he or she is a part. Items such as the following should be known: history of the school and community, traditions, curricular offerings, economic status, philosophy of education, industrial development, size, political structure, and problems and projected future growth. These factors will have implications for the type of students to be taught, the parents with whom the teacher will work, the community of which the teacher is to be a part, and the social, political, and educational climate within which the teacher must work. A more de-

tailed analysis of the school and community are discussed in Chapters 1 and 2.

PROBLEMS OF BEGINNING TEACHERS CITED BY DIRECTORS OF PHYSICAL EDUCATION

A representative number of directors of physical education in school systems across the nation were surveyed to determine what they feel are the most difficult problems faced by beginning teachers. Since these administrators had an opportunity to observe beginning teachers as they embarked on their professional careers, their experiences should be of value in helping new teachers to have a good start. The thinking of these administrators may be summarized under the following headings: organization, teaching, teacher-student relationships, teacher-teacher relationships, and making adjustments.

Organization

Many of the problems of beginning teachers are caused by poor organization, which can easily be corrected. Some of the beginning teachers are not accustomed to moving large groups of students from one place to another and from one formation to another. They are not thoroughly familiar with the various methods of class organization for various activities. Sometimes they are poorly organized in respect to uni-

Fig. 10-2. Teacher-student relationships are important. (Hurst-Euless-Bedford Public Schools, Hurst, Texas.)

forms, lockers, towel fees, and many routine duties important to the efficient running of a physical education program.

Problems concerned with organization can be easily remedied if the beginning teacher will study them, become familiar with various types of organization, and ask questions and the help of experienced teachers.

Teaching

The beginning teacher is sometimes a very excellent performer in various physical education activities, and it is hard for him or her to realize that some students have no idea how to throw or jump or perform other basic skills. Often too much time is spent in teaching games rather than teaching basic fundamentals and skills. Often the new teacher does not have the ability to completely involve the class in the activity. Sometimes there is a tendency to teach the units the teacher is interested in and does well, and to minimize those in which he is weak.

The beginning teacher needs to put into practice the tools he or she has learned during undergraduate training. This includes presenting skills within the ability of the pupil, utilizing appropriate teaching techniques, making lesson plans, and finally, recognizing one's own shortcomings in

some areas of physical education and trying hard to correct deficiencies through in-service training.

Teacher-student relationships

Discipline and both personal and professional relationships are involved in teacher-student relationships. Students will frequently test the authority of the new teacher, and sometimes the teacher does not meet the test. Discipline problems may arise, and the teacher may fail to face them directly and, instead, refer the students to the principal's office. The teacher may expect too much from the students, the students may not be adequately motivated, or the teacher may show favoritism to certain students, especially athletes.

The beginning teacher needs to establish rapport with pupils, which requires the ability to be both firm and pleasant, as well as consistent, to know boys and girls as human beings rather than just so many "numbers," and to establish friendships with pupils without becoming "one of them." Establishing rapport in this manner requires further effort on the part of the new teacher if he or she is replacing another teacher who had been extremely well liked and respected by the pupils.

The beginning teacher should recognize that sometimes disciplinary problems are a result of the teacher's lack of planning and class organization. The teacher will be respected much sooner by boys and girls if he can handle the discipline himself rather than passing it on to the principal's office.

Teacher-teacher relationships

Physical education, including sports, tends to isolate teachers of physical education from the rest of the building and often from colleagues in other subject areas. As a result, some beginning teachers fail to realize the importance of participating in general building activities with all teachers, attending faculty meetings regularly, and becoming an integral part of the faculty.

From the very beginning the new teacher should become acquainted with other members of the faculty, work cooperatively with them, share committee responsibilities, attend faculty meetings, and be respected by all.

Making adjustments

The beginning teacher often finds facilities, staff, equipment and other conditions on the job to be far below his expectations and far from ideal. He should realize that teachers do not always have ideal situations in which to teach and in fact, very few of them do; many are faced with poor equipment, limited facilities, changing weather conditions, and other substandard conditions.

The new teacher must adjust to the position, the school, other teachers, school policies, procedures, and routines. Regardless of the situation, the conditions that prevail should be accepted as a challenge to excellent teaching in spite of limitations. The teacher should follow through on the many duties, responsibilities, and "chores" for which he is responsible. He should make an adjustment to existing policies and to the curriculum, with its inherent demand for skillful budgeting of time. The teacher should recognize his responsibility to professional physical education standards and

also to the students, faculty, and school of which he is a part.

Planning is necessary—even the teacher of long experience needs at least a brief written plan as a protection against forgetfulness or wasting time. A teacher's responsibility involves actually teaching the student *how* to perform an activity or a skill; merely telling a pupil *what* to do, or simply supervising activities in a gymnasium is not enough. Rules and regulations should be established and followed. Accidents may occur when rules are not followed. Exercising foresight will help to prevent problems and is preferable to trying to get out of predicaments. For example, the climbing ropes should be tied up before the class period starts so that it will be unnecessary to shout at the students who are swinging on them after class has begun. Finally, the teacher should practice a little self-evaluation each day and then faithfully try to eliminate weaknesses and expand on strengths.

SELECTED PROFESSIONAL PROBLEMS CITED BY BEGINNING PHYSICAL EDUCATORS

A few of the more common professional problems experienced by the beginning physical educator, with recommendations for meeting them, are the following: (1) discipline, (2) working effectively with colleagues, (3) lack of respect for physical education, (4) inequitable use of facilities, (5) problems peculiar to men and women physical educators, and (6) extra school assignments.

Discipline

Lack of discipline is one of the most common problems cited by beginning physical educators in the secondary school. Poor neighborhoods, parental neglect and indifference, overcrowded classes, student transiency, low economic conditions, and pampered children have been cited as contributing factors. Teachers have mentioned that some students are guilty of inattention, unpreparedness, smoking, cutting classes, refusing to follow instructions, talking, and many other infractions.

If a teacher is to be a success in his or her profession, classes must be conducted in an orderly manner, and the teacher must have the respect of the pupils. Part of the difficulty in regard to discipline problems may be caused by the youthful appearance of the teacher and the desire on the part of the students to test the new teacher.

Some beginning teachers are more sensitive than others about the reasons why discipline problems arise. For example, one teacher stated that poor planning on his part was quickly recognized by the pupils, causing many of his discipline problems. Another teacher noted that in some schools the beginning teacher must work three times as hard as an experienced instructor in order to establish proper student-teacher relations. A third teacher related that the previous teacher was not respected, which made it more difficult for him to work effectively. A fourth teacher made an excellent point when she said that she did not understand the boys and girls with whom she was working. She pointed out that she lacked knowledge of their stages of growth and development, and therefore of what to expect at each age level. She recognized that this problem could be alleviated only by a thorough study and understanding of the physical, mental, social, and emotional characteristics of children and youth.

Experienced teachers have recommended many techniques that should be helpful to the physical educator in working with groups of students:

1. Be firm when first meeting a group. It is easy to relax after a good relationship has been established, but it is difficult to gain control over a group that has not known discipline.

2. Maintain poise with a noisy group. Call for silence and then wait for the order to be obeyed. If necessary, call to one or two individuals to be quiet. This will often have the desired effect on the class.

3. Use a whistle only when necessary.

Blow it sparingly, but require attention whenever it is used.

4. Wait for silence before talking. A murmur can multiply quickly if it is not stopped.

5. Know the pupils well in order to determine the best approach to each individual.

6. Maintain self-control. No situation should be allowed to deteriorate into a personal duel with the children.

7. Give all pupils a feeling of belonging. Show the boys and girls that they are all part of the group and will receive your interest and attention.

8. Be liberal in praise. Every child wants to be praised by the teacher, and accomplishment should be recognized.

9. Be friendly and relaxed. The atmosphere that the teacher establishes in class will be quickly copied by the pupils.

10. Be sympathetic. Show an awareness of the difficulty of the stunt or skill and encourage the child to continue.

11. Know the subject matter; have a sense of humor; have the courage of your convictions; work for challenging, exciting programs; and be consistent, fair, and democratic.

12. Know the pupils' interests, abilities, parental and family backgrounds, and achievements.

13. Make physical education activities interesting, meaningful, and vital.

14. Find out what the pupils' problems are, and try to help them solve their difficulties.

Working effectively with colleagues

A problem frequently cited by beginning teachers is the problem of working effectively with other members of the department of physical education and with other faculty members. One beginning teacher commented that it was particularly difficult to gain the cooperation of older teachers because they were inflexible. Another teacher said that some colleagues do not cooperate because a new teacher is too ambitious and too much of an "eager beaver." Another teacher believed that physical education teachers are frowned upon as not being very scholarly. Finally, another teacher commented that being young and inexperienced makes it difficult to adjust— one is looked upon more as a student than as a faculty member.

Probably the comment of one beginning teacher on this problem is the best advice that can be given. She said, "Whether or not you get along with colleagues depends upon you."

Human relations can be effective when a person is considerate, tries to help others, is not overly critical, listens to the advice of others, becomes a member of the team, and tries in every way to contribute effectively to the achievement of the goals of the organization.

It is important for the new teacher to understand that the experienced instructors have amassed practical knowledge in addition to their formal training, which places them well ahead of teachers just out of college. There are many techniques that can be learned from colleagues. The beginning teacher should watch closely and select the methods that can be of value.

The new teacher should try to follow accepted procedures and systems, fitting into the existing pattern as much as possible. Being willing to work, anxious to learn, and able to get along increases the possibility of obtaining quick acceptance by colleagues.

Another aspect of this problem is the distribution of the work load. There is the question of whether the new teacher should carry a heavier or a lighter load than the older teachers and do more or less committee work at first.

The new teacher should willingly accept assignments of teaching and nonteaching duties, but he should feel free to ask questions when there is some phase of the program or duties that is not clear. New teachers often run into difficulty because they are afraid to ask questions. They think this would indicate ignorance, and instead of seeking the answers, they blunder ahead,

making mistakes and intensifying problems.

Each teacher is primarily responsible for his or her own preparation for the job. There is also the responsibility of the administrator, however, to help prepare the new teacher for the experiences to be encountered. Some steps that administrators can take that in the opinion of their Association[3] would benefit a beginning teacher include those listed here:

1. To provide all the necessary pertinent information
2. To establish workshops for new teachers
3. To assign an adviser for each new teacher
4. To hold seminars for new teachers
5. To have new teachers observe excellent teaching
6. To demonstrate teaching techniques to improve skills

Lack of respect for physcal education

Sometimes physical educators are referred to as "muscular woman" or "muscle men" or given other uncomplimentary names. The effect of this situation is to separate these teachers from other teachers, who are considered educators. It is important to break down this stereotyped thinking. Only when administrators, colleagues, and the public, in general, understand the true purpose and philosophy of physical education will this thinking change.

Physical educators should be educators first. They should exemplify well-educated people. They should be interested in the total development of students—not just their physical development. Although the work may concern itself with the physical more than the work of other teachers, it should not deter them from an appreciation of the importance of giving high priority to the mental development of youngsters, recognizing that the physical is only a means to an end. The end must be the education of the total child.

The dress of physical educators as well

as their manners will help to support or disprove the stereotype. The working uniform should be restricted to the gymnasium. The teacher would not, of course, be expected to change clothes every time he leaves the gymnasium for a few minutes, but he should be properly attired for every school function, whether it is an assembly, a faculty meeting, or a conference, as well as for just going home. Furthermore, in all actions the physical educator should try to show that he or she is a well-mannered, cultured, educated human being who ranks on the same level with other educators.

Another major task for the teacher is to interpret the program of physical education wherever he or she goes. There is much misunderstanding in regard to the goals and values of the profession. All phases of the program—classes, adapted programs, intramural and extramural activities, and interscholastic athletics—should be interpreted correctly, together with their specific worth in the educational program for students.

The physical educator must be a professional person in every respect. This means joining local, state, and national organizations, recruiting outstanding personnel for the profession, continually seeking opportunities for self-improvement, being an effective teacher, continually keeping abreast of the latest developments and thinking in the field, and being a good public relations ambassador for physical education. If each physical educator would fulfill his responsibilities in these areas, physical education would soon be respected throughout the country.

Inequitable use of facilities

The use of the available facilities, according to many beginning teachers, seems to be a common problem throughout the country. Several beginning teachers point out that too often the women's department is asked to give up facilities in favor of the varsity interscholastic program. It may be that a separate gymnasium or field is not available for a girls' intramural program, or

that, because of the varsity schedule, the area is free only during the late afternoon hours or once a week. The equipment shared by both departments may also be divided inequitably. Finally, the budgetary allotments may be apportioned in such a way that the men's department obtains the lion's share and the women's department a bare minimum. The underlying causes may be the following:

1. There may be little administrative enthusiasm for the girls' program. Such a problem may take considerable time to correct, and the new teacher must work slowly and patiently to build up a more favorable administrative attitude. It may be that a solution can be reached by gaining the cooperation of the men's department. An effort should also be made to build up student and community interest in the girls' program. When interest is aroused, it may be possible to convince the administrator of the importance and value of the program, recognizing that the men's program should not suffer to accomplish the needed changes. The positive aspect of improving the women's program should always be emphasized. New teachers should be careful not to criticize another department.

2. Lack of understanding by the men's department may be apparent. Once again it is necessary to organize the best possible program and to stimulate interest among the girls. If the men's department is approached with an obvious understanding of the problems regarding time, space, practice, and other needs, but with some realistic suggestions, it may be possible to set up a schedule that can provide for all groups that need the gymnasium.

Problems peculiar to men and women physical educators

Men physical educators experience many different types of problems when beginning to teach. They may be required to take on additional responsibilities in the community, working with recreation, church, and various youth groups. If they are married, there are extra responsibilities that require additional funds when starting salary schedules do not adequately provide for family considerations. A beginning teacher may not be assigned teaching and coaching duties in accordance with his or her wishes.

There are many problems faced by the beginning male teacher, but the most common seems to be associated with an over-emphasis on interscholastic athletics. The pressures involved in sports, when they are increased by local newspapers, radio, television, community, and alumni influence, place undue importance on this phase of the physical education program. The physical educator wants to be an effective teacher in his regular classes and intramural activities but finds that community pressures often force him to spend a disproportionate amount of time on the interscholastic athletic program. Under such conditions the teacher should steer a steady course, realizing that he is associated with educational, rather than professional, athletics. The coach who puts a winning team above all else, tries to pressure teachers to keep boys eligible, teaches how to win at any cost, is rude to officials, is not completely honest, and closes his eyes to improper conduct, will be a credit neither to his school nor to the profession of physical education. There are many valuable contributions that sports can make to the student, such as teamwork, skill, sportsmanship, respect for ability, and greater understanding of the value and place of sports in our society. These worthy goals must receive the main emphasis as the total physical education program for all students is kept in proper focus.

Women physical educators also have many problems with which to contend during their first year on the job. Some of these, including inequitable use of facilities, have been mentioned. Other problems may involve her professional as well as her personal life.

Male physical education teachers frequently receive extra pay for extra coaching duties, but the time spent by female teachers with the girls' intramural and interscholastic programs often remains unrecognized. When an unequal pay scale exists, the female physical education instructor—together with other teachers in the school who devote extra work to the band, orchestra, dramatic group, school newspaper, or other activity—should strive to impress the administration with the need for added salary benefits.

The beginning female teacher may find an obvious lack of interest in physical education among secondary school girls. The students may be more interested in dates and in their hair and social obligations than in physical education. They do not want to become strong and athletic. If the girls' program is to have appeal to girls, characteristics of femininity should be fostered. Secondary school girls are interested in developing their feminine charms and their skills—not their muscles. The teacher should exemplify grace, poise, and femininity, along with fine coordination and body control, so that physical education can be recognized as developing such attributes of beauty. The personal appearance of the teacher, her attitude toward her work, and the appearance of her office and the locker room should contribute to the overall picture. Setting a feminine example attracts interest among students who may otherwise be lost to the program.

Personal problems may also confront the beginning teacher. If she is married, there is the problem of time to devote to the home. Physical education requires long hours, and home life may be neglected. Good planning and organization in the home as well as at school may relieve this situation. For the unmarried teacher, either too much socializing in the evening or too much fretting about domestic problems may interfere with her work at school. The teacher who enjoys her work, however, finds that self-preoccupation disappears as soon as the morning bell sounds and that the problems of the students replace her own.

Not all the problems presented here will be faced by all new female teachers, but some of them will be present. The teacher who keeps in mind her responsibilities to her students, school, and profession, gets along with others, and does her best work should encounter little difficulty.

Extra school assignments

One of the most pressing problems facing beginning teachers of physical education is the extra duties required during the school day. It is not uncommon for the physical educator to be assigned to supervise a lunchroom period, to keep an eye on the entrance or exit where the students congregate, to handle traffic at school functions, to manage school dances, to monitor study halls, or to supervise the parking lot. Too often the number and type of such assignments place an unfair burden upon the teacher, sometimes to such a degree that they interfere with his or her primary responsibility as a physical educator. It is important, of course, to perform all duties to the best of one's ability. It is also reasonable to point out to the administrator in charge those instances when such assignments affect teaching, infringe upon hours that could be put to better professional use, or take an unfair amount of a teacher's free time.

SELECTED ADMINISTRATIVE PROBLEMS CITED BY BEGINNING PHYSICAL EDUCATORS

The beginning physical educator will encounter many problems that may be classified as administrative in nature. These problems involve administrative responsibilities and decisions of chairmen of departments, principals, superintendents of schools, and other persons who work in similar capacities in school systems. These responsibilities and decisions have important implications for the physical education program. Therefore, the teacher of physical education must be alert to the problems involved and continually interpret to those in administrative positions the philosophy, needs, and policies that are necessary if physical education is to make its greatest contribution to the students.

The administrative problems discussed

Fig. 10-3. The physical educator is often required to take charge of planning festive occasions as an extra assignment. (Walt Whitman High School, South Huntington Schools, New York.)

in this section are encountered by many beginning physical education teachers, and they involve facilities, budget, scheduling, grouping of pupils, class size, time allocation, and legal liability.

Facilities

Enrollments are continually expanding from coast to coast, and as a result school construction is at an all-time high. Therefore, many physical educators will be asked for their recommendations concerning facilities needed. Furthermore, as a specialist in this area the beginning teacher should know the basic facility requirements, adaptations that can be made to improve the program, and the best way to proceed in developing an adequate physical plant.

It is important that the beginning teacher know what a good physical education plant should contain in the way of standard equipment, adequate locker areas, and offices, including size require-

Fig. 10-4. The beginning teacher should know what equipment a good physical education plant should contain.

ments. This knowledge will be of help, especially if the plant is to be remodeled or enlarged or a new school is to be built. It is the responsibility of the physical educator to be able to work with the architects to make economical and sound suggestions. It is also important for the physical educator to know what is wrong with the existing plant so that he or she may take the necessary precautions when planning a program. A number of good sources for information regarding the physical plant may be found in the list of selected readings at the end of the chapter.

Gymnasiums and auxiliary facilities

The type, size, and number of gymnasiums should reflect the number of participating individuals, the variety of activities to be conducted, the number of desired teaching stations, official court sizes, the number of spectators, and the need for enjoyable and safe activity participation. It is preferable for a gymnasium to be in a separate wing in the school building in order to minimize the possible disturbance to other classrooms, as well as to have the gymnasium readily available for after-school use without the necessity of opening the entire building.

Below are listed some facility problems, with suggestions for alleviating the difficulties.

Problem

Only one small gymnasium is available for use by both boys and girls.

Solution

One solution would be to alternate weeks in the gymnasium—one week for the boys and the next for the girls. During the spring and fall this would not present a great handicap because one group can be out-of-doors. During the winter months, it would be advantageous to have coeducational classes once or twice weekly. The remaining days of alternating weeks can be spent in a classroom—discussing the rules, techniques, and strategy of sports; the value of physical education and physical fitness; leisure-time activities; and health instruction. It may also be possible to use some other indoor area for physical education when the gymnasium is not available.

Scheduling the physical education classes under such conditions presents problems. The number of students and of physical education classes per week, the length of periods, and the activities to be taught must all be considered in arriving at the best solution. It may be possible to schedule classes in such a way that when the boys of a class are taking physical education the girls are assigned to home economics, typing, or some other class program, and that when the girls are scheduled for physical education the boys are assigned to shop, mechanical drawing, etc. This, again, would depend upon the school, the number of pupils, and scheduling difficulties.

Problem
No gymnasium is available.

Solution
In the event that no gymnasium is available, there is no great problem as long as the weather is fair. Classes may be held out-of-doors. When bad weather comes and classes must move indoors, classroom periods might be used for discussions, as mentioned above. There are also some other areas that can be used for physical activity.

Multipurpose room (or large, uncluttered area). The multipurpose room is usually larger than a regular classroom. It has no permanent furniture, the ceiling is usually at a regular height, and the lighting fixtures are often without protection. It can be used for tumbling and apparatus work, relays, games of low organization, mimetics, testing, and other limited activities. At a nominal expense, the light fixtures and windows can be screened and the room used for additional selected activities.

Classrooms. It is possible to make use of an empty classroom or two for indoor physical activity if there is no multipurpose room available. There would not be enough room for running games, but there would be sufficient space for tumbling and apparatus work, for recreational activities such as table tennis, bat-back, and handball, and for some basketball where a goal-hi could be used or possibly a basket and backboard permanently installed. With some ingenuity and modification, other activities may also be conducted.

Other areas. It is also possible to practice track work in the hallways or in the basement areas.

A modified physical education program can be conducted without a gymnasium. An important consideration in the use of any area is to plan for the *safe* use of the facility, limiting activities to those that can be conducted without fear of accident. In such planning, it will always be necessary to take into account the features listed below.

1. Obstructions. Make provision to have obstructions covered, or establish a floor plan to avoid any activity near them. Be sure that the students are conscious of these obstructions.

2. Lighting. Secure larger bulbs or more fixtures, if needed, in order to provide sufficient light for the activity area.

3. Ventilation. Be conscious of temperature. Be sure that vents or radiators are covered or protected and that the students are made aware of them.

4. Composition of the floor. Consider those activities that would be applicable to wood, tile, or concrete floors and make selections accordingly.

Locker, shower, and drying areas

It is important that the physical education plant have adequate locker, shower, and drying rooms. Refer to the books on facilities at the end of the chapter for necessary and standard requirements.

Where there are insufficient locker facilities it will be necessary to work out a plan for their most efficient use. It is possible to have students double up or to assign certain grades permanent gymnasium lockers, while the other students have lockers only during their physical education period. It may be advisable to switch at some time during the year to equalize this advantage.

Dirty, dark, unpainted, unappealing locker rooms often can be brightened, cleaned, painted, and made more attractive. Where there is no locker room, it will be necessary to find an area that can be utilized for changing into gymnasium uniforms. This may be a vacant classroom, storage area, or lavatory. It is also possible to have the pupils wear their uniforms under their school clothes if there is no area available for changing. This should be the last resort, however, because it violates a basic use of the uniform. Students should be able to change out of sweaty or dirty clothes before returning to a classroom.

The problem of shower and drying rooms is very simple. Either there are facilities or there are not. If there are showers, it is important that they be used. If not, a dry rubdown should follow each activity period. In some cases perhaps a sponge bath may be feasible.

Special activity areas

There should be teaching stations in addition to the gymnasium—for use in conducting many physical education activities. These may include rooms for remedial or adapted activities, apparatus work, weight lifting, wrestling, rhythms, squash, handball, fencing, or any other activities of particular interest. A recommended size for an auxiliary gymnasium is 40 by 60 by 24 feet.

It is possible to convert regular classrooms for certain of these special activities. Some of these rooms would need special equipment—such as ladders, bars, ropes, pulley weights, or mats—in order to properly conduct the activities. Facilities needed will depend upon the interests, abilities, and desires of the students, as well as upon the comprehensiveness of the program, the availability of staff, and the accessibility of rooms.

Outdoor areas

When outdoor facilities are planned, it is highly desirable to have them located convenient to the gymnasiums and locker areas and also to have them available for year-round use by the community.

The size of outdoor areas will vary from 10 to 40 acres. On the junior high school level the facilities should be adequate for a girls' program of archery, volleyball, tennis, and hockey and a boys' program of soccer, touch football, baseball, speedball, softball, golf, and track. The senior high school field should also allow for field hockey, lacrosse, football, and baseball, as well as ample space for other activities in the regular physical education class.

When a school playfield is not available, it is still possible to have outdoor activities. Some schools may be in the vicinity of a park or recreational play area that would be satisfactory. It may be necessary to have double periods of physical education, to allow time for travel to and from this area. It will be necessary to receive permission from the school administration and the park or recreation department for the use of such space. Another alternate site may be the school parking area. It is possible that lines could be painted on asphalt and cars limited to a certain section in order to allow room for the physical activities. It

Fig. 10-5. Outdoor play areas should be convenient to gymnasiums and locker areas. (Lincoln High School, Yonkers, N. Y.)

may also be possible to use the school's grassy areas. As a last resort it may be necessary to use the street adjacent to the building. In such a case it would be essential to have the street closed, at least during school hours. No physical education class should be limited to indoor classes all year long.

An adequate physical plant can help in developing a good physical education program. A poor plant, however, does not mean that there will necessarily be a poor program. In most cases it will be as good as the physical educator and the school administration want it to be.

Budget

In every school system, equipment and supplies are purchased each year for use in the schools. There are many things a teacher can do to secure the proper supplies and/or equipment needed for the program.

There are generally two sources of money for physical education items: (1) the board of education and (2) organizations within the school.

An allocation from the board of education may consist of money allotted directly to the physical education department or given to the principal to divide among all the departments in the school. The usual procedure for using this money is for the teacher to requisition the needed items, obtain the principal's approval, and send the requisition to a central purchasing agent for processing and purchase. This procedure centralizes the purchasing power and often brings increased value for each dollar spent.

There is frequently some type of athletic association and/or other student organization that handles the proceeds from the sale of school General Organization memberships, athletic contests, dramatic or music presentations, the school store, and other fund-raising affairs or activities. This money is used to support many of the school activities, as well as for the purchase of special supplies or equipment. It is a source of funds for items the central purchasing agent may not approve for payment out of tax money, as well as for special items that must be obtained quickly. The faculty adviser can explain the procedure for his particular school.

If the necessary funds are not available through these channels, there are still other means of obtaining equipment and supplies. The ingenuity of physical education teachers and pupils working together, with the cooperation of other teachers and the school administration, can solve many problems.

A small list of items that can be constructed at little or no expense in the shops or the backyard includes the following: starting blocks, hurdles, vaulting standards, crossbars, backboards, batons, chinning bars, a form of parallel bars, mat trucks, sideline markers, yardline sticks, goal flags, charging sled, and football dummies. It is also possible to call upon the home economics department to sew and clean uniforms and upon the art department for publicity purposes. Special fund-raising drives can be organized, with the proceeds earmarked for specific needs. These may include a cake sale, a white elephant sale, or a dance.

Scheduling

The importance of proper scheduling cannot be overemphasized. A school that schedules physical education classes in a manner to meet the needs and interests of the students will usually have a good program.

Scheduling should be done according to a plan. The plan for scheduling should be based upon (1) the number of students taking the course, (2) the number of teachers available to teach the course, and (3) the number of rooms or teaching stations available. This plan should provide for early scheduling of physical education.

Since English, history, the sciences, mathematics, and physical education are required of all students, it seems logical to assume that these subjects should usually be scheduled first. Physical education and science laboratory periods should also be given particular consideration because there are usually fewer physical education teaching stations and science laboratories available than rooms for other subjects. If a sound progression in physical education is to be maintained, it is important that class size be approximately the same and that homogeneity by grade be a minimum prerequisite to scheduling. The physical educator should inform the administration of the sound reasons that make it important to give physical education early attention in setting up the school program.

In scheduling for physical education, every student should be included. This, of course, is based on the premise that the responsibility of the physical education department to adapt the program for the atypical child will be carried out.

Grouping

When considering how to group pupils for physical education, there are many problems that must be thought through before a decision is reached.

It is widely accepted that classes should be homogeneous. In physical education the real question is "homogeneous in what respect?" Various groupings can be made, depending upon the criteria used: grade, sex, age, health, physical fitness, ability, motor capacity, speed, strength, endurance, or interests, for example. The American Association for Health, Physical Education, and Recreation[4] points out that the need for grouping students homogeneously has long been recognized, but the inability to scientifically measure such important factors as ability, maturity, interest, and capacity has been a deterrent to accomplishing this goal. They state that the most common procedure for grouping today is by grade or class.

The ideal grouping plan will take into consideration all the factors that affect performance—intelligence, capacity, ability, interest, knowledge, age, height, weight, etc. It is not administratively possible,

Platnick's Photo Service, Hempstead, L. I.

Fig. 10-6. Students will learn more in a swimming class if grouped homogeneously, according to degree of skill.

however, to utilize all these factors in many schools.

Some form of grouping is essential to provide the type of program that will promote educational objectives and protect the student. On the secondary level the most feasible procedure appears to be to schedule classes by grade and then to organize subgroups within the regular physical education class. Classification within the physical education class can be based on such factors as age, height, intelligence, interests, motor ability, and motor capacity.

Size of classes

The size of physical education classes will vary greatly from school to school, and it may also vary from class to class within any one school. The number of pupils in each class has implications for teacher effectiveness.

Criteria to determine class size

When considering the size of classes, it is essential to consider the number of teaching stations, the supplies and equipment, and the size of the area, as well as the number of available teachers.

Many of the same principles that are applicable in an English class also apply in the gymnasium. Obviously, the effectiveness of both the English teacher and the physical education teacher will be seriously hampered if there is an excessive number of pupils. Individual attention is limited, and many children must "sink or swim" on their own. Organization of a large class takes more time, discipline may be a greater problem, and the administrative structure of the class must be more formal. Furthermore, there is less opportunity to help meet the individual interests and needs of the children.

In recommending proper class size to an administrator, the American Association for Health, Physical Education, and Recreation suggests that the number of pupils in a class should not exceed 35.[4] LaPorte's committee suggests 35 as a suitable size for activity classes—and not more than 45. This group also recommends that the size of remedial and corrective classes should be 20 to 25 and should never exceed 30.[5]

What to do with large classes

On the senior high school level, the problem of scheduling is a difficult one because students have individual programs. Each program is made to suit the individual student's needs. In the junior high school, it is sometimes a simpler process because of the block system, in which a group of students is scheduled as a unit and goes to different teachers as a unit.

One technique suitable for handling large classes is the use of student leaders. The effective use of trained pupils to assist in the management and organization of large classes can prove helpful. The students may be trained with a leaders' club that meets during a regular club period, after school, or both. With the assistance of these students it will be possible to institute an active squad work program. It will also be possible for the teacher to work with selected groups while the others are busy under the direction of their leaders. The responsibility for the class, however, always rests with the teacher. It is important for the teacher to oversee all activities, even though he or she may spend a major part of a class period with a particular group or groups.

Time

Standards for time allotment vary. In a survey of state requirements, the differences ranged from no specific time requirements for physical education, in some states, to minimum daily requirements. Recently, more educators and administrators have realized the importance of a minimum daily period of physical education.

The amount of time spent on physical education depends on the length of the other class periods, which may vary from 30 to 60 minutes. When figuring the amount of physical education a student receives, the time needed for dressing and showering should be taken into consideration. For boys, this would be approximately 5 to 7 minutes at the beginning of a period and about 7 to 13 minutes at the end of the period. It is usually necessary to add a few extra minutes for girls, particularly if hair must be dried. This means as little as 15 to 20 minutes of actual activity on the gymnasium floor. In some situations, it would be advisable to have two double periods weekly rather than five single periods. Considering a basic 45-minute period, the school that schedules five daily periods of physical education weekly may total as little as 125 minutes of physical activity per week. In the same school, by using two double periods each week, it is possible to have 150 minutes of physical activity while allowing the same amount of time for showering and dressing.

The time advantage that can be achieved by double periods should be considered, even though the thinking of most educators is for a continuity that can be achieved only through a daily period of physical education. Another consideration is the status achieved when physical education is scheduled on the same basis as English, the sciences, history, and mathematics. It is important for the physical educator to analyze the situation in his own school and recommend the policy that will best meet his particular situation.

Legal liability

A high school student who charged that he had been paralyzed as a result of negligence after an injury in a football game recently was awarded over $200,000. This is only one of many cases of legal liability that regularly occur in physical education programs.

With the growth in physical education programs throughout the country, there has been a resultant increase in the problems involving legal liability. The very nature of physical activity involves a certain amount of risk and hazard, and for their own welfare, teachers must be aware of their responsibility and liability for any accident.

Defining liability

A teacher's liability is "tort" liability; that is, it is "liability for personal or property injuries caused through the defendant's negligence. . . . Any tort action involves proof of four elements: that the defendant owed a duty to avoid unreasonable risk to others, that the defendant failed to observe that duty, that the failure to observe that duty caused the damage which occurred, and that damage in fact occurred to plaintiff . . ."[*]

Negligence. Negligence can be defined as something that a reasonable person would not do or the failure to do something that a reasonable person would do. There can be no legal liability unless there is negligence. Negligence must be shown. If one did not foresee a danger of accident as a reasonably prudent person should, there is negligence. Another condition demands an unfulfilled duty toward the injured person. Every teacher has such a duty because he or she is acting *in loco parentis* (in place of a parent).

Following are types of conduct[†] that constitute negligent acts:

1. Appropriate care is not used by the teacher. Example: An instructor permits a student to use the trampoline without stationing spotters.

2. The circumstances under which the activity is done creates risks, although it is done with due care and caution. Example: Two softball games are played on opposite ends of an area that is not large enough to permit overlapping outfielders.

3. The teacher is indulging in an act that involves an unreasonable risk of direct and immediate harm to others. Example: The physical education instructor places a boy

---

[*]From Fahr, Samuel M.: Legal liability for athletic injuries, Journal of Health, Physical Education, and Recreation 29:12, Feb. 1958.
[†]Based on types of conduct that create unreasonable risks to others, from Harper, Fowler V.: A treatise on the law of torts, Indianapolis, 1938, Bobbs-Merrill Co., Inc., pp. 171-176.

at a certain position to mark where the shot put landed. The instructor puts a shot that hits the boy's head.

4. The teacher sets in motion a force, the continuous operation of which may be unreasonably hazardous to others. Example: A person, without justification, frightens a horse or dog that becomes uncontrollable.

5. The teacher creates a situation that is unreasonably dangerous to others because of the likelihood of the action of a third person or inanimate forces. Example: The instructor permits a student to ride a bicycle on a playground crowded with other pupils. The result is an injury to another student.

6. The teacher entrusts dangerous devices or instruments to persons who are incompetent to use or care for such instruments properly. Example: The instructor permits students to use fencing foils without supervision.

7. The teacher neglects a duty of control over third persons who, by reason of some incapacity or abnormality, he knows to be likely to inflict intended harm upon others. Example: The instructor fails to supervise and control the conduct of a boy who is a bully in the play area.

8. The teacher fails to employ due care to give adequate warning. Example: The instructor, although he is responsible for supervision, absents himself or herself from the area. In another example, a student is struck by a car when crossing the street between the gymnasium and the athletic field. Negligence is found because no crosswalk was provided, no safety instruction was given to the students, and no warning signs for motorists were posted.

9. The teacher fails to exercise proper care in looking out for persons who he has reason to believe may be in danger. Example: The teacher does not clear the students from the area directly behind the batter in a baseball game.

10. The teacher fails to employ appropriate skill to perform acts undertaken. Example: The teacher is unable to perform first aid when it should be administered.

11. The teacher fails to make adequate preparation to avoid harm to others before entering into an activity where such preparation is necessary. Example: The instructor permits students to use the horizontal bar without a mat underneath.

12. The teacher fails to inspect and repair equipment or mechanical devices used by others. Example: The teacher fails to inspect flying rings and other hanging equipment periodically.

How to avoid negligence. It should be obvious that the best way to avoid negligence is to use common sense and insist upon safety rules at all times. Some necessary rules include the following:

1. Clear a playing area of all obstacles (equipment and obstructions).

2. Inspect all equipment regularly.

3. Lock up apparatus when it is not in use.

4. Have a health examination for all competitors.

5. Never permit a boy or girl to participate who may be injured.

6. Instruct in safety rules before permitting participation in an activity.

7. Employ spotters at all times.

8. Repair, remove, or do not use defective equipment.

9. Have ample insurance coverage at all times.

10. Never leave a class alone.

11. Always use protective equipment in contact activities.

12. Be sure the activity is suitable for the age level.

13. Do not force a student to participate in any activity that involves the hazard of personal injury.

14. Administer first aid when necessary.

15. Do not treat injuries.

16. Request, in writing, the repair of any hazardous conditions.

17. Insist that all participants wear proper uniforms at all times.

Defenses against negligence. In order for damages to be awarded, it is necessary for the plaintiff to prove that the negligence involved resulted in, or was directly con-

Fig. 10-7. The individual assumes some risk when participating in physical education activities.

nected to, the injury. The legal defense against such a charge may be any of the following:

1. Act of God. A condition occurs that is beyond the control of man.

2. Assumption of risk. When participating in an activity that involves certain risks, that individual assumes responsibilities for those risks. There is still, however, the responsibility for effective leadership and safe equipment and facilities.

3. Contributory negligence. The injured person does not act as a reasonably prudent person of his age should act. In this case the negligence of the teacher is canceled. Every person is expected to maintain a reasonable amount of self-protection.

4. Proximate cause of injury. The negligent act must be the direct and immediate cause of injury. If the negligent act was only indirectly or remotely concerned with the injury, the claim will be disallowed.

Teacher liability

Teachers are liable for their own negligence. The doctrine of *respondeat superior,* however, can relieve them of liability. This doctrine holds that employers are liable for torts of their employees committed within the scope of their employment. In Iowa,

the State Supreme Court ruled that a teacher is not liable for charges while carrying on a government function, even though he is guilty of negligence. Some states, such as New York, New Jersey, and Connecticut, have "save harmless statutes," which permit the payment, out of school funds, of damages arising through the negligence of teachers or other employees of the school district.

Many teachers, particularly physical educators, purchase liability insurance from private companies. The American Association for Health, Physical Education, and Recreation has recently made available a policy that will protect its members from liability while engaging in any activity sponsored by the school or organization. The best means of avoiding any legal liability, however, is to make good use of the basic safety factors previously mentioned.

Insurance

Since schools require boys and girls to actively participate in physical education, they have a moral responsibility to protect them financially against injury. Staff members, because of the nature of their work and the need for protection against accidents and negligence, also need coverage.

Some kind of insurance program should therefore be carried. Some factors to consider in such a protective insurance program are listed below.

1. All children and staff members should be covered in both class and out-of-class activities.

2. Prior to the selection of an insurance policy, a study should be made of school needs and problems, the various types of policies offered by different companies, and the insurance program that best meets the local situation.

3. Insurance policies should provide sufficient funds to cover doctor's fees, hospital expenses, x-ray examinations, dental care, etc.

4. Commercial plans should be explored, together with athletic association plans and other plans. Although commercial plans may be more expensive, they may provide better coverage.

5. In many cases the nonallocated form of policy is the more desirable, since benefits will be paid up to a specific amount regardless of the type of injury, whereas an allocated policy limits the benefits for each type of injury—such as a broken arm, etc.

6. Staff members and other employees should also have insurance coverage.

7. The approved American Association for Health, Physical Education, and Recreation Income Protection and Public Liability Programs offered to members of the Association, in cooperation with Mutual Benefit Health & Accident Association, should be explored. Some of the benefits, as listed by the Association, are the following:

> Rates are substantially lower than comparable coverage offered on an individual basis.
> Disability benefits are doubled during hospital confinement.
> Accident benefits are payable up to a lifetime, with house confinement never required.
> Sickness benefits are payable up to five years, with house confinement required only during vacations or leaves of absence.
> Eligible members may apply for coverage up to the age of 65 years.

HOW TO FAIL SUCCESSFULLY

It was pointed out at the beginning of this chapter that the first year of teaching is the most critical. Many beginning teachers fail because they have not adequately equipped themselves for the job or because they did not function effectively after they were on the job. There follows a student checklist entitled "How to Fail Successfully," which appeared in *The Physical Educator*.[6] After this checklist is included a formula for success that should be studied and followed by every beginning physical educator who wants to be successful in the profession.

How to fail successfully*

Place a plus in front of the statement if it is true about you; a zero if false.

1. I do just enough work to get by.
2. I wouldn't think of doing more than is expected of me.
3. I think teachers have favorites.
4. When I violate a rule I always get caught. Others get by.
5. I don't make a special effort to find out what is expected of me.
6. I spend as little time as possible working on subjects I don't like.
7. I don't have any study plan. Nor do I have any method of checking myself to see that I am doing each day what is required.
8. I don't make a special effort to do my work neatly or accurately.
9. I get to class as late as possible—just in time to escape tardiness.
10. I get set to rush out of the room as soon as the warning bell rings.
11. I am not interested in keeping the building looking nice. I wouldn't think of picking up a piece of paper on the floor.
12. I am not particularly interested in my personal appearance.
13. I don't try to do exactly what the teacher expects of me.
14. I don't try to see things from the teacher's point of view.
15. I never compliment a teacher on any of his or her many fine qualities.
16. I am not concerned about the success of other students. I am solely interested in myself.
17. I do not try to be cheerful. I prefer to spread gloom.
18. I don't try to see the good points of my fellow students.
19. I know I am perfect.
20. I expect perfection in others.

---

*From The Physical Educator **15**:19, March, 1958.

21. I think others should look out for my welfare.

22. I always put off until tomorrow what I don't have to do today.

23. I think others are to blame for my failure.

24. I believe I am inferior. Others are more fortunate.

25. I am satisfied with myself. I don't need to do anything to improve.

Scoring: The greater the number of plus answers the more successful you are in the Art of Failure.

A FORMULA FOR SUCCESS

H. Harrison Clarke[7] has worked out a formula for success, about which every physical education teacher should do some thinking:

$$PS = (I.P)(3PI + 2HW + PB)(CP)^n$$

PS is for professional success
 I is for intelligence
 P is for preparation
PI is for personal integrity
HW is for hard work
PB is for professional breaks
CP is for careful planning.*

An understanding of the ingredients of this formula will do much to minimize the problems that a new teacher may encounter.

POINTS TO REMEMBER

1. The possibility of avoiding many potential problems by investigating before accepting a position
2. The probability that discipline will be your major professional problem
3. Some problems directed toward the teacher as a member of the physical education department, not to him personally
4. The necessity of coordination between the male and female physical education departments
5. The need for the member of the physical education department to be an educator first
6. How to conduct a program when the facilities are limited
7. Sources of money for equipment and supplies and procedures for using the money
8. Why physical education classes should be scheduled early in developing the school's master plan
9. The need for homogeneity in physical education classes
10. Proper class size and how to subgroup for good instruction
11. Information regarding the legal liability of teachers

PROBLEMS TO THINK THROUGH

1. Why is the problem of acceptance of great importance to any beginning teacher?
2. How can one best prepare for the first day of teaching?
3. What do you anticipate as your greatest problem upon entering the teaching profession? Why?
4. Select any secondary school and determine how the facilities could be improved at a minimum expense. Use only the land and buildings available. What long-range major changes would you recommend?
5. How are supplies and equipment purchased in the school that you attended? Can the system be improved? How?
6. What are the advantages of having a physical education class containing students from the same grade?
7. Explain what a teacher should do when an accident occurs.
8. Compare the advantages of having five single physical education periods weekly with those of having two double periods weekly.

CASE STUDY FOR ANALYSIS

Unfavorable working conditions, as well as low salaries, are causing many teachers to leave the profession. Some of these conditions relate to the size of classes, the length of the daily schedule and worksheet, and clerical duties and after-school obligations. Determine the degree to which adverse conditions prevail in a school system of your choice. Analyze factors that contribute to these conditions. How may the beginning teacher help to combat this problem?

EXERCISES FOR REVIEW

1. What are some techniques that are beneficial in working with large groups?
2. What school duties may be assigned to a beginning teacher?

*From Clarke, H. Harrison: A formula of success for the professional student, Journal of Health, Physical Education, and Recreation **25**:35, Dec., 1954.

3. Why is the orientation period important for good teaching?
4. Of what value are interscholastic activities to the student and the school?
5. How can the female physical education teacher avoid being labeled as the "girls' coach"?
6. What can the physical educator do if there is no gymnasium available in the school?
7. What areas can be used to change into uniforms in the absence of a locker room?
8. How can a physical education class have out-of-doors activities without a playing field?
9. What departments in the school can help to minimize physical education expenses?
10. What size should physical education classes be?
11. How may student leaders help the physical educator?
12. List ten negligent acts in physical education. Give an example of each.
13. What are the legal defenses against negligence?

REFERENCES

1. Wey, G. W.: Why do beginning teachers fail? National Association of Secondary School Principals Bulletin **35**:55, Oct., 1951.
2. Kleinman, Lou: The relationship between job selection by beginning teachers and subsequent teacher adjustment, doctoral thesis, New York University, 1959.
3. Commission on Staff Relations in School Administration, American Association of School Administrators: Staff relations in school administration, 33rd yearbook, Washington, D. C., Feb., 1955, The Association.
4. American Association for Health, Physical Education, and Recreation: Administrative problems in health, physical education and recreation, Washington, D. C., 1953, The Association.
5. LaPorte, W. R.: The physical education curriculum (a national program), Los Angeles, 1955, University of Southern California Press.
6. How to fail successfully, The Physical Educator **15**:19, March, 1958.
7. Clarke, H. Harrison: A formula of success for the professional student, Journal of Health, Physical Education, and Recreation **25**:35, Dec., 1954.

SELECTED READINGS

American Association for Health, Physical Education, and Recreation: Administrative problems in health, physical education and recreation, Washington, D. C., 1953, The Association.
American Association of School Administrators: Staff relations in school administration, 33rd yearbook, Washington, D. C., 1955, The Association.
Bucher, Charles A.: Administration of school and college health and physical education programs, ed. 4, St. Louis, 1967, The C. V. Mosby Co.
Bucher, Charles A.: Foundations of physical education, ed. 5, St. Louis, 1968, The C. V. Mosby Co.
Bucher, Charles A., and Reade, Evelyn: Physical education and health in the elementary school, ed. 3, New York, 1970, The Macmillan Co.
Clarke, H. Harrison: A formula of success for the professional student, Journal of Health, Physical Education, and Recreation **25**:35, Dec., 1954.
Fahr, S. M.: Legal liability for athletic injuries, Journal of Health, Physical Education and Recreation **29**:12, Feb., 1958.
Harper, Fowler V.: A treatise on the law of torts, Indianapolis, 1938, Bobbs-Merrill Co., Inc.
Knapp, Clyde, and Jewett, A. E.: The physical education student and beginning teacher, New York, 1957, McGraw-Hill Book Co.
Lamb, Marion M.: Your first year of teaching, New Rochelle, N. Y., 1956, South-Western Publishing Co.
MacConnell, James D.: Planning for school buildings, Englewood Cliffs, N. J., 1957, Prentice-Hall, Inc.
National Association of Secondary School Principals: Health, physical education and recreation in the secondary school, Washington, D. C., 1960, The Association.
National Council on School House Construction, Peabody College, Nashville, Tenn.
National Education Association: Planning facilities for health, physical education and recreation, revised edition, Washington, D. C., 1956, The Association.
Pierce, David A.: Saving dollars in building schools, New York, 1959, Reinhold Publishing Corp.
Sudell, R., and Waters, D. T.: Sports buildings and playing fields, London, 1957, B. T. Batsford, Ltd.
Sumption, Merle R., and Landes, Jack L.: Planning functional school buildings, New York, 1957, Harper & Brothers.
Voltmer, E. F., and Esslinger, A. A.: The organization and administration of physical education, ed. 3, New York, 1958, Appleton-Century-Crofts.
Westkaemper, Richard B., and Scott, Harry A.: From program to facilities in physical education, New York, 1958, Harper & Brothers.

chapter

11

The physical educator and teaching style

Courses in methods and materials in professional preparation curricula are typically concerned with instructing the future physical educator in how to teach a particular skill, how to correct student errors in skill performance, and how to direct the practice of a skill. Such courses may be said to be skill-centered. For example, the methods of teaching soccer are taught as a unit, and then the methods unique to other team, individual, and dual sports are taught as independent units. Methods and materials courses are also concerned with patterns of class organization for the teaching of a skill. The future physical educator learns where to place the left-handed student, how to line the students up for instruction so that they do not face into the sun, and the most efficient methods of moving from lines to semicircles to rows for various drills and lead-up games.

Rarely do methods and materials courses consider the individuality and creativity of the teacher, and even more rarely do they take into account the individuality of the student to whom the methods will be applied. These courses do, however, serve an essential purpose as part of the professional preparation curriculum. They do introduce the future physical educator to

effective methodology in both teaching and class management, and they do help to prepare for the student teaching experience. What methods and materials courses frequently do not do is to provide the future teacher with experiences in developing a system of teaching that is unique to himself.

DEFINITION OF THE TERM "TEACHING STYLE"

Teaching style and teaching methodology are two separate yet complementary phenomena. Teaching methodology is based on a standard philosophy of physical education and on the objectives of the physical education program. A physical educator's style of teaching is an expression of himself as an individual and is related to his personal philosophy and objectives. A physical educator adapts his methodology to his teaching style rather than the reverse. A physical educator who teaches "according to the textbook" does not have a teaching style of his own. A physical educator may, however, follow a syllabus explicitly without compromising his teaching style.

We may thus define teaching style as an observable phenomenon that is an expres-

Fig. 11-1. Teaching style is an expression of oneself as an individual. (Ames High School, Ames, Iowa.)

sion of the physical educator's individuality in relation to his stated philosophy and program objectives. Additionally, a physical educator's teaching style is reflected in his methodology of teaching and in his class organization and management.

KINDS OF TEACHING STYLE

There are two basic kinds of teaching style: teacher-centered and student-centered. There are many varying and overlapping styles both among physical educators and within the individual physical educator, but one or the other style will predominate, as a way of thinking, for a single teacher.

Teacher-centered style

The teacher-centered physical educator is often described as autocratic. He states his philosophy of physical education in terms of his personal relationship to his profession, and his personal conception of the goals of his profession in relation to his own teaching. His program objectives are stated in terms of what he wishes to accomplish as a teacher, and his evaluation is made in relation to what he has accomplished through his program. For example,

the teacher-centered physical educator might list some of the daily objectives of a unit in basketball in the following manner:

1. To teach the dribble
2. To teach the hook shot
3. To teach foul shooting

The autocratic physical educator will evaluate the basketball unit as a successful learning experience if he has indeed taught the dribble, the hook shot, and foul shooting, *and* has taught his class to perform these skills to a common standard. The satisfaction for the autocratic physical educator, then, is based not on student success but on teacher accomplishment in terms of teacher-centered objectives. The program evaluation is not derived from observing student success but rather from an analysis of the teaching and its effectiveness in terms of student learning.

The teacher-centered physical educator is somewhat of a perfectionist and expects that all his students will be able to perform a certain skill in the same way. He does realize that not all students have the ability to meet a single standard of performance, but his teaching is frequently geared to those students who can measure up to the physical educator's criteria for success.

This teacher tends to feel that he has failed as a teacher when a student falls short of the expected goal. The teacher-centered physical educator strives to guide his students toward the response or action he views as being the correct one in any given situation. In a rules quiz, for example, all the students may correctly answer that there are nine players on a baseball team. They may not know why there are nine players or what the players' duties are, but they have given the correct response, and that accomplishes the goal.

The teacher-centered physical educator is generally a rather rigid individual, and his rigidity is transferred to the teaching situation. His classes tend to be dull rather than exciting, and his students are more often externally motivated by fear of failure than by an inner-directed desire to succeed. This physical education stylist is often the delight of supervisors and administrators because he demands excellent discipline and maintains tight control over his classes. It is difficult to be able to state accurately, however, whether or not the students in such classes derive any enjoyment from their physical education experience.

In a teacher-dominated physical education class, the instructor is most likely to follow tried and tested methodology rather strictly. This teaching stylist feels that only proven methods and techniques will work, and he resists innovation because he feels that it threatens his effectiveness as a teacher. He sometimes refers to educational innovations as fads that will not be fully accepted because their lasting value has not been demonstrated. A capsule analysis of this stylist would state that he has had one year of teaching experience that has been repeated "x" number of times.

The teacher-centered physical educator is less interested in the individual student than in the student group. He frequently views a class as simply a group of bodies that need to be physically educated. For this reason, the teacher-centered physical educator is less apt to know his students by name than to know them by their physical abilities. He frequently can describe accurately the tumbling, softball, or other skills of the fourth student in the second squad, but he may not know the student's name. His students often feel that they are less important to the teacher than the condition of the gymnasium floor, the cleanliness of the locker room, or the height of the grass on the playing field.

The teacher-centered physical educator is chiefly concerned with the cognitive areas of teaching, and less often with the affective areas. He chooses the body of knowledge he will impart to his students and is interested only in their grasp of it as knowledge. He depends on observable motor skills and the scores on written and skill tests to tell him whether or not the knowledge is being absorbed. He is not particularly interested in whether or not his students appreciate, enjoy, or want to participate in certain physical education activities. The right of choosing the activities to be engaged in are reserved for teacher, and the activity is taught for the sake of the activity.

The teacher-centered stylist feels that he must conform to the philosophy of the school administration, and this is frequently a traditionalist philosophy. Thus, the physical educator believes that it is also his duty to have his students conform, and he feels that this can be accomplished only through a traditional teaching style. In the gymnasium or on the playing field it is the physical educator who demonstrates new skills, and the students are expected to mimic the instructor's technique. Student evaluations are thus subjectively arrived at in relation to their ability to conform, not only in regard to techniques of performing skills, but in the areas of behavior and attitude as well. The results of written tests are sometimes discounted if they diverge either way from the physical educator's subjective evaluation of the student.

This style of teaching physical education often helps to stereotype the field as one that stands apart from the rest of the school program. The teacher-centered physical educator is primarily concerned with his relationship to his own field only, and tends not to keep abreast of changes in general education. He does not regard changes in general education any more seriously than he regards changes in physical education as being important to his own teaching and professional growth.

Intramural and interscholastic sports programs and physical education clubs are also influenced by the teacher-centered physical educator in much the same way as the class program is influenced. Often, the intramural and club activities offered are not decided on the basis of student need and interest, but rather on the basis of what the physical educator thinks the students ought to have.

Under the teacher-centered approach, a student may be barred from joining clubs and intramural teams if he also has an interest in other school clubs and activities. In some instances, a student whose band rehearsal makes him a few minutes late for a club meeting or game may find himself locked out of the gymnasium or locker room. The teacher-centered physical educator tends to theorize that the student cannot be seriously interested in the after-school program in physical education if he does not make the effort to arrive at the activity on time. This labels the student as a nonconformist in the eyes of the teacher and effectively drives the student away from after-school physical education activities. In some secondary schools, this lack of a cooperative relationship on the part of the physical educator with other school activities results in a marked failure of the intramural and club programs in physical education. Students will seek out, and participate in, those school activities which answer their needs and interests, and welcome them as individuals who have something to contribute.

With the teacher-centered physical educator, intramural teams in a rigid setting are frequently highly coached. Contests are instructional extensions of the class period rather than games played purely for enjoyment. The physical educator will supervise very closely, and at times he will remove a student from a game if he feels that the student is not "giving his all." He may also stop a contest to correct the skill errors of several players. Frequently, the physical educator will have formed the teams and appointed a captain for each without any student participation, and he will exercise the right to shift players from one team to another.

In varsity sports, the teacher-centered physical educator will dominate the game completely. The physical educator in his role as coach will decide all lineups and lineup changes, and direct all game strategy from the bench. In a sport such as football, for example, the coach will send the plays in to the quarterback rather than letting the quarterback direct the offense. A game in which this kind of team goes on to victory is another example of guiding students to the response desired by the teacher. The victory serves as a proof, for the physical educator, of the worth of the teacher-centered style of teaching, but such a victory makes a questionable contribution to the physical, mental, emotional, and social growth of the players involved.

Student-centered style

The student-centered physical educator is sometimes thought of as a democratic teacher. The student-centered physical educator's philosophy is stated in terms of the relationship of physical education to the total educational field and its goals. He conceives of the goals of physical education as running parallel to those of general education. The student-centered physical educator's program objectives are stated in terms of student needs and interests, and his evaluation is based upon how well his program has succeeded in meeting those needs and interests. He might list some of the daily objectives of a unit in tennis in the following manner:

1. To be able to execute the forehand

2. To be able to serve

3. To be able to play a game of doubles

The student-centered physical educator will be pleased with this unit if, among the other basic tennis skills, his students can return the forehand shot into the playing court, serve well enough to keep the ball in play, and cooperate with a partner in playing a game of doubles. This physical educator is not satisfied with teaching minimal skills. Rather, he desires to have his students learn skills as well as they can so that they will find success and pleasure in physical activity. He does not attempt to develop champion players in a sport such as tennis, but he is instead concerned with the ability of his students to be able to play a recreational game of tennis, even if it is played on a beginning level. The student-centered physical educator does not expect or demand that all students attain a common level of skill; rather, he desires that each student attempt to reach his own potential. The satisfaction for this stylist is based on student success in terms of student-centered objectives. The program evaluation is derived from an observation of student success and from an objective analysis of the teaching in relation to its ability to meet student needs and interests. This physical educator uses his evaluation as a guide to adaptations and modifications that might help him to meet student needs even more effectively.

The student-centered physical educator is especially cognizant of differences in student ability, and avoids setting common criteria for skill performances. Instead, he prefers to devise charts or other devices that show the beginning, intermediate, and advanced level of performance for each skill or combination of skills. Each student can use these criteria to judge his own progress and performance and to attempt to

Fig. 11-2. There are various types of teaching styles. (Ames High School, Ames, Iowa.)

move from the beginning to the more advanced levels according to his individual potential. Thus, each student progresses at his own most comfortable rate and can thus find success that is meaningful to him as an individual. Because there are no artificial or induced standards toward which each student must strive, there is less chance for failure. The student-centered physical educator attempts to gear his teaching to each individual in the class rather than to any one similarly skilled group of individuals. The teaching is then on a more personalized basis, and there is a decided emphasis on remedial help for those who need it, as well as on coaching tips for those who are more advanced. The student-centered physical educator strives to help his students reach their own goals in regard to motor skill ability.

The student-centered physical educator is usually very flexible. In the teaching situation he will alter or adapt a lesson if he sees that it is not accomplishing its purpose. He will frequently make other on-the-spot changes if his class seems unusually tired or if a dreary day leads to student lethargy. He will devise unique games or activities that will help to rekindle student interest and enthusiasm, or he will place a unique lesson in the program merely to provide a break in routine. His classes are exciting to watch, and his students are enthusiastic about the class because they find it stimulating and challenging. These students have an inner motivation to succeed because they are encouraged to operate as individuals and to succeed as individuals. This helps them to discipline their own behavior. At times, this physical educator is criticized by supervisors and administrators because the noise emanating from the gymnasium or playing field is interpreted as a lack of control on the part of the physical educator, rather than being recognized as the sounds of boys and girls responding enthusiastically to their physical education experience. Discipline is an undertone—not a fear-inducing characteristic of the class period.

The student-centered physical educator welcomes innovations because he feels that he is contributing to his students, to his profession, and to his own professional growth through the use of the latest techniques and methodology. He will, for example, adopt the principles of movement education, giving them an objective and sufficiently lengthy trial before accepting them as a permanent part of his program, or rejecting them because they make a questionable contribution to his students. He judges innovations on student relevance rather than on how they relate to him as a teacher. This stylist also appreciates traditional methodology, but he does not view it as unchanging or unchangeable. Each new school year represents new techniques and methodologies to be tested, new activities to introduce, new individuals to guide through the physical education experience, new challenges to be met, and new personal experiences to be gained.

The student-centered physical educator is interested in each student as an individual, and realizes that physical education makes a unique contribution to the individual that is made by no other phase of the school program. This physical educator knows each student by name, and can accurately describe each student's physical education needs, interests, and abilities. He is interested in his students as whole human beings, and willingly gives of his time for individual guidance and counseling. His students prize him as a teacher because they know that he views them as the most important part of the physical education program.

This physical educator attempts to teach his students to think for themselves, to be creative, to express themselves, and to ask questions. He is concerned with the cognitive objectives of physical education, but he is also especially concerned with the affective objectives. He is vitally interested in having his students become aware of the values of physical activity and the varieties of physical activity. He wants them to enjoy and appreciate physical activity, to seek out new activities, and to participate in them on their own. This teacher employs a conceptual approach to physical education so that his students will be able to base their knowledge of physical activity on scientific understanding. When new activities are introduced or new units initiated, the students understand the value of, and need for, that activity, aside from the fact that the activity is required by a syllabus.

The student-centered physical educator believes in a balance of activities presented in a logical progression, but he also very strongly feels that his students should be able to select the activities that appeal to them. Rather than dictating the activity for each unit, the physical educator will present his students with a list of several activities that will fulfill the same student needs as indicated by their motor ability and physical fitness test scores. If there is more than one teacher, the class may be divided into two interest groups. If there is only one teacher, the class may decide to select one activity, or the classes may be so arranged that two activities can be covered. Some student-centered physical educators will extend the number of class periods allocated to a unit in order to assure meeting the needs and interests of the students.

The student-centered physical educator is also interested in conforming to administrative dicta, but he does not view this as a hindrance to his program or to his desire to utilize the latest thinking in physical education. Before adopting any new method or technique that might be viewed as radically different, he will present his plan to his superiors for approval, showing how he hopes that the innovation will make the physical education experience more meaningful for his students. This physical educator further realizes that there are many alternatives in teaching, and is willing to test any alternative that seems pertinent and logical. He also knows that his performance of a skill is not necessarily the best way for his students to perform it. He takes variations in body build, flexibility, strength, endurance, and experience into account, and enlists students to demonstrate a variety of techniques for their fellow classmates. This helps his students to understand that there is more than one acceptable technique in performing a skill.

Student evaluations, for the student-centered physical educator, are based on many objective measures. He does not believe that a single grade should be given to a student, especially when the grade is expected to include skill, attitude, and behavioral outcomes. This physical educator prefers to evaluate his students in a written, comprehensive statement that is more meaningful than a letter or number grade. Some secondary schools have permitted their physical education staffs to devise a separate physical education evaluation form based on just such a statement, and including places for noting test scores and other factors. Such evaluation forms give a total picture of student progress.

The student-centered physical educator is interested in his own field as well as in the other areas of the curriculum. He reads professional journals and attempts to understand the changes being made in general education. He views education and physical education as dynamic, and he is aware of their many interrelationships and interdependencies. Through his reading and meetings with other professionals, he strives to grow as a teacher in conjunction with the growth of education and physical education as professional fields of endeavor.

Intramural and interscholastic sports, as well as physical education clubs, are student-centered when the physical educator is student-centered. The intramural and club activities offered are directly related to student needs and interests. There are frequently different programs for students in different grades. For example, in the fall season ninth-grade girls may be offered soccer and speedball, while senior girls may be offered field hockey and lacrosse. Similarly, ninth-grade boys may have programs in soccer and track events, while there is a touch football and field event offering for senior boys.

The student-centered physical educator wants his students to be interested in all phases of the school program. He will work cooperatively with the art, drama, or music teachers to plan a schedule of after-school events that will not conflict, or he may set aside a special day for students whose diversity of interests makes cooperative scheduling difficult.

Intramural teams are organized by the students under the supervision of the physical educator, and captains are elected by the vote of team members. The games are played for their recreational value, regardless of the skill levels of the various players. While the intramural program is considered to be an extension of the class program, it is regarded not as a teaching-learning situation but as an opportunity for each student to practice his skills and to enjoy the use of them in an activity of his own choosing. Team lineups, substitutions, and the conduct of the intramural games will be student-directed. The teacher will supervise, but he will never control or dominate the games.

Varsity sports will also be student-directed. Although the physical educator will be directly responsible, as coach, for the overall administration of the team, the players themselves will take the most important role. Lineups, lineup changes, and game strategy will evolve from a dialogue between the players and the physical educator. Additionally, the quarterback in football or the catcher in baseball will have the responsibility for calling the game plays, with the physical educator suggesting plays only when the situation demands it. In victory, the glory belongs wholly to the players, and in defeat they will have learned invaluable lessons that will lead to future victories. The student-centered approach makes a definite contribution to the physical, mental, emotional, and social growth and development of the students and athletes in such a program because student initiative is the key note.

Teacher-centered style vs. student-centered style

Both the teacher-centered physical educator and the student-centered physical educator are equally knowledgeable about their subject matter. It is only their *approach* to teaching this subject matter that really differs. While the subject matter is the prime focus of the former, the latter focuses on the student in the teaching-learning situation.

Neither style of teaching is perfect, nor is either free of disadvantages. Both styles have their merits, and both have been used successfully by many different teachers of many different subjects. Each style has been described from a puristic, theoretical point of view so that differences would be more easily recognized and understood, but it must be remembered that teachers tend to borrow elements of both styles and incorporate them into their own unique teaching systems.

In practice, physical educators may shift from style to style, depending on the particular lesson. In teaching team and dual sports, the physical educator may use an approach that is closer to the teacher-centered style, and he may do this for a variety of reasons. For example, he may have a class, or several classes, that have not developed the maturity required for a student-centered approach, or the physical educator may want to teach a skill and have only a limited amount of time. This same physical educator may find that these same classes benefit most from the student-centered approach when its use is limited to such creative-expressive activities as dance, tumbling, gymnastics, swimming, and other individual sports. It is also possible to use the teacher-centered style during one part of a class period and the student-centered style during another part of the same class period.

A physical educator may use the teacher-centered style in his class program, and in a varsity coaching situation but prefer the student-centered style for the intramural and club program, or the reverse may be true. Any number of combinations of teaching style may be observed in the individual physical educator, depending upon the activity, the needs of the students, and the physical educator's assessment of the most appropriate style for the situation.

The two teaching styles are not exclusive, and they do overlap. A physical educator may, in fact, state his objectives and goals in student-centered terms, yet instruct through the teacher-centered style. However, the predominating style in use at the time will be readily identifiable to the observer.

PHILOSOPHY AND TEACHING STYLE

There are five major philosophies that direct education and educational thought and influence teaching style. These philosophies are idealism, realism, pragmatism, naturalism and existentialism. The ability to understand the key concepts of these philosophies and to relate these concepts to education helps a physical educator to articulate a philosophy of his profession and guides him in developing a teaching style that reflects his personal philosophy.

Idealism and teaching style

Idealism is a heritage from the ancient Greek thinkers and philosophers. The idealist places universal ideas at the center of the universe, and says that these ideas represent absolute and universal reality. Further, the idealist believes very strongly in man's powers of reasoning and intuition.

In regard to education, the idealist feels that the quest for knowledge is inner-directed and that the creativity and thought processes of the student are personal to him. The role of the teacher is to supply a learning atmosphere and mold the mind of the learner.

The idealist regards physical education as more than a purely physical experience. He expects the physical education program to provide opportunities for mental, social, and emotional growth as well. The idealist would strongly support a physical education program that encouraged student initiative and creativity and furthered his intellectual attainment. Having the student understand the *why* of the activity would be approved. The teacher would be looked upon as the possessor of all culture and worthy of emulation by the student. The emphasis would be centered upon seeing how nearly the pupil could achieve the ideal.

Realism and teaching style

Realism as a philosophy took hold as an entity during the late nineteenth and early twentieth centuries, although its roots are as old as those of idealism. The realist places the laws of nature at the center of the universe and supports the scientific method as the best way of seeking and gaining knowledge.

Mathematics and science are, to the realist, the core of the educative process. The educative process as a whole is thought of as a system of learning how to acquire knowledge, acquiring knowledge, and putting knowledge to use. The role of the teacher is to be objective in methodology, testing, and student evaluation. The development of standardized tests was influenced by the philosophy of realism.

The realist values physical education because he feels that the physical education experience helps the student to learn to adjust to the world. The outcome of the activity in terms of student adjustment is of prime importance to the realist. He would prefer a scientifically formulated program that follows a logical sequence. However, any activities offered in the program would have to be justified as valuable on the basis of scholarly research. The realist believes strongly in the drill method of teaching and in teacher demonstration. He would require that student evaluations be derived from the results of objective tests. The realist would approve of a physical education program that had a teacher strong in scientific procedures but whose personality and views did not play a part in the learning procedure.

Pragmatism and teaching style

Pragmatism is considered to be an American philosophy in its modern concept. The word pragmatism was first used in the 1800's, the approximate time this philosophy began to evolve out of its earlier form, which was known as experimentalism. Pragmatism is the philosophy associated with John Dewey.

The pragmatist is a flexible man who believes in change, in man's integration with his world, and in the scientific method. The pragmatist places experience at the center of his universe because he feels that man cannot know, or prove, anything that he has not personally experienced.

Dewey said that experience is the key to learning and that the problem-solving method gives the student the experience he needs in order to learn. The pragmatist stresses individual differences between students and demands a student-centered school. The role of the teacher is to inspire, guide, and lead the student through a variety of problem-solving activities.

The pragmatist demands a physical education program that meets the needs of the individual student. A wide variety of activities, with emphasis on creativeness, is of prime importance. Rigidity and formality, which are inherent in drills and exercises, would not receive the approval of the pragmatist. He believes in providing activities that arise from the interests and experiences of the student and in adapting the activity to the student. He also prefers that students sample innovative activities, that they be involved in deciding curriculum content, and that they participate as equals in program planning. The pragmatist would accept only a physical educator who is a purist in the student-centered style.

Naturalism and teaching style

Naturalism is the oldest philosophy known to the western world. It shares many of the concepts of realism and pragmatism because it has had a strong influence on the development of these philosophies.

The naturalist places at the center of the universe only those things which exist in actuality. In other words, only material, or physical, things have significance. The naturalist values society as a whole but is more concerned with each man as an individual.

Naturalist thought has influenced the development of the educational philosophies of realism and pragmatism. The naturalist desires a student-centered school in which the educational process is geared to the growth, needs, and interests of each individual student. The problem-solving method is important to the naturalist, who feels that the role of the teacher is to guide the student through the process of investigation by the use of example and scientific demonstration.

The naturalist believes in a wide variety of physical activity and in vigorous exercise. All activities in his program must be geared to the student as an individual rather than as part of a larger group. The program should follow the natural pattern of the student's growth and development. The naturalist strongly disapproves of intense group competition, although he does approve of intramural programs, providing that the competition is controlled. He states that no activity should be introduced unless the student is ready for it and has expressed a need for it and an interest in it. This philosophy would much prefer the purely student-centered stylist but would accept a strongly student-centered stylist who has some traces of the teacher-centered style in his approach. In the latter case, the naturalist would suggest that the physical educator attempt to adapt his methods entirely to the student-centered style.

Existentialism and teaching style

Existentialism emerged as a philosophy in the late nineteenth century but did not receive significant recognition until after World War II. Existentialism is a thoroughly modern philosophy.

The concept of the individuality of man forms the core of existentialism. The existentialist believes that each man guides his own destiny, determines his own system of values, and occupies a place that is superior to that of the society at large.

The existentialist says that education is an adventure in the discovery of self and that the schools must be totally student-centered so that the individual student will not be hindered in his attempts at discovery. The existentialist advocates that the student be given full freedom to learn what he is interested in learning at the time he is interested in learning it. The student selects not only the subject matter but the method through which learning will take place. Norms, standardized tests, and group tests would be entirely eliminated in favor of an individual evaluative process. The role of the teacher is to monitor the learning environment and to supply the needed tools and opportunity for learning, as well as to serve as a stimulus for the student.

In regard to physical education, the existentialist would prefer a balanced and varied program that has something for everyone. Additionally, the existentialist would prefer that each student have freedom in the choice of activities and that he be responsible for disciplining himself, guiding his own learning, and evaluating his own progress. The teaching approach most preferred by the existentialist is that of the physical educator who is completely student-centered.

DEVELOPMENT OF A TEACHING STYLE

A teaching style develops gradually and is unique to each physical educator because of the myriad individual variations and shadings that may be applied to a style. There are various influences, however, that affect the development of an individual's teaching style. Two of the most important influences are the undergraduate professional preparation program and the student-teaching experience. A third influence is the philosophy of the school system in which the beginning teacher matures.

Influence of the undergraduate professional preparation program

It is in the undergraduate years that the future physical educator first explores the

Fig. 11-3. Teaching style develops gradually. (Ames High School, Ames, Iowa.)

nonactivity aspects of physical education. Courses in the history and philosophy of education and physical education, in principles and practice of physical education, and in organization and administration of physical education form a foundation of understanding and comprehension of the breadth and depth of the field. Through such courses the future physical educator begins to form a personal philosophy of physical education. He is often required, as an adjunct to these courses, or in methods and materials courses, to formulate a series of objectives for physical education, to plan course outlines and curriculum content, and to write lesson plans.

The philosophy and teaching style of the undergraduate instructors have a profound influence on the development of the student's teaching style. In general, a department will decide upon how the students in that department are to write their objectives and construct the lesson plans that will carry out these objectives. The decision may dictate student-centered terminology or teacher-centered terminology, or some kind of compromise terminology. However, the point is too infrequently made that there is more than one way of writing objectives and that there is more than one style of teaching that will carry out the objectives satisfactorily. Experience in teaching gained in methods courses further influences and reinforces the dictated teaching style. It is this method of phrasing objectives and this style of teaching that is brought to the student-teaching experience.

Influence of the student-teaching experience

The student-teaching experience is often described as the culminating experience of the future physical educator's undergraduate preparation. This culminating experience is at times a traumatic one for the student teacher, but it is an invaluable experience because it provides an opportunity for further development of, or drastic modification in, teaching style.

Not all the master teachers associated

with a particular undergraduate school will state their objectives or design their lesson plans in exactly the same way. There may be many variations, and the student teacher who has begun to develop a student-centered style may find that his master teacher advocates a rigidly teacher-centered style. These stylistic differences can be a source of friction between the student teacher and the master teacher. It is typically the student teacher who adapts his teaching style in order to gain the approval of the master teacher and in order to ensure a favorable evaluation at the end of the student-teaching experience.

The master teacher has an obligation to the student teacher but an even stronger obligation to his students. Secondary school students are adaptable, and a change in teaching style at the beginning of a new unit will not have a detrimental effect on the students. A change in the middle of a unit could be less than beneficial. It is of no value to the student teacher to follow the example of the master teacher without question. Conferences between the two individuals can open doors to understanding, however, and may result in an enjoyable and worthwhile experience for both the master teacher and the student teacher.

Influence of the philosophy of the school system

The beginning teacher may or may not have a well-defined teaching style, depending upon the strength of his undergraduate experience and his willingness to express himself as an individual in the teaching situation. The initial weeks of full-fledged teaching give the beginning teacher an opportunity to amalgamate his undergraduate and student-teaching experiences.

In a one-teacher department, the beginning teacher will be free to test both teaching styles and to make adaptations, modifications, and compromises. Where there are several teachers in a department, the probationary teacher may be required to adhere to a preferred departmental style. In either case, the philosophy of the school system as a whole will give the beginning teacher clues as to how much innovation he can attempt.

The beginning teacher may find that he is free to innovate and to teach by any style he wishes. He may find that he must shift his teaching style frequently until he finds a style that he considers most comfortable and to which his students react best. An experienced teacher, too, will modify and change his teaching style from time to time as student needs and interests change.

IDEAL TEACHING STYLE

There is no one ideal teaching style. Each physical educator may find that the suitability of a particular teaching style depends on the circumstances and the teaching situation.

Teaching style must be the physical educator's unique expression of his role in relation to the role of his students. The value system of the students balanced against the value system of the physical educator will help to influence the choice of a teaching style.

Teaching style should be viewed as dynamic rather than static. As student needs change, and as the profession of physical education grows, the teaching style should be adapted to keep abreast of this growth and change. Fear of attempting the new and untried impedes the professional growth of the physical educator, but a willingness to be flexible enhances the physical educator as a professional member of a professional field of endeavor.

POINTS TO REMEMBER

1. The teacher should be able to exercise his individuality and creativity.
2. The student should be able to exercise his individuality and creativity.
3. A physical educator's style of teaching is an expression of himself as an individual.
4. Teaching style is an observable phenomenon.
5. The teacher-centered physical educator is often autocratic.

6. The student-centered physical educator tends to be democratic.
7. The physical educator's philosophy of education influences his teaching style.
8. There is no ideal teaching style.

PROBLEMS TO THINK THROUGH

1. How can methods and materials courses be changed so that they take more cognizance of individual teaching styles?
2. How closely aligned are teaching style and teaching methodology?
3. How can the area of affective learning take place more effectively under the teacher-centered style?
4. How can we objectively evaluate teaching style in terms of student need?
5. How can we justify the teacher- or coach-dominated activity or sport in terms of contributions to student creativity and initiative?
6. How can a physical educator determine whether his teaching style is unique to himself?

CASE STUDY FOR ANALYSIS

A student teacher finds that his teaching style and that of his master teacher are directly opposite. The student teacher feels that he is obligated to follow the example set by the master teacher, but he wishes to test his own theories, methods, and style of teaching. He hesitates to assert himself because he fears that he may be given a poor evaluation as a result. What steps should he take to resolve his dilemma?

EXERCISES FOR REVIEW

1. What are the characteristics of the teacher-centered style?
2. What are the characteristics of the student-centered style?
3. Under what circumstances should a physical educator change his teaching style?
4. How do the individual philosophies of education influence teaching style?
5. What factors help to determine the development of a teaching style?
6. Show why it is true that teaching style is dynamic rather than static.

REFERENCES

1. Davis, Elwood Craig: Philosophies fashion physical education, Dubuque, Iowa, 1963, Wm. C. Brown Co.

2. Mosston, Muska: The integration of a style of teaching with the structure of the subject matter, National College Physical Education Association for Men, 70th Proceedings, 1966.
3. Raths, Louis E., Wasserman, Selma, Jonas, Arthur, and Rothstein, Arnold M.: Teaching for thinking, Columbus, Ohio, 1967, Charles E. Merrill Books, Inc.
4. Shumsky, Abraham: In search of teaching style, New York, 1968, Appleton-Century-Crofts.

SELECTED READINGS

Bloom, Benjamin (editor): Taxonomy of educational objectives, Handbook I: Cognitive domain, New York, 1956, David McKay Co., Inc.

Bruner, Jerome S.: Toward a theory of instruction, Cambridge, Mass., 1966, Harvard University Press.

Conant, James B.: The American high school today, New York, 1959, McGraw-Hill Book Co.

Conant, James B.: The education of American teachers, New York, 1963, McGraw-Hill Book Co.

Durant, Will: The story of philosophy, New York, 1961, Washington Square Press, Inc.

Koerner, James D., The miseducation of American teachers, Baltimore, 1965, Penguin Books.

Krathwohl, David R., Bloom, Benjamin S., and Masia, Bertram B.: Taxonomy of educational objectives, Handbook II: Affective domain, New York, 1964, David McKay Co., Inc.

BOOKLETS, PAMPHLETS, AND ARTICLES

Abernathy, Ruth: Implications for physical education in the current reexamination of American education, Journal of Health, Physical Education, and Recreation 32:19, Jan., 1961.

American Association for Health, Physical Education, and Recreation: Becoming a better teacher (special journal feature), Journal of Health, Physical Education, and Recreation 32:17, April, 1961.

Barton, Helen M.: Creativity in team sports, Journal of Health, Physical Education, and Recreation 34:33, Nov.–Dec., 1963.

Fischer, Louis: Teaching style and religion in the classroom, The Educational Forum 32:211, Jan., 1968.

Fox, Philip S.: Student teaching: the culminating experience, Journal of Health, Physical Education, and Recreation 35:39, April, 1964.

Gaffney, Matthew P.: If I were a dictator, Journal of Health, Physical Education, and Recreation 32:23, Feb., 1961.

Holbrook, Leona: Education is our business, Journal of Health, Physical Education, and Recreation 37:19, April, 1966.

Hyman, Ronald T.: Teaching: triadic and dynamic, The Educational Forum 32:65, Nov., 1967.

Katz, Jeffrey M.: Seniors view their student teaching, Kappa Delta Pi Record 4:75, Feb., 1968.

Lemen, Mildred: Implications of the problem-solving method for physical educators, Journal of Health, Physical Education, and Recreation 37:28, March, 1966.

Mand, Charles L.: The case for a bold, new physical education experience, Journal of Health, Physical Education, and Recreation 33:39, Sept., 1962.

Romney, Golden: Creative teaching, Journal of Health, Physical Education, and Recreation 32:17, Oct., 1961.

Roundy, Elmo Smith: Problems of and competencies needed by men physical education teachers at the secondary school level, Research Quarterly of the AAHPER 38:274, May, 1967.

Smith, Hope M.: Motor activity and perceptual development: some implications for physical educators, Journal of Health, Physical Education, and Recreation 39:28, Feb., 1968.

Wickstrom, Ralph L.: The lost art of teaching physical activities, Journal of Health, Physical Education, and Recreation 32:26, Nov., 1961.

part

four

Teaching physical education

Yonkers Public Schools, Yonkers, N. Y.

chapter 12

The teaching-learning process

The teaching-learning process implies a duality of effort between the student and the teacher. The student learns from all the factors in his environment, but it is the school that is primarily responsible for formal learning through the educative process. Teaching and learning are synchronized into a process that is ongoing, developmental, and dynamic in nature. The teaching-learning process has many phases, each of which is vitally important to the process of education.

TEACHING

Learning is generally defined as an observable change in behavior. Teachers attempt to bring about positive behavioral changes through their classroom involvement with the student. To enhance learning, a teacher strives to provide the student with a favorable classroom environment that is conducive to learning. Teaching carries with it a twofold responsibility: the structuring of the learning material, and the provision of a desirable learning atmosphere. The structuring of the learning material will be dealt with in depth in the next chapter. This chapter is concerned with aspects of the learning environment itself.

Nature of a favorable environment

If the teaching process is to be enhanced, several environmental factors need careful consideration. Each factor stems from basic individual needs and may be categorized according to four major areas of concern:

1. Physical needs
   a. Heat. Temperatures should be maintained within a comfortable range so that students do not become drowsy from too much heat or overstimulated from too much cold.
   b. Light. Proper lighting in all classroom areas protects and aids students' vision.
   c. Ventilation. Proper circulation of fresh air is important to the health and comfort of everyone in the classroom.
   d. Equipment. Equipment should be in safe condition, adequate to the number of students in the class, and of the proper size and weight for the particular age level.
   e. Facilities. Adequate and safe facilities are a necessity for proper conduct of classes.
2. Emotional needs—A positive approach should be maintained in the handling of students and their problems. The National Association for Mental Health lists several factors essential to good mental health that have significance in the school situation:
   a. Acceptance. The student should feel that he is accepted as a person of worth by his teachers and his peers.
   b. Security. The student should know what is expected of him as a person and as a student.

Fig. 12-1. The student learns from all the factors in his environment. (Guymon Junior High School, Guymon, Okla.)

c. Protection. The student should not be made to feel that either his peers or his teachers have marked him as a failure or potential failure.

d. Control. The student should understand and abide by proper standards of good conduct and courteous behavior.

e. Independence. The student should feel that he has the freedom to express himself as an individual as long as he does not impinge on the rights of others.

f. Guidance. The student's efforts and successes need to be constructively criticized, praised, and recognized.

3. Social needs—Democratic group processes recognize both the larger group and the individual within the group.

a. Cooperation. Through cooperative efforts with his peers the student should feel that he is making an individual contribution to the larger group.

b. Competition. Through controlled competition with his peers the student should feel gratification in success, experience the adventure of competing, gain pride in accomplishment, and know the satisfaction that comes from wholehearted effort.

c. Grouping. Through grouping techniques students should be placed in groups where they will feel most comfortable and where they will be encouraged to work to their capacity.

d. Rapport. Good teacher-student relationships help the student to feel that he is respected as an individual.

4. Intellectual needs—Not all students' intellectual needs can be met in the same way, and not all students function best in a single kind of learning situation. Some students learn best in a democratic environment where they are encourged to be creative through a problem-solving approach. These students have the maturity to be able to conceptualize knowledge and come to their own conclusions through personal discovery. Other students function best in a rather rigidly teacher-dominated situation because they are not as yet ready to help guide their own learning. A single classroom may contain either type of student, or students who alternate between the two systems, depending on the material to be learned. Only through a comprehensive knowledge of each student can the teacher determine how each individual learns best and adapt the teaching methods as the need dictates.

Creation of a favorable environment

The preceding discussion outlines the basic factors necessary for the creation of an environment in which learning may take place. Yet each of these components must be combined so that an effective teaching-learning atmosphere is created. If, for example, each factor is present save one, the atmosphere will not be as conducive to the educational process as it might be. An overheated gymnasium, a poorly ventilated locker room, or a teacher who concentrates only on the students with high motor skill ability will each have a negative effect on the teaching-learning atmosphere. The physical needs, such as heating, lighting, and ventilation, are often only minor problems that can be corrected at once if difficulties arise. However, the social, emotional, and intellectual needs of the students need much more care and attention. The complexity of these needs and their interdependencies demands far greater consideration from the teacher and far more time and effort. Meeting these needs usually is possible only through the establishment of effective teacher-pupil re-

Chester Studios, Inc., New York

Fig. 12-2. Motivation is an inducement to action. (Yonkers Public Schools, Yonkers, N. Y.)

lationships. Unless the teacher is willing to become sincerely involved with his students, effective learning cannot take place, no matter how ideal the physical environment may be. This genuine involvement with the student sets the teacher apart from the teaching machine and gains for him or her professional respect. Good teacher-student relationships provide one of the most vital keys to successful teaching and learning. This particular relationship is probably most noticeable in the physical education classroom or on the athletic field, where the physical educator is not only a teacher of skills but a counselor of students as well.

Effective teacher-student relationships

The establishment of effective teacher-student relationships is dependent directly on the individuals involved in the educative process. The teacher must enjoy teaching, be patient and firm, know the subject matter, and know the growth and developmental characteristics of the students, as well as their needs and interests. A survey

of secondary school students revealed that the outstanding characteristic a teacher should possess is understanding.

Students who are willing to listen, to learn and put forth effort to improve, are highly desirable from the standpoint of the teacher. The student's ability to cooperate and to impose a degree of self-discipline also helps to establish classroom rapport.

Effective teacher-student relations are frequently a direct outgrowth of the style of teaching or type of classroom control utilized by the teacher. For example, two teachers in charge of similar teaching situations might exhibit totally different personalities and require entirely different behavioral characteristics from their students. While one teacher might be autocratic, demanding immediate and strict obedience to directions and commands, the other might be a more informal disciplinarian who expects a measure of self-control from the students. The first teacher described would demand respect from the students and would teach in a cold atmosphere, while the second teacher would command the respect of the students and maintain a warm relationship with them.

There are three major categories of classroom control that relate to the effectiveness of the teaching situation. Two have been briefly described in the preceding paragraph, but there is also the *laissez-faire* type of teacher who elicits still a different kind of control.

1. Autocratic control. The teacher dominates the classroom and the students, gives commands, and expects high standards to be met in regard to discipline.

2. Laissez-faire control. The students are given almost complete freedom within the classroom while the teacher simply observes or monitors the situation. Little is required in the way of discipline, and the class is frequently out of control.

3. Democratic control. The students share in all of the classroom processes and are expected to be able to exert some self-discipline.

The type of physical education teacher who fits each of the above descriptions is familiar to most observers. The autocrat is the domineering, drill-sergeant type: The laissez-faire physical educator is the one who merely throws out the ball to let the students play as they will: The democratic teacher tends to listen to the students and share the planning for the class with them. Although learning does take place in all three situations, the democratic physical educator would be the one most likely to have developed the warmest rapport with the students, and would be the most understanding of the students and their individual needs.

Individualized approach

At the present time in education, trends in all subject-matter areas point toward meeting individual student needs. Students are being offered opportunities for independent study and research, and are taking a larger share in their own education and its direction.

This individualization of programming requires stepping down from the command

Fig. 12-3. The teacher should have a knowledge of each of the students in the program. (Ames High School, Ames, Iowa.)

style of teaching and giving over some of the responsibility for learning to the students themselves. In the academic classroom, learning tasks are assigned that are more within range of the individual's capabilities and potential—the learning is not geared solely to the needs of the larger group. In physical education, testing helps to determine individual activity needs, and goals may be recognized and needs met more meaningfully.

Examples of individualized programming in physical education can be seen in a class where each student is given the freedom to work independently on the skills within an assigned unit, attempting to improve according to his own capacities and abilities. In a basketball unit, for example, some more-highly skilled students might work on shooting ten consecutive foul shots, while students of lower ability might work at another basket on simply improving their shooting technique in order to make a single successful shot.

To accomplish this type of teaching, the teacher must have a comprehensive knowledge of each of the students in the program. He must know the students' needs, their interests, and their individual abilities. While this individualized approach requires greater effort on the part of the teacher, there are many rewards in terms of student learning and teacher effectiveness.

LEARNING

Learning is a change or alteration in behavior and in general depends upon three major factors: heredity, the home environment, and the learning opportunities provided by the school. A recent study of high school students indicated that their high academic standings were 70% attributable to heredity, while the home and the school contributed 30%.[1]

Heredity

Nature versus nurture as a contributing factor in personality development has long fascinated educators and psychologists. They are especially interested in the extent to which the genetic makeup of an individual affects the outcome of his developmental nature. Present-day knowledge has now reached the point where science feels that genetic makeup will someday be able to be altered so that individuals can be produced who have desired, predetermined characteristics. In their studies of the makeup of intelligence, psychologists are finding that it may be possible to control portions of the intellect through the administration of such agents as ribonucleic acid. The significance of these discoveries holds many implications for education and physical education. Teachers need to remain up-to-date on discoveries and advances in these vital areas. Teachers need to know how these changes will affect the classrooms of the future and the physical abilities of the students of the future.

Home environment

Community and governmental agencies have long been striving to improve the environmental factors that serve as strong educational forces. Better homes, better jobs, better wages, and improved working conditions have been denied large segments of the population. In the typical middle-class home, books and conversation are a part of life and a way of life. In the homes of the disadvantaged, books are a rarity, and the home can be of little aid in preparing the child for school and an education. A few significant advances have been made in respect to the disadvantaged. Project Head Start, for example, is believed to be a help in preparing preschoolers for their first formal educational experience by offering the childhood experiences that are lacking in the home. Improved living conditions for the lower socioeconomic groups may someday in the future make these homes vital contributors to the educational process. Teachers need to realize that not all students come from homes in which education is a potent force, and that not all students are prepared for the challenge of school.

The school

As time goes on, computerized education may bring about great changes in the structure of the school. Through computers, a student may be able to obtain references from sources across the country or retrieve information in a short period of time rather than spend hours of research in a variety of books and reference materials. The teacher may become more of a guide through the machine-controlled process, giving the praise and encouragement, and the personal help, that the machine cannot give. Some of these changes have already come about in school systems, but until computers are utilized on a national scale, the school will still depend on the teacher and his training and abilities. In spite of the move toward computers, the teacher will still be the center of the educational process, for it is the teacher who must decide what the machine can do for each student, and it is the teacher who must evaluate what the machine is doing for the student. It is also the teacher who provides the human factor, upon which good teaching and learning will always depend.

The school must ask itself what vital conditions and characteristics of a learning situation most influence a student during the developmental years. By knowing these determinants the school can adjust and adapt to future educational developments in every curricular area. By knowing the determinants of learning, the school will better be able to meet its responsibilities to its students.

Learning process

Learning does not take place simply because the proper atmosphere exists or because the physical tools for learning, such as books, pencils, or athletic equipment, are available. In order for learning to take place, there must first of all be an individual who is motivated to learn, incentives that will increase the motivation, challenges that make reaching the learning goal an adventure, and continued effort on the part of the individual to overcome the challenges and arrive at the goal.

While all individuals are capable of learning, not all individuals learn at the same rate or in the same manner. Not all learners can be reached by a common methodology or teaching style. Many different kinds of learning styles have been identified, and learners tend to use each of these styles in varying degrees, depending on the material or concepts to be learned. Some learners are completely verbal-oriented, for example, while other learners succeed best when the problem-solving technique is used. Memorization, concept formation, and trial-and-error learning are other examples of learning styles.

The incentives offered for learning are vital to the educational process because they enhance motivation. Grades for achievement, placement in a higher ability group, and teacher praise and recognition are forms of incentives that are commonly used in education.

The challenges presented to the learner also help to increase the individual's motivation to solve a learning problem. If a learning task is too easy and the goal is reached without much effort on the part of the learner, very little real learning can take place. As the individual overcomes a variety of challenges that are set in his path, and as he draws closer to his goal, he learns—that is, each individual's success in overcoming a challenge is a true learning experience. However, no challenge should be so difficult that eventual goal attainment is made an impossibility.

In order to learn and to retain what he has learned, the individual must put forth a continued effort in order to overcome the challenges in his path and in order to arrive at his goal. A learner may experience failure in his first attempts at learning, but as he continues to try, he will reach a successful response in a given situation. As the learner continues to put forth effort, he will continue to make more and more successful responses that lead to goal attainment.

Fig. 12-4. The law of readiness is important for effective learning. (Hurst-Euless-Bedford Public Schools, Hurst, Texas.)

Thorndike set forth three laws of learning: the law of readiness, the law of exercise, and the law of effect.

The *law of readiness* in learning refers to the developmental, or maturational, level of the individual. Learning will take place more readily and effectively if the desired response can be successfully accomplished. Just as an infant may not learn to walk until his development readies him for the task, so is learning later in life dependent on the readiness of the learner.

The *law of exercise* refers to the necessity of continual practice of a given response to ensure learning. When a satisfying response is repeated in answer to a given stimulus, learning will take place. By the same token, when a response is not repeated frequently, forgetting, or loss of learning, may take place.

The *law of effect* in learning refers to the satisfaction which ensues when an appropriate response is given. A satisfying response is more likely to be repeated than a response that brings dissatisfaction to the individual.

Thorndike's association theory has been one of the most respected in education.

Thorndike believed that learning involved conditioned responses through habit-formation where a given stimulus (S) produced a response (R) through the establishment of a bond, or association. Teaching involves providing the stimulus to produce a desired response. The relationship of Thorndike's particular theory of learning to current teaching practices in physical education is readily observable. In terms of the learning of skills for various physical education activities, it is logical to assume that learning will take place more readily if the student is developmentally able to acquire a particular skill (the law of readiness). For example, a young student with inadequate muscular development would be unable to perform such tasks requiring strength as chin-ups or a softball throw for distance.

Regarding the law of exercise, the practice and drilling on skills such as the hockey dribble and basket-shooting have long been utilized as an effective means of learning. It should be pointed out that practice of an incorrectly performed skill also leads to learning, but of an undesired sort. The physical education teacher must remain alert to correct form whenever the practice of a skill is involved. It follows that correct responses result in desirable skill performances, such as baskets that score, home runs, and touchdown passes. In physical education the law of effect is readily applicable. Satisfaction with points scored or with winning performances easily leads to learning of required skills according to successful patterns.

Improved timing and automatic, well-conditioned responses are vital to physical education activities, so that tense, exciting situations, emotional stress, or other factors will not inhibit performance. For this reason, another facet of this conditioned response theory of learning also enters into teaching. The idea of overlearning, or reinforced learning as it is sometimes called, develops out of the continued-practice aspect of learning. The nature of overlearning skills in physical education assures controlled performances under stressful conditions. The ability to overlearn, to concentrate total effort, becomes the mark of a competitor, who exhibits highly developed skill learning.

Cognitive theory of learning

In opposition to the response theory of learning there emerged a different approach, known as the cognitive theory, which developed from the Gestalt system of psychology. Kohler and his followers in psychology defined learning as a sudden insight or reconstruction of a pattern of action. This insight takes place when a background of information suddenly unfolds itself into a totality, or a new whole, that is comprehensible to the student.

The cognitive theory of learning can be applied to physical education. For example, the process of learning complex tumbling stunts or the skills needed in highly organized team sports can be explained in terms of the theory. A participant in the game of football needs to understand the total purpose and process of the game if his play in a particular position during the game is to prove effective. He needs overall

insight into the development of the plays. For this reason, in the teaching of team sports the whole-part-whole method of teaching is frequently utilized. The basic outline of the entire game is introduced to the class, elementary game play is allowed, and then fundamental skills are practiced for later improvement of the game situation. By using this whole-part-whole method, the teacher is trying to develop a total *gestalt,* or picture, of the game in the student's mind, to help him visualize and learn the game patterns. The same theory can be applied to the learning of complex diving and tumbling stunts, in which the performer needs to have a complete picture clearly established in his mind before attempting to perform the stunt. The ability to combine the twists with the somersaults in mid-air is the result of an understanding of the whole stunt as well as of its parts.

Further refinements of the cognitive approach to learning are distinguishable in contemporary educational concepts. John Dewey and, later, Kirkpatrick, believing that experience is a great teacher, promoted the problem-solving approach to learning. This approach is finding increased favor in all subject-matter areas at the present time. They theorized that teachers should organize a wide variety of experiences and then leave the children free to think, hypothesize, and create their own behavioral patterns.

This "heuristic" learning, as it is also called, in which the child is free to make discoveries for himself, makes the learner a true participant in the learning process and generates excitement in his own self-education. Such experiences match the democratically controlled type of classroom, in which the student seeks his own level of top performance in accordance with his abilities.

The problem-solving approach to instruction in physical education may be found also in the current trend to "movement education," discussed in Chapter 16. According to this approach, fundamental movements are used as a basis for skill instruction. Teachers allow students the freedom to search for and find patterns most satisfying to them as individuals. Instead of telling the student to shoot a foul shot with two hands, the teacher allows the individual to attempt the shot in every conceivable combination of motions. By arriving at his own conclusions of what is the most satisfying method for him, the student achieves more complete and longer-lasting learning.

Conceptualization is another aspect of learning that is finding increased importance in education today. It is thought that total concepts formulated by the individual continue to guide and pattern his behavior long after school years are completed. Thus, it is hoped that providing students with basic concepts will result in a more meaningful educational background. In physical education this type of teaching has not yet been highly developed, but growing out of the problem-solving approach to learning will come basic concepts in skills and movement. From these fundamentals will be developed concepts basic to teaching all aspects of physical education.

For greater clarification of the learning process in physical education, it is necessary for teachers to define more specifically exactly what is to be learned. To attain the goals of physical education the student experiences a program of activities, each of which requires participation and development of skill. Learning in physical education requires the learning of skills. How is this accomplished? What is the more specific learning process that is required for the acquisition and improvement of motor performances?

Motor learning

The term "motor learning" is generally used in reference to the improvement of a motor performance or the development of a skill. For example, when, through practice, a golfer improves his putting skill, an archer improves his aim, or a pitcher improves his delivery, motor learning has taken place.

Movement is a fundamental aspect of human behavior, and skills may be categorized in several different ways. Two frequently used categories of skills are types of action, and function.

Motor skills, as they relate to types of action, may be divided into fine versus gross motor skills or into sensory versus perceptual motor skills.

Fine motor skills are those requiring manual dexterity, such as typing, whereas *gross motor skills* involve large-muscle activity, as in running.

Sensory motor skills are those which develop as a result of the sensory cues (feeling, tasting, hearing, seeing, and smelling). Serving a volleyball would involve a sensory cue, for example. *Perceptual motor skills* are developed whenever the perceptual process is involved (judgments concerning speed, depth, and background information). In archery, both types of skill are involved, because cues of feeling and seeing are used, as well as judgments concerning distance and point of aim.

Motor skills may also be categorized according to their function in human existence. Whereas some motor skills are essential for normal existence (walking, self-care), others may be classified in terms of their self-improvement or educational values (reading, writing), and others are recreational in nature. Physical education skills would be classified generally in this latter division.

How does a student learn a motor skill? Is motor skill ability inherited or acquired? Is it transferable from one type of activity to another? Researchers are only just beginning to find answers to some of these questions.

Process of motor learning. Motor learning involves the establishment of pathways within the complex neuromuscular system of the human body. The very simplest human movement, such as clapping the hands, involves a pathway that may be divided into three distinct parts: the sensory, the connecting, and the motor neurons. These neurons form a neural pathway to bring about muscular innervation, making the hands come together. Neuromuscular skills are merely different sets of pathways that have been established through practice. The following questions immediately come to mind concerning the development of skill.

1. *Are all skills acquired, or are some movements inherited?* Some movements may be categorized as inherited. For example, under normal circumstances, individuals walk, and they perform "swimming" movements in the water. Refinements of these motions can be acquired. Examples include hopping, skipping, and stroking in the water. Other inherited movements include those reflexes which are automatic and involuntary by nature, such as the knee jerk, eye wink, and breathing.

2. *Once learned, are motor skills always remembered?* Retention of motor skills is dependent on many factors. Those skills which are easily acquired, are natural, are used frequently, or are "overlearned" usually remain with an individual for a long period of time. For example, riding a bicycle, swimming, skating, and throwing are rarely forgotten. The degree of perfection in performance may vary, but usually a well-refined skill may be reacquired in a relatively short period of time.

3. *How much should a skill be practiced?* The amount of practice necessary to learn a skill depends on the individual, his quickness at acquiring the skill, and the degree of perfection desired. It has been found helpful to practice a motor skill in a series of a few attempts, followed by rest, and then to return to a series again. By distributing practice and rest intervals, neural pathways may be developed and stabilized.

4. *What about injuries?* In injuries where muscle tissue has been damaged, usually rest will allow a return to normal functioning. In instances where nerve endings are damaged, new neural pathways may need to be established, and relearning may take a little longer.

5. *Of what value is mental practice?* Mental practice refers to preperformance thinking about the skill to be performed, in terms of its parts and the total result. By establishing a mental image, teachers have been able to improve performances of skill by students in classroom situations. For this reason physical educators should consider carefully the word cues used in teaching and should recognize the value of going over, step by step, the execution of a skill with students prior to performance.

A great deal remains to be learned about the importance of one other essential factor related to learning: that one vital element which pushes one student to learn and improve, while another student, given the identical set of instructions, under the same conditions, does not learn or improve. Some identify this basic ingredient as *desire*, whereas others label it *motivation*. In either case, it has been recognized as the most important factor in the learning situation.

Motivation

The place of motivation in the learning process is indeed distinctive. It has been described as "that which gives both direction and intensity to human behavior."[*] Recent studies of all types of students, from dropouts to overachievers, have led investigators to certain conclusions about the motivated student:

1. Girls tend to be more positively motivated than boys.

2. Students from more favorable socioeconomic situations are better motivated.

3. Motivation to learn appears to be a fairly stable and constant phenomenon.

4. There can be too much motivation. We need optimal rather than maximal motivation.[2]

Recognizing these factors about motivation, the teacher must provide external motivation for those students who need it.

[*]From Frymier, Jack R.: Motivating students to learn, NEA Journal **57**:37, Feb., 1968.

Because styles of learning vary—some are visual, some aural, and others physical—the teacher must attempt to reach each individual student in class.

Sources of motivation vary and are generally found to be one of two types: intrinsic or extrinsic. Both play an important part in the teaching-learning process and need to be understood by the teacher.

Intrinsic motivators. Intrinsic motivators are factors found within the individual which prompt him to practice, review, and improve in any phase of learning. A sincere desire to learn, because of a genuine need to use the material or skill, is probably one of the greatest forces promoting learning. When a student strives to improve his own performance for his own sake—when he believes it is important to him personally to know how to swim or to play golf, for example—then he will be more likely to master the subject and retain his skills.

Intrinsic motivation brings about the more desirable type of learning: learning that will not be disturbed by the emotional tensions of competition or external stress. This type of motivation produces learning which in and of itself is its own greatest reward. The student recognizes his own improvement and is satisfied with the results of his efforts. The transfer of knowledge is more likely to take place when learning is self-motivated. The student who drives himself to a better performance in one skill area, such as ball-handling, will probably do better in other ball games as a result. Transfer and retention of knowledge and skill are a vital aspect of any educational endeavor, and the teacher should strive to promote this type of learning.

How does the teacher foster intrinsic motivation to promote learning? Educators generally believe that students who share in the planning of their programs of study are more likely to have a greater interest in it. The goals and objectives students set for themselves are usually those which they will sincerely strive to attain. Teachers who establish goals and objectives that take into account the needs and interests of their students, and who allow students to share in their specific program planning, can surely expect greater and more effective learning to result.

Extrinsic motivators. While some students are perhaps more highly motivated from within, teachers realize that extrinsic motivational factors are not without value. Grades, awards, trophies, and point systems fall into the category of extrinsic motivators—factors that originate outside the individual. There are some students who will work hard just to earn the coveted "A" or the trophy which the school awards. When the student does this work, learning takes place.

Pressure from the peer group may also be classified as an extrinsic motivator. The desire of adolescents to be a part of the team or a star on the athletic field promotes much learning in physical education.

A third extrinsic motivator is especially important for a teacher to understand and use. In simplest terms, genuine praise may do more to promote individual learning than all the ribbons or medals the school can provide. When a student knows he is performing correctly, several things happen: he continues to perform in the same manner, thereby creating a pattern of automatized movement in performing a skill, he feels pleased with himself, and he develops a positive self-image that further promotes the learning process. Educators generally agree that punishment (fear or threat) in some way actually shatters the entire learning situation and disturbs the total teaching-learning process. This seems to hold true for every age level, in all subject-matter areas. Particularly, though, it is applicable to physical education, in which a confident self-image, plus a skilled performance (achieved through practice that has been guided by constructive criticism and praise), combine to help produce better physically educated individuals.

In connection with this discussion of intrinsic and extrinsic motivational factors, it is interesting to speculate about the apt-

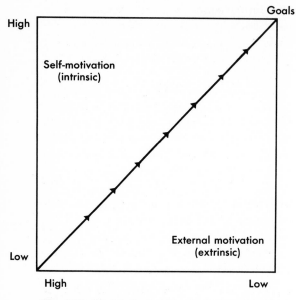

Fig. 12-5. Motivation.

ness of Fig. 12-5. Assuming that individuals are motivated both from within and without in an inverse relationship, consider as ideal those students whose intrinsic motivation is so high that overall goals of education are nearly achieved. Students fall somewhere on this line as they approach this general purpose of education. It is for teachers in their role as planners, organizers, and motivators to move students upward on this ladder, or scale, toward effective behavior.

In the words of Winston L. Prouty, United States Senator from Vermont:

> The mission of education ought to be to give each child the chance to work at his own level and to progress as far and as fast as his ability to learn permits.*

In summary, it should be remembered that students learn with or without stimulating material and with or without suitable environments. The source of such powers of learning is the internal motivational force. However, good teaching can further stimulate and enhance learning. Some learning may take place with little or

---

*From Prouty, Winston L.: Exceptional children —the neglected legion, NEA Journal **55**:25, March, 1966.

no desire on the part of the student, but such knowledge does not remain with him long.

It is the teacher's responsibility to provide the motivational force in a suitable environment with stimulating materials. This is teaching.

POINTS TO REMEMBER

1. A definition of learning
2. An understanding of the association theory of learning
3. An understanding of the *gestalt* theory of learning
4. The differentiation between intrinsic and extrinsic motivation
5. The importance of readiness to learning
6. The value of rapport in the teaching-learning process

PROBLEMS TO THINK THROUGH

1. Of what value is a knowledge of theories of learning?
2. Why is there no one answer to the problems of how to teach?
3. In what situations, if any, would an autocratic type of classroom atmosphere be necessary? A *laissez-faire* type?
4. What types of motivational devices may a teacher use in handling special cases such as the obese? The awkward? The brilliant? The retarded? The handicapped?

CASE STUDY FOR ANALYSIS

After careful observation of three different teaching situations, make a comparison in writing of what has been seen in terms of the where, when, what, who, and how of teaching. Pay particular attention to the motivation of students and the type of rapport established by the teacher. What suggestions may improve the existing situation?

EXERCISES FOR REVIEW

1. What is learning?
2. Explain three types of teacher control prevalent in a classroom.
3. Define and explain several types of motivators.
4. What environmental factors enhance learning? Why?
5. Differentiate between the *association* theory and the *gestalt* theory of learning, and apply each to teaching in physical education.

REFERENCES

1. Coyne, Walter A.: Presidential scholars, American Education 3:6, 1967.
2. Frymier, Jack R.: Motivating students to learn, NEA Journal 57:2, Feb., 1968.

SELECTED READINGS

Association for Supervision and Curriculum Development: Theories of instruction, Washington, D. C., 1965, The Association.

Bucher, Charles A.: Foundations of physical education, ed. 5, St. Louis, 1968, The C. V. Mosby Co.

Cowell, Charles C., and France, Wellman L.: Philosophy and principles of physical education, Englewood Cliffs, N. J., 1963, Prentice-Hall, Inc.

Cratty, Bryant J.: Movement behavior and motor learning, ed. 2, Philadelphia, 1967, Lea & Febiger.

National Association of Physical Education for College Women and National College Physical Education Association for Men: Motor learning, Quest, monograph VI, Spring, 1966.

Oxendine, Joseph B., Psychology of motor learning, New York, 1968, Appleton-Century-Crofts.

Seagoe, May V.: A teacher's guide to the learning process, ed. 2, Dubuque, Iowa, 1961, Wm. C. Brown Co.

Singer, Robert N., Motor learning and human performance, New York, 1968. The Macmillan Co.

BOOKLETS, PAMPHLETS, AND ARTICLES

Berlin, Irving N.: Special learning problems of deprived children, NEA Journal 55:22, March, 1966.

Bigge, Morris L.: Theories of learning, NEA Journal 55:18, March, 1966.

Blackie, John: How children learn, NEA Journal 57:40, Feb., 1968.

Brunner, Catherine: How and what to teach the very young child, NEA Journal 57:44, Feb., 1968.

Dawson, Kenneth E., and Norfleet, Morris: The computer and the student, NEA Journal 57:47, Feb., 1968.

Foreman, Kenneth E.: Stretching the mind, Journal of Health, Physical Education, and Recreation 36:19, May, 1965.

Frances, Sister Marian, SNJM: Establishing teacher-student rapport, NEA Journal 55:19, Oct., 1966.

Frymier, Jack R.: Motivating students to learn, NEA Journal 57:37, Feb., 1968.

Idzerda, Stanley J.: A good teacher is a good teacher, NEA Journal 55:15, Nov., 1966.

Jackson, Philip W.: The way teaching is, NEA Journal 54:10, Nov., 1965.

Lockhart, Aileene: Conditions of effective motor learning, Journal of Health, Physical Education, and Recreation 38:36, Feb., 1967.

Lockhart, Aileene: What's in a name?, Quest, monograph II, Tucson, Ariz., Spring, 1964.

Oxendine, Joseph B.: Generality and specificity in the learning of fine and gross motor skills, The Research Quarterly 38:86, March, 1967.

Ray, Henry W.: Freeing pupils from the sit-look-listen syndrome, NEA Journal 56:8, April, 1967.

Riessman, Frank: Styles of learning, NEA Journal 55:15, March, 1966.

Smith, Hope M.: Motor activity and perceptual development, Journal of Health, Physical Education, and Recreation 39:28, Feb., 1968.

VanDalen, D. B.: Philosophical profiles for physical educators, The Physical Educator 21:113, Oct., 1964.

Vincent, William John: Reinforcement theory—its implications for the teaching of gymnastics, The Physical Educator 21:166, Dec., 1964.

White, Mary Alice: Speculations on the child's world of learning, NEA Journal 55:20, March, 1966.

13

Methods
of
teaching

Teaching causes a change in behavior (learning) through the relationship established between teacher and student. This relationship is the result of the preparation and presentation of materials in a manipulated situation, the *method* being selected by the teacher. The term method, therefore, refers to the structuring of an educational setting in order that learning may take place. Methods include a variety of educational presentations, such as the lecture and the demonstration, each one appropriate for a specific teaching purpose. Selection of the appropriate method by the teacher during the preliminary planning stages of a unit is an important aspect of effective teaching.

The terms "methods" and "techniques" of teaching are frequently confused. *Methods* of teaching are ways of presenting material to students, while the *techniques* of teaching have reference to the tools or devices employed by the teacher to carry out successfully the method already selected. For example, if a demonstration of a skill has been planned as an introductory method, an appropriate technique might be a particular seating arrangement or lighting effect to be used during the dem-

onstration. The technique makes the method more effective and enhances learning. Whereas methods are generalized approaches to the presentation of material, techniques are specific to circumstances in the particular class session and are developed through experience by a teacher over a period of time.

FACTORS AFFECTING THE SELECTION OF METHOD

The proper selection of an appropriate teaching method involves consideration of several factors. While class size, equipment, and facilities merit some thought, these factors are more often considered in connection with organization of the class. Methods of teaching are determined by the nature of the activity itself, the particular purposes or goals to be achieved, and the age level and ability of the group.

Nature of the activity. The wide variety of activities included in a well-rounded physical education program necessitates utilization of different teaching methods, depending upon the nature or type of activity. Teaching an individual stunt such as a handspring requires a personal approach to improve an individual's performance,

Fig. 13-1. Teaching method involves consideration of several factors.

Fig. 13-2. High school girls in dance. (New York City Schools.)

while teaching offensive team tactics requires total group knowledge. Therefore, the selection of a method must take into account the nature of the activity. The nature of physical education activities may be differentiated in the following manner:

1. *Team sports:* Activities in which three or more players combine together to compete against a group consisting of a similar number of opponents. Scores are attributed to each group.

2. *Individual and dual sports:* Activities in which a single individual competes against a single opponent, or two players compete against two opponents. Scores of two players (partners) may be combined.

3. *Rhythms:* Activities in which a steady measured beat (vocal or instrumental) accompanies movement patterns, both axial and locomotor. Patterns may be performed singly, in pairs, or in groups.

4. *Aquatics:* Activities that take place in the water. These may be competitive, synchronized, instructional, or recreational in nature.

5. *Gymnastic activities:* Individual, self-testing activities in which tumbling skills and special apparatus are used. Individual scores may be totaled to determine team points.

6. *Track and field activities:* Individual self-testing activities in which running skills and speed are tested, as well as jumping and throwing power. Individual scores may be totaled to determine team points.

7. *Winter activities:* Activities that take place on snow and ice during the winter months. These may be individual or team endeavors.

8. *Games of low organization:* Activities in which all individuals participate freely with a single purpose in mind, such as tagging another player or trying to hit him with a ball.

For the purposes of this chapter on methodology, activities will be categorized according to the above distinctions.

Nature of the group goals. The nature of the group goals is an extremely important element to be considered in teaching methods. What do the students themselves expect to learn and achieve in a particular unit of work? In basketball, for example, they all want to play the game and to improve their skills only through playing. The creative teacher needs to develop exciting drills for skill practice, thus improving abilities of the individuals and upgrading game play while maintaining class enthusiasm.

Frequently the teacher needs to determine student objectives and goals for classwork. Providing an opportunity to hear students express their interests and desires will often bring out special individual hopes. Some girls may want to lose weight, and boys may want to improve game skill. Meeting these individual goals, revealed through democratic group processes, makes physical education a more meaningful experience for all.

Nature of the group. It is important to keep in mind the characteristics and interests of the students in the class. The differences between boys and girls, their physi-

Fig. 13-3. The characteristics and interests of students will help to determine methods. Mimetics. (Hartsdale Public Schools, Hartsdale, N. Y.)

cal abilities, their interests, and their attitudes all need consideration if teaching methods are to be appropriate. For example, on the junior high level, a variety of methods should be utilized to appeal to the students' widespread interests and to their need for change. Whereas a lengthy lecture would serve only to bore these younger students, it might be appreciated as a time-saver by older adolescents. The ability level of the students also needs clarification when methods are selected. Advanced students move rapidly through introductory and review sessions in a unit and should move on quickly into the advanced skills presentations.

In the discussion that follows, teaching methods are charted according to their appropriateness to the major areas of a physical education program. Methods are generally categorized according to phases within a teaching unit:

1. Methods of introducing the unit
2. Methods of improving physical skills
3. Methods of achieving social objectives
4. Methods of promoting intellectual learning
5. Methods of closing the unit

A section on definitions of terms follows the presentation of methods. Differentiation will be made for large and small classes to some extent, although this problem is handled in Chapter 18. Also, indications will be made of variations for boys and girls, for older and younger students, and for differing skill levels, whenever appropriate.

In schools where teams of teachers are organized, it should be pointed out that methodology as presented here remains unchanged. It is still the final presentation of material by an individual teacher which produces the causal relationship for teaching. Selection of methods may be the result of team consultation or of individual preference.

It should also be realized at the outset that teaching is an individual process, and no exact pattern for teaching can be de-

fined. A teacher must bring common sense and judgment plus knowledge and skills to the school situation, and must combine these attributes to provide worthwhile learning experiences. Appropriate teaching methods can be selected by the teacher only in accordance with a particular school situation, and no outsider can prescribe that choice. Past experiences naturally aid greatly in making decisions about teaching methodology. New teachers should try out the various methods presented in this chapter to determine which are the most effective for them. They must evaluate their work and strive to improve their methods on the basis of each teaching experience, for only in this way does experience truly help to make better teachers.

METHODS OF TEACHING TEAM SPORTS

Team sports are the favorites of boys and girls, and are taught extensively throughout the upper levels of a progressive program of physical education.

The values of football, softball, soccer, hockey, and the many other team sports are numerous. The physical skill and fitness benefits, the intellectual opportunities, and social organization all combine to make team sports an excellent educational experience.

Because of these inherent values and their widespread appeal, physical educators should strive to present team sports to students in a manner that will provide meaningful experiences to the greatest number. Thoughtful selection of methods will accomplish this end. There are certain teaching problems which are unique to this area of team sports, such as the different skill requirements of various positions and the complexities of annual rule changes. These and similar problems require special consideration.

Problems unique to the teaching of team sports

1. *How should class time be divided between the teaching of game skills and ac-*

tual playing of the game itself? In teaching team sports the *whole-part-whole* approach is generally thought to be the most effective. This theory uses the word "whole" to include the entire picture of the game, and the word "part" refers to basic skills or elements that make up the total game. When a team sport is introduced to a physical education class, it is helpful during the first class session to provide an overall picture of the total game, perhaps through a demonstration game or film version. This should be followed by the selection of basic skills for practice, and then the skills can be used in game situations. As the unit progresses, individual skills may be stressed through drill practice for part of the period, with the closing minutes of the class being devoted to actual game play. The game situation should itself be a learning experience through proper coaching and suggestions from the sidelines.

An attempt should be made for all members of a class to experience the game situation, even though in large classes it is sometimes difficult to organize. When the importance of skills is understood in terms of their application to the game itself, stu-

dents are more interested in improving them. Without adequate skills, the playing of the game becomes frustrating to students. Therefore, a teacher must carefully balance the introduction of skills and game play in classes, for the greater satisfaction of all the students.

2. *How should skills that are specific to certain positions in a team sport (e.g., pitching in baseball) be included in the unit?* At the junior high school level it is usually appropriate to teach students the fundamental skills essential to a particular sport. This provides each student with an opportunity to determine his own strengths and weaknesses, and to appreciate the difficulties of all the skills required to play in sports. When more advanced skill progressions are introduced in high school, special groupings may be more meaningful, based on the interests and abilities of the individual.

3. *How should theories of position play be presented and opportunities provided for students to play various positions?* Theories of position play should be presented with the use of such teaching aids as chalkboards, magnetic game boards, and films.

Fig. 13-4. Girls' physical education class. (Manchester High School, Manchester, N. H.)

Table 6. Methods of teaching team sports—baseball, basketball, football, hockey, lacrosse, soccer, speedball, volleyball

	Methods	*Purposes*	*Group goals*	*Differences in large and small classes*	*Differences between boys and girls*	*Differences between age levels*
Methods of introducing unit	Lecture Demonstration Verbal explanations	To introduce activity to entire class	To understand game as a whole	Less formal in small classes Easily adaptable to large classes		In junior high school, more time is needed for orientation but in small, short sessions
Methods of improving physical skills	Demonstration Performance: drill, mimetics, criticism Review Assignment Problem-solving	To improve physical skills, physical fitness	To improve skills related to game	Careful organization needed for most effective drilling in large classes (See Chapter 18)	Boys more interested in perfecting skills than girls	Progressive, from known to unknown
Methods of achieving social objectives	Problem-solving Discussion Supplementary team organization Verbal explanation	To promote safety consciousness, teamwork, cooperation, good sportsmanship	To develop team spirit, winning effort	In large classes good student leaders should be developed		In junior high school, teams and captains should be changed frequently
Methods of promoting intellectual learning	Lecture Verbal explanation Evaluation: oral, written Assignments Problem-solving Discussion Review	To teach history, rules, strategy, tactics, etiquette, related facts of sport	To understand rules of game, and offensive and defensive strategy			Intellectual or associated learnings should be stressed with older high school students
Methods of closing unit	Supplementary special events: tournament between squads or classes Evaluation: skills, knowledge	To provide special opportunity for game play for everyone To measure progress of class	To have exciting tournament To measure progress	Use shorter time units in larger classes		

It is particularly helpful to slow learners to have diagrams of football plays or basketball strategy outlined visually in front of them. Also, very large groups can be instructed efficiently and effectively with the use of these aids.

Opportunities to play in various positions should be provided, particularly at the junior high level, when specific sports skills are being developed. This may be done through squad assignments and position changes after short innings or baskets, or after a specified number of downs or goals. For example, in baseball or softball, outfielders and infielders may exchange positions after each inning or after each out is made, if time is limited.

4. *How should opportunities for creative thinking be provided?* The strategy and team play necessary in team sports provide the perfect media for allowing students the freedom to create new plays, new tactics for offensive and defensive positions, and new rules. Teachers should welcome such contributions and foster their application to game situations, rather than coaching every play.

METHODS OF TEACHING INDIVIDUAL AND DUAL SPORTS

A wide variety of activities is included in the area of individual and dual sports.

Their values are numerous in terms of challenges to the individual to develop and improve physical skills, some of which will have later use in leisure-time activities.

Individual and dual sports have long been a part of the American way of life. Recent years have seen the mushrooming of business interests in some of these sports, to match the increase in leisure time being enjoyed by people in every walk of life. Of particular importance to physical educators has been the establishment of the Lifetime Sports Foundation. Through its research and financial resources, programs in five "lifetime" sports (archery, badminton, bowling, golf, and tennis) have been developed for the promotion of instruction in schools and communities. Working through state professional associations and utilizing physical educators, this foundation has sponsored clinics for teachers of these sports all over the country.

Recreational and combative activities, also included in this category, have been finding their place in physical education programs. Often some of these activities are included on an elective basis or as part of the coeducational program. Teaching must be structured on an individual basis in this area to be effective, and class organization is the key to success.

Table 7. Methods of teaching individual and dual sports—archery, badminton, bowling, fencing, golf, recreational sports, tennis, wrestling

	Methods	Purposes	Group goals	Differences in large and small classes	Differences between boys and girls	Differences between age levels
Methods of introducing unit	Lecture Demonstration Verbal explanation Discussion	To provide general understanding of total sport	To learn the game	Less formal in small classes		In junior high school, a brief acquaintance with many sports should be programmed

Table 7. Methods of teaching individual and dual sports—archery, badminton, bowling, fencing, golf, recreational sports, tennis, wrestling—cont'd

	Methods	*Purposes*	*Group goals*	*Differences in large and small classes*	*Differences between boys and girls*	*Differences between age levels*
Methods of improving physical skills	Evaluation Performance: drill, mimetics, criticism Review Assignment Demonstration Problem-solving	To improve physical skills, physical fitness	To acquire skills and fitness necessary to play game for pleasure	Difficult to individualize instruction in large classes Use leaders Formalized instruction in large classes		In junior high school, only basic skills needed to play game should be introduced Advanced skills in high school
Methods of achieving social objectives	Lecture Discussion Verbal explanation Supplementary: team, squad organization Problem-solving	To promote safety consciousness, recreational skills, partnerships, co-operation, good sportsmanship	To learn to play with partner comfortably To learn spotting, safety techniques To do well in competition	Formal methods used in larger classes Easily adapted to small classes	Coeducational experiences may be provided in some of these activities	
Methods of promoting intellectual learning	Lecture Demonstration Verbal explanation Evaluation: oral, written Review Assignment Problem-solving Discussion	To teach history, rules, etiquette, game tactics, scoring, partner play, strategy	To learn strategies, scoring, etiquette, rules governing play for recreational enjoyment			Progressive, from simple to more difficult More extensive coverage in high school
Methods of closing unit	Evaluation: knowledge, skill Supplementary special events: tournament	To provide opportunities for scoring games, participation in games or meets, evaluation of progress	To try skills in game situation To measure self-progress To do well in competition	Tournament play will require longer time in large classes unless playing time is shortened		

Problems unique to the teaching of individual and dual sports

1. *With limited equipment and facilities, how can individual sports be taught to large classes?* Basic instructional techniques can be provided to large groups simultaneously. For example, ninety students in a gymnasium might go through the motions of forehand stroking in tennis. Through mimetics and formalized instruction, a beginning can be made. However, individualized instruction and actual game play would probably be limited to one squad, and squads would need to rotate to the instructor's station, while in other areas squad leaders may organize related activities.

2. *Should boys' and girls' classes be combined for instruction in individual sports?* There is no reason why boys and girls should not learn many of these recreational activities in combined classes. The skills involved in archery, golf, shuffleboard, etc. can be taught and learned in a coeducational setting, so that more efficient use can be made of the physical education staff. Social objectives can also be accomplished in this manner. At the junior high school level, where socializing techniques have not yet become as sophisticated as in high school, learning of skills might be impeded by mixed classes. Therefore, at this age level, coeducational classes might be more successful when recreational playing, rather than the learning of skills, is the purpose.

METHODS OF TEACHING RHYTHMIC ACTIVITIES

Because of the important values accruing to all participants, rhythmic activities should continue to be included throughout the secondary school program. The educational and recreational objectives of physical education find quick fulfillment in a well-conducted program of folk, square, and other dancing activities. The opportunities for creativity and the grace, poise, and balance required in modern dance are particularly appealing to girls. Other rhythmic activities, such as hoop work, rope jumping, and ball handling, are becoming increasingly popular for girls as a result of increased enthusiasm for gymnastics.

The magical force that rhythm provides to teaching makes it especially capable of bringing unity, cooperative effort, and satisfaction to even the largest classes.

Problems unique to the teaching of rhythmic activities

1. *What should be done to improve motivation for folk and square dancing?* Secondary school students often profess a dislike for these activities, but in reality the boys and girls enjoy the opportunity of being together. Making classwork fast-paced and progressively difficult should help to keep their interest level high. The active, sincere participation and effective leadership of the boys' teacher will ensure the cooperation of the boys in the program.

2. *To what extent should perfection in technique be developed in rhythmic activities?* Rhythmic activities should be performed to be appreciated. However, standards of perfection should vary in terms of the purposes of the group. Performance of folk and square dancing requires knowledge of foot patterns so that members of the square, set, or circle can keep pace with the group and not cause confusion. Perfection is not necessarily a goal, unless an exhibition is planned.

Skills involved in ball-bouncing routines and in hoop and rope work necessitate a higher degree of perfection for performance. The interaction of movements requires it. Similarly, the exhibition of creative modern dance routines requires additional practice toward perfection. However, rehearsals can be held during after-school hours if a special program is planned.

The degree of perfection sought compares inversely with the amount of material covered in teaching rhythmic activities. Whenever many folk and square dances

Table 8. Methods of teaching rhythmic activities—folk, square, social dancing, modern dance, rhythmic activities

	Methods	*Purposes*	*Group goals*	*Differences in large and small classes*	*Differences between boys and girls*	*Differences between age levels*
Methods of introducing unit	Demonstration Review	To introduce new movement patterns to be included in unit To review what is known	To understand what new movement will be encompassed in new unit			
Methods of improving physical skills	Demonstration Verbal explanation Performance: drill, mimetics Review Problem-solving Evaluation	To extend physical skills for improved responses To permit experimentation To determine present level of ability	To improve physical abilities for better usage To develop new movement patterns, new responses	In large classes make appropriate use of space, alternate groups	Boys should strive to improve strength and power moves Girls should improve balance, grace, poise	
Methods of achieving social objectives	Supplementary groupings Problem-solving	To promote social cooperation To improve understanding of others	To work together cooperatively	Exchange positions of sub-groupings frequently Rotate groups in sub-groupings, if necessary	Some activities may be coeducational (folk, square, social dancing)	Change positions frequently in junior high school
Methods of promoting intellectual learning	Lecture Discussion Problem-solving	To learn historical, cultural background To provide problems for thoughtful solution To experiment with time, space, force	To study place of types of dance in cultures To develop new dimensions in terms of environment		Boys need to be motivated	In senior high school, new meanings and dimensions can be created in movement
Methods of closing unit	Evaluation Supplementary special events: exhibition	To determine progress of class To present program	To demonstrate dances that have been learned To participate in program			

Fig. 13-5. Rhythmic activity.

are introduced to students, polished execution is apt to be sacrificed. A higher degree of skill and perfection would be achieved by a group that limits itself to a smaller number of routines for the purpose of exhibition.

METHODS OF TEACHING AQUATICS

The new high school complexes under construction today generally include swimming facilities, while older high schools are making use of the new portable swimming pools and air bubbles to provide aquatics in physical education. Teachers of physical education must be prepared to instruct some, if not all, water sports.

The aquatics program has many values. Physical exercise, endurance, and fitness, as well as techniques for personal safety, come immediately to mind. Moreover, the specialized skills necessary for synchronized swimming, lifesaving, and scuba diving are finding increased favor among today's adolescents. Surfing has captivated the interest of swimmers of all ages on both coasts, and the tremendous upsurge of interest in boating and recreational water sports has not only provided impetus to the acquisition of swimming skills but has created a responsibility for schools to educate students in all phases of aquatics.

Problems unique to the teaching of aquatics

1. *With such a widespread differentiation in swimming skill, from rank beginner to lifesaver, how should instructional swimming be taught?* It is true that a wide variation of swimming skill is usually found in a physical education class, and since instruction in swimming skills has been established as the goal, the teacher should divide the group according to ability. The American Red Cross categories of swimmers are helpful for this purpose: beginners, advanced beginners, intermediates, swimmers, and advanced swimmers. Advanced swimmers could sometimes assist the teacher in teaching skill progressions to novices. Because water safety is of utmost importance, the teacher should seek all types of qualified assistance for lifeguarding purposes.

2. *How should excuses from swimming class be handled?* This is one of the most difficult problems in teaching swimming. Colds in both boys and girls during the winter, the menstrual cycle of girls, plus their concern over getting their hair wet, continually interfere with the teaching program, and necessitate special regulations for swimming class. Ideally, the program should be so interesting that the students do not want to miss swimming class. However, there are always some students who are less motivated toward swimming than others. Provision should be made for those excused from swimming activity to make up their class work after school on other days. During class they should assist as lifeguards, trying to learn through observation, and then help with towels and suits in the locker room.

3. *Should activities such as synchronized*

Table 9. Methods of teaching aquatics—swimming, synchronized swimming, recreational swimming (water polo), scuba diving, lifesaving, competitive swimming

	Methods	*Purposes*	*Group goals*	*Differences in large and small classes*	*Differences between boys and girls*	*Differences between age levels*
Methods of introducing unit	Evaluation Lecture Demonstration Verbal explanation Discussion	To divide group into ability groups To instill safety consciousness	To learn safety rules, personal safety skills in water			Some activities too advanced for junior high school leve
Methods of improving physical skills	Demonstration Performance: drill, critical analysis Review Problem-solving Evaluation: diagnostic skill tests	To determine present abilities To improve skills, fitness	To improve fitness, endurance, coordination, safety skills	Individualized instruction essential	Girls more interested in synchronized phases than boys	Watch for fatigue, cold in younger students
Methods of achieving social objectives	Lecture Supplementary: grouping Discussion Verbal explanation Problem-solving	To provide safety procedures To encourage participation, teamwork, cooperation	To create teamwork, group synchronization To acquire recreational skills		Instructional classes are generally not coeducational Lifesaving and other elective courses may be combined	
Methods of promoting intellectual learning	Problem-solving Evaluation Assignments Discussion Demonstration	To create swimming routines To teach lifesaving knowledge, physiological dimensions To broaden interests in swimming	To learn synchronized swimming routine To learn how to care for others in water To learn about scuba diving equipment, methods	Problem-solving harder to use in large classes Assignments useful in large classes	Problems of buoyancy differences in boys and girls	In older groups stress physical laws and physiological principles of swimming
Methods of closing unit	Evaluation Supplementary special events: swimming meet	To measure progress in skills To evaluate progress in skills applied	To measure progress To participate in swimming meet or synchronized swimming program To go scuba diving on a lake			

swimming, scuba diving, and lifesaving be open only to advanced students? The American Red Cross requires students to pass a preliminary test for admission into the standard lifesaving course. However, in the case of synchronized and competitive activities, the school should provide opportunities for interested beginners to learn these special skills. Advanced groups limited to swimmers of greater proficiency should also be established to further develop their talents and interests.

METHODS OF TEACHING GYMNASTICS

Interest in gymnastics has been steadily increasing in this country over the past decade. This has been evidenced by the addition in the curriculum of gymnastics for girls, by the development of gymnastic teams, and by the competitive meets scheduled on local, regional, and nationwide levels.

The teaching of gymnastics is usually structured according to Olympic activity outlines, with tumbling providing the basis for learning more advanced skills and performing with apparatus. The teacher needs to devote a great deal of time to the development of good tumbling skills before introducing the trampoline, rings, parallel bars, and so forth. Particular attention needs to be paid to the establishment of good safety habits. From the outset of the unit, instruction should be offered in proper care and handling of mats, safety checks for equipment, and spotting techniques for partners. Rules for participants must be observed by all students if the unit is to meet with success.

Teachers should not overlook the valuable teaching assistance offered by the emphasis on, and publicity surrounding, the Olympics. Students can gain invaluable knowledge by watching taped versions of Olympics performers. Striving to compete within the limitations imposed by Olympic standards is also an excellent educational device.

Gymnastics, with its variety of activities,

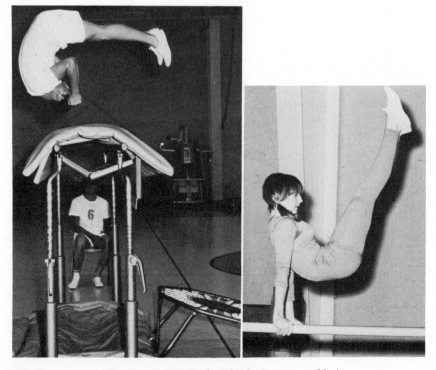

Fig. 13-6. Gymnastics. (Guymon Junior High School, Guymon, Okla.)

Table 10. Methods of teaching gymnastics

	Methods	*Purposes*	*Group goals*	*Differences in large and small classes*	*Differences between boys and girls*	*Differences between age levels*
Methods of introducing unit	Lecture Demonstration (with aids) of individual activities simultaneously or in separate class periods Verbal explanation Discussion	To introduce various events in gymnastics	To learn about activities included in unit		Boys' events: rings, horizontal bar, parallel bar, vaulting, floor exercise, trampoline Girls' events: uneven parallel bars, balance beam, floor exercise, vaulting,	
Methods of improving physical skills	Evaluation: physical skills Performance: drill, criticism Review Assignment Demonstration Problem-solving	To improve physical skills, physical fitness qualities necessary for performance	To acquire skills To improve physical fitness qualities	In large classes, smaller groups should be stationed with leaders at other activities	Girls tend to improve balance, poise, grace Boys need strength	Basic tumbling moves must be learned first
Methods of achieving social objectives	Discussion Demonstration Performance Supplementary (grouping) Problem-solving	To learn safety techniques, spotting for each other To promote individual effort teamwork	To care for safety of each other To do well in competition To cooperate	In large classes student leaders should assist with equipment and class organization		In junior high school, students enjoy working in pairs or small groups
Methods of promoting intellectual learning	Lecture Demonstration Problem-solving Verbal explanation Evaluation: oral, written	To learn about current champions To study principles of movement To motivate individual	To understand how to improve own performances To determine own capacities, try to improve			In senior high school, students should learn about physical laws governing balance, movement
Methods of closing unit	Evaluation: oral, written Supplementary special events: gymnastic meet, program	To measure progress To attempt competition or performance of events	To measure own progress To perform for others			

provides opportunities to improve several important qualities and characteristics. Strength, balance, and control come immediately to mind when tumbling stunts are considered. For girls it is vital to point out the excellence in poise, grace, and beauty of movement that characterizes the balance beam and floor exercise routines. It is these very qualities which have helped to advance the popularity of gymnastics in recent years. The appeal that gymnastics has to the individual who wishes to try to improve himself cannot be underestimated.

Problems unique to the teaching of gymnastics

1. *How can a teacher supervise various gymnastic activities effectively and simultaneously?* A teacher must give careful consideration to planning activities in gymnastics in order to keep safety first and foremost. A single teacher cannot supervise more than one activity at a time. Therefore, older students or students with advanced ability should be utilized whenever possible. If outside assistance is not available, activities should be coordinated in such a way that the instructor is free to supervise that activity which requires his personal attention, and other students should be able to lead running, exercises, or squad games that are less hazardous in nature.

2. *How does a teacher motivate the poorly skilled students in gymnastic activities?* The student who is awkward, overweight, or in some other way unable to feel comfortable in gymnastics needs the special attention of the instructor. The very simplest tumbling skills and locomotor combinations should be acquired first, in order that the student may feel capable and satisfied. Simple floor exercise routines can be developed to enable that student to participate and then to improve.

METHODS OF TEACHING TRACK-AND-FIELD ACTIVITIES

Track and field, with its variety of events, has a widespread appeal to stu-

dents. Each participant will be able to find one or more activities particularly suited to him, either in field events or in running. Track and field is like gymnastics in this respect, as well as in terms of its demands on the individual to try to improve his own performance. In track and field the student is actually competing against himself, to better his own record in minutes or feet or inches. Success is therefore a measure of individual effort and work, and an accomplishment of which to be extremely proud.

The values of track-and-field activities are numerous. Elements of physical fitness are an inherent aspect of track events (speed, endurance, strength, agility), and the benefits to the cardiovascular system are acknowledged by doctors as well as physical educators.

Here again the Olympics have added greatly to the significance of these activities and to our knowledge for improvement of performances. Teachers should take advantage of the information thus gained and should utilize all available data for motivational and educational purposes.

Problems unique to the teaching of track-and-field activities

1. *How does one teacher supervise many activities in one class period?* When track-and-field activities are introduced to a large class, it is sometimes helpful to discuss each activity separately and to allow all the students to become acquainted with the teaching hints required for that particular skill. When all the events to be included in the unit have been covered, the teacher might suggest squad assignments at the various stations for practice, with leaders to assist.

2. *Should all students learn to perform all events in track and field?* At the junior high school level it is generally a good idea to have all the students experience a wide range of events, as in track and field. Selection of specific skills to perfect might wait until the high school years, after determin-

Table 11. Methods of teaching track and field activities

	Methods	*Purposes*	*Group goals*	*Differences in large and small classes*	*Differences between boys and girls*	*Differences between age levels*
Methods of introducing unit	Lecture Demonstrations (with aids) of individual activities simultaneously or at different class periods Verbal explanation Discussion	To introduce many track-and-field activities efficiently	To learn about activities		Girls' events may not include longer distances, hurdles, pole vault	In junior high school, should learn about all the activities included in this area Specialization in higher grades
Methods of improving physical skills	Evaluation: physical skills Performance: drill, mimetics, criticism Review Assignment Demonstration Problem-solving	To improve physical skill, physical fitness qualities	To acquire skills necessary for events To improve physical fitness qualities	In large classes individuals will need outside practice		In junior high school, there should be experimentation of various styles of performance, e.g., styles of roll for high jump
Methods of achieving social objectives	Discussion Supplementary (grouping) Problem-solving	To promote safety consciousness, teamwork, independent effort, group cooperation in competition	To learn safety procedures To do well in competition	In large classes use of group leaders necessary		
Methods of promoting intellectual learning	Lecture Demonstration Verbal explanation Evaluation: oral, written Review Assignment Problem-solving	To promote understanding of successful styles of movement needed for various activities, according to body build To study current record holders	To understand how to improve own performance through knowledge of physical laws, body types, etc.			In high school, students should learn about physical laws and forces behind successful patterns of movement

Continued.

Table 11. Methods of teaching track and field activities—cont'd

	Methods	Purposes	Group goals	Differences in large and small classes	Differences between boys and girls	Differences between age levels
Methods of closing unit	Evaluation: oral or written, of knowledge, skill Supplementary special events: track meet	To measure progress To apply learning to competitive situation	To measure progress To utilize learning in competitive situations			

ing those activities which seem to be best suited to the individual.

3. *How can scores be recorded most effectively in large classes?* It is impossible for a single teacher to keep an accurate record of each individual in a large class. Therefore, squad leaders might be made responsible for recording performances, or individuals themselves might keep track of their own scores on individual record cards.

METHODS OF TEACHING WINTER ACTIVITIES

Winter activities can be classified as team sports (ice hockey), recreational sports (sledding and skiing), and even rhythmical activities (figure skating). However, the elements of ice and snow add to the teaching situation rather unique problems that need consideration.

A basic groundwork of information, preliminary exercises, and land drills should be offered in preseason classes, in order that no time will be lost once appropriate ice-and-snow conditions exist. For example, in figure skating, mimetic practice of the difficult school figures, including correct shoulder and hip rotation, helps to clarify mental images of skills prior to execution on the ice. In skiing, practice of weight-shifting and edging is helpful. Safety information and tips on the care of equipment can be discussed in class lec-

tures, and team strategies for ice hockey can be developed, with forwards and defensemen.

As soon as appropriate conditions exist, students should be allowed opportunities to try their skills on the slopes or the ice. Instruction will need to be individualized as much as possible by grouping students according to abilities and interests. These activities may easily be conducted on a coeducational basis, with the exception of ice hockey.

Problems unique to the teaching of winter activities

How can equipment be provided for students? The nature of winter activities requires special equipment (skis and skates) that precisely fits each individual student. Just as each student should provide his own sneakers for the gymnasium, so it seems logical to assume that students should try to obtain their own skates and ski boots, if possible. This is necessary both for safety reasons and for improved learning conditions. It is very difficult to try to learn to skate on skates that are too large or too small, or on skis that cannot be properly adjusted to the boots. With the added danger of slipping and falling in these activities, a properly fitted ski boot or skate is essential. Because this equipment is expensive and requires special waxing and sharpening, winter activities are gener-

Table 12. Methods of teaching winter activities—ice hockey, skiing, skating

	Methods	*Purposes*	*Group goals*	*Differences in large and small classes*	*Differences between boys and girls*	*Differences between age levels*
Methods of introducing unit	Lecture Discussion Demonstration Verbal explanation	To teach about care of equipment To determine goals for unit and each individual	To understand purpose of unit To select areas of interest			
Methods of improving physical skills	Verbal explanation Performance: mimetics, drill, criticism Evaluation: skill test Review Problem-solving	To teach basic skills involved in activities To improve performance	To improve abilities To enjoy recreational aspect of activities	Individualized instruction, if at all possible	Boys generally engage in ice hockey Girls enjoy rhythm, balance, grace, control of figure skating	
Methods of achieving social objectives	Supplementary (grouping) Discussion	To promote group enthusiasm To teach safety skills, consideration for others	To get along with each other To learn how to watch out for others and care for them		Skiing and figure-skating classes should be coeducational	
Methods of promoting intellectual learning	Lecture Discussion Assignment Problem-solving	To teach about historical aspects, rules, growth, and development of sports	To learn rules of hockey To understand competitive regulations governing skiing and skating			
Methods of closing unit	Evaluation: skill tests Supplementary: program, competition	To provide opportunity to perform To evaluate progress	To perform in program or competition To evaluate self-progress			Competition scaled by age-level groupings

ally optional parts of programs of physical education, to be enjoyed by those able to provide items essential for instruction.

METHODS OF TEACHING GAMES OF LOW ORGANIZATION

In most circumstances, games of low organization are part of the elementary physical education program. However, there are certain occasions when they serve a distinct purpose within the secondary program.

It should be noted here that games of low organization involve any number of players in large-muscle activities. Rules and explanations are minimal, while activity level is optimal for all participants. Therefore, these activities are useful when the teacher desires a large segment of the class to enjoy activity while one squad is elsewhere receiving special instruction. Dodge-ball games, tag games, keep away, and mass soccer are types of activities requiring basic skills. Teams can be quickly devised to suit the needs of the situation, and activity can be started immediately. Fun and satisfaction are derived, and occasionally these, too, should be considered as

Fig. 13-7. Swedish ball routine involving bouncing, throwing, and catching, with free movement of body. (Colorado Springs Public Schools, Colorado Springs, Colo.)

important outcomes of the physical education program.

Problems unique to the teaching of games of low organization

How often should these be included in the program? In the junior high school, games of low organization can be utilized frequently, for this age level still enjoys the freedom allowed in these activities. Older students in secondary school will lose interest more rapidly because of the lack of real challenge and necessity for intellectual response. Occasional inclusion in the program will be successful, however.

DEFINITION OF TERMS

Lecture. The lecture may be used frequently in physical education to present such topics as current events, history and development of a sport, rules, and etiquette. A lecture should be addressed to a group in such a way that all can hear and see the speaker. Preferably, it should be brief and to the point if the lecture is to be followed by active participation, because students are generally anxious to "get on with the game." However, a lecture in which a quantity of information is presented to a large class in an auditorium or a classroom setting becomes an advantageous and efficient use of time.

Demonstration. It is reasonable to expect a physical educator to demonstrate effectively most of the skills being taught. This does not imply expertness in every sport but a basic, sound background in fundamental skills. In addition to the teacher's

Table 13. Methods of teaching games of low organization

	Methods	Purposes	Group goals	Differences in large and small classes	Differences between boys and girls	Differences between age levels
Methods of introducing unit	These are supplementary activities (instruction would not be in units)					
Methods of improving skills	(Skills would already have been acquired) Performance	To provide practice for large numbers simultaneously	To play games	More adaptable in large classes		
Methods of achieving social objectives	Supplementary (grouping)	To play together cooperatively for activity	To play for fun together	More adaptable for large classes		Highly popular in junior high school
Methods of promoting intellectual learning						Not challenging enough for senior high school
Methods of closing unit	(None)					

demonstration, there are many excellent audiovisual instruments that are available and that enable the student to see a skill performed clearly and accurately. A well-illustrated high school physical education textbook can also be useful. When a skill is demonstrated before the class, certain important factors should be kept in mind:

1. The demonstration should be well planned so that all important points are firmly fixed in the teacher's mind.

2. The demonstration should be organized so that all students are able to see and hear well, and if student assistants are used, they should know the purposes and procedures necessary to show effectively the particular skill under study.

3. All necessary equipment and materials should be on hand so that no time is wasted once the demonstration is begun, and so that the time is used most effectively.

4. Helpful pointers for proper performance of the skill should be given. The skill should be analyzed according to its basic parts and then shown in its entirety. In teaching a new skill, emphasis should be on the right way to do it—not the wrong way.

A demonstration lesson may be in the form of an actual performance by a group, or a filmed or taped presentation of the subject may be given. The factors defined above are applicable to this situation as well as to a demonstration by a single individual.

Verbal explanation. In physical education verbal explanations are used extensively for introduction and analysis of skills. Whereas a lecture provides a formal, lengthy presentation of material, verbal explanations are generally brief, concise descriptions. Frequently this method is combined with a demonstration of a particular skill, prior to practice by the class, or it may be used in connection with rule discussions or settling squad disputes. By taking advantage of teachable moments for brief explanations about proper group cooperation and consideration, a teacher may

promote genuine learning in social development.

The importance of the carefully chosen "word cues" in teaching should be stressed here. The creation of a correct mental image prior to physical execution of a movement sets the stage for the successful performance of the task. Telling students to use fingertips on a volleyball may produce the desired results, but describing the ball as a "hot potato to be tapped away quickly" should be more effective.

Discussion. In leading a discussion, the teacher will find that it is important to keep in mind the exact points to be stressed. Questions should be prepared in advance in order to guide the direction to be taken. All students should feel that their contributions are welcome, and the teacher should try to draw out opinions from students who may otherwise remain silent. Timing is another important consideration, for a discussion that drags on too long may lose its impact.

Discussions are often more effective than verbal explanations. By using thought-provoking questions and good discussion techniques, the physical education teacher can help the entire class to arrive at a greater understanding of learning experiences, such as team play and tactics, or to improve its attitudes toward health, safety, or exercising. However, worthwhile discussion demands time, whereas verbal explanation may be quite brief. The values derived for the students should be the determining factor if a choice must be made between these two valuable methods.

Performance. Performance is the backbone of physical education, because students learn by doing. Therefore, opportunities must be provided for students to participate to the fullest possible extent in the activities included in the program. Frequently, the *mimetic technique* is used when new skills are introduced prior to actual performance. This technique provides an opportunity to "get the feel" of a movement through imitation in a simulated experience. For example, the hockey dribble may be acted out with or without hockey sticks at the beginning of the unit. Clever word pictures and rhythmic patterns assist students in kinesthetically feeling the desirable action. Mimetic drills may also be used as warm-up exercises at the beginning of a class period.

The use of *drills* is another valuable method of providing opportunities for performance of skills in physical education. Mastery of skills through practice and automatization is essential to satisfaction in game play, and the proper conduct of drills provides an efficient and effective teaching method.

Drills in physical education can be as dull as memorizing a multiplication table, or they can be nearly as much fun as the game from which they are derived. For real learning to take place they should be as interesting as possible, and this of course requires planning on the part of the teacher. The following principles are important when planning drill formations:

1. Drills should be an outgrowth of the game situation. This gives meaning to the drill. The students are not asked merely to kick a ball, for example, but are instructed to kick the soccer ball through the goal posts for a score.

2. Drills should allow maximum participation for all class members. A student has a turn to practice more frequently if the class is divided into many units of a small number of students. For a teacher to make as many practice units as possible, all available equipment must be put to use. These two factors (the size of the class and the available equipment) must be considered when planning drills.

3. Drills should be interesting and fun. Adding the competitive element to a drill formation or scoring points for adapted techniques makes the drill much more fun while the student is trying to learn a skill.

4. Drills should allow for both individual instruction and total supervision. In setting up drill formations the teacher must remember his or her responsibility for the entire group and must therefore be able to supervise all working areas. At the same time, individual instruction should be given to students needing special help. Thus, in both instances proximity to the groups is essential.

5. Drills should be varied frequently to prevent boredom or loss of interest. Changing drill formations—for example, from the shuttle type to the circle—can be stimulating, which is necessary, particularly with junior high school students. However, every change must be planned so that time is not wasted unnecessarily in going from one lineup to another. For example, if groups are in four equal lines, it would be very difficult to set up three circles, and wasteful to follow this change by going back to four units again. Groups should remain fairly constant, and formations should change smoothly from one to another.

6. Drills should not take the whole class period. Classes will lose interest in the perfection of skills if no opportunity to test them in the appropriate game situation is allowed.

7. Drills should progress from the simple to the more difficult. Drills should start with simple formations—either review old skills or practice new ones in simple form. When formations and patterns are changed, the skills should be made increasingly difficult or combined with other skills to maintain interest and utmost effort in participation.

The necessity of drills in teaching physical education is great, but for them to be most effectively used, they must be carefully and thoughtfully planned with all these factors in mind. Some teachers find it more satisfactory to teach one skill at a time, but others—feeling that good student leaders can direct skill practices—set up groups in order to provide for drilling on different skills at the same time. Under the direction of leaders, groups can rotate to different skill stations until all students have had practice within each assigned area. Such a procedure would depend, of course, upon the equipment and practice areas available, as well as upon effective leadership, but it would promote leadership and develop group responsibility and cooperation. This same division of groups may even be used on an elective basis, with students selecting the drill they need to practice most, and then rotating.

Constructive analysis. Constructive criticism of performance is another essential method of teaching for improvement of skills. Positive suggestions to students of ways in which they might change their batting stance or follow-through, to name two examples, have been found to be more helpful than negative statements of "No, not that way!" Personal, individual attention indicates the sincere interest of the teacher toward the student and helps to motivate him to improve his performances.

Evaluation. Evaluation becomes a method of teaching when it benefits the students by giving them an opportunity to measure their own progress and learning during a unit. Student evaluations may be accomplished through oral questioning, written tests, or physical skills and fitness testing. When tests are administered at the beginning and at the end of a unit, students are motivated to work harder for improvement. Students want to know the bases upon which they are judged; through testing they know what is expected of them and can rate themselves in comparison to their own previous scores. Testing and other methods of evaluation are discussed further in a separate chapter, but their usefulness as a method of teaching requires mention here. In connection with oral questioning as a method by which students profit from the class session, the following techniques for effective questioning should be understood.

1. Questions should be clearly stated so that they may be easily understood.

2. Questions should challenge the thinking of the students and require well-thought-out answers, not a mere "yes" or "no."

3. Questions should provoke contributory answers, not foolish responses.

4. Credit for a partially correct answer should be given. Sarcasm or ridicule should never be a teacher's tool for responding to improper answers.

5. Questions and answers should not be repeated by the teacher. The teacher should expect full attention from the group, so that such repetition is unnecessary. The teacher may, however, ask for a restatement of an answer by another member of the class to ensure complete understanding.

6. Questions should be directed to the class as a whole before an individual is called upon, in order to keep the attention of the entire class.

If these general suggestions are followed, a question period can be made a very worthwhile learning experience for all members of the class, even though they may not all have an opportunity to answer or contribute.

Assignments. Assignments, or homework, belong in a physical education program, and much learning can be accomplished if they are effective. For example, students who are weak in performance of some of their physical skills should be encouraged to devote additional time to improve and develop their abilities. This is especially true where daily physical education classes are not scheduled. The spending of valuable time in explaining rules and giving other information can be avoided if assignments using supplementary rule sheets or rule books are made. Some teachers may want to require notebooks on sports, sports personalities, or other outside reading, either as makeup work or as enrichment opportunity for students temporarily unable to participate, or for athletically gifted students. Students need to be aware of the wealth of material available today about all of their sporting interests, and they should share it with their classmates if time and opportunities permit.

Problem-solving. The problem-solving approach to teaching has received great impetus recently from the current emphasis placed on encouraging independent and creative thinking. In all educational pursuits the development of the initiative of the individual is sought, with environmental freedoms and experimental opportunities being forcefully provided.

Physical educators are recognizing that students at the high school level can gain new insights into skill analysis, game situations, and especially movement experiences through this teaching method. It is felt that whenever freedom in movement permits personal recognition of a better way to perform a physical skill, such as throwing a ball for distance, after trials of many different ways, such a conclusion or result remains longer with the student. The permanent change in behavior is real learning because it is self-directed. The teacher's role in this method of teaching is one of setting up the situation and allowing freedom of experimentation. Students are led to experiment on their own and to think for themselves in answering a given problem. The problem may involve a physical skill, such as throwing a ball, or a game strategy, such as team plays for forwards shooting baskets or soccer goals, or it may involve the definition of movement in time and space as part of a creative experience in dance or movement education. The key to success with this method lies in the individual student's ability to feel free to experiment and to experience, and it is the teacher who provides this freedom.

Supplementary learning experiences. Other situations that cannot be classified as methods of teaching provide learning opportunities and expose students to learning experiences. One major source for students is their *observation* of the class, their friends, and of the results of events occurring in the classroom. It has long been recognized that little children learn more from each other, in swimming, for example, than from what they are told. In the same way, older students can learn by observing class details. A teacher can promote specific observations through directions to individuals. For example, in a basketball unit, where so often only a few players may actually participate in the game situation at one time, the remaining students may be instructed to analyze the players on the floor, or just one player, perhaps, in terms of floor mistakes, movement under the basket, ball-handling ability, or guarding techniques. A teacher promotes learning by following the class observations with discussions with the class as a whole.

Another supplementary learning experience stems from *team organization.* Opportunities for leadership and fellowship—for cooperating and working with others for the greater good—are the direct results of the squad or team setup used in physical education classes. By working with students and by managing teams, a teacher can improve social attitudes and promote attainment of social objectives. Differences in backgrounds, as well as cultural and racial distinctions, can be erased on the playing field or in the gymnasium, providing that the teacher works constructively toward this goal. *Special events* also provide supplementary learning. At the close of a teaching unit, competitive tournaments, visitation of demonstrations, and special presentations or programs by selected individuals permit additional learning. Often it is the inclusion of these special events which makes physical education one of the outstanding features of a high school program. Students remember the tournament, the speaker, or the modern dance program, for example, that made the physical education class outstanding.

POINTS TO REMEMBER

1. Methods used in teaching physical education should relate specifically to the established goals.
2. Many different methods may be utilized in teaching classwork. Most of them may be combined or interchanged to provide variety in class structure, although some of them may be used only for accomplishment of specific objectives.
3. Certain principles underlie the choosing of methods in preparation for teaching a class,

and these must be kept in mind for the development of an effective teaching situation.

4. The daily class in physical education is the most important factor in teaching and therefore must be carefully planned and thought out in advance. Students may participate in planning this phase, as well as all phases of the program, if departmental organization permits.

5. The selection of methods depends on age level and developmental level of the class, as well as facilities and space, size, and time factors.

PROBLEMS TO THINK THROUGH

1. A new teacher of physical education, just added to the department, finds the year's program already formulated. In what ways can he or she (a) allow pupils to help in the planning within that program, and (b) convince the department that cooperative pupil-teacher planning can be utilized in an overall schedule?

2. This same new teacher finds that, while the physical fitness and physical skills objectives are being adequately met, the other goals—knowledge, appreciation, and social development—are not being stressed by other members of the staff. In what way can he or she work for the attainment of these goals?

3. In what way can leaders be most effectively used in the instructional phase of the program?

4. How much use should be made of assignments, or "homework"?

5. How can a teacher emphasize the importance of students' evaluation of their own classwork?

6. Which goals of physical education have counterparts in the everyday living experiences of students, and how can a teacher ensure transfer of learning for them?

7. What place does motivation have in daily classwork, and how does a teacher promote it?

CASE STUDY FOR ANALYSIS

The newly appointed and only teacher in the girls' (or boys') high school department is responsible for teaching physical education classes three times a week to class groups ranging from twenty-four to forty-eight students. The administration has given the teacher a free hand to organize the curriculum, and no particular philosophy of education is expected to be followed.

Prior to his first class session this new teacher learns that previous course construction was entirely teacher controlled. What introduction to class work should be given to the classes, and how would the classes be conducted for the first teaching unit? For later units? With what purposes in mind?

EXERCISES FOR REVIEW

1. Formulate three drills to be used in teaching beginning soccer that would be progressive and require little change-over time.

2. Devise a set of leading questions to be used in starting a group discussion on teamwork in basketball.

3. Outline the format of a softball (baseball) notebook to be assigned to tenth-grade students.

4. Write out an explanation of the foul-shooting technique.

5. Describe three mimetic warm-up exercises and appropriate commands related to tennis strokes.

6. Observe the teaching of a class and evaluate the methods used.

7. When ten or twelve students are playing a game of full-court basketball, in what way can the remaining students in the class be effectively and purposefully occupied?

8. Plan a series of review questions to be answered orally by a class studying volleyball.

SELECTED READINGS

Bookwalter, Karl W.: Physical education in the secondary schools, Washington, D. C., 1963-1964, Center for Applied Research in Education.

Bucher, Charles A.: Foundations of physical education, ed. 5, St. Louis, 1968, The C. V. Mosby Co.

Bucher, Charles A.: Physical education for life, St. Louis, 1969, Webster Division, McGraw-Hill Book Co.

Cowell, Charles C., and France, Wellman L.: Philosophy and principles of physical education, Englewood Cliffs, N. J., 1963, Prentice-Hall, Inc.

Daughtrey, Greyson: Methods in physical education and health for secondary schools, Philadelphia, 1967, W. B. Saunders Co.

Kozman, Hilda C., Cassidy, Rosalind, and Jackson, Chester O.: Methods in physical education, ed. 4, Dubuque, Iowa, 1968, Wm. C. Brown Co.

Miller, Arthur G., and Massey, M. Dorothy: A dynamic concept of physical education for secondary schools, Englewood Cliffs, N. J., 1963, Prentice-Hall, Inc.

Shepard, Natalie Marie: Foundations and principles of physical education, New York, 1960, The Ronald Press Co.

BOOKLETS, PAMPHLETS, AND ARTICLES

Baley, James A.: Teaching the spike in volleyball, Journal of Health, Physical Education, and Recreation **35**:57, Nov.–Dec., 1964.

Beggs, David W., and Buffie, Edward G.: Invention, innovation and Physical Education, Journal of Health, Physical Education, and Recreation **35**:19, Oct., 1964.

Cutler, Ralph: Dance for high school boys and girls, Journal of Health, Physical Education, and Recreation **35**:36, April, 1964.

Edwards, Marigold: Why should I strive? and Neal, Patsy: What more could one ask? Competition, Journal of Health, Physical Education, and Recreation **37**:28, Jan., 1966.

Gambelli, Frank E.: Circuit training in the junior high school, Journal of Health, Physical Education, and Recreation **38**:93, March, 1967.

Geisler, Fred W.: Volleyball, Journal of Health, Physical Education, and Recreation **37**:48, Jan., 1966.

Hertzke, George E.: A team-teaching approach to physical education, The Athletic Journal **47**:76, March, 1967.

Keiser, Helen A.: Volleyball circuit training, The Physical Educator **24**:69, May, 1967.

Lemen, Mildred: Implications of the problem-solving method for physical educators, Journal of Health, Physical Education, and Recreation **37**:28, March, 1966.

Rasch, Philip J., and Kroll, Walter: Safe wrestling, Journal of Health, Physical Education, and Recreation **36**:32, March, 1965.

Santoro, Joel T.: Advantages of team teaching for physical education, The Physical Educator **24**:73, May, 1967.

Vogelsinger, Hubert: Soccer, Journal of Health, Physical Education, and Recreation **37**:31, Jan., 1966.

Whitehead, Robert J.: Boys, basketball, and books, Journal of Health, Physical Education, and Recreation **35**:26, Nov.–Dec., 1964.

Wickstrom, R. L.: In defense of drills, The Physical Educator **24**:38, March, 1967.

Methods and materials for teaching the atypical student

A beginning physical educator soon discovers that the students in a single physical education class cannot accurately be said to form a homogeneous group. While all the boys or all the girls in a single physical education class may be in the same secondary school grade, and while all of them may fall within a certain narrow age range, they will not possess the same physical and mental abilities. Not all of them will have developed to the same levels of emotional and social maturity. A large majority of these students will fall into the classification "average," or "normal," for their age and grade. Other students will deviate considerably from their peers on a physical, mental, emotional, or social measure, or on a combination of these measures. This latter group may be said to be atypical.

The atypical student in physical education presents a challenge to the teacher, for he may fall into any of several different categories. The culturally disadvantaged child is atypical, as are the physically gifted student, the creative student, and the awkward student with low motor ability. Atypical groupings also include emotionally disturbed students and mentally retarded students, as well as physically handicapped students. Each of these groups needs a strong and well-planned physical education experience. In schools where facilities and teaching personnel are available, adapted programs are developed especially to meet the needs of the atypical student. More often, the atypical student is thrust into a regularly scheduled physical education class. The physical educator must then be prepared to make both program and instructional adaptations to meet his special physical education needs.

It is a rare secondary school that does not have at least a few atypical students on its class rolls. It is a definite possibility that someday each physical educator may have to teach at least some students who fall outside the norm. Each physical educator should know how to best provide for the atypical student.

THE CULTURALLY DISADVANTAGED STUDENT

Culturally disadvantaged students have always made up a segment of the school population, but it is only recently that they have become a real concern to various communities and to the school serving these communities. It is a common error for the public to associate only the black child

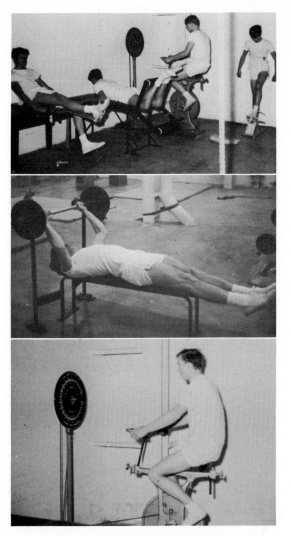

Fig. 14-1. Program for atypical students. (Oconomowoc Senior High School, Oconomowoc, Wis.)

with cultural deprivation. Professional educators, especially, must realize that cultural deprivation crosses all color lines and ignores none of them.

The culture of poverty is especially apparent in the large urban centers. In 1960 one in three city children was classified as culturally disadvantaged in estimates made by the Ford Foundation. At the present time an estimated 50% of the children living in cities are culturally disadvantaged. Many of the inhabitants of Appalachia, suburban communities, and isolated small towns and rural villages all across the United States are culturally disadvantaged.

Characteristics of the culturally disadvantaged student

The culturally disadvantaged student feels isolated from the mainstream of life. His home and neighborhood environment is a negative influence that destroys his confidence, robs him of a chance for success, and defeats any aspirations he may have. The goals of middle-class culture, as represented by the school, seem to be unreachable goals to someone who lives in the culture of poverty.

A culturally disadvantaged student may not achieve success in school because the cultural standards of the school and the home environment are usually inconsistent. Even schools in ghetto areas are staffed by teachers who represent the middle-class segment of society.

In a classroom situation the culturally disadvantaged student is unable to compete successfully scholastically, emotionally, or socially. Because reading and conversation have not been encouraged at home, he is severely restricted in his ability to communicate. He finds it extremely difficult to use logic or form concepts, or think in abstract terms. The culturally disadvantaged student is, for these reasons, often behind his proper grade level in achievement. He frequently attains low scores on intelligence and standardized tests because these tests are not designed to measure him accurately. As the culturally disadvantaged student continues to meet failure, he loses any motivation he may have had to achieve, and his levels of ambition and aspiration continue to decline.

Continual failure in the classroom negatively affects the school behavior of the culturally disadvantaged student. His short attention span, emotional instability, excitability, and restlessness often contribute to disruptive behavior patterns.

Educational needs of the culturally disadvantaged student

Many culturally disadvantaged students come from itinerant families. The children of migratory workers, in particular, will attend several different schools throughout the course of a single school year. Other culturally disadvantaged families are mobile because they constantly search for higher-paying jobs or better living conditions. This mobility further increases the educational deprivation of the culturally disadvantaged student.

Educational curricula for the culturally disadvantaged cannot be conventional middle-class curriculums with conventional middle-class objectives and goals. The teacher cannot employ traditional middle-class methodology and impose middle-class standards of discipline. The traditional and conventional approaches to education do not help the culturally disadvantaged student to rise out of his poverty; they only succeed in driving him deeper into his narrow existence.

Many authorities have criticized the unrealistic educational atmosphere to which the culturally disadvantaged student is systematically exposed. On the elementary school level, especially, it is pointed out, reading books and textbooks illustrate and espouse a way of life that is totally alien to the culturally disadvantaged. It is further noted that if the student does indeed continue his education in a secondary school, the curriculum choices offered are really only weak attempts to resolve long-standing educational inequities. On the secondary school level the culturally disadvantaged student is sometimes arbitrarily channeled into a terminal vocational program, without regard to his hidden potential for seeking a higher education and a professional career.

Educators are constantly seeking to adjust curricula or to introduce innovative curricula that will better serve the culturally disadvantaged. As yet, definitive answers as to how a curriculum can realistically meet the needs of culturally disadvantaged students have not been found. However, educators have been able to identify three broad curriculum designs in secondary education for the disadvantaged. These three educational patterns may be termed remedial education, curriculum adjustment, and methodological modification. These patterns are not mutually exclusive.

Remedial education is a genuine need of the disadvantaged, but an entire secondary school curriculum cannot be based on such a program. However, many communities are engaged in out-of-school remedial education through such programs as Project Head Start, Project Mid-Start, and Upward Bound.

Curriculum adjustment involves a slowing down of the educational pace. Curriculum content is identical for all segments of the school population, but classes made up of disadvantaged students spend proportionately greater amounts of time in each subject area. A regularly paced class will cover a unit of work in mathematics, for example, in many fewer class periods than will a slower-paced class of disadvantaged students. In these latter classes, discipline is very rigid—a concession to the teacher but not necessarily the most conducive atmosphere for the students. This slower method of teaching makes a questionable contribution to the disadvantaged student. It does not guarantee that educational or vocational needs are being met. However, it does allow the student to move into regularly paced classes when his ability permits, and to move more slowly in those courses where he needs to increase his confidence and knowledge.

Methodological modifications are nothing more than the extreme adaptation of existing standard courses, or are specially designed standard courses. This educational technique is sometimes known as "tracking." When this method of educating disadvantaged students is adopted, the curriculum is made up almost entirely of vocationally oriented subject matter designed to prepare the student for the job market. Very few courses with a purely academic orientation are included in the programs, which effectively closes the door on higher education. For example, courses in mathematics will be geared toward learning to

Table 14. Nonwhite public school population in 48 major cities, 1965-1966 school year*

City	Non-white K-12 population as percentage of total K-12 population	Percentage of total Negro elementary students in schools 90% to 100% Negro	Percentage of total Negro elementary students in majority Negro schools	Percentage of total white elementary students in schools 90% to 100% white
New York	28.4	20.7	55.5	56.8
Chicago	*52.0*	*89.2*	*96.9*	*88.8*
Los Angeles	21.0[1]	39.5[3]	87.5[3]	94.7[3]
Philadelphia	*55.1*	*72.0*	*90.2*	*57.7*
Detroit	*55.5*	*72.3*	*91.5*	*65.0*
Baltimore	*61.0*	*84.2*	*92.3*	*67.0*
Houston	34.0	93.0	97.6	97.3
Cleveland	*49.0*	*82.3[4]*	*94.6[4]*	*80.2[4]*
Washington	*88.0*	*90.4*	*99.3*	*34.3*
St. Louis	*60.0*	*90.9*	*93.7*	*66.0*
Milwaukee	21.2	72.4	86.8	86.3
San Francisco	43.0	21.1	72.3	65.1
Boston	26.0	35.4	79.5	76.5
Dallas	24.0[2]	82.6	90.3	90.1
New Orleans	*63.0*	*95.9*	*96.7*	*83.8*
Pittsburgh, Pa.	36.7	49.5	82.8	62.3
San Antonio	13.0	65.9	77.2	89.4
San Diego	13.0	13.9	73.3	88.7
Seattle	15.2	9.9[5]	60.4[5]	89.8[5]
Buffalo	32.1	77.0	88.7	81.1
Cincinnati	*40.0*	*49.4*	*88.0*	*63.3*
Memphis	*52.0*	*95.1*	*98.8*	*93.6*
Denver	13.0	29.4	75.2	95.5
Atlanta	*52.0*	*97.4*	*98.8*	*95.4*
Minneapolis	6.0	..	39.2	84.9
Indianapolis	32.1	70.5	84.2	80.7
Kansas City, Mo.	*40.9[1]*	*69.1*	*85.5*	*65.2*
Columbus, Ohio	26.0	34.3	80.8	77.0
Phoenix	12.0	NA	NA	NA
Newark	*53.8*	*51.3*	*90.3*	*37.1*
Louisville	*41.9*	*69.5*	*84.5*	*61.3*
Portland, Ore.	8.6	46.5	59.2	92.0
Oakland	*50.6*	*48.7*	*83.2*	*50.2*
Fort Worth	22.0	NA	NA	NA
Long Beach	*76.6[1]*	*NA*	*NA*	*NA*
Birmingham	*57.7*	*NA*	*NA*	*NA*
Oklahoma City	16.8	90.5	96.8	96.1
Rochester, N. Y.	20.1	43.6	74.6	65.5
Toledo	25.9[1]	NA	NA	NA
St. Paul	6.0	34.4[3]	64.2[3]	93.9[3]
Norfolk	36.0	NA	NA	NA
Omaha[1]	17.8	47.7	81.1	89.0
Miami	*45.7*	*91.4*	*94.4*	*95.3*
Akron	25.0	40.9[3]	68.1[3]	26.6[3]
Jersey City	39.6	NA	NA	NA
Dayton	36.0	NA	NA	NA
Tulsa	15.2	90.7	98.7	98.9
Wichita	14.3	63.5	89.1	94.8

* From Alsop, J., Schwartz, R., Pettigrew, T., and Smith, M.: Ghetto schools—problems and panaceas, The New Republic, 1967.

This table requires two comments. In the first place, the given percentages of nonwhite school populations do not include Puerto Ricans. Thus they grossly understate the true dimensions of the ghetto school problem in several major cities. *Per contra*, they do include children of Asian origin. Hence they overstate the problem in one or two cities, such as San Francisco and Los Angeles, which have large populations of Chinese- and Japanese-Americans. Second, the figures themselves are almost certainly on the low side. In Washington, for instance, the Negro percentage of the school population is given as 88. Last year, however, the true percentage was 90.3, close to 93% in the primary and elementary schools and 85.6% in the high schools.

[1] City and school district are not coterminus. [2] Does not include kindergarten. [3] 1963–1964 data.
[4] 1962–1963 data. [5] 1964–1965 data.

make change, while courses in English will concentrate on writing a business letter or going to an interview. In the former there will be no attempt to teach the concepts of secondary school mathematics, such as algebra and geometry, and in the latter there will be no attempt to teach literature or theme writing. In some secondary schools, placement of a student in a program of this sort is undertaken in spite of the student's personal aspirations or untapped academic ability that might be revealed through exposure to a more academic curriculum.

These three systems seem to have more disadvantages than advantages, but they will be continued to be used until better methods are found to reach the needs of these youth in secondary schools. Culturally disadvantaged students do need vocational training, but they also need to be free to select courses that meet their individual needs and interests. The culturally disadvantaged student will not succeed educationally if all his courses are dictated, or if he is confined by a tracking system or is otherwise educationally isolated. The secondary schools must be as dedicated to educating culturally disadvantaged students as they are to educating the more advantaged segments of the school population.

The physical educator and the culturally disadvantaged student

In the physical education classroom the culturally disadvantaged student can be given an opportunity to meet success. Physical activity has a strong appeal for these youngsters, whether they are students in a school in their neighborhood or community or part of the student body in a school in an advantaged area.

The physical educator is the most important single factor in a secondary school physical education program for the disadvantaged. The physical educator must have a sincere interest in these students and must be willing to assume the responsibility for physically educating them. He should have an adequate background and

special training in general education and physical education courses concerned with teaching the disadvantaged. These courses will help him come to a fuller understanding of the culturally disadvantaged student and the educational problems this student faces. The physical educator must have the ability to develop rapport with culturally disadvantaged students so that he can better respect, understand, and help these students. The physical educator must be able to provide an enriched program that will help to motivate the culturally disadvantaged student to make the best use of his physical, intellectual, and creative abilities.

The physical education program and the culturally disadvantaged student

The school physical education program frequently is the only supervised physical activity program for the culturally disadvantaged student. These students usually do not have a neighborhood recreational facility available, and must conduct their sports and games on unsupervised streets or in dangerously littered lots. The school physical education experience must be designed to afford this student the physical education and recreational activities that are denied him elsewhere.

1. *The physical education program must be carefully tailored to meet the needs and interests of the students.* Culturally disadvantaged students enjoy vigorous activity as well as creative and self-testing activities. There must be a wide choice of activities offered so that these students can select not only those experiences they find pleasurable but also those in which they can find success. As fundamental challenges are met successfully, new challenges must be presented in a logical progression.

2. *The physical education program must be designed to increase the physical fitness and motor skill abilities of the students.* The program should include activities that will help the students to increase their physical fitness levels. Lack of structured programs outside the school denies culturally disadvantaged students the opportu-

nity to participate in a regular program of physical activity, which often prevents them from maintaining even minimal fitness levels. Motor skill abilities are also often minimal simply because some students may never have had the benefit of a good physical education program in school.

3. *There must be provision for suitable competition.* Culturally disadvantaged students need and enjoy competition. Competitive sports and games must be a part of the class program, but time must also be allotted for the individual to compete with himself in order to raise a physical fitness test score or to improve in a skill performance. Intramural programs are an invaluable extension of the class program, and the culturally disadvantaged student should be encouraged to participate. Likewise, culturally disadvantaged students should be encouraged to seek membership on interscholastic teams.

4. *The program must provide for carry-over interests.* The culturally disadvantaged need to develop a background in the lifetime sports. Swimming, dancing, and tennis, as well as other recreational activities such as bowling, should be included among the lifetime sport activities offered.

5. *Equipment must be carefully purchased to suit the program.* There should be records, a phonograph, and a variety of rhythm instruments. Culturally disadvantaged students enjoy rhythmical activities and find that they are successful in such areas as dance, gymnastics, and tumbling, where they can demonstrate their creativity and express their individuality. Many warm-up activities, as well as many games, can be done to a musical accompaniment.

6. *The program must allow for each student to be treated as an individual.* Culturally disadvantaged students are especially conscious of their individuality, and the program should allow ample opportunity for self-expression and creativity. Teacher recognition and praise for the most minor accomplishment is of utmost importance to the continued success of these students.

7. *The program should help to instill good health habits and attitudes.* Where possible, showers should be available to the students. Each student should be provided with an individual locker, and cleanliness and proper maintenance of uniforms should be required.

8. *The size of classes should be so arranged that discipline is easy to maintain.* Secondary school physical education classes are frequently overcrowded, and discipline is a major problem. If possible, culturally disadvantaged students should not be in a large class because little teaching takes place, and because the individual student becomes lost in the mass. These students need and want to follow firm, consistent, and appropriate disciplinary standards. As much as any student, they must know what is expected of them and should be made to conform to the standards. However, any disciplinary standards imposed must relate directly to the students. Artificial standards will result in a total lack of discipline.

9. *The physical education program should attempt to instill values that will extend into the classroom situation.* Through the activities of physical education, culturally disadvantaged students can obtain a release of tension in an acceptable way. They can also learn, from the give-and-take of sports, how to get along with others, and will become more aware of the needs, abilities, and talents of their classmates. If these experiences are provided in the physical education class, at least some of the lessons will be transferred to the academic classroom.

10. *The program should be correlated with the general education program of the school.* Through physical education activities much general educational knowledge and many such skills and abilities can be enhanced. Through folk dances, for example, it is possible to acquaint the student with the dress and customs of various cultures. This knowledge will help a class in history to become more interesting to the student, and will help him to develop pride

in his own culture. Through a sport such as baseball, mathematics can be brought to life. The students will be able to see the relationship between mathematics and its uses for such practical purposes as determining baseball batting averages, computing team won-lost percentages, and understanding angles so that this knowledge can be applied to laying out a baseball diamond.

THE PHYSICALLY HANDICAPPED STUDENT

The physically handicapped student may have a temporary disability, such as a broken arm, or he may be in a postoperative stage of recovery. Other physically handicapped students suffer from more permanent disabilities, such as blindness, deafness, or irremediable orthopedic conditions. The range of physical handicaps extends from minor to major in severity, and directly affects the kinds and amounts of participation in physical activity.

Whatever the disability, a physical education program should be provided. Some handicapped students will be able to participate in a regular program of physical education with certain minor modifications. A separate, adapted program should be provided for those students who cannot participate in the basic instructional program of the school. The physically handicapped student cannot be allowed to sit on the sidelines and become only a spectator. He needs to have the opportunity to develop and maintain adequate skill abilities and fitness levels.

There are about three million children and youth between the ages of 4 and 19 years in the United States who are physically handicapped in varying degrees. About 500,000 of these handicapped individuals are of secondary school age. These figures are based on estimates made by the Bureau of the Census through its ongoing United States National Health Survey. Many authorities feel, however, that accurate statistics have not as yet been made available, and that the number of physi-

cally handicapped youth may be somewhat higher than these estimates. Further, these surveys sometimes classify mental retardation under the broad category of physical handicaps.

Many of the more severely handicapped secondary school children attend special schools where their unique needs can be met by highly trained staff members. The remainder are enrolled in the public secondary schools. It is this latter group with which the physical educator must be especially concerned.

Characteristics of the physically handicapped student

The presence of a physical handicap does not mean that the student has an attending mental handicap, although this is sometimes true. Physical handicaps may stem from congenital or hereditary causes, or may develop later in life through environmental factors, such as malnutrition, or from disease or accident. Sometimes negative psychological and social traits develop because of the limitations imposed on the individual by a severe physical handicap.

A physically handicapped student is occasionally ignored or rebuffed by classmates who do not understand the nature of the disability, or who ostracize the student because his disability prevents him from participating fully in the activities of the school. These attitudes toward handicapped persons force them to withdraw in order to avoid being hurt, which results in their becoming further isolated from the remainder of the student body. Some experts have noted that the limitations of the handicap often seem more severe to the observer than they in fact are to the handicapped individual. When this misconception occurs, the handicapped student must prove his abilities in order to gain acceptance and a chance to participate and compete on an equal basis with his nonhandicapped classmates.

The blind or deaf student, or the student with a severe speech impairment, has different problems from those of the orthopedically handicapped student. The student who is partially sighted, blind, deaf, or has a speech impairment cannot communicate with great facility. The orthopedically handicapped student is limited in the physical education class but not necessarily in the academic classroom. The student with vision, hearing, or speech problems may be limited in both the physical education classroom and the academic classroom.

Educational needs of the physically handicapped student

Physically handicapped students in general have the same academic needs, interests, and abilities as do their nonhandicapped peers. While special arrangements must be made for students who have speech, hearing, or visual disabilities, these students are capable of competing successfully in the classroom atmosphere.

Physically handicapped students need preparation for vocations, technical schools, or college. They can contribute to the school through participation in social and service activities. They are far less limited in the general education program and activities of the school than in the physical education program.

The physical educator and the physically handicapped student

There is a lack of physical educators who are specifically trained to teach the physically handicapped. School systems find that the cost of providing special classes taught by specially trained physical educators is prohibitive. Where there are no special classes, the physical educator must provide, within the regular instructional program, those activities which will meet the needs of the handicapped student. Further, placing the physically handicapped student in a regular physical education class will help to give him a feeling of belonging. This advantage is not always possible where separate, adapted classes are provided.

To be able to provide an adequate pro-gram for physically handicapped students, the physical educator needs special training. Advanced courses in anatomy, physiology, physiology of activity, and kinesiology are essential, along with special work in psychology and adapted physical education. The professional preparation curriculum should also include courses in movement education and body mechanics.

The physical educator must have an understanding of the physical disability of each handicapped student and must be aware of any psychological, social, or behavioral problems that may accompany the disability. The physical educator must know the capacities of each handicapped student so that he can provide him with an individualized program.

The physical education program and the physically handicapped student

No two physically handicapped students will have the same limitations in regard to the activities of the physical education program. Under no circumstances can the physical educator diagnose the disability and prescribe a physical activity program. This must be accomplished by the student's physician. The physician's recommendations for students whose conditions have been previously diagnosed should be followed. If in the course of the year the physical educator observes that a student seems to have some kind of physical handicap that is not noted on the record cards of the school, the physical educator must refer the student to his family physician or the proper agency through the normal administrative process of the school. After the disability has been medically diagnosed and activity recommendations made, it becomes the responsibility of the physical educator to provide the proper program.

Some handicapped students will be able to participate in almost all the activities that nonhandicapped students enjoy. Blind students, for example, have successfully engaged in team sports where they can receive aural cues from their sighted teammates. Some athletic equipment manufacturers have placed bells inside game balls, and the blind student is then able to rely on this sound as well as on the supplementary aural cues. Ropes or covered wires acting as hand guides also enable the blind student to participate in track-and-field events. Still other activities, such as swimming, dance, calisthenics, and tumbling, require little adaptation or none at all, except in regard to heightened safety precautions.

In general, deaf students will not be restricted in any way from participating in a full physical education program. Some deaf students experience difficulty in activities requiring precise balance, such as balance-beam walking, and may require some remedial work in this area. The physical educator should be prepared to offer any extra help that is needed.

Other physically handicapped students will have a variety of limitations and a variety of skill abilities. Appropriate program adaptations and modifications must be made in order to meet this range of individual needs. The following general guidelines are helpful in physically educating the physically handicapped on the secondary school level:

1. *Cooperate with the physician in plan-ning each student's program.* The physician is the individual most knowledgeable about the history and limitations of a student's handicap. He is therefore in the best position to recommend a physical activity program for the student.

2. *Test the motor skill ability and physical fitness levels of each student.* The student's abilities and levels of fitness should be tested in areas where medical permission for participation has been granted. This will not only ensure a proper program for the individual but will help in placing the student in the proper class or section of a class.

3. *Keep the program under constant evaluation.* Careful records should be kept showing the student's test scores, activity recommendations, activities engaged in, and progress through the program. In this way, the physical educator will know whether the program is reaching its objectives, the student will be able to discuss his progress with the physical educator, and the school health team and the student's physician will be able to be kept up-to-date on the student's progress and needs.

4. *Keep the adapted and regular programs as similar as possible.* Where the two programs are totally divergent, the physi-

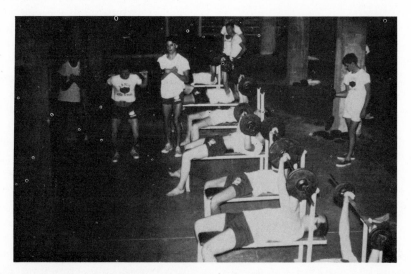

Fig. 14-2. A program for building up physical deficiencies. (Hurst-Euless-Bedford Public Schools, Hurst, Texas.)

cally handicapped student is isolated from his classmates. When the programs are as similar as possible, the handicapped student can be made to feel a part of the larger group and will gain self-confidence and self-respect. Similarity in the programs will also effectively serve to motivate the physically handicapped student.

5. *Provide challenges for the student as he progresses.* Physically handicapped students need the challenge of a progressive program. They welcome the opportunity to test their abilities, and should experience the fun of a challenge and the success of meeting it.

6. *Provide time for extra help.* Handicapped students should be given an opportunity to seek extra help and extra practice after school hours. During this time they can benefit from more individualized instruction than is possible during the class period.

7. *Select activities on an individual basis.* Although several handicapped students in a single class may be able to participate in several activities in common, they may not have a common interest in these activities. The fitness level of each student and his ability, recreational needs, sex, and age, as well as his interests, will help to determine the activities the student will engage in pleasurably.

8. *Adapt the activity to the student rather than the student to the activity.* The student's disability determines the activities in which he can participate. Therefore, any modifications or adaptations that are made must be made in the activity.

9. *Provide safe facilities and safe equipment.* Safe facilities and safe equipment are essential in any physical education program. Extra safeguards must be taken when a physical education class includes physically handicapped students.

10. *Provide suitable extra class activities.* Experts feel that physically handicapped students are placed in an unduly hazardous situation when they engage in highly competitive activities. Intramural and club programs should be provided, but they must be of such a nature that physically handicapped students can enjoy them in a safe, controlled atmosphere that precludes the danger of injury.

THE MENTALLY RETARDED STUDENT

There are special schools in many states that serve mentally retarded students either on a residential basis or a day-care basis. Public secondary schools also offer specially designed curricula and employ teachers who have the comprehensive background and training needed to teach in programs for the retarded. In some public schools, special physical education classes are offered for these students, while in still other schools, mentally retarded students participate in the regularly scheduled physical education classes.

Mental retardation can be a result of hereditary abnormalities, a birth injury, or an accident or illness that leads to impairment of brain function. There are degrees of mental retardation, ranging from the severely mentally retarded, who require custodial care, to the educable mentally retarded, who function with only a moderate degree of impairment.

Each year in the United States more than 126,000 babies are born who have some degree of mental retardation. At present, there are more than seven million mentally retarded children and adults in the United States.

Many agencies are conducting research in the field of mental retardation in an attempt to discover the causes of mental retardation, the nature of mental retardation, and the methods through which it may be prevented. Some agencies are operating innovative training schools for mentally retarded students. The Joseph P. Kennedy, Jr., Foundation is spearheading much of the research concerned with mental retardation and is also a leader in providing camping and recreational programs for the mentally retarded. The Kennedy Foundation has also sponsored training programs for teachers of the mentally retarded. The United States Government has sponsored an experimental physical education program for the mentally retarded at the Austin State School in Austin, Texas. This program is cooperatively conducted by a staff of special education teachers, specially trained physical educators, vocational rehabilitation technicians, and architectural engineers. A special program and special equipment have been designed especially for use with the mentally retarded. Climbing devices, obstacle courses, and unique running areas, as well as a swimming pool, are part of the special facilities. The objectives of this program include social and personal adjustment, as well as the development of physical fitness, sports skills, and general motor ability.

Characteristics of the mentally retarded student

Mentally retarded students show a wide range of intellectual and physical ability. The experts seem to agree that a mentally retarded child is usually closer to the norm for his chronological age in physical development than in mental development. Some mentally retarded students are capable of participating in a regular physical education class, while others have been able to develop only minimal amounts of motor ability. In general, the majority of mentally retarded students are two to four years behind their normal peers in motor development alone.

Despite a slower development of motor ability, mentally retarded students seem to reach physical maturity faster than do normal boys and girls of the same chronological age. Mentally retarded children tend to be overweight and to lack physical strength and endurance. Their posture is generally poor, and they lack adequate levels of physical fitness and motor coordination. Some of these physical problems develop because mentally retarded children have had little of the play and physical activity experiences of normal children. The problems of some mentally retarded youngsters are further multiplied by at-

tendant physical handicaps and personality disturbances.

A mentally retarded student does not have the ability to think in the abstract or to remember isolated facts well. A short attention span, a tendency to overreact emotionally, and a low threshold of irritability also contribute to the classroom problems of the mentally retarded student. While not all mentally retarded students have the same personal characteristics, some of them also tend to be very restless, destructive, and impulsive.

Educational needs of the mentally retarded student

Mentally retarded students need a sound foundation in educational skills. Many of them will seek, and be able to hold, jobs at the conclusion of their secondary education, and there must be vocational training courses for them. Girls in particular need and enjoy courses in home economics, while both boys and girls benefit from instruction in money management and the techniques of using the telephone and writing acceptable letters.

While special classes are usually conducted in many subject areas of the school curriculum, it has been found that the mentally retarded student can join with his peers in some subjects. Vocational and shop courses, art, music, home economics, and physical education are a few of the subjects in which mentally retarded students can find success outside of the special class. Likewise, the mentally retarded student can enjoy intramural activities and school clubs and can contribute to special events, school committees, and service organizations.

The physical educator and the mentally retarded student

The mentally retarded student requires a physical educator with special training, special skills, and a special brand of patience. Such a student lacks confidence and pride and therefore needs a physical educator who will help him to change his negative self-image. The physical educator must be able to provide a program designed to give each student a chance for success. The goals of the program cannot be so high that they are unreachable.

The physical educator must be ready to praise and reinforce each minor success. He should be capable of demonstrating each skill and giving simple and concise directions, and he must be willing to participate in the physical education activities with the students. Discipline must be enforced and standards adhered to, but the disciplinary approach must be a kind and gentle one.

The physical educator must be especially mindful of the individual characteristics of each mentally retarded student. Students who need remedial work should be afforded this opportunity, while students who can succeed in a regular physical education program should be placed in such a class or section. Above all, the physical educator must remember that he cannot proceed with a class of mentally retarded students in the same manner as he would proceed with a class of students with average intelligence and physical ability.

The physical education program and the mentally retarded student

Most mentally retarded students need to be taught how to play. They are frequently unfamiliar with even the simplest of childhood games and lack facility in the natural movements of childhood, such as skipping, hopping, and leaping. They are often seriously deficient in physical fitness and need work in postural improvement. Further, mentally retarded students find it difficult to understand and remember game strategy, such as the importance of staying in the right position, and cannot relate well to the rules of sports and games.

The majority of mentally retarded students need a specially tailored physical education experience. For those who can participate in a regular physical education class, care must be taken that these stu-dents are not placed in a situation where they will meet failure. In a special physical education class, the mentally retarded student can be exposed to a variety of physical education experiences. Physical fitness and posture improvement, along with self-testing activities and games organized and designed according to the ability and interests of the group, will make up a vital part of the special program. In such a class, activities can be easily modified and new experiences introduced before interest wanes. Research has indicated that specially tailored physical education classes can help mentally retarded students to progress very rapidly in their physical skill development.

Physical education can make a very positive contribution to the mentally retarded. Not only must the program be a suitable one, but the physical educator must also be adequately prepared and emotionally and intellectually dedicated to teaching these students.

1. *The program should provide opportunities for increasing physical fitness.* Mentally retarded students do not initiate play experiences or seek out physical activity. Lack of a regular program of physical exercise, as well as lack of understanding of the need for such a program, means that the mentally retarded student is typically lacking in physical fitness. A sound program that includes physical fitness activities can help these students to become more physically fit.

2. *Provide a background of basic motor activities.* Movement education is especially suited to mentally retarded students. These students have often not engaged in the natural play activities of childhood and need to develop their gross motor skill abilities in order to be able to find success in some of the more sophisticated motor skills.

3. *Provide a wide variety of self-testing activities.* Mentally retarded students enjoy even the smallest success in physical activity. Giving such a student an opportunity to compete against himself will help him to

AAHPER-KENNEDY FOUNDATION

SPECIAL FITNESS TEST for the mentally retarded

A manual explaining the purpose of this test, administrative procedures, and how to record and use the results is available from:

AAHPER
NEA PUBLICATIONS—SALES
1201 SIXTEENTH STREET, N.W.
WASHINGTON, D. C. 20036

($1.00 per copy)

It presents graphs showing changes in the performance of retarded children with age, national norms for educable retarded boys and girls 8 to 18 years of age, and suggestions for improving their physical fitness.

It is highly recommended that anyone using this test obtain a copy of the manual.

Special Fitness Record Forms (score cards) are also available (5¢ each)

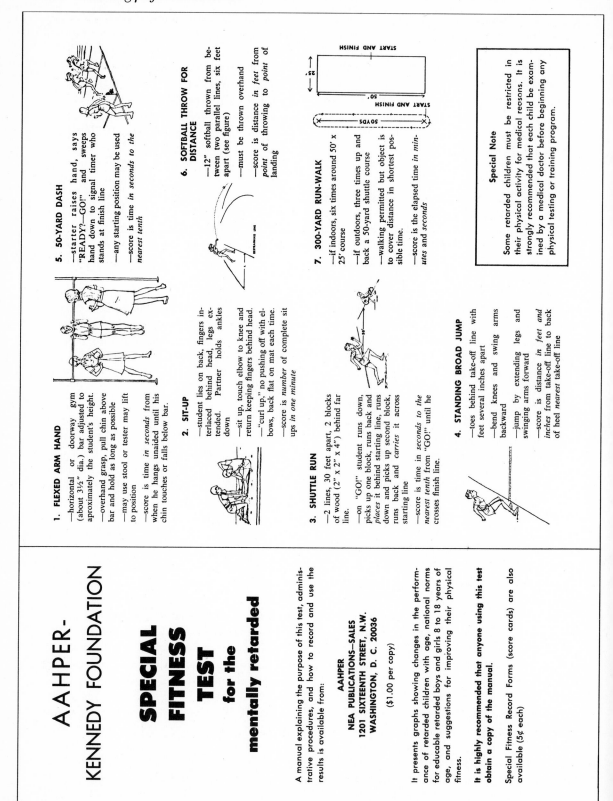

1. FLEXED ARM HAND

—horizontal or doorway gym (about 3½" dia.) bar adjusted to approximately the student's height.

—overhand grasp, pull chin above bar and hold as long as possible

—may use stool or tester may lift to position

—score is time *in seconds* from when he hangs unaided until his chin touches or falls below bar.

2. SIT-UP

—student lies on back, fingers interlaced behind head, legs extended. Partner holds ankles down

—sit up, touch elbow to knee and return keeping fingers behind head.

—"curl up," no pushing off with elbows, back flat on mat each time.

—score is *number* of complete sit ups *in one minute*

3. SHUTTLE RUN

—2 lines, 30 feet apart, 2 blocks of wood (2" x 2" x 4") behind far line.

—on "GO!" student runs down, picks up one block, runs back and *places* it behind starting line, runs down and picks up second block, runs back and *carries* it across starting line

—score is time *in seconds to the nearest tenth* from "GO!" until he crosses finish line.

4. STANDING BROAD JUMP

—toes behind take-off line with feet several inches apart

—bend knees and swing arms backward

—jump by extending legs and swinging arms forward

—score is distance *in feet and inches* from take-off line to back of heel *nearest take-off line*

5. 50-YARD DASH

—starter raises hand, says "READY?—GO!" and sweeps hand down to signal timer who stands at finish line

—any starting position may be used

—score is time *in seconds to the nearest tenth*

6. SOFTBALL THROW FOR DISTANCE

—12" softball thrown from between two parallel lines, six feet apart (see figure)

—must be thrown overhand

—score is distance *in feet* from *point* of throwing to *point* of landing

7. 300-YARD RUN-WALK

—if indoors, six times around 50' x 25' course

—if outdoors, three times up and back a 50-yard shuttle course

—walking permitted but object is to cover distance in shortest possible time.

—score is the elapsed time *in minutes and seconds*

Special Note

Some retarded children must be restricted in their physical activity for medical reasons. It is strongly recommended that each child be examined by a medical doctor before beginning any physical testing or training program.

STANDARDS FOR AAHPER SILVER AWARD

(Qualified by achieving the standard on any five test items)

GIRLS

Age	Flexed Arm Hang (sec.)	Sit Ups (no.)	Shuttle Run (sec.)	Standing Broad Jump (ft.—ins.)	50-yd. Dash (sec.)	Softball Throw (ft.)	300-yard Run-Walk (min.—sec.)
8	5	13	15.0	3' 1"	11.3	27	1:34
9	6	15	14.2	3' 4"	10.5	34	1:33
10	8	17	13.3	3' 10"	9.3	41	1:23
11	7	18	12.9	4' 0"	9.1	46	1:23
12	5	19	12.2	4' 3"	8.8	56	1:18
13	5	18	12.3	4' 3"	8.9	57	1:16
14	6	20	12.1	4' 6"	8.7	63	1:15
15	5	20	12.0	4' 6"	8.6	65	1:20
16	5	21	12.1	4' 8"	8.6	67	1:18
17	4	20	12.5	4' 9"	9.0	62	1:22
18	7	20	12.2	4' 9"	9.0	61	1:20

BOYS

Age	Flexed Arm Hang (sec.)	Sit Ups (no.)	Shuttle Run (sec.)	Standing Broad Jump (ft.—ins.)	50-yd. Dash (sec.)	Softball Throw (ft.)	300-yard Run-Walk (min.—sec.)
8	7	16	14.0	3' 4"	10.5	43	1:33
9	8	17	13.1	3' 10"	9.9	58	1:24
10	8	20	12.6	3' 11"	9.2	66	1:20
11	11	22	11.9	4' 6"	8.9	80	1:15
12	12	24	11.6	4' 10"	8.3	95	1:12
13	10	25	11.3	5' 0"	8.2	104	1:10
14	13	26	11.0	5' 3"	8.0	112	1:07
15	12	31	11.2	5' 9"	7.5	137	1:01
16	17	29	11.1	6' 1"	7.3	154	0:59
17	17	30	10.6	6' 2"	6.9	159	0:56
18	25	31	10.6	6' 6"	7.1	159	0:57

STANDARDS FOR AAHPER GOLD AWARD

(Qualified by achieving the standard on any five test items)

GIRLS

Age	Flexed Arm Hang (sec.)	Sit Ups (no.)	Shuttle Run (sec.)	Standing Broad Jump (ft.—ins.)	50-yd. Dash (sec.)	Softball Throw (ft.)	300-yard Run-Walk (min.—sec.)
8	10	18	13.8	3' 8"	10.1	33	1:28
9	11	21	12.9	3' 9"	9.1	46	1:24
10	13	25	12.1	4' 5"	8.8	52	1:16
11	12	24	11.9	4' 8"	8.4	65	1:15
12	10	24	11.5	4' 11"	8.1	71	1:09
13	11	22	11.6	4' 10"	8.3	72	1:10
14	12	25	11.3	5' 1"	8.2	86	1:08
15	11	25	11.0	5' 1"	8.0	84	1:12
16	11	24	11.2	5' 3"	8.1	82	1:11
17	10	24	11.7	5' 3"	8.2	81	1:13
18	10	24	11.5	5' 3"	8.5	84	1:11

BOYS

Age	Flexed Arm Hang (sec.)	Sit Ups (no.)	Shuttle Run (sec.)	Standing Broad Jump (ft.—ins.)	50-yd. Dash (sec.)	Softball Throw (ft.)	300-yard Run-Walk (min.—sec.)
8	11	20	12.6	3' 9"	9.4	57	1:23
9	13	23	12.1	4' 5"	8.9	73	1:17
10	16	26	11.8	4' 8"	8.5	81	1:13
11	19	27	11.1	5' 1"	8.2	99	1:08
12	19	30	11.0	5' 4"	7.9	114	1:05
13	19	30	10.8	5' 6"	7.7	125	1:04
14	22	30	10.4	5' 11"	7.4	142	1:00
15	26	34	10.7	6' 4"	7.1	159	0:58
16	29	34	10.2	6' 9"	6.9	181	0:55
17	29	35	9.8	7' 2"	6.3	176	0:51
18	39	36	9.9	7' 1"	6.5	187	0:52

STANDARDS FOR KENNEDY FOUNDATION CHAMP AWARD

(Qualified by achieving the standard on all seven test items)

GIRLS

Age	Flexed Arm Hang (sec.)	Sit Ups (no.)	Shuttle Run (sec.)	Standing Broad Jump (ft.—ins.)	50-yd. Dash (sec.)	Softball Throw (ft.)	300-yard Run-Walk (min.—sec.)
8	14	22	13.0	3' 10"	9.6	36	1:26
9	16	25	12.4	4' 1"	8.8	58	1:19
10	16	29	11.9	4' 8"	8.5	59	1:12
11	17	27	11.5	5' 0"	8.2	75	1:13
12	14	28	11.1	5' 4"	7.8	82	1:06
13	14	25	11.2	5' 1"	7.9	81	1:07
14	16	27	11.0	5' 6"	7.8	95	1:04
15	15	27	10.6	5' 6"	7.8	94	1:06
16	14	26	11.0	5' 7"	7.9	97	1:05
17	13	27	11.1	5' 6"	7.9	98	1:10
18	13	28	11.2	5' 8"	8.1	93	1:09

BOYS

Age	Flexed Arm Hang (sec.)	Sit Ups (no.)	Shuttle Run (sec.)	Standing Broad Jump (ft.—ins.)	50-yd. Dash (sec.)	Softball Throw (ft.)	300-yard Run-Walk (min.—sec.)
8	15	22	12.4	4' 1"	9.1	61	1:22
9	19	27	11.9	4' 9"	8.6	85	1:14
10	21	29	11.4	4' 11"	8.2	89	1:08
11	24	29	10.9	5' 4"	8.0	108	1:05
12	25	32	10.7	5' 6"	7.5	123	1:03
13	25	33	10.5	5' 10"	7.5	140	1:00
14	32	34	10.1	6' 4"	7.1	151	0:56
15	33	36	10.3	6' 9"	6.9	181	0:56
16	37	38	9.9	7' 0"	6.5	188	0:52
17	34	38	9.6	7' 5"	6.1	187	0:49
18	49	38	9.7	7' 4"	6.3	204	0:49

For boys and girls who achieve the CHAMP standards on all seven test items and engage in at least 30 hours of sports and recreational activity.

Fig. 14-3

gain confidence and pride in accomplishment.

4. *Provide a carefully structured, progressive program.* Mentally retarded students have the same physical activity needs as do normal students. A progressive program will help to interest and motivate them in a variety of physical activities.

5. *Provide opportunities for competition in games of low organization.* Mentally retarded students enjoy the give-and-take of competition, but any competition must be geared specifically to their needs and abilities. The experience of competing will aid in the development of desirable social traits.

6. *Introduce new activities at the beginning of a class period.* Mentally retarded children tire easily and have a short attention span. New activities will be learned more easily and will be enjoyed more before fatigue sets in and while interest is still high.

7. *Provide for a choice of activities.* This will help the mentally retarded student to feel that he is important. Further, if a choice of activities is offered, motivation, morale, and discipline will remain higher.

8. *Provide for lifetime recreational skills.* These skills are essential for any student, but mentally retarded students, especially, need to learn the value of recreation. Through specially designed intramural and club programs, additional recreational experiences can be introduced.

9. *Stress positive health and safety habits.* Provide each student with a locker and require that proper care be taken of the physical education uniform. Where possible, provide time in the program for showers. Stress should be placed on the relationship between health and physical activity. Safety must be constantly stressed in all activities and must be related to other phases of the school program.

10. *Keep accurate, up-to-date records.* Records will help in guiding the student and in assessing his abilities and limitations. The students' parents are also interested in their progress, and keeping them informed of gains will help to establish good public relations. Accurate and complete records will be invaluable to the student's guidance counselor, the school health team, and the student's personal physician. Complete records will also help the physical educator in making an objective evaluation of the program.

THE DISRUPTIVE STUDENT

The disruptive student may suffer from deep-seated emotional disturbances, or he may simply be in need of guidance and counseling to help him resolve less serious problems that lead to his disruptive behavior. Some students who dislike school will be disruptive in classes even though there is no serious emotional problem involved. In any case, the disruptive student presents special problems for the physical educator, who must be concerned not only with teaching but also with the safety of the students in the class.

A single disruptive student can have a disastrous effect on the conduct of a class as well as on the behavior of the rest of the students in that class. Effective teaching cannot take place when discipline deteriorates.

Characteristics of the disruptive student

Emotionally unstable students have difficulty in maintaining good relationships with their classmates and teachers. Some of their abnormal behavior patterns stem from a need and craving for attention. Sometimes the disruptive student exhibits gross patterns of aggressiveness and destructiveness. Other emotionally unstable students may be so withdrawn from the group that they refuse to participate in the activities of the class, even to the extent of refusing to report for class. In the case of physical education, the disruptive student may refuse to dress for the activity when he does report. These measures draw both student and teacher reaction, focusing the desired attention on the nonconforming student.

Emotionally unstable students are often restless and unable to pay attention. In a physical education class they may poke and prod other students, refuse to line up with the rest of the class, or insist on bouncing a game ball while a lesson is in progress. These are also ploys to gain attention, and the student behaves similarly in the academic classroom for the same reason.

Some disruptive students may have physical or mental handicaps that contribute to their behavior. Others may be concerned about what they consider to be poor personal appearance, such as extremes of height or weight, or physical maturity not in keeping with their chronological age. Still other disruptive students may simply be in the process of growing up and are finding it difficult to handle their adolescence.

Educational needs of the disruptive student

The disruptive student is in need of guidance and counseling. The school cannot impose discipline on the disruptive student before the causes for his behavior have been ascertained. The school has many services available to it through which it can help the disruptive student. School psychologists can test the student, and social welfare agencies can assist by working with both the student and his family. Case studies of the student and conferences with all the student's teachers can be invaluable in determining his needs. The school health team will also have pertinent information to contribute, as will the student's guidance counselors. Conferences with the student also help to open the doors to understanding.

The school cannot take the responsibility for arbitrarily expelling or suspending the disruptive student without first carefully and comprehensively examining the causes for his behavior. Expulsion or suspension often serve to heighten the negative feelings of the student and make it more difficult to draw the student back into the life of the school.

The physical educator and the disruptive student

If the physical educator is faced with many disruptive students in a single class, he must first examine himself and his relationship to that class. The physical educator's rapport with the entire class, his relationships with individual students, his disciplinary standards, and his program will all affect student behavior to some degree.

If negative student behavior stems from some aspect of a student's personality, then the physical educator must take positive steps to resolve the problem so that teaching can take place. The physical educator must deal with each behavioral problem on an individual basis, and seek help from the school personnel best equipped to give aid. The student's guidance counselor will have information that will be of help to the physical educator. A conference with this individual may reveal methods that have proved effective with the student in the past. Further, the observations made by the physical educator will be of value to the guidance counselor's continuing study of the student.

The physical educator will find that not all disruptive students are continual and serious behavior problems. As much as teachers, students have their good and bad days. The physical educator should have a private conference with the student whose behavior suddenly becomes negative, and try to understand why the student has reacted in a way unusual for him. Such a conference will lead to mutual understanding and often help to allay future problems with the same student.

Much of the physical educator's task is student guidance. In individual cases of disruptive behavior, the physical educator should exhaust all his personal resources in order to alleviate the problem before enlisting aid from other sources. Any case of disruptive behavior demands immediate action on the part of the physical educator to prevent minor problems from becoming major ones.

The physical education program and the disruptive student

A majority of secondary school pupils enjoy physical activity and physical education. They look forward to the physical education class as one part of the school day in which they can express themselves and gain a release of tension in an atmosphere that encourages it. For this reason, the student who is disruptive in the classroom is often one of the best citizens in the physical education class.

Physical education is in a unique position to help the disruptive student. Most students profit from the activities of physical education, and through their actions in this phase of the school curriculum, it is possible for teaching personnel to gain many insights into student behavior.

1. *Know each student by name, and as an individual.* Individual knowledge of each student is of utmost importance in physical education, and in understanding individual behavior patterns. Recognizing a student's needs and problems early in the school year will help to prevent future behavior problems.

2. *Be certain that students understand the behavior required of them.* While physical education classes are conducted in a less formal manner than classroom subjects, this does not mean that lower standards of behavior are acceptable. Students should know what the standards are on the first day of class and should be expected to adhere to these standards in all future classes.

3. *Discipline must be firm and consistent.* When rules are rigid one day and relaxed the next, students will not know how to react. Discipline must be enforced in a firm and consistent manner for all students during all classes.

4. *Discuss behavioral problems with the individual student.* Respect for the individual student is a necessity. No student likes to be criticized or embarrassed in front of his peers. When a student is singled out from a group and used as a disciplinary example, the atmosphere in the class will deteriorate. Respect for the student means maintenance of respect for the teacher. If disciplinary matters are handled on a one-to-one basis, rapport is enhanced.

5. *Expect good behavior from all students.* If the disruptive student knows that the physical educator expects him to behave in a bizarre manner, he will react in just this way. Good behavior should be expected until the student acts otherwise.

6. *Try to ensure that the disruptive student will be successful in the physical education class.* Constant failure only abets disruptive behavior. If a student is known to be hostile and disruptive, an attempt should be made to avoid placing him in situations where he feels inadequate and shows this in his behavior. If, for example, a disruptive student does not run well, he may still make a superior goalie in soccer, a position that would not require him to run.

7. *Give praise as often as possible.* If the disruptive student has a special skill talent, ask him to demonstrate for the class. This will give him the recognition and attention he needs. Give praise for a skill that is well performed, and notice the minor accomplishments of the student.

8. *Allow the student to help with equipment.* Make the position of equipment leader a reward rather than a punishment. See that each deserving student, including the disruptive ones, receive this honor when they merit it.

9. *Welcome the disruptive student to intramural and club activities.* No student is going to participate in extra class activities unless he really wants to do so. Set behavioral standards for these activities and open them to all students in the school who meet the standards. Acceptance into a club or participation on an intramural team may help the disruptive student gain self-respect and peer recognition and approval.

10. *Keep the student's guidance counselor informed of his progress.* The guidance counselor should know of any progress made by the pupil. Too often these individuals are informed only of failures or increasing behavior problems. Progress in

one area of the school curriculum may have a positive effect on progress in other areas of the curriculum.

THE POORLY COORDINATED STUDENT

Well-coordinated students are the bright lights of the physical education class. Often held up as examples by the physical educator, they find success easily and receive much individual attention because they respond well to instruction and coaching. There is another segment of the school population, however, that needs individual instruction even more—the awkward, uncoordinated students who are frequently left to learn skills as best they can.

The student with low motor ability is often ignored by the physical educator. He is unpopular with his classmates because he is considered a detriment in team sports. He is undesirable as a partner in dual sports and therefore is paired with equally uncoordinated and awkward partners. The student with low motor ability needs special attention so that he can improve his physical skill performances, derive pleasure from success in physical activity, and gain a background in lifetime sports.

Physical education makes special arrangements for the physically handicapped, the mentally retarded, and the athlete. Very little is done for the poorly coordinated student.

Characteristics of the poorly coordinated student

The poorly coordinated student exhibits a measurable lack of physical ability. Less often considered is the psychological effect of the student's physical inabilities. The poorly coordinated student who is not given special help in the secondary school often becomes the adult who abhors any physical activity and is reticent about participating in adult recreational activities.

Poorly coordinated students are usually placed in regular physical education classes when they have no mental or physical handicaps. The only concession made to their problem is through ability grouping in schools where facilities and personnel are adequate. Even then, ability grouping sometimes is used only to separate the "duds" from the "stars," thus increasing the poorly coordinated student's feelings of inadequacy. The poorly coordinated student may be held up to ridicule by fellow students as well as by physical education teachers, who tend to use him as an example of how not to perform a physical skill.

The poorly coordinated student will resist learning new activities because the challenge this presents offers little chance for success. The challenge of a new skill or activity to be learned may create such tension within the student that he becomes physically ill. In other instances this tension may result in negative behavior.

Poor coordination may be the result of several factors. The student may not be physically fit, he may have poor reflexes, or he may not have the ability to use mental imagery. For some reason such as a lengthy childhood illness, the poorly coordinated student may not have been normally physically active. Other poorly coordinated students will enter the secondary school physical education program from an elementary school that lacked a trained physical educator, had no facilities for physical education, or had a poor program of physical education. A single factor or a combination of any of them will help to retard motor skill development.

Educational needs of the poorly coordinated student

The physical education program frequently motivates students with specific problems to perform better in the academic classroom by offering an opportunity for success in physical activity. This process may work in reverse with the poorly coordinated student. A student's dread of his physical education class will have a detrimental effect on his ability to perform well in the classroom. Both his behavior and his academic achievement may be adversely affected.

When classroom performance declines, it is the classroom teacher who will become aware of the problem first. As with any other student problem, the first step in resolving that problem is a conference with the student and then with the student's guidance counselor. It may be only through such conferences that the cause of the problem is revealed and the physical educator made aware of his contribution to the problem. Unless the physical educator is made aware of the problem, steps cannot be taken to remedy it. Many problems of this nature in a single school cast shadows of doubt on the value of the physical education program, its philosophy, and objectives. If measures are not taken to adequately resolve the problems, poor relations will develop between the physical educator, the student body, the remainder of the school faculty, the administration, and the community.

The physical educator and the poorly coordinated student

The physical educator must understand child growth and development and formulate a physical education program that is based on sound principles of growth and development. A knowledge of adolescent growth and development and of adolescent psychology is also an essential prerequisite to teaching on the secondary school level. Additionally, the physical educator must be able to use his knowledge to select activities and devise progressions that are appropriate to the age and grade level of the students in the program.

In working with poorly coordinated students the physical educator must exercise the utmost patience. He must know why the student is poorly coordinated and be able to devise an individual program for him that will help him to move and perform more effectively. The physical educator must be sure that the student understands the need for special help, and should try to motivate him to succeed. When a skill is performed with even a modicum of improvement, the effort must be praised and the achievement reinforced.

With a large class and only one instructor, there can be relatively little time spent with each individual. The buddy system, in which a poorly coordinated student is paired with a well-coordinated partner, often enables both students to progress faster. Immediate successes will not be forthcoming for the poorly coordinated student, and the physical educator must be careful not to push the student beyond his limits. An overly difficult challenge, coupled with the fatigue that results from trying too hard, may result in retarding, rather than accelerating, improvement. Any goal set for the poorly coordinated student must be a reachable goal.

The physical educator has a very definite responsibility to the poorly coordinated student. Poor attitudes concerning physical activity can too easily be carried over into adult life. If these negative attitudes can be reversed by the physical educator early in the student's secondary school career, the student may find that he will be motivated to develop abilities in several of the lifetime sports.

The physical education program and the poorly coordinated student

The objectives of the program for poorly coordinated students will not differ from the objectives of any physical education program, but the emphases will lie in different areas, and many activities will be modified or adapted as the need arises.

Before a program is devised, the status of the students will need to be known so that their individual abilities and needs can be identified. Physical fitness and motor ability testing must be ongoing phases of the program. Through the physical education program the students must come to realize that their special needs are being met because they are as important as the well-skilled students in the eyes of the physical educator.

1. *Carefully weigh the advantages and disadvantages of ability grouping.* Separating students into ability groups may cause poorly coordinated students to feel that they are being pushed out of the way. If

ability grouping is used, they must receive adequate instruction and a meaningful program, and have equal access to good equipment and facilities.

2. *Select the proper activities.* If a student has poor eye-hand or eye-foot coordination, he will not succeed in such activities as tennis or soccer. Activities must be chosen that suit the abilities of the students and at the same time help them to develop the needed coordination.

3. *Offer a varied, interesting, and progressive program.* Work on improving fitness and self-testing activities should form only a part of the program. Games of appropriate level, rhythmics and dance, and such activities as swimming and archery will help to stimulate and maintain interest.

4. *Offer a club program for all students.* Physical fitness clubs, swimming clubs, and other clubs open to all students will benefit poorly coordinated students. If ability grouping is used in class, a common club program will help to remove the stigma of separateness.

5. *Include competition in the program.* With carefully arranged teams and schedules in an intramural program, poorly coordinated students can be given a chance to compete on their own level. Preparation for intramural competition should be a part of the class program.

6. *Include some activities of a coeducational nature.* Dancing in particular lends itself to coeducational instruction. When classes can be combined and coeducational instruction offered, poorly coordinated students have an opportunity to develop social skills.

7. *Group students on a flexible pattern.* Different groupings for different activities will stimulate interest and provide students with a variety of partners.

8. *Provide for upward progression.* Reassess the students periodically to see how they are progressing. When an adequate level of success has been attained in a particular activity, move the student into a faster-moving and more highly skilled group.

9. *Involve the students in program planning.* Offer a selection of activities that will appeal to poorly coordinated students, and guide their selections in relation to their abilities.

10. *Provide for lifetime sports skills.* Swimming and dance are ideal for future recreational use. Poorly coordinated students need a background of lifetime sports skills to help them offset the tensions that will arise in their lives and receive the fullest enjoyment from life. Rather than attempting to develop championship-level skills, these students need to develop enough skills to be able to appreciate and engage voluntarily in physical activity.

THE PHYSICALLY GIFTED OR CREATIVE STUDENT

By what criteria do we judge the gifted or creative student in physical education? Is it the boy who captains the basketball team, the girl who scores the most goals for the field hockey team, or is it the boy who wins a state gymnastics title or the girl who aspires to a career as a professional danger? Is it the student who decides to be a professional physical educator? The gifted or creative student in physical education has a combination of many qualities, the depth of each quality varying with the individual. Gifted and creative students in physical education are atypical because they also need a specially tailored physical education experience.

In this section we are not concerned with the secondary school student who is gifted intellectually. These students may also be gifted physically, but some intellectually gifted students have only low or average motor ability. We are concerned here with the student who is exceptional because of his or her motor skill abilities, and who perhaps is also gifted intellectually.

Characteristics of the physically gifted or creative student

The physically gifted student is not the student who is a star athlete in one sport or activity. The physically gifted student has superior motor skill abilities in many activities and maintains a high level of physical fitness. He may be a star athlete, but in general he is simply a good all-around performer. In a game situation, he always seems to be in the right place at the right time.

The physically gifted student learns quickly and requires a minimum of individual instruction. He is usually enthusiastic about physical activity and practices his skills of his own volition. Any individual instruction he does require is in the form of coaching rather than remedial correction. The physically gifted student has a strong sense of kinesthetic awareness and understands the principles of human movement. The student may not be able to articulate these latter two qualities, but observation by the physical educator will reveal that the student has discovered how to exploit his body as a tool for movement.

The physically creative student also has a well-developed sense of kinesthetic awareness and knows how to use his body properly. This student is the girl who dances with ease and grace or who is highly skilled in free exercise. It is the boy who is the lithe tumbler or gymnast. These students develop their own sophisticated routines in dance, tumbling, gymnastics, apparatus, and synchronized swimming. They may or may not be extraordinarily adept in other physical education activities but are as highly teachable as are the physically gifted.

Educational needs of the physically gifted or creative student

The physically gifted student or the physically creative student may or may not exhibit similar extraordinary abilities in the academic classroom. Physical talent, creativity, and intelligence are not necessarily correlated, although they may be. A student who is doing very poorly academically may be the superior student in physical education, or he may be superior in all phases of the secondary school program.

For the academically gifted student, most secondary schools offer honors courses, opportunities to conduct independent research, or courses that lead to college credits. Where a student shows exceptional talent in physical education but none in the classroom, appropriate measures must be taken to discover, and perhaps remedy, the cause of this disparity. Exceptional students in physical education should be identified to the guidance personnel by the physical educator in a conference, since grade reports will reveal a superior mark only, and reveal little of the student as an individual. Guidance personnel should be informed of these exceptional students as early in the school year as a reliable and valid judgment can be made.

The physical educator and the physically gifted or creative student

The beginning physical educator, especially, may find it difficult to teach a student who seems to possess many more physical abilities than the teacher. However, there is no student in a secondary school who knows all there is to know about an activity. Students' knowledge is limited by what they have been taught or have learned on their own. Many experiences will still be new to them.

The physically gifted student or the physically creative student may not have attempted a wide range of activities—he may have experienced only those activities offered in the school physical education program. Both the physically gifted and the physically creative student, as well as the average student, will be stimulated and challenged by the introduction of new activities. The creative student in dance may be introduced to a new kind of music, or the boy who is skilled on apparatus may enjoy adding new moves to his routines. The athlete may be a good performer, but he may need to become a better team player. He may rely on his superior skills rather than on a complete knowledge of the rules and strategies of sports and games.

The physical educator has a contribution

to make to each student in the physical education program. The challenges presented by students of exceptional ability will help to keep the physical educator alert, stimulated, and enthusiastic about his teaching.

The physical education program and the physically gifted or creative student

A well-planned physical education program will be adaptable to the needs of all the students it serves. Before the program can be definitively developed, however, the specific needs, limitations, and abilities of the students in the program must be defined. The activities offered must be adapted to the needs of the students, since the students cannot be adapted to the program. Objectives are not achieved in the latter manner.

The exceptional student needs a structured program of physical activity, since this is a vital part of his mental, social, emotional, and physical development. Some schools have made it a policy to excuse athletes from the activity program when their varsity sport is in season. This is a disservice to the student, especially when the varsity sport and the unit being taught in class are different. A student benefits from physical activity in a regular program. The physical educator can keep the interest of the exceptional student high by adopting some tested methods.

1. *Develop a leaders' program.* This type of activity has proved valuable in many secondary schools. Leaders can assist the physical educator in innumerable ways and develop a sense of responsibility for the program because they are directly involved. Members of leaders' clubs have served as gymnastics and tumbling spotters in classes other than their own and can assist as officials in both the class program and during intramural contests. Members of leaders' clubs thus still participate in the activities of their own class but at the same time receive the benefit of extra exposure to activities.

2. *Utilize audiovisual materials.* Movies, filmstrips, loop films, and slides interest and benefit all students, but by watching these materials the exceptional student can compare his performance with those of experts, gain new insights into skills, and discover new techniques of performing skills.

3. *Provide special challenges.* Textbooks in physical education are not in wide use in secondary school physical education programs. While all students could benefit from the use of a textbook, special outside readings, assignments, and research problems would provide an additional challenge for the exceptional student. The senior author (C. A. B.) of this book has written a new physical education textbook for high school boys and girls, *Physical Education for Life,* which should be especially helpful.

4. *Encourage the exceptional student to assist in his own class.* Many of the highly skilled or creative students will be able to assist students who have low motor skill abilities. By working on a one-to-one basis, the amount of individualized instruction will be increased. The student with low motor ability will receive the special assistance he needs, and the gifted student will be helped to realize that not all students possess high levels of ability.

5. *Assign the student to coaching responsibilities.* The exceptional student can assist in the intramural program by acting as a coach on a day when his team is not playing. Coaching a team will help the student to become more cognizant of the importance of team play, sportsmanship, and the need for rules. Such coaching, however, should be done under the close supervision of the physical educator.

6. *Provide challenges within the program.* A skilled gymnast would not benefit from a beginning unit in tumbling. If his class is on this unit, the exceptional student can be assigned to work on advanced skills or on an advanced routine. A girl who shows great creativity in dance can be assigned to design a new dance or to devise some new steps.

POINTS TO REMEMBER

1. Every physical educator will at some time have to teach at least a few atypical students.
2. There are many different categories of atypical students.
3. Physical education has a strong appeal for the culturally disadvantaged.
4. Physically handicapped students may exhibit a wide range of disabilities.
5. Some mentally retarded students can participate in regular physical education classes.
6. A disruptive student may affect the safety of a physical education class.
7. A poorly coordinated student may become a behavior problem if he does not receive special assistance.
8. The physically gifted or physically creative student can benefit from participation in regular physical education classes.

PROBLEMS TO THINK THROUGH

1. Should the objectives of physical education be the same for all secondary school students?
2. What is the advantage of having specially trained physical educators for special students?
3. What are the advantages and disadvantages of having special physical education classes for atypical students?
4. What special concern should physical education have for the student with average physical ability?
5. How can physical education best deal with the resistive student?
6. What implications does ability grouping have for the atypical student?

CASE STUDY FOR ANALYSIS

You are a beginning physical educator in a medium-size secondary school, and the only member of your department. (There is one teacher for the boys and one for the girls). On the first day of activity in the fall, you notice that one of your students is refusing to put on the physical education uniform. The remainder of your class is dressed for activity and ready to report to the playing area. What steps will you take to resolve this problem?

EXERCISES FOR REVIEW

1. What special responsibilities does the physical educator have for the atypical student?
2. How can the physical educator best adapt his program to the needs of the mentally retarded student?
3. What special physical education needs does the creative student have?
4. To what other resources can the physical educator turn when he needs assistance in understanding and working with the atypical student?
5. Through what means outside of the class program can physical education contribute to the atypical student?
6. What special challenges does the physically gifted student present?

REFERENCES

1. Bucher, Charles A.: Foundations of physical education, ed. 5, St. Louis, 1968, The C. V. Mosby Co.
2. Daniels, Arthur S., and Davies, Evelyn A.: Adapted physical education, New York, 1965, Harper & Row, Publishers.
3. Riessman, Frank: The culturally deprived child, New York, 1962, Harper & Row, Publishers.
4. Schurr, Evelyn L.: Movement experiences for children, New York, 1967, Appleton-Century-Crofts.

SELECTED READINGS

Bucher, Charles A.: Physical education for life, St. Louis, 1969, Webster Division, McGraw-Hill Book Co.
Conant, James B.: Slums and suburbs, New York, 1964, New American Library.
Cratty, Bryant J.: Social dimensions of physical activity, Englewood Cliffs, N. J., 1967, Prentice-Hall, Inc.
Fantini, Mario D., and Weinstein, Gerald: The disadvantaged: challenge to education, New York, 1968, Harper & Row, Publishers.
Harrington, Michael: The other America, New York, 1962, The Macmillan Co.
Information Center–Recreation for the Handicapped: Recreation for the handicapped, a bibliography, Carbondale, Ill., 1965, Southern Illinois University.

BOOKLETS, PAMPHLETS, AND ARTICLES

AAHPER Project on Recreation and Fitness for the Mentally Retarded: Challenge, May, 1968, American Association for Health, Physical Education, and Recreation.
Activity programs for the mentally retarded, Journal of Health, Physical Education, Recreation, 37:24, April, 1966.

Bode, Mary Jane: You are my sunshine, American Education 4:16, May, 1968.

Carlton, Lessie, and Moore, Robert H.: Culturally disadvantaged children can be helped, NEA Journal 55:13, Sept., 1966.

Duggar, Margaret P.: Dance for the blind, Journal of Health, Physical Education, and Recreation 39:28, May, 1968.

Frankel, Esther C.: Toward a rebirth of creativity, Journal of Health, Physical Education, and Recreation 38:65, Nov.–Dec., 1967.

Hayden, Frank J.: Physical fitness for the mentally retarded, Toronto, Canada, 1964, Rotary Clubs.

Hilsendager, Donald R.: The Buttonwood Farms project, Journal of Health, Physical Education, and Recreation 39:46, March, 1968.

Information Center–Recreation for the Handicapped: ICRH Newsletter (all issues).

The Joseph P. Kennedy, Jr., Foundation: A Guide for day camps, and recreation programs for the retarded, Washington, D. C., The Foundation.

Kretchmar, Robert T.: The forgotten student in physical education, Journal of Health, Physical Education, and Recreation 31:21, May–June, 1960.

Moynihan, Daniel P.: The discarded third, Look 30:27, May 17, 1966.

New York State Division for Youth: Youth Service News 19:1, Winter, 1967-1968.

The Program Aids Co., Inc.: A physical fitness program for special education, Newsletter for Leaders in Health, Physical Education, Athletics, and Recreation 5:4, March, 1968.

Slader, Carl V.: A workable adaptive program, Journal of Health, Physical Education, and Recreation 39:71, Jan., 1968.

Stein, Julian U.: A practical guide to adapted physical education for the educable mentally handicapped, Journal of Health, Physical Education, and Recreation 33:30, Dec., 1962.

Williams, F. Neil: Physical education adapts to the visually handicapped, Journal of Health, Physical Education, and Recreation 35:25, March, 1964.

Methods and materials
for
developing physical fitness

The term "physical fitness" has been defined and interpreted in many different ways during the past few years. There are some persons who believe that physical fitness refers only to body building and motor performance. Others, including most physical educators, prefer to think in terms of *total fitness* of the individual—physical, social, emotional, and intellectual fitness— and recognize this as the more valuable educational goal.

Physical educators have a very real responsibility to their students and the community in the area of physical fitness and its role in total individual fitness. Increased public awareness and curiosity about what is being done in the schools have forced teachers in this field to come up with concrete programs and answers. However, the public does not yet realize that physical fitness is but a part of the total fitness picture, and thus teachers have a dual educational role: explaining to students and to parents alike the overall story of total fitness and one of its components, physical fitness.

The current high level of interest in fitness is the result of a massive campaign sponsored by the President's Council on Youth Fitness, established first during President Eisenhower's administration, and later changed by President Kennedy in 1961 to the President's Council on Physical Fitness. It is now known as the President's Council on Physical Fitness and Sports. Under the leadership of such men as Shane McCarthy, Bud Wilkinson, Stan Musial, and James A. Lovell, Jr., the Council has attempted to raise the standards and level of physical fitness of people across the entire country. Their nationwide campaign reached out in many different educational areas, striving to accomplish the following:

1. To improve programs of physical education, with increased emphasis on physical fitness
2. To increase state leadership and supervision of physical fitness and sports programs
3. To increase the number of school personnel doing physical education work
4. To conduct regional clinics in physical fitness
5. To establish demonstration centers in schools where high-level fitness programs were organized
6. To develop adult fitness programs
7. To improve standards in Armed

Forces testing and training programs
8. To publish pamphlets, booklets, and other resource materials
9. To inform the public and develop their interest in physical education through advertising in public media

Statistics indicate the remarkable effectiveness of the Council's work. Not only have physical education programs been improving, but the number of teaching specialists has increased, state supervision and leadership has been extended, and the physical fitness levels of students has substantially improved. Many states now have a governor's physical fitness council or commission. Fitness programs for cycling, swimming, jogging, and running specified distances have been developed, with badges and awards issued across the country to those who qualify.

Yet physical educators and Council members realize that only a beginning has been made. Other statistics indicate that much more has to be done—in the many states that do not yet have full-time people employed in the department of education to supervise the program, and in the nearly 40% of schools where no daily physical education classes are held for all students.

In March of 1968, former President Johnson changed the Council's name to President's Council on Physical Fitness and Sports, and raised the Council to a cabinet-level post. This was done for the purpose of extending the scope of the Council and promoting sports and fitness in America.

TEACHING PHYSICAL FITNESS

The task of teaching physical fitness is a difficult one, particularly in regard to teaching adolescent students. The following reasons account for this:

1. Lack of interest. Adolescent girls are sometimes more interested in "feminine

Fig. 15-1. Several methods used in developing physical fitness in high school students. (Oak Ridge High School, Oak Ridge, Tenn.)

fancies" than physical pursuits, and boys often want to become star athletes without extensive effort.

2. Lack of understanding. Adolescents do not fully understand the term "physical fitness" as it relates to their growth and development, and their all-round health and total performance.

3. Lack of uniformity. Physical fitness is an individual attainment and cannot be achieved by a total group through an identical process.

Furthermore, the very nature of physical fitness requires maintenance. It is not a fact, like the multiplication tables, which once learned may be set aside. Physical fitness is a condition that must be maintained. Healthful attitudes toward fitness must be developed in students, along with an appreciation for its significance.

Achievement of physical fitness is another difficulty, for fitness itself varies in relation to the individual's personal requirements. The scholar needs physical skills different from those of the football player and therefore requires a different level of fitness. However, the basic components of fitness—such as good posture, desirable health habits, and social, emotional, and mental well-being—are necessary for all. It is the responsibility of the physical education teacher to promote the development of these components to their fullest degree. Students must be made aware of their need for physical fitness and led toward achievement of this goal. This should

Platnick's Photo Service, Hempstead, L. I.

Fig. 15-2. Building physical fitness through swimming.

be done through both the instructional and the noninstructional phases of the total physical education program.

INSTRUCTIONAL PROGRAM

There are many methods and techniques useful for teaching adolescents in the area of physical fitness. The instructional program itself should contain definite steps for appraisal, guidance, and testing throughout the school year, and related discussions, assignments, and studies should be included for special emphasis.

Teaching methods and techniques*

Appraisal. The appraisal of physical fitness in secondary school is an important teaching method that serves many purposes. Appraisal of fitness provides the teacher with a picture of the fitness level of each student, each class unit, and the overall school population. These data may then be helpful in determining individual student needs and the needs of the total program. Statistics on speed, accuracy, and other components of fitness should be used throughout the year to aid in program planning and to promote fitness. (See Chapter 19.)

The process of appraisal shoud be very beneficial for the student. It should provide an understanding of the true nature of fitness. Having endurance, efficiency, and coordination enough to complete satisfactorily the everyday tasks required in high school should be recognized as one of the fitness objectives. Students also need to recognize that physical fitness is not the same for each individual, and this attitude may be promoted through the appraisal process. Furthermore, appraisal helps to motivate students toward improvement of their own physical abilities. Instead of mistaking physical fitness for mere muscular strength, they see that exercise can be fun and that it is necessary for proper growth and development and healthy resistance to disease.

---

* See also Chapter 19 on Evaluation.

Many materials have been developed for appraisal of physical fitness. They will be discussed in greater detail later in the chapter. However, it should be noted here that some of the physical fitness tests include norms, or scoring scales, for evaluation of physical performance. These are helpful in student appraisal, because they offer a more precise technique for comparing scores of students of the same age, height, and/or weight. Students, too, prefer to picture their own test results in terms of the achievements of hundreds of their peers, instead of just their classmates. Norms also serve as an excellent educational device for many students.

Norms do not provide the total picture in the assessment of physical fitness, however. A physical education teacher should be cautious in applying norms since these scores vary according to the basis used for their development (age, height, etc.). One study indicates that both physique (height and weight) *and* developmental level (accelerated, normal, or retarded growth pattern) are important determinants in physical performance levels. Norms that do not consider the overweight factor, for example, may be scaled too high for accomplishment by such persons.[2]

Another study of 7,600 boys and girls, 10 to 18 years of age, analyzed the relationship of age, height, and weight to performances in the California Physical Fitness Test. Results brought about recommendations that *age* be used as a basis for test norms, for steady progress was shown by students each year in nearly all test items.[3]

Obviously, more research is needed in this area of testing physical fitness and establishing norms for guidance. The physical educator should recognize the limitations while taking advantage of values.

Guidance. The teaching program should provide an opportunity for individual guidance of students in the area of physical fitness. This may be done in connection with the appraisal program, with individual conferences scheduled for each student to discuss personal problems and weak-

Record form for identification of physically underdeveloped pupils

Teacher _____   School year _____

Period or section _____   Date of 1st test _____

School _____

Girls

Name of pupil	Modified pull ups ages 10-17; 8			Sit ups ages 10-17; 10			Squat thrust ages 10-17; 3			Remarks*
	1st test		Retest	1st test		Retest	1st test		Retest	
	Pass	Fail	Date passed	Pass	Fail	Date passed	Pass	Fail	Date passed	

*Enter here any conditions, e.g., obesity, posture, etc., that may affect physical performance.

Fig. 15-3. (Courtesy Guymon Junior High School, Guymon, Okla.)

nesses. When a teacher is able to offer this personal attention to each student and can suggest exercises and methods of improvement, the boy or girl consciously puts forth effort to improve.

Group guidance in the general aspects of physical fitness should also be included in the instructional program through a unit of study. For girls, stress should be placed on proper posture and good body mechanics in daily activities—that is, in standing, sitting, walking, lifting, carrying books, studying, and so on. By appealing to the girls' desire to be attractive and to develop balance, grace, and poise in movement, the teacher may motivate these students toward improved fitness. A unit for boys should stress increasing their achievement levels in strength, endurance, flexibility, accuracy, balance, and other physical traits. In this way they, too, are motivated toward improving physical fitness. A successfully taught unit should have carryover value not only into daily life but also into college and later years, by developing a wholesome attitude toward fitness and its importance in effective living.

Guidance in physical fitness should not only be included as a unit of study for students but should also be emphasized in each class in the *daily* instructional program. The value of daily calisthenics and warm-up exercises should be stressed in terms of their role in developing physical fitness. A study comparing the physical fitness of Japanese children to boys and girls in Iowa showed that Tokyo children scored higher in nearly all motor performance tests. Furthermore, it was shown that Japanese students had longer and more frequent physical education classes in which to develop these skills.[4] Students in this country must recognize the importance of daily workouts for developing and maintaining a high level of performance in physical fitness activities. Guidance of this kind is of utmost importance to students while in school, for then in later years, as they organize themselves for adulthood, exercise will form an integral part of daily living.

Testing. Testing should be a regular part of the total physical education program, and testing for physical fitness should be included as one phase of evaluation. The materials for testing different components of physical fitness are extensive. Many of the established tests have been developed for men because of the emphasis on physical training necessary for the armed services, but some are suitable for use with boys in secondary schools. A few tests have

been adapted for girls and have comparative norms that are valuable in the secondary school program. One of the best tests for both boys and girls is the Physical Fitness Test Battery developed by the American Association for Health, Physical Education, and Recreation. The motivational and educational value of these tests should be recognized here, however, for they are definitely a vital teaching technique for physical fitness.

Discussion. Students in secondary school should have an opportunity to discuss various aspects of physical fitness as part of their instructional program. Related problems such as dieting, relaxation, and menstruation are topics that arouse much interest in girls. Narcotics and alcohol studies provide excellent learning possibilities for both boys and girls. Special studies in these and similar subjects related to physical fitness in everyday life should be a regular part of the instructional program.

Assignments. Homework assignments on fitness that are coordinated with the regular instructional program should be given. These assignments may be in the form of improving performance of particular physical fitness exercises such as push-ups or sit-ups, or they may be in the form of readings related to this particular subject. Studying about young girls and boys who have accomplished unusual feats in athletics is both interesting and inspiring to adolescents. In schools using teaching teams, wherein students have an opportunity to do independent research, this topic of physical fitness may well be a personal assignment.

The senior author of this book has recently written a physical education textbook for high school students, entitled *Physical Education for Life.* It devotes considerable space to the subject of physical fitness and how it can be developed and maintained.

Other techniques. In order to emphasize physical fitness in the instructional program, there are a few supplementary techniques that are particularly helpful. The use of audiovisual aids is an excellent way to stimulate student interest. Bulletin boards, performance charts, exceptional records, and similar devices serve as reminders when displayed prominently. In addition, having the students conduct drills and take turns in leading the class allows an unforgettable personal experience in promoting physical fitness. Of most importance, however, is making physical fitness enjoyable, for when students see that activities are fun, they will profit more fully from the instructional program.

Materials for teaching and testing physical fitness

At the present time the quantity of materials for teaching physical fitness continues to increase as a result of nationwide interest, fostered by the President's Council on Physical Fitness and Sports, and increased emphasis on health status, drugs, and medical care. Physical educators have found greater interest in and reception for their programs among parents and lay people and have found it an ideal time to expand and extend their programs and facilities.

There is a wealth of material presently available to teachers for use in physical education classes. Following are some of the better-known physical fitness test batteries and exercise programs that have been developed recently as part of the campaign for fitness.

1. *Youth Physical Fitness*—suggested elements of a school-centered program, President's Council on Youth Fitness, July, 1961, Superintendent of Documents, Washington, D. C. 40¢.

Part One—A discussion of the current concept and foundations of physical fitness programs, including suggested standards for instruction and complementary programs.

Part Two—Suggested tests and activities and developmental exercises for boys and girls, grades 4 to 12. Standards for different age levels are included with suggested test items, all of which have been adapted from the AAHPER test.

2. *Youth Fitness Test Manual*, American Association for Health, Physical Education, and Recreation, Washington, D. C., 1965, $1.00.

This booklet contains explanations for the administration of seven suggested test items, together with percentile scores for boys and girls at different age levels.

The Association has also developed record forms for this testing program, and special awards and emblems that may be presented to participating students.

3. *Vim*—A complete exercise plan for girls 12 to 18 years of age, and

4. *Vigor*—A complete exercise plan for boys 12 to 18 years of age, President's Council on Physical Fitness, May, 1964, Superintendent of Documents, Washington, D. C., 25¢ each.

These booklets contain helpful hints and facts about fitness for youngsters and include a daily exercise plan suitable for them to follow.

5. *Adult Physical Fitness*—A program for men and women, President's Council on Physical Fitness, Superintendent of Documents, Washington, D. C., 35¢.

This is an adult program for home exercising with which the teacher should be familiar.

6. *Royal Canadian Air Force Exercise Plans for Physical Fitness*—5BX, for men; 10BX, for women, Queen's Printer and Controller of Stationery, Ottawa, Canada, Revised, 1962, $1.00.

This, too, is an adult home exercise plan with which the teacher should be familiar.

7. *Physical Fitness for Girls*, by William Hillcourt, and

8. *Physical Fitness for Boys*, by William Hillcourt, A *Golden Magazine* Special, New York, 1967, Golden Press, Inc., $1.00.

There are many other materials available in the area of physical fitness. Many state departments of education have developed their own testing instruments (California, Oregon, Washington, Iowa, Virginia, New York), as have some cities (Tucson, Denver, Omaha, Louisville, Kansas City). A movie entitled *Why Physical Education?** which has been produced for use in junior and senior high schools, discusses physical fitness and total fitness as the goal of physical education programs.

Other new films and materials related to physical fitness are listed below.

Films

Girls Are Better Than Ever (13½ min.) Free
Modern Talking Picture Service
1212 Avenue of the Americas, New York, N. Y. 10036

Time of Our Lives (27 min.) Free
Associated Films, Inc.
600 Madison Avenue, New York, N. Y. 10022

Badhe Chalo (11 min.) Express postage collect
Information Service of India
Film Section
3 East 64th Street, New York, N. Y. 10021

**Why Physical Education?* 16 mm., sound and color, 14 minutes, $150.00, produced by Wexler Film Productions, available from Henk Newenhouse, Inc., 1017 Longaker Road, Northbrook, Ill.

Rhythmic Ball Exercises (1966) (13 min.) Free
Embassy of Finland
Press Section
1900 Twenty-fourth St. N. W., Washington,
D. C. 20008
Physically Fit (Don Schollander) (4½ min.) Free
Modern Talking Picture Service
(As above)
Focus on Fitness (19 min.) Free
Eastman Kodak Co.
Audio-Visual Service
343 State Street, Rochester, N. Y. 14650

Materials	Single price	Per 100
Adolescent Years		
As Others See Us	$.15	$.08
How Teens Set the Stage for Smoking	.10	.02
Why Girls Menstruate	.10	.02
Fitness		
Physical Fitness	$.05	.02
Exercise and Fitness	.05	.02
Safeguarding the Health of the Athlete	.05	.02
Seven Paths to Fitness	.10	.02
Tips of Athletic Training (vols. I-VI)	.05	.02

American Medical Association, 535 N. Dearborn St., Chicago, Ill. 60610

The physical fitness checklist included here is another helpful educational tool for teachers interested in this type of material for their students.

Chapter 17 contains other movies and records, listed according to manufacturers, which may be useful in the area of physical fitness. The bibliography at the end of this chapter includes several new booklets, pamphlets, and articles that provide much helpful information. It should be noted here that the American Association for Health, Physical Education, and Recreation is an excellent source for all kinds of supplementary materials on fitness, as is the President's Council on Physical Fitness and Sports. Teachers should also investigate their own state departments of education, for not only have testing programs been initiated from their offices but also publications on courses of study, programs, and clinic suggestions.

A physical fitness checklist

Medical aspects   Yes No
  1. Thorough dental and health examination each year ___ ___
    a. Fit heart and circulatory system, digestive system, nervous system, etc. ___ ___
    b. Proper body development, according to age and sex (height and weight, etc.) ___ ___
  2. Correction of remediable health defects, i.e., vision, hearing, overweight, etc. ___ ___

Physical activity
  1. At least 1½ to 2 hours a day spent in vigorous physical activity, preferably outdoors ___ ___
  2. Adequate muscular strength and endurance* ___ ___
  3. After running 50 yards, heart and breathing return to normal rates within 10 minutes ___ ___
  4. Average skill in running, jumping, climbing, and throwing ___ ___
  5. Control of body in activities involving balance, agility, speed, rhythm, accuracy ___ ___
  6. Skill in recreational activities, i.e., arts and crafts, bowling, dancing ___ ___

Posture
  1. When student is standing upright, string dropped from tip of ear passes through shoulder and hip joints and middle of ankle. ___ ___
  2. When student is sitting in a chair, trunk and head are erect, weight balanced over pelvis, or trunk slightly bent forward. ___ ___
  3. When student is walking, slumping is avoided, body is in proper balance, and excessively wasteful motions of arms and legs are eliminated. ___ ___

Health habits
  1. Rest: at least 8 hours of sleep each night ___ ___
  2. Diet: four servings daily from each of the four basic food groups ___ ___
    a. Meat, poultry, fish, and eggs
    b. Dairy products
    c. Vegetables and fruits
    d. Bread and cereals
  3. Cleanliness
    a. Daily bath ___ ___
    b. Teeth brushed after every meal ___ ___
    c. Clean hair, nails, and clothing ___ ___
  4. Abstain from use of tobacco and alcohol ___ ___

Isometrics

Recently, widespread attention has been focused on isometrics, an exercise system developing one particular facet of physical fitness—strength. Physical education teachers should understand the principle behind

---

*The school health or physical education teacher can help to determine proper standards.

isometrics and recognize its values and limitations, in order to place isometrics in its proper perspective within the physical education program.

Definition. Isometrics is a series of exercises designed to develop strength in particular muscle groups. In isometrics muscle groups are contracted against an immovable force, or resistance, and "held tight" before relaxing after a count of six to ten. The tension produced in the muscles increases their strength through this isometric contraction. Isometric contractions should not be confused with isotonic, or dynamic, contractions, in which the muscle groups work against a resistant force that is overcome, as in weight lifting.

Values. An important value of isometric exercise is conditioning. Through daily application of isometrics, muscles learn to work efficiently and effectively in performance of activity. It is believed that increased muscular strength improves speed, power, and flexibility, all of which are important components of body conditioning and fitness. For this reason, isometrics has gained in popularity not only in school programs but also in amateur and professional athletics as well.* It is important, however, to evaluate carefully the equipment and literature that are flooding the market on isometrics.

Isometric exercises are also valuable in a corrective, or remedial, program of physical education. Whenever a student has identifiable weakness in specific muscle groups, such as arm and shoulder muscles, isometric routines are particularly helpful.

Limitations. Certain limitations exist in the isometric program of exercise when it is

applied to a school program of physical education. As has been previously stated, the value of isometrics lies in meeting *individual* needs for strengthening and conditioning. In large physical education classes it would be very difficult to individualize this program sufficiently for instructional purposes.

Furthermore, while students may become motivated at first with this new approach to exercising, enthusiasm may soon be lost if no tangible results are seen. Dynamometers, machines that measure strength, are not standard equipment in most schools, and students may not recognize their actual progress without them.

Also, emphasis should not be placed merely on isometrics to the exclusion of other physical fitness objectives. Isometrics, like weight lifting, has specific values that should be utilized whenever possible, within the limits of proper programming for physical fitness.

OUT-OF-CLASS PROGRAM

The noninstructional program, which includes all activities held outside the regularly scheduled physical education class, is equally important to the promotion of physical fitness. The intramural and extramural activities, clubs, demonstrations, contests, and other activities all serve to focus student attention on physical pursuits.

Intramural activities

The intramural program should be available to as many students as possible. By providing an interesting and exciting program of intraclass games in a wide variety of sports and in an atmosphere in which all students believe their participation is welcome, the teacher is able to increase the overall interest in physical fitness and skills.

Extramural activities

A program of interscholastic competition serves to heighten the interest of boys and girls, and their efforts to make the honor

---

*Some manufacturers have even developed special exercise kits, charts, and handbooks of isometrics. Ideas, Inc., Box 730, Isometric Division, 118 Grand Ave., Laramie, Wyo.; and American Fitness Programs, 212 Gilmer, Johnson City, Tenn., are only two of several sources, and many new books are being published on this subject, one of which is Wallis, Earl L., and Logan, Gene A.: Isometric exercises, Englewood Cliffs, N. J., 1964, Prentice-Hall, Inc. The senior author's book, *Physical Education for Life,* lists many excellent isometric and isotonic exercises for high school boys and girls.

squads or varsity teams induce improvement in physical fitness at the same time.

Clubs

There are several clubs that may be sponsored by the physical education department to provide benefits for physical fitness. The cheerleaders, baton twirlers, and drill team, and the gymnastics, tumbling, cycling, and physical fitness clubs all require many attributes of physical fitness for performance. The avid interest that many students have in these types of activities should be developed. Leaders clubs and modern dance groups also have a definite part in the physical education program, and membership should be open to all interested students.

Demonstrations

Public demonstrations and performances of club activities, such as those of the modern dance group, not only improve the physical fitness of participants but also serve to increase the interest in and appreciation of these activities.

Contests and campaigns

Sometimes a special contest or campaign to promote good posture or a similar component of physical fitness is an excellent technique for arousing and enhancing interest. Student planning as well as participation in such events should be fostered to gain the most value from them.

Organizations

Organizations such as an athletic association, Hi-Y, or scouting and explorer troops may serve to promote fitness both among its members and on a school-wide basis as well.

Outings

Field trips, clinics, and outdoor camping expeditions are very popular with students, and they provide fitness experiences not otherwise available. The physical education teacher should try to sponsor such events whenever feasible.

Awards

For students who have shown much improvement or have performed exceptionally well in specific areas of physical fitness, a ribbon or small award may be presented. The American Association for Health, Physical Education, and Recreation has special awards and certificates that may be given in connection with the ad-

Fig. 15-4. Cheerleaders club. (White Plains High School, White Plains, N. Y.)

Fig. 15-5. Outdoor camping expedition builds physical fitness. (San Diego County Schools, San Diego, Calif.)

ministration of their physical fitness test, as previously mentioned.

Cosponsored activities

Much interest can be stimulated with coeducational activities sponsored by both the boys' and the girls' departments or with special events sponsored cooperatively with community organizations. The local Dads Club or Chamber of Commerce is generally interested in physical fitness activities and willingly conducts field days, contests, and sports days. The physical education teachers should work with the leaders of these organizations to ensure proper management and supervision for the benefit of the students.

POINTS TO REMEMBER

1. The physical fitness goal of physical education requires special emphasis because of increased national concern in this area.
2. The instructional program of physical education should be geared to physical fitness through methods of teaching that include appraisal and guidance.
3. The additional teaching techniques of testing and assignments should stress physical fitness in the instructional program.
4. The noninstructional program should em-

phasize fitness through its many components.
5. Students in secondary school need to be guided in physical fitness to become aware of its importance to everyday living.
6. Students need to realize the individuality of physical fitness and should understand their own personal requirements in this area.

PROBLEMS TO THINK THROUGH

1. How can the results of the appraisal of physical fitness be most effectively used for the benefit of the students?
2. In a community that sponsors few recreational programs, how may the physical education department of the secondary school promote community-wide interest in physical fitness activities?
3. The administration of a secondary school is disturbed about students smoking on school property, contrary to regulations. Students and some members of the community are in favor of a student smoking lounge. In what ways may the physical education department combat this trend?
4. In a small secondary school there is only one teacher of girls' physical education and one teacher for the boys. Activities after school are therefore limited to the supervision and facilities available to these two instructors.

How may an adequate intramural program be set up that would promote physical fitness for the greatest number of students?

5. What methods may be used to improve physical fitness in students scoring low on appraisal?

6. In what ways may individual personal guidance be offered to students needing special attention in physical fitness work?

CASE STUDY FOR ANALYSIS

The physical education department in a large secondary school plans to promote a year-long campaign for physical fitness, not only for students in the school but also for the community-at-large. The administration has approved the idea and offered some financial assistance to back their campaign. What steps would the staff take in carrying out their campaign within the instructional program? In the noninstructional program? In the community? What special activities and events may be sponsored? In what ways may students become involved in the program?

EXERCISES FOR REVIEW

1. What are the advantages and disadvantages in running a physical fitness appraisal program more than once during a year?

2. What particular objectives should be established for a unit on physical fitness with eighth-grade girls? Boys?

3. What aspects of physical fitness should be stressed in team sports? Individual sports? Formal activities? Rhythms? Aquatics?

4. What exercises are particularly valuable for developing strength? Endurance? Flexibility? Balance? Other components of physical fitness?

5. What types of charts and diagrams would serve effectively to motivate students in physical fitness?

6. What current outside reading materials may be valuable homework for high school students?

7. In what ways may a leaders club assist the physical education teacher in testing and promoting physical fitness?

8. What types of awards would be appropriate for performances in physical fitness?

9. What topics for discussions in physical fitness would be of particular interest to high school girls? Boys? Both?

10. What are the advantages and disadvantages to choosing a "most physically fit" boy and girl?

REFERENCES

1. President's Council on Physical Fitness: Four years for fitness 1961-1965, a report to the President, Washington, D. C., 1965. U. S. Government Printing Office.

2. Wear, C. L., and Miller, Kenneth: Relationships between physique and developmental level to physical performance, Research Quarterly 33:4, Dec., 1962.

3. Espenschade, Anna S.: Restudy of relationships between physical performance of school children and age, height and weight, Research Quarterly 34:2, May, 1963.

4. Ikeda, Namiko: A comparison of physical fitness of Children in Iowa, U. S. A., and Tokyo, Japan, Research Quarterly 33:4, Dec., 1962.

SELECTED READINGS

American Association for Health, Physical Education, and Recreation: The growing years—adolescence, Fifth Yearbook, Washington, D. C., 1962, The Association.

American Association for Health, Physical Education, and Recreation: Fitness series, Washington, D. C., The Association.

Athletic Institute: Exercise and fitness, Chicago, 1962, The Institute.

Athletic Institute: Health and fitness in the modern world, Chicago, 1962, The Institute.

Bucher, Charles A.: Foundations of physical education, ed. 5, St. Louis, 1968, The C. V. Mosby Co.

Cureton, Thomas Kirk: Improving the physical fitness of youth, Monographs of the Society for Research in Child Development, Inc., Serial no. 95, Yellow Springs, Ohio, 1964, The Antioch Press.

President's Council on Physical Fitness: Adult physical fitness, Washington, D. C., U. S. Government Printing Office.

President's Council on Physical Fitness: Vigor, Washington, D. C., U. S. Government Printing Office.

President's Council on Physical Fitness: Vim, Washington, D. C., U. S. Government Printing Office.

President's Council on Physical Fitness: Youth physical fitness, Washington, D. C., U. S. Government Printing Office.

BOOKLETS, PAMPHLETS, AND ARTICLES

AMA and AAHPER Joint Committee on Exercise and Fitness: Health problems revealed during physical activity, Journal of Health, Physical Education, and Recreation 37:6, Sept., 1967.

Bender, Jay A., Kaplan, Harold M., and Pierson, Joy K.: Injury control through isometrics and isotonics, Journal of Health, Physical Education, and Recreation 38:26, Feb., 1967.

Brooks, Betty Willis: Views of physical fitness from four educational philosophies, The Physical Educator **24**:31, March, 1967.

Collins, George J.: Physical achievements and the schools, bulletin 1965, no. 13, Office of Education, U. S. Department of Health, Education, and Welfare.

Cooper, Kenneth H.: How to feel fit at any age, Reader's Digest, March, 1968.

Doherty, J. Kenneth: The nature of endurance in running, Journal of Health, Physical Education, and Recreation **35**:29, April, 1964.

Flint, Marilyn M.: Selecting exercises, Journal of Health, Physical Education, and Recreation **35**:19, Feb., 1964.

Hillcourt, William: Physical fitness for girls, New York, 1967, Golden Press, Inc.

Hillcourt, William: Physical fitness for boys, New York, 1967, Golden Press, Inc.

Hunsicker, Paul A., and Reiff, Guy G.: A survey and comparison of youth fitness, 1958-1965, Journal of Health, Physical Education, and Recreation **37**:23, Jan., 1966.

Marshall, James W., and McAdam, Robert E.: A buddy plan of active resistance exercise, Journal of Health, Physical Education, and Recreation **35**:76, March, 1964.

McCarthy, Jean: Fitness for activity, The Physical Educator **22**:154, Dec., 1965.

Pennington, G.: Fitness honor roll, The Physical Educator **21**:173, Dec., 1964.

Ponthieux, N. A., and Barker, D. G.: Relationship between socioeconomic status and physical fitness measures, The Research Quarterly **36**:464, Dec., 1965.

Ponthieux, N. A., and Barker, D. G.: Relationship between race and physical fitness, The Research Quarterly **36**:468, Dec., 1965.

Rosenstein, Irwin, and Frost, Reuben B.: Physical fitness of senior high school boys and girls participating in selected physical education programs in New York State, The Research Quarterly **35**:403, Oct., 1964.

Steinhaus, Arthur H.: Fitness beyond muscle, The Physical Educator **23**:103, Oct., 1966.

Weiss, Raymond A.: Is physical fitness our most important objective? Journal of Health, Physical Education, and Recreation **35**:18, Feb., 1964.

Yarnall, C. Douglas: Relationship of physical fitness to selected measures of popularity, The Research Quarterly **37**:286, May, 1966.

16

Methods and materials
for
movement education

The traditional curricula of our secondary schools are currently being challenged by the students they serve. These traditional curricula are gradually being replaced by innovative and flexible educational experiences that attempt to meet the real needs of the students. The new focus in secondary education is on individual creativity and individualized learning. Some subject areas of the secondary school curriculum utilize teaching machines and other technological hardware in an attempt to individualize the learning experience. These technological advances have helped to create many changes in the methodology of teaching. Physical education has not resisted these changes. Secondary school physical education programs are emphasizing the individual through comprehensive instruction in the lifetime sports and through a renewed concentration on all phases of the creative-expressive activities, such as dance and gymnastics. This increased awareness of the individual and of the individual's creativity has made education for movement a vital part of the newly developing curricula in physical education.

THE ORIGINS OF MOVEMENT EDUCATION

Movement education has been misunderstood, misinterpreted, and at times misused within physical education programs in the United States. Movement education is not a recent development, nor is it synonymous with dance. Movement education has been a part of physical education curricula in English schools for many years and is closely aligned with the *movement exploration concepts* integral to dance. Movement education as a foundational phase of the physical education curriculum can be traced historically to the theories of the dancer Rudolf Laban. After fleeing Germany for England during World War II, Laban established an Art of Movement Center bearing his name. Like the kinesiologists, Laban was a student of human movement. He believed that each individual possesses inherent natural movements, and felt that through rigid and formal exercises man loses his ability to move freely and easily. Conversely, Laban said, experiences in spontaneous and exploratory movement would help individuals to reach their potential for efficient and effective movement through increased kinesthetic awareness.

Prior to World War II, physical education in English schools stressed formal gymnastics. During World War II England revised both its educational philosophy and its educational structure. Courses and teaching methodology were updated, and education for movement was made the central focus of physical education programs. English children are educated in movement from the earliest school years. When the concepts of the movement education approach to physical education reached the United States in the late 1950's, they were first inserted into basic instructional programs for women on the college level. Frequently, courses entitled "Movement Education" bore little resemblance either to Laban's principles or to the movement education methodology developed in England. Rather, these first attempts to educate for movement were closely correlated with the objectives, techniques, and methodologies associated with existing courses called "Body Mechanics," "Movement Fundamentals," or similar titles. These early courses in programs for college women used movement as a tool primarily to reeducate the body. The system of movement education as developed in England uses the body as a tool for enhanced motor skill development, beginning with the natural movements of childhood as the foundation for all bodily movement.

Since 1960, many articles and books have been written and published in the United States that focus directly on movement education. Research is being conducted, and several pilot programs in elementary schools are well under way. Through these media, professionals are developing an understanding of movement education and its proper application within physical education curricula in the schools of the United States. Further, a corps of experts in the specialized area of movement education is being developed, and these individuals are giving freely of their knowledge and experience to other physical educators. At the present time, these advances are helping to make movement education one of the most significant new trends in the field of physical education.

WHAT IS MOVEMENT EDUCATION?

Everything an individual does involves bodily movement of some sort. Movement

Fig. 16-1. Movement education has great potential for enhancing human physical performance. (Walt Whitman High Schools, South Huntington Schools, New York.)

education attempts to help the individual to become mentally as well as physically aware of these movements. Thus, movement education is based on a conceptual approach to human movement. That is, the better able the individual is to mentally understand a movement pattern, the easier it will be for him to develop physical skills. For example, softball is frequently a popular team sport taught on the secondary school level. Many girls and some boys never develop the mental ability to throw well because physical errors in the position of the throwing arm only, or errors in foot position only, are corrected at the teacher's suggestion. Through movement education, the position of each body segment in relation to the whole body is perceived by the student intellectually before the physical skill is attempted. When the student is intellectually aware of the position of his body as an entity, rather than considering his body to be made up of independent segments, physical skill learning is enhanced.

The experts do not agree on a single definition for movement education. They do agree, however, that movement education is dependent on physical factors in the environment and on the individual's ability to intellectually and physically react to these factors. Through movement education, the individual develops his own techniques for dealing with the environmental factors of force, time, space, and flow as they relate to various movement problems. The mental and physical skill development of the individual is of prime concern to the movement educator, rather than the common skill development of an entire class or group.

THE UNIQUENESS OF MOVEMENT EDUCATION

How does the methodology of movement education differ from the traditional methodology of physical education? As much as physical education has traditionally been taught through structured classes, classes in movement education are also structured.

It may seem that movement education is nothing more than a haphazard approach to traditional physical education in relation to skill teaching and learning, but this is far from the case. In many instances, movement education classes involve a more highly structured approach and demand more of the teacher in regard to concrete philosophy, sound objectives, logical progressions, and understanding of proper techniques and methodology, as well as creative ability.

Movement education employs the problem-solving approach. Each skill that is to be explored presents a challenge to the student. Learning results as the student accepts and solves increasingly more difficult problems. For this reason, the natural movements of childhood are considered to be the first challenges that should be presented to the student. Movement educators feel that adult problems in physical skill performance are the result of poor habits developed in early childhood. While most children spend their preschool years in uninhibited running, jumping, leaping, climbing, twisting and other such vigorous activities, it is pointed out that these movements eventually become stereotyped. Children do not, on their own, explore a variety of movement patterns. Through movement education, the child is encouraged to walk or run or otherwise move at different speeds, in different directions, and on different levels. He is encouraged to exploit physical obstacles, such as an inclined plane or even another person, and to incorporate them into his own unique movement patterns. The child gains confidence and enjoyment in the use of his entire body for movement, and begins to develop an intellectual understanding of the capabilities of his body and how they differ from the capabilities of the bodies of others. These understandings, developed as physical skill develops, helps to form a basis for more efficient and effective physical movement in later years.

Traditional physical education emphasizes the learning of specific skills through

Fig. 16-2. Traditional physical education emphasizes the learning of specific skills through demonstration, drill, and practice. (Left, Mount Pleasant Senior High School, Wilmington, Dela.; right, Peabody Demonstration School, George Peabody College for Teachers, Nashville, Tenn.)

demonstration, drill, and practice. Movement education emphasizes the learning of skill patterns through individual exploration of the body's movement potential. These two approaches to skill learning are not in opposition to each other. Movement education does not supplant learning that takes place in traditional physical education programs. Movement education does help the student to develop a better foundation for the learning of the more sophisticated skills. Education in movement is the first step in becoming a physically educated person.

THE PLACE OF MOVEMENT EDUCATION IN THE PHYSICAL EDUCATION CURRICULUM

In the English schools, movement education begins in the first grade and is the sole vehicle through which physical education is taught in the elementary schools. In English secondary schools, girls continue to be educated in movement, but this is interwoven with the learning of specific sport skills. Secondary school boys concentrate on learning specific sports skills taught by traditional methods. However, both the boys and the girls have acquired a sound understanding of movement, and this knowledge facilitates their motor skill learning and performance.

Movement education teaches proper use of the body as a tool for movement. It is not concerned with the rules of specific sports and games, with the strategy involved in playing a game, or with teaching the mechanics of playing, for example, first base in softball or center in basketball. These areas of knowledge are the province of traditional methodology. Through movement education the student discovers the leverage, balance, force, and speed required to kick a soccer ball, dribble a basketball, execute a forward roll, or throw a softball. Through traditional physical education, the student learns the applications of these and other skills.

Particularly on the secondary school level, we find boys and girls who do not perform physical skills well. They may lack confidence, or they may not be motivated to perform well simply because they have never experienced the satisfaction of a well-performed skill. These uncoordinated boys and girls may be physically capable of a good performance but may not intellectually understand the physical criteria of a good performance. These students need to be educated and/or reeducated in movement.

Movement education should be an ongoing part of physical education curricula. It should not be used as a short-term phase of the program inserted to bridge the change-over from indoor to outdoor seasons or to fill a gap of several lessons between different units of study. Movement education need not, on the secondary school level, fill an entire class period. It can be used during each class period to replace formal warm-ups or calesthenics. With careful and thoughtful planning on the part of the teacher, the principles of movement education can be used to introduce new sports skills or scientific concepts of skill performance, replacing demonstration and drill. In this way, teacher-directed learning can move toward student-conceptualized learning, thus enhancing not only the physical but the intellectual objectives of physical education programs. Through the movement education method, students perform as individuals, and their performance depends in a large degree on their creativity and problem-solving ability.

THE ROLE OF THE TEACHER IN MOVEMENT EDUCATION

In traditional physical education programs, the physical educator explains a skill, demonstrates it, and directs student drill and practice. The teacher corrects errors in performance as the students strive to perfect the skill in relation to what they have seen and been told. The movement educator does none of these things.

A movement educator sets the problems and challenges for his students, guides the students through a thinking process, observes their attempts at solving the problem, and asks questions and stimulates their thinking through discussions of the problem. The movement educator improvises unique equipment where needed and avoids demonstrating or using formal patterns of class organization, such as circles, lines, or rows.

Whereas the physical educator sets the standards for the performance of a particular skill, the movement educator helps each student to become motivated to perform at his own peak of ability. Whereas the physical educator evaluates a student on the performance of a skill, the movement educator asks each student to evaluate his own performance and suggest his own ideas on how he can improve his performance. Whereas the physical educator tells a student that his headstand is unsteady because his head and hands are too closely aligned, and shows the student the proper alignment, the movement educator asks the student to suggest how he might change the alignment of his body parts to stabilize his headstand. In this way, the student may attempt several unsatisfactory alignments before discovering the most stable one, but he will intellectually understand the physical adjustments he has made. This understanding will transfer to other skill learnings. The movement educator guides his students toward success by helping them to evaluate their own performance and by providing encouragement to each student as he or she seeks to solve a problem in movement.

Where traditional physical education methodology is speech-centered, movement education is activity-centered. The movement educator employs a problem-solving approach and allows the individual student to use his creativity to solve the problem. The movement educator neither dictates a solution to a problem in movement nor demonstrates the performance of a skill. Because there can be no stereotyping of a performance or imitation of the teacher's

Fig. 16-3. Movement education is activity-centered.

performance, the student is free to establish his own most comfortable movement patterns. The student is guided into using his body as the prime tool for movement rather than conceiving of his body as a force to be overcome before movement can take place.

MOVEMENT EDUCATION IN THE SECONDARY SCHOOL

Secondary school students can reap the benefits of movement education experiences whether or not they have been exposed to this method in the elementary school. Movement education lends itself to all phases of the physical education curriculum on all levels and can be adapted to use with all activities. The modification and adaptation of method will seem far stranger to the physical educator than to the student.

It would be difficult, if not impossible, to revert to the use of the natural activities of childhood in a secondary school situation. However, movement education can be employed on this level to introduce new skills, and it can be tailored to help in correcting performance errors in familiar skills. Further, most secondary schools offer units in dance. Dance and movement education depend both on the creativity of the individual and on his use of his body in relation to the time, space, force, and flow of a move-

ment or series of movements. Both dance and movement education are often described as systems of nonverbal communication.

The techniques and methods peculiar to movement education are suited to use with secondary school boys and girls alike. If a unit in soccer is being introduced and the dribble or pass is to be learned, the teacher may ask his students to discover on their own how many different ways they can use their feet, with the exception of the toe, to propel the ball. The students are then given ample time to explore this problem. The teacher circulates from student to student, observing their progress. If the teacher should discover that a student persistently contacts the ball with only one foot, he will ask a question that will help the student to discover not only that he can use both feet but that there are advantages to be gained from doing so. At the end of the exploratory period, the teacher will call his students together and ask several of them to demonstrate the techniques they have discovered. Student evaluations and suggestions will be elicited, with the teacher guiding the discussion through questions. After this brief period, the teacher may ask the students to attempt to find out how they can keep the ball in motion while maintaining control of it. A third problem for the same class period may involve a problem in passing the ball back and forth with a partner over an increasing distance, while a final problem may be concerned with asking the students to discover how they can stop a rolling ball using their feet and legs only. Student demonstrations and discussions would follow each problem-solving period of the class time, and the class would be concluded by using these newly discovered skills in a teacher-created lead-up game. The use of relays would not be suitable since they emphasize competition between groups rather than focusing on the achievement of the individual.

The movement education approach also lends itself to apparatus activities. Freedom of use and movement on equipment, with appropriate regard to safety, can precede problems in mounting, using the piece of apparatus, and dismounting. This approach gives each student an opportunity to succeed, since no specific movement patterns are required or demanded. In teaching the use of the trampoline, for example, an initial problem might be to move across the trampoline in any way the students desire. Some may roll across, some may choose to bounce across, and others will go on all fours, while still others will create their own unique method. All these methods deserve teacher praise for a problem correctly solved. From this beginning, students may be asked to find out in how many different ways they can bounce on the bed of the trampoline. Through exploration and student demonstrations and discussions, use of the arms and legs for control and height will be understood and perfected, leading to the learning of the proper use of, and skills unique to, the trampoline. Skill learning will thus have been guided by the teacher, but the skills will have been discovered by the students themselves.

These two examples show how movement education can be used on the secondary school level to introduce new skills. Movement education can also be used effectively to perfect and improve performance in skills that have been learned previously. The physical educator begins with the observation stage and has the student suggest how he can improve his performance through the exploration of a variety of new stances, positions, or techniques.

Movement education on the secondary school level is an invaluable tool for use with the student who does nothing well in physical education. By being encouraged to explore skills rather than having to mimic stylized patterns, this student can attain a measure of success and become motivated to proceed and progress at his own pace.

Those secondary school students who have been educated in movement in their secondary school years will benefit from a continuation of this training. Further, they can be of inestimable aid to the secondary school physical educator who wishes to teach skills through the principles of movement education in situations where a majority of students have had no prior movement education experiences.

Movement education is not a panacea that will make a highly skilled performer out of a student who is poorly skilled. It does offer a means through which the physical educator can assist the student in forming an intellectual concept of the skill to be performed or perfected. When corrections or adjustments are verbalized or demonstrated by the physical educator, the student need only attempt to mimic the physical movements, often totally disregarding any intellectual understandings that underlie the physical act.

Individual analysis of problem-solving situations is the basis for movement education. Rather than telling or showing students how to perform, the teacher guides the students through a series of possible responses as they seek solutions that are individually appropriate. In traditional physical education, the teacher is a director, commander, and evaluator, while in movement education, the teacher is a questioner, a guide, and an observer.

The high school boy and girl will find

Fig. 16-4. Movement education can be used on the secondary school level to improve performance in skills. (Left, Peabody Demonstration School, George Peabody College for Teachers, Nashville, Tenn.; right, Spartanburg Public Schools, Spartanburg, S. C.)

the senior author's new textbook, *Physical Education for Life,* an informative resource on movement education. The basis of physical movement and how it can be applied to physical activities are discussed in detail in this book.

STUDENT EVALUATIONS IN MOVEMENT EDUCATION

In traditional teaching methodology in physical education, the teacher sets the standards for the performance and evaluates student performance in relation to these standards. In the movement education approach to teaching physical education, standards may be applied to a skill performance, but the ways in which these standards are attained are quite different.

Every student in a movement education program sets his own goals, but because the students are reacting as individuals, they are not only directing their own learning but disciplining their learning as well. A skilled performance is thus judged not by a single standard for an entire class but by a series of standards that reflects the individual standards and differences of each of the members of the class. The physical education class becomes a laboratory experience in which the student is not only encouraged, but given the freedom, to test a variety of solutions to a performance problem before arriving at his personal answer to that problem. When a student is given such experiences, the satisfactions gained from a successful performance help to motivate him to accept increasingly more difficult performance challenges. Each student can experience success because each solution attempted is a step toward the personal goals set by the student. The movement education approach helps to eliminate the fear of failure and of ostracism or criticism for failure to meet a common standard. Students achieve on their own level and derive fun and satisfaction from their physical education experience.

Evaluations in movement education can be achieved objectively and realistically. Program objectives will be student-centered and student-achieved. For each activity within the physical education class program, including the team, dual, and individual sports and activities, and physical fitness and dance units, there can be a

Table 15. A progressive program

Area	Elementary	Junior high school	Senior high school
I. For developing skills	To develop movements necessary for basic sports skills (run, throw, catch)	To extend areas of basic skills in a wide variety of activities	To perfect techniques and capacities in basic skills
II. For physical skills	To understand basic components of physical fitness	To increase physical fitness levels through continued movement experiences	To improve and maintain physical fitness levels through movement experiences
III. For creative expression	To provide opportunity to respond freely to a variety of stimuli	To provide opportunity to experiment with many complex movements	To innovate and create new movements and new experiences
IV. For communicative experiences	To provide imaginative and dramatic opportunities	To provide more complex ideas for communication in terms of time, space, force	To innovate and create new relationships with environment
V. For understanding scientific principles	To understand basic function of balance and gravity	To develop greater understanding of forces of gravity in relation to static and dynamic movement	To understand physical laws governing motion, force, and balance as they apply to movement

movement education approach. Within this framework, student progress can be measured on an individual basis in a cooperative student-teacher effort. Written tests concerned with intellectual understanding of the scientific principles of skill performance can be employed. Physical skill tests designed to measure individual achievement, as well as physical fitness tests, can also be applied to the evaluative process. Students on the secondary school level are capable of self-evaluation through student-teacher conferences. By combining these and other methods, a truer and more meaningful evaluation of each student's progress toward becoming a physically educated person can be derived. Total involvement of the student in all phases of the program will serve to enhance not only student achievement but the accomplishment of the program objectives as well.

MOVEMENT EDUCATION AND THE EXTRA-CLASS PROGRAM

Movement educators avoid group competition on the elementary school level. On that level, the student competes with himself to improve his own performance and understanding of it. Games are used, but the competitive aspects are eliminated as much as possible. Games are a means through which newly learned skills can be practiced and correct performance reinforced.

On the secondary school level, competition is a necessary part of many traditional programs. Students enjoy competition, and it serves as a stimulus to them. Within the regular class program, where movement education is employed, sports and games can be played competitively as soon as the students are satisfied that they have achieved sufficient skill ability to enjoy competition.

Intramural programs should be open to all students in a school. Participation in an intramural program should precede a student's membership on an interscholastic or varsity team. The movement education approach used in the class program will help each student to become more aware of the value of participating in sports and games of his own choosing outside the class program requirements. Students will also better understand the qualities needed for membership on the more highly competitive teams. Movement education programs help to complement and supplement the extra-class offerings of secondary school physical education programs.

POINTS TO REMEMBER

1. Movement education is a significant new approach to teaching secondary school physical education.
2. Movement education frees the individual student to work and progress at his own pace.
3. Movement education helps the student to better understand the physical laws that govern human movement.
4. Opportunities for creative expression and exploration are an invaluable aspect of movement education.
5. Physical skills are developed through an individualized problem-solving technique.

PROBLEMS TO THINK THROUGH

1. On what basis should a student be graded when the movement approach to teaching physical education is utilized?
2. Is the movement approach applicable for all the goals and objectives of physical education programs on the secondary school level?
3. Are movement education experiences equally vital for secondary school boys as well as girls?
4. Does the movement education approach offer a new means of motivating those secondary school students who are resistive to physical education?

CASE STUDY FOR ANALYSIS

A class of high school freshmen has scored low on initial physical fitness tests. The teacher has also observed that the students do not exhibit adequate levels of motor ability on a variety of skill tests. Intellectually, the class as a group expresses disinterest in and distaste for physical education. The first unit of instruction for these students will be track-and-field activities. How can the teacher interest and motivate these students as well as help them to improve their fitness scores and skill abilities?

EXERCISES FOR REVIEW

1. How does the problem-solving method of teaching help movement education to succeed?
2. In what ways can the area of dance contribute to movement education?
3. How does movement education correlate with traditional programs of physical education in secondary schools in the United States?
4. Compare the role of the teacher in traditional physical education with the teacher's role in movement education.
5. How can movement education help students to develop confidence in their skill performances?

REFERENCES

1. Allenbaugh, Naomi: Learning about movement, NEA Journal **56**:48, March, 1967.
2. Howard, Shirley: The movement education approach to teaching in English elementary schools, Journal of Health, Physical Education, and Recreation **38**:31, Jan., 1967.
3. Kleinman, Seymour: The significance of human movement: a phenomenological approach, NAPECW Report, p. 123, 1962.
4. NAPECW and NCPEAM, Quest, Monograph II, Tucson, Ariz., 1964.

SELECTED READINGS

Barrett, Kate R.: Exploration—a method for teaching movement, Madison, Wis., 1964, College Printing and Typing Co., Inc.
Broer, Marion R.: Efficiency of human movement, Philadelphia, 1966, W. B. Saunders Co.
Bucher, Charles A.: Foundations of physical education, ed. 5, St. Louis, 1968, The C. V. Mosby Co.
Bucher, Charles A.: Physical education for life, St. Louis, 1969, Webster Division, McGraw-Hill Book Co.
Cratty, Bryant: Movement behavior and motor learning, Philadelphia, 1964, Lea & Febiger, 1964.
Diem, Lieselott: Who can? Frankfort, Germany, 1962, Wilhelm Lempert, Publisher.
Hackett, Layne C., and Jenson, Robert G.: A guide to movement exploration, Palo Alto, Calif., 1966, Peek Publications.
Hoye, Anna Scott: Fundamentals of movement, Palo Alto, Calif., 1961, The National Press.
Schurr, Evelyn L.: Movement experiences for children, New York, 1967, Appleton-Century-Crofts.
Souder, Marjorie A., and Hill, Phyllis J.: Basic movement foundations of physical education, New York, 1963, The Ronald Press Co.
Torrance, E. Paul: Rewarding creative behavior, Englewood Cliffs, N. J., 1965, Prentice-Hall, Inc.

BOOKLETS, PAMPHLETS, AND ARTICLES

Boyd, Barbara, Cox, Gloria, Ghens, Carol, and Williams, Sandra: Whatever happened to basic movement skills? Journal of Health, Physical Education, and Recreation 37:21, May, 1966.

Cratty, Bryant J.: On the threshhold, Quest, Monograph VIII, Spring (May), 1967.

Estes, Nolan: Encouragement for innovation, NEA Journal 55:30, Dec., 1966.

Lemen, Mildred: Implications of the problem-solving method for physical educators, Journal of Health, Physical Education, and Recreation 37:28, March, 1966.

Little, Billy Jean: Creativity in physical education, The Physical Educator 24:75, May, 1967.

Locke, Lawrence F.: The movement movement, Journal of Health, Physical Education, and Recreation 37:26, Jan., 1966.

Oberteuffer, Delbert, Tillotson, Joan S., and Ulrich, Celeste: Dance as an art form, Journal of Health, Physical Education, and Recreation 35:19–21, Jan., 1964.

Torrance, E. Paul: Seven guides to creativity, Journal of Health, Physical Education, and Recreation 36:26, 1965.

Wagner, Ann: A basic concept of physical education, The Physical Educator 21:169, Dec., 1964.

Wyrick, Waneen: Purposes and usefulness of balls in creating rhythmic exercises, The Physical Educator 23:120, Oct., 1966.

chapter

17

Resources and materials
for teaching*

The use of teaching aids and materials is a method of teaching that supplements the learning process. Students who are not stimulated by other teaching methods may be motivated by films, charts, or other resource materials, and highly skilled students may broaden the scope of their knowledge by studying enrichment materials. Well-chosen teaching aids are of special value in teaching the culturally disadvantaged or other students whose formal experience with physical education has been limited. Acquaintance with the wealth of outside resources and information from which all members of a class may benefit is an invaluable aid in teaching, and the physical educator should make good use of such information.

In recent years considerable progress has been made in regard to teaching aids. The equipment and tools have been vastly improved and the resources and services greatly extended so that all schools may take advantage of these instructional materials.

In this chapter suggestions concerning valuable audiovisual aids, special aids, reading materials, outside resources, and sources of supplies are offered. The principles to be followed when using these mate-

rials are included at the beginning of the chapter to serve as a guide for the teacher in making proper use of them.

PRINCIPLES GOVERNING THE USE OF TEACHING AIDS AND MATERIALS

When selecting audiovisual aids or other resources and materials, the teacher of physical education should consider certain principles that make utilization of these aids effective and valuable. The similarity between these principles and those suggested in other methods of teaching should be noted, for the aim in each case is to create a worthwhile learning situation.

1. *Materials should be carefully selected and screened.* The teacher should preview the materials to make sure they are appropriate for the unit and age level and that they present information in an interesting and stimulating manner. For instance, a basketball slide film that is geared for boys would probably not be suitable for use in a girls' class.

2. *Proper preparation of materials should be made.* The teacher should check all equipment that may be necessary for the presentation of materials, to make sure that it is in operating condition. Record players and movie projectors, in particular, need to be carefully checked before they are used.

*See also Appendix.

Fig. 17-1. The presentation of materials should be planned and integrated into the lesson. (Hartsdale Public Schools, Hartsdale, N. Y.)

3. *The presentation of materials should be planned and integrated into the lesson.* Students should be properly introduced to the materials so that they know what to expect and so that they understand their relationship to the unit of study.

4. *Materials should be presented to the students in a proper learning situation.* Students should be located so that all may hear, see, and learn from the material being presented to them. They should realize that they will be held responsible for the information being presented.

5. *Materials should be varied.* Different types of materials should be chosen for presentation, to stimulate the varying interests of the students. A teacher using films or slide films exclusively does not take full advantage of supplementary materials available for widespread appeal.

6. *Use of supplementary materials should be limited.* The teacher should place a reasonable limit on the use of extra teaching materials to maintain a balance between supplementary learnings and those gained from regular instructional materials.

7. *Care should be taken to avoid excessive expenses.* A reasonable part of the instructional budget should be set aside for supplementary materials. This amount should be in accordance with the emphasis placed on this phase of the teaching program.

8. *Records and evaluations of materials should be maintained.* All supplementary materials should be carefully evaluated and records kept on file for future reference. This should save the unnecessary expense involved in reordering or duplicating materials and in maintenance of outdated materials.

By following these principles the teacher is able to supplement learnings with materials that are valuable and interesting to the students.

A recent study by one of the author's students was concerned with current practices and trends in the use of audiovisual media for the teaching of motor skills in professional physical education programs. This study has implications for secondary school physical education programs in that it reveals the number of responding schools

Fig. 17-2. Audiovisual aids. (Evergreen Park High School, Evergreen Park, Ill.)

that offer or require a course in audiovisual media and techniques in their professional preparing programs.

The researcher developed and mailed a questionnaire that was returned by sixty-three physical education directors in a variety of colleges and universities. Of these respondents, five required a course in audiovisual media and techniques, while thirty-five offered such a course on an elective basis. A total of fifty-four of the individuals answering the questionnaire indicated that they felt that audiovisual media serve as a valuable supplement to instruction in the learning of motor skills.

The study also found that video taping is increasing in use as an instructional tool. The audiovisual media used with the most frequency by the respondents in this study were, in order of frequency, 16 mm. and 8 mm. films, loop films, cartridge films, chalkboards, wall charts, slide films, filmstrips, and instructional television.

CLASSIFICATION OF RESOURCES AND MATERIALS

On the pages that follow, three categories of materials are discussed in terms of their purposes, problems, and specific resources. Suggestions are listed under *reading materials, audiovisual aids,* and *special*

aids, and while these are recent and fairly inclusive listings, new types of materials are always being placed on the market. Teachers should be on the lookout for the very latest items available, as listed in journals, catalogs, and advertisements.

Reading materials

Purposes

To provide up-to-date information and enrichment materials on all aspects of the program.

Problems

To keep track of materials and assignments. A check-out system should be developed so that the teacher may know where materials may be located. In addition, some method of annotating particularly beneficial articles or resources should be devised, thus simplifying assignments.

Types

1. *Textbook:*
Bucher, Charles A.: *Physical Education for Life,* St. Louis, 1969, Webster Division, McGraw-Hill Book Co.

The text for high school boys and girls provides information about physique, posture, physical skills, physical fitness, safety and first aid, and the body in motion. The book also includes basic instruction about twenty different sports and activities. Additional information is provided on the purchase and care of equipment. The textbook is both informative and motivating and is an excellent means of giving high school students a rich physical education experience.

2. *Articles* (research, historical, educational, informational, or supplementary):

All-American Athlete, Dept. J., 801 Palisade Ave., Union City, N. J. 07087

Athletic Journal, Athletic Journal Publishing Co., 1719 Howard St., Evanston, Ill. 60202

The Coach, Lowe and Campbell Athletic Goods, 1511 Baltimore Ave., Kansas City, Mo. 64108

Coach and Athlete, 1421 Mayon St., N. E., Atlanta, Ga. 31324

Dance Magazine, 268 West 47th St., New York, N. Y. 10036

Journal of Health, Physical Education, and Recreation, 1201 Sixteenth St., N. W., Washington, D. C. 20036

Recreation, National Recreation Association, 8 West 8th St., New York, N. Y. 10011

Research Quarterly, The, 1201 Sixteenth St., N. W., Washington, D. C. 20036

Scholastic Coach, Scholastic Magazine, Inc., 33 West 42nd St., New York, N. Y. 10036

Sports rule books and digests

U. S. Gymnast Magazine, P. O. Box 53, Iowa City, Iowa 52240

3. *Booklets, pamphlets, and catalogs* (educational and supplemental information about health, safety, and related areas):

American Association for Health, Physical Education, and Recreation, 1201 Sixteenth St., N. W., Washington, D. C. 20036

American School and University, Product Catalog File, American School Publishing Co., 470 Fourth Ave., New York, N. Y. 10016

The Athletic Institute, 805 Merchandise Mart, Chicago, Ill. 60654

American Medical Association, 535 N. Dearborn St., Chicago, Ill. 60610

Metropolitan Life Insurance Co., 1 Madison Ave., New York, N. Y. 10010

National Dairy Council, 111 N. Canal St., Chicago, Ill. 60606

Science Research Associates, 259 E. Erie, Chicago, Ill. 60611

Audiovisual aids

Purposes

To give information to a large group at one time in such areas as skill breakdowns, game play, techniques and rules of sports, and enrichment materials; to provide musical or other rhythmical accompaniment.

Problems

To keep an accurate and up-to-date file on current materials, with evaluative suggestions. Individual file cards are helpful for this purpose. Large school systems and new schools generally maintain departments for audiovisual instruction, with personnel specifically hired for the maintenance, distribution, selection, and follow-up of all equipment and materials in this area.

Types

1. *Motion pictures.* Motion pictures for use in physical education classes are available in every area. They may be purchased in color or black-and-white, or rented for nominal fees. Catalogs issued by film companies contain listings of films

Fig. 17-3. Audiovisual aids. (Peabody Demonstration School, George Peabody College for Teachers, Nashville, Tenn.)

available for rental or purchase, and generally include brief descriptions of the films themselves to help the teacher in making selections. Teachers should have on hand the following excellent catalogs:

Health, Physical Education, and Sports Films (1967-1969), Visual Aids Service, Division of University Extension, Champaign, Ill. 61820

Educators Guide to Free Films (published annually), Educators Progress Service, Randolph, Wis. 53956

Guides are also available for filmstrips and for tapes, scripts, and transcriptions.

The first is a catalog of films (see following partial listing) from all the various rental agencies, categorized by individual sports and related areas. Films may be rented through this university service.

The *Educators Guide* is an index of free films, listing names, titles, and companies where such films are available.

Other film companies that distribute educational films (whose listings would be found in the catalogs suggested above) include the following:

Association Films, Inc., 600 Madison Ave., New York, N. Y. 10022

Ideal Pictures, Inc., 1010 Church St., Evanston, Ill. 60201

Modern Talking Picture Service, 1212 Avenue of the Americas, New York, N. Y. 10036

School Film Service, 549 West 123rd St., New York, N. Y. 10027

A partial listing of films available for rental through Visual Aids Service, Division of University Extension, University of Illinois, Champaign, Ill. 61820:

Archery

Archery for Girls
Archery Fundamentals

Archery Instruction and Safety
Bows and Arrows
Introduction to Field Archery

Baseball

Baseball for Millions
Baseball Instruction: Base Running
Baseball Instruction: Batting and Bunting
Baseball Instruction: Catching
Baseball Instruction: First and Third Basemen
Baseball Instruction: Outfielding
Baseball Instruction: Pitching
Baseball Instruction: Shortstop and Second Baseman
Batting Fundamentals
Batting Stars of Baseball
A Boy, a Bat and a Baseball
Catching Fundamentals
Catching in Baseball
Circling the Bases
Democracy of Baseball
Hitting in Baseball
Infield Play at First and Third
Lou Gehrig's Greatest Day (You Are There)
Official Baseball
Play Ball, Son
Throwing in Baseball

Basketball

Basketball for Boys: Fundamentals
Basketball for Boys: Team Play
Basketball for Girls: Fundamental Techniques
Basketball for Girls: Game Play
Basketball for Millions
Basketball Fundamentals (second edition)
Basketball Strategy for Girls
Basketball Techniques for Girls
Girls' Basketball for Beginners
Official Basketball
Play Championship Basketball
This Is Basketball
Understanding Basketball

Bowling

American Bowls
Bowling Aces
Bowling Fundamentals
Splits, Spares, and Strikes

Dance

American Square Dance
Canada Dances
Dance Demonstration
Dance Festival
Dance Your Own Way
Dancer's World
Indian Dances
Introduction to Dance
Let's Dance
Modern Dance
Social Dancing
Square Dancing

Football

Ball Handling in Football
Blocking in Football
Football Fundamentals: Blocking and Tackling
Football Kicking Techniques

Official Football
T Formation (Basic Plays)
T Formation (Open Plays)
Tackling in Football
This is Football

Golf

Building Your Golf Swing
In the Rough
Pitch and Run—Pitching and Sand Shots
Play Better Golf, Part I (Fundamentals)
Play Better Golf, Part II (Advanced)
Putting
Welcome to Golf

Gymnastics

Advanced Tumbling
Beginning Tumbling
Gymnastics: Fundamentals and Techniques, Part I
Gymnastics: Fundamentals and Techniques, Part II
Gymnastics: Side Horse Exercises
Intermediate Tumbling
Rhythmic Exercises
Simple Stunts
Trampoline Fundamentals

Softball

Girls, Let's Learn Softball
Softball for Boys
Softball for Girls
Softball Fundamentals

Sports, Miscellaneous

Badminton Fundamentals
Fundamentals of Badminton
Fundamentals of Soccer
Handball Fundamentals
Soccer—Let's Play
Soccer for Girls (revised edition)
Speed-a-Way
Speedball for Girls
Table Tennis

Swimming and diving

Advanced Swimming
Anyone for Diving?
Beginning Swimming
Crawl Stroke
Diving Fundamentals
Dolphin Kick
Fundamentals of Swimming
Matt Mann's Swimming Techniques for Boys
Matt Mann's Swimming Techniques for Girls
New Magic of Swimming
Safe Swimming
Springboard and Front Approach
Springboard Diving
Swimming and Diving Aces
Swimming for Beginners

Tennis

Advanced Tennis
Beginning Tennis
Court Favorites (Tennis)
Fundamentals of Tennis

Technique of Tennis
Tennis—Elementary Fundamentals
Tennis—Intermediate and Advanced Fundamentals
Tennis for Beginners
Tennis Tactics
Tennis Techniques

Track and Field

Bannister Wins the Mile Run (You Are There)
Dashes, Hurdles, and Relays
The Discus
Distance Races
Fundamentals of Running
Fundamentals of Track and Field
High Jump
The Hurdles
Middle Distances
Pole Vault
The Relays
Running Broad Jump
Shot Put
The Sprints
This Is Track and Field

Volleyball

Fundamentals of Volleyball
Play Volleyball
Volleyball Drills and Techniques
Volleyball for Boys
Volleyball for Women
Volleyball Skills
Volleyball Strategy for Girls
Volleyball Techniques for Girls

Winter Sports

Introduction for the Art of Figure Skating
Ski Thrills

Wrestling

Scientific Unarmed Self-Defense: An Exposition of the Ancient Asian Esoteric Arts
Wrestling: Basic Skills, Part 1—Starting Positions and Takedowns
Wrestling: Basic Skills, Part 2—Escapes and Reversals
Wrestling: Basic Skills, Part 3—Breakdowns into Pinning Combinations

2. *Slide films.* Slide films have been developed for rental and purchase purposes on both a sound and silent basis. Rental prices are generally $2.50 or $3.50. Prices for purchase depend on the number of slide film units, ranging from $13.75 for one or two units, to $69.00 for six or eight units without the record. The accompanying record adds another five or ten dollars to the price.

An outstanding source of full-color slide films is The Athletic Institute, 805 Merchandise Mart, Chicago, Illinois 60654. To rent their slide films, contact must be made with Ideal Pictures, Inc., at one of their regional offices:

102 West 25th Street, Baltimore, Md. 21218
58 E. South Water St., Chicago, Ill. 60601
1840 Alcatraz Ave., Berkeley, Calif. 94703.

Slide films are available in thirty-four sports,

including beginning archery, beginning badminton, beginning baseball, beginning bowling, campcraft, beginning fencing, beginning golf, beginning table tennis, gymnastics, beginning soccer, beginning softball, swimming, beginning tennis, track and field, beginning volleyball, and beginning wrestling, plus individual recreational sports such as fishing, ice skating, skiing, and judo. Excellent booklets (75¢ for students) accompany each of these slide films.

3. *Learning loops.* 8 mm. learning loops may be purchased from The Athletic Institute, at approximately $9.00 per loop, and an 8 mm. loop film projector is also available directly from the Institute. These loops are an excellent device for specific instruction in skill performance. They are available in each individual event in track and field for men, track and field for women, gymnastics, and tennis.

4. *Loop movies.* Loop movies consist of several 16 mm. loops spliced together, end to end, for continuous projection. They are available for purchase from Champions on Film, 3666 South State St., Ann Arbor, Mich. 48104, with prices ranging between $20.00 and $50.00. These films cover such subjects as basketball, wrestling, swimming, baseball, golf, tennis, trampoline, and track.

5. *Television.* Although educational television (ETV) has met with widespread appeal at various age levels in all phases of the curriculum, its usage as a teaching technique in physical education is still rather limited. A study by the National Center for School and College Television surveyed ETV stations, state ETV networks, and several closed-circuit facilities to determine the status of health and physical education courses on television. The results of their questionnaires indicated that only fifty-five telecourses were broadcast for use at elementary, secondary, and college levels. The 9% of telecourses geared to the secondary level generally dealt with health problems, and one dealt with golf. (This survey was based on materials presented over television during the 1965-1966 school year.)

Conferees engaged in this study agreed that the full potential of television had not yet been reached, and recognized that recent developments in physical education, such as movement efficiency and sensory-perceptual experiences, contained concepts adaptable to television production. Their outlook should be noted by all teachers of physical education, in order that further research and application of this teaching aid can be fully utilized in the future.*

6. *Video tape.* Video tapes are finding increased usage in many educational endeavors and are being recognized as an invaluable teaching aid in physical education activities. Several purposes illustrate the adaptability of this special type of recording device. It may be used in the following ways:

a. To video-tape sports performances for later study with still frames, for closer analysis of action

*NCSCT News, supplement no. 4, National Center for School and College Television, Box A, Bloomington, Ind. 47401.

b. To supervise several outdoor play areas from one location through a closed-circuit television monitoring device

c. To provide objective evaluation of an individual performance, such as diving or trampolining, through instant replay

d. To build up a school library of tapes for specific instructional purposes at later dates

These are only a few of the instructional possibilities of this versatile teaching tool. Its popularity will continue to increase because of its adaptability, the ease with which it may be operated, and its effectiveness. Current problems caused by tapes that fit improperly in some machines are being solved.

One source of equipment is Concord Electronics Corporation, 1935 Armacost Ave., Los Angeles, Calif. 90025, makers of audio tape recorders, video tape recorders, closed circuit television, and communications products.

7. *Phonographs and audio tape recorders.* For extensive use in physical education classes, phonographs and audio tape recorders must be durable, portable, and provided with discrete volume controls. Transportation and storage of this valuable equipment may be a problem if safe closet space is not available relatively near the gymnasium. The following are well-known manufacturers:

Newcomb Audio Products Co., Dept. JO-10, 6824 Lexington Ave., Hollywood, Calif. 90028

Rheem Califone Corp., 5922 Bowcroft St., Los Angeles, Calif. 90016

8. *Records* (available in all speeds, some in unbreakable nylon materials, for teaching all rhythmic activities):

Canadian F.D.S., 605 King St., W. Toronto 2B, Ontario, Canada

Cheviot Corp., Dept. J-11, Box 34485, Los Angeles, Calif. 99034

Dance Record Center, 1159 Broad St., Newark, N. J. 07114

Dance Records, 1438 Springvale Ave., McLean, Va. 22101

Folkraft Records, 1161 Broad St., Newark, N. J. 07114

Freda Miller Records, Dept. J, Box 383, Northport, N. Y. 11768

Hoctor Records, P. O. Box 38, Waldwick, N. J. 07463

Honor Your Partner Records, Educational Activities, Inc. (formerly Square Dance Associates), P. O. Box 392, Freeport, N. Y. 11520

R.C.A. Victor Educational Records, 155 East 24th St., New York, N. Y. 10010

Rhythms Production Records, Whitney Building, Box 34485, Los Angeles, Calif. 99034

Russell Records, P. O. Box 3318, Ventura, Calif. 93003

Stepping Stones, 2506 Overland Ave., Los Angeles, Calif. 90064

Windsor Records, 5530 J. Rosemead Blvd., Temple City, Calif. 91780

9. *Drum* (dance drum, bongo drum, and similar percussive devices). Drums are used extensively to provide rhythmical measures for creative activities. They should be kept in a dry place, for extreme dampness causes loss of tone. In such instances, placing the drum on a radiator for a few minutes restores tensity. The Fred Gretsch Mfg. Co., 60 Broadway, Brooklyn, N. Y. 11211, makes a handy dance drum at a reasonable price.

Special aids

Purposes

To provide graphic, illustrative material to students, in an interesting and educational manner.

Problems

To find time to utilize displays effectively, to change displays for added interest, and to keep up-to-date with current events. Student assistants should be utilized to prepare and maintain the displays.

Types

1. *Charts, diagrams, and photographic materials* (for materials in several different sports):

Coordinated Program Chart Co., 2604 North Stevens St., Spokane, Wash. 99205

Division for Girls' and Women's Sports, American Association for Health, Physical Education, and Recreation, 1201 Sixteenth St., N. W., Washington, D. C. 20036

Easy Post, P. O. Box 425, Normal, Ill. 61761

Nissen Corp., 930 27th Avenue, S. W., Cedar Rapids, Iowa 52416

Physical Education Aids, P. O. Box 5117, San Mateo, Calif. 94402.

2. *Bulletin boards and chalkboards* (cork or beaver board, stationary or movable). These are excellent teaching devices, both for educational and motivational purposes. They should be colorful, interesting, neat, clear, uncluttered, and changed often. School administrators generally provide these materials.

3. *Magnetic boards* (blank-surfaced boards suitable for specific sports, such as soccer, football, or basketball, or all-purpose types of boards, suitable for all sports). These boards are excellent teaching devices for team sports. Although the initial expense ($19.00 to $50.00) seems rather steep at first, the lasting value of this item over several years makes it a worthwhile investment. The following are suppliers:

Jaconda Mfg. Co., Dept. HP, 5449 Hunter St., Philadelphia, Pa. 11931

The Program Aids Co., Inc., 550 5th Ave., New York, N. Y. 10036

OUTSIDE RESOURCES

Outside resources available to supplement the classroom teaching include professional personnel, community activities, and clinics.

Professional personnel

Purpose

To provide an interesting incentive to students by having a visiting professional demonstrate, teach, or discuss a sport or related experience.

Problems

To plan and organize for thorough effectiveness and safety. Pre-planning with the guest is essential, and preparation with students allows them to gain more fully from the experience.

Types

The directors and personnel of professional organizations such as the National Golf Foundation, United States Lawn Tennis Association, and Amateur Athletic Association.

Community activities

Purposes

To promote good public relations with the community and to provide additional activities for student participation.

Problems

To find time to plan and organize carefully the various details of the activities with community leaders.

Types

Recreational activities (tennis meets); PTA-sponsored special events and programs; benefit athletic demonstrations.

Clinics

Purposes

To provide additional and valuable learning experiences to students attending these clinics, either as participants or observers. Taking an honor team, a leaders club, or an entire class to a special program of this type offers information and an opportunity for appreciation which they never forget because of the specialized nature of the experience.

Problems

Planning, organizing transportation, obtaining parental permission, and providing supervision of the students. In many schools definite procedures for taking students on field trips are outlined, and they should be carefully followed.

Types

Special games and programs put on by visiting professional clubs (basketball or football teams); special clinics sponsored by local or state teaching organizations; traveling college groups and community organizations.

MATERIALS FOR TEAM SPORTS
Outstanding reading materials

National Federation of State High School Athletic Associations, 7 South Dearborn St., Chicago, Ill. 60603:

Official Football Rules (National Alliance edition)	$0.45
Football Case Book (Official Interpretations)	0.80
Football Handbook	0.45
(Combination price, $1.50)	
National Basketball Rules (Federation edition)	0.45
Basketball Case Book (Official Interpretations)	0.80
Basketball Handbook	0.45
(Combination price, $1.50)	
Baseball Rules	0.45
Baseball Case Book	0.80
Baseball, Umpires Manual	0.45
(Combination price, $1.50)	
Football Officials' Manual	0.45
Basketball Officials' Manual	0.45
Basketball Rules Simplified and Illustrated	0.80
High School Football Rules Simplified and Illustrated	1.30

Division for Girls' and Women's Sports, American Association for Health, Physical Education, and Recreation, 1201 Sixteenth Street, N.W., Washington, D. C. 20036:

Basketball Guide (243-07778)	$1.25
Field Hockey–Lacrosse Guide (243-07238)	1.25
Soccer-Speedball Guide (243-07240)	1.25
Volleyball Guide (243-07786)	1.25
Softball Guide (243-07838)	1.25

Division of Athletics, AAHPER (above address):
Speedball for Men (241-07818)	1.50

Slide films

The Athletic Institute, 805 Merchandise Mart, Chicago, Ill. 60654:

	Sound	Silent	Rent
Baseball (7 units)	$72.50	$61.50	$3.50
Basketball (7 units)	63.00	52.75	3.50
Basketball (girls; 8 units)	71.75	60.50	3.50
Field Hockey (5 units)	49.00	40.50	3.00
Soccer (3 units)	37.75	32.25	2.50
Softball (8 units)	80.25	69.00	3.50
Volleyball (4 units)	42.50	37.00	3.00

Student manual for each sport	$0.75
Instructor's guide	2.00

Note: Rental prices do not include shipping charges. Rental of these filmstrips must be ordered through Ideal Pictures at one of the following addresses:

1840 Alcatraz Ave., Berkeley, Calif. 94703
1558 Main St., Buffalo, N. Y. 14209
417 N. State St., Chicago, Ill. 60610

Special charts (techniques)

Division for Girls' and Women's Sports, American Association for Health, Physical Education, and Recreation, 1201 Sixteenth St., N. W., Washington, D. C. 20036:

Basketball (12 charts) (243-06878)	$1.50
Softball (11 charts) (243-06874)	1.50
Volleyball (11 charts) (243-06886)	1.50

MATERIALS FOR INDIVIDUAL SPORTS
Outstanding reading materials

Division for Girls' and Women's Sports, American Association for Health, Physical Education, and Recreation, 1201 Sixteenth St., N. W., Washington, D. C. 20036:

Archery-Riding Guide (243-07232)	$1.25
Bowling-Fencing Guide (243-07760)	1.25
Tennis-Badminton Guide (243-07242)	1.25
Recreational Games and Sports (243-07554)	1.00

National Federation of State High School Athletic Associations, 7 South Dearborn, Chicago, Ill. 60603:

Wrestling Officials' Manual	$0.50

Slide films

The Athletic Institute, 805 Merchandise Mart, Chicago, Ill. 60654:

	Sound	Silent	Rent
Archery (4 units)	$42.50	$36.75	$3.00
Badminton (6 units)	56.75	49.25	3.00
Bowling (4 units)	42.50	37.00	3.00
Campcraft (4 units)	51.75	46.25	3.00
Cycling (8 units)	89.75	78.75	3.50
Fencing (4 units)	51.75	46.25	3.00
Golf (6 units)	65.00	55.00	3.50
Judo (6 units)	73.50	65.00	3.50
Table Tennis (2 units)	26.00	23.25	2.50
Tennis (6 units)	62.50	54.00	3.50
Wrestling (5 units)	65.00	56.75	3.50

Student manual with each sport	$0.75
Instructor's guide	2.00

Note: Rental price does not include shipping charges. For rental procedures, see instructions under "Materials for Team Sports," slide film listings.

Lifetime Sports Education Project, American Association for Health, Physical Education, and Recreation, 1201 Sixteenth St., N. W., Washington, D. C. 20036:

Golf Group Instruction (245-07738)	$ 8.00
Tennis Group Instruction (245-07742)	8.00
Gym-Bowl Instruction Kit (245-07712)	15.00
Gym-Bowl Teacher's Manual (245-07714)	1.00

Special aids (technique charts and posters)

Division for Girls' and Women's Sports, American Association for Health, Physical Education, and Recreation 1201 Sixteenth St., N. W., Washington, D. C. 20036:

Badminton (12 charts) (243-07842)	$1.50
Tennis (12 charts) (243-07844)	1.50

Lifetime Sports Education Project, AAHPER (above address):

Golf Group Instruction (6 posters) (245-07740)	$9.00
Tennis Group Instruction (6 posters) (245-07744)	9.00
Ideas for Badminton Instruction (245-07754)	1.00
Ideas for Golf Instruction (245-007756)	1.00
Ideas for Tennis Instruction (245-07758)	1.00

Harvard Table Tennis Co., 265 Third St., Cambridge, Mass. 02142:

Harvard Table Tennis Teacher (booklet)	Free
Harvard Table Tennis Tournament (charts)	Free

Fencing/Judo & Karate Equipment, Castello's, 30 East 10th St., New York, N. Y. 10003:

Catalog	Free

MATERIALS FOR AQUATICS
Outstanding reading materials

Division for Girls' and Women's Sports, American Association for Health, Physical Education, and Recreation, 1201 Sixteenth St., N. W., Washington, D. C. 20036:

Aquatics Guide (243-07776)	$1.25

Slide films

The Athletic Institute, 805 Merchandise Mart, Chicago, Ill. 60654:

	Sound	Silent	Rent
Competitive Swimming (3 units)	$34.25	$28.75	$2.50
Diving (3 units)	45.25	39.50	3.00
Life-Saving (3 units)	30.75	25.25	2.50
Skin and Scuba Diving (6 units)	79.75	71.25	3.50
Swimming (4 units)	32.00	26.50	2.50

Note: Provisions for rental as listed under "Materials for Team Sports."

Student manual	$0.75
Instructor's guide	2.00

Special aids

Division for Girls' and Women's Sports, American Association for Health, Physical Education, and Recreation, 1201 Sixteenth St., N. W., Washington, D. C. 20036:

Aquatics—Swimming and Diving Charts (18)	$2.00

Youngjohn Enterprises, Inc., P. O. Box 4522, Cleveland, Ohio 44124
Instructional swimming charts (11)

11″ × 14″ size	$ 3.50 per set
23″ × 17½″ size	14.95 per set

American Red Cross (local chapters)
Charts, skill sheets, instructional materials Free

MATERIALS FOR TRACK AND FIELD
Outstanding reading materials

National Federation of State High School Athletic Associations, 7 South Dearborn St., Chicago, Ill. 60603:

Track and Field Rules	$0.65

Division for Girls' and Women's Sports, American Association for Health, Physical Education, and Recreation, 1201 Sixteenth St., N. W., Washington, D. C. 20036:

Track and Field Guide (243-07840)	$1.25

Slide films

The Athletic Institute, 805 Merchandise Mart, Chicago, Ill. 60654:

	Sound	Silent	Rent
Track and Field (9 units)	$60.50	$46.50	$3.50
Track and Field (girls) (2 units)	18.00	15.25	2.50

Note: Provisions for rental as listed under "Materials for Team Sports."

Student manual	$0.75
Instructor's guide	2.00

Special aids (awards and emblems)

American Association for Health, Physical Education, and Recreation, 1201 Sixteenth St., N. W., Washington, D. C. 20036:

Junior High School Emblems (242-06832)	$0.40 ea.	$4.60 doz.
Senior High School Emblems (242-06834)	0.45 ea.	5.25 doz.

Embroidered Emblem Patches (places in meet)

First place (242-06836)	$0.20 ea.	$2.20 doz.
Second place (242-06838)	same	same
Third place (242-06840)	same	same

MATERIALS FOR GYMNASTICS
Outstanding reading materials

Division for Girls' and Women's Sports, American Association for Health, Physical Education, and Recreation, 1201 Sixteenth St., N. W., Washington, D. C. 20036:

Gymnastics Guide (243-07782)	$1.25

Slide films

The Athletic Institute, 805 Merchandise Mart, Chicago, Ill. 60654:

	Sound	Silent	Rent
Gymnastics (for girls and women) (4 units)	$44.50	$38.75	$3.00
Trampolining (3 units)	35.50	30.00	2.50
Tumbling (3 units)	31.00	25.25	2.50
Tumbling (advanced) (3 units)	37.25	31.75	2.50

Student manual	$0.75
Instructor's guide	2.00

Note: See previous procedures regarding rental, as indicated under "Materials for Team Sports."

Special aids (technique charts)

Nissen Corporation, 930 27th Ave., S. W., Cedar Rapids, Iowa 52406:

Boys

Side Horse	$1.00 ea.
Parallel Bars	1.00 ea.
Still Rings	1.00 ea.
Horizontal Bar	1.00 ea.
Long-Horse Vaulting	1.00 ea.
Free Exercise	1.00 ea.

Girls

Side-Horse Vaulting	1.00 ea.
Uneven Parallel Bars	1.00 ea.
Balance Beam	1.00 ea.
Free Exercise—Balancing and Beginning Tumbling	1.00 ea.
Free Exercise—Acrobatics and Intermediate Tumbling	1.00 ea.

MATERIALS FOR WINTER SPORTS
Outstanding reading materials

Division for Girls' and Women's Sports, American Association for Health, Physical Education, and Recreation, 1201 Sixteenth St., N. W., Washington, D. C. 20036:

Outing Activities and Winter Sports (243-07784)	$1.25

United States Figure Skating Association, 178 Tremont St., Boston, Mass. 02158

Figure Skating Educational Kit, by Mary Maroney	$1.00

Slide films

The Athletic Institute, 805 Merchandise Mart, Chicago, Ill. 60654:

	Sound	*Silent*	*Rent*
Ice Skating (4 units)	$49.75	$44.25	$2.50
Skiing (6 units)	56.25	48.00	3.50
Student manual			$0.75
Instructor's guide			2.00

Note: Rental procedures as listed under "Materials for Team Sports."

MATERIALS FOR RHYTHMS

American Association for Health, Physical Education, and Recreation, 1201 Sixteenth St., N. W., Washington, D. C. 20036:

Selected articles on dance (243-06938)	$1.25
Dance Production (243-06924)	1.00

Educational Activities, Inc., Box 392, Freeport, N. Y. 11520:

Keynotes to Modern Dance (course, records)	$27.95
Musical Ball Skills (manual, records)	11.95
Rhythmrix (manual, records)	11.95
Dances Without Partners (album 32, 33)	11.95 ea.
Basic Popular Music	5.95

Class management
and
control

Oconomowoc Senior High School, Oconomowoc, Wis.

Class management
and
control

CLASS MANAGEMENT

Good class management is essential in every phase of teaching. It is perhaps even more important in physical education because of the extensive equipment, facilities, and records involved and the larger class sizes that often exist. Because of the partial loss of class time needed for dressing and showering procedures, the remaining minutes must be put to the very best use if an effective teaching program is to result. This can be done only through good class management.

Class management, then, is synonymous with creating a teaching situation. From the point of view of the teacher, it means providing time and opportunity for teaching, and for the student it means promoting self-management and self-responsibility for the benefit of the class. When these two objectives are accomplished, the teacher is ready to teach and the students are ready to learn.

Class management includes all the necessary procedures and routines that are a part of the daily instructional program. Roll call, excuses, and showers all require certain procedures to make the most efficient use of the time available. Yet class management should not be confused with actual teaching methods, for instruction is not the issue here. The organization, or arrangement, of the class so that instruction takes place most effectively is the major concern.

The main purposes of good class management are as follows:

1. To make the most effective and efficient use of class time
2. To ensure the safety of the group through class routines and procedures
3. To provide a controlled classroom atmosphere in which instruction may take place
4. To promote self-discipline and self-motivation on the part of each individual in the class
5. To develop within the students a sense of responsibility toward themselves and toward each other
6. To enhance rapport between teacher and student that will promote learning
7. To create a group spirit in which each individual feels good within himself and feels comfortable with his group
8. To recognize and provide for the needs and interests of each individual within the group

9. To make the most effective use of the teacher's time and energy
10. To provide the most effective organization and arrangement of the class in order that instruction may be given and learning will take place

Good class management is brought about through careful and thoughtful planning on the part of the teacher with the students. This mutual and cooperative planning should be the backbone of class organization so that students willingly maintain the standards they have established. They understand and respect the mutual benefits that will be derived by the entire class, and in a sense they manage themselves. This is class management at its best.

The teacher's role in developing this ideal type of class management is one of guidance and leadership during the planning periods and orientation of students at the beginning of the school year. Advance preparation, class orientation, and class procedures are the main areas with which the teacher must be concerned. These three topics will receive detailed attention in the first part of this chapter.

Advance preparation

Early preparation includes the many details which the physical education teacher

should organize before school opens in the fall. The opening program, the equipment, the lockers, records, and the schedule all need to be prepared. This readiness is a basic step to good class management, for it prepares the teacher in advance, and he or she is then able to devote full attention to the requirements of the students when they arrive.

Program planning

An outline of the program for the year should be formulated on the basis of the departmental objectives and curriculum. Plans for the opening unit and the first week of school should be drawn up completely, so that the teacher knows exactly what needs to be accomplished in the first meeting of all classes. In schools in which team teaching exists, the team should sketch general areas of programming and duty assignment. The working out of details, such as specific skill needs of a group, should be delayed until students and teachers plan together.

Equipment and facilities

All equipment and facilities should be checked with the inventory made the year before. The teacher should make sure that all necessary repairs have been completed and that everything is ready and safe for

Fig. 18-1. Good class management is brought about through careful and thoughtful planning. (Yonkers Public Schools, Yonkers, N. Y.)

use. This also includes playing fields, gymnasiums, and permanent equipment. The special equipment needed for the first teaching unit, whether it concerns hockey, soccer, or football, should be taken from storage and placed in an appropriate place where it is easily accessible. The teacher will thus be prepared to make use of it as soon as the class is organized.

Locker room

Necessary preparations should also be made in the locker room. A check to ensure that the lockers are clean and in working order will save much confusion. It is very frustrating to assign a locker to a student, only to find that it does not work and that the whole process must be repeated.

If there are bulletin boards in the locker rooms, they should be attractively prepared with appropriate pictures and materials. When the students come into the locker room and see these careful preparations, they will realize that the teacher is enthusiastic and ready to go to work, and they, too, will become motivated.

Class lists and records*

The physical education teacher will find the new class lists very helpful. Preparing record files and grade books ahead of time saves a great deal of confusion later on. It is usually quite difficult to find time to take care of these clerical duties once school has begun. There are always many other urgent matters that require immediate attention, and the paper work remains undone. The mental attitude of the teacher is greatly improved, too, when these details have been cared for beforehand.

Schedules

The final detail that should be given attention before school opens is the teaching schedule. Any changes or errors that occur should be taken care of in advance of the initial class meetings to prevent confusion in the minds of the students. At this time

*See also Appendix.

the scheduling of practice periods and the use of facilities should be cooperatively worked out by the men's and women's departments so that the after-school program can be organized without delay. This includes the games scheduled with other schools, for although the men's program may be outlined well in advance, the women's after-school program must then be coordinated with the men's program.

Class orientation

Proper orientation of each physical education class is exceedingly important because it affects the outcome of all the classwork throughout the year. It is during the first week of school that the students are introduced to all phases of physical education work and are made aware of their personal responsibilities for successful completion of the course. This period of orientation includes student registration and locker assignment, and group planning sessions and discussions.

Registration of students

Usually at the first class session some form of class registration is necessary. The information required and the form of registration vary, depending on the uses to which the registration is put. Customarily it is thought valuable to have on file the following items about each student:

Name
Address
Home telephone number
Age and birthday
Locker number and combination
Health status
Record of fee payments
Activities (electives, intramural activities, honor teams)
Test scores and achievement records
Awards, varsity letters

Only a part of this information is taken during the registration period. Other factors, such as electives and awards, would be reported at the appropriate time. By maintaining a personal record of each student from year to year, an overall picture of his accomplishments is readily available.

The form on which information is recorded should be a printed card with spaces outlined on both sides, where appropriate details may be filled in. The cards may be used to call the roll until squad cards are made out (if this is the general procedure), and then they may be filed in the physical education office.

Locker assignment

Another item of business that can be taken care of during the orientation period, when students do not yet have uniforms and sneakers available for participation, is the assignment of lockers. This routine procedure becomes difficult when combinations to built-in locks must be explained, but even in such instances no more than one class period should be necessary to accomplish this task.

Locker rooms are generally organized according to a regular pattern, with rows of lockers and benches arranged alternately. The room itself should be well lighted and ventilated and kept as clean as possible. There are several different types of lockers used in school locker rooms: baskets, long lockers, half-size lockers in two tiers, and combinations of baskets or small lockers, with one large dressing locker. In each of the above cases locks may be built in, with the teacher having a master list of combinations and a master key, or individual locks may have to be provided by the students. If students provide the locks, the teacher must keep an accurate record of students' locker combinations, for many occasions arise when it is essential that the teacher have access to all lockers.

The major point to be kept in mind when assigning lockers is the spacing of class members. Aisles and sections must not be overcrowded, to guard against accidents and facilitate dressing as rapidly as possible. The teacher may also wish to assign lockers in a pattern designed to promote class unity by breaking up cliques.

Lockers may be selected by the individuals in the class or specifically assigned by the teacher, but whichever method is used, it should be consistently followed by the teacher with all class groups. The choice of method depends on class size, locker room conditions, and departmental procedures that may have been established.

Group planning

The teacher may wish to devote part of one of the orientation periods to a discussion of the physical education program so that the students will understand the objectives and purposes of the program and have an opportunity to ask questions concerning it. The teacher should prepare in advance a general outline of points to be used in the discussion, to ensure that all phases of the program are covered.

The extent of the discussion depends largely upon the course of action the teacher intends to follow. During orientation a discussion of the year's program by the students may bring out suggested elective units or special requests in regard to the intramural and interscholastic programs. On the other hand, the teacher may use the time to introduce the program the particular class will be following, as determined by departmental organization. The nature of the discussion will depend on the degree of flexibility in program arrangement, as determined by the philosophy of the department in respect to student planning.

During the discussion period, time should be taken to determine, through class suggestion and selection, the rules and regulations that will be a necessary part of classwork. The students themselves should establish a code of conduct for the locker room, the showers, roll call, and other class situations in order to give them an opportunity to realize the need for such codes and to accept their own regulations more willingly.

The teacher must carefully moderate the discussion so that all individuals have an opportunity to express opinions and to ensure the level of discussion is a worthy one.

This may also be an appropriate time for the election of class helpers, leaders, or captains. Valuable pointers on the qualifications of leaders may be brought out at this time, again in the form of a class discussion.

Class procedures

Good management of a class is brought about by giving considerable attention to many small details covering teacher and student behavior. The suggestions that follow govern all phases of a single class period except the actual instruction of the class. It is this class organization, however, which is the key to promoting a valuable instructional period; therefore, these small details cannot be overlooked. Important factors in class procedure include locker room regulations, roll call, shower procedures, costume regulations, excuses, and before-class readiness.

Before class

When students come to a class in physical education the teacher should be completely prepared for them. Personally, the teacher should be properly dressed for class and stationed in the locker room, where students may easily locate him or her for advice or questioning. Plans for the class organization should be fixed in the teacher's mind, and all equipment should be in readiness.

The students should come to class in an orderly fashion, just as they proceed to all school classes. This businesslike atmosphere should continue throughout the dressing time.

Locker room regulations

Locker room regulations, determined and enforced by the class, should include the following.

Benches. Benches between lockers should remain clear of books and clothing to prevent these items from being crushed, pushed around, or lost. Benches are to be used to sit on while changing.

Books. A special place should be set aside where students may put their books. Usually they may easily be placed on top of the lockers, provided the lockers are not too high. This prevents any damage or loss to this important property.

Clothing. All clothing should be hung up neatly in long lockers, and shoes should be placed on the floor of the locker. This protects the clothing and prevents it from becoming dirty or damaged. Even where half-size lockers are used, this regulation should be enforced. Lockers should be closed and locked during classes to ensure the protection of all belongings.

Valuables. Valuable jewelry and wallets should, of course, be locked inside a locker during physical education. Some teachers require all jewelry to be put away in this manner, thus preventing damage to or loss of the jewelry or possible injury to students by some types of costume jewelry.

Lights. Locker room lights should be turned out when all students proceed to the gymnasium. A member of the class should be given this particular responsibility, and the job should be shared by many students during the course of the year.

Routine. The routine within the locker room should merely be a matter of changing clothes in the quickest and easiest fashion. Strict silence is usually not necessary, but students should attend to the business at hand without any undue nonsense or fooling around. Loud and raucous behavior would not be in accordance with regular school conduct.

Time. The time allotted for changing clothes before class should be established by the students in the orientation week discussions. Customarily, five minutes is sufficient for all students to change and proceed to their places.

Costume

The costume, or gym uniform, varies in style, shape, and color; the requirements governing its use, preferably established by the groups concerned, may also vary, from rigid to loose restrictions. The following considerations are pertinent:

Types of uniforms. Girls' uniforms range from one-piece gym suits with a skirt or short type of bottom to a two-piece outfit of blouse and shorts. Boys' uniforms are generally shorts and a T-shirt, perhaps marked by the school insignia.

Requirements. Besides determination of the basic outfit, there should be requirements about sneakers, socks, and sweatshirts for all participants in physical activity. All students should be required to dress in these items for every class. Furthermore, all clothing should be clearly labeled with the owner's name, with either indelible ink, chain stitching, or name tags.

Improper preparation. Definite regulations should be established regarding a "penalty" for not fulfilling all requirements concerning uniform. Students should realize their responsibilities in this matter and understand the consequences of not meeting them.

Laundering. It is very important to set definite time periods at which clean uniforms are required. For girls in classes meeting twice a week, a clean uniform is probably necessary every two or three weeks. For boys, the time period may have to be shorter. Effective means of checking on clean uniforms, probably during roll call, should be established to ensure enforcement of this requirement.

Roll call

A teacher is legally responsible for the group in his or her charge and should therefore keep an accurate record of attendance for each class session. In physical education an exact system of recording should be devised because of the variation in student participation. Symbols are needed to denote excuses, uniform cuts, absences, tardiness, and similar situations. Roll call can become a very complicated and time-consuming process and therefore needs careful consideration, to further good class management.

Methods for roll call. Teachers of physical education have devised various means of calling roll, for the purpose of saving time and promoting efficiency. Some of the better methods are worthy of attention.

1. Number check. The students are assigned a certain number and must be standing on it when roll is taken. The numbers are painted, in order, along the sidelines of the gymnasium floor, and the teacher merely notes vacant numbers.

2. Number call. The students are given a certain number which they must call out at the appropriate time. Numbers not mentioned are then noted by the teacher as absent.

3. Roll call. The teacher calls out the names of all students and listens for their responses.

4. Squad call. Names of the students are checked according to organized squads, with leaders assisting the teacher by

Fig. 18-2. Girls' physical education uniforms vary from school to school. (Hartsdale Public Schools, Hartsdale, N. Y.)

checking attendance, uniform cuts, and so forth.

Each of the above methods has its values. However, the first suggestions are rather impersonal, and a more friendly atmosphere can be promoted through the use of the last method. Furthermore, the use of student leadership—while requiring more time on the part of the teacher for instruction and training—has the advantage of fostering good leadership qualities.

Systems for roll call. There is no established rule about when class roll should be taken or what symbols should be used. It is customary for attendance to be taken at the beginning of a class period so that a report of students absent from class but not listed on the daily absence list may be sent to the office. This is an important function of every teacher, for truancy is against state law. Offenders must be discovered as soon as they are found absent from any part of the school day. Besides fulfilling legal responsibility by taking roll at the beginning of the class, the teacher will find proceeding from roll call formations to the next setup a convenient way of organizing the group for instruction. Taking roll in the middle of the period may interrupt drill practice, and sometimes there is not enough time at the end of the period, no matter how closely the lesson is planned.

In regard to the use of symbols, most teachers develop their own systems. The main criteria that should be kept in mind are speed, clarity, uniformity, and exactness. If leaders are used, they must be able to understand all the necessary variations, and in the case of a teacher's absence the substitute should be able to interpret the system. Symbols most often required cover the following items:

Absence
Tardiness
Excuse
    Office
    Illness
    Observing
Uniform cut
    Suit
    Sneakers
    Not clean

Safety. Roll call is a very convenient time for checking on safety regulations. This important factor needs special emphasis in physical education, and it is at this point in the daily lesson that equipment rules and safety regulations can be reviewed. Each class member should know and accept his personal responsibilities for the safety of others, and the teacher can promote this attitude easily at this time.

Excuses from class

The problems concerning temporary and permanent excuses from class are always prevalent in physical education. Methods of handling these problems depend upon the size of the department, the facilities available, and the determination of the teacher. Above all, the philosophy of the department stands behind the procedure in these cases.

Basic philosophy. Ideally, a good physical education program should include some kind of modified or adapted activities program for individuals who are injured, disabled, or recently recovered from illness. Limited activities under these circumstances should be prescribed by a physician and administered by the teacher. Because most physical education teachers have studied the adapted program, it is possible for them to carry out such instructions. When this type of program is in operation, there is no need for temporary or permanent excuses.

Unfortunately, limitations in facilities, time, and personnel prevent the inclusion of this type of program in many situations, and teachers must try to make adaptations within their own class programs.

Methods of handling excuses. Temporary or permanent excuses from physical education class may be accepted by the teacher but should be authorized by the school health department. This prevents a student from being excused from class for a reason that is not valid, and it channels health problems through the nurse or doctor, who should be aware of all health deficiencies. Some teachers send excused students directly to a study hall if they have no alternate program established within their classes and no adapted program is available. Theoretically, excused students should change from their street clothes whenever possible and participate in as much of the regular class activity as possible. Whenever a particular activity is more than the student should undertake, he should have a specific assignment related to classwork, which he must complete during that time.

Work assignments. Work assignments for excused students may take many forms, depending upon the activity engaged in by the class. Students should be engaged in a purposeful activity such as keeping score, taking notes on the class, or charting a player's position in a team game. More difficult tasks may include writing team plays, marking a specific position, creating a dance or skit, or reading a special assignment for a later report to the class. If it is possible to assign a remedial type of exercise, with permission of the physician, this should be done. Whatever course of action is taken, the teacher needs much time and great patience to motivate excused students to spend class time wisely and to help them achieve educational objectives.

Showers

The amount of time allotted for dressing at the close of the physical education class depends upon the shower requirement. Because of the health-teaching opportunity provided by a showering program, all students should be required to meet this regulation. Certain rules must be established in this regard, however, and procedures for enforcement set up.

Regulations. A well-run showering program demands certain restrictions for efficiency and safety, and consistency in their application is essential. Towels, too, may become a problem unless properly handled.

In respect to the time necessary for efficient showering, twelve to fifteen minutes is the usual amount. However, this can only be relative to the number of students

in the class and the number of shower stalls available. Girls generally require a longer period of time to shower than boys, so this should also be considered.

Because of the danger of slipping on a wet locker room floor, students should dry completely in the drying area, which is usually constructed adjacent to the showers. If none exists, the teacher should designate a particular portion of the locker room, near the shower exit, as "for drying only." In connection with safety, it is also essential that soap, deodorants, and other personal items be kept in unbreakable plastic containers.

The problem of towels can best be solved when the school provides them. Each student is then given a clean, dry towel that is returned at the end of the period. When students bring their own towels from home, they frequently allow them to mildew in the lockers, for lack of proper drying and cleaning. Squad captains should assist the teacher in the collecting and counting of towels, especially when towels are rented and the teacher is responsible for the exact number of towels supplied by the rental company.

Enforcement. If showers are required of all students, the teacher must have a method of enforcing this regulation. One of the easiest methods is to send students into the showers by squads, using leaders to help in checking off the squad members.

There is one exception to the regulation of required showering, and this relates to girls who are menstruating. In schools where no individual shower stalls and dressing areas are provided, these girls should be instructed to sponge off carefully at the sinks while partially dressed. In addition, a doctor's excuse from showering should be honored. All other students well enough to be in school and to participate in physical activity should be required to take a shower.

Grading

Grading in physical education, as in any academic subject, is a very difficult matter.

It should be kept in mind that the purpose of grading is to report an individual's progress both to that individual and to his parents. Each must understand exactly what the grade represents if it is to have any real meaning and subsequent effect. It must be pointed out that a grade in physical education represents many different factors—not skill alone. Further, it is the percentage accorded to each of these factors, as well as the form of the grade, that must be given consideration by the teacher. For an extensive discussion of these topics, see Chapter 19.

Cumulative records*

Record keeping in physical education, as in every field of endeavor, is a time-consuming process. However, time devoted to this aspect of the program is well spent if the material collected is pertinent, useful, and up-to-date. These are the main considerations regarding the records that should be kept, and they should help determine what materials are to be included.

The registration card spoken of in connection with class orientation is the basic item to be included in the individual record file. Each year a new registration card is added to the file with necessary and up-to-date information. Other data that should be on file—either on the same card if there is room, or separately—should include, according to Voltmer and Esslinger,[1] the following items:

Health information: medical excuses, changes
Activities: clubs, electives, intramural activities, etc
Grades: term and final marks, test scores
Attendance
Awards and honors
Teacher information: character notes and references

The gathering of too much information that will serve no purpose is always a danger. However, good records, efficiently kept from year to year, provide an accurate picture of an individual's growth and development and a meaningful basis for determining his particular needs.

*See materials in Appendix.

Problems and interruptions

Flexibility in the management of classes should be a byword for all teachers but particularly for physical educators. Many unforeseen occurrences create interruptions in the established school routine, and the teacher who can remain flexible and adapt suddenly yet wisely is a real master. There are several types of interruptions that merit attention: assemblies, class outings, fire drills, and injuries. (Weather may sometimes cause an interruption if the teacher has not considered it when planning.)

Assemblies. In schools where a combination auditorium-gymnasium is used, assemblies become a major source of interruptions. Book week, the science fair, and special examinations are all held in the auditorium, in addition to the regular assembly programs. Even when assemblies do not interfere with the scheduled physical education classes, the chairs may have to be put up or taken down. In this event the physical education teacher must have alternate plans to follow: written work, the use of audiovisual materials, or discussion. Fortunately, in good weather classes can be held outdoors and this problem is removed.

Class outings or trips. When class groups are taken on special field trips or outings, the physical education teacher is often left with half a group. In this instance the regular classwork should be adapted to the smaller group.

Fire drills and shelter drills. Safety drills are essential in all schools, and regular, prescribed procedures should be followed when such drills occur during physical education class. Instructions are usually issued by the administration as to where the groups should exit. The teacher is responsible for his or her particular group and must see that orders are carried out. These drills are a source of confusion when they occur at the end of a period, at a time when students are changing. The teacher should try to point out this difficulty to the principal so that the situation may be avoided.

Injuries. Injuries occur even in the safest situations and cause much distress to students in class. The teacher must be assured and calm in following regular accident procedures. All instructions—to send for the nurse, carry out activity, or dismiss the class—should be given with unruffled authority, to prevent students from becoming unduly alarmed or excited and perhaps from creating further danger because of thoughtless actions.

Characteristics of good class management

Careful observation of a single physical education class should reveal to a large extent the degree of management the teacher has promoted. Thoughtful analysis of the conduct of the students and their application to the day's work should point out certain characteristics of good class management. The following questions provide a guideline for such an analysis:

1. How much time is used in locker room procedures before class? After class?

2. How much time is required to check attendance?

3. How much time is required for students to become organized into working groups?

4. Are the students properly prepared for participation?

5. Are the students motivated to improve and are they engaged in purposeful activity?

6. Do the students display eagerness? Enthusiasm? Cheerfulness? Attentiveness? Respect?

7. Are *all* students thoughtfully engaged in some form of activity related to the unit or classwork for that day?

8. Do the students display an understanding of the purpose(s) of the day's lesson?

9. Are the students aware of their responsibilities for the safety and welfare of the group?

10. How much time is consumed by the teacher in *repetition* of directions?

11. Is the teacher's attention constantly directed toward individual questioners and disturbing groups? Or is his or her attention directed toward the supervision of all groups and assistance to some?

12. Do the students reveal satisfaction

Fig. 18-3. Careful observation of a physical education class will reveal to a large extent the degree of management the teacher has promoted. Physical education class in swimming. (Richwoods Community High School, Peoria Heights, Ill.)

from active participation at the close of the class period?

CONTROL

It was pointed out in the first part of this chapter that good class management sets the stage for instruction. The situation might then be described as teacher-controlled. In contrast, when routines and procedures are not understood and students do not know what is expected of them, confusion and chaos often are created. Discipline problems result from lack of control, a control imposed from without (the teacher) or within (the student). In either circumstance, instruction cannot effectively be introduced until proper controls are reinstated.

Incidence of discipline problems

Problems of misbehavior and violence have been increasing both inside and outside of schools. In a recent survey of crime rate, the National Education Association was told that of the five million arrests made by the FBI in 1964, 20.5% were of youths under 18 years of age. Juveniles were found to be involved in more than one third of the crimes solved by the police in the same year.[2] In studying misbehavior within schools, eight out of ten teachers reported confiscating weapons, and fourteen of those surveyed indicated violence had occurred in their schools. Furthermore, teachers indicated that misbehavior erupted in music, physical education, and activity courses more often than in other subject areas, generally because of overcrowded conditions. The median class size in junior high school physical education was 36.6, and in senior high school it was 38.8, higher than in any other subject.[3]

Discipline

It has been said that if education is changing behavior, discipline is controlling it for the purpose of education.

Methods of controlling behavior are many and varied, but the effectiveness of a single method may be determined only in terms of the resultant change. Was it a desirable change? Was the resulting change the one originally intended? For example, if, in handling a misbehavior problem, the teacher wins the student's compliance but produces within him hatred for the activity, has the original goal been met?

Handling discipline problems

Self-discipline is a developmental goal for each individual, as are self-respect, self-control, and independence of thought, action, and deed. Ideally, the adolescent moves along a continuum toward selfhood, where fewer and fewer limitations need to be imposed from the external environment. Conversely, the less mature student requires discipline and controls from others to help him along the way.

The teacher must recognize the developmental nature of this goal and strive to handle discipline problems with consideration for the makeup of the individual and the scope of his actions. Most teachers prefer to handle misbehavior problems themselves, particularly when infractions are fairly mild. In cases where the degree of misbehavior is more severe, the teacher should follow school procedures already established for such circumstances. Reporting occurrences to the administration is the general course of action taken in most schools. Assignment to detention hall, removal from class, or dismissal from school may be necessary. Ultimately, however, dismissal merely removes the problem from the situation, rather than helping the student find ways to improve his behavior.

Corporal punishment

One of the most controversial issues in education today surrounds the question of using corporal punishment to solve discipline problems. Such action is allowed by some administrators but forbidden by others. Teachers should be aware of established policies in this regard and should not violate them under any circumstances. Should a teacher not be in agreement with a particular policy, it would be better for him to effect a change in the policy itself rather than to openly defy it. It is interesting to note that, in a survey of teacher opinion, over 58% of several hundreds polled responded in favor of corporal punishment, while 34% were opposed.[4]

Other techniques

Other, less severe techniques of handling discipline problems include written assignments, reading assignments, oral reports to the class, additional exercising, work tasks, makeup classes, and a failing grade. Weighing such factors as the age of the student, the seriousness of the infraction, and the number of infractions by an individual helps to determine the choice of technique. A teacher needs to be consistent in meting out penalties, but consideration of the individual case should be the strongest determinant. For example, if two boys are caught creating a disturbance of some kind, and one of the boys is a constant troublemaker while the other is generally helpful, the resulting penalties might be different for each student.

The teacher also needs to keep in mind encroachments on his own time schedule each time penalties are determined. Having to read long dissertations (that may have been copied from a book) benefits neither the student nor the teacher, and having to stand around while students run additional laps wastes the instructor's time as well as breeds contempt for running in the minds of the offenders.

From this discussion it may be seen that no cardinal principles exist to guide a teacher in handling discipline problems. The burden remains with the individual teacher to be fair and effective while treating the student with consideration and respect. Humiliation, degradation, threats, and fear accomplish little toward motivating a student along desirable lines.

Prevention of problems

Just as the best defense is often described as a strong offense, so effective discipline might begin with prevention of

problems. Students should not be given a chance to misbehave.

Ideally, students should not want to misbehave. The realistic teacher tries to prevent their even thinking about foolish behavior by making sure that (1) they are having too much fun, (2) they are too busy, (3) they are too much interested in what is going on, (4) they are working too hard to improve, and (5) they want a good grade.

Under these circumstances control is enforced under the careful guidance of the instructor *through the students themselves.* Group discipline and self-discipline are in action here, rather than teacher-imposed regulations. Several keys to the development of this type of control may be deciphered here. Awarding of grades might be included as one of them, but for students who do not care about grades, and there are always a few, this factor would not be effective. (See motivation discussion in Chapter 12.) Effective planning and organization, as previously discussed, are certainly contributing elements to controlling the class session. However, the vital factor underlying the successful teaching picture can be found with the group itself. It is the power of the group that prevails. A creative teacher utilizes the dynamics of group interaction and the group process to reap benefits for each class member.

Grouping

Current thinking in education reflects a widespread interest in the problem of grouping. There are many who feel that *age* continues to be the best determinant for class grouping. In another report from a junior high school principal, claims were made for the successful application of *height* as a measure of development, and therefore maturity, for grouping of students. For the most part, however, the trend seems to be toward ability grouping. It was Conant's feeling that groups should be homogeneous in all subject matter areas except twelfth-grade American Government courses. In physical education, ability grouping has frequently been utilized in swimming courses, but grouping by skill level within other classes seems to be finding increased favor.

Methods of grouping. Several methods of grouping need study in terms of their advantages and disadvantages for physical education classes. It should be pointed out that methods of grouping can and should vary, depending on the teacher's purposes, the activity, the age group and size of the class, and the working units required for the course. The basic philosophy of the program also enters into consideration. The teacher needs to remember that successful teams or squads promote real enthusiasm and motivation in activities, and for this reason, appropriate grouping becomes a key factor in instruction. In a school in which teaching teams are used, groups may be selected according to activity, choice, need, or ability, depending on the unit of study. For example, in a very large high school in which 400 students are assigned to 10 physical education teachers, groups would be divided on an entirely different basis from that which would be used in a small school in which only 25 students meet for class during a single period. At the junior high level it is important to change groupings frequently to motivate and stimulate the students' changing interests. Many factors need consideration, and no single method of grouping answers the problems found in various teaching situations for physical education programming.

It is the responsibility of the physical education teacher to choose the method of grouping that is most appropriate to his or her teaching situation. Consideration must first be given to the desirability of possible *types* of groups as well as to the several *factors* that also determine the final selection of a method of grouping.

Types of groups. Methods of grouping may be classified according to the type of *control* that determines the selection of the group. Control may be in the hands of the teacher or the student, or it may be left to chance. Each type of grouping has its own particular advantages and problems, and each should be considered carefully by the

teachers when he is grouping a class for instruction.

Teacher-controlled methods of grouping. In the teacher-controlled type of grouping the teacher determines the groups. Teams or squads are selected according to scores on fitness tests, according to a particular skill or ability such as basket-shooting or speed, or on the basis of some other single underlying factor, such as height or weight. The teacher then distributes students on different squads into either homogeneous or heterogeneous groups.

Homogeneous groups

Samples
1. Low, average, and highly skilled gymnasts
2. Slow, average, and fast runners
3. Tall, medium, and short students

Advantages
1. The teacher knows individual needs in the area under study.
2. The teacher can select teaching methods appropriate to the levels and abilities of a particular group.
3. Individual students feel at home in their group when the abilities of all are similar.
4. Opportunities for leadership are provided students in the low and medium groups which otherwise may not be available.
5. The teacher may control cliques of students through their distribution on teams.
6. Students formulate realistic assessments of their own abilities and may be motivated to improve.

Problems
1. It is an unrealistic classroom setup; groups are not generally composed of people of like ability.
2. There may be a lack of motivation and incentive among some students in the lower groups.
3. There may not be adequate leadership in low ability groups.
4. Teachers may have a difficult time finding opportunities to retest and change groups of students showing improvement.
5. Record keeping and evaluation of students may become complicated if groups change frequently within a unit.

Heterogeneous groups

Samples
1. Highly skilled students evenly distributed
2. Tallest players evenly distributed
3. Leaders evenly distributed

Advantages
1. The teacher controls the distribution of students of high, average, and low skills to make even teams.
2. The teacher may control cliquishness in the same manner.
3. Leadership in all groups may be assured.
4. Students of high ability are motivated to

assist others on their own team, and those of low ability are motivated to improve.

5. Opportunities are provided for students to learn how to work together effectively with others.

Problems

1. Students dissatisfied with the group may be resentful and blame the teacher.

2. It is a very time-consuming method of grouping for the teacher because it requires much thought and preparation; well-balanced teams may not be the result.

3. A team or squad that does not perform well together immediately loses its spirit instead of trying harder to work together.

4. It is difficult to teach groups composed of different levels of skills.

Note: Schools presently engaged in the team-teaching approach have found teacher-controlled methods of grouping most helpful in dividing large classes into smaller study groups.

Student-controlled methods of grouping. In the student-controlled method of grouping, students select the teams. Captains previously elected by the class or appointed in some other manner select the members of their own teams. This may be done in front of the group or separately at a different time or place. Another method of grouping in this manner is to have captains select only part of their teams and allow the remaining students an opportunity to divide themselves evenly on teams of their choice.

Advantages

1. Captains are generally well-respected individuals and good leaders, for they have been elected by the group or otherwise selected for their abilities.

2. Initial selections by the captains generally provide an even distribution of highly skilled players to effect balanced teams.

3. Team spirit is promoted because players are generally pleased about being chosen or having an opportunity to select their own team.

Problems

1. Students waiting to be chosen by captains often feel left out and uncomfortable while hoping to be selected.

2. This is a time-consuming method if the entire class waits for teams to be selected.

3. The teams that result from this method are not necessarily balanced.

4. Cliques are not necessarily broken up by this method.

5. Some animosity may develop between students and captains.

Note: This method may be used most effectively to select teams for tournament games in ending a special unit of study, such as basketball or volleyball, especially if captains select entire teams without the class in attendance.

Methods controlled by chance. In this type of grouping, chance is the determining factor. Teams or squads are formed on the basis of homeroom groups or from numbers drawn from a hat. The system of lining students up and having them number off by "threes" or "fours" is frequently used. The line itself then offers a new factor of control, in that students may be lined up by alphabet, by height, or just haphazardly. The resulting teams are all heterogeneous in nature.

Advantages

1. Groups are realistic and competitive.

2. Skilled players assist others in their group.

3. Intraclass games and tournaments are usually interesting.

4. Students learn to play and get along well with all other students in their class.

5. Groups may be created and changed quickly and easily.

6. Many leadership opportunities are allowed if terms are changed often and if individuals are not allowed to serve as leaders a second time.

7. The teacher maintains standards of fairness and equality, because chance is the controlling factor.

Problems

1. It is difficult to meet the needs and interests of the individuals in these groups.

2. Teaching methods may not be appropriate for all students.

3. Teams may come out unbalanced, thereby hampering class tournaments and games.

Note: A teacher must vary methods used for selecting groups, for students are quick to catch on to repetitive methods. For example, if a teacher always divides groups by having students number off by fours, the students will soon begin to station themselves at intervals of fours as they line up.

These various methods of grouping have their advantages and problems. Before selecting the type of grouping most suitable to his or her teaching situation, the teacher needs to evaluate several other related factors.

Other factors involved in grouping

1. *How many squads or teams should be established?* The teacher should keep in mind the ultimate goal of providing the most practicing opportunities possible by creating the most groups according to equipment. The activity itself, the number of students, the number of teachers, and the facilities and teaching stations availa-

ble are all determinants in answering this initial question. The samples given in Table 16 indicate the different numbers of teams that may result because of the difference in the situation, not the activity.

2. *With which type of working groups may the objectives for physical development best be met in this unit?* Some units of study may require special groupings for drills, e.g., forwards and guards in basketball, defensive and offensive players in football, and heavyweight and lightweight students in wrestling. Therefore, the teacher must determine whether heterogeneous or homogeneous groupings would be more suitable for the activity.

3. *With which type of working groups may the objectives for social development in this unit best be met?* Teams providing oppotunities for leadership and for establishing harmonious relationships may result from selections made by either teachers or students. Perhaps there are special cliques that need to be separated for a more smoothly functioning class, and the teacher may therefore prefer to control the groupings for a particular unit.

4. *With which type of working groups may the objectives for intellectual development best be met?* Homogeneous groups may understand certain types of instruction more quickly when it is geared to each group's particular level. For example, rules and historical development of games may be learned more quickly by groups of lower abilities when audiovisual aids (charts, magnetic boards, etc.) are utilized in teaching. However, lectures would probably be suitable in giving this information to other groups.

5. *With which type of grouping may the objectives for emotional development in this unit best be met?* With a class of highly stimulated junior high school girls, for example, who are just being introduced to the game of speedball, squads may best be selected by the teacher in order to maintain calm and control. Then, at the end of the unit, the students may select teams for a tournament to climax the unit.

The teacher must weigh the answers to these questions before deciding which method to follow in grouping the class. The problem of heterogeneous versus homogeneous grouping in education has been and still is being argued from many different viewpoints. However, each teacher must determine the most suitable method in the existing circumstances.

SUMMARY

Good class management in physical education is the result of many factors. Planning, orientation, procedures, and grouping are all vitally important elements both for the prevention of discipline problems and for the promotion of instruction. Other contributing factors include the selection of class leaders and interaction between groups, which have intangible results yet promote the overall aim of education.

POINTS TO REMEMBER

1. There are certain preparations that should be made before school begins in the fall.
2. Methods of orienting a class to physical education work during the first week of school should be planned.
3. Students should participate in the formulation of codes of conduct in the locker room and gymnasium.
4. Methods and regulations should be established to minimize danger in the locker room when administering a shower program.
5. Methods and procedures for taking attendance should be efficient, clear, and concise.
6. Types of records kept in physical education

Table 16. Factors involved in grouping

Activity	Number of students	Number of teachers	Teaching stations and equipment	Squads/ members
Volleyball	48	1	2 courts 8 balls	4/12
	120	2	2 courts 8 balls	8/15
Basketball	60	1	6 goals 10 balls	6/10
	120	2	6 goals 10 balls	10/12

should be purposeful, up-to-date, and complete.

PROBLEMS TO THINK THROUGH

1. What health items would it be important to include in an individual's record card?
2. To what extent should students participate in forming rules and regulations for class routine, and to what extent should the teacher's word be law?
3. Considering that the teacher is legally responsible for the students in his charge, should a leader or class assistant be responsible for taking attendance?
4. What reasons are in favor of having captains select teams openly, so that all members of the class know the order in which they are chosen? Against?
5. What should a physical education teacher do in a situation in which the school nurse sympathetically hands out excuses from physical education class too frequently?

CASE STUDY FOR ANALYSIS

In a large high school there are four men and three women physical education instructors teaching all pupils in grades nine through twelve. In the present situation no adapted physical education is taught except for the small amounts the individual teachers are able to give excused pupils in the regular class periods. How should a new teacher coming into this setup be prepared to handle excused students in his own class? How should he work to improve the situation? What materials and information would he need?

EXERCISES FOR REVIEW

1. Design an all-purpose registration card to be used for the orientation period and for permanent records.
2. Construct a list of regulations necessary for a locker room and shower setup and indicate what responsibilities could be given class leaders.
3. How many costume "cuts" should be allowed a student during each grading period before lowering his grade?
4. What key questions may be asked a group of students in leading a discussion to determine class standards?
5. What assignments may be given to students excused from a basketball class, to be completed while observing class?

6. What are the advantages and the disadvantages of grouping a class of students into squads on the basis of skills?

REFERENCES

1. Voltmer, E., and Esslinger, A.: The organization and administration of physical education, New York, 1967, Appleton-Century-Crofts.
2. National Education Association: Student behavior in secondary schools, 1964, Washington, D. C., 1965, Research Division, The Association.
3. National Education Association: Class size in secondary schools, National Education Association Research Bulletin **43**:1, Feb., 1965.
4. National Education Association: What teachers think, Washington, D. C., 1965, The Association.

SELECTED READINGS

Bucher, Charles A.: Administration of school and college health and physical education programs, ed. 4, St. Louis, 1967, The C. V. Mosby Co.
Bucher, Charles A.: Foundations of physical education, ed. 5, St. Louis, 1968, The C. V. Mosby Co.
Bucher, Charles A.: Physical education for life, St. Louis, 1969, Webster Division, McGraw-Hill Book Co.
Conant, James B.: The comprehensive high school, New York, 1967, McGraw-Hill Book Co.
Dexter, Genevieve: Teachers' guide to physical education for girls in high school, Sacramento, Calif., 1957, California State Department of Education.
Long Beach Public Schools: Guide to the teaching of physical education and junior high school girls, Long Beach, Calif., 1956, Board of Education.
National Association of Secondary-School Principals: Health, physical education, and recreation in the secondary school, Washington, D. C., May, 1960, The Association.
Shepard, Natalie Marie: Foundations and principles of physical education, New York, 1960, The Ronald Press Co.
Torrance, E. Paul: Rewarding creative behavior, Englewood Cliffs, N. J., 1965, Prentice-Hall, Inc.
Van Dalen, Deobold B., and Van Dalen, Marcella M.: The health, physical education, and recreation teacher, Englewood Cliffs, N. J., 1956, Prentice-Hall, Inc.

BOOKLETS, PAMPHLETS, AND ARTICLES

Adams, Philip C., Jr.: Ability grouping in junior high school, Journal of Health, Physical Education, and Recreation **35**:83, May, 1964.
American Association of School Administrators, Association for Supervision and Curricular Development, National Association of Secondary-School Principals, and Department of Rural Education: A climate for individuality, NEA Journal **55**:34, Nov., 1966.

Bettelheim, Bruno: Grouping the gifted, NEA Journal **54**:8, March, 1965.

Cawelti, Gordon: High-school ability grouping programs, The Bulletin of the National Association of Secondary School Principals **47**:34, March, 1963.

Coffey, Margaret: Some unorthodox thoughts about showers, Journal of Health, Physical Education, and Recreation **37**:29, May, 1966.

Committee on Exercise and Physical Fitness of the American Medical Association: Classification of students for physical education, Journal of Health, Physical Education, and Recreation **38**:16, Feb., 1967.

Cratty, Bryant J., and Sage, Jack N.: Effect of primary and secondary group interaction upon improvement in a complex movement task, Research Quarterly **35**:265, Oct., 1964.

Gnagey, William J.: Controlling classroom behavior, Washington, D. C., 1965, Department of Classroom Teachers, American Education Research Association, of the National Education Association.

Hall, J. Revis, Killebrew, Katherine, and Lewis, Nellie Mae: Personalizing instruction, NEA Journal **55**:36, Nov., 1966.

Howard, Alvin W.: Discipline: three F's for the teacher, The Education Digest **31**:25, Sept., 1965.

Joyndt, Louis: Time savers, The Physical Educator **21**:159, Dec., 1964.

Muster, Karl W.: These techniques work for me, NEA Journal **56**:16, Sept., 1967.

National Education Association, Research Division: Student behavior in secondary schools, 1964, Washington, D. C., 1965, The Association.

National Education Association, Research Division: What teachers think, Washington, D. C., 1965, The Association.

National Education Association: Class size in secondary school, NEA Research Bulletin **43**:1, Feb., 1965.

Nelson, Wayne E.: Take time to teach student leaders, Journal of Health, Physical Education, and Recreation **37**:22, April, 1966.

Olson, Willard C.: Ability grouping: pros and cons, The PTA Magazine **60**:24, April, 1966.

Pearl, Arthur: Are you sure pupils are better off at school? Nation's Schools **78**:46, Aug., 1966.

Wolfson, Bernice J.: Individualizing instruction, NEA Journal **55**:31, Nov., 1966.

part

six

Evaluation

Spartanburg Public Schools, Spartanburg, S. C.

Pupil evaluation
and
grading

Physical education teachers have the responsibility of evaluating the degree to which they are accomplishing professional objectives. This process of evaluation should cover two general areas: pupil achievement, which includes the progress report or grade, and program administration. In Chapter 20 details of the evaluation of program administration and teaching are discussed, whereas in the present chapter the main topic is pupil evaluation and grading.

Evaluation of pupil achievement should determine to what extent program objectives are being met. Evaluation should reveal levels of student development toward each of the four major goals: physical fitness, physical skills, knowledge and appreciation, and social development. The results of this evaluation process should serve many purposes. Besides providing a basis for grading pupil progress, evaluation techniques should also provide essential information for the motivation, guidance, and grouping of students and for program planning and curriculum building.

Current emphasis on meeting individual needs has increased the importance of these evaluative techniques, particularly

for the purpose of identifying exceptional children. In order for the orthopedically handicapped, gifted, and retarded children to receive equal opportunities in education, special adapted programs, both in physical education and in general education, are being developed to meet their particular needs.

There are many techniques of evaluation that are useful in measuring pupil achievement. Selection of a particular instrument depends on several factors, including time, facilities, and type and purposes of information sought. Physical education teachers must devise a program of evaluation suitable to the philosophy and objectives of their particular school situation and physical education program. However, at least a minimum program of evaluation should be instituted to fulfill the teachers' responsibilities in this area. Larson and Yocom[1] suggest that a minimum program of measurement and evaluation in physical education include the following:

A. Evaluation of pupil achievement
  1. Physical fitness
    a. Medical examination
    b. Physical fitness test
  2. Physical skills
    a. General test of motor ability

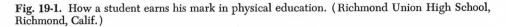

YOU EARN YOUR MARK IN PHYSICAL EDUCATION

(You earn **6** points a day for full participation)

Participation and Health - - - - - - -	240 points
Skills (ability) - - - - - - - - -	60 points
Knowledge of the Rules - - - - - -	20 points
Maximum Total - - - - - -	320 points

A - - 320 - 306	**Bonus Points—**		
B - - 305 - 286	Class Intramural Champ	-	10
C - - 285 - 261	Leader in Decathlon	- -	5
D - - 260 - 241	Satisfactory Captain	- -	10
F - - 240 - Below	Oiler Leader - - - -		15

Make-Up — 6 points a week on scheduled day.

Fig. 19-1. How a student earns his mark in physical education. (Richmond Union High School, Richmond, Calif.)

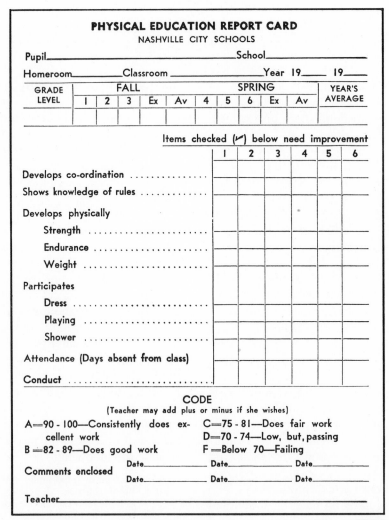

PHYSICAL EDUCATION REPORT CARD
NASHVILLE CITY SCHOOLS

Pupil_____School_____

Homeroom_____Classroom _____Year 19_____ 19_____

GRADE LEVEL	FALL					SPRING					YEAR'S AVERAGE
	1	2	3	Ex	Av	4	5	6	Ex	Av	

Items checked (✔) below need improvement

	1	2	3	4	5	6
Develops co-ordination						
Shows knowledge of rules						
Develops physically						
Strength						
Endurance						
Weight						
Participates						
Dress						
Playing						
Shower						
Attendance (Days absent from class)						
Conduct						

CODE
(Teacher may add plus or minus if she wishes)

A=90 - 100—Consistently does excellent work

B =82 - 89—Does good work

C=75 - 81—Does fair work

D=70 - 74—Low, but, passing

F=Below 70—Failing

Comments enclosed   Date_____ Date_____ Date_____

Date_____ Date_____ Date_____

Teacher_____

(Front)

Fig. 19-2. Physical education report card. (Nashville City Schools, Nashville, Tenn.)

3. Knowledge and appreciation
   a. Teacher-made tests
4. Social development
   a. Observation
B. Evaluation of program administration (according to standards established by leading authorities)
   1. Class program
   2. Adapted program
   3. Interscholastic sports
   4. Intramural activities
   5. Administration

   Each to be evaluated
   in terms of:

   a. Activities   e. Participation
   b. Leadership   f. Records
   c. Facilities   g. Research
   d. Equipment   h. Budgetary allotments

A more comprehensive program of measurement and evaluation would include several other testing techniques, such as sports skill tests, attitude and interest inventories, checklists, and questionnaires. The development of a program of evaluation adequate for a particular school situation takes a great deal of careful thought and study on the part of the staff. Furthermore, the relationship of the results of the evaluation process to the individual report card is another area of great concern.

Methods and materials for evaluation of pupil achievement and various systems of

ATTITUDES AND PRACTICES	Items checked (✔) below need improvement					
	1	2	3	4	5	6
SOCIAL						
Uses self-control						
Is courteous in speech and action						
Co-operates						
Cares for property (incl. textbooks)						
Is considerate toward others						
Respects and obeys school rules						
WORK						
Makes good use of abilities						
Follows directions promptly						
Completes each task						
Works independently						
Uses initiative						
HEALTH						
Maintains personal cleanliness						
Maintains correct posture						
Obeys safety precautions						

PARENT'S SIGNATURE

1. _____
2. _____
3. _____
4. _____
5. _____
6. _____

(Back)

Fig. 19-2, cont'd. For legend see opposite page.

Student ....

.... 19........... - 19......

Grade

RICHWOODS COMMUNITY HIGH SCHOOL

Progress Report in Physical Education

Teacher .... Counselor ....

1st pd.	2nd pd.	3rd pd.	Sem. exam	Sem. avg.	4th pd.	5th pd.	6th pd.	Sem. exam	Sem. avg.	Units crdt.

EXPLANATION OF MARKING SYSTEM

Achievement—Grading for actual work done by the student

A—94-100—Excellent   D—70-77—Below Average
B—86- 93—Above Avg.   F—Below 70—Failure
C—78- 85—Average   E—Conditional
       Inc.—Incomplete

ACTIVITIES INCLUDED IN GRADING PERIODS

ACTIVITIES	1	2	3	4	5	6
Flicker Ball						
Flag Football						
Soccer						
*Field Hockey						
*Speed Ball						
*Campcraft						
Basketball (beginning) (advanced)						
Volleyball (beginning) (advanced)						
Tumbling (beginning) (advanced)						
Apparatus (beginning) (advanced)						
Wrestling (beginning) (advanced)						
Handball						
Badminton						
Recreational Games						
*Fundamental Rhythms—Modern Dance						
Track and Field						
Softball						
Archery						
Golf						
Co. P.E. Social Dance						
Co. P.E. Square Dance						
Co. P.E. Volleyball & Rec. Games						
Driver Training (Classroom)						
Health Education (Classroom)						
*Indicates Girls' Activity Only						

GRADING PROCEDURE

The six week grade is evaluated in the following areas:
1. Performance of Skills
2. Knowledge of Skills and Physical Fitness
3. Social Attitudes including cooperation, sportsmanship, and leadership
4. Hygiene conditions (uniforms, showers), and attendance.

PHYSICAL FITNESS TESTS
(Based on National Norms)

	Trial 1 (Fall)		Trial 2 (Spring)	
	Score	% ile	Score	% ile
Pull-Ups (Boys) (shoulder strength)				
Modified Pull-Ups (Girls) (shoulder strength)				
Sit-Ups (abdominal strength)				
Shuttle Run (agility)				
Standing Broad Jump (leg power)				
50-Yard Dash (speed)				
Softball Throw (arm power)				
600-Yard Run-Walk (endurance)				

The National Norms and Scores are based on Age, Weight, and Height.

PARENT'S SIGNATURE

Your signature means only that you have seen this report.

1st Period..

2nd Period..

3rd Period..

4th Period..

5th Period..

Each absence, however short, interferes with the student's progress.

(Front)   *(Back)*

Fig. 19-3. Progress report in physical education. (Richwoods Community High School, Peoria Heights, Ill.)

reporting pupil progress are presented and discussed.

METHODS AND MATERIALS FOR EVALUATING PUPIL ACHIEVEMENT

An evaluation program of pupil achievement should be designed to determine level of achievement in relation to the four principal objectives of the physical education program. The following testing techniques, resources, and materials, plus methods of devising tests, are included in the goal area where they are most suitable and applicable.

Organic development of physical fitness

Medical examination. A medical examination should be given to each student once a year by a competent doctor, and a cardiovascular test should also be administered once a year if possible.

Physical fitness tests. Physical fitness tests

Fig. 19-4. Skills need to be tested in physical education. Girls' trapeze skills. (Centennial High School, Pueblo, Colo.)

should be given early in the school year and in the spring as well. The results of such tests help determine the degree of fitness of the pupils, provide the teacher with a basis for student classification for instructional purposes, and indicate the progress of the students toward attainment of this objective. Several test batteries, such as the AAHPER Physical Fitness Test Battery,[2] have been devised for measurement in this area; they were discussed in Chapter 15.

Physical skills

Because a major portion of the physical education class is devoted to the teaching of skills, many skill tests in each of the various sports have been developed. They cover a wide range of age levels and grades in some sports, while in other activities there may be no suitable test available. General tests of physical capacity and motor efficiency have also been developed for evaluation of student performance and capacity.

Suggested general skills tests. In the past, leaders in the field have devoted much time and research to testing *motor educability, motor capacity, physical capacity, motor ability,* and *motor efficiency.* These terms may appear at first to be synonymous with physical fitness. The beginning teacher should understand, however, that the work done in each of these areas is not to be confused with recent physical fitness testing. Some of the former tests measured inherent aptitudes of pupils, while others measured achievement in basic motor skills. The beginning teacher wishing to use some of these tests should become familiar with the various kinds of tests and the purposes of each—the following, for example: (1) Rogers Strength Test,[3] (2) California Physical Fitness Pentathlon,[4] (3) McCloy's General Motor Ability and Capacity Test,[5] (4) Larson Muscular Strength Test,[6] (5) Illinois High School Physical Condition Test,[7] and (6) Indiana Physical Fitness Test for High School Boys and Girls.[8]

These are a few of the many tests available to the teacher of physical education for testing general skills. Reference to the original works of the authors will provide directions necessary to the administration of these tests.

Suggested sports skills tests. Leaders in the field of physical education have developed testing instruments for skills in such sports as the following: archery, badminton, baseball, basketball, bowling, football, golf, gymnastics, handball, field hockey and ice hockey, riding, rhythms, figure skating, soccer, softball, speedball, squash, stunts and tumbling, swimming, tennis, and volleyball. Descriptions of these tests, including age level, equipment needed, and administrative directions, are given in one or more source books.[3, 5, 9, 10]

Other suggestions for testing may be found in the individual sports rule books, current literature, periodicals, and booklets on sports. In looking over these tests the teacher finds that certain basic skills necessary to the games themselves have been

AAHPER SPORTS SKILLS TESTS

CLASS COMPOSITE RECORD

Teacher ____________ Class ____________ Date ____________

School ____________ City ____________

A

NAMES	Age	1		2		3		4		5		6		7		8		9		10	
		Score	%	Score	%	Score	%	Score	%	Score	%	Score	%	Score	%	Score	%	Score	%	Score	%

CLASS COMPOSITE RECORD

Fig. 19-5. Shown on this and the following two pages are the record forms for skills tests. The squad score card, **B**, is to be filled out as the test is given. Note that scores for the various test items are recorded in different ways. The class composite record, **A**, has space for recording the raw score and the percentile score, which is determined by using tables. (See Table 17.) The personal data sheet, **C**, has room for several tests; the profile, **D**, can be used for several tests also, by using pencils of different colors.*

*All the record forms shown on these pages are available from the American Association for Health, Physical Education, and Recreation. Order from NEA Publications-Sales, 1201 16th St., N.W., Washington, D. C. 20036.

Sports Skills Squad Score Card (242-07704), 3¢ each
Sports Skills Class Composite Record (242-07702), 5¢ each
Sports Skills Personal Data and Profile Record (242-07700), 3¢ each

Discount of 10% for 2 to 9 copies; discount of 20% for 10 or more.

selected, and the testing procedures that have been devised for these skills are closely related to the game situation. Suggested methods for rating or scoring individual performances on a specified number of trials, as well as norms for grade level performances, are usually included. Limitations to the use of these tests exist, however, for in many instances too much time is required for their administration, their reliability or validity is questionable, or the norms listed may be for the college years. It is necessary to study these prepared tests carefully, therefore, to determine their suitability or adaptability to a particular teaching situation.

Perhaps the most significant new development in the area of skill evaluation is being promoted under the sponsorship of the American Association for Health, Physical Education, and Recreation. Their Re-

search Council has been working to devise tests and norms for effective evaluation of boys and girls, grades five through twelve, in physical education programs across the United States. When completed, this total project, which includes instructional manuals, will include skill tests for the following:

Archery	Lacrosse
Badminton	Soccer
Baseball	Softball
Basketball	Swimming
Field hockey	Tennis
Football	Track and field
Golf	Volleyball
Gymnastics	

The sports skills test manuals are very helpful not only for testing purposes but for instructional pointers as well. Sample class composite record forms, data forms, and profile forms (see Table 17) are available from the Association.

SQUAD SCORE CARD

Fig. 19-5, cont'd. For legend see opposite page.

AAHPER SPORTS SKILLS TESTS — Softball — PERSONAL DATA RECORD

Name: Joan Dean
School: Kennedy Jr. High   City: Rising Sun, Maryland

	1.		2. Test Periods 3.		4.			
Date	4/8/67		4/21/68					
Age	12		13					
Grade	7		8					
Height	4' 10"		4' 11"					
Weight	100		105					
TESTS	Score	%	Score	%	Score	%	Score	%
1. Distance throw	70	50	76	50				
2. Accuracy throw	9	60	11	65.				
3. Pitching	6	60	8	60				
4. Speed throw	23.1	55	21.4	60				
5. Fungo Hitting	19	75	20	75				
6. Base running	14.6	70	13.9	75				
7. Field...	16	85		75				

PERSONAL DATA RECORD

C

AAHPER SPORTS SKILLS TESTS — Softball — PERSONAL PROFILE RECORD

Name: Joan Dean
School: Kennedy Jr. High   City: Rising Sun, Maryland

Code
1968 ————
1969 ————

PERSONAL PROFILE RECORD

D

Fig. 19-5, cont'd. For legend see p. 338.

Teacher-made tests. When acceptable testing devices are not available, teachers may want to originate sports skills tests that are appropriate and accurate for their teaching situations. This is a long and involved process, but the following suggestions may be helpful when developing sports skills tests for personal use.

1. The sport should be analyzed to determine and select skills for measurement.

2. Special procedures should be devised for the administration of a test of a skill or skills.

3. A preliminary test should be administered to a group and a check made to see if those of acknowledged superior ability score higher than others in their performances.

4. If the above check suggests validity, complete rating of the group should be made and the validity coefficient computed.

5. The test results should again be checked, this time against the rules of the game from which the skill was taken, with higher scorers playing against lower scorers.

6. Retesting should be done on one group to compute the reliability coefficient.

7. The raw scores from the test should be converted to some type of comparable scoring system to make results most useful.[11]

A teacher following these procedures can be fairly sure that the results of the test are valid and reliable.

Other testing techniques. Sports skills tests are only one method of evaluating physical skills. In some types of activities there are no objective tests available for use, and more subjective measures must be made. There are also some skills which in themselves are impossible to measure objectively. Other techniques, such as

Table 17. Softball throw for distance (girls)* (percentile scores based on age/test scores in feet)

Percentile	Age							Percentile
	10-11	12	13	14	15	16	17-18	
100th	120	160	160	160	200	200	200	100th
95th	99	113	133	126	127	121	120	95th
90th	84	104	112	117	116	109	109	90th
85th	76	98	105	109	108	103	102	85th
80th	71	94	98	104	103	98	97	80th
75th	68	89	94	99	97	94	93	75th
70th	66	85	90	95	93	91	89	70th
65th	62	81	86	92	88	87	87	65th
60th	60	77	83	88	85	84	84	60th
55th	57	74	81	85	80	81	82	55th
50th	55	70	76	82	77	79	80	50th
45th	53	67	73	79	75	76	77	45th
40th	50	64	70	76	72	73	74	40th
35th	48	61	68	73	70	70	72	35th
30th	45	58	64	69	67	67	69	30th
25th	43	55	62	66	64	63	66	25th
20th	41	51	60	61	61	60	63	20th
15th	38	48	56	57	58	56	60	15th
10th	34	43	51	52	54	51	55	10th
5th	31	37	43	43	49	45	50	5th
0	20	20	20	20	20	10	10	0

*From Softball for girls, skills test manual, Washington, D.C., 1966, American Association for Health, Physical Education, and Recreation, p. 37.

teacher ratings and progress charts, must be used.

Teacher ratings are generally necessary in evaluation of the form used in completing a skill. For example, diving, ski jumping, and figure skating must be judged partially or totally on the basis of form. In addition, the form used in batting, shooting baskets, playing tennis or badminton, hockey dribbling, and swimming is important to the level of achievement and must be judged by teacher rating. The teacher must therefore determine a scale for judgment—1 to 5 or 1 to 10—and establish specific standards for rating individual performance. When more than one judge is used, averages of ratings are computed and more acceptable results are obtained.

Teacher ratings are also necessary in the evaluation of creative movement or performance. Establishing certain criteria, or evaluative standards, provides a basis for rating on a predetermined point scale by the teacher or judges. Criteria such as use of space, use of body, use of focus, use of types of movement, and degree to which the given problem was solved should be developed by the teacher and explained to the students involved in the test.

Student progress in a particular skill is another factor that is sometimes difficult to measure. In some sports, such as bowling and archery, the scores themselves may be used to indicate improvement. The teacher can keep a record of scores on charts to measure individual progress. Charts are also useful in measuring progress, because keeping track of the number of baskets shot and missed or the number of goals attempted will result in an indication of performance skill and progress.

However, the performance of each individual must be assessed separately when charts are used to determine improvement for grading purposes. Some students may intentionally score low early in the season, in order to exhibit great progress when tested at the end of the unit. Also, several students may have identical progress scores, such as three more baskets on the second testing round. The teacher must then consider which student making a score of three evidenced greater improvement: the low scorer who managed to make three more baskets or the expert who scored high originally, yet still increased his score by three. Only by evaluating each student performance individually can a teacher make proper use of charts in grading.

Knowledge and appreciation

In the area of knowledge and appreciation, tests differ from those of physical fitness and skills—in that an intellectual process is involved, rather than a motor performance. Standardized written tests are available in some of the sports and may be found in rule books and source books of the various sports. Unfortunately, many standardized tests are constructed for the college level. Teachers may therefore have to devise their own tests, using either the oral, essay, or objective form. In so doing, the teacher can be certain that the test covers assigned materials and that it is suitable for the age level being tested.

Principles of test construction. There are certain principles of test construction that should be followed when developing an original written knowledge test.

1. The items selected should cover the entire subject matter, with emphasis placed on the most important facets of the game.

2. The length of the test should be related to the time available for testing.

3. The test should be appropriately worded and geared for the age level to be tested.

4. Directions should be simple and clear.[11]

Techniques of testing. There are several different techniques that may be utilized in test construction. True-and-false items, matching questions, sentence completion, multiple-choice, and diagrams, as well as short essays, may be combined to make an interesting and comprehensive examination of knowledge.

The following are a few suggestions as to the exact wording of objective tests. Teachers may not realize the importance of a single word in a written test until a student points out some confusion or misinterpretation.

1. Questions or test items should be worded so as to avoid ambiguity and triviality.

2. Statements should be simple and direct, not tricky, involved, or based solely on opinion.

3. Words such as *never, always, none,* or *all* should be omitted in sentences requiring true or false answers.[5]

Knowledge tests are generally developed in objective form, but evaluation of appreciation requires other techniques. To determine attitudes and opinions in physical education, the teacher will find that short-answer questionnaires, opinion polls, and surveys are useful. These testing techniques are not designed to determine factual comprehension, as knowledge tests are, but to discover student preferences in the area of program content or their attitudes toward class conduct. Results of these tests, therefore, are not computed on an individual basis but are used to determine overall class opinions or estimations. Because of the personal nature of these testing techniques, the forms are, of necessity, teacher-made. Construction of these questionnaires or surveys depends on the information sought and the purposes to be served.

Administration of tests. When a written test is administered, directions should be read aloud as well as written on the test paper. A few questions as to the timing or scoring of the test may be answered, but they should be limited. Following the signal "go," no further questions or talking should be allowed. Nothing is more disconcerting to the teacher or the students than unnecessary questioning. If directions are clear and the test is well constructed, a satisfactory examination should result. The period is then worthwhile, and the students will acknowledge the value of a written test in physical education.

Social development

Social development is a goal of the physical education program that also requires evaluation, but unfortunately, it is one aspect that is often neglected by teachers. The social development of the adolescent is a complex process, as was pointed out in Chapter 3. However, various techniques of testing have been devised to measure some of its aspects: social adjustment, attitudes and interests, social efficiency, and social status.

Testing social adjustment. Measurements of social adjustment may be made through the administration of standardized inventories (such as the Bell Adjustment Inventory) that have been developed specifically for this purpose. Such inventories should be used cautiously, however, and the results regarded only as clues to or indications of adjustment problems. The guidance department of a large school system is probably better equipped to administer and interpret these tests, but the physical education teacher should be familiar with them. A list of some of the other tests for social adjustment includes the following: Science Research Associates Inventory, Minnesota Multiphasic Personality Inventory, Washburne's Social Adjustment Inventory, and the Bernreuter Personality Inventory. These tests are usually concerned with common adolescent problems or worries about the home, health, friends, and so on. Such tests or inventories are for general educational use, not for physical education personnel alone; therefore, the school psychologist or guidance counselor should be consulted in regard to this phase of testing.

Testing attitudes and interests. The guidance department should also be able to assist the physical educator in testing the attitudes or interests of adolescents. Attitudes may be measured in different ways. As examples, three techniques are mentioned: (1) teacher evaluation (observation of students, with an anecdotal record being kept by the teacher), (2) opinion polls, and (3) rating scales. The physical education teacher should ask for the assistance of other teachers, and particularly of the guidance personnel, in this type of testing. Teachers work together because of a mutual interest in student problems, and sharing the test results promotes greater understanding among all concerned. This type of faculty cooperation would apply also to interest inventories such as the Strong Vocational Interest Blank, or the Kuder Preference Record. The development of social interests, attitudes, and adjustment, while being a goal of physical education, is also a general educational goal, and testing them is the concern of the entire teaching staff.

Two scales developed specifically for testing attitudes in physical education are the Adams scales.[15] Students are asked whether they agree or disagree with such statements as "Physical education gets very monotonous," and "Physical education is my favorite subject."

Testing social efficiency. In regard to testing social efficiency, rating scales have been developed by leaders in the field of physical education specifically for use within the program. Three are listed.

1. The McCloy test consists of rating, on a scale of 1 to 5, nine character traits.[12]

2. B. E. Blanchard devised a frequency rating scale for measuring character and personality in physical education classes.[13]

3. O'Neel published a rating scale for high school boys in physical education classes.[14]

In these three tests, ratings of the frequency of behavior are measured by observer judgment. By referring to the original sources indicated, the teacher may learn the techniques of administering these tests for social efficiency.

Testing social status. Sociometrics is the measurement of social relationships as determined by use of a sociogram. The sociogram is useful in physical education as a method of teaching and of testing the social status of individuals in a class, team, or squad. The results of the sociogram point out the natural leaders in the groups and the outsiders trying to become members. When the device is used more than once with the same group, a comparison of the results indicates social growth or change. A sociogram may be taken, for example, by asking all members of a team to list two people whom they would most like to have as their friends, with their choices limited to a given group or team. Results may be pictured with arrows pointing to the names listed, as shown in Fig. 19-6.

It may be interpreted from the particular sociogram shown here that John is the strongest leader, with Bill following closely behind. John, Larry, and Ed seem to form a rather small social clique, while Bill, who would like to join them, returns friendship with Fred only. It may be said also that

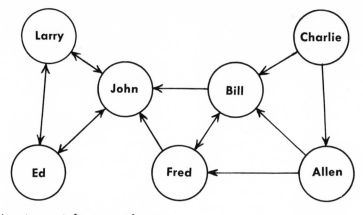

Fig. 19-6. A sociogram indicates social status.

Allen may be trying to break up this friendship, and that Charlie, who was chosen by no one, would be happy with either Bill or Allen for a friend.

An indication of social development in such a group would be the movement of Charlie and Allen into an acceptable position in the group and the enlargement of the clique so that friendships are more spread out. A second sociogram would then show partial proof of social development and accomplishment through teamwork in whatever the group activity may have been. This is a simple technique of testing social development. It is useful as a tool in teaching because it indicates social interactions and points out possibly dangerous cliques, as well as those individuals who need assimilation into the group. The teacher, knowing this, can gear teaching to avoid social upsets and to improve social relationships.

Problems in evaluating student achievement

The testing of student achievement and the analysis of results necessary for their future application are essentials of the teaching program. For the new teacher, five main problems stem from this responsibility: (1) allotting time for testing, (2) selecting tests, (3) administering tests, (4) keeping records, and (5) using the results.

Allotting time. The time necessary for adequate evaluation of students' achieve-

ments must be set aside as a regular part of the teaching program. In situations where classes meet every day, one class period every other week may be devoted to testing. When classes meet only two or three times a week, the teacher should plan for evaluation procedures at least at the beginning and end of each unit of study in order to obtain accurate records of growth and progress.

Selecting tests. In selecting tests the new teacher should survey the available instruments to determine if they are pertinent to his or her particular school situation. Proper selection of tests helps to overcome the problems of large classes, short periods, and individual rating needs. Because good organization and wise use of leaders also help to eliminate loss of valuable time, the beginning teacher should plan testing periods very carefully in order to make the most of them. Testing itself is a teaching method, with its promotion of good performances and its motivational purposes, and time taken for evaluation is therefore not wasted.

In selecting a test for administration to a class, the teacher should be concerned with five elements of the particular test: validity, objectivity, reliability, norms, and administrative feasibility. If the test is satisfactory in all these respects, the teacher may be assured that the results will be accurate.

Validity. The test should measure what it is supposed to measure. If the teacher is measuring balance, for example, the test should measure balance, and not some other physical characteristic, such as speed or endurance.

Objectivity. The scoring of the test should be exact and well defined, and as free as possible from personal opinion or subjective judgment. If two or more judges evaluate the performances of a class group, their answers or scores should be similar. This is an important factor in testing, and it affects the students to a great extent. They recognize the value of exact scoring methods for particular performances, and generally prefer them to scaled value-judgments.

Reliability. The testing device should consistently produce the same results. If a test were repeated under very similar conditions with the same group, the results should be equivalent—with the better performers again scoring high, etc. Extraneous factors such as practice, distance, or time should not influence the results.

Norms. The test should have an accepted scale of performance scores normal for particular age levels and groups. Norms are useful for comparison of the achievements of one group with those of a similar group. Norms are valuable, however, only if they are based on a large population, which ensures a wide range of performance levels.

Administrative feasibility. It should be possible to administer a test to a class group without too much expense, loss of time, or other complication. It is logical to expect that testing student achievement consumes a reasonable amount of time, expense, and consideration. Evaluation should not, however, result in excessive loss of teaching time, to the detriment of the program. This factor often determines the feasibility of administration of a particular type of test. Taking into account class size, available equipment, and length of class periods may eliminate an otherwise sound testing device.

Making the selection of a testing instrument according to these five factors is necessary if accurate and worthwhile results are to be obtained. The teacher of physical education should take great care in surveying available tests before making a final choice.

Administering tests. The feasibility of administering a particular instrument of testing is not the only consideration involved prior to selection. Other factors unrelated to the test itself may become problems during test administration and therefore need to be anticipated by the teacher.

1. *What provisions can be made in regard to changing climactic conditions?* For example, in a test for accuracy in archery or punting in football, wind direction and velocity may be a disturbing factor. Can retests be administered?

2. *What provisions can be made for makeup testing of pupils who may be absent on the day the test is given?* Will time be set aside after school, or during the regular class program to accommodate these pupils? Will the identical test be given, or will a substitute be used to prevent preparation on the basis of rumors or gossip?

3. *What provisions can be made to correct errors made by student assistants, in timing, for example, or in scoring test results?* Will retesting solve this problem, or will the advantage of previous practice produce a higher score by the testee?

4. *What provisions can be made for the maintenance of testing targets, line markers, etc., during the test administration?* Chalk lines frequently become blurred or erased during test administration. Can masking tape be used, or is it possible to assign a student leader the task of keeping lines or circles visible?

5. *What provisions can be made for students who err throughout the entire test, either through a misunderstanding of the directions or through a lack of sufficient time?* Should such students automatically fail because of their unacceptable performances, or should they be allowed the opportunity to take the test again in the makeup period?

These are questions that the teacher

must answer when administering tests, whether they be written or performance tests of student achievement.

Keeping records. The clerical duties attached to the testing program pose other difficulties. Records should be kept up-to-date and new test results constantly analyzed in terms of student progress and program planning for most effective use. The teacher must take time to do this if the true values of evaluation are to be realized.

In order to ease this difficulty somewhat, schools have been making use of community volunteers, or teacher-aids, to free regular teachers from these clerical duties, which consume so much time. The physical education teacher should investigate this possibility in regard to record-keeping. The form of the record itself may help to make the task less burdensome. Samples of such forms are included in the appendix materials at the end of the book. Some schools have been finding the use of IBM cards to be a real help in solving the problem of recording test results. The Evergreen Park Community High School uses this system to record physical fitness test results and to send reports home as well. A sample card is seen in Fig. 19-7.

It may also be helpful for the teacher to maintain a record file of evaluative tests used, adding comments concerning possible success or problems involved in their administration. This procedure would prevent repetition of testing with unsuitable instruments.

Using test results. The results of all types of tests of student achievement should be put to use if the process of evaluation is to have any direct value for the students. There are several ways in which this may be done, and the choice depends on the purpose of the particular test.

Tests administered at the beginning of a unit—whether skill, knowledge, or fitness tests—serve as prognostic devices to determine the needs of the group in relation to that specific activity. The teacher should interpret test results immediately and use them in planning the unit of study. Special groups may need to be formed on the basis of skills, or a special area of the activity may need emphasis because of a general weakness of the group. The motivational aspect of prognostic tests is also a valuable teaching tool.

Tests administered in the middle of a unit serve a diagnostic purpose, since results can indicate to the teacher those areas wherein teaching has not been sufficiently clear to make learning complete. The teacher then knows that the remaining

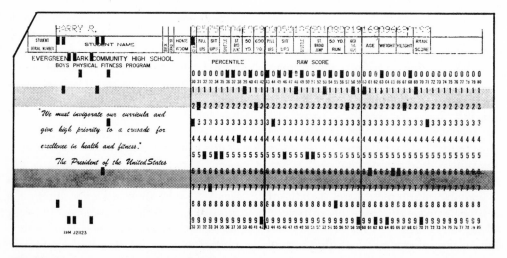

Fig. 19-7

class sessions need to include review and clarification of ideas to cement learning.

Tests at the close of a unit of study indicate pupil progress and achievement. When they are compared with preliminary tests, a vital measure of improvement and effort is obtained.

Evaluation of student achievement should do more than produce figures of present status. It should promote improvement of this status. This can be accomplished only through appropriate use of accurate test results.

Scores on all tests administered within a given unit, course of study, or semester should be averaged and combined with other determinants to equal a student's grade for that particular report period. The problems of using test results and developing a grading system are extremely important ones, and the physical education teacher must consider them very carefully and thoughtfully.

METHODS AND MATERIALS FOR GRADING

Grading in physical education is a complex process, for a single grade represents many different facets of pupil achievement —all of them important. In simplest terms, a grade is a teacher's (or teachers') estimation of pupil status. It may take several different forms, it may be arrived at by many different techniques, and it may serve many purposes.

Purposes of grading

In general, a grade serves two primary purposes: it informs the student of his present status, and it also notifies the parents. Grades may also serve several subsidiary functions: (1) a motivational device for some students, (2) a guide to program planning and regrouping of students, because grades identify areas of strength and weakness in the curriculum and in the youngsters, and (3) a basis for counseling students, for abrupt changes in a student's grades would probably be indicative of problems. Unfortunately, grades are some-

times used as a threatening device to push or force students into activity, which is not a desirable purpose of grading.

Principles of grading

To be of real value, a grade in physical education should be developed according to certain well-defined principles:

1. It should be representative of an individual pupil's achievement in relation to the established objectives of physical education. Comparison of achievement with other students should be avoided.

2. It should be developed on the basis of all four objectives of physical education. Emphasis should be placed on physical skills and physical development to the same degree that these factors are stressed in the program of instruction.

3. It should be understood by the student. He or she should know its components, the method of derivation of the grade, and how the factors were weighted.

4. It should be understandable to parents. It should be explicit enough so that the objectives of the program are clearly defined.

5. It should be expressed in the same manner as grades in other subject matter areas throughout the school. This not only facilitates record keeping and transfer of credits but also places physical education on the same level as other subjects.

6. It should be determined on the basis of several different evaluative techniques. Both subjective and objective measurements should be used.

7. It should be fair—a just estimation of the student's achievement and proper consideration should be given to other factors, such as improvement, effort, sportsmanship, and citizenship.

Methods of grading

There are several methods utilized in grading, not only in the field of physical education but also throughout the general educational complex in this country. Some examples include the following:

1. Letter grades: A, B, C, D, and E or F
   H, S, and U
   P and F
2. Numerical grades: 1, 2, 3, and so forth
3. Explanatory paragraphs
4. Checklists: often used to check weaknesses in such areas as effort, improvement, or citizenship

Problems in grading

In physical education the main problem is trying to arrive at a single grade that truly represents the pupil's achievement toward the various objectives. To what degree should performance and ability be weighted in relation to achievement in knowledge and social development? Some teachers believe that the former should have twice the value of the latter, because physical skills and development are the primary *raison d'être* of a program of physical education. Others believe that all four objectives should be considered equally.

Another problem in grading centers around improvement. To what degree should improvement in skills affect the final grade? Should the student who has low motor ability but who shows real improvement in a sports unit be rated in the same manner as the highly skilled individual who merely loafs along throughout the unit?

A third question arises out of the procedures necessary in physical education class. Should credit for grading be given for having a clean gym suit, for being dressed for participation in every class, for showering, and for attendance? In addition, there is the problem of effort in physical education class. How does a teacher determine maximum effort, and is such effort accorded an automatic "A"? These are some of the questions the physical educator must answer before developing a grading system suitable for use in his or her school situation.

Dr. Lynn McCraw of the University of

Table 18. Proposed plan for grading*

Components	Weightings	Instruments

Attitude in terms of
  Attendance
  Punctuality
  Suiting out
  Participation
	5% to 25%	Attendance and other records
		Teacher observation

Skills in terms of
  Form in execution of skill
  Standard of performance
  Application in game situation
	20% to 35%	Objective tests
		Teacher observation
		Student evaluation

Physical fitness with, emphasis on
  Muscular strength and endurance
  Cardiovascular-respiratory
    endurance
  Agility
  Flexibility
	20% to 35%	Objective tests
		Teacher observation

Knowledge and appreciation of
  Skills
  Strategy
  Rules
  History and terms
	5% to 25%	Written tests
		Teacher observation

Behavior in terms of
  Social conduct
  Health and safety practices
	5% to 25%	Teacher observation
		Student evaluation

*From McCraw, Lynn W.: Principles and practices for assigning grades in physical education, Journal of Health, Physical Education, and Recreation **35**:2, Feb., 1964.

Texas proposes a plan for grading that offers some solutions to the above problems (Table 18).

Ideally, the report card should be clear, concise, accurate, and explicit. It should show achievement in physical skills, general ability, social development, and all the objectives that were stressed throughout the program. Perhaps more than one grade is necessary to clarify the many facets of the program for the parents.

It is always revealing to discuss the problem of grading with the students themselves, to determine what elements they feel a physical education grade should encompass, and to allow them to estimate a grade for themselves. In a survey of high school girls, it was interesting to note that those whom the teacher rated "A—" or "A" ranked themselves only "B" or "B+," while students whom the teacher ranked "C—" or lower often rated themselves above the teacher's estimate. This typifies the attitudes of many students towards themselves: those who do little often think they deserve more, while those who put forth real effort rarely feel that they are deserving.

In a survey of eighth graders, who were asked about the components of a physical education grade, the element cited with greatest frequency was effort. One astute remark made by an eighth-grade girl included the following observations:

> I think that physical education should be graded, but not on a scale, just by the level that one person can reach by himself. It is up to the physical education teacher to get to know her students and learn just how far their abilities go, and then grade each person on the basis of how much he or she is improving. This could probably best be done by having a place on the report card where the physical education teacher can make a statement about the child's improvement.

The chart shown in Fig. 19-8 depicts another method by which various factors might be weighted in determining an individual's grade. Ability factors, such as physical fitness, game skills, knowledge scores, etc., are included in percentages along vertical lines, while attitudes, adjustment, and improvement are diagrammed

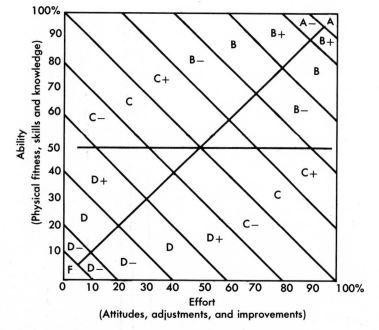

Fig. 19-8. Evaluation chart.

along the horizontal percentage line. If a student ranks in the 50th percentile in ability and in the 80th percentile for his attitudes and effort, his final grade would be "C+." On the other hand, a student with excellent physical skills and high ability who loafs during class period, putting forth little or no effort, would fall into the "C" range.

Grading in team teaching

Grading in schools using teaching teams for instruction has been a difficult problem to solve. It has been found that members of the teaching teams must formulate criteria for grades together in order to provide consistency throughout the school. The master teacher in charge of a particular unit, such as volleyball, is responsible for all grades during that grading period, and the helping teachers turn their grades in to him for compilation. In this way a student accumulates several grades in many areas during one grading period. Teachers who have taught under this system seem to believe that it works out satisfactorily for everyone concerned.

POINTS TO REMEMBER

1. There are many important factors to be considered when selecting tests for evaluation, such as validity and reliability.
2. There are many types of tests useful in evaluating pupil achievement in the four goals of physical education.
3. Teacher-made tests of knowledge and skills must be constructed according to certain principles.
4. A system of grading should be developed on the basis of certain well-defined principles
5. A grade should be a true measure of pupil status and should be expressed in a form similar to that used in other academic areas in the school.

PROBLEMS TO THINK THROUGH

1. Should skill tests be administered both at the beginning of a sports unit and at the end? What factors should be considered in planning them?

2. Should a written knowledge test be given at the close of every sports unit?
3. When should physical fitness testing be done—at the beginning, middle, and/or end of the year?
4. Should tests of social development be given within a single sports unit? What type? At what other times of the year may they be given?
5. Under what circumstances may teacher-made tests be more valuable than standardized tests?
6. Of what value are tests of social interests and attitudes?
7. To what uses may the results of physical fitness tests be put?
8. A student of low motor ability would probably never be graded higher than a "C" in physical education class.

CASE STUDY FOR ANALYSIS

A high school physical education program consists of classes that meet twice a week. The department wishes to gather factual evidence that would point up to the administration the need for expanding the program and convince them of the value of a daily class in physical education. What evaluation techniques would be useful to promote this argument?

EXERCISES FOR REVIEW

1. Define validity of a test, and explain.
2. Define reliability of a test, and explain.
3. Devise a sample knowledge test of volleyball rules for seventh grade girls or boys.
4. Administer one physical fitness test item to a group and compare the scores with national norms.
5. Prepare a set of directions to be given orally before administering a written knowledge test to a class.
6. Select a specific skill essential to the game of basketball and devise a simple test for measuring its performance.
7. Look up a standardized skill test in one of the source books and evaluate its suitability for use in a nearby high school.
8. Make a sociometric study of a group or team presently established and evaluate the individual status of participants.

REFERENCES

1. Larson, Leonard A., and Yocom, Rachael D.: Measurement and evaluation in physical,

health, and recreation education, St. Louis, 1951, The C. V. Mosby Co.

2. Hunsicker, Paul: AAHPER physical fitness test battery, Journal of Health, Physical Education, and Recreation **29**:24, Sept., 1958.
3. Clarke, H. Harrison: Application of measurement to health and physical education, Englewood Cliffs, N. J., 1967, Prentice-Hall, Inc.
4. California physical fitness pentathlon, Bulletin of the California State Department of Education **11**:8, Nov., 1942.
5. McCloy, C. H., and Young, N. D.: Tests and measurement in health and physical education, ed. 3, New York, 1954, Appleton-Century-Crofts.
6. Larson, L. A.: A factor and validity analysis of strength variables and tests with a test combination of chinning, dipping, and vertical jump, Research Quarterly **11**:82, Dec., 1940.
7. Illinois high school physical condition test and standards of performance, bulletin no. 6, Sept., 1944, Office of Public Instruction, Health, and Physical Education Department.
8. State of Indiana: Physical fitness manual for high school boys, bulletin no. 136, 1944, Department of Public Instruction.
9. Mathews, Donald K.: Measurement in physical education, ed. 2, Philadelphia, 1963, W. B. Saunders Co.
10. Scott, M. Gladys, and French, Esther: Evaluation in physical education, St. Louis, 1950, The C. V. Mosby Co.
11. Stroup, Francis: Measurement in physical fitness, New York, 1957, The Ronald Press Co.
12. McCloy, C. H.: Character building through physical education, Research Quarterly, Oct., 1930.
13. Blanchard, B. E.: A behavior frequency rating scale for the measurement of character and personality in physical education classroom situations, Research Quarterly, May, 1936.
14. O'Neel, F. W.: A behavior frequency rating scale for the measurement of character and personality in high school physical education classes for boys, Research Quarterly, May, 1936.
15. Adams, R. S.: Two scales for measuring attitude toward physical education, Research Quarterly **34**:1, March, 1963.

SELECTED READINGS

Bovard, John F., Cozens, Frederick W., and Hagman, E. Patricia: Tests and measurements in physical education, ed. 3, Philadelphia, 1949, W. B. Saunders Co.

Cowell, Charles C., and Schwehn, Hilda M.: Modern principles and methods in high school physical education, Englewood Cliffs, N. J., 1958, Allyn & Bacon, Inc.

Downie, N. M.: Fundamentals of measurement: techniques and practices, New York, 1958, Oxford University Press.

Hunsicker, Paul: AAHPER physical fitness test battery, Journal of Health, Physical Education, and Recreation **29**:24, Sept., 1958.

Hunsicker, Paul: Physical fitness tests, Journal of Health, Physical Education, and Recreation **28**:21, 68, Sept., 1957.

Joint Committee (Brownell, Clifford L., chairman): Administrative problems in health, physical education and recreation, Washington, D. C., 1953, American Association for Health, Physical Education, and Recreation.

Jordan, A. M.: Measurement in education, New York, 1953, McGraw-Hill Book Co.

Larson, Leonard A., and Yocom, Rachael D.: Measurement and evaluation in physical, health, and recreation education, St. Louis, 1951, The C. V. Mosby Co.

Latchaw, Marjorie, and Brown, Camille: The evaluation process in health education, physical education, and recreation, Englewood Cliffs, N. J., 1962, Prentice-Hall, Inc.

McCloy, Charles H., and Young, Norma D.: Tests and measurement in health and physical education, ed. 3, New York, 1954, Appleton-Century-Crofts.

Mathews, Donald K.: Measurement in physical education, ed. 3, Philadelphia, 1968, W. B. Saunders Co.

National Research Council, American Association for Health, Physical Education, and Recreation: Measurement and evaluation materials in health, physical education, and recreation, Washington, D. C., 1950, The Association.

Oliva, Peter F.: The secondary school today, Cleveland, Ohio, 1967, The World Publishing Co.

Scott, M. Gladys, and French, Esther: Evaluation in physical education, St. Louis, 1950, The C. V. Mosby Co.

Smithells, Philip A., and Cameron, Peter E.: Principals of evaluation in physical education, New York, 1962, Harper & Row, Publishers.

Stroup, Francis: Measurement in physical fitness, New York, 1957, The Ronald Press Co.

Torrance, E. Paul: Rewarding creative behavior, Englewood Cliffs, N. J., 1965, Prentice-Hall, Inc.

Wandt, Edwin, and Brown, Gerald W.: Essentials of educational evaluation, New York, 1957, Henry Holt & Co.

BOOKLETS, PAMPHLETS, AND ARTICLES

American Association of Health, Physical Education, and Recreation: Sports skills test manuals (archery, basketball, football, softball), Washington, D. C., 1966-1967, The Association.

Boyd, Clifford A., and Waglow, Irving F.: The individual achievement profile, The Physical Educator **21**:117, Oct., 1964.

Fabricius, Helen, Hanson, Dale, Singer, Robert, and Solley, William H.: Grading in physical education, Journal of Health, Physical Education, and Recreation **38**:34, May, 1967.

Jorndt, Louis C.: Point systems—motivational devices, The Physical Educator **23**:19, March, 1966.

Lawrence, Trudys: Appraisal of emotional health

at the secondary school level, Research Quarterly **37**:252, May, 1966.

Liba, Marie R., and Loy, John W.: Some comments on grading, The Physical Educator **22**:158, Dec., 1965.

National Education Association: Reports to parents, National Education Association Research Bulletin **45**:51, May, 1967.

Oxendine, Joseph B.: Social development—the forgotten objective? Journal of Health, Physical Education, and Recreation **37**:23, May, 1966.

Piscopo, John: Quality instruction: first priority, The Physical Educator **21**:162, Dec., 1964.

Teacher and program evaluation

Evaluation of pupil achievement is only one part of the program of evaluation. According to the minimum standards of evaluation outlined in Chapter 19, the entire program of physical education must be carefully analyzed. The ultimate purpose of this step is to improve all phases of the program for the benefit of the students. This includes determining areas of weakness in the program, effecting curriculum changes, and expanding and improving facilities. Such changes can best be brought about when facts and figures resulting from concrete evaluation indicate a real need to the administration of the school.

Administrators today are taking a very close look not only at programs but also at teachers themselves. Recent advances in education, such as teaching teams, have necessitated development of more accurate methods of rating teachers and their abilities. In this chapter the two important factors, teacher evaluation and program administration evaluation, are discussed.

TEACHER EVALUATION

Teacher evaluation is an integral part of the overall process of evaluating program administration, but recently this phase has received particular emphasis. Methods and techniques measuring teacher effectiveness and ability have been greatly expanded, and information concerning a teacher's personal history and growth has acquired greater importance, as evidenced by the bulging record folders filed in principals' offices.

Increased stress on the teacher and teaching has resulted from many factors. Educators today have recognized more and more the importance of the teacher-pupil relationship and therefore have been more concerned with the personality patterns of individual teachers. Then, too, with rapidly increasing school populations and pressures of admission into colleges, the effectiveness of teaching has assumed greater importance and as a result has been more carefully scrutinized. Other factors, such as merit pay schedules and teaching team programs, have forced principals and supervisors to differentiate teachers of superior quality. One other factor behind this movement of teacher evaluation—organization and administration of education—today has become "big business" in the economic and political sense of the words. Increased community pressures and criticisms of educational policies and procedures have brought about the need for greater professionalism among educators. Extensive appraisal of teachers and teaching has been one result of this trend.

Evaluation of teachers and their effectiveness involves several steps. As in other phases of evaluation, school systems vary in the extent and degree to which they fulfill this need. In general, however, a teacher's personal record file would include information regarding the following:

A. Personal status
    1. Health and physical status
    2. Intellectual abilities
    3. Social and emotional stability
B. Professional status
    1. History
    2. Experiences
    3. Teaching effectiveness
    4. Relationship with pupils
    5. Relationship with colleagues
    6. Relationship with the profession
    7. Relationship with the community*

The process of evaluation—that is, the actual collection of information—should encompass opinions from several sources. The teacher himself should be responsible for some self-evaluation; other sources are the administrator and colleagues.

Personal status

Health. A teacher should be in good health and physical condition. A majority of schools require periodic health examinations and chest x-ray films. The rigors of teaching demand a healthy, vigorous person, particularly in the field of physical education. However, physical perfection is not necessarily a requisite of any teaching position. There are countless handicapped persons who have been effective teachers in spite of their handicap. (A decade ago the New York City schools had a regulation stating that vision of all swimming teachers had to be nearly 20-20 and that no person wearing corrective lenses could be hired for this activity. However, this restriction has been lifted.)

Intellectual abilities. A teacher should be well-educated, well-read, and able to apply knowledge to everyday pursuits. Many schools require evidence of this ability, expecting prospective teachers to take the National Teachers Examination or the Teacher Education Examination Program. Other statistics are also used, such as col-

lege entrance examination scores and transcripts of college records.

Social and emotional stability. A teacher should be a well-adjusted person, finding contentment in his surroundings while making contributions to it. Administrators have several instruments and methods available to them for comprehensive appraisal of teachers' personalities. The Minnesota Teacher Attitude Inventory,[1] the Minnesota Multiphasic Personality Inventory,[2] and the Rorschach Test[3] are some of the well-known tests that may be used. Other methods are observations, interviews, anecdotal records, and student opinion.

Professional status

Preparation. A teacher should have a broad knowledge of educational psychology and history and be particularly well schooled in the special subject matter of his choice. Administrators are particularly interested in the teacher's professional preparation and expect teacher-training institutions to make recommendations on the basis of fair and honest appraisal techniques. Grades in the major field and in student-teaching work may be of particular importance.

Experience. A teacher should seek outside experiences that are both broadening and educational to expand the background brought to a teaching position. Administrators generally take a close look at all summer experiences, such as counseling and recreation work, as well as travels in assessing a teacher's experiences. Past experiences in the teaching field are naturally important aspects that would be studied also.

Teacher effectiveness. A teacher should be able to apply knowledge and teaching techniques to the classroom situation and be able to communicate effectively with the students.

Methods of appraisal

Administrators have several methods of appraisal available for use in this important aspect of teacher evaluation.

---

*See Chapter 10.

Observation. Administrators may make personal assessments of a teacher's abilities through several periodic visitations to class. Criteria such as those listed in class management would be helpful (i.e., control of the class, type of discipline used, attitude of the youngsters, etc.).

Student opinion. A periodic checkup of student opinions may be used to determine specific qualities of teaching. Students may be asked to rate teachers (1 to 4, or poor to excellent) on such factors as use of sarcasm, cheerfulness, preparation, discipline, etc. The Morris Trait Index[4] is another survey that may be used by students.

Evaluation results. Scores on tests and evaluation procedures may be used to appraise outcome of teaching to a certain degree. However, when more than one teacher serves in a department, such a method would not be applicable.

Anecdotal record. An administrator may keep track of problems that come to his attention as a result of a particular teacher's classroom activities. Complaints from students or teachers would fall into this category. (For example: Where was the teacher when those boys started that fight in the locker room? Or why are students always late to classes following gym class?)

Standardized instruments. An administrator may use one of several standardized evaluation charts to appraise teacher effectiveness. For example, Beecher's Teaching Evaluation Record,[5] the Purdue Teachers Examination,[6] or the Ohio Teaching Record[7] may be used by the administrator himself, or he may request or require his teachers to file a self-evaluation sheet, such as the Haverhill Evaluation Inventory.[8]

Relationship with pupils. A teacher should promote a proper relationship with students. Administrators may estimate teacher-pupil relations through simple techniques, including observation. Requests for a particular teacher to serve as a chaperone or as a sponsor for a club activity might be indicative of that teacher's relationships. Also, complaints from students and/or parents should be given due consideration by administrators, in case they are justified.

Relationship with colleagues. A teacher should establish good working relationships with his fellow teachers and immediate supervisors. An administrator may record a teacher's contributions at teachers meetings, at workshops, or on voluntary committees. Holding an elective office in a faculty association, credit union, or committee would certainly be an indicator of status among one's associates, and administrators would take note of this.

Relationship with profession. A teacher should maintain a continuing interest in the profession and seek ways of making a contribution to its advancement. Administrators may become acquainted with a teacher's professionalism through his or her activities in local, state, and/or national organizations (committee work and office-holding). Within the school an administrator may look for innovations and changes in teaching techniques and programming. He may also check a teacher's familiarity with the current literature in education, through requesting a list of books recently read, journal subscriptions, etc., for this, too, is a measure of professionalism.

Relationship with the community. A teacher should promote good school-community relations through contacts with parents, agencies, clubs, and businesses. Administrators recognize that good public relations are a vital force between a school and its community. Each teacher should foster good school-community relations, which, by their very nature, involve a two-way process. The teacher should show evidence of loyalty to the school and its administrative policies and practices—at PTA functions, board meetings, etc.—and he should be a loyal contributor to the community, working for its betterment through cooperation with and promotion of its interests, such as the Memorial Day Parade, the summer recreation program, etc.

The appraisal practices set forth here are not intended to be an absolute formula. They are merely suggestions of possible practices that individual school systems may employ. Three other points should be emphasized in this regard:

1. Administrators generally evaluate all teachers in a similar manner. Physical education teachers should not expect special considerations because they have winning teams or bring in valuable gate receipts.

2. Administrators generally evaluate all teachers in a similar manner, but consideration would naturally be given to length of experience in a particular school situation. The beginning teacher would not be expected to evidence the same degree of effectiveness or competency as the teacher with five or ten years of experience in that school.

3. Standards of evaluation are themselves indicative of the school's expectations. For example, submitting weekly lesson plans or not smoking on the job are regulations with which a prospective teacher may not wish to comply. A teacher who does not agree with the standards expected of him or her in a school situation would probably be more effective in another school system.

The National Education Association has published a booklet in which inferior and superior standards in all phases of school administration are compared. In the section on staff personnel policies and procedures, the following description is given of superior evaluation procedures:

> Although special emphasis is placed upon probationary teachers, every professional employee is evaluated on a continuing basis and shares responsibility for such evaluation. The primary purpose of evaluation is looked upon as the improvement of performance and is in no way related to salary. The school system conducts in-service workshops for the orientation and training of personnel responsible for evaluation, and takes this responsibility into consideration in determining work load and staff requirements. Procedures, evaluation forms, and guides are developed on the basis of cooperatively developed standards of performance and job descriptions. Criteria of evaluation are explicit, are written, and are made known to all staff members at the beginning of each school year. Criteria appropriate to each professional task are used for the evaluations. Each observation and evaluation includes a consultation between the staff member and the evaluator. Various techniques are used, including evaluations by more than one evaluator. Staff members sign and receive copies of written evaluations, and review and appeal procedures are in operation.*

PROGRAM ADMINISTRATION EVALUATION

Evaluation of program administration may be a yearly procedure, handled by members of the department for the purpose of curriculum organization, or it may be an examination of the whole school by a visiting team of specialists from the state department or professional association for the purpose of accreditation. The process of evaluation itself involves rating or judgment of the program according to selected criteria and standards. Standardized forms have been developed to evaluate all phases of the physical education curriculum. Excerpts from some of these forms are included in this chapter:

1. LaPorte health and physical education scorecard no. II for junior and senior high schools and four-year high schools[9]
2. National Study of Secondary School Evaluation (1960): Evaluative criteria for boys' physical education (D-14) and Evaluative criteria for girls' physical education (D-15)[10]
3. Educational Policies Commission: Checklist on school athletics[11]

Where standardized tests are not available to judge program administration, criteria based on authoritative textbook sources or the judgment of two or more experts in the field must be established.

The following are sample questions that may be formulated for teacher rating of program administration. They may either be answered poor, fair, good, or excellent, or be scored on a scale of 1 to 10. All areas of the program are listed, and questions are raised concerning the various factors.

Class program

1. Does the teaching program devote equitable time to team sports, individual

*From National Education Association: Profiles of excellence, Washington, D. C., 1966, The Association, p. 54 .

sports, rhythms and dance, and gymnastic activities?

2. Are the available equipment and facilities adequate to allow maximum student participation?

3. Are reasonable budgetary allotments made for the class teaching program?

4. Are accurate evaluation procedures carried out and are worthwhile records kept?

5. Are minimal participation requirements met by all students?

6. Are students meeting proper physical education requirements in regard to dressing and showering?

7. Are proper safety measures taken in all activities?

8. Are opportunities for developing student leadership being afforded in the class program?

Adapted program

1. Do adequate screening procedures determine all possible participants in this program?

2. Are adequate facilities, equipment, time, and space made available to the program?

3. Are proper supervision and instruction afforded each individual participant?

4. Is medical approval obtained for each individual's regimen of activity?

5. Do participants engage in some of the regular class work, as well as remedial classes, when advisable?

6. Are careful records and progress notes kept on each student?

7. Is the financial allotment to the program reasonable?

8. Does student achievement indicate the value of the program?

Intramural and extramural programs

1. Are intramural and extramural sports offered to all students in as many activities as possible?

2. Has participation in these programs increased during the past year?

3. Is maximum coaching supervision available to players?

4. Is adequate financial assistance given to this phase of the program?

5. Are accurate records maintained concerning the participants, their honors, awards, and electives?

6. Does the reward or point system emphasize the joys of participation rather than stress the value of the reward?

7. Is equipment well cared for and properly stored to gain the most use from it?

Fig. 20-1. Are interscholastic sports available to all students? (Lincoln High School, Yonkers, N. Y.)

8. Are competitive experiences wholesome and worthwhile for all participants?

Interscholastic program

1. Is financial support for this program provided by the physical education budget?

2. Is there equitable financial support for all sports in the interscholastic program?

3. Are interscholastic sports available to all students, boys and girls alike?

4. Are adequate health standards being met in respect to number of practices and games, fitness of participants, and type of competition?

5. Is competition provided by schools of a similar size?

6. Is the program justifiable as an important educational tool?

7. Are academic standards for participants maintained?

8. Are good public relations with the community furthered through this program?

Aquatics

1. Are maximum instruction and participation opportunities made available to all students?

2. Is superior care taken in cleaning and maintaining the pool area—with proper checks on water chlorination, temperature, and filter system?

3. Is adequate supervision by qualified personnel available at all times?

4. Are health standards of cleanliness and rules requiring freedom from infection enforced at all times?

5. Are proper safety regulations enforced at all times?

6. Does student achievement indicate value of the program?

7. Are competitive swimming and diving events properly officiated and controlled?

8. Is swimming on the intermediate level a requirement for graduation?

Administration

1. Is the teaching staff well qualified and capable of carrying out the program?

2. Is the program run efficiently, with little loss of teaching time or space, and is maximum use made of facilities?

3. Are professional standards maintained as to class size and teacher assignment?

4. Is the departmental organization on a democratic basis, with all members sharing in the decisions?

LA PORTE HEALTH AND PHYSICAL EDUCATION SCORECARD NO. II FOR JUNIOR AND SENIOR HIGH SCHOOLS AND FOUR-YEAR HIGH SCHOOLS*

Name of school _____ Address _____
Junior, Senior, or 4-year school _____ Principal _____
Rating for school year _____ Rated by _____ Date _____
Number of students enrolled: Boys _____ Girls _____

Scorecard summary	*Possible score*	*Actual score*
1. Program of activities	30	
2. Outdoor areas	30	
3. Indoor areas	30	
4. Locker and shower areas	30	
5. Swimming pool	30	
6. Supplies and equipment	30	
7. Medical examination and health service	30	
8. Modified-individual (corrective) activities	30	
9. Organization and administration of class program	30	
10. Administration of intramural and interschool athletics	30	

*From LaPorte, William, Ralph: Health and physical education scorecard no. II for junior and senior high schools and four-year high schools, Los Angeles, 1942, University of Southern California Press.

5. Do members of the staff have a professional outlook, attend professional meetings, and keep up with the latest developments in the field?

6. In what areas have scientific tests and research been made for contribution to the profession?

These are just a few sample questions that may be used in evaluating program administration. The key to successful evaluation of this type lies in the follow-up steps for improvement.

Whenever possible, a standardized evaluation form should be utilized. The La-Porte scorecard no. II, developed several years ago, includes questions in ten general areas. However, only two sample questions, selected from the first five areas, appear in the excerpt shown on pp. 358 and 359.

Sample questions

1. Program of activities
    a. Content of core and elective programs is distributed over gymnastics, rhythms, aquatics, individual sports (including defense activities), and team sports. (Not less than 6% of time to each of the five types = 1; not less than 9% = 2; not less than 12% = 3)
    b. Daily participation in physical and/or health education class instruction periods of from 45 to 60 minutes is required of *all* students. (Two days a week = 1; four days = 2; five days = 3)
2. Outdoor area
    a. Total available field and court playing space varies from two to ten or fifteen acres, according to size of school. (Minimum of two acres, and one additional acre for each added unit of five hundred students (boys and girls) = 1; minimum of two acres, and one additional acre for each additional unit of four hundred students = 2; minimum of two acres, and one additional acre for each additional unit of three hundred students = 3)
    b. Sufficient playing fields are marked off and equipped (for multiple use in field hockey, field ball, soccer, softball, speedball, touch football, etc.) to accommodate all outside peak load classes (for both boys and girls). (Fair facilities = 1; good facilities = 2; excellent facilities = 3)
3. Indoor areas
    a. One or more gymnasium areas sufficient for boys' and girls' inside class activities (according to size of school) (for common use of apparatus, boxing, corrective activity, fencing, gymnastics, rhythms, tumbling, and wrestling) are available and are appropriately equipped, as well as properly heated, lighted, and ventilated. (Standards approximately met = 1 to 2; fully met = 3)
    b. Gymnasium floors are of hardwood; lines are properly painted; walls are smooth and clear; paint is a light, neutral color; radiators and drinking fountains are recessed; ceiling height is between 18 and 22 feet. (Standards approximately met = 2; entirely met = 3)
4. Locker and shower area
    a. Locker rooms (sunny and well ventilated) provide free floor space, exclusive of lockers, adequate to care for peak load of use. (Peak load equals largest number of students dressing in any one class period.) (8 sq. ft. per pupil = 1; 10 sq. ft. = 2; 12 sq. ft. = 3)
    b. Individual locker facilities are provided for all students. (Box lockers or narrow vertical lockers = 1; combination box and dressing lockers = 2; half-length, standard-size lockers, or self-service basket system, combined with full-length dressing lockers for peak load = 3)
5. Swimming pool
    a. Adequate swimming facilities are available for all students (both boys and girls). (Off-campus facilities, closely adjoining = 1; small pool [less than 1250 sq. ft.] on school grounds = 2; large pool [over 1250 sq. ft.] on school grounds = 3)
    b. Pool construction provides proper acoustics; suitable scum gutters; nonslip decks; white tile or other light finish on sides and bottom; underwater lighting if pool is used at night; bottom of pool clearly visible at all times of operation. (Standards approximately met = 1 to 2; fully met = 3)

Total scores:

100 = fair-minimum.	200 = good-average.	300 = superior-ideal.

A second well-known evaluation instrument was developed by the National Study of Secondary School Evaluation. Questions shown on pp. 360 and 361, for both the boys' and girls' programs, are similar, and samples of their criteria are included.

The Educational Policies Commission has developed a checklist on school athletics that could easily serve as an evaluation instrument in this one area. The checklist shown on p. 361 is a very small sample of this type.

EVALUATIVE CRITERIA

NATIONAL STUDY OF SECONDARY SCHOOL EVALUATION—1960

BOY'S PHYSICAL EDUCATION (D-14); GIRLS' PHYSICAL EDUCATION (D-15)*

Part I. Checklist on organization (sample)
1. Physical education required of all grade levels of secondary school.
2. Physical education classes meet ------ periods per week.
3. Physical education classes are ------ minutes in length.
Supplementary data
1. Number excused for physical education class ------.
2. Describe procedures for excusing boys (girls) from class.
Evaluations (Excellent, 5; Very good, 4; Good, 3; Fair, 2; Poor, 1)
1. To what degree are physical education activities provided for all boys (girls)?
2. Do time allotments of the program meet instructional needs satisfactorily?
3. How satisfactory are controls and safeguards for all athletic activities?

Part II. Nature of offerings (sample)
Evaluations
1. How adequate is *variety* of experiences to meet physical education needs of all boys (girls)?
2. How adequate is *content* of experiences to meet physical education needs of all boys (girls)?
3. How satisfactorily do experiences provide for present and future leisure-time needs?
4. How adequately does the program provide for desirable activities in terms of individual physical education needs?

Part III. Facilities (sample)
Evaluations
1. How adequate is space indoors?
2. How adequate are facilities outdoors?
3. How adequate is quantity of permanent equipment?
4. How adequate is quality of permanent equipment?
5. How adequate are provisions for health, safety, and sanitation?

Part IV. Direction of learning (sample)
A. Evaluations of instructional staff
1. How adequate is the preparation of the staff for teaching physical education?
2. How adequate is the preparation of the staff for conducting a balanced intramural and interschool program?
3. How adequate is the preparation of the staff for conducting school and community recreational activities?
B. Evaluations of instructional activities
1. Adequate planning and preparation?
2. Data of health appraisal used?
3. Instructional needs adapted to individual needs?
4. Health and safety considered?
5. Desirable social and emotional development?
6. How effective is teaching?
C. Evaluations of instructional materials and equipment
1. Reading and reference materials adequate?
2. Quantity of materials adequate?
3. Quality of materials adequate?
4. To what extent are materials accessible to boys (girls)?

---

*From National Study of Secondary School Evaluation: Evaluative criteria, Washington, D. C., 1960, The Study.

Part IV. Direction of learning (sample)—cont'd
  D. Methods of evaluation
    1. Are the methods of evaluation comprehensive?
    2. Are the results of evaluation used?
    3. Are students of promise in physical education identified?
Part V. Outcomes
  A. Evaluations: Does the program . . .
    1. Develop knowledge and understanding of physical education activities?
    2. Develop skills in body mechanics and physical education activities?
    3. Provide activities to carry over into leisure time?
    4. Develop interest and skill for adult leisure?
    5. Develop desirable habits of cleanliness and good grooming practices?
    6. Promote desirable social and emotional behavior (both spectators and pratici-
       pants)?
    7. Develop strong, healthy, well-coordinated bodies?
Part VI. Special characteristics of the program
    1. Most satisfactory elements of the program
    2. Areas of greatest need
Part VII. General evaluation
    1. Is the program of physical education consistent with the philosophy?
    2. Does the program of physical education meet the needs of the students?
    3. Does the program of physical education identify the problems of the students?

CHECKLIST ON SCHOOL ATHLETICS*

Checklist of 100 questions to be marked:

Yes, No or Unknown   Agree   Disagree   Uncertain

Sample questions
1. Facilities
    a. Does your board of education provide adequate facilities in athletics for *all* students?
    b. Do girls share equally with boys in the use of your school's athletic facilities?
2. Personnel
    a. Are all who coach athletic teams in your school competently trained and certified as
       teachers?
    b. Do the athletic coaches have professional training in physical education equivalent to
       a minor or more?
3. Intramural programs
    a. Does every student in your school system have opportunity for participating in a variety
       of intramural sports?
    b. Is the intramural sports program conducted as an integral part of the total program of
       physical education and not as a "feeder" system for interscholastic athletics?
4. Junior high school policies and programs
    a. Is the athletic program for junior high school pupils suited to the needs of children
       who are undergoing rapid changes in physical growth?
    b. Does the athletic program in junior high school consist primarily of sports organized
       and conducted on an intramural basis?
5. Athletics for girls
    a. Does the school athletic program for girls provide opportunities for all girls to par-
       ticipate according to their needs, abilities, and interests?
    b. Are facilities for girls' athletics provided in accordance with the requirements of the
girls' program, and not on the basis of causing minimum inconvenience to the boys' program?

*From The Educational Policies Commission: School athletics: problems and policies, Ameri-
can Association of School Administrators, Washington, D. C., 1960, The Association.
  Printed copies in leaflet form may be purchased from the Office of The Educational Policies
Commission, 1201 Sixteenth Street, N. W., Washington, D. C. 20036. Price: 10 cents each;
2 to 9 copies, 10% discount; 10 to 99 copies, 25% discount; 100 or more copies, 33⅓% discount.

Whichever method of program evaluation is selected, it should be realistic, functional, and continuous, in order to fulfill its major purposes of benefiting the students.

POINTS TO REMEMBER

1. Teacher evaluation is a growing responsibility of administrators.
2. Evaluation is a continuing process.
3. Steps involved in teacher evaluation encompass every aspect of a teacher's personal and professional status.
4. Program evaluation may be accomplished within a school system or by a visiting team of specialists.
5. All evaluation procedures must take into account special factors related to the particular community involved.

PROBLEMS TO THINK THROUGH

1. To what extent should self-rating procedures be included in a teacher's personal record file?
2. What is the primary purpose of program evaluation?
3. Should the teaching staff be informed of the methods of teacher evaluation in use within their school system?
4. For what reasons would test scores be evidence of effective teaching? For what reasons would they not?
5. Should a teacher be well-liked by students in order to be an effective teacher?

CASE STUDY FOR ANALYSIS

A large new suburban high school is preparing for a visitation from the state accreditation committee. The physical education department is expected to collect concrete evidence of student achievement in all phases of the program. What materials would provide concise information for this purpose?

EXERCISES FOR REVIEW

1. Take a survey of at least ten people by asking them to list in order of importance the five most important qualities of a good teacher. Make a composite listing of these qualities.
2. Compare the complete evaluation instruments presented partially in this chapter and note differences.
3. Evaluate as completely as possible a high school in the college community.
4. Interview a teacher, and on the basis of that discussion, write a description of the teacher's personal and professional status. What key questions may be used?

REFERENCES

1. Cook, Walter W., Leeds, C. H., and Callis, R.: Minnesota Teacher Attitude Inventory manual, New York, 1951, Psychological Corporation.
2. Hathaway, S. R., and McKinley, J. C.: Minnesota Multiphasic Personality Inventory manual, rev. ed., New York, 1951, Psychological Corporation.
3. Beck, Samuel J.: Rorschach's test: I, Basic processes, ed. 2, New York, 1949, Grune & Stratton, Inc.
4. Morris, Elizabeth H.: Morris Trait Index L, Bloomington, Ill., Public School Publishing Co.
5. Beecher, Dwight E.: The evaluation of teaching: backgrounds and concepts, Syracuse, N. Y., 1949, Syracuse University Press.
6. Kelley, Ida B., and Perkins, Keith J.: How I teach, Purdue Teachers Examination, Educational Test Bureau, Minneapolis, 1942, Educational Publishers, Inc.
7. Ohio Teaching Record, anecdotal observation form, 2nd rev. ed., Columbus, 1945, College of Education, Ohio State University.
8. Haverhill Public and Vocational Schools: Evaluation inventory, Haverhill, Mass., The Schools.
9. LaPorte, William Ralph: Health and physical education score card no. II for junior and senior high schools and four-year high schools, Los Angeles, 1942, University of Southern California Press.
10. National Study of Secondary School Evaluation: Evaluative criteria, Washington, D. C., 1960, The Study.
11. Educational Policies Commission: School athletics: problems and policies, American Association of School Administrators, Washington, D. C., 1954, The Association.

SELECTED READINGS

American Academy of Physical Education: Professional contributions no. 4, November, 1955, Washington, D. C., 1956, The Academy.
American Association for Health, Physical Education, and Recreation: Measurement and evaluation materials in health, physical education, and recreation, Washington, D. C., 1950, The Association.
Bookwalter, Karl W., and Bookwalter, Carolyn W.: Purposes, standards and results in physical education, Indiana University, 1962, Bureau of Educational Studies and Testing, School of Education.
Bucher, Charles A.: Foundations of physical education, ed. 5, St. Louis, 1968, The C. V. Mosby Co.

Cole, Luella: Psychology of adolescence, ed. 3, New York, 1948, Rinehart & Co., Inc.

Havel, Richard C., and Seymour, Emery W.: Administration of health, physical education, and recreation for schools, New York, 1961, The Ronald Press Co.

LaPorte, William Ralph: The physical education curriculum, ed. 6, Los Angeles, 1955, College Book Store.

Larson, Leonard A., and Yocom, Rachael D.: Measurement and evaluation in physical, health and recreation education, St. Louis, 1951, The C. V. Mosby Co.

Latchaw, Majorie, and Brown, Camille: The evaluation process in health education, physical education, and recreation, Englewod Cliffs, N. J., 1962, Prentice-Hall, Inc.

Smithells, Philip A., and Cameron, Peter E.: Principles of evaluation in physical education, New York, 1962, Harper & Row, Publishers.

BOOKLETS, PAMPHLETS, AND ARTICLES

Brian, George: Evaluating teacher effectiveness, NEA Journal 54:35, Feb., 1965.

Howsam, Robert B.: Facts and folklore of teacher evaluation, The Education Digest 29:13, March, 1964.

Malone, Wayne C.: A checklist for evaluating coaches, Coach & Athlete 29:42, Oct., 1966.

National Education Association: Methods of evaluating teachers, NEA Research Bulletin 43:12, Feb., 1965.

National Education Association: What teachers and administrators think about evaluation, NEA Research Bulletin 42:108, Dec., 1964.

Simpson, Ray H., and Seidman, Jerome M.: Student evaluation of teaching and learning, Washington, D. C., 1962, American Association of Colleges for Teacher Education.

Vander Werf, Lester S.: How to evaluate teachers and teaching, New York, 1960, Holt, Rinehart & Winston, Inc.

Records and forms
for
physical education

G A A Point System Name _____																	Hr	R	S	R	S	Hr	R	S	R	S
	Year				Year				Year				Year				Remarks								
	F	W1	W2	S	F	W1	W2	S	F	W1	W2	S	F	W1	W2	S	Awards Received								
Archery																	Award				Date				
Badminton																	1								
Basketball																	2								
Bowling																	3								
Dance																	4								
Field day																	5								
Golf																									
Hockey																									
Riflery																									
Saddle																	Responsibilities								
Softball																									
Speedball																									
Swimming																									
Table Tennis																									
Tennis																									
Volleyball																									
Total																									
Grand Total																	☆ Received Trophy								

Field and court diagrams

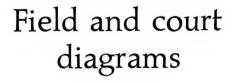

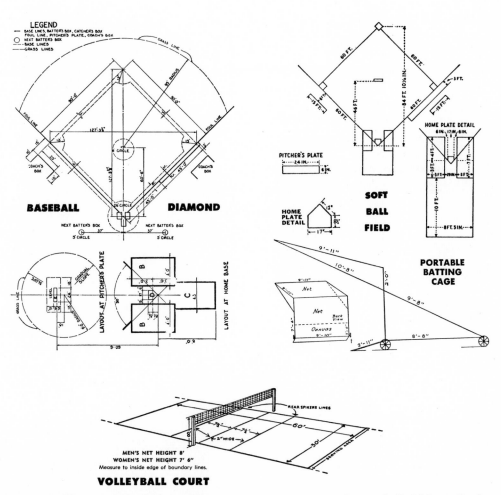

(From Athletic Field and Court Diagrams; courtesy Lowe and Campbell Athletic Goods, Kansas City, Mo.)

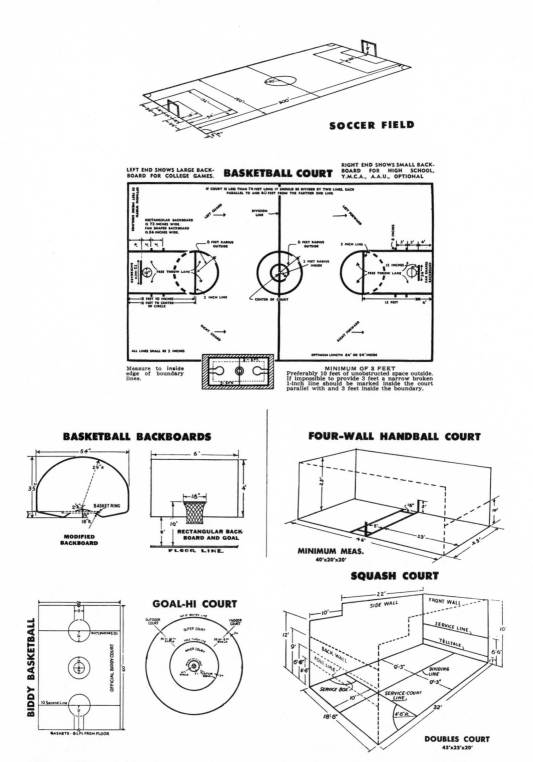

(From Athletic Field and Court Diagrams; courtesy Lowe and Campbell Athletic Goods, Kansas City, Mo.)

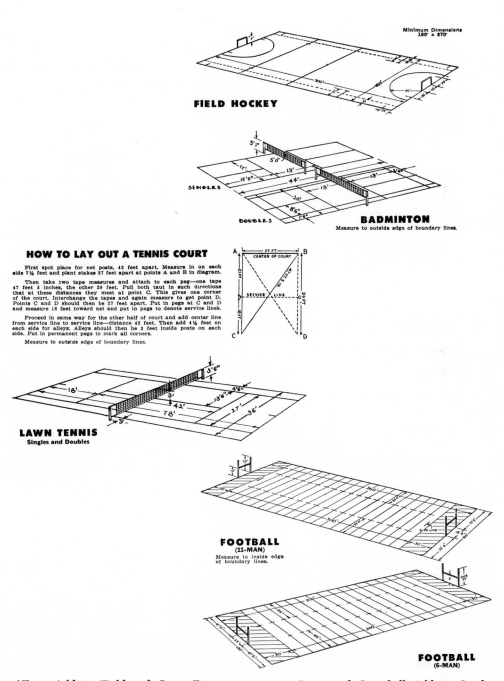

FIELD HOCKEY

BADMINTON
Measure to outside edge of boundary lines.

HOW TO LAY OUT A TENNIS COURT

First spot place for net posts, 42 feet apart. Measure in on each side 7½ feet and plant stakes 27 feet apart at points A and B in diagram.

Then take two tape measures and attach to each peg—one tape 47 feet 5 inches, the other 39 feet. Pull both taut in such directions that at these distances they meet at point C. This gives one corner of the court. Interchange the tapes and again measure to get point D. Points C and D should then be 27 feet apart. Put in pegs at C and D and measure 18 feet toward net and put in pegs to denote service lines.

Proceed in same way for the other half of court and add center line from service line to service line—distance 42 feet. Then add 4½ feet on each side for alleys. Alleys should then be 3 feet inside posts on each side. Put in permanent pegs to mark all corners.

Measure to outside edge of boundary lines.

LAWN TENNIS
Singles and Doubles

FOOTBALL
(11-MAN)
Measure to inside edge of boundary lines.

FOOTBALL
(6-MAN)

(From Athletic Field and Court Diagrams; courtesy Lowe and Campbell Athletic Goods, Kansas City, Mo.)

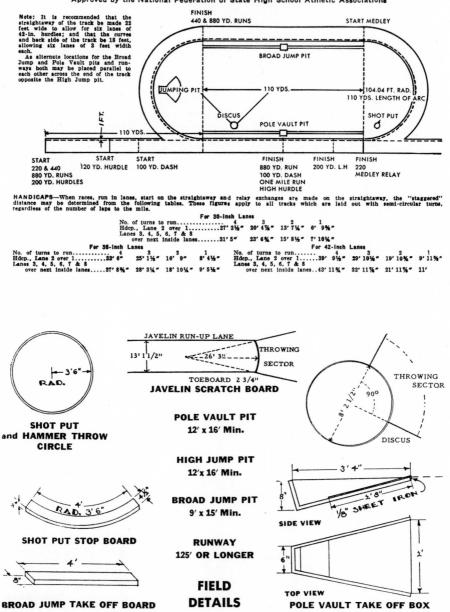

QUARTER-MILE TRACK

Approved by the National Federation of State High School Athletic Associations

Note: It is recommended that the straightaway of the track be made 22 feet wide to allow for six lanes of 42-in. hurdles; and that the curves and back side of the track be 18 feet, allowing six lanes of 3 feet width each.

As alternate locations for the Broad Jump and Pole Vault pits and runways both may be placed parallel to each other across the end of the track opposite the High Jump pit.

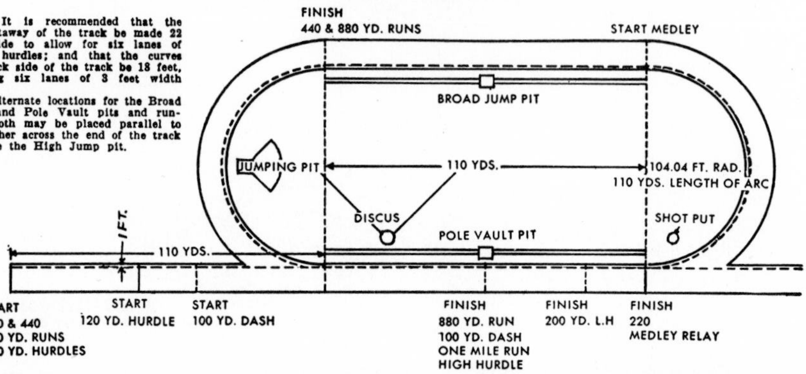
FINISH
440 & 880 YD. RUNS
START MEDLEY
BROAD JUMP PIT
JUMPING PIT
110 YDS.
104.04 FT. RAD.
110 YDS. LENGTH OF ARC
DISCUS
SHOT PUT
POLE VAULT PIT
1 FT.
110 YDS.
START
220 & 440
880 YD. RUNS
200 YD. HURDLES
START
120 YD. HURDLE
START
100 YD. DASH
FINISH
880 YD. RUN
100 YD. DASH
ONE MILE RUN
HIGH HURDLE
FINISH
200 YD. L.H
FINISH
220
MEDLEY RELAY

HANDICAPS—When races, run in lanes, start on the straightaway and relay exchanges are made on the straightaway, the "staggered" distance may be determined from the following tables. These figures apply to all tracks which are laid out with semi-circular turns, regardless of the number of laps to the mile.

For 30-Inch Lanes

No. of turns to run	4	3	2	1
Hdcp., Lane 2 over 1	27' 2½"	20' 4⅞"	13' 7¼"	6' 9⅝"
Lanes 3, 4, 5, 6, 7 & 8 over next inside lanes	31' 5"	23' 6¾"	15' 8½"	7' 10¼"

For 36-Inch Lanes

No. of turns to run	4	3	2	1
Hdcp., Lane 2 over 1	33' 6"	25' 1½"	16' 9"	8' 4½"
Lanes 3, 4, 5, 6, 7 & 8 over next inside lanes	37' 8⅜"	28' 3¼"	18' 10¼"	9' 5⅛"

For 42-Inch Lanes

No. of turns to run	4	3	2	1
Hdcp., Lane 2 over 1	39' 9½"	29' 10⅛"	19' 10¾"	9' 11⅝"
Lanes 3, 4, 5, 6, 7 & 8 over next inside lanes	43' 11¾"	32' 11⅞"	21' 11⅞"	11'

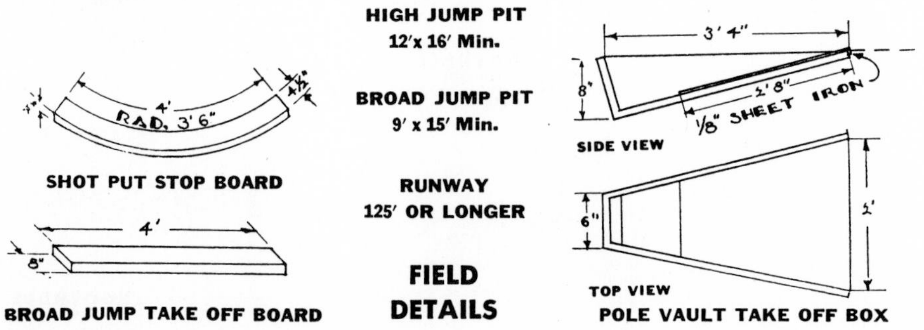
3'6"
RAD.
SHOT PUT
and HAMMER THROW
CIRCLE
JAVELIN RUN-UP LANE
13' 1 1/2"
26' 3"
THROWING
SECTOR
TOEBOARD 2 3/4"
JAVELIN SCRATCH BOARD
THROWING
SECTOR
90°
8' 2 1/2"
DISCUS
POLE VAULT PIT
12' x 16' Min.
HIGH JUMP PIT
12' x 16' Min.
BROAD JUMP PIT
9' x 15' Min.
RUNWAY
125' OR LONGER
4'
RAD. 3'6"
SHOT PUT STOP BOARD
4'
8"
BROAD JUMP TAKE OFF BOARD
FIELD
DETAILS
3' 4"
8"
2' 8"
1/8" SHEET IRON
SIDE VIEW
6"
2'
TOP VIEW
POLE VAULT TAKE OFF BOX

(From Athletic Field and Court Diagrams; courtesy Lowe and Campbell Athletic Goods, Kansas City, Mo.)

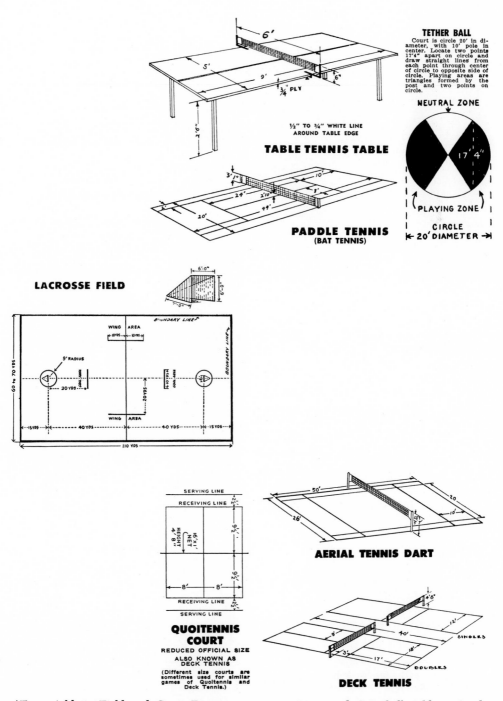

TETHER BALL

Court is circle 20' in diameter, with 10' pole in center. Locate two points 17'4" apart on circle and draw straight lines from each point through center of circle to opposite side of circle. Playing areas are triangles formed by the post and two points on circle.

½" TO ¾" WHITE LINE
AROUND TABLE EDGE

TABLE TENNIS TABLE

PADDLE TENNIS
(BAT TENNIS)

LACROSSE FIELD

QUOITENNIS COURT

REDUCED OFFICIAL SIZE
ALSO KNOWN AS
DECK TENNIS

(Different size courts are sometimes used for similar games of Quoitennis and Deck Tennis.)

AERIAL TENNIS DART

DECK TENNIS

(From Athletic Field and Court Diagrams; courtesy Lowe and Campbell Athletic Goods, Kansas City, Mo.)

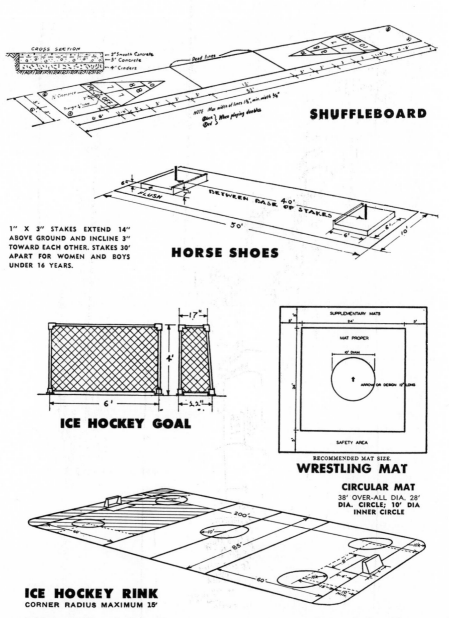

SHUFFLEBOARD

HORSE SHOES

1" X 3" STAKES EXTEND 14"
ABOVE GROUND AND INCLINE 3"
TOWARD EACH OTHER. STAKES 30'
APART FOR WOMEN AND BOYS
UNDER 16 YEARS.

ICE HOCKEY GOAL

WRESTLING MAT

CIRCULAR MAT
38' OVER-ALL DIA. 28'
DIA. CIRCLE; 10' DIA
INNER CIRCLE

ICE HOCKEY RINK
CORNER RADIUS MAXIMUM 15'

(From Athletic Field and Court Diagrams; courtesy Lowe and Campbell Athletic Goods, Kansas City, Mo.)

Tournament drawings

ROUND ROBIN TOURNAMENT

In this simple but efficient method, each team plays every other team once with the final standing determined on a percentage basis.

The following formula will apply to any number of teams, whether the total is odd or even. With an odd number of teams there is the same number of rounds; with an even number of teams there is one less number of games than teams.

FOR ODD NUMBER OF TEAMS

Assign to each team a number and then use only the figures in drawing the schedule. For example, in a league with 7 teams start with 1, putting down figures in the following order:

7	6	5	4	3	2	1
6-1	5-7	4-6	3-5	2-4	1-3	7-2
5-2	4-1	3-7	2-6	1-5	7-4	6-3
4-3	3-2	2-1	1-7	7-6	6-5	5-4

Note that the figures go down on the right side and up on the left. No. 7 draws a bye in the first round and the others play as indicated. With an odd number of teams, all numbers revolve and the last number each time draws a bye.

FOR EVEN NUMBER OF TEAMS

With an even number of teams the plan is the same except the position of No. 1 remains stationary and the other numbers revolve about it until the original combination is reached. For example, with 8 teams:

1-2	1-8	1-7	1-6	1-5	1-4	1-3
8-3	7-2	6-8	5-7	4-6	3-5	2-4
7-4	6-3	5-2	4-8	3-7	2-6	8-5
6-5	5-4	4-3	3-2	2-8	8-7	7-6

Two things only must be remembered: (1) With an even number of teams, No. 1 remains stationary and the other numbers revolve. (2) With an odd number of teams, all numbers revolve and the last number each time draws a bye.

LADDER TOURNAMENT

In a ladder tournament the competition is arranged by challenge and the tournament requires a minimum of supervision. A player may challenge either of the two players above him in the ladder. If the challenger wins, he exchanges places with the loser in the ladder. All challenges must be accepted and played at an agreed time. Players draw for positions in the ladder; a starting and closing date for the tournament must be announced. Each player carries his handicap against all players, in case handicaps are used.

TABLE TENNIS

1
2
3
4
5
6
7
8
9
10

PYRAMID TOURNAMENT

The pyramid tournament is similar to the ladder tournament except the design allows for more participating and challenging. After the original drawings are made any player may challenge any other player in the same horizontal row. If he wins he may then challenge anyone in the row above, the two change places in the pyramid.

TOURNAMENT SCHEDULE CALCULATOR

Teams Entered	Byes Top	Byes Bottom	Single Elim. No. Games	Double Elim. No. Games	Round Robin No. Games
4	0	0	3	6 or 7	6
5	1	2	4	8 or 9	10
6	1	1	5	10 or 11	15
7	0	1	6	12 or 13	21
8	0	0	7	14 or 15	28
9	3	4	8	16 or 17	36
10	3	3	9	18 or 19	45
11	2	3	10	20 or 21	55
12	2	2	11	22 or 23	66
13	1	2	12	24 or 25	78
14	1	1	13	26 or 27	91
15	0	1	14	28 or 29	105
16	0	0	15	30 or 31	
17	7	8	16	32 or 33	
18	7	7	17	34 or 35	
19	6	7	18	36 or 37	
20	6	6	19	38 or 39	
21	5	6	20	40 or 41	
22	5	5	21	42 or 43	
23	4	5	22	44 or 45	
24	4	4	23	46 or 47	
25	3	4	24	48 or 49	
26	3	3	25	50 or 51	
27	2	3	26	52 or 53	
28	2	2	27	54 or 55	
29	1	2	28	56 or 57	
30	1	1	29	58 or 59	
31	0	1	30	60 or 61	
32	0	0	31	62 or 63	

(Round Robin Tournament, Ladder Tournament, and Pyramid Tournament from Athletic Field and Court Diagrams; courtesy Lowe and Campbell Athletic Goods, Kansas City, Mo.; Tournament Schedule Calculator courtesy Boys' Physical Education Department, New Trier Township High School, Winnetka, Ill.)

DOUBLE ELIMINATION TOURNAMENT

Two defeats eliminate an entry in this tournament. The losers in the first rounds move into the losers' bracket. The teams which advance farthest in either bracket meet each other in the final game. Should the winner of the losers' bracket defeat the winner of the first round bracket, the teams are rematched for the championship when one team will have lost two games.

Byes are distributed in the first round of the original elimination brackets as in a single elimination tournament, but in the first round of the losers' brackets byes must be arranged to avoid giving a second bye to an entry that has already had a bye. Also, at all stages of the losers' bracket, avoid pairing entries that have met in earlier rounds, if possible.

This type tournament is seldom used unless the entries are eight or less in number. If more than eight entries, double the process and the two winners meet for the title.

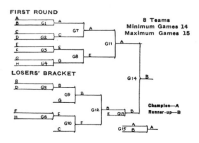

8 Teams
Minimum Games 14
Maximum Games 15

Formula for total number of games, with N representing Number of entries: 2(N-1)=**Minimum Games to Play;** 2(N-1)+1=**Maximum Games to Play.**

TYPES OF TOURNAMENT DRAWINGS

There are several different kinds of bracket arrangements that may be used in conducting tournament competition and the type of elimination is usually determined by several factors: (1) The type of activity. (2) The number of entries. (3) The amount of playing time. (4) Playing space and equipment. (5) Age of participants. (6) Officials available.

With a large number of entries it is sometimes desirable to run a combination tournament. For example: A double elimination—single elimination tournament. The winners of the double elimination brackets compete in a single elimination tournament to determine the ultimate champion.

Number of Byes. The first step before making a drawing for the bracket arrangement is to determine the number of entries.

When the number of competitors is 4, 8, 16, 32, 64 or 128, or any higher power of "2," they shall meet in pairs. When the number of competitors is not a power of "2" there shall be byes in the first round. For example: If there are 13 entries, a bracket of 16 with three byes is required. The purpose of having byes is to bring into the second round a number of competitors that is a power of "2." To determine the number of byes subtract the number of competitors from the next higher power of "2"; to determine the number of competitors in the first round subtract the number of byes from the total number of competitors. If the byes are an even number one half of them shall be placed at the top of the draw and one half at the bottom of the draw; if they are unevenly numbered there should be one more bye at the bottom than the top. The byes at the top half shall be the names first drawn. The next names drawn shall be placed in the first round. The byes in the bottom half are drawn last.

Seeding the Draw. It is a common practice to select the best teams or individuals and place them in the bracket so that they will not meet in the early rounds of the play. Two or more entries may be seeded—usually the four best are selected in a sixteen bracket and eight in a thirty-two name bracket. The seeded entrants are usually placed in the 1st, 5th, 9th, 13th, etc., bracket positions. The No. 1 and 4 seeded teams are generally placed in the first and fifth positions of the top bracket and the No. 2 and 3 seeded teams in the ninth and thirteenth positions of the lower bracket; or No. 1 and 3 in the upper with No. 2 and 4 seeded teams in the lower half.

CONSOLATION TOURNAMENT

There are two types in general use: The consolation type tournament is generally used only when the number of entries is 8 or 16. In No. I bracket arrangement only the losers in the first round of play compete for consolation title. In No. II, the losers in all the rounds except the final of the upper bracket compete for 3rd and 4th place.

In both tournaments every team plays at least two games before being eliminated.

FIRST ROUND BRACKET—16 ENTRIES

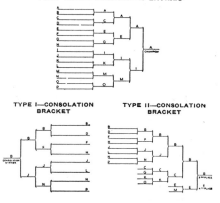

SINGLE ELIMINATION TOURNAMENT

If the contestants are of equal strength or their strength is not known, have a drawing for positions in the bracket. If the strength is known, seed the best teams so they will not meet in the early rounds. Place the seeded entries in the 1st, 5th, 9th, 13th, etc., positions.

All BYES must occur in the first round of play. The total number of games played is always one less than the number of entries. To determine the number of games that the winner would have to play count the powers of two in the number of entries, e. g., with 32 entries the winner plays 5 games.

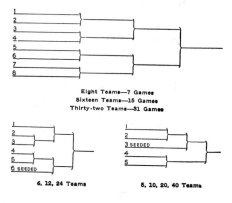

Eight Teams—7 Games
Sixteen Teams—15 Games
Thirty-two Teams—31 Games

6, 12, 24 Teams   **5, 10, 20, 40 Teams**

(From Athletic Field and Court Diagrams; courtesy Lowe and Campbell Athletic Goods, Kansas City, Mo.)

Health and adapted physical education forms

The following forms and records have been selected from the authors' files. School systems across the country which developed these forms are to be commended for their work.

	GRADE	AGE	Forward Head	Head Tilt	Forward Shoulder	High Shoulder	Body Torque	Body List	Kyphosis	Scoliosis	Lordosis	Pelvic Tilt	Tibial Torsion	Knock-Knee	Bowleg	Hyperextended Knee	Pronation	Flatfeet	Obesity	General Faulty Posture	Psychological	Refer Private Physician	Special Class	Regular Class	
C O D E:																									**SCHOOL**
+ Slight/Mild 1																									
++ Moderate 2																									**DATE**
+++ Severe 3																									
R Right																									
L Left																									**REMARKS**
Examining Doctor																									
1.																									
2.																									
3.																									
4.																									
5.																									
6.																									
7.																									
8.																									
9.																									
10.																									
11.																									
12.																									
13.																									
14.																									
15.																									

:ma - 2/14/63:500

Health Service
HEALTH CONSULTATION REQUEST

Date_____19 __

We are requesting the examination of

_____   _____
Name   School

because of the following causes:

_____

_____

_____

_____
Signature

_____
Position

(Front)

The findings of our examination of the bearer are_____

_____

_____

_____

Recommendation_____

_____

_____

_____M. D.
Director of Health Service

(Back)

SPECIAL ADAPTATION FOR PHYSICAL EDUCATION PROGRAM

All pupils registered in the schools of New York State are required by the Education Law to attend courses of instruction in physical education. These courses are required to be adapted to meet the needs and/or improve his condition.

The physical education program is flexible, involving many forms of indoor and outdoor activities. The following is a general list of activities included in the physical education program at the Rye High School during the school year:

____Football	____Touch Football	____LaCrosse	____Soccer
____Basketball	____Volleyball	____Softball	____Speedball
____Pole Vaulting	____Weight Lifting	____Baseball	____Wrestling
____Archery	____Tennis	____Apparatus	____Swimming
____Calisthenics	____Free Exercises	____Mimetics	____Self-testing Stunts
____Trampoline	____Tumbling	____Track	____Badminton
____Running Games	____Bowling	____Shot Put	____Golf
____Square Dancing	____Rhythms and Dances		____Social Dancing

THE EXAMINING PHYSICIAN WILL RECOMMEND THE ABOVE ACTIVITIES IN WHICH YOU MAY PARTICIPATE BY A (✓) MARK.

(Front)

TO THE EXAMINING PHYSICIAN: This pupil has come to you for
( )   Evaluation of a known condition
( )   Recheck of a known condition
( )   Care of a current condition

In order that we may best meet the present needs of this pupil, please fill out both sides of this card and return it to the SCHOOL NURSE TEACHER at the Rye High School.

Pupil's Name_____ Date _____

Findings:

This is to certify that I have examined the above pupil and recommend adaptation to the physical education program as indicated on the reverse side of this card for the period checked below.

	Weeks	Months	Indefinitely	School year
( ) No restrictions				
( ) Partial restrictions	____	____	____	____
( ) Total restrictions	____	____	____	____

Comments:

Signature of Examining Physician_____Tel. No._____
Note: This report will be attached to the pupil's school health record and a duplicate made for the physical education office.

(Back)

```
Adviser_____

Student_____

        Please report at the Nurse's Office as
soon as possible regarding:_____

_____


                        Thank you,

                        _____R.N.

                        _____R.N.

Date_____
```

```
                    GIRLS' GYM

            Please excuse_____,

adviser _____ from showers because

of _____

until _____

        She is under treatment _____.  She is

not under treatment _____.   Thank you.

                        _____


Date _____
```

(Courtesy Girls' Physical Education Department, New Trier Township High School, Winnetka, Ill.)

_____Teacher _____

JUNIOR HIGH SCHOOL GROWTH RECORD

_____ School_____ Year _____ Date

HEALTH, SAFETY AND PHYSICAL EDUCATION	NOV.	JAN.	APR.	JUNE
1. Shows cooperative spirit				
2. Respects personal and public property				
3. Recognizes and accepts responsibility				
4. Is courteous				
5. Makes good use of time and materials				
6. Uses health knowledge				
7. Practices safety				
8. Shows skill in activities				
9. Shows leadership				

(Front)

Department of Physical Education
PUPIL EXERCISE CARD

Name _____ Date_____ Period_____

1. _____
2. _____
3. _____
4. _____
5. _____
6. _____
7. _____
8. _____
9. _____
10. _____

(Front)

HEIGHT AND WEIGHT CARD

Name_____ Teacher_____ Period_____
Grade_____

Date			Date										
Age			Weight										
Height			— + %										
Weight			Date										
Average			Weight										
— + %			— + %										

Remarks:

PHYSICAL EXAMINATION PERMIT

(This appointment must be kept. No
excuse will be considered adequate.)

Adviser_____ Date_____

_____
is to be excused from class at_____
to have a physical examination.

Boys report to the training room in
the gym. Girls report to the Nurse's
Office, room 205.

Time student completed examination__

Released by:_____

Time student returned to class_____

Signature of teacher_____

_____
The teacher who receives this permit
should return it to the adviser who
should check to see that the time
interval is reasonable.

(Courtesy Health Department, New Trier Township High School, Winnetka, Ill.)

DEPARTMENT OF PHYSICAL EDUCATION FOR GIRLS

Dear Parent:

      For many years, the Girls' Health and Physical Educa-
tion Department has had a policy to protect the eyes of those
girls who wear glasses. It has been our practice to ask the
girl to remove the glasses. However, if the use of the glasses
makes a great deal of difference, we ask the girl to protect
her glasses and her eyes by wearing glasses guards. Unfortunately,
since these guards are not things of beauty nor comfortable to
wear, we do have an occasional student who refuses to wear them.
In such instances we have taken particular care to explain the
reasons for the policy and why it is important. The answer
usually is that the student will take full responsibility for
any accident which might occur; obviously, however, this is no
substitute for protection.

      We want you to understand our policies in protecting
students' eyes and ask you to urge your daughter to cooperate
in wearing glasses guards for her own protection. You will
agree, we believe, that we have tried to take every precaution.

      We are sure that you understand our position and that
you will urge your daughter to take advantage of the protection
which is provided.

                     Yours very truly,

                     Instructor, Girls' Health and
                     Physical Education Department

NAME_____
Last   First

BODY MECHANICS INSPECTION CARD — GIRLS

School					Living with Parents?_____	
					(Yes - No)	
Grade	B	A	B	A	B	A
Date (Begin. of Sem.)						
Age (Yrs. & Mo. - 14⁸)						
Height (Inches)						
Weight						
Average Weight						
— or + %						
Constipation						
Menses: Reg. - Days						
Dysmenorrhea						
Foot Inspection						
Swim. — Physician's Recommendation						
Current History (Illness, etc.)						
Physician's Recommendation						
Correction Needed						
Remarks						

PREVIOUS HISTORY
(Age or Date)

Menses Onset...................

Accidents, Operations,
Serious Illness, etc.

Feet						
Body Alignment						
Miscellaneous						
Posture Test Grade						

CODE: 1st Sem. — B = Blue Pencil   DEVIATION FROM NORMAL — 1. Slight
2nd Sem. — A = Red Pencil   (Red or Blue Lines & Marks)   2. Medium
3. Severe

(Front)

	B	A	B	A	B	A
Health Instruction						
First Aid Record						
Swim Test						
Physical Education Record						
Miscellaneous Record						
Assigned to: Class Instructor Period						
Withdrawn (Mo. & Yr.)						

Junior High Honor
Health Club

Notes:

(Back)

THE STATE EDUCATION DEPARTMENT
DIVISION OF HEALTH AND PHYSICAL EDUCATION

FORM FOR USE WHEN MAKING SPECIAL ADAPTATIONS
OF PHYSICAL EDUCATION TO MEET INDIVIDUAL PUPIL NEEDS

....*School*

To Dr .... *Family Physician*   *Date*..............................

Regarding the physical education activities of your patient..,

we shall appreciate your cooperation in filling out this blank and returning it at your earliest

convenience to..., principal of

....school.

All pupils registered in the schools of   are required by the Education Law
to attend courses of instruction in physical education.   These courses are required to be adapted
to meet individual pupil needs.   This means that a pupil who is unable to participate in the
entire program should have his activities modified to meet his needs and/or improve his condition.
Specific activities are provided for children who are below par physically and require special
attention for the following conditions:

(*Check the condition which applies to this pupil*)

.... Postoperative	.... Defective posture (functional)
.... Convalescent	.... Flabby musculature
.... Cardiac	.... Foot defects
.... Faulty nutrition	.... Others (specify)
.... Early fatigue	

The following is a general list of activities included in the physical education program:

V	M	N			V	M	N		
....	....	....	Apparatus						
....	....	....	Athletics		....	....	....	Swimming	V=Vigorous
....	....	....	Dual combat		....	....	....	Recreational sports	M=Mild
....	....	....	Self-testing stunts		....	....	....	Marching tactics	N=None
....	....	....	Calisthenics and free exercises				....	Quiet games	
....	....	....	Mimetics				....	Corrective exercises	
....	....	....	Rhythms and dances				....	Rest	
....	....	....	Running games					....	

This is to certify that I have examined...
and recommend that he should participate only in the activities that are checked above for a
period of...............weeks.

Remarks: ....

....

....   *Date*............................
Family Physician

NOTE.   This report will be attached to the child's school health record and a duplicate made for the
physical education office.

DEPARTMENT OF PHYSICAL EDUCATION FOR GIRLS

To the Examining Physician:

The administration of our high school wishes to cooperate with the family physician in its endeavor to provide the girls of the school with healthy and well-coordinated bodies. We feel that our physical education program is sufficiently flexible and broad enough in its scope to provide each student who is physically capable of attending school with some form of beneficial exercise.

There will naturally be some students in whom a period of rest alone is advisable. However, these should be extremely few in number. In our restricted physical education classes rest, relaxation, mild games, and posture work are stressed, and it is possible to adapt the work to the individual's strength.

Our department of physical education would greatly appreciate any suggestions that the physician has to offer and would welcome the privilege of conferring with him concerning the beneficial possibilities of their program in building the strength of his patient.

In order that the school may fulfill its purpose, we are asking all physicians whose patients are physically unable to participate in our physical education program or need their activity limited to fill out the accompanying blank.

We greatly appreciate your help and cooperation.

Yours very sincerely,

Superintendent

(Courtesy Girls' Physical Education Department, New Trier Township High School, Winnetka, Ill.)

```
                   DEPARTMENT OF PHYSICAL EDUCATION FOR GIRLS


  Name_____, _____ Adviser_____
           (Last)              (First)

  I have examined the above-named student and recommend that she be allowed
  to participate only in those activities which have not been crossed out.

       A. Strenuous         B. Intermediate        C. Mild

       Basketball           Badminton              Archery
       Field hockey         Baseball               Corrective or posture
       Games--relay races   Corecreational games     exercises
       Intramural swimming  Deck tennis            Restricted class
       Lacrosse             Gymnastic exercises      Croquet
       Lifesaving           Horeseback riding      Individual exercises
       Rhythmic dancing     Recreational leadership  Modified games
       Speedball            Social dance           Quiet social games
                            Swimming               Relaxation
                            Tennis                 Table tennis
                                                   Walking

  If the condition of the above-named student is such at the present time
  that complete rest is desirable during physical education classes, please
  indicate this and the number of days for which the student should continue
  in rest._____

  Up to the date of_____, please restrict this student's activ-
  ities as indicated above.  She is under my care for_____.
                                                          (Ailment)

  I would further like to suggest that the Department of Physical Education
  could contribute to the well-being of this girl in the following manner:

  _____

  _____


                          Signed_____
                                     (Examining Physician)

                          Address_____

  Date_____      Telephone_____
```

(Courtesy Girls' Physical Education Department, New Trier Township High School, Winnetka, Ill.)

DEPARTMENT OF HEALTH AND PHYSICAL EDUCATION FOR BOYS

Student's name_____Address_____Telephone_____

Adviser_____

The range and latitude of the health and physical education program at our high school is so varied that every pupil able to be in school should derive benefit from some phase of this program. Daily classes of 40 minutes, with about 15 minutes for undressing, showers, and dressing, leaves 25 minutes for actual activity.

Please check (✓) either generally or individually the types of physical education which you recommend for this pupil.

STRENUOUS( )	MODERATE ( )	MILD ( )
__ Basketball	__ Bag punching	__ Badminton practice
__ Boxing	__ Club swinging	__ Corrective exercises
__ Calisthenics	__ Practice hand ball	__ Free throwing
__ Hand ball	__ Running and walking	__ Horseshoes
__ Commando course	__ Shooting baskets	__ Playing catch
__ Rope climbing	__ Swimming (noncompetitive)	__ Swimming (recreational)
__ Running half mile	__ Table tennis	__ Tennis practice
__ Soccer	__ Tennis practice	__ Throwing at target
__ Swimming (competitive)	__ Tossing medicine balls	__ Walking
__ Tumbling--gymnastics	__ Touch football	__ _____
__ Wrestling	__ Volley ball	__ _____
__ _____	__ _____	__ _____

If the condition of this student is such at present that complete rest (recumbent position in bed) is desirable during his physical education class period, please indicate this and give the number of days he should continue these supervised rest periods._____

If any other information should be given for the welfare of this boy, add same here or feel free to call Mr._____ any school day at the high school, Central 1-2400.
_____
_____

Up to the date of_____please restrict this student's activities as indicated above. He is under my care for_____
_____

                              Signed_____
                                        (Examining Physician)

                              Address_____

Date_____   Telephone_____

(Courtesy Boys' Physical Education Department, New Trier Township High School, Winnetka, Ill.)

DEPARTMENT OF PHYSICAL EDUCATION FOR BOYS

| (Last name) | (First name) | (Adviser) | (Form secured) | (Form returned) |

Physician's <u>Partial or Complete</u> Waiver <u>for</u> Swimming

I have examined the above-named boy and recommend that his swimming be restricted as indicated below (please check):

The present required physical education swimming program for this boy includes every_____ within the following dates:_____

This boy may engage in STRENUOUS ( ) MODERATE ( ) MILD RECREATIONAL ( )
swimming, but

        He should not dive. ....( )

        He should not put his head under water. .....( )

        He may swim but should wear a nose clip. ....( )

This boy should NOT participate in any swimming. ....( )

Please list any other restrictions and <u>reasons</u> for same with <u>time</u> involved so
that a program may be arranged to his advantage.

_____
_____
_____
_____

Signed_____ Telephone_____ _____ Date_____
        (Physician)   (Exchange)   (Number)

<u>To Be Filled Out By Student</u>

Have you participated in swimming classes previously at this school?_____

Check below the approximate distance you are now capable of swimming:

        None ....( )

        One length of pool, 25 yd. ....( )

        Two lengths of pool.........................( )

        100 yd. or more ....( )

                Signed_____
                                (Student)

Note: Nonswimmers are often admitted to the pool from three to five times per
week with individual help, resulting in rapid improvement. We live in an
area where swimming is almost a "must" for fun, health, and safety. Don't
miss this wonderful opportunity.

This form, properly filled out and signed, is to be returned to the BOYS'
HEALTH OFFICE.

(Courtesy Boys' Physical Education Department, New Trier Township High School, Winnetka,
Ill.)

GIRLS' HEALTH AND PHYSICAL EDUCATION DEPARTMENT

Name_____   Date_____

Homeroom_____ R_____ S_____

    A notification has been received from the Health Service which specifies
that your classification for participation in physical education and G.A.A.
intramurals is the following:

Classification	Activity Requirements
____ A	Regular physical education--no limitation in G.A.A. intramurals
____ B	Regular physical education--no G.A.A. intramural participation without special permission from Health Service
____ Special	Assigned to special class which does not have activities demanding strenuous or prolonged exertion-- no G.A.A. intramurals without special permission from Health Service
____ Rest	Assigned to rest in Health Service--no G.A.A. intra- murals
____ Dropped	No physical education; program changed, to report to homeroom--no G.A.A. intramurals without special permission from Health Service
____ No physical education until further notice	Excused temporarily and to report to homeroom--no G.A.A. intramurals without special permission from Health Service

    If your classification is anything except "A" you are <u>not</u> to participate
in any G.A.A. intramural activities after school unless special permission
is granted by the Health Service. This is your official and latest classification and is now in effect.

                              Chairman, Girls' Health and
                              Physical Education Department

Dear Parents:

The health inspection given to all students has a
twofold purpose:

1. To make certain insofar as possible that
no student having a serious physical condition
participates in the regular physical education
program until such conditions be remedied.

2. To discover possible conditions which
should be called to the attention of both you and
your family physician.

This inspection might reveal a temporary situation
such as a throat condition, which might have improved
between the time of the school inspection and your family
physician's examination at a later date.

On the other hand, every year follow-up examinations
have shown that certain of the conditions brought to light
by the school inspection are serious and require immediate
attention.

Attached to this letter you will find mention of the
special health situation which we suggest be brought
immediately to the attention of your family physician.

Very sincerely yours,

Superintendent

PHYSICAL EXAMINATION RECORD

NAME_____ ADVISER_____ TELEPHONE_____ PHYSICIAN_____

LAST   FIRST

PARENT OR GUARDIAN_____ ADDRESS_____ DENTIST_____

PLEASE CHECK IF YOU HAVE HAD THE FOLLOWING DISEASES

Chickenpox	Whooping Cough	Mumps	Scarlet Fever	Typhoid Fever	Diphtheria	Rheumatism	Tonsilitis	Vaccination for Smallpox	Diphtheria Immunization	Measles

BIRTH DATE

What operations have you had?_____
Give type of operation and dates_____
What serious injuries have you had?_____
Specify injury and date_____
Remarks_____

		Weight	Height	Weight	Height	Weight	Height	Weight	Height
Date									
Age									
Weight									
Development									
Nourishment									
SKIN	Acne								
	Ringworm								
	Planatar Warts								
EYES	Vision R L	R L	R L	R L					
	Exophthalmos								
	Conjunctiva								
EARS	Hearing R L	R L	R L	R L					
	Discharge R L	R L	R L	R L					
	R L	R L	R L	R L					
	Cerumen R L	R L	R L	R L					
NOSE	Obstruction								
SINUSES									
MOUTH									
THROAT	Tonsils								
	Advise Removal								
	Removed								
NECK	Thyroid								
	Pulsation of Vessels								
CHEST									
LUNGS	Palpation								
	Percussion								
	Auscultation								

(Continued Below)   (Continued Below)

HEART	Murmurs						
PULSE	At Rest						
	After Exercise, 20 hops						
	After 2 Min. Rest						
SPINE AND POSTURE							
ABDOMEN							
HERNIA							
GENITALS	Varicocele						
	Hydrocele						
NERVOUS SYSTEM	Speech Defect						
	Coordination						
	Tremor						
FEET							
SUMMARY	Classification						
	Reason						
	Length of Time						
	Comments and Suggestions						
	Excused from Swimming						
	How Long?						
	Excused from Showers						
	How Long?						
REMARKS							

Class "A"—Unrestricted physical education activity.
Class "B"—Regular physical education but no intramural competition.
Class "C"—Restricted physical education activity (special classes).
Class "D"—Supervised rest.

X—Means defect present.
XX—Means defect needs attention—parents notified.
XXX—Means defect needs immediate attention—parents notified.

(Courtesy Health Department, New Trier Township High School, Winnetka, Ill.)

PART I   NAME   SEX M F   DATE OF BIRTH   PLACE OF BIRTH

HEALTH RECORD

| ADDRESS | PHONE | ADDRESS | PHONE | ADDRESS | PHONE |

FATHER   NAME   BIRTHPLACE   MOTHER   NAME   BIRTHPLACE

SCHOOL   PLACE   COUNTY   PHYSICIAN / TO BE CALLED IN EMERGENCY   NAME   PHONE

HISTORY

	DATE		DATE		DATE		DATE
CHICKEN POX		SORE THROAT		TBC. IN ASSOCIATES		OPERATIONS	
MEASLES		RHEUMATIC FEVER		WHOOPING COUGH			
GERMAN MEASLES		HEART DISEASE		RUNNING EARS		TONSILLECTOMY	
MUMPS		INF. PARALYSIS				SERIOUS INJURY	
DIPHTHERIA		PNEUMONIA					
SCARLET FEVER		TUBERCULOSIS					

PREVENTATIVE AND CONTROL MEASURES

IMMUNIZATIONS	DATE	TESTS	DATE	COLOR PERCEPTION	
SMALL POX		TUBERCULIN			
DIPHTHERIA		CHEST X-RAY			

PART II   ANNUAL HEALTH EXAMINATION RECORD

AGE												
GRADE												
DATE OF PHYSICIAN'S EXAM.												
ATTENDANCE												
SCHOLASTIC RATING *												
HEIGHT												
WEIGHT												
EYES — V.A.-C R												
V.A.-C L												
V.A.-C BOTH												
V.A.-S R												
V.A.-S L												
V.A.-S BOTH												
OTHER DEFECTS												
EAR — HEARING SCORE (DECIBELS) R												
HEARING SCORE (DECIBELS) L												
OTHER DEFECTS												
NUTRITION												
TEETH — TEMPORARY												
PERMANENT												
GUMS												
TONSILS												
NOSE												
GLANDS — CERVICAL												
THYROID												
OTHER (SPECIFY)												
HEART												
LUNGS												
ORTHOPEDIC — STRUCTURAL DEF.												
POSTURE												
FEET												
SKIN (NON-COMMUNICABLE)												
HERNIA												
NERVOUS SYSTEM (SPECIFY IF EPILEPSY)												
SPEECH												
GENERAL CONDITION*												
SIGNATURE OF PHYSICIAN												

CODE: N or blank space no defect found; x, observation (not to be reported or followed); xx, Defect (to be reported and followed); xxx, Severe Defect (report and immediate follow-up); I, irremediable defect (already followed); S.R., Supplementary Record; *Good, Fair, Poor; **V.A., visual acuity; o, with Glasses; s, without Glasses.

NOTE: The Physician's signature is a guarantee that the indicated examination is complete.

(over)

(Front)

PART III	PART IV	PART V	PART VI
RECOMMENDATION OF PHYSICIAN FOR FOLLOW-UP AND/OR MODIFICATION OF SCHOOL PROGRAM	TREATMENT OF DEFECTS (DATE AND INITIAL)	ILLNESS ABSENCE CAUSE AND DURATION	SUMMARY OF OBSERVATION OF TEACHERS AND OTHERS

NAME		SEX-M.F.		EYE	EAR	NUT	TEETH		GUM	TONS	NOS	GLANDS		HRT	LUN	ORTHOPEDIC			SKN	HER	N.S.	S.P.	G.C.	FILE NO.
							TEM	PER				CER	THY			STR	POS	FEET						

(Back)

Physical education activity, skill, and squad forms

The following forms and records have been selected from the authors' files. School systems across the country which developed these forms are to be commended for their work.

Co-Educational P. E.

Last Name	First Name		Period	Section	Standing

INDICATE YOUR CHOICE (1 for first, 2 for second, etc.)

10th Grade	11th Grade	12th Grade
	Badm't'n & P'g P'g - ____	Archery - - - - ____
Dancing - - - - ____	Dancing - - - - ____	Badm't'n & P'g P'g - ____
		Dancing - - - - ____
Sports - - - - ____	Sports - - - - ____	Sports - - - - ____
_____ - - - - ____	_____ - - - - ____	Tennis - - - - ____
_____ - - - - ____	_____ - - - - ____	_____ - - - - ____

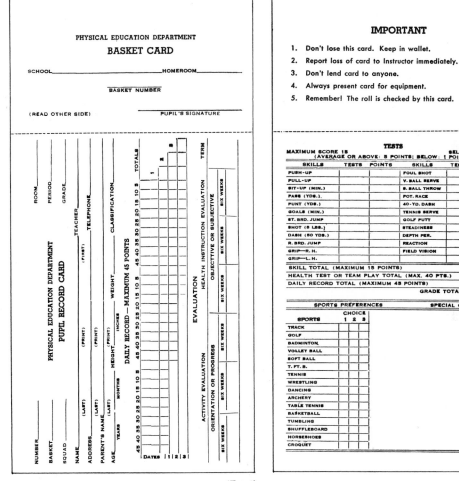

(Front)   *(Back)*

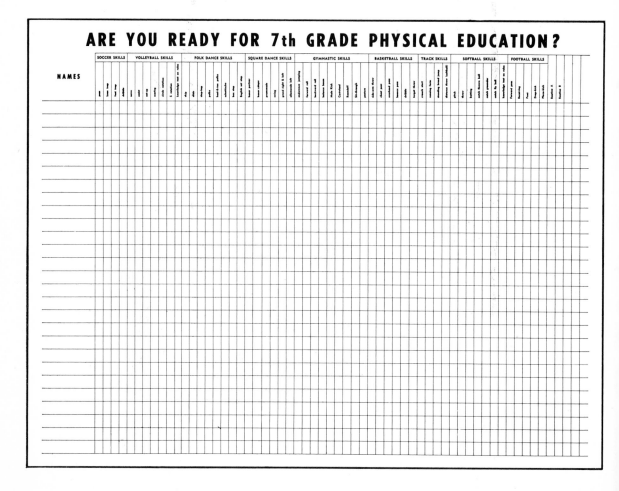

Name								Date of Birth		Date of Entry			
						PHYSICAL EDUCATION RECORD — GIRLS							
Address				New Address					New Address				
Grade	7	8	9	10	11	12		Grade	7	8	9	10	11	12
Teacher's Initials								Absences						
Citizenship								Excuses						
Preparation								Medical						
Class Work								Grade		COMMENTS				
Leadership								7						
Rhythms Modern Dance														
Square & Folk Dance														
Social Dance								8						
Tap Dance														
Athletic Games Basketball														
Field Hockey								9						
Soccer & Speedball														
Softball														
Volleyball								10						
App., Stunts, Tumb.														
Aquatics														
Archery								11						
Badminton & Tennis														
Adapted Activities								12						
Intramurals								Grade	7	8	9	10	11	12
Tests Standing Broad Jump								Height						
Chins (Reg. or Mod.)								Weight						
Get up—Pick up														
Burpee								Final Gr.						

DEPARTMENT OF PHYSICAL EDUCATION

JUNIOR HIGH POINT CARD - GIRLS

NAME_____JUNIOR HIGH SCHOOL

		DATE	ATHLETIC ACTIVITY									LEADERSHIP										HEALTH							RUNNING TOTAL	GRAND TOTAL
CERTIFICATE			VOLLEY BALL	BASKET BALL	SOCCER	SPEED BALL	SOFT BALL	OTHER ACTIVITIES	OTHER ACTIVITIES	OTHER ACTIVITIES	SUMMER PLAYGROUNDS	GAA PRES.	GAA ASSTS.	COLOR CAPT.	SQUAD LEADER	MONITOR	OFFICIALS	TEAM CAPT.	CHAMPIONSHIP TEAMS	CHAMPIONSHIP TEAMS	GRADE A IN P. E. CLASS	ORTHOPEDICS	HONOR HEALTH CLUB	BEG. ARC	INTER. ARC	SWIMMER ARC	ADV. SWIM. ARC	J.A.R.C. LIFE SAVING		
EMBLEM																														
CHEVRONS																														
LETTER																														
STARS																														
YR.	TCH.	GRADE																												
		7B																												
		7A																												
		8B																												
		8A																												
		9B																												
		9A																												

1000 POINTS_____

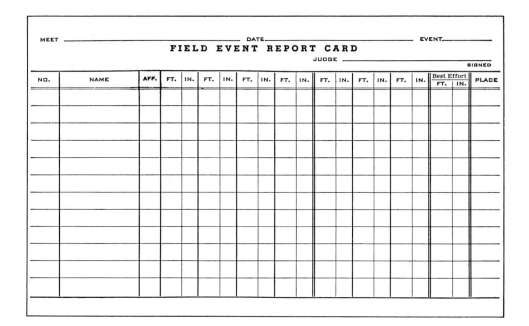

MEET _____ DATE_____ EVENT_____

FIELD EVENT REPORT CARD

JUDGE _____

SIGNED

NO.	NAME	AFF.	FT.	IN.	FT.	IN.	FT.	IN.	FT.	IN.	FT.	IN.	FT.	IN.	FT.	IN.	Best Effort FT.	Best Effort IN.	PLACE

PHYSICAL EDUCATION RECORD

Name _____   **Counselor** _____

Grade Year	Class	Per	Teacher	Health Finding	Date	Recommendation	Correction	G. A. A.

Remarks:

SENIOR SCHOOL GOAL SHEET

Pupil's Name ....

SKILLS — ATHLETIC AND GYMNASIUM (Boys)

Seventh Grade 19____ 19____		Eighth Grade 19____ 19____		Ninth Grade 19____ 19____	
Gymnastic Skills **Can do in good form—**		**Can do in good form—**		**Gymnastic Skills** **Can do in good form—**	
1. Forward roll	_____	1. Handstand against wall	_____	1. Spinning wheel	_____
2. Backward roll	_____	2. Cart Wheel	_____	2. Hand spring	_____
3. Head Stand	_____	3. Handspring, with mat	_____	3. Touch tow jump	_____
4. Full squat	_____	4. Forward roll, over 2 men	_____	4. Forward roll — over 3 men	_____
5. Double forward roll	_____	5. Rope climb, using feet	_____	5. Rope Climb — without feet	_____
6. Walk balance beam forward	_____	6. Standing rope jump	_____	6. Fence vault shoulder high	_____
backward	_____	7. Running high dive Chest high	_____	7. Running rope jump	_____
7. Half lever rings	_____	8. Support half lever parallel bars	_____	8. Cut off on bars	_____
8. Running high dive	_____			9. Cut off on rings	_____
9. Travel on bars	_____	9. Complete Piroette	_____	10. Travel 7 rings	_____
10. One leg squat	_____	10.	_____	11. Inverted push up against wall	_____
11.	_____	11.	_____	12. Double knee circle horizontal bar	_____
12.	_____	12.	_____	13.	_____
				14.	_____
Athletic Skills **Football**		**Athletic Skills** **Football**		**Athletic Skills** **Football — Accuracy**	
Drop kick	_____ ft.	Center ball — 5 yds. 5/6	_____	Drop kick 3/6	_____
Place kick	_____ ft.	Center ball — 8 yds. 4/6	_____	Place kick 3/6	_____
Forward pass	_____ ft.	Catch punts	_____	Forward pass 3/6	_____
Punt	_____ ft.	**Defensive formations**		Punt 3/6	_____
Basketball		7-2-2	_____		
Push pass	_____	6-3-2	_____	**Basketball**	
One hand pass	_____	**Offensive Formations** Single wing back	_____	Foul shot 5/10	_____
Bounce pass	_____	Double wing back	_____	Goal Shots 7 in 30 seconds	_____
One hand bounce pass	_____	T formation	_____		
Push shot	_____	**Soccer**		**Boxing**	
Foul shot	_____	Dribble and pass	_____	Stance — on guard	_____
Volleyball		**Basketball**		Shifting of feet	_____
Serve	_____	Properly executes Reverse pivot	_____	Left lead to body, and guard	_____
Return	_____	Dribble and shoot	_____	Left lead to head, and guard	_____
Baseball		**Wrestling**		Box 2 — 1 minute rounds	_____
Throws ball correctly	_____	Standing position	_____		
Catches ball correctly	_____	Take-downs	_____	**Track**	
Track		Pinning holds	_____	Run — 50 yds. 7 2/5 sec.	_____
Start	_____	Wrestle — 3 minutes	_____	Running broad jump, 13'	_____
High jump	_____ ft. _____ in.	**Baseball**		Running high jump, 3'9"	_____
Broad jump	_____ ft. _____ in.	Bunt and run	_____	Discus throw 50"	_____
Shot put	_____ ft. _____ in.	Run bases against time	_____	Shot put (8 lb.) 28'	_____
Baton passing	_____	Accurate base throwing	_____	Organizes and officiates at a team game	_____
Sprint	_____	Time of running	_____	Time of running	_____
Distance	_____	Time of running	_____	Time of running	_____
Push ups	_____	Time of running	_____	Time of running	_____
Push ups	_____				
Push ups	_____				
Push ups	_____				

BP-1M-10-51

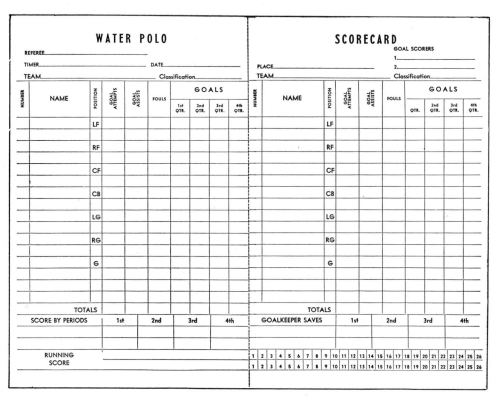

(Front)

(Back)

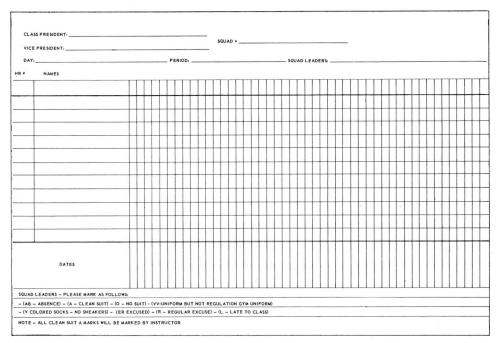

(Front)

CLASS PRESIDENT: _____   SQUAD # _____

VICE PRESIDENT: _____

DAY: _____   PERIOD: _____   SQUAD LEADERS: _____

HR #   NAMES

DATES

SQUAD LEADERS – PLEASE MARK AS FOLLOWS:

– (AB – ABSENCE) – (A – CLEAN SUIT) – (O – NO SUIT) - (VV-UNIFORM BUT NOT REGULATION GYM UNIFORM)

– (V COLORED SOCKS – NO SNEAKERS) – (ER EXCUSED) – (R – REGULAR EXCUSE) – (L – LATE TO CLASS)

NOTE – ALL CLEAN SUIT A MARKS WILL BE MARKED BY INSTRUCTOR

DAYS_____   PERIOD_____   LEADERS_____

SQUAD NO._____

NAMES

JAN, JUNE

WRITTEN TESTS | CITIZENSHIP | CLASS WORK | SHOWERS | TOTAL CLEAN SUITS | BASKETBALL | 20 FREE THROWS | BASKETS 1 MIN. | APPARATUS STUNTS-TUMBLING AVE. | BUCK | ELEPHANT | ROPE VAULT | RINGS | HORSE | TRAVELING RINGS | PHYSICAL FITNESS AVE. | SQUAT THRUST | S. B. JUMP | PULL UPS | AGILITY RUN | K W | FINAL GRADE JANUARY | FINAL GRADE JUNE

(Back)

Accident forms

The following forms and records have been selected from the authors' files. School systems across the country which developed these forms are to be commended for their work.

GIRLS' HEALTH AND PHYSICAL EDUCATION DEPARTMENT

Re: Accident Report

Student injured_____ H.R._____

Date of injury_____ Time_____

Description of important details of accident:

Treatment or care by Health Service, if any:

Instructor or coach's follow-up:

                              (Signed)_____

       (Use reverse side if additional space is necessary.)

REPORT OF ACCIDENT

Date_____ 19____   Hour_____

Name of child_____ Age_____

Address_____

Reported by_____

Nature of accident_____
_____
_____
_____

Witnesses--names and addresses_____
_____
_____

Statements of witnesses_____
_____
_____
_____
_____

Reason for injured being at site of accident_____
_____
_____

Name of teacher in charge and statement of circumstances_____
_____
_____

First aid_____
_____
_____

Name of physician_____

Name of hospital_____

Follow-up_____
_____
_____
_____
_____
_____

STANDARD STUDENT ACCIDENT REPORT FORM
Part A. Information on ALL Accidents

1. Name: _____ Home Address: _____
2. School _____ Sex M ☐; F ☐. Age: _____ Grade or classification: _____
3. Time accident occurred· Hour _____ A.M., _____ P.M. Date: _____
4. Place of Accident   School Building ☐   School Grounds ☐   To or from School ☐   Home ☐   Elsewhere ☐

5. NATURE OF INJURY				**DESCRIPTION OF THE ACCIDENT**
Abrasion	_____	Fracture	_____	How did accident happen? What was student doing? Where was student?
Amputation	_____	Laceration	_____	List specifically unsafe acts and unsafe conditions existing. Specify any tool,
Asphyxiation	_____	Poisoning	_____	machine or equipment involved. _____
Bite	_____	Puncture	_____	_____
Bruise	_____	Scalds	_____	_____
Burn	_____	Scratches	_____	_____
Concussion	_____	Shock (el.)	_____	_____
Cut	_____	Sprain	_____	_____
Dislocation	_____			
Other (specify)	_____			

PART OF BODY INJURED				
Abdomen	_____	Foot	_____	_____
Ankle	_____	Hand	_____	_____
Arm	_____	Head	_____	_____
Back	_____	Knee	_____	_____
Chest	_____	Leg	_____	_____
Ear	_____	Mouth	_____	_____
Elbow	_____	Nose	_____	_____
Eye	_____	Scalp	_____	_____
Face	_____	Tooth	_____	_____
Finger	_____	Wrist	_____	_____
Other (specify)	_____			

6. Degree of Injury: Death ☐ Permanent Impairment ☐ Temporary Disability ☐ Nondisabling ☐
7. Total number of days lost from school: _____ (To be filled in when student returns to school)

Part B. Additional Information on School Jurisdiction Accidents

8. Teacher in charge when accident occurred (Enter name) _____
   Present at scene of accident: No· _____ Yes: _____

9. IMMEDIATE ACTION TAKEN			
First-aid treatment	_____	By (Name):	_____
Sent to school nurse	_____	By (Name):	_____
Sent home	_____	By (Name):	_____
Sent to physician	_____	By (Name):	_____
		Physician's Name:	_____
Sent to hospital	_____	By (Name):	_____
		Name of hospital:	_____

10. Was a parent or other individual notified? No. ___ Yes. ___ When. _____ How: _____
    Name of individual notified: _____
    By whom? (Enter name): _____
11. Witnesses· 1. Name: _____ Address: _____
              2. Name· _____ Address: _____

12. LOCATION	**Specify Activity**		**Specify Activity**	**Remarks**
Athletic field	_____	Locker	_____	What recommendations do you have for pre-
Auditorium	_____	Pool	_____	venting other accidents of this type? _____
Cafeteria	_____	Sch. grounds	_____	_____
Classroom	_____	_____ shop	_____	_____
Corridor	_____	Showers	_____	_____
Dressing room	_____	Stairs	_____	_____
Gymnasium	_____	Toilets and		_____
Home Econ.	_____	washrooms	_____	_____
Laboratories	_____	Other (specify)	_____	_____

Signed: Principal: _____ Teacher: _____

(National Safety Council—Form School 1)   Printed in U.S.A. Rep. 200M—25302

REPORT OF INJURY OR ACCIDENT OCCURRING ON SCHOOL PROPERTY

School_____   Note: 5 reports should be made out:
                                          3 copies for Superintendent's
Date_____   office, 1 copy for Medical Office,
                                          and 1 copy to be kept at the school.
Time_____

Name of pupil_____   Age_____ Reporting Room_____

Address_____

Description of place where accident occurred:_____

State briefly but completely what happened, giving names of witnesses,
addresses and signatures, if possible:_____
_____
_____
_____

Description of injury:_____
_____
_____

By whom was aid rendered?_____

When and how were parents informed?_____

Disposition of case (home, hospital, etc.):_____

Method of transportation:_____

When was attending physician called?_____ At whose request_____

Name of physician:_____

                    Signature_____

SUBSEQUENT REPORT: By whom?_____ Date_____

When did pupil return to school duties?_____

Extracurricular activities of pupil:_____

        (a) Before accident:_____
_____

        (b) After accident:_____
_____

                    Signature_____

LIABILITY ACCIDENT NOTICE
(Not Automobile)

Name of Company	Policy No.	Name and Location of Agent

			COVERAGE DATA			Policy Dates:	
Limits	Liab.	Med. Pay.	Elevator	Products	Contr.		Other (Specify)
B. I.							
P. D.							

Insured

Name   Phone

Address

Location of Insured Premises

Time and Place

Date and Time of Accident

Location

Injured Person

Name   Age

Address

Occupation

Employed by:

What was injured doing when hurt?

The Injury

Nature and extent of injury

Where was injured taken after accident?

Probable disability   Has injured resumed work?

Property Damage

Owner   Address   Phone

List damage   Estimated cost of repair $

Witnesses

Name   Address   Phone

Description of Accident

Date: _____

Signature of Agent   Signature of Insured

Use reverse side for diagram and any other information of importance in reporting the accident

Physical education test and achievement forms

The following forms and records have been selected from the authors' files. School systems across the country which developed these forms are to be commended for their work.

PHYSICAL FITNESS PENTATHLON			SCHOOL										LAST NAME		FIRST			IN	
			AVALON		POLY														
			DEWEY		WILSON														
			JORDAN																

No.	Inst.	Pd.	Stand. Broad	Score	Rope Climb	Score	300 Run	Score	Bar Snap	Score		Score	Ht.	Wt.	Age	Exp.	Class	Total Score	Gr.
1																			
2																			
3																			
4																			
5																			
6																			
7																			
8																			
9																			
10																			
11																			
12																			

STANDARD PERFORMANCE

Class	Minimum	Average	Superior	Excellent
A	200	255	295	375
B	190	240	280	360
C	180	230	270	350
D	170	220	260	340

AVERAGE SCORE

DATE

Sophomore Yr.		
Junior Yr.		
Senior Yr.		

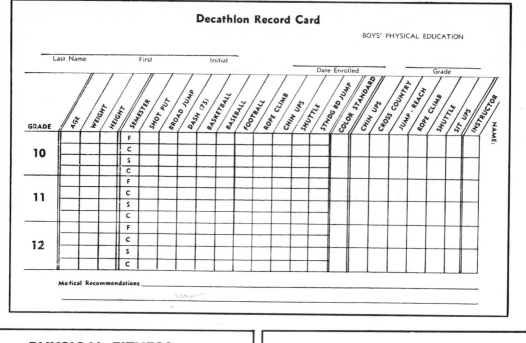

Decathlon Record Card

BOYS' PHYSICAL EDUCATION

	Last Name	First	Initial	Date Enrolled	Grade

GRADE				SEMESTER	AGE	WEIGHT	HEIGHT	SHOT PUT	BROAD JUMP	DASH (75)	BASKETBALL	BASEBALL	FOOTBALL	ROPE CLIMB	CHIN UPS	SHUTTLE	STNDG BD JUMP	COLOR STANDARD	CHIN UPS	CROSS COUNTRY	JUMP - REACH	ROPE CLIMB	SHUTTLE	SIT UPS	INSTRUCTOR NAME:
10				F																					
				C																					
				S																					
				C																					
11				F																					
				C																					
				S																					
				C																					
12				F																					
				C																					
				S																					
				C																					

Medical Recommendations _____

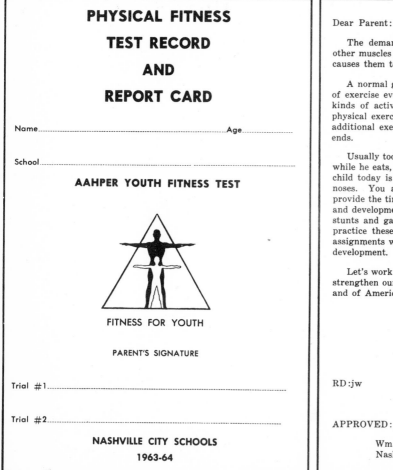

PHYSICAL FITNESS
TEST RECORD
AND
REPORT CARD

Name...Age...........................

School...

AAHPER YOUTH FITNESS TEST

FITNESS FOR YOUTH

PARENT'S SIGNATURE

Trial #1...

Trial #2...

NASHVILLE CITY SCHOOLS
1963-64

Dear Parent:

The demand that vigorous exercise makes on the heart and other muscles and on the body systems such as lungs, nerves, etc., causes them to grow stronger.

A normal growing child is said to need from two to five hours of exercise every day. The school day is so crowded with other kinds of activity that only a small part of the day is given to physical exercise. Therefore, we are asking your help in giving additional exercise time to your child after school and on weekends.

Usually too many of the child's waking hours are spent sitting, while he eats, listens, reads, rides, watches, writes or waits. The child today is literally staging a sit-down strike right under our noses. You and your child's teacher by working together can provide the time and the activity necessary for the proper growth and development of your child. The teacher will teach the skills, stunts and games and with your encouragement, your child will practice these activities at home together with the active work assignments which we hope you will also provide for their proper development.

Let's work together to put an end to this "sit-down" strike and strengthen our children and the future security of our community and of America.

Respectfully yours,

Robert Dunkerley
Robert Dunkerley
Director of Physical Education

RD:jw

APPROVED: *Wm. Henry Oliver*
Wm. Henry Oliver, Superintendent
Nashville City Schools

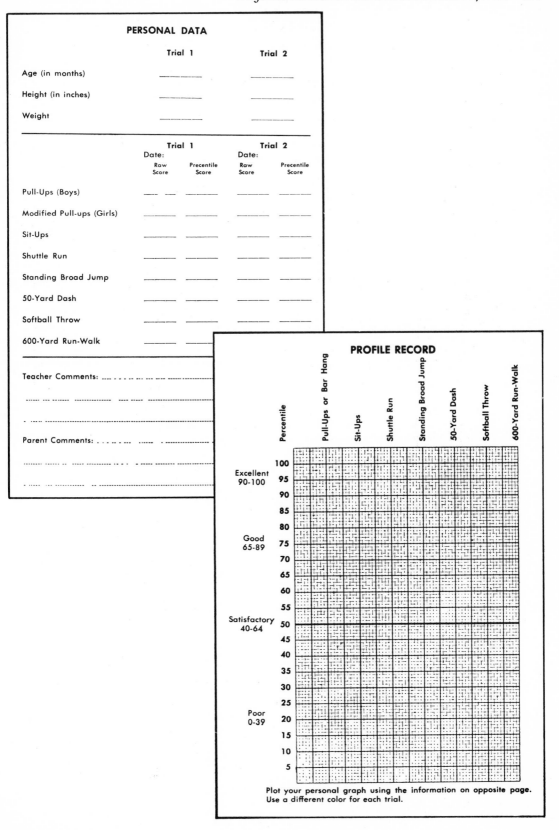

PERSONAL DATA

	Trial 1	Trial 2
Age (in months)	_____	_____
Height (in inches)	_____	_____
Weight	_____	_____

	Trial 1 Date:		Trial 2 Date:	
	Raw Score	Precentile Score	Raw Score	Precentile Score
Pull-Ups (Boys)	___ ___	___ ___		
Modified Pull-ups (Girls)	_____	_____	_____	
Sit-Ups	_____	_____	_____	
Shuttle Run	_____	_____	_____	
Standing Broad Jump	_____	_____	_____	
50-Yard Dash	_____	_____	_____	
Softball Throw	_____	_____	_____	
600-Yard Run-Walk	_____	_____		

Teacher Comments: .... - . --- --- --- --- ---------------

...... --- ------- -------------- ---- ----- -----------

. ---- ------- ---------- --------------------------------

Parent Comments: . . - -- --- ------ . ------------------

...... --- --- -------- -- ----- -------- ------------

. --- ----- ------ -- ---------------------------------

PROFILE RECORD

Plot your personal graph using the information on opposite page. Use a different color for each trial.

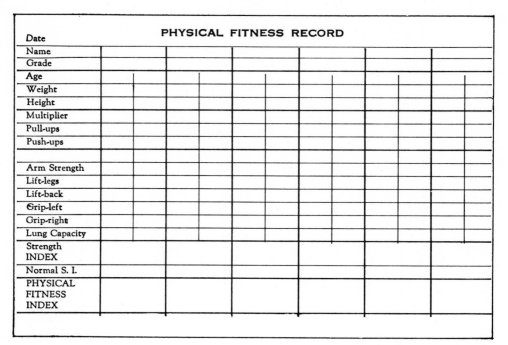

Date	PHYSICAL FITNESS RECORD					
Name						
Grade						
Age						
Weight						
Height						
Multiplier						
Pull-ups						
Push-ups						
Arm Strength						
Lift-legs						
Lift-back						
Grip-left						
Grip-right						
Lung Capacity						
Strength INDEX						
Normal S. I.						
PHYSICAL FITNESS INDEX						

(Front)

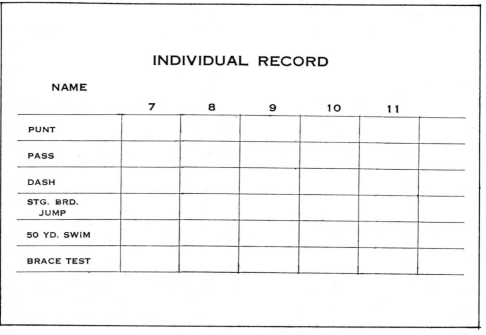

INDIVIDUAL RECORD

NAME

	7	8	9	10	11	
PUNT						
PASS						
DASH						
STG. BRD. JUMP						
50 YD. SWIM						
BRACE TEST						

(Back)

A CITIZENSHIP GUIDE SHEET

The selection shall be based on the service the pupil has rendered to the home room or to the school and on the general quality of his citizenship.

I. Attitudes of cooperation in the home room, classroom, and school
   A. Honesty
      1. Does not cheat during an examination
      2. Can be trusted to handle school funds
      3. Returns lost articles that he finds
      4. Tells the truth regardless of consequences

   B. Loyalty
      1. Does many important <u>little</u> jobs for the good of the school
      2. Behaves publicly in such a manner as to reflect credit to his school

   C. Dependability
      1. Works faithfully at everything he does
      2. Cooperates with teachers in and out of the classroom
      3. Willingly accepts assigned duties

   D. Sportsmanship
      1. Plays fair and square in all situations
      2. Takes defeat without making excuses
      3. Compliments others when they do well
      4. Keeps his temper even when competition is keen

   E. Conduct
      1. Obeys school rules
      2. Accepts deserved punishment without complaint
      3. Admits it when he has done something wrong
      4. Considers the good of the class and does not attempt to monopolize the teacher's time or class discussion

   F. Personal attitudes and self-improvement
      1. Makes new students feel welcome
      2. Shows respect to adults and classmates
      3. Has understanding and sympathy for weaknesses and failures of others
      4. Respects his own property, the property of others and of the school
      5. Does his schoolwork to his best ability

II. Activity and voluntary participation in home room and school activities
   A. Interest in service to the school through activities and clubs
   B. Support of home room activities such as parties, meetings, and intramural games
   C. Support of worthy causes such as Community Fund, Red Cross Drive, Christmas Project, etc.
   D. Support of school functions such as dances, plays, etc.

It is not expected that a pupil should have participated or excelled in <u>all</u> of the above items.

Citizenship Committee

NAME (Print)		Last		First		DATE OF BIRTH		Y	M	D	X
Date of Test											
GRADE											
AGE	y	m	y	m	y	m	y	m	y	m	y	m
WEIGHT		—		—		—		—		—		—
HEIGHT		—		—		—		—		—		—
$\left(\frac{Wt.}{10} + Ht.\text{-}60\right)$ MULTIPLIER	—		—		—		—		—		—	
PULLUPS		—		—		—		—		—		—
PUSHUPS											
ARM STRENGTH											
LIFT—BACK											
LIFT—LEGS											
GRIP—LEFT											
GRIP—RIGHT											
LUNG CAPACITY											
STRENGTH INDEX											
NORMAL S. I.											
PHYSICAL FITNESS INDEX											
Classification											

REMARKS

(Front)

Date						
SPECIAL NOTATIONS SCHOOL-MED. Examination						
CORRECTIVE DATA						
Weight-(Actual)						
" -(Chart)						
POSTURE						
FOOTBALL						
HOCKEY						
SOCCER						
BASKETBALL						
BASEBALL						
TRACK—FIELD						
TENNIS						
ARCHERY						
SOFT BALL						
HIKING						
SWIMMING						
TUMBLING						
HANDBALL						
BOXING						
CROSS COUNTRY						
TOTAL						
ABSENCES (Previous Year)						
LONG ILLNESS						
GENERAL SCHOLASTIC ACHIEVEMENT (Previous Year)						

(Back)

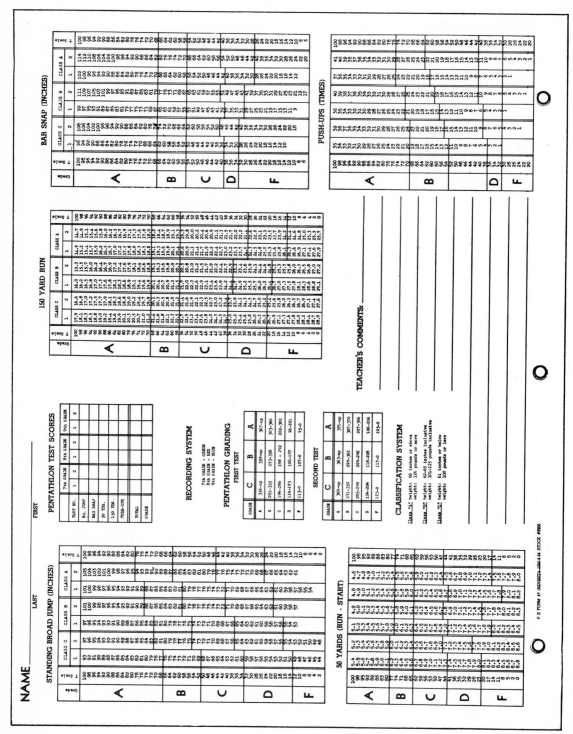

(Front)

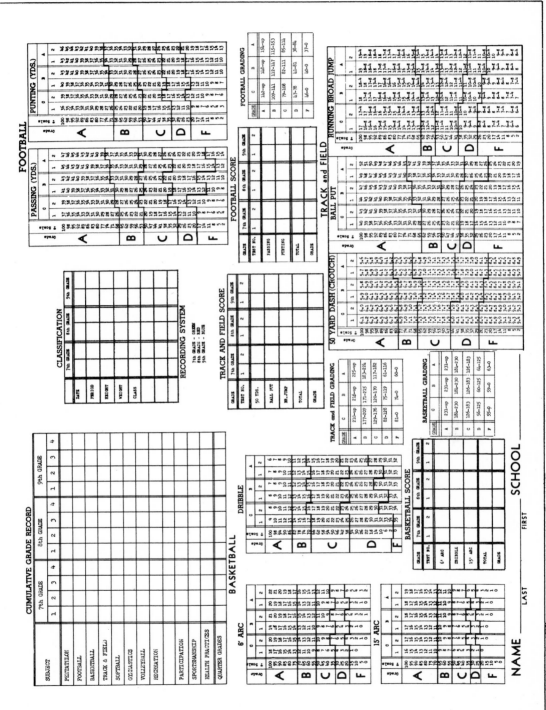

(Back)

SENIOR HIGH SCHOOL GOAL SHEET

7th, 8th and 9th Grades

Pupil's Name ....

PHYSICAL FITNESS — ATHLETIC PARTICIPATION

We believe that physical health is as important as mental health and that neither of the two can function to capacity unless the other is in proper balance. For this reason a definite program of physical education is carried on. This program is extensive for the majority, but intensive for the individual who has definite and specific needs. This sheet is an attempt to set forth in objective terms the physical fitness of the individual child so far as it can be measured and to give a record of the intramural sports in which he has participated.

Physical Fitness Index *

	Seventh Year 19........ 19........	Eighth Year 19........ 19........	Ninth Year 19........ 19........
Fall			
Spring			

NORMAL PHYSICAL FITNESS INDEX IS 1.00.

Posture * *

Fall			
Spring			

Intramural Participation

Football			
Speedball			
Soccer			
Basketball			
Volleyball			
Baseball			
Track			

* The Physical Fitness Index is a number arrived at by a rather complicated formula which has been worked out over a period of years and through extensive research in children's physical abilities. It is an attempt to give, in one symbol, an expression of the physical tone of the individual. Since it takes into consideration many separate strengths, as well as height, weight and age, it is not only significant as regards the individual in comparison with people of his own structure, but it also gives an opportunity to discover any inherent weakness and to plan for its remedy. The members of the Physical Education Department will be glad to go into this matter in detail if you will call on them.

** Posture is stated as excellent, good or poor. This is done to bring to the individual's attention his habitual posture, for it is only by conscious effort that any change can be brought about. The members of the Physical Education Department will be glad to consult with you regarding this matter.

SENIOR SCHOOL

Department of Physical Education
Boys, Grades 10-11-12

Pupil's Name .... · Teacher ....

Advisers: Grade 10 ....   Grade 11 ....   Grade 12 ....

Objectives of the Program:
1. To develop skills necessary for the satisfactory participation in the various sports, both group and individual.
2. To aid in the development of organic strength and physiological health through physical education activities.
3. To improve attitudes toward the social values of athletics, such as cooperation, fair play and self discipline.
4. To develop an attitude of awareness of desirable postural habits and practice.

	GRADE 10 — Date 19.... 19....	GRADE 11 — Date 19.... 19....	GRADE 12 — Date 19.... 19....
1st GOAL PERIOD	1. Football Skills — Completion of Skill Tests ...... 2. Soccer Skills ...... 3. Coeducational Activities ...... 4. P.F.I. Score ...... (Self Evaluation Only) 5. Preparation and Attitude	1. Football Skills ...... (Senior Football Decathlon) 2. Soccer Skills ...... 3. P.F.I. Score ...... (Self Evaluation Only) 4. Preparation and Attitude	1. Football Skills ...... (Senior Football Decathlon) 2. Soccer Skills ...... 3. P.F.I. Score ...... (Self Evaluation Only) 4. Preparation and Attitude ......
2nd GOAL PERIOD	1. Basketball Skills ...... (Completion of Skill Tests) 2. Gymnastics ...... (Rings, Parallel Bars and Vaulting Box) 3. Coeducational Activities ...... 4. Preparation and Attitude	1. Basketball Skills ...... (Completion of Skill Tests) 2. Gymnastics ...... (Rings, Parallel Bars and Vaulting Box) 3. Preparation and Attitude	1. Basketball Skills ...... (Completion of Skill Tests) 2. Gymnastics ...... (Rings, Parallel Bars and Vaulting Box) 3. Preparation and Attitude ......
3rd GOAL PERIOD	1. Tumbling ...... 2. Volleyball Skills ...... 3. P.F.I. Score ...... (Self Evaluation Only) 4. Preparation and Attitude	1. Volleyball Skills ...... (Class Tournament) 2. Gymnastics ...... (Rope Jump, Ropes, Tumbling) 3. P.F.I. Score ...... (Self Evaluation Only) 4. Preparation and Attitude	1. Volleyball Skills ...... (Class Tournament) 2. Gymnastics ...... (Rope Jump, Ropes, Tumbling) 3. P.F.I. Score ...... (Self Evaluation Only) 4. Preparation and Attitude ......
4th GOAL PERIOD	1. Track Skills 100 Yd. Dash ...... 880 Yd. Dash ...... High Jump ...... Broad Jump ...... Shot Put ...... 2. Softball Skills ...... (Class Tournament) 3. Preparation and Attitude ...... Accumulated Points for Block "B"	1. Track Skills 100 Yd. Dash ...... 880 Yd. Dash ...... High Jump ...... Broad Jump ...... Shot Put ...... 2. Softball Skills (Class Tournament) 3. Individual Sport Orientation (Golf and Tennis) ...... 4. Preparation and Attitude ...... Accumulated Points for Block "B"	1. Track Skills 100 Yd. Dash ...... 880 Yd. Dash ...... High Jump ...... Broad Jump ...... Shot Put ...... 2. Softball Skills (Class Tournament) 3. Instruction in Golf and Tennis ...... 4. Preparation and Attitude ...... Total Points Block "B" ...... Yes ☐ No ☐

DEPARTMENT OF PHYSICAL EDUCATION
ATHLETIC REPORT

School_____ Sport_____ Game No._____

Game with_____ Played at_____

Date_____ Score_____ Opponents_____
(Your Score)

Referee_____ Umpire_____ H. L._____
Rating of officials: (Use numerals: 1—excellent, 2—good, 3—fair, 4—poor)

Attendance_____ Receipts_____ Guarantee (Paid)_____

Received_____

Weather conditions_____ Principal's lists were (not) exchanged_____

	PLAYER (Full name)	NO.	POSITION	LIST TOTAL PARTICIPATION			REMARKS
				Quarters	Innings	Events	
1							
2							
3							
4							
5							
6							
7							
8							
9							
10							
11							
12							
13							
14							
15							
16							
17							
18							
19							
20							
21							
22							
23							
24							
25							

Scorer_____ Record compiled by_____

Time_____ Signature of Coach_____

Physical education
attendance and excuse forms

The following forms and records have been selected from the authors' files. School systems across the country which developed these forms are to be commended for their work.

P. E. EXCUSE

....

Last Name (*Print*) First Name   HR   Period

DATE: REASON   SIGNATURE

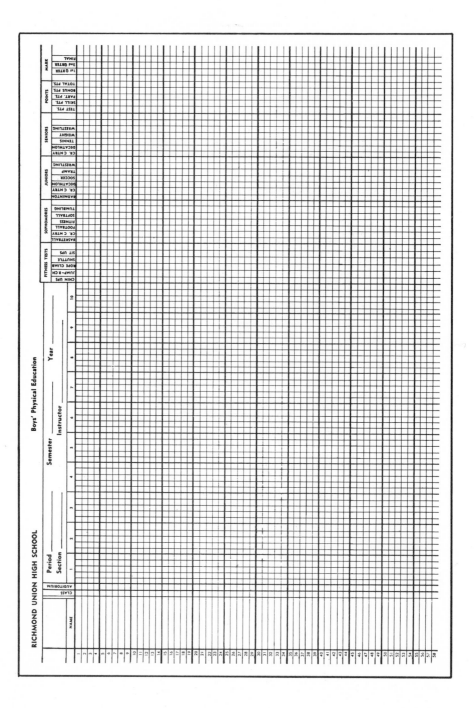

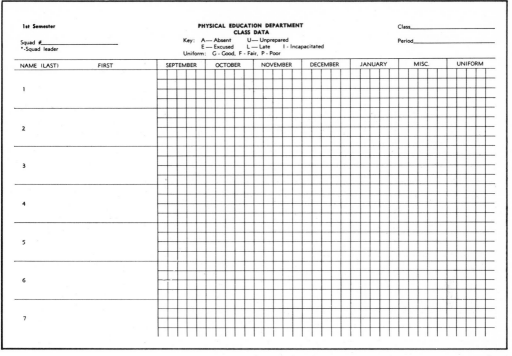

(Front)

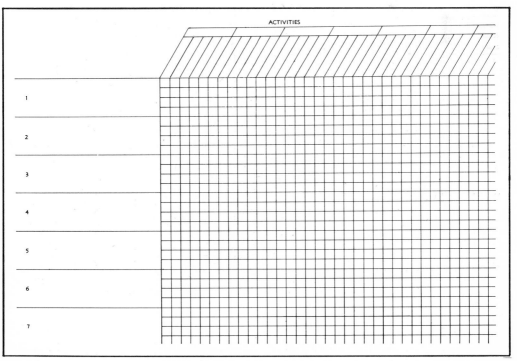

(Back)

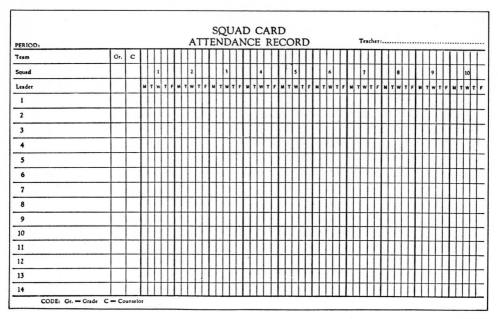

(Front)

(Back)

APPOINTMENT SLIP

Date................................ Room.............. Range.............. Seat..............

....
Name

Please see me as soon as possible, or at..

Place.............................. Signed...

Please bring this slip with you

ATTENDANCE CARD

Name _____ H.R._____ R___ S____

Address _____ Telephone _____

Parents/Guardians _____ Evanston _____
or (City) _____

1st att.	1	2	3	4	5	6	7	8	9	10	11	12
2nd att.	1	2	3	4	5	6	7	8	9	10	11	12

1st Sem. Health Ed. _____

2nd Sem. Health Ed. _____

1st Sem. Physical Ed.	Med. Ex._____	**2nd Sem. Physical Ed.**
Period_____ Gym_____	_____	Period_____ Gym_____
Teacher _____	Feet:	Teacher _____
Suit - label	1 - OK___ I___ P___	**Suit** - label
Shoes - label		**Shoes** - label
S. Shirt - label	2 - OK___ I___ P___	**S. Shirt** - label

Time Issued		
PERIOD TARDINESS	**TIME ISSUED }**	Class
	PERIOD TARDY SLIP	
Name_____	NAME_____	
Adviser_____	ADVISER_____	
Period_____ Class		Issued by
	REASON_____	
Issued } by }_____	PERIOD_____	
	This slip to be collected by the teacher and returned to the office. TEACHER'S SIGNATURE_____	

(Courtesy New Trier Township High School, Winnetka, Ill.)

NEW ENROLLEE

Date_____   Girls Phys. Ed._____
Name_____   　　　　H.R._____
　　Period_____
　　Room_____   Teacher_____
　　Feet checked_____   P.X. appt._____
　　Cards:
　　　Attendance_____   Padlock_____
　　　Activity_____   Yellow_____
　　Year_____   Credit_____

　　　　　　　　　　　　Class List

CHANGE OF PROGRAM

Date _____   Girls' Phys. Ed. _____

Name _____   H.R. _____

    Periods — from _____   to _____

    Teachers — from _____   to _____

    Locker changed _____   Act. card _____

Drop _____   Note: _____

Left _____

Completed _____

Double _____

Make-up _____   Atten. _____   Class List _____

PHYSICAL EDUCATION EXCUSE

NAME ....

GRADE .... ADVISOR .... GYM PERIOD ....

DATES—EXCUSED FROM .... TO ....

DOCTOR ....

REASON ....

....

NO PHYS. ED. ....

MODIFIED PROGRAM

　　　FULL PROGRAM EXCEPT COMPETITIVE SPORTS ....

　　　PARTICIPATION EXCEPT ....

SCHOOL SCHEDULE ADJUSTMENT, IF ANY ....

....

Name..
　　　　　　　　(Last)　　　　　　　　　(First)　　　　　　　(Second)

Home
Address.. Home
　　　　　　(No.)　　　　(Street)　　　　　(Village)　　Tel. No.....................................

Name of { Parent*
　　　　　 or
　　　　　 Guardian* } ....
*Cross out one　　　　　　　　　(Last)　　　　　　　(First)　　　　　(Second)

Business Address...
　　　　　　　　　　(No.)　　　　　　　(Street)　　　　　　(City)

If office is in large bldg. } Indicate— { ....
　　　　　　　　　　　　　　　　　　(Name of Building)　　　(Bus. Tel. No.)

Parent's　　　　　　　　　　　　Family
Occupation.. Physician...................................
　(Name of firm or institution with which connected)

Date of　　　　　 Place of
Your　　　　　　　 Birth ....
Birth　　　　　　　　　　　　　(City)　　　　　　　　(State)

　　How far can you swim? Check distance:　Not at all ☐　25 yards ☐　100 yards ☐

JUNIOR

CLASS	19 SEPT.	OCT.	NOV.	DEC.	19 JAN.	FEB.	MAR.	APR.	MAY	JUNE
M.										
T.										
W.										
TH.										
F.										

PERIOD ( )　　　　　CREDIT ( )　PERIOD ( )　　　　　CREDIT (

SENIOR

CLASS	19 SEPT.	OCT.	NOV.	DEC.	19 JAN.	FEB.	MAR.	APR.	MAY	JUNE
M.										
T.										
W.										
TH.										
F.										

PERIOD ( )　　　　　CREDIT ( )　PERIOD ( )　　　　　CREDIT (

WAIVER	WITHDRAWAL	RE-ENTRANCE		
LAST NAME	FIRST NAME		ADVISER	S. NO.

ADVISER

FIRST NAME

LAST NAME

(Front)

(Courtesy Boys' Physical Education Department, New Trier Township High School, Winnetka, Ill.)

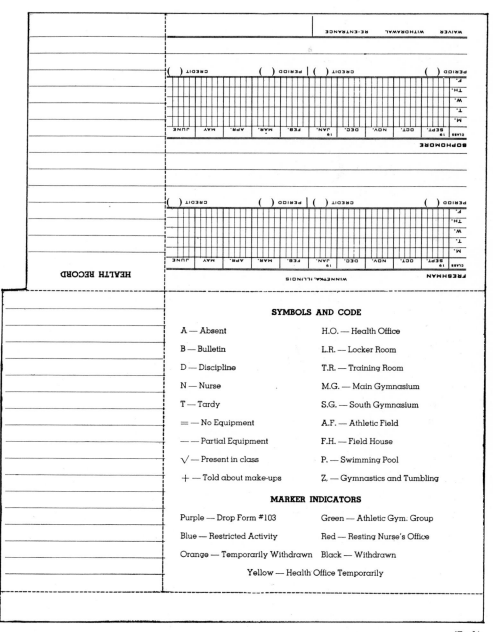

HEALTH RECORD

SYMBOLS AND CODE

A — Absent   H.O. — Health Office

B — Bulletin   L.R. — Locker Room

D — Discipline   T.R. — Training Room

N — Nurse   M.G. — Main Gymnasium

T — Tardy   S.G. — South Gymnasium

= — No Equipment   A.F. — Athletic Field

— — Partial Equipment   F.H. — Field House

√ — Present in class   P. — Swimming Pool

+ — Told about make-ups   Z. — Gymnastics and Tumbling

MARKER INDICATORS

Purple — Drop Form #103   Green — Athletic Gym. Group

Blue — Restricted Activity   Red — Resting Nurse's Office

Orange — Temporarily Withdrawn   Black — Withdrawn

Yellow — Health Office Temporarily

(Back)

(Courtesy Boys' Physical Education Department, New Trier Township High School, Winnetka, Ill.)

Physical education equipment forms

The following forms and records have been selected from the authors' files. School systems across the country which developed these forms are to be commended for their work.

	Belt	Jersey	Pants	Game Jersey	Nurmi Shirt	Helmet	Sweat Shirt	Sweat Pants	Socks	Shoes	Warm-Ups	Supporter Pads	Pads Hip	Shoulder	

Last Name — **First**

Home Room   Locker   Lock   Phone No.

Sport

Checked Out   Checked In

**BOYS' PHYSICAL EDUCATION
EQUIPMENT CARD**

428

INVENTORY							
Date	Manufacturer	Dealer	Cat. No.	Total on Hand	Number Purchased	Cost	Comment

(Front)

Year	New	Good	Fair	Obs.	Total	Numbers or Sizes								

(Back)

Boys Equipment Card

NAME:_____ ACTIVITY:_____ DATE:_____
         (LAST NAME FIRST)

ARTICLE	BLACK	ORANGE	WHITE
SHOES			
PANTS (PRACTICE)			
JERSEY ''			
HIP PADS – SLIDE			
SHOULDER PADS			
THIGH PADS			
T SHIRT			
SUPPORTER			
SOCKS – STOCKINGS			
JERSEY (GAME)			
PANTS ''			
WARMUP – JACKET			
WARMUP – PANTS			
HOOD			
HELMET – CAP			

HOME ROOM _____

AGE _____ HT. _____ WT. _____

YEAR IN SCHOOL _____

LOCKER # _____

TELEPHONE # _____

ADDRESS _____
_____

SIGNATURE:

MISCELLANEOUS:

NEW TRIER TOWNSHIP HIGH SCHOOL - WINNETKA, ILLINOIS
BOYS' PHYSICAL EDUCATION DEPARTMENT

Report of Broken or Missing Equipment

_____ _____   1 2 3 4   _____
(Date) (Period)   (Class)   (Instructor)
       Broken --------------"X"   Missing ---------------"O"

Badminton Racket - - - ( )   Soccer Ball - - - - - - - ( )
Basketball - - - - - - ( )   Speedball - - - - - - - - ( )
Handball - - - - - - - ( )   Table Tennis Ball - - - - ( )
Handball Gloves - - - ( )   Table Tennis Paddle - - - ( )
Softball - - - - - - - ( )   Tennis Racket - - - - - - ( )
Softball Bat - - - - - ( )   Touch Football - - - - - ( )
_____   - - - - ( )   Volleyball -- - - - - - - ( )

Student _____ Adviser _____

Remarks _____
_____
_____
_____

Form PE-11

HEALTH AND PHYSICAL EDUCATION DEPARTMENT

<u>Annual Inventory of Physical Education Supplies and Equipment</u>

Below is list of supplies and equipment for recording inventories. It is divided into two sections: supplies and equipment. The first refers to materials that are consumed in current use, and their service life is relatively short. The second refers to all articles that have permanent usefulness over a period of time and are not consumed or destroyed in their use. Check all supplies and equipment in both sections, adding any items that are not listed.

- -

Compiled by_____ School_____Year_____

Supplies	Items on Hand	Add'l Items Rec'd	Total 1 & 2	New	Good	Poor	Dis- carded	Total 3 to 6
	1	2		3	4	5	6	
ARCHERY								
Arm Guards								
Arrows								
Bowstrings								
Bows								
Finger Tabs								
Quiver								
Target Faces								
Targets								
Target Stands								
BADMINTON								
Nets								
Presses								
Racquets								
Shuttlecocks								
BALLS								
Baseballs								
Basketballs								
Cage								
Footballs, junior								
Footballs, official								
Footballs, touch								
Golf, practice								
Golf, game								
Handball								
Hockey, practice								
Hockey, game								
Medicine								
Paddle Tennis								
Rubber Play Balls, large								
Rubber Play Balls, medium								
Rubber Play Balls, small								
Soccer								
Softballs								
Table Tennis								
Tennis								
Volleyballs								

Name_____ Room_____
        First   Middle   Last

Locker_____ Lock_____ Date_____
        Number   Number

My signature above is in recognition of the agreement that in consideration of the free use of a school locker during this school year I agree to use the above-numbered lock on my duly assigned locker only, to keep my locker locked when not necessarily open, to maintain my locker in good condition, and to forfeit all rights to this lock if left at school after the close of examinations in June.

A lock may be redeemed by the school at the time the purchaser leaves school provided it is turned in by the person who originally purchased it from the school.

From whom was this lock purchased?_____

GIRL'S PADLOCK CARD

_____First Name)_____(Middle Name)_____(Last Name)_____

YEAR	ROOM-R-S	PERIOD	LOCKER	PADLOCK	COMBINATION

EQUIPMENT RECORD CARD
TO BE RETURNED TODAY

Name_____ Teacher_____ Period_____

No.	Article	No.	Article	No.	Article
	Archery, Arm Guard		Handball		Sponge Ball
	Archery, Arrow		Hockey Ball		Tape Measure
	Archery, Bow		Hockey Sticks		Table Tennis Net
	Archery, Glove		Jacks - Ball		Tennis Ball
	Badminton Racket		Jump Rope		Tether Ball
	Badminton Shuttlecock		Marbles		Timer (Stop Watch)
	Basketball		Pick-up Sticks		Whistle
	Bean Bag		Ping Pong Ball		
	Checkerboard		Ping Pong Paddle		
	Checker Men		Playground Ball		
	Chest Protector		10" 16"		
	Chinese Checkers		Quoits		
	Clip Board		Softball		
	Darts		Softball Bat		
	Deck Tennis Rings		Shin Guards		
	Dominoes		Shuffleboard Cue		
	Eye-glasses Guard		Shuffleboard Disc		
	Goal Guards		Shuttlecock		
	Golf Ball		Shuttle Loop		
	Golf Club		Soccer Ball		

EQUIPMENT ISSUE

Date..

I .... have

accepted school property ....

.... (write in article and its number)

and agree to return it clean and in good condition or pay for said uniform.

Signed ....

H. R. #

Home Phone #   Home Address...

GIRLS' HEALTH AND PHYSICAL EDUCATION DEPARTMENT

Equipment--Inventory and Condition

Activity_____   Date_____

School year 19__ - 19__   Season_____   Done by_____

	NUMBER			
	Total Usable	New	Used	Discarded

Recommendations for following season

    1. Repair

    2. Purchase

DEPARTMENT OF HEALTH AND PHYSICAL EDUCATION

Re: Lost Property Report

Student owner_____ H.R._____ R___ S___

Date of loss_____ Time_____ Period_____

List missing articles:

Description of known details:

Instructor's follow-up:

(Signed)_____

(Use reverse side if additional space is necessary.)

EQUIPMENT CHECKOUT RECORD

Player_____ Home Room_____

Address_____ Phone_____

Class_____ Height_____ Weight_____ Age_____

Parents Waiver_____ Examination_____ Insurance_____

Football   Cross Country   Basketball   Swimming   Wrestling

Baseball   Track   Tennis   Golf

	Out	In	Game Equipment	Out	In
Blocking pads			White jersey		
Shoulder pads			Maroon jersey		
Hip pads			White pants		
Thigh pads			Maroon pants		
Knee pads			Warm-up pants		
Helmet			Warm-up jacket		
Shoes			Stockings		
Practice pants					
Practice jersey					

I hereby certify that I have received the above-listed athletic equipment and will return same not later than the day following the last game of the season for the sport checked.

Signature_____

BOYS' PHYSICAL EDUCATION DEPARTMENT

Equipment Inspection

Please write on this sheet the names of boys not wearing clean gym clothing. Also give the advisers' names. Thank you.

Inspection may involve any day with special emphasis on each MONDAY. The instructor should place his initials following the date of each recording.

Date	Instr. Init.	Boy's Name	Adviser	Dirty Clothes	Partial Equipment	Torn Clothing	*Borrowed Equipment

*Borrowed equipment with or without owner's consent should always be followed up with a discipline note.

(Courtesy Boys' Physical Education Department, New Trier Township High School, Winnetka, Ill.)

EQUIPMENT INVENTORY

Sport_____   Date_____

	Reconditioned	Stored	Total	Remarks
Uniforms				
Varsity jerseys				
Green				
White				
J.V. jerseys				
Green				
White				
Varsity pants				
J.V. pants				
Shoes				
Hip pads				
Shoulder pads				
Rib pads				
Thigh guards				
Knee pads				
Belts				
Helmets or caps				
Practice pants				
Practice jerseys				
Scrimmage vests				
Sliding pads				
Over socks				
Under socks				
Equipment				
Balls				
New				
Used				
Bats				
New				
Used				
Bases				
Dummies				
Nets				
Masks				
Protectors				
Leg guards				
Mits				
Watches				
Score cards				
Shot puts				
Discus				
Starting blocks				
Hurdles				
Rings				
Poles				
Cross bars				
Batons				
Stands				

Signed_____

BASKETBALL

Name_____   Address_____

Homeroom_____   Date_____   Phone_____

Medical_____   Permission_____   Insurance_____

Height_____   Weight_____   Age_____

Deposit received_____   Deposit returned_____

Equipment Issued	Equipment Returned
1. Game shirt	
White_____	
Purple_____	
2. Game pants	
White_____	
Purple_____	
3. Warm-up jacket_____	
4. Warm-up pants_____	
5. Reversible "T" shirt_____	
6. Sneakers_____	
7. Knee pads_____	
8. Other_____	

Signature_____

Remarks:

Dear Mr. and Mrs.

_____, who is in my _____ period class in
physical education, has not:

    ____ Bought her padlock and had her locker assigned

    ____ Bought or presented her complete equipment--
         regulation suit, tennis shoes, and sweatshirt

    ____ Marked all her equipment with her first initial
         and last name (Markings should be embroidered
         above the pocket on the gym suit and in a similar
         place on the sweatshirt; name tapes are accept-
         able.)

    Our equipment for physical education is as necessary as
the textbook for English. Anyone is at a distinct disadvantage
without required equipment. I am sure you will do all that you
can to see that your daughter's deficiencies as indicated above
are corrected at once.

    Please feel free to call me about this or any other
matter.

             Sincerely,

                 Instructor, Girls' Health and
                 Physical Education Department

Miscellaneous physical education forms

The following forms and records have been selected from the authors' files. School systems across the country which developed these forms are to be commended for their work.

Athletic Permit

Name of Student ....

Parents' Waiver

To Whom It May Concern:

This is to certify that my son/daughter.. (please write his/her name) has my permission to train for and participate in Athletic Honor Team Games / Tigerettes / Cheerleaders (underline particular activity) at White Plains High School. I assume for myself full responsibility should any accident occur to him/her either in training for such activity or in game performances, or in traveling to and from various schools where this activity is carried on.

Signature .... Parent

Date ....19......

Pupil's Name.. Gr..........................

Permission is hereby given to .... to
                                                        Pupil's Name
participate in the After-School Play Program for the

.... season. I understand (he) (she) will
          Fall, Winter, Spring

participate in .... on .... of each
                    Activity   *Days*

week from about .... to ....
                        Hour   *Hour*

Date ....
                                                Parent or Guardian

Enrollment in this program is voluntary. However, once enrolled regular attendance
is-expected unless prevented for reasons of health or family plans. The pupil is
expected to notify the activity supervisor of the reason for each absence.

Details of each season's program are given each pupil to take home in September
of each year. Another copy will gladly be sent on request.

RICH TOWNSHIP HIGH SCHOOL

EAST CAMPUS

Athletic Award

196___ 196___

THIS IS TO CERTIFY THAT

_____
NAME

HAS MET THE REQUIREMENTS FOR

THE_____ LETTER IN_____
    VARSITY, SOPH, FRESH, MGR.   (SPORT)

SIGNED_____ SIGNED_____
        DIRECTOR OF ATHLETICS   COACH

DEPARTMENT OF PHYSICAL EDUCATION

Date_____ 19__

I am willing to have my son/daughter participate in the afterschool activities carried on by the Department of Physical Education. I hereby give my consent for _____, a pupil in the _____ School, to play _____ during the season of 19___. I shall not hold the Board of Education nor any of its employees responsible for the payment of any bills incurred because of accident or injuries to my son/daughter due to athletics or traveling to and from games or practice periods.

_____
Signature of Parent or Guardian

PHYSICIAN'S STATEMENT

I have examined _____ and believe that he is in condition to participate in any of the following sports.

Football	Baseball	Swimming	Obstacle racing
Soccer	Ice hockey	Tennis	Heavy apparatus
Basketball	Handball	Golf	Giant ball
Track and field	Volley ball	Badminton	Field hockey
Cross country	Canoeing	Tumbling	Speed ball

Signature_____M.D.

Date_____

SAMPLE RECOGNITION LETTERS

My dear Mike,

Physical Education has come pretty hard
for you, Mike, but you've always been willing
to tangle with it in a good try. Never have
you sacrificed your fine sense of the neat and
the appropriate to the false standards of haste
or carelessness.

Your class and home room spirit has been
fine too, Mike, and I want you to know that I
appreciate it.

Yours sincerely,

_____

Dear John:

I wish to commend you for your splendid
work and fine cooperation. You have helped
greatly in making our year successful.

It has been a real pleasure to work with
you as a member of the intramural basketball
team.

Sincerely yours,

_____

Dear Bob:

It is a pleasure to send you this letter
in recognition of the fine effort you have put
forth in a subject which you have found very
difficult.

May you always attack new problems with
as much determination and may you become more
and more successful in your physical education.

Sincerely yours,

𝕲. 𝕬. 𝕬.

_____

has earned membership in the Girls' Athletic Association of

.... High School until _____

_____President

_____Secretary

She now has_____points toward_____

Certificate of Award
TO

_____
OF

_____
for Meritorious participation in

_____

SEASON_____

_____   _____
PRINCIPAL   DIRECTOR

Girls' Athletic Association

Homeroom _____

Year _____

| Sport | Points | | | | | Remarks |
	Fall	Winter I	Winter II	Spring	Trophy Points	Trophies Received
Archery						
Badminton						
Basketball						
Bowling						
Dance						
Field Day						
Golf						
Hockey						
Riflery						
Saddle						
Softball						
Speedball						
Swimming						
Table Tennis						
Tennis						
Volleyball						
Total						
Grand Total						

BASIS FOR THE EVALUATION OF TEACHING SERVICES

I. <u>Teacher-Pupil Relationships</u> (A teacher who works well with pupils)

1. Shows respect for the personal worth of each pupil
2. Seeks to understand pupil behavior before making evaluative judgments
3. Is sympathetic, kind, patient--yet firm
4. Respects confidences
5. Respects the individual differences in children and provides learning situations in his classroom to meet these differences
6. Gains the acceptance and respect of pupils

II. <u>Evidence of Instructional Skill</u> (A teacher who is effective in his teaching)

1. Is competent in the subjects he teaches
2. Uses a variety of materials and teaching techniques
3. Stimulates pupils to think critically
4. Adapts instructional methods and materials to the abilities and interests of individual pupils
5. Develops and uses effective techniques of evaluation
6. Makes extent and purpose of assignments clear
7. Maintains an attractive and stimulating classroom environment

III. <u>Evidence of Classroom Control and Management</u> (A teacher who controls and manages his class successfully)

1. Provides a well-controlled democratic environment
2. Enters into pupils' activities without dominating them
3. Encourages children to work to capacity without undue tension
4. Exercises care for the safety and health of pupils
5. Shows ability to organize
6. Is able to handle behavior problems without emotional upsets or emotional extremes

IV. <u>Teacher-Staff Relationships</u> (A teacher who works well with his associates)

1. Promotes good will among individuals and groups
2. Serves on committees and participates in other group projects
3. Carries his share of school responsibilities willingly and cheerfully; readily responds when called upon to assume extra responsibilities
4. Is alert to ways in which he can improve conditions in the school and helps others cheerfully
5. Goes through regular "channels" on matters affecting the welfare of associates or of the institution
6. Gains the respect of his associates
7. Is prompt and accurate with reports

(cont'd)

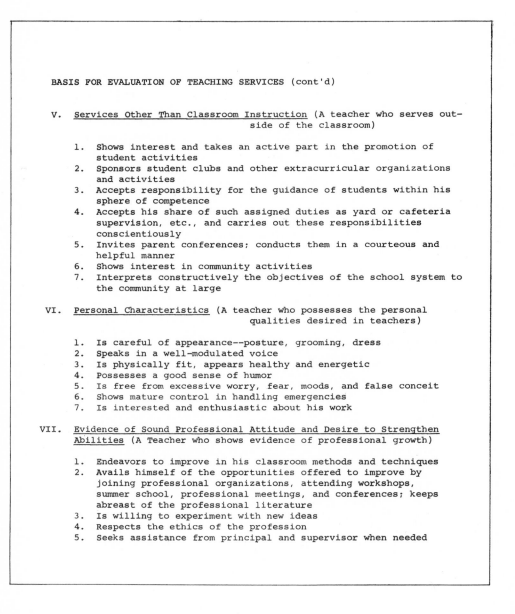

BASIS FOR EVALUATION OF TEACHING SERVICES (cont'd)

V. <u>Services Other Than Classroom Instruction</u> (A teacher who serves out-
                                                      side of the classroom)

    1. Shows interest and takes an active part in the promotion of
        student activities
    2. Sponsors student clubs and other extracurricular organizations
        and activities
    3. Accepts responsibility for the guidance of students within his
        sphere of competence
    4. Accepts his share of such assigned duties as yard or cafeteria
        supervision, etc., and carries out these responsibilities
        conscientiously
    5. Invites parent conferences; conducts them in a courteous and
        helpful manner
    6. Shows interest in community activities
    7. Interprets constructively the objectives of the school system to
        the community at large

VI. <u>Personal Characteristics</u> (A teacher who possesses the personal
                                      qualities desired in teachers)

    1. Is careful of appearance--posture, grooming, dress
    2. Speaks in a well-modulated voice
    3. Is physically fit, appears healthy and energetic
    4. Possesses a good sense of humor
    5. Is free from excessive worry, fear, moods, and false conceit
    6. Shows mature control in handling emergencies
    7. Is interested and enthusiastic about his work

VII. <u>Evidence of Sound Professional Attitude and Desire to Strengthen
      Abilities</u> (A Teacher who shows evidence of professional growth)

    1. Endeavors to improve in his classroom methods and techniques
    2. Avails himself of the opportunities offered to improve by
        joining professional organizations, attending workshops,
        summer school, professional meetings, and conferences; keeps
        abreast of the professional literature
    3. Is willing to experiment with new ideas
    4. Respects the ethics of the profession
    5. Seeks assistance from principal and supervisor when needed

Physical education
checklist

THE STATE EDUCATION DEPARTMENT
DIVISION OF HEALTH AND PHYSICAL EDUCATION

CHECK LIST FOR PHYSICAL EDUCATION

Education assumes a responsibility to pass on our cultural and social inheritance and to equip children and youth physically, mentally and emotionally for living in a changing world. This process involves (1) recognition of the needs of the individual in terms of the principles of pupil growth and development, (2) organization and administration of the curriculum for most effective use in the realization of its purposes as established by these needs and (3) continuous evaluation of the program to insure systematic progress toward the realization of the objectives of physical education and the purposes of education.

Physical education recognizes this concept of education and has a unique contribution to make in meeting these needs for the self-realization of the individual through the activities in its program. The beneficial effects of exercise and activity, however, are produced only when activities of the right type and amount are provided under qualified personnel. The methods and techniques used in the conduct of these activities need to be such that not only are these physical and organic needs met but opportunity is provided for growth in the development of social behaviors, habits, attitudes, emotional stability.

In order for individuals to function as contributing members of a democracy it is essential that they learn self-discipline in relation to the group through the development of those qualities which are essential to democratic living such as cooperation, leadership, fellowship, good sportsmanship etc. It is also essential that they develop (1) strength to be ready for tasks encountered in everyday routine and in emergencies, (2) stamina to continue necessary tasks without undue fatigue, and energy to participate in recreation activities after a day's work, (3) cardio-respiratory endurance for sustained effort in activities involving motion of the entire body, (4) agility to be able to make wide ranges of movement easily, (5) speed to be able to move rapidly when personal safety demands it, (6) control to coordinate body movement skilfully, (7) knowledge and skill in a wide variety of recreational activities to insure continued participation.

The check list has been prepared to help school officials and interested citizens' groups to judge their physical education programs in terms of the basic elements needed to reach the objectives stated above and to stimulate planning in terms of pupil needs and local conditions. It should enable communities to identify the strength and weaknesses of their physical education programs and to direct attention to areas needing further study and action for improvement. The check list is designed for such self-appraisal use. It is not for a report to the Department.

These elements are grouped under eight main headings:

Program activities	Personnel
Program planning	Facilities
Evaluating	Safety and sanitation
Scheduling	Budget

Continued on next page.

(From New York State Department of Education, Division of Health, Physical Education, and Recreation.)

I The program provides a broad variety of activities to serve all pupils.

  1 Informal activities such as singing games, simple circle games, creative activities (games of invitation and imagination) and games of hunting, fleeing and chasing type. Yes .... No ....

  2 Games of simple organization such as kickball, dodgeball, relays etc. Yes .... No ....

  3 Team games, such as basketball, volleyball, softball, soccer etc. Yes .... No ....

  4 Individual and dual games, such as badminton, tennis, horseshoes etc. Yes .... No ....

  5 Gymnastics, such as stunts, tumbling, apparatus. Yes .... No ....

  6 Rhythms and dancing, such as folk, square, social. Yes .... No ....

  7 Winter sports, such as skating, skiing, snowshoeing. Yes .... No ....

  8 Body mechanics and correctives. Yes .... No ....

  9 Swimming and water safety. Yes .... No ....

  10 Extraclass, interschool and intramural activities (boys and girls)

    a An organized extraclass program is provided for pupils in upper elementary grades. Yes .... No ....

    b All athletic activities are an integral part of the physical education program. Yes .... No ....

    c The intramural program is well organized and attractive to the extent that most of the pupils willingly participate. Yes .... No ....

    d Girls' interschool activities are limited to sports days, invitation games and other invitation activities. Yes .... No .... Girls' rules are used in the conduct of these activities. Yes .... No ....

    e Interschool activities for boys below the seventh grade are limited to sports days and invitation games. Yes .... No ....

II The program is planned in terms of community needs and of the growth and development needs of pupils.

  1 The purposes of education and objectives of physical education are used to guide planning. Yes .... No ....

  2 The activities are introduced at the appropriate grade and growth level. Yes .... No ....

  3 There is a written master plan which provides for progression and continuity in the instruction. Yes .... No ....

  4 Planning for the program is shared by administrator and staff. Yes .... No .... By staff and pupils. Yes .... No .... With citizens' groups. Yes .... No ....

III Provision is made for evaluating the program by determining the growth and progress of pupils.

  1 Records of pupil status and progress are maintained with reference to the following:

    a Physical fitness. Yes .... No ....

    b Knowledge and skill in activities. Yes .... No ....

    c Social growth and group relationships. Yes .... No ....

  2 Appropriate evaluative methods are used to determine pupil progress in the above-mentioned items.

    a Recognized standards. Yes .... No ....

    b Teacher-made tests or measures. Yes .... No ....

    c Anecdotal report. Yes .... No .... Teacher observation. Yes .... No ....

IV The school schedule provides for the following:

  1 A daily period of physical education instruction for each pupil. Yes .... No ....

  2 Pupils grouped for such instruction according to their grade or growth level. Yes .... No ....

3 Classes of uniform size. Yes .... No .... Small enough to provide good working groups (a maximum of 40 pupils is recommended). Yes .... No ....

4 Additional classes for those who need remedial (corrective) work. Yes .... No ....

5 Restricted program for pupils physically unable to participate in regular program of activities. Yes .... No ....

6 Equitable scheduling of facilities between boys andgirls for both class and extraclass activities. Yes .... No ....

V Qualified personnel is provided to conduct a well-rounded program.

1 Sufficient personnel is provided to meet the class instruction and laboratory requirements in accordance with the needs of pupils as outlined in the Regulations of the Commissioner. (A physical education teacher for each 240 elementary or 190 secondary pupils is recommended.) Elementary: Yes .... No .... Secondary: Yes .... No ....

2 A qualified director (where there are five or more on the staff) or a department head (four or less on staff) is available to provide necessary administrative and supervisory services. Yes .... No ....

3 Continuous professional growth of staff is provided for through:

a Regular staff conferences. Yes .... No ....

b Attending general faculty meetings. Yes .... No ....

c Attending local, zone and state meetings and workshops. Yes .... No ....

d Recent graduate study in physical education and related fields. Yes .... No ....

e A well-equipped professional library. Yes .... No ....

f Professional visits to observe programs in other schools. Yes .... No ....

4 Girls' program is conducted by a woman teacher. Yes .... No ....

5 Additional faculty assistance is provided for intramural program.
Girls: Yes .... No .... Boys: Yes .... No ....

For interschool program.
Girls: Yes .... No .... Boys: Yes .... No ....

VI The physical education and recreation facilities permit a well-rounded program for all pupils.

1 Teaching station indoors for every 240 pupils enrolled. Yes .... No ....

2 Sufficient dressing space for largest class. Yes .... No ....

3 Dressing locker for each pupil in largest class. Yes .... No ....

4 A gymnasium storage locker for every pupil enrolled above the 4th grade. Yes .... No ....

5 At least one shower head for every five pupils in the largest class. Yes .... No ....

6 A well-drained, suitably located body-drying area. Yes .... No ....

7 Storage space for apparatus. Yes .... No .... Equipment and supplies. Yes .... No ....

8 Suitable office space for each physical education teacher. Yes .... No ....

9 A swimming pool. Yes .... No ....

10 Remedial (corrective) room. Yes .... No ....

11 All-weather paved area adjoining building for primary grades' use. Yes .... No ....

12 Separate apparatus and play area for smaller children. Yes .... No ....

13 Separate playing fields for Intermediate grades. Yes .... No .... Secondary girls. Yes .... No .... Secondary boys (class and intramurals). Yes .... No .... Interschool sports. Yes .... No ....

14 Court area for tennis. Yes .... No .... Badminton. Yes .... No .... Volleyball. Yes .... No ....

Continued on next page.

15 Area for archery. Yes .... No .... Horseshoe pitching. Yes .... No .... Golf instruction. Yes .... No ....

16 Shed or other building for the storage of outdoor equipment. Yes .... No ....

17 The elementary school is planned to function as a neighborhood center and the high school as a community center. Yes .... No .... This planning is shared with citizens' groups. Yes .... No .... Park officials. Yes .... No .... Planning officials. Yes .... No ....

VII Provisions are made for healthful and safe conduct of physical education activities.

1 A thorough annual medical examination is provided for all pupils. Yes .... No ....

2 All candidates for interschool teams are given a special examination at the beginning of each sport season. Yes .... No ....

3 Subsequent examinations within each sport season are given when needed. Yes .... No ....

4 All participants in the more vigorous sports are provided with adequate protective equipment. Yes .... No ....

5 There is a regular safety check on all equipment and apparatus. Yes .... No ....

6 Gymnasium floor is kept clear of apparatus and equipment when not in use. Yes .... No ....

7 Good care, proper use and orderly storage of equipment are provided. Yes .... No ....

8 Fields are properly maintained for maximum and safe use. Yes .... No ....

9 Clean and sanitary conditions prevail in all areas. Yes .... No ....

10 An appropriate towel service is provided. Yes .... No ....

11 Protection Plan or other accident insurance coverage is provided for the physical education classes. Yes .... No .... Interschool teams. Yes .... No .... Intramural groups. Yes .... No ....

VIII The physical education budget is adequate and there is an equitable distribution of funds between the different activities of the program.

1 The annual budget request for physical education is prepared on the basis of a careful inventory and the complete needs of the program to be provided for the school year. Yes .... No ....

2 Essential equipment is available for physical education. Yes .... No .... If not, the purchase of needed items is planned for. Yes .... No .... Available instructional supplies are satisfactory in quantity to permit maximum and simultaneous pupil participation in any one activity. Yes .... No .... The supplies provided permit instruction in a broad variety of activities. Yes .... No ....

3 Sufficient funds have been allocated for travel, protective equipment and other necessary expense in connection with: Boys' interschool activities. Yes .... No .... Boys' intramural activities. Yes .... No .... Girls' invitation games. Yes .... No .... Girls' intramural activities. Yes .... No ....

4 Funds are provided for attendance at professional meetings and conferences by staff members. Yes .... No ....

Index